ADVENTURES OF THE
MAD MONK
JI GONG

About the Translator

John Shaw during his twenty year U.S. Marine Corps career served part of that time as a Chinese/Japanese/Korean interpreter. He was stationed in China for two tours totaling six years and visited China twice after those tours. During his first visit he came across the tales of Ji Gong in a bookstore. After scanning the book, he bought a copy having decided it would be interesting to read. He read the entire book and then thought it would be enjoyable to translate the first half. He immersed himself in this project at a leisurely pace over several years.

Publisher's Note

During the process of translating this classical Chinese work, John Shaw was fortunate to have the invaluable expertise and input of his wife, Mrs. Sara Janet Shaw, a former professional editor, in all editorial matters. Together they worked as a team to make this manuscript highly accessible and interesting for English readers.

GUO XIAOTING

ADVENTURES OF THE MAD MONK JI GONG

Translated by John Robert Shaw

Introduction by Victoria Cass

TUTTLE Publishing

Tokyo | Rutland, Vermont | Singapore

Published by Tuttle Publishing, an imprint of Periplus Editions (HK) Ltd.

www.tuttlepublishing.com

ISBN: 978-0-8048-4322-5

Distributed by

North America, Latin America & Europe
Tuttle Publishing
364 Innovation Drive
North Clarendon
VT 05759-9436, USA
Tel: 1 (802) 773 8930
Fax: 1 (802) 773 6993
info@tuttlepublishing.com
www.tuttlepublishing.com

Asia Pacific
Berkeley Books Pte Ltd
61 Tai Seng Avenue #02-12
Singapore 534167
Tel: (65) 6280 1330
Fax: (65) 6280 6290
inquiries@periplus.com.sg
www.periplus.com

Japan
Tuttle Publishing
Yaekari Building 3rd Floor
5-4-12 Osaki Shinagawa-ku
Tokyo 1410032, Japan
Tel: (81) 3 5437 0171
Fax: (81) 3 5437 0755
sales@tuttle.co.jp
www.tuttle.co.jp

17 16 15 14   5 4 3 2 1   1404MP

Printed in Singapore

Table of Contents

Introduction

"Among those whom I like or admire, I can find no common denominator, but among those whom I love, I can; all of them make me laugh."

W. H. Auden

THE great Buddhist divinities of China have marked an austere passage through history. Arhats of immense dignity—severe gods of wisdom—left sacred texts; patriarchs founded grand temple complexes so that their doctrines might live; and martyred men and women sacrificed their own limbs as signs of devotion. These lions of the faith are the saints of Buddhism, famed for their miracle tales. But Ji Gong—the saint in this book—is not that saint; and that is not his story. Ji Gong is a god of the streets—a drinker, a trickster, a city magician who lives among shopkeepers and traveling merchants, among the impoverished scholars, street hustlers and courtesan-prostitutes, all with survival tales and hard-luck stories. He is their exorcist, their avenger; he is a streetwise hero, the common man's patron saint.

Ji Gong was born in Hangzhou, perhaps in the year 1130, during the Song Dynasty (960–1279). However, only one Song Dynasty biographer, Chan Master Jujian, found him worthy of mention, and the Master's account is mercifully short.[1] Lord Ji studied at the great Lingyin Monastery, an immense temple compound that still ranges solemnly up the steep hills above Hangzhou. The Chan masters of the temple instructed him in the infamously harsh practices of their sect, but failed; the young monk, following in the steps of other great ne'er-do-wells and holy fools of Chinese religions, managed the one distinct accomplishment revealed in this account: he got himself fired. He left the monastery, became a wanderer with hardly a proper jacket to wear, and achieved renown—not in the temples, but in the wine shops.

If this were the only version of this monk's life, he would have vanished, as did the thousands, perhaps millions, of other lowly disciples; but

---

1. Meir Shahar, *Crazy Ji, Chinese Religion and Popular Literature* (Harvard University Asia Center, 1998), 24.

Ji Gong's story was hijacked. It was claimed by generations of city dwellers—900 years of entertainers and the entertained—who seized on this
tale of defiance and trickster humor among the Hangzhou taverns, giving
the simple account both life and bulk. Indeed, the full might and weight
of the storyteller profession—its multiple clans and guilds, its steely mem-
bership practices, and its decades of training starting in childhood—was
thrown behind the lore of Ji Gong. This ignominious monk assumed center stage in the cycle of accounts; accounts that multiplied and expanded
as city life in China expanded. Later chroniclers gave him many names:
Ji of the Dao, the Living Buddha, the Hidden Recluse of the Qiantang
Lake, the Chan Master, The Drunken Arhat, Elder Brother Square Circle,
Abbot Ji, and his most familiar and suitable rubric: Crazy Ji.

The author of our version, Guo Xiaoting, lived in the late 1800s and
into the twentieth century, coming happily to the tales almost a millennium after Ji Gong lived. Guo Xiaoting wrote *The Complete Tales of Lord
Ji* in the 1890s, editing the raft of material from popular performances,
mimicking in some measure the storyteller's gimmicks and voice. Nor
was Guo Xiaoting embarrassed about his lowly sources. For another of
his works, he bragged that the long performances of storytellers—two-
month stagings were not unusual—were his source.[2] And although many
of these sorts of claims are specious—an attempt by intellectuals to evade
the charge of producing frothy literatures—this one seems to have been
true. *Ji Gong* does, in fact, reveal the world of the Beijing storyteller as the
century changed in 1900: where restaurants and theaters offered the tales,
and where Guo Xiaoting—in retirement—earned a living.

Thus, though the original tale and early versions of *Ji Gong* tell of
Hangzhou life, where the famous Lingyin Monastery presides, the
900-years-later version—our version—though set in Hangzhou, has the
look, smells, and—above all—sounds of Beijing. Within Guo Xiaoting's
tale and John Shaw's translation, not only does the monk Ji Gong emerge,
but so also do the lives and places of Guo Xiaoting's own world. We see
the alleyways and temple grounds, the lowlife and high ambitions of the
men and women of China of the late 1800s and early 1900s, a curbside
capsule of the late Qing Dynasty as it teetered on the brink of collapse.

---

2. Shahar, *Crazy Ji*, 117.

Six years after Guo Xiaoting published a second installment of the *Ji Gong* tales, the Outer City District Police for the city of Beijing compiled a survey.[3] In 1906 the "First Statistical Survey of the Security Administration" (*Jingshi waicheng xunjing zongting diyici tongjishu* 京師 外城 巡警 總廳 第一次統計書) reported that there were 347 restaurants, 308 courtesan-entertainer halls, 301 inns, 246 teahouses (where operas were performed), and 699 opium dens: all in a single district of Beijing. These were not the only place where people gathered. Temple complexes housed thousands of religious clerics and disciples and offered holiday fairs and popular performances. Grand compounds served the thousands of visiting merchants; they used the extensive banking institutions[4] to monitor their investments. Businesses of all levels dominated the streets of Beijing; at the turn of the century, when *Ji Gong* was published, there were over 25,000 commercial establishments.[5] Of course, the poor numbered in the thousands: soup kitchens, homeless shelters, and programs for temporary employment helped some.[6] The police did not simply observe this activity; Beijing was the most policed city in the world. A network of officers supervised the city through the night in a series of watchmen's contacts. "The beating of drums, bells, and bamboo boards enabled policemen to be part of a sweep through the streets and lanes … part of an elaborate choreographed system … that kept officers always within earshot of each other."[7] Members of the British Macartney mission in 1793 complained of being kept awake by the continual clapping and clopping.[8]

This was a city of size and scale. Foreigners were astounded; Father Pierre-Martial Cibot thought Beijing "the most peopled in the universe."[9] The estimates varied from one to three million inhabitants, depending on the inclusion of the extensive suburbs. The inns and restaurants, so carefully recorded by security officials, reflected this scale. One restaurant, a "publick house" visited by the Scotsman John Bell, was "the largest

3. Susan Naquin, *Peking, Temples and City Life, 1400–1900* (University of California Press, 2000), 638.
4. Susan Naquin and Evelyn Rawski, *Chinese Society in the Eighteenth Century* (New Haven, Yale University Press, 1987), 101.
5. David Strand, *Rickshaw Beijing, City People and Politics in the 1920s* (Berkeley, University of California Press), 104.
6. Naquin, *Peking*, 641–643.
7. Alison Dray-Novey, "Spatial Order and Police in Imperial Beijing," *Journal of Asian Studies* 52, no. 4 (November 1993): 896.
8. Dray-Novey, "Spatial Order and Police in Imperial Beijing," 896.
9. Dray-Novey, "Spatial Order and Police in Imperial Beijing," 889, note 2.

of that sort I ever saw; and could easily contain six or eight hundred people. The roof was supported by two rows of wooden pillars ... the great
part was filled with long tables, having benches, on each side, for the
accommodation of the company."[10] Traders, artisans, factory workers,
bosses and laborers, and the institutions—from temple compounds to
marketplaces, big and small—shaped the nature of Beijing. This was a
city with a city ecology: a city that had its own order and rhythm, with
thriving subcultures of interlocking occupations. To be sure, the Manchu
dominated the capital—laws were becoming increasingly strict on separation of races—but city patterns held the contours of life in Beijing.

Thus for Guo Xiaoting's audience, *The Complete Tales of Lord Ji* presents a tour of the places, sounds, and customs of Beijing on the brink of
the twentieth century. Readers would have been quick to hear the Beijing
slang; shopkeepers lived and worked in and among the neighborhood
hutong (the Beijing term for alley); a sly Daoist monk would be likely to
yuan (Beijing slang for "cheat," a word that is at the heart of many plot
twists). Red fruit (*hongguo*)—sweetened hawthorn fruit—was a Beijing
snack available in the novel; and Beijing buildings, not the palaces or
temples, but the *sihefang*—courtyard homes—sheltered the novel's residents.[11] If the city sights and sounds matched the Beijing cityscape, so did
the characters. Some were generic city dwellers, but some were clearly
northerners familiar to a nineteenth-century reader. Pipe smokers greeted
one another in teahouses; pipe smoking was a popular diversion never
seen in Hangzhou of the Song Dynasty.[12] A typical Beijing entertainer—
the *pingshu* performer—makes his appearance in the novel. This artist
was a typical northern "clapper-style" teller of rough-and-tumble tales of
heroes and bandits.[13] And if the citizens of *The Complete Tales* were northerners, they were also plain people. A few rich and mighty sit on the narrative outskirts—usually to threaten, occasionally to reward; but
workaday Beijing is the setting, and Beijing citizens the cast.

Beijing is clearly the common man's city. Though great walled compounds dominated old Beijing, Ji Gong's Beijing is permeable. It is a city
with a horizontal sight line; traded goods move through the streets like

---

10. John Bell (1691–1780), *Travels from St Petersburg in Russia to Diverse Parts of Asia*, vol-
    ume II (Glasgow, University of Edinburgh), 54.

11. Shahar, *Crazy Ji*, 116.

12. Carol Benedict, *Golden-Silk Smoke, A History of Tobacco in China, 1550–2110* (Berkeley,
    University of California Press, 2011), 18–21.

13. Shahar, *Crazy Ji*, 116–118.

fish through shoals. When a precious talisman disappears from a friend's keeping, Ji Gong learns of its progress. The talisman was stolen by members of the White Coin Gang, and then sold to the manager of the Old Studio Antique Shop (for 30 ounces of silver); then it is sold to Prime Minister Qin (for 500 ounces of silver!). Finally, it is taken through the gate of Prime Minister Qin's estate and hung in the upper story of a fine pavilion. This slick circulation is managed, Ji Gong is told, "in a matter of hours, while you were drinking with your friends."[14] As goods move, so do travelers. As readers, we are on foot in this vital city; no need for the grander forms of travel. When Ji Gong threads his way through this peculiar urban marriage of Hangzhou and Beijing, we can follow him at a good crisp walk.

Enter the ghost.

> His skin was a light sickly purple in color, his eyebrows heavy and long, shading his widely spaced eyes. With his hands he dragged the long chains with which he was bound and the heavy lock that fastened them together. His tangled hair was tied in a loose knot and his beard was like trampled grass.
>
> Prime Minister Qin gazed at him. "Alas!" Yes, it was his adoptive father and patron, Qin Guai, returning home as a baleful ghost!...
>
> "My old father!" exclaimed Prime Minister Qin. "I thought that you would have been in heaven long ago. Who would have thought that you could still be suffering in the underworld!"
>
> Qin Guai answered, "Son, for your father's sake, while you are yet in the world of light occupying your high position, return to the path of virtue before father and son-in-law go down in the stormy sea."[15]

You might expect an evasive view of morality in *The Complete Tales of Lord Ji*, for these characters rely on peasant cunning. But the mournful voice of Qin Guai's ghost tells another story. Ji Gong has here summoned

14. Guo Xiaoting, *Ji Gong Quan Zhuan* 濟公全傳 (Nanjing: Fenghuang, 2008), chapter 5.
15. Guo Xiaoting, *Adventures of the Mad Monk Ji Gong*, trans. John Shaw (Tuttle Publishing, 2014), chapter 10.

an agent of retribution laced with the terrors of filial guilt. And despite the low humor and humble streets, the moral code of Ji Gong is rigorous, his punishments sure and certain. The retribution meted out in this scene is exquisitely personal. The ghost-father shames the avaricious son; a wrenching humiliation abases the prime minister. Indeed, if the Confucian bureaucracy named itself a moral patriarchy with the Son of Heaven residing at the top, the horizontal landscape of nineteenth-century Beijing had its parallel forms of rectitude. Beijing life occupies, in *The Complete Tales*, a moral landscape, where a harsh and deeply ingrained vision shapes events, although these codes may have varied from what the Emperor recommended.

Ji Gong governs an ad hoc clan of the righteous oppressed. He pulls the threads of karmic connections, wrestling the high and mighty out of their compounds. Abuse of office, sexual violence against the weak, humiliation of the ordinary, and even the never-trivial crime of snobbery are always punished. The code is simple: decency. Though none of the characters is grand, all of them are armed with a pitch-perfect sense of probity. Even small gestures are governed by the sense of a refined doctrine. Decorum reaches to the smallest scale: "Even though at first the monk looked like nothing more than a beggar, to save Zhao Yuanwai's face Li Guoyuan could not do otherwise than go forward to offer a ceremonial greeting."[16] As with the rites (*li*) of fine society, this is the *li* of the counter-tradition, constituting a powerful bond, clan-like and rigorous. Shopkeepers, courtesans, and monks—denizens of Beijing—use the words "sister" and "brother" deliberately. "When Li Guoyuan saw that it was Zhao Wenhui, he immediately went forward, raising his clasped hands in greeting, and said, 'I have been looking forward to seeing you, Elder Brother.'"[17] These kinship terms color the fabric of the novel; they signal bonds that, once made, are never broken. Loyalty was paramount.

The aristocrats of these clans of the streets are Ji Gong's warriors. Dyed through and through with righteousness (*yi* 義), they are the moral police of the Beijing streets, the elder-brother patriarchs of the Beijing *hutong*. In reality they are an odd mismatch of bodyguards, martial-arts stage-performers, and bandits. But, of course their mismatch-outsider status is a point of pride, all of them suffering from a failure to know their place in society. These warriors call themselves men and women of the "water-

---

16. Guo Xiaoting, *Ji Gong Quan Zhuan*, chapter 5.
17. Guo Xiaoting, *Ji Gong Quan Zhuan*, chapter 5.

ways and greenwood" (*jianghu lülin* 江湖綠林). As outsiders they are proud to know each other by secret signs: an arc made by a weapon, an odd word used in greeting, some trick of appearance; with a simple gesture, kinship is recognized. Ji Gong himself is the chief among his band of defiant rogues. His skills are the most powerful; he is the godly (*shen* 神) version of this cast. But with his magic, lowly characters, though banished from power, are sanctioned—literally—by an eccentric, though intrinsically lucid, divine authority. *The Complete Tales* make something magical and deeply moral out of the city and its clash of circumstances. Guo Xiaoting, along with the centuries of performers of the Ji Gong epic, manufactured in this book a comic bible, appropriating a saint who was out and about in their midst, and clearly available: for, as the Song biographer has told us, Ji Gong was conveniently out of work.

In 1900, the same year that Guo Xiaoting published his second installment of *The Complete Tales of Lord Ji*, the city of Beijing was under siege. The forces of Germany, Japan, England, Russia, the United States, Italy, and France had taken Beijing; they had marched through the massive city gates, taken control of the foreign legation, and seized the Imperial Palace. The army of foreign soldiers had driven out the court; in April of that year, the Empress Dowager fled the palace dressed as a peasant. Nor did the troops stop there; they had arrived to punish the Boxer rebels. These rebels were a band of the displaced poor that had attacked Christian missions "to save China." Indeed, the Boxers had an implacable hatred of foreigners. Thus, there followed a vicious European response; this was divine retribution. Emperor William II of Germany declared, "Peking should be razed to the ground!" When the troops left for China, he urged his men, "Show no mercy! Take no prisoners."[18] Nor did they; foreign troops razed villages and executed thousands of peasants and peasant soldiers.

Not that this chaos was isolated. As the century ended, massive failures marked China's political life. In 1894 sections of the empire were ceded to Japan, and Germany in the same decade received sections of Shandong. From the court to the bureaucracy, to universities, to fine

---

18. Jean Chesneaux, Marianne Bastid, and Marie-Claire Bergere, *China from the Opium Wars to the 1911 Revolution* (New York, Random House, 1976), 334.

estates of educated gentry, all the structures of a well-policed world were in disarray: leading to the year 1911, when 2,000 years of dynastic governance convulsed in failure, toppling like a mountain into revolution and civil war. China was at one of the most terrible tipping points in history.

Within this maelstrom, in 1900, Guo Xiaoting wrote his second installment of *The Complete Tales of Lord Ji*. In these violent years Guo takes us, with apparent insouciance, through an odd-fellow comic narrative. Ji Gong is the curbside comedian of China. He typically plays the fool; temple statues portray him with an idiot's grin. But from that vantage point he is a master of the fine art of ridicule, as he exposes the grand as grandiose. And if he is a fool, he is a holy fool. Meir Shahar, in his wonderful book *Crazy Ji*, has linked Ji Gong to other lunatic eccentrics in Chinese religion. "Crazy shamans, eccentric Daoists, wild Buddhists, and carefree poets" have all "played an important role in the religion and art of China."[19] Ji Gong's madness has obvious method. It invokes the elemental, engaging what Robert Torrance called "the subversive and even anarchical sense of life."[20] He is a comic hero whose outrageous laughter evokes the sense of nature's raw authority; Crazy Ji conveys a sense of "heightened vitality, of challenged wit and will."[21]

The horrors of 1900 notwithstanding, Ji Gong's brand of comedy had an audience. Tales of rogues—or *picaros*—was a booming industry. For the entire Qing Dynasty, into the time of civil war of the 1910s and 1920s, readers loved the picaresque. Popular presses in Beijing and Shanghai produced the tales of Monkey, the comical demon-queller from *Journey to the West*; other episodic tales were also popular. Journeys to the North, to the South and to the East were available as well.[22] Still more rogues emerged from these original adventures. Pigsy from *Journey to the West* had his own story cycle. The band of heroes from the *Enfeoffment of the Gods* had dedicated readers. Even the magistrate Judge Bao appeared in these story cycles as a comic eccentric, a master of disguise.[23] Of course, readers and listeners thrilled to the epic cycle *Shuihu zhuan,* or *Water Margin*. They knew precisely the weaponry, the costumes, the strategies, and the famous lines of all 108 heroes. When Russian diplomat Egor Petrovich Kovelevsky

---

19. Shahar, *Crazy Ji*, 43.

20. Robert Torrance, *The Comic Hero* (Cambridge, Harvard University Press, 1978), 11.

21. Torrance, 11, citing Susan K. Langer.

22. Robert Hegel, *Reading Illustrated Fiction in Late Imperial China* (Stanford: Stanford University press, 1998), 51–63.

23. Anne E. McLaren, *Popular Culture and Ming Chantefables* (Leiden, Brill, 1998), 170–183.

perused the bookstores of Beijing in 1850, he found that the "back rows of the (book) shops are usually crowded with novels ... The greatest fame is enjoyed by the old novels, which are reprinted in hundreds of editions."[24] He was right, as we know from the numbers. Aside from the storyteller scripts and storyteller imitations, there were the smoothly narrated novels, and then there were reprints, sequels, and spin-offs, with single chapters expanded into new books entirely. This was a good crop to harvest. No wonder Guo Xiaoting came out with *The Complete Tales of Lord Ji*, Part II, in 1900.

The picaresque tales that flew off the back shelves were not always well received by the court, however. Imperial censors, in fact, found the "old novels" to be deeply troublesome. Light-hearted and comical though they may be, novels were considered polluting. Censors looked at fiction and saw rebellion. Novels had a terrible reputation. *Water Margin*, though a favorite throughout the Qing, was subjected to heavy-handed censorship. Ambassador Kovelevsky, in his visit to the Beijing bookstore, may have noticed the numbers, but he did not notice the laws. *The Laws and Codes of the Great Qing* (*Da Qing lùli* 大清律例) labeled the book "licentious"; adventure tales undermined that well-ordered cityscape laid out in the police survey. The Qing legal code was clear: "All bookshops that print the licentious story *Water Margin* must be vigorously sought out, and the work prohibited. Both the woodblocks and the printed matter should be burned. In case [it is discovered that] this book is being made, and ... should [an official] himself engrave it, he shall be stripped of office entirely."[25]

If the officials monitored publishers, they monitored ordinary citizens as well. The reading public for these tales of adventure had an official category: "stupid" (*yu* 愚). Those who bought vernacular texts or who listened to storytellers were called *yufuyufu* (愚夫愚婦)[26]—stupid men and stupid women. This official view was more than demeaning, it was damning. The word "stupid" (*yu* 愚) had the connotation of politically dangerous, as in stupefying, deluding, or corrupting. Officials laced their descriptions of local leaders with such terms, accusing them of *yumin* (愚民), deluding the masses. The empire's unsavory elements were bracketed together: the practitioners of cults, the malcontents, the tumultuous, as well as the writers and readers of fiction.

24. Lillian M. Li, Allison J. Dray-Novey, and Haili Kong, *Beijing, From Imperial Capital to Olympic City* (New York, Macmillan, 2007), 92.

25. Hegel, 30–31.

26. McLaren, 285.

This fearful view of popular fiction was not without real bite. Popular fiction and all books were monitored with malign precision. Censors had terrible means at their disposal. When the *Abbreviated History of the Ming History* was published, censors were repelled by some few passages. The author foolishly linked the Manchu people to other "barbarian" peoples. The book itself was quickly suppressed, but the censorship was extended. Those connected with the project were tracked down. The publishers were tried, convicted, and executed, and "those who had merely purchased the book" were punished as well. "Seventy individuals were put to death and their families exiled, their estates confiscated."[27] This is censorship at an impressive level.

The imperial watchdogs and culture police were a ready posse. Fiction could stir up rebellion. In this, as it turns out, they were right. Readers of Qing fiction were truculent. They mimicked their heroes, used gangster argot, practiced swordplay, and gathered and plotted against the state. Mimicry was not the only issue, however. Heroes of the picaresque were considered gods. Ji Gong, in particular, was an unruly saint. The same Boxer rebels who surrounded Beijing in 1900 practiced the cult of Ji Gong.[28] Missionary observers had seen young Boxer soldiers in cult practices: "After greeting the deities and taking their places respectfully on either side of the altar, the little boys suddenly began to look sickly, with red faces and staring eyes; they foamed at the mouth; they began to shout and laugh."[29] These rituals inspired the Boxers. Northern China was a vast terrain of the displaced and desperate; flood, disease, and imperial incompetence had created an impoverished and unstable population, a mob of "hungry, discontented, hopeless idlers," as the American ambassador noted.[30] This northern mob, however, coalesced through cult practices. Ji Gong and other heroes of the waterways and greenwood gave them divine legitimacy.

---

27. Susan Naquin and Evelyn S. Rawski, *Chinese Society in the Eighteenth Century* (New Haven: Yale University Press, 1989), 15.
28. Shahar, *Crazy Ji*, p. 172. Also see Shahar for discussion of reading fiction as religious practice, 6–7. Also see Joseph Esherick (1988), *The Origins of the Boxer Rebellion* (University of California Press), 1988.
29. Chesneaux, Bastid, and Bergere, 342.
30. Larry Clinton Thompson, *William Scott Ament and the Boxer Rebellion: Heroism, Hubris, and the Ideal Missionary* (Jefferson, NC: McFarland, 2009), 30.

Vibeke Bordahl has traced the long histories of "schools"—the specific lines—of storytellers. She has collected performance lineages going back as many as seventy-eight generations. Storytellers of *Water Margin* passed down their knowledge in one famous clan for two hundred years.[31] The Ji Gong stories have had their own great lineage. From storyteller performances to storyteller scripts, to smooth narratives by Qing writers, to contemporary movies, and then to TV shows, Ji Gong has lasted a millennium. He has, in fact, fared better than Confucius. Not that this is surprising. When the court and its revered texts and malign proclamations were abandoned, the oral tradition survived. Performers retained the lore of Ji Gong in their prodigious memories. Nor was Ji Gong a mere entertainer. Though he may be charged with the crime of comedy, his signature off-kilter view is compelling. Indeed, off-kilter has its uses. His anarchical intelligence offers us a refracted view of a difficult age, an age of corrupted authority and unmoored lives—a world in which the Empress had to flee the city dressed as a peasant. The late Qing was not a time for the great lions of history, but was "a world too numbed for tragedy and too disillusioned for glory."[32] Comedy sits in that vacuum, providing an apparently blithe view from the sidelines.

Günter Grass revealed that he preferred the style of the "Spanish and Arab picaresque"; the jester's version reflects the world "in concave and distorting mirrors."[33] Indeed, the picaresque attracts those who live with violence. The talent of the jester for comical escape, offers a model, if not of victory, then at least of survival, as playing the rogue offers useful cover.

Victoria Cass
Baltimore, Maryland

---

31. Vibeke Bordahl and Jette Ross, *Chinese Storytellers' Life and Art in the Yangzhou Tradition* (Boston, Cheng and Tsui, 2002), 68.

32. Torrance, 10.

33. Maya Jaggi, "Slaughterhouse Lives," review of *Pow* by Mo Yan, trans. Howard Goldblatt, *Literary Review* 406 (February, 2013): 47.

CHAPTER 1

Military Finance Officer Li visits Buddha and begs for a son; an immortal lohan descends to earth and begins anew the cycle of reincarnation

THE patchwork robe made for Guang Liang, the newly elected super-intendent of the monks at the Monastery of the Soul's Retreat at Linan, was placed on display before daybreak. It was arranged on a high-backed armchair placed on a low platform to the west of the altar before the huge statue of the boddhisatva Guan Yin. In the morning when the sun shone through the door, it illuminated each scrap of precious brocade and every bit of exquisite embroidery with the unusually fine stitching that made the robe a dazzling ceremonial vestment.

The monks had begged for these scraps at the gate of every great fam-ily in Linan, the twelfth-century capital of the Southern Song Dynasty of China. The monastery was the most important temple in the empire and, as the monks explained, Guang Liang would some day almost certainly become its abbot when the old abbot was no more. People had gladly contributed not only material, but also money for the sewing, which was done at the finest shop in Linan.

In the first two hours of its showing, most of the monks, with the exception of the abbot, had seen the robe. Soon wealthy matrons would be pointing out their bits of brocade to their friends, but before that could happen, the robe suddenly disappeared. No one knew where it had gone, but all the monks guessed that Dao Ji, the Chan (Zen) monk, had taken it, and he was missing.

Who was this Dao Ji? He was the son of a military officer, Li Maoqun. Li was usually addressed as Li Yuanwai. Most respected gentlemen were called *yuanwai* in the time of the Southern Song Dynasty. In the fourth year of that dynasty (1131 C.E.), Li was living not far from the capital Hangzhou, more commonly called Linan in those times.

Li was registered as a native of the Tiantai district in Taizhoufu, a pre-fecture in the east-central portion of the province of Zhejiang. His wife was called Wang Shi, meaning a wife from the Wang family, since women usually continued to be called by their maiden names after marriage.

This couple loved the virtuous life. Li Yuanwai was extremely kind to others and not unduly severe toward the soldiers he commanded. Because of this, his reputation as a good officer was widespread. At home he was pleasant and generous, and outside his home he helped those in danger and relieved those in distress with padded clothing in winter and draughts of medicine in summer. When Li Yuanwai walked along the street, people generally called him Virtuous Li, but a few among them disagreed, saying, "If he is truly virtuous, why is there not a son?"

Li Maoqun overheard this talk, so later, when his wife saw him come home sad and dejected, she asked why he was unhappy. Her husband said, "When I was strolling in the street, almost everyone was calling me Virtuous Li, but among them there were some who said privately, but so that I could hear, that, if I were truly good it would not be possible for me to be without a son. I think that heaven has its spirits and the Buddha has his spirits, and if we ask, it is in their power to permit us to have a child."

"Why not take a second wife or buy two concubines and have a son and a daughter?" urged his wife.

Her husband said, "Oh, my wife, it is wrong to say such words. How could I do such a stupid thing! My wife, you are only approaching forty. You can still give birth to sons or daughters. You and I will purify ourselves by fasting and bathing for three days and then go to the Guojing temple on Tiantai mountain, beyond Yongning village. There we will worship Buddha and beg for a son. If heaven above has eyes, you and I, husband and wife, may still have a child."

"Very good," said Wang Shi.

Li Yuanwai selected a date, and with his wife riding in a cart while he rode a horse, they and their party of servants reached the foot of Tiantai mountain. They looked up at the mountain rising up to meet the clouds, its peaks standing erect, the dense forests and the Guojing temple halfway to the top. When they reached the outside of the temple, they saw how large and high the monastery gate appeared. Inside there were two towers, one for the drum and one for the bell. Just beyond was the purification hall for the guests, the hall for reading the sutras or scriptures of Buddhism, and a large building with twenty-five rooms for storing the complete religious library of Buddhism, the *Tripitaka*.

Li Yuanwai got down from his horse. From within, the monks came out to greet the couple. At the great hall they were offered tea. The master of the temple, old Abbot Gong, came himself to welcome them and took them to each place where they were to burn incense. Husband and wife first went to the imposing Hall of Treasures and prayed. They knelt to ask the immortal Buddha to bless them, saying, "As we renew the incense, teach us a thousand times ten thousand times that we may have a son. If Buddha, the founder, will manifest his spirit, we will make extensive repairs to an old temple and fashion a golden image. This is our prayer." On they went, burning incense at each place.

When they reached the Lohan Hall, containing images of *lohan* (disciples of Buddha), they also burned incense. When they were standing in front of the fourth *lohan*, they saw the image slip from its pedestal. Since the words "fall to earth" when used by Buddhists also means "be born into the world," the senior priest Gong said, "Your prayer is answered! Your prayer is answered! You will certainly have an honorable son. When the day comes, I will come to wish you happiness."

Li Yuanwai returned home with his wife and servants. Without knowing it, his wife became pregnant and after some months gave birth to a boy. At the time of the birth, a red light seemed to fill the courtyard and there was a strong odor of a strange perfume. Li Yuanwai was extremely happy, even though the newborn cried continuously, never ceasing straight through to the third day.

On this third day, just as the relatives and friends in the community came to offer congratulations, some neighbors came in to say that Abbot Gong of the Guojing monastery had come personally to give the official his kind regards and offer his good wishes.

Li Yuanwai went to welcome him and Abbot Gong said, "I can see that you are very happy. Is your son well?"

"From the time he was born, he has cried without ceasing," Li Yuanwai replied. "I feel very anxious about this. Does the revered monk have some subtle way to cure this?"

Abbot Gong said, "It is easily managed. If you will go into the house and carry your son outside, I will take a look, and then I will understand the cause."

Li Yuanwai said uneasily, "The child is not yet a full month old. I am afraid it will not be right to carry him outside."

Abbot Gong said, "There will be no harm. Simply wrap him loosely in a robe. The three lights of the sun, moon, and stars will not harm him."

As soon as Li Yuanwai heard this reasonable suggestion, he went quickly and carried the child out. The boy, who was born with an attractive face, clear-cut features, and a pleasant personality, was still crying without stopping. As soon as Abbot Gong came over and looked at him, his crying mouth stretched into a smile.

The old monk stroked the top of the child's head with his hand and said, "Do not smile. Do not smile. I know your past history, you coming and I going. How can the great provincial families be so confident of their futures?"

The child immediately stopped crying, and the monk said, "May I take a disciple's name and give it to him as a remembrance? He would be called Li Xiuyuan—meaning 'Li who restores those harmed by malevolent influences, either from their own previous incarnations or from the wrongful acts of others.'"

Li Yuanwai assented and carried the child inside. A little later the father came out, saying that food was prepared for the monk.

The relatives and friends scattered and soon senior monk Gong also left.

Li Yuanwai hired a wet nurse to assist in caring for the child. The child grew and became strong.

Light is like an arrow, the days and months like a weaver's shuttle. The years passed with the parents hardly aware of them, and Li Xiuyuan reached the age of seven. They had never intended that he should simply gather with the village boys, idly talking and laughing. So his parents decided that his studies should begin. An old graduate, Du Qunying, was hired to teach the boy at the instructor's home. There were two others in the class. One was Han Wenmei, the son of Han Wenzheng, a military man, filial and upright, from Yongning village. The other was Wang Shi's nephew, Wang Zhuan, who lived in Jiuning village. He was the son of Wang Anshi, the commander of a military unit. Wang Zhuan was eight years old.

The three boys studied together and truly enjoyed one another's friendship. Li Xiuyuan was the youngest, but he never forgot what had once passed before his eyes. He advanced rapidly as he studied, and surpassed ordinary students in talent. Master Du thought this remarkable, and often said to people that he had waited long for such a talent as that of Li Xiuyuan.

When he reached the age of fourteen, Li Xiuyuan had great skill in reciting passages from the *Four Books* of the philosopher Confucius, as well as the *Five Classics,* and numerous works of other ancient Chinese philosophers discussing Confucianism. Together with the two others, Wang and Han, he was constantly composing poems and reciting them in a loud voice.

That year they were thinking of taking the provincial examinations as degree candidates. But Xiuyuan's father fell sick and could not get out of bed. He was in a serious condition, too ill to be aware of what other people were doing. Someone sent for Wang Anshi, his wife's younger brother, to come to his bedside.

Li Yuanwai said, "My dear brother, I will not be long in the world of men. Your nephew and your older sister will need you to take care of them. Xiuyuan cannot always be a student. I have made arrangements for him to marry a girl of the Liu family in the Village of the Thousand Gates. She has no one living in her immediate family. I depend upon you, younger brother, to manage everything regarding this."

Wang Anshi said, "Husband of my older sister, let your heart be at rest and take care of your illness. You need not instruct me further. I will take care of the matter myself."

Li Yuanwai also said to Wang Shi, "Dear wife, I am fifty-five years old now and so cannot be said to be dying young. After I die, above all things take care of our boy and teach him to become famous. Even though my soul is beneath the dreadful Yellow Springs, I will be joyous."

Finally he gave Xiuyuan several sentences of instruction, but alas, his heart was in turmoil and his mouth and eyes closed in death. As soon as Li Yuanwai died, the family wept together.

Officer Wang helped with all the details of the bereavement. Since Xiuyuan remained in mourning, he could not take part in the examinations. That year Wang Zhuan and Han Wenmei both obtained their *Xiucai*, or bachelor's degrees, and both families were congratulated.

In the home of Wang Shi there was an upper room that the family called the meditation tower. There, a record was kept of the family's financial and other affairs up to each year's end. This would be written in the form of a table and offered up to heaven together with the bills of account, without hiding the truth and keeping nothing back. There Li Xiuyuan began to develop an interest in the study of Daoism. The practice of this religion often included elements of herbal medicine, alchemy, numerology, exorcism, and black magic. Whenever he saw one of the Daoist scriptures, he would read it through without stopping.

Two years passed, and his mother fell sick and died. Li Xiuyuan wept for her alone. Officer Wang helped and managed the funeral arrangements.

Until the age of eighteen Li Xiuyuan continued to like Daoist books. When in that year his mourning was completed, he changed from his mourning clothes and immediately left home. He had been contemplating the red dust of mortality, his broken world, and his various problems. All the affairs at home were being taken care of by his uncle and did not need his attention. Li Xiuyuan went to the family grave, burned some sheets of paper spirit money, left a note for Officer Wang, and then immediately went away.

When Officer Wang had not seen him for two days, he sent a man to look for him. The man did not find the nephew, but he did find the note. Officer Wang opened the note and read, "Xiuyuan has left. You need not look for him. In some other year we will meet and you will know the result."

Because Officer Wang knew that his nephew had recently been going to the Anguan temple in the neighborhood to study Buddhism and Daoism, he sent someone there to look for the boy. However, the people at the temple had not seen him. Wang also sent men to put up white placards in various places. On them he had written that any person who came with Li Xiuyuan to his home would be given one hundred ounces of white silver in reward; and any person who knew where the boy actually was and sent a letter about him would be given fifty ounces of silver. After three months, Uncle Wang and his people still had no idea where Xiuyuan had gone.

After Li Xiuyuan had broken contact with his home, he wandered aimlessly to nearby Linan. When he had spent all his money, he went into a temple and asked to leave the world. The monks there, however, did not dare to keep him because he was obviously a runaway from a good family.

Li Xiuyuan next went to the Monastery of the Soul's Retreat that occupied a large tract of ground facing the city from across the West Lake, considered to be one of the most beautiful spots in China. There he asked to see the master of the temple.

The abbot, Yuan Kong, a Buddhist of the ninth degree, was aged and feeble, but his mind was still strong and his understanding profound. When Xiuyuan was brought before him, the old monk knew at once that the youth was the reincarnation of the golden-bodied *lohan* who subjugates tigers and dragons. *Lohan* were commonly believed to be powerful spirits of former teachers of Buddhism, filled with infinite compassion. However, in order to enter Nirvana, the state of having attained enlightenment and the freeing of the self, these *lohan* had to pass through countless reincarnations because of the burden of their human faults.

The abbot could not change the direction of the boy's destiny, but he could help him with his teaching. The abbot was master of nine different schools of Buddhism. He, therefore, was able to train a disciple in whichever of these denominations seemed most suitable. After observing Xiu-yuan's natural gifts and disposition, the old man decided that the boy should become a Chan monk, "Chan" being the Chinese pronunciation of "Zen" in Japanese. The abbot named him Dao Ji, meaning "salvation through Buddhist wisdom." He would no longer use the name Xiuyuan.

Chan Buddhism stressed meditation, but it also laid great emphasis on using insight and rational thinking to solve problems and find practical solutions. Chan monks during the Song dynasty had already earned a reputation for challenging Buddhist rules and ignoring conventional social behavior.

> Even in tranquil courtyards bright with flowers,
> You dare not say all's well. Though walls and gates
> Be higher than the tallest tall man's head,
> Malicious spirits that may hear such words
> Will fly like locusts to invade each quiet spot.

> Confucian duties, Daoist spells
> And Buddha's promise of release from karma's chains
> Together share the minds of thoughtful folk.

> Both heaven and hell with countless gods and demons
> Mirror the earth in all its vast complexity.
> Souls of the dead roam ceaselessly
> Until they may be born on earth once more.

> On earth among the living, wandering monks of Chan
> Respect what seems the best in every discipline,
> Yet mock pretense and all external trappings
> And work mysteriously to gain their ends.

The prevailing practice in the Monastery of the Soul's Retreat was more conservative, however, and many of the monks felt that this Chan novice was pursuing ideas contrary to their own. It was inevitable that he should be criticized, and even taunted. Once, while meditating, he remained so long in concentration that he became confused and disoriented. As a result, some of the others began to call him Ji Dian, meaning "Mad Ji." Thereafter the rumor persisted, and even spread beyond the monastery, that he was indeed insane.

In spite of efforts to destroy his reputation, he afterward became known as Ji Gong by many people outside the monastery. During some earlier dynasties, "Gong" had been the title of a duke. Thus, when people called him Ji Gong, it was very much like calling him High and Noble

Lord Ji. It was a title reserved for those most revered and appreciated.

As for the young Dao Ji, he passed through his three years of training, ignoring the taunts. He received his certificate and became a full-fledged monk. Even then, however, he was not accepted by the other monks, and his isolation from them grew.

Here and there about the monastery Dao Ji observed that individuals had little hoards of money that they had kept from the offerings of the visiting faithful. This all too common practice of subtracting a percentage of everything that fell into one's hands was called a "squeeze." The monks used their squeeze for new robes or sandals, or for some extra food beyond the day's single meal.

Every few days Dao Ji would take the money from one or two of the little hoards and disappear from the monastery. He would spend the money in restaurants dining on dishes made with meat and fish and drinking wine, all of which he particularly loved. When people used to say to him that monks should eat only vegetarian meals, he responded with half-concealed mockery, saying, "The founder of Buddhism left us a verse which goes, 'Some improve their hearts but neglect their mouths; others help their mouths but neglect their hearts.' If I only improve my heart but neglect my mouth, then I would be failing to maintain my body and so be ungrateful to Guang Liang, the superintendent of the monks, who is like my father and mother who gave me this body."

After a day or two in the city, he would return and, except for attending the noon meal, he would usually spend his time studying alone in the upper part of the Great Memorial Pagoda.

Shortly before this period, the superintendent of monks was transferred to another temple. The monks chose one of their group, Guang Liang, to be the new superintendent. He ranked next to the abbot in authority. Guang Liang was just a little bit fat from the tidbits he snatched between meals, and his smooth, moon-shaped face had a look of calm and benign authority. However, Dao Ji knew that the new superintendent was a man without learning and that there was certainly nothing holy about him. Dao Ji could see nothing in him except an ambitious desire to control the great Monastery of the Soul's Retreat.

The old abbot who had been Dao Ji's teacher was a wise and saintly man. The thought that Guang Liang would one day take the place of the abbot was intolerable to Dao Ji. When the costly silk patchwork robe was placed on display before being presented to Guang Liang by the monks, Dao Ji waited for his chance. When no one was watching, he stole the

robe and pawned it. That night he feasted in the city. In the morning he
returned and pasted the pawn ticket high on the monastery gate.

When Superintendent Guang Liang saw that the robe was gone, he
sent the monks looking for it everywhere. The monks were not permitted to paste announcements or anything else on the monastery gate, so
when some of them saw the piece of paper pasted high on the gate, they
removed it. When they saw what it was, they took it to redeem the robe.
Guang Liang meanwhile went to the master of the temple, the abbot, and
complained: "The crazy monk in this temple is not peaceful and virtuous
according to our rules. He constantly steals all the monk's clothing, money,
and other things. These actions call for severe measures! We must control him now and punish him for his offenses!"

The master of the temple, Yuan Kong, countered: "Dao Ji has no stolen goods in his possession; he cannot be punished. What you should do
is carry out a secret investigation and, if there is evidence of theft, bring
him to me."

Superintendent Guang Liang dispatched two acolytes to keep Ji Gong
under secret observation. Ji Gong was sleeping in the Hall of Great Treasures with his head on the altar table. The two little monks, Zhi Ching
and Zhi Ming, exercising great caution, watched him each day. One day
they saw him come out stealthily from the great hall and go around looking everywhere for some time. Afterward he looked in at the hall, went
back inside, and came out again, walking furtively. He was holding close
to his chest an old mat wrapped around something. Just as he was walking along the center of an old alley between some buildings in the temple
grounds, he saw Zhi Ching and Zhi Ming, who said, "Good Ji Dian, what
did you steal now? You can stop thinking about getting away." Going over
and thrusting out their arms, they caught Ji Gong and went at once to the
rooms of the master of the temple.

The superintendent of the monks first said to the abbot, "The temple
master knows that here in an eminent temple Ji Dian has failed to obey
the regulations. Since he has stolen temple property, he must be punished
according to our laws."

When the master of the temple, Yuan Kong, heard this, he thought
to himself: "Dao Ji, if you have stolen temple property, I cannot ask them
to accept this. Even though I would like to give you sanctuary, there is
nothing I can say." Then he said to the others, "Just have the people bring
him forward."

When Ji Gong came into the front room of the master of the temple he said, "Oh, there you are, Elder Monk. I have been meditating." Whenever he saw the senior monk, Ji Gong spoke in this manner. Yuan Kong for his part did not require him to kneel and touch his forehead to the ground in the traditional kowtow.

The abbot said to him, "Dao Ji, you have not been keeping the temple rules. You have stolen temple property. How shall you be punished?"

"Destroy his garments, his rice bowl, and the certificate of his Buddhist vow! Send him out of the temple! Do not authorize him to be a monk!" exclaimed the superintendent of the monks.

The old master of the temple said to himself, "I will simply censure him severely." He then said to Ji Gong, "Dao Ji, take out the things that you have stolen and show them to us."

"Teacher, they are truly taking advantage of me. I have been sleeping in the Hall of the Great Treasures. While I was sweeping the floor, I noticed that there was no trash container, so I was carrying everything out in my arms. Wait and I'll show you." Having said this, Ji Gong loosened the flat silken cords that tied the matting, and with a thunderous noise the dirt and dust from inside fell to the floor.

The master of the temple, in an extremely angry voice, said, "Superintendent Guang Liang, you have maliciously accused a good person of stealing. This merits severe censure. Beat the sounding board and call the monks together. Instruct them that the entire temple must be thoroughly swept."

The monks all assembled hurriedly, each one paying no attention to anyone else and each making a great deal of noise. In the confusion, Ji Gong walked out of the temple unnoticed. He went out through the monastery gate, down the mountainside, and into the forest near the West Lake.

CHAPTER 2

Dong Shihong sells a daughter to bury a relative;
the living lohan rescues a virtuous man

Where does the Spirit dwell?
From home you need not part.
The way's not deep or far.
A spring's beneath your heart.
There's help for those who seek;
Don't be ashamed to ask
Nor fear that you may not
Be equal to the task.

AS Ji Gong walked into the forest beside the West Lake, he suddenly saw a man preparing to hang himself. The monk understood at once a great deal about the man, having made a quick estimate of the man's natural inclination to goodness.

The man was surnamed Dong, with the personal name of Shihong, and his native place was Qiantang prefecture in the province of Zhejiang. His unusual filial piety was shown in his treatment of his mother, who was named Qin Shi, because she came from the Qin family. He had lost his father early in life. Dong Shihong's wife, Du Shi, had died young, leaving a daughter named Yujie, who was very intelligent and bright.

Dong Shihong was an artisan who beat gold into sheets of gold leaf. When his daughter was eight years old, his mother, Qin Shi, became bedridden with a severe illness. Though he took care of her, the family was poor, and he was unable to manage its affairs. Therefore he pawned his daughter, Yujie, to go as a serving maid in the home of scholar Gu in exchange for fifty ounces of silver. He used the money to take care of the old lady.

When his mother did not see Yujie, she asked, "Where is my granddaughter?"

Dong Shihong said that she had gone to stay with her aunt. His mother's sickness worsened; she was unable to get up for seven days, and suddenly she was dead. He then had to use the few ounces of silver remaining for her funeral.

He then went to the town of Jiangfu and there worked continuously, carrying the heaviest load of work possible. With great difficulty he accumulated the sixty ounces of fine silver ingots needed to repay the original amount he had borrowed, plus interest. At last, he thought, he could redeem his daughter and take her back to the family home.

Along the road he talked to no one. When he reached Linan, he stayed overnight at the Yuelai Inn outside the Qiantang gate. He had his silver with him. The next day he walked on to Baijiajuan and began asking about senior graduate Gu. The neighbors all said that old master Gu had been promoted to the foreign office, and they did not know where he was performing his official duties. When Dong Shihong heard this, it was as if he had been standing at the top of an immensely tall pagoda and had lost his footing.

At the bank of the Qiantang River, he asked all the workers who pulled the old decaying barges up and down the river whether they remembered moving the household furniture of official Gu. No one knew which way the eminent master Gu had gone, nor did they know what had become of Dong Shihong's daughter.

When Dong Shihong came to the outside of the Qiantang gate, he had a few drinks in his sorrow at the India Street Inn. Hardly knowing it, he became drunk and entered the land of dreams. Waking, he left the inn, and shortly after stopped to look around. Without realizing it, he had taken the wrong road and was lost himself. He had also lost the silver ingots. Somehow, just as he had awakened, he had touched his clothing and the silver had fallen out. The shock of this discovery was overwhelming, and he was unable to endure the realization.

As he walked toward the forest, the more he thought, the more life lost its flavor. He thought he would never be able to see his daughter's face again. Existence had become worse than death. He felt that he was suffering the consequence of a terrible sin. Thinking these thoughts as he walked into the forest, he unwound the long sash from around his waist and made it into a noose, intending to hang himself.

Suddenly he saw coming toward him from the opposite direction a Buddhist monk who was saying to himself, "Dead, dead! Once dead and that's the end. Death is better than living. I want to hang myself, so I have taken off my sash. Now I want to tie it up in the tree."

Dong Shihong was quite surprised to hear this. Raising his head, he saw that the monk presented a most unseemly appearance.

> Head unshaven, face unwashed,
> Drink-blurred, slanting, blinking eyes;
> Whether stupid or acting so,
> Or dangerously mad,
> His tattered clothing full of holes,
> His long sash tied into a noose,
> And monks' shoes worn to shreds,
> With legs half bare and ankles red,
> He'd waded streams and crossed the hills,
> As if there were no obstacles
> And all were level ground.
> Here among China's rivers and lakes,
> Between the earth and the sky,
> He wandered as he must.
> He did not meditate chant.
> By some admired, by some despised,
> Drinking and eating fish and meat,
> Carousing through the night or day,
> He charmed his friends, dismayed his foes,
> And many wrongs he put to right.

When Dong Shihong heard the monk say, "I want to hang myself. I just want to put the noose around my neck and hang," Dong quickly went over to him. "Monk, why do you seek to shorten your life?" he asked.

Ji Gong replied, "My teacher spent three long years instructing me while living on the contributions of the worshippers. Putting aside a little day by day and month by month, it was very difficult to get together five ounces of silver. Finally I received my teacher's orders. He sent me to buy two monks' garments and two monks' hats. I like to drink wine very, very much. In the wine shop, because I greedily drank two extra measures of wine, I got tipsy, then drunk, and then very drunk, and lost the five ounces of silver. I intended to go back to the temple to see my teacher, but then I was afraid that the old monk would be angry. The more I thought about it, the angrier I became. I kept thinking 'What a life! A story without a title!' Therefore I want to hang myself."

When Dong Shihong heard this, he said, "Monk, you may be distressed about a few ounces of silver, but not to the point of dying. I still have five or six ounces in odd bits of silver in my bag. I am already a dead man, and there is no reason for me to keep them. Come, I will give you these five or six ounces and help you." Thrusting out his hand, he gave a small purse to the monk.

The monk took it in his hand, laughed, "Ha! Ha!" and said, "This silver of yours, however, is not such a good kind as mine was. Besides, it's all broken up into different-sized pieces."

When Dong Shihong heard this, he was not very happy, and thought to himself, "I did a bit of pointless charity in giving you that silver, since you complain that it is no good." Then he said to him, "Monk, go and use that to pay back the money."

The monk assented and said, "I'm going."

Dong Shihong thought to himself, "This monk absolutely does not understand the customs of the world concerning favors asked and done. I gave him this silver that he did not appreciate and that he said was not good. Then, when he was going, he didn't even ask my name and didn't know enough to thank me. Truly he is of an uncouth generation. Anyway, as for myself, I am about to die."

Just as he was feeling resentful, he saw the monk coming back, and heard him say, "As soon as I saw the silver, I forgot everything else and didn't even ask the kind gentleman's honorable name and why he is here."

Dong Shihong told him the entire story about losing the silver ingots. The monk said, "Ah, you also lost some silver. Since father and daughter cannot see each other, you hang yourself. Well I'm going."

When Dong Shihong heard this, he said, "This monk really doesn't understand proper courtesies. He doesn't know how to talk to people."

He saw the monk walk five or six steps and then come back saying, "Dong Shihong, are you really going to die, or are you pretending?"

Dong Shihong said, "What if I am really going to die?"

The monk said, "If you are really going to die, you can do me a genuine favor. The complete outfit of clothing you are wearing is worth five or six ounces of silver, and you are leaving it for the wolves to eat and the dogs to gnaw. What a useless waste! Take your clothes off and give them to me. You dropped into the world naked; go out the same way. Wouldn't that be better?"

When Dong Shihong heard this speech, his entire body began to shake, and he said, "A good monk you are! You really understand friendship! As a casual friend, I gave you several ounces of silver. I have been burning paper to call up a devil!"

The monk clapped his hands, and laughing loudly said, "Very good! Very good! You must not get excited. I only asked you. You lost your money, so you were going to die. Fifty or sixty ounces of silver do not amount to anything. I will take you to find your daughter and cause you and your daughter to come back together. Flesh and bone reunited. How about it? Congratulations!"

Dong Shihong said, "Monk, I lost the money to redeem my daughter—if I don't have the money, how is it possible that we can be reunited?"

The monk answered, "It's all right. I have a way. You come with me."

Dong Shihong asked, "Monk, where is your temple? Where can one find it, and what are your honorable names?"

Ji Gong replied, "I came to the West Lake hurriedly from the Monastery of the Soul's Retreat. My name is Dao Ji. People call me Ji Dian, the mad monk."

Dong Shihong realized that the monk did not speak in an unrefined manner. Rewinding the sash around his waist, Dong Shihong asked, "Where did you say you were going, Teacher?"

Ji Gong said, "Walk!" Turning, he led Dong Shihong straight ahead. The monk was singing a mountain song:

> Walk, walk, walk and roam, roam, roam.
> There is no better way than this to pass the spring and fall.
> Now today I feel how good it is to be a monk.
> Now I do regret those years I had to spend in toil.
> Now I see that love is an illusion.
> Now I feel that wives are all a snare.
> What can equal crossing fields and rivers?
> What can equal the gourd in my bare hands?
> What can equal the sound of wind and rain?
> What can equal the slowly fading day?
> Happy now from morn to night and no one cares about me.
> Never a vexation, never something sad.
> Hemp sandals striding over field and stream,
> Ragged monk's robe and head as smooth as satin.
> I can be gentle or I can be hard.
> Outside my body there's a world of new delights.
> It doesn't matter if the earth wants skulls and bones.
> Caring not for heaven, stopping not for earth,
> Happy as a powerful prince,
> I can sing songs and make them up as well.
> I can doze whenever I am tired,
> Then when I wake, I can quickly go again
> Back to the world's affairs.

The monk went on with Dong Shihong through the Qiantang gate into Linan and stopped inside a small lane. There he spoke to Dong Shihong, saying, "You stand here inside this lane. Don't wander off. In a little while, a person will ask you your birthday and your age. Just answer him. Today I am going to bring you two, father and daughter, face to face, flesh and bone back together."

Dong Shihong agreed and said, "Saintly monk, you are most compassionate and kind."

The monk turned his head and looked. On the north side of the road was a large gateway. Inside the gateway stood twenty or thirty of the household's people. From the tablet hung above the gate, he knew that it was the home of a government official.

The monk proceeded up the steps and said, "Excuse me, gentlemen. Is this the house of the Zhao family?"

The household people, glancing quickly, saw that he was a poor monk and said, "You are not wrong. Our master is named Zhao. What are you doing here?"

The monk replied, "I have heard people say that the old lady of your honorable house is sick in body and gravely sinking, and that it is feared that she may die. I came especially to see your master and to offer a cure for the old lady."

When the family's people heard the monk's words, one of them said, "Monk, your arrival is most opportune. You are not wrong about what you have heard. Because the young master of the house became seriously ill, the old mistress was so concerned about the child that she became disturbed and fell ill. A great many doctors have come to see her, but there has been no sign of improvement. The master of the house, Zhao Wenhui, is most filial toward his mother, and from the first, when he saw the old lady's illness grow more serious, invited famous medical men to come."

The man continued, "There is a *yuanwai* named Su whose personal name is Beishan. In his home there is also an old lady who became sick. They invited a gentleman named Li Huaiqun, who is well versed in herbal medical science, to examine her. The master of the house has just now gone to the Su home to invite that gentleman to come here."

Even as he spoke, a group of horsemen came riding up with three men at the front. The first, a good-looking man riding a white horse, wore a square cap on his head topped by a jade flower with two ribbon streamers. On his body he wore the blue satin leisure coat of a gentleman. It was embroidered with a design of bats and butterflies. This man was Li Huaiqun, a cousin of Zhao Wenhui.

The second wore a double-butterfly treasure-blue jacket and a blue satin gentleman's cap with three embroidered blue flowers. He wore a soft blue satin leisure garment and black palace-style shoes. His face was like the waning moon, eyebrows compassionate and eyes benevolent. Three long strands of beard, blown by the wind, went sweeping across his chest. This was Su Beishan.

The third was also dressed like a wealthy official with a white face, long beard, and handsome features.

When the monk had finished looking at them, he went over and, stopping the horses, said, "Will the three gentlemen go more slowly? I have been waiting for you for some time."

Zhao Wenhui, the third of the three riders, seeing the monk walk into the road, said, "We have urgent business, monk; we have invited this gentleman to cure my old mother's illness. You should come to solicit funds on another day. Today it is not possible to talk with you."

The monk said, "Not possible, you say! But, I am not soliciting alms. Today I heard it said that the force of the illness influencing the old lady in your residence has grown more severe. I have made a vow to treat those who have become ill, wherever they may be. Today I came with the special intention of treating your mother's illness."

Zhao Wenhui said, "The gentleman I have invited here is the most famous doctor of the present age. You can go away. We are not using you."

As soon as the monk heard this, he turned his head and, looking at Li Huaiqun, said, "Sir, even though you are a famous doctor, I can still teach you what illness one kind of medicine can cure."

Doctor Li asked, "What kind of medicine are you talking about, monk?"

Ji Gong asked in return, "What illness can be cured by biscuits hot out of the oven?"

Doctor Li replied, "I don't know. They are not among the herbal medicines."

The monk laughed. "Ha! Ha! You don't even know one of the most important principles and still dare to call yourself a famous doctor! Biscuits that come out of the oven cure hunger. Isn't that right? You didn't know that! I had better come with you into the Zhao home and help you."

Li Huaiqun said, "Good! Monk, you just come with me."

Zhao Wenhui and Su Beishan could not very well keep him back—the only thing they could do was to go on through the gateway with the monk. When they entered the old lady's house and sat down, they were given tea by the house servants.

Doctor Li examined the old lady and said that she had a collection of bloody mucus in her throat, and that she could not become well except by expectorating it. The old lady was advanced in years. Both her spirit and her blood were deficient, so medicine could not be used. Official Zhao was then asked whether there was anything else he wanted the doctor to do.

Zhao Wenhui said, "Sir, my field is not medicine, but I know that there are famous doctors. You may recommend someone in addition, if you choose."

Doctor Li said, "Here in Linan there are only two outstanding doctors—myself and Tang Wanfang. Those people that he can cure, I can cure; those that he cannot, I also cannot. We two have the same capabilities."

When they had conversed just to this point, Ji Gong spoke up. "You need not all become alarmed. First, let me look at the old lady."

Zhao Wenhui was first of all a caring son, and as soon as he heard the monk's words, he said, "Good. Come and look." Li Huaiqun also wanted to observe the monk's capabilities.

When Ji Gong approached the old lady, he patted her twice on the head and said, "Old lady, you are not going to die. Your head is still hard."

Li Huaiqun asked, "What are you saying, monk?"

Ji Gong said, "I will summon the phlegm and make it come out, and then everything will be all right." Going around to the front of the old lady, he said, "Phlegm, phlegm, come out quickly! You're blocking up the old lady enough to kill her."

Doctor Li laughed, but just as he said, "Isn't that a bit unprofessional?" he saw the old lady cough up a mouthful of mucus.

Ji Gong put out his hand with a piece of medicine in it, saying, "Bring me a bowl of water." It was brought to him by one of the household servants.

Zhao Wenhui looked and asked, "Monk, what is that medicine? Can it cure my mother's illness?"

Ji Gong laughed loudly, and holding out the medicine in his hand answered, "This medicine that I carry has endless uses. It completely cures numerous symptoms of many diseases. It is the Eight Treasure Pill to Restore the Dead. It is by no means one that may lie loosely with other medicines." After Ji Gong had spoken, he placed the pill in the bowl, saying, "The old lady is in this state because of anxiety. Now that she is relieved of the mucus she will grow stronger. Very soon she will fall into a stupor and not awaken immediately. Wait and take good care of her. As she takes the medicine, some good results will be seen immediately."

As soon as Zhao Wenhui heard this, he realized that Ji Gong had an extensive medical background and that he had explained the cause exactly. Excitedly he began to speak: "Saintly monk, you are really too kind. It was because my mother was so fond of the child that she became ill with anxiety. I have a boy aged six who is suffering from a retributive illness. He complains of a wrong having been done to someone else, but no one knows what it is. He is still in a delirium and has not awakened. When my mother became disturbed about the boy, her throat became congested. If, my teacher, you are to cure my mother completely, I must also ask the monk to cure my little child."

Since the old lady had now awakened, the monk had her drink the medicine, and she recovered completely. Zhao Wenhui went to her and paid his respects. In addition, he kowtowed to the monk and asked him to cure his son.

Ji Gong said, "It is also not difficult to cure your son. It is, however, necessary that we obtain one thing. After that I can manage the cure very well."

Zhao Wenhui asked what that necessary thing was. Ji Gong would not be hurried nor pressured into explaining that the thing needed to make the entire family of Zhao Wenhui well again was to bring Dong Shihong and his daughter together.

CHAPTER 3

The arts of Chan cure illness in the Zhao home; Buddha's laws operate in secret to end sorrows

AFTER Ji Gong had restored the mother of Zhao Wenhui to health, there was still the six-year-old son to attend to. Ji Gong said, "I can cure him, but there is a supplementary element which is difficult to find. This is needed to introduce the other medicine. There must be a fifty-two-year-old man who must also have been born on the fifth day of the fifth month, and a nineteen-year-old girl born on the fifth day of the eighth month. The tears of these two people can be combined into a medicine. Then I can make the cure complete."

Su Beishan and Li Huaiqun could see that the monk truly had a remarkable lineage. They asked the monk where he lived and what honorable names he was called. He answered each of their questions.

Zhao Wenhui went outside and sent people to search for a fifty-two-year-old man had been born on the fifth day of the fifth month.

At first they asked among those in the household itself and in the homes of relatives and friends nearby. They found no one. If the age was right, the birthday was wrong. If the month and day were right, the year was wrong. The crowd kept searching until they reached the gate. There they saw a man standing outside whose years seemed to be about half a hundred. One of the family, Zhao Liansheng, quickly went over to him and raising his clasped hands in greeting asked, "May I ask Brother's name?"

He replied, "My surname is Dong, and my personal name is Shihong. My family came from Qiantang. I am waiting here for a man."

The family member asked, "Is the elder brother fifty-two years old?" The answer was "You are not wrong." Again the family member questioned him. "Were you born on the fifth day of the fifth month?" Again the answer was "You are not wrong." The family member, quickly taking him by the hand, said, "Master Dong, you come with me. The head of our household has invited you to come in."

Dong Shihong asked, "How does your honorable household head know me? Tell me and I will go with you."

The family member then explained in detail the reason for the search and the need for the supplementary medicine. Dong Shihong then went in with him. There he saw Ji Gong, Zhao Wenhui, and the others. The family member introduced him to everyone.

Ji Gong said, "Now, quickly find the nineteen-year-old girl who was born on the fifth day of the eighth month."

As soon as Dong Shihong heard the age and birthdate, which were the same as those of his daughter, his heart moved swiftly. Just then he saw one of the household people come in who said, "Auntie Gu found that the slave girl, Spring Maid, is nineteen and was born on the fifth day of the eighth month, and has called her."

Then Dong Shihong saw a girl come in from outside. As soon as he saw that it was his own daughter, his heart was filled with anguish, and his tears began to fall. When the girl saw that it was her father, she also started crying.

The master of the household where she originally had been was named Gu. At that time he had only recently returned from the diplomatic corps. When Scholar Gu had been given a new post, Auntie Gu and Spring Maid had become part of the Zhao household. Father and daughter were each weeping bitterly as they saw the other's face.

The monk laughed, "Ha! Ha!" and exclaimed, "Excellent! Excellent! Today I have made three for one, and how delightful the three are!" Putting out his hand, he received the medicinal tears. Holding them in his palm, he called for a household person to dissolve the medicine in water. Ji Gong then had them wash young Master Zhao with the mixture. In a little while, the boy's facial expression became normal, his delirium was gone, and his illness was completely cured.

The monk told Zhao Wenhui the entire story of how Dong Shihong had lost the money and had been about to hang himself and how he, Ji Gong, had saved him and brought father and daughter together.

Zhao Wenhui rewarded Dong Shihong by giving him one hundred ounces of silver and allowing him take his daughter away with him. Afterward, Zhao Wenhui would buy another serving maid for his father's sister.

When Li Huaiqun questioned the monk, he learned for the first time that Ji Gong was a senior monk of the Monastery of the Soul's Retreat. Su Beishan went over and greeting the monk ceremoniously, inquiring, "May I ask as a great kindness that you cure my own mother's illness?"

The monk stood up and replied, "I will go to your home now."

Su Beishan said, "Very good!"

Zhao Wenhui could not very well detain Ji Gong. Bringing a hundred ounces of white silver, he offered it to the monk to buy some more clothes. The monk said, "If you wish to thank me, come closer," and then he whispered something into Zhao Wenhui's ear.

Zhao Wenhui said, "Teacher, please rest assured that on that day I will be there." Then he asked Su Beishan whether he had asked anyone to treat the illness of his mother.

Su Beishan replied, "Actually I have invited a great many gentlemen, but all have turned out to be useless. Recently one who is truly a living saint of the medical profession, Tang Wanfang, treated her, but I have seen no improvement in her condition. I also asked Dr. Li to treat her, but he, too, was not effective. They all say that older people cannot be helped when the vitality and blood are deficient. I also with all my heart rely on the will of heaven. Today I was able to meet this saintly monk who was fated to help this old lady to recover from an illness that has been truly hard to bear."

At Su Beishan's home, which was known as the "Green Bamboo Studio," they entered and went into the western courtyard. There they came to the door of a spacious house of five sections on the north side. When they were seated inside, they could see the old lady, Su Beishan's mother, lying on a bed.

There were several old women and slave girls standing in attendance who found the monk's torn and ragged clothing quite ridiculous. Their laughter was more than Ji Gong could tolerate. "You should stop laughing at this clothing of mine and listen to what I say. Those who laugh at the monk's torn clothes have neither eyes nor face." (Meaning they lack both perception and self-respect.)

The household people offered tea. Ji Gong took out a piece of medicine and held it in his hand. As soon as Su Beishan perceived its black color, resembling betel nut, and its strange repellent odor, he reached out for it. Taking the unfamiliar pill in his hand, he asked, "What is the name of this medicine?"

Ji Gong answered, "This is a subtle medicine that I possess as a monk. It is called the pill of fate. If a person is about to die and takes this medicine of mine, life will return. It is also the pill of movement and understanding."

Su Beishan used water to dissolve the pill and gave the mixture to his mother to drink. In a short time the old woman had completely recovered from her illness.

Su Beishan directed someone to prepare wine and invited the monk into the library, where they sat drinking wine and discussing ancient and present affairs. Ji Gong revealed to Su Beishan the splendor of his erudition and the aspirations hidden within his breast. Su Beishan than knew that Ji Gong was one who transcended the great men of the world. Su Beishan begged Ji Gong to become his teacher, and wanted to give him new clothing. But the monk would accept nothing, saying, "If you wish to thank me, it need only be as it is between us at present. Now I must go."

Su Beishan said, "My teacher, here it will always be as if this were your worldly home. When you wish to come, you may live here."

The monk replied, "Nicely said. Today I will return to the temple." He left the Su household, and in the street began singing as he walked on his way.

> Where now are the sounds of their laughter?
> Where are the flowers and brilliant brocades?
> Where are those years we once were so joyous?
> Lonely tombs echo back my cry.
> Though I grieve for my old companions,
> I must follow the light of truth.
> May I flee the world and its pleasures;
> May the world only pass me by.

So Ji Gong returned to the temple. The superintendent of the monks, Guang Liang, wanted to destroy Ji Gong. Guang Liang was holding a grudge because Ji Gong had stolen his robe and also had played a trick on him with a bundle of dust and dirt that the superintendent had thought was an object stolen by Ji Gong.

Guang knew that Ji Gong slept in an upper room of the Great Pagoda, and sent one of the acolytes to make sure that Ji Gong was there—and, if he was, to burn him to death during the night.

The first time that the fire was set, Ji Gong had risen to relieve himself, and the water he made showered the little acolyte on the head and put out the fire.

When the little acolyte started a fire the second time, the high, blazing flames were seen at once. The multitude of monks in the temple cried out: "This is terrible! Quick, let us put out this fire! That crazy monk Dao Ji is up in the Great Pagoda sleeping and will be burned to death—perhaps he can be saved."

Superintendent Guang Liang thought that this time he had been able to burn the mad monk to death. Although no one knew it, Guang Liang was just savoring this delight when he saw Ji Gong coming out of the Great Hall of Treasures. He was laughing loudly, saying, "When men call upon men to die, heaven may be unwilling; but when heaven calls upon men to die, there does not seem to be any difficulty."

When Superintendent Guang Liang saw that Ji Gong was not dead, he was most unhappy. He went to the temple master and told him, "We are now obliged to punish Ji Dian for the burning of the Great Pagoda."

The old temple master replied, "The fact that the Great Pagoda caught fire was the will of heaven. How can it be attributed to Dao Ji?"

The superintendent answered the temple master saying, "Nations have the law of kings; temples have the Buddhist rules. In this temple, when one person has a lamp lighted, everyone has a lamp lighted according to the time specified—such as when they come together to eat, and when they go to their rest at night. Dao Ji keeps his lamp burning all night and makes it burn like a supernatural fire. This is against Buddhist rules and he should be punished for that. He should be sent out of the temple and not be allowed to be a monk."

The old temple master said, "The punishment you recommend is too severe. He could be sent to collect alms for the restoration of the Great Pagoda. Have Dao Ji called to see me."

Not long after, Dao Ji was seen to come in and stand in front of the temple master, greeting him and saying, "Reverend Temple Master above, I press my palms together in greeting."

The temple master said, "Dao Ji, you have not been keeping the Buddhist rules and as a result the Great Pagoda has burned. I am sending you to solicit funds to repair this building. Ten thousand ounces of silver are needed for the task. Ask your brother teacher to specify how many days you should be given."

Ji Gong asked, "Brother teacher, how many days would you give me?"

The superintendent of the monks asked, "Can you raise ten thousand ounces of silver in three years?"

Ji Gong replied, "It won't do—it's too long. You must say some time less."

The superintendent asked, "Can you raise ten thousand ounces of silver to repair the Great Pagoda in one year?"

Ji Gong replied, "It won't do. It's still too long. You can come down a little more—try again."

The superintendent said, "Half a year."

Ji Gong shook his head and said to come down a little more.

The superintendent said, "One month."

Ji Gong said it was still too long.

The superintendent asked, "Can you raise ten thousand ounces of silver in one day?"

Ji Gong retorted, "If ten thousand ounces of silver can be raised in one day, you go and raise it! I can't!"

All the monks discussed the matter together and said that there should be a limit of one hundred days. They asked Ji Gong to go out and solicit funds. If he were able to raise the ten thousand ounces of silver in that time, he would triumph. He would have paid his debt and that would be the end of his punishment.

Ji Gong agreed, and every day went out to solicit funds. In the vicinity of Linan there were countless young monks taking pledges as they begged for the salvation of all souls. Either pretending to be stupid or acting terrified, not one of them would raise his eyes from his signature book to look at Ji Gong.

One day near the Monastery of the Soul's Retreat, on the rear slope of the Flying Cliff Mountain, where there were hares, deer, foxes, and cranes, Ji Gong saw two hunters. He stopped them on the road saying, "What are your honorable names and where are you going?"

One of the men replied, "I am Chen Li; my nickname is 'The Man with the Beautiful Whiskers'. That man is my sworn brother, Yang Meng, who suffers from a mysterious illness. We are going to hunt hares on the mountain and then return. May we ask who is the teacher?"

Ji Gong explained, laughing loudly, and then remarked, "Every day you are on the mountain hunting hares. In order to preserve your life, you terminate the life of other things."

Yang Meng and Chen Li realized that the monk was a superior recluse and knelt to offer greetings, asking Ji Gong to be their teacher and saying, "We two from now on will change our occupation and will henceforth seek our living by acting as armed escorts for travelers."

The monk said, "Good! Soon your business will be flourishing."

After the two had gone, the monk went into the monastery. He spent his days drinking and no longer solicited alms. The superintendent did not press him, thinking that when the time limit had passed, it would be a fine thing to have Ji Gong sent away out of the monastery.

The days went by, first slowly and then swiftly, until over a month had passed. Ji Gong had not collected one ounce of silver. One day he noticed

that none of the temple monks were nearby. Ji Gong went into the hall
where the image of Wei Tuo, an ancient Hindu ruler, was located. He con-
templated the ruler's benign face.

In its bright gold leaf, the image of Wei Tuo seemed like that fabulous
dancing phoenix which was said to herald and protect a just and benevolent emperor. So, it was believed, had the spirit of this ancient Vedic king
of the Hindus come to herald and protect the Lord Buddha and to assist
him in his teaching that all reality was one and that the goal of each
believer should be to transcend the limitations of the individual. The kind
and reassuring face of the image was like that of the bodhisattva Guan Yin,
she who was the essence of passionate enlightenment. The light glinted
from the helmet and chain-link armor of the image. About its waist was
an embroidered sash, the ends of which seemed to wave and ripple in the
wind. On its feet were green and black military boots, and in its hand it
held the diamond-headed scepter for subduing every repugnant and
malevolent spirit.

After a time Ji Gong said, "Venerable Wei Tuo, guardian spirit, go with
me and help me." Stretching out his hands, the monk picked up the image
of Wei Tuo, left the temple, and started walking through the region of
West Lake.

People passing him on the road said, "I have seen monks soliciting
funds. There were some carrying great chains, some beating wooden fish
gongs, but none wandering about while carrying an image of the guardian spirit."

The monk laughed loudly and said, "You haven't opened your eyes.
Speak softly. This is our temple's transportation officer." When they heard
what the monk had said, they all laughed.

Suddenly, as Ji Gong looked ahead, he could see a trail of black smoke
rising in the sky. He halted and clapped his hands three times saying,
"Excellent! Excellent! How can I ignore this?" Going forward, he saw that
on the north side of the street there was an inn that sold wine and food.
It was a building of two stories named the Drunken Sage Tower. On the
wooden tablet above the door was written:

> A hundred poems flowed
> From Li Taibo's brush
> While he was drinking
> In his Changan inn.
> Great Tang Minghuang was bored
> And sent his barge for him.

> But Li Taibo insisted that he was
> Merely a spirit in a jug of wine
> And sent the emperor's messenger
> Back to him alone.

On either side of the door were lines of characters reading, "The drunkard's universe expands," and "In the wine pot, days and moons grow long."

Inside Ji Gong heard a ladle rattle. He pulled aside the door curtain and asked, "May I trouble you, innkeeper?"

The innkeeper, taking Ji Gong to be an ordinary monk soliciting funds, said: "We in here will next give money on the fifteenth."

Ji Gong said, "Right, we will next do business on the fifteenth."

Standing outside the door, he saw three men coming from the east. They were the owner of a rice and provision shop and his guests. Ji Gong thrust out his arm and said, "If you three want to eat a meal, they will next be open in here on the fifteenth." As soon as the three men heard this, they went to another place.

After three or four other parties had come and had all been stopped and turned away by Ji Gong, the innkeeper came out and asked very angrily, "What do you mean by stopping all my customers?"

Ji Gong replied, "I wanted to eat a meal, and when I started through the door, you told me to return on the fifteenth. I knew then that only on the fifteenth would you start serving food."

When the innkeeper heard this, he said, "I thought you came to solicit funds. Only because of this I said that on the fifteenth I would give money to the Buddhists and the Daoists. Do you understand?"

Ji Gong said, "No, I came to eat a meal."

The innkeeper said, "Please come in."

Ji Gong carried the image of Wei Tuo into the back room, sat down at a long table, ordered several kinds of dishes, and drank four or five pots of wine. When he had finished, he called the waiter to calculate the bill. Altogether it amounted to a string of six hundred and eighty cash, a cash being a copper coin with a square hole in the center so that it could be strung on a string. A cash was worth a very small fraction of a cent.

Ji Gong said, "Write it on my account, and another day when I eat, I will pay both bills together."

CHAPTER 4

Liu Taizhen is deluded by the arts of Chan;
Li Guoyuan goes to breakfast and
loses a prince's tally

> Thoughts of her he loves
> As moonlight strikes the wall,
> How gentle were her ways,
> How beautifully she read.
> Her angry passion now,
> Her strange and swift assaults,
> She does not hear his voice
> Nor recognize his face.
> He does not know the cause.
> Betrayed by one she loved.
> The doctors come and go;
> They cannot find the cure.

AFTER the monk had left the wine shop and was walking along on his way, it occurred to him to visit the Shrine of the Three Virtues and see Liu Taizhen, the Daoist. At the same time he was conscious of the effects of wrongdoing upon someone elsewhere in the vicinity. He directed his spiritual light toward it, clapped his hands, and nodded his head saying, "How can I ignore it? May I be like the Master of Power, Wen Shu Bodhisattva!"

Muttering the words, "Dao, Dao," he went on to the Shrine of the Three Virtues outside the Qingbo gate. There he noticed that the wooden tablet advertising exorcisms had been taken down and that the place looked rather forlorn and quiet. The monk knocked twice.

As for the Daoist, after returning to his shrine from the Zhou family house, he used some of the silver that he had been given as the result of Ji Gong's kindness to redeem the various articles he had pawned. He told an apprentice Daoist boy to take down the sign announcing the availability of exorcisms. He also told him: "If anyone comes again to invite me to chase out a ghost, you are to say that I have gone into the hills to search for medicinal herbs."

The little attendant nodded his head and agreed. Then the old Daoist went into his room at the back of the shrine and began reading his books to relieve his boredom. The boy was playing in the courtyard when he heard someone knocking at the gate and went to open it. Looking out, he saw a poor, ragged monk standing there. The Daoist boy asked, "Who is wanted?"

Ji Gong said, "I am looking for the venerable Daoist Liu of your household, to go to our place to chase ghosts. I am inviting him to exorcise and to cure sickness."

The Daoist boy said, "He can't. Our teacher has gone into the hills to gather herbs. It is not certain how many days it will be before he comes back."

Ji Gong said, "You go in there to that old Daoist looking at his book and mention that the old man is here, and then he will see me."

When the little attendant heard this, he was speechless for a moment and thought to himself, "Huh! How did he know my teacher was at home reading?" Then he said quickly, "Just wait here, monk."

Then he hurried back to tell the old Daoist. "Teacher, there is a poor monk outside who said he was inviting you to chase a ghost and purify a house. I told him you had gone to pick herbs, and he said, 'Go in to the old Daoist looking at a book and mention that I have come,' and that you would see him."

The old Daoist was quite surprised and remarked, "Probably it's the old man."

The boy said, "That's right. The monk said to tell you that the old man had come."

The Daoist immediately went to look outside. Naturally it was Ji Gong. The Daoist quickly spoke. "Where did you come from, venerable sir? Your student kowtows to you."

"Good," said Ji Gong. "You have led me hither. I came to your shrine to sit for a while and ask you about a certain matter. Since you are no longer exorcising evil spirits and purifying homes, I wondered what the teacher and his several followers were doing to feed themselves."

The old Daoist said, "Teacher, ordinarily I simply try to cure illness or do anything to get a bowl of rice to eat. Since coming back from the home of the Zhou family, I have been so frightened. How would I dare to perform exorcisms? My shrine really does not have any income. Perhaps, venerable sir, you may have some suggestion. While we are talking, please come in and sit down."

The monk said, "I could teach you some formulas for obtaining wealth, if you could learn. Then if you wanted gold or silver, you could simply recite them. If you wanted good clothing or good food, it would come as soon as you started to recite."

The old Daoist said, "If I could only study this, it would be excellent. I would not study anything else. Teacher, venerable sir, please help me to perform such alchemies."

The monk said, "You could not perform them now. To be able to perform such things, first you must bump your head against the ground in a kowtow one thousand times a day for forty-nine days. You must recognize me as your teacher. You must kneel on the ground and recite the Sutra of the Eternal in Time. Then kowtow and stand and repeat 'O Mi To Fu.' That is counted as one time."

The Daoist said, "I will do it. I will kowtow one thousand times a day, if only at the end of the forty-nine days I will be able to have whatever I ask for. Then I want to do it."

The monk said, "That is still not enough. When I want to drink wine, who will go for it?"

The old Daoist replied, "I will have one of the boys get it for you."

The monk said, "I like to eat meat at each meal. Who will go and buy it for me?"

The Daoist said, "I will go and buy it. Morning and evening pastries, three meals a day, I will take care of it all."

The monk said, "Then we will start early tomorrow morning. But first send out one of your boys to buy some crude spirits and several dishes of food. I will drink first."

The old Daoist quickly called an apprentice to go and buy wine and some prepared dishes.

The next morning the monk proposed an idea. They would use two old flat-bottomed baskets and buy one thousand yellow beans. The monk would sit on a rush mat. The Daoist would recite the Sutra of the Eternal in Time, knock his head against the ground once, then recite "O Mi To Fu." Then he would take one yellow bean out of the yellow basket and put it into the red basket. In this way he would remember.

After the old Daoist had knocked his head against the ground several tens of times, his back ached and his legs were very painful. When he had knocked two hundred, he noticed that the monk had shut his eyes and seemed to be taking a nap. The old Daoist thought, "I'll take a double handful and knock a few times less." When he saw that the monk really seemed to be sleeping soundly, he quickly took a double handful and put it into the red basket.

The monk opened his eyes and said, "You are an odd one! Trying to practice the spiritual arts by stealing on the sly! Knock harder!" With that he snatched the beans out of the red basket, taking out more than three hundred.

After the old Daoist had kowtowed for five or six days, the silver that he had saved up was all spent. The monk kept calling for someone to go and buy wine and prepared dishes. The Daoist told the apprentice, "Do not take my Daoist robe yet; pawn the gold hairpin. After I have mastered the formulas, I will get it back." The boy pawned it, and they ate for another five or six days, and again there was no money.

The old Daoist called the manager of the pawn shop and asked him to take the tables, chairs, and stools from the great hall of the shrine. After that there are really no words to describe what went on for what amounted to one month and six days. The last thing that the Daoist had managed to save was his one pair of pants. The apprentices also had lost most of their clothing. Finally the Daoist said to the monk, "Teacher, I really have no money. Teach me the magic formulas now so that I can get something for us to eat."

The monk said, "If I had been able to work that kind of magic, why do you think I would have had you bringing me wine?"

"Ah, that is true," said the Daoist when he heard this. "Teacher has hoodwinked me. What is to be done?"

The monk said, "If you have no money, I will be gone."

The Daoist said, "After the saintly monk is gone, I and my apprentices will starve to death."

"I will teach you some hocus-pocus that you can master," said the monk.

"What hocus-pocus?" asked the Daoist.

The monk replied, "Om Ma Ni Pad Me Hum."

The Daoist did not understand what he had heard and said, "Oh, that is gibberish. You are just making noises."

"That's right," said the monk. He repeated it three more times until the Daoist was able to say it. The monk then told him to kneel in the courtyard and repeat it. Just as the Daoist was saying, "Om Ma Ni Pad Me Hum," Ji Gong, who was standing behind him, pointed at the ground with his finger, and a little piece of the brick paving flew up and hit the Daoist on the head, causing a small red lump to appear.

"What happened?" The Daoist asked.

Ji Gong answered, "As soon as you started reciting hocus-pocus, the brick looked at you and then hit you. That is because of your power in reciting."

"I am not going on," The Daoist protested.

"Do not worry," said Ji Gong, "I will teach you a few safe phrases. When you see any bricks, just say, 'Bricks, you are above me and I will respect you. I will not recite hocus-pocus, and you will not get up and hit me.'"

"Teacher, what shall I do?" the Daoist asked.

Ji Gong told him, "I will give you my monk's robe to put on and the hat to wear and teach you several phrases. Go to the Su Embankment at the West Lake near the Qiantang gate. There you will find a place called the Cold Spring Pavilion. Go up there and stand, saying loudly three times, 'Li Guoyuan, Li Guoyuan need not go to the Monastery of the Soul's Retreat at the West Lake to find Ji Gong. Give me your ten ounces of pure silver, and you will still have three hundred and sixty cash left.'"

The old Daoist did not want to go, but there was not a cash at the shrine, so he went. Every time he had gone out before, his clothing had been very handsome and correct. Today the old Daoist had no choice. He put on the monk's old, ragged robe and asked, "Teacher, if I do go there and say these words three times, will the silver just fall?"

The monk replied, "Just keep your mind on getting there and calling out the words loudly three times. Then there will be someone who will question you. We monks have an expression, 'Take a small donation.' It will be enough to take care of you for your lifetime."

The Daoist had no choice but to go. He left the Shrine of the Three Virtues with his head bowed, fearing to meet someone he knew.

Along the street there were many neighbors who knew the Daoist. Some of them seeing him commented: "Isn't that the venerable Daoist Liu from the Shrine of the Three Virtues? How could he have come to this condition? The tables seem to have turned. It could not have been anything else—he must love gambling."

The old Daoist heard them but could not very well answer. He walked on until he came to the Su embankment at the West Lake and the Cold Spring Pavilion. There was a major highway at that place and a great many people passing to and fro. The old Daoist stood at the pavilion and called out, "Li Guoyuan need not go to the Monastery of the Soul's Retreat to look for Ji Gong. Give me the ten ounces of pure silver you have, and you will still have three hundred and sixty cash left."

The Daoist called this out three times and attracted the attention of a great many people. All of them started talking. Some said that the old Daoist had gone mad. Others said that he was looking for Li Guoyuan.

Just as this discussion was taking place, two men walked up through the crowd. One of them was saying to the other, "Dear brother, is that Ji Gong, or someone that looks like him?"

The two moved closer. The one in front seemed from his clothing to be a wealthy man. The other, a younger man, appeared cultured and elegant. As the two looked at the old Daoist, the first said, "You! Old Daoist, have you harmed or killed Ji Gong and taken from him those clothes that you are wearing?"

"I certainly have not harmed or killed Ji Gong. He has harmed me! He has eaten me down to my last pair of pants!" the old Daoist protested. "What are the names of you two honorable gentlemen?"

The cultured and elegant younger man was Li Guoyuan. His home was in the fourth *hutung*, a narrow alley, of the Green Bamboo Forest that was in the southern part of Linan. The family was at one time wealthy, and he himself was a literary graduate. He had taken a wife from the Lin family, a virtuous young woman, very dear to him. For no apparent reason she was stricken with a mental illness. A great many gentlemen had been invited to examine her, but with no helpful results. Li Guoyuan was very depressed by this.

He had a friend named Li Chunshan who acted as a private tutor in the home of a high official named Du. One day early in the morning Li Guoyuan went to see Chunshan. While the two were discussing their personal affairs, Li Guoyuan mentioned that his wife had become mentally ill and that, although they had invited several doctors to examine her, she was no better.

Li Chunshan said, "In the household shrine of High Official Du, there is a prince's tally. It is a scroll that was once sent by an emperor to one of his sons as a symbol that his father had chosen him to be the next emperor. This tally has been a treasured possession of the Du family for several generations. On this tally are the eight trigrams, symbols used to repel evil, and the characters 'five thunders' are shown. Perhaps it is an invocation to the Thunder God, a protector of mankind against the demons that cause illness. I will ask if I can lend it to you. If he won't lend it, I will simply take it and give it to you to use. If you hang it in your home for two hours, it will drive out all evil spirits."

Li Guoyuan said, "Just as soon as this tally cures my wife's illness, I will return it."

Li Chunshan went to the Du family shrine, and, opening a chest, secretly removed the prince's tally and brought it outside. It was in a small case of precious cedar.

Li Chunshan said, "This is a treasured heirloom of the Du family. I secretly borrowed it to let you take it, but a thousand times ten thousand be careful! Hang it for two mornings and it will drive out the evil spirit. Then get it back to me."

Li Guoyuan said, "I will bring it back tomorrow." Taking the tally, he said goodbye.

But as he walked away by himself, he thought, "Oh! We didn't have breakfast!" Originally they had intended to eat together, but as soon as they started talking about the scroll, they forgot all about it. "It's not convenient for me to go home and eat now. Just ahead there is a restaurant on the north side of the road. I will go in and look."

Inside the place was full of wealthy friends of his. Everyone stood up and called, "Graduate Li, come and drink with us."

Li Guoyuan said, "Do not shout, gentlemen. I have to talk to someone." He went to the back room and found a table. After he had called for wine and drunk two cups, he thought to himself, "Everyone called to me in greeting, and I didn't greet anyone. That was wrong of me." He quickly got up and went to say a word to his friends.

When he had finished speaking to them, he turned and went back to his table. Suddenly his eyes widened in fright, and his mouth dropped open in an idiotic expression. The demon-chasing, five-thunders, eight-trigram prince's tally was gone!

CHAPTER 5

Zhao Wenhui goes to the West Lake to visit Ji Gong; the drunken Chan master explains celestial bargaining

AFTER Li Guoyuan had greeted his various friends and returned to find that the borrowed scroll was not to be seen, he could no longer drink any of his wine, nor eat the food. He thought to himself, "If I had lost anything but the scroll, I could make some sort of repayment, but there is nowhere that this kind of thing can be purchased. This is a treasured family heirloom of the Du family. If news of this gets out, how could my friend, my elder brother, not lose his position?"

He then quickly called the manager to reckon the amount of the bill, telling him to put it on his account. The manager asked why he had not eaten. Li Guoyuan said, "I have some important business to do."

Without any further talk, he hastened home and calling several trusted people of his household together, he told them: "While I was eating in such and such a wine shop just now, I lost a prince's tally consisting of a scroll with the eight trigrams and the characters 'five thunders' as a prayer to ask the help of the Thunder God. Go around and see whether you can find out which gang the thief belonged to, and whether you can get someone to buy the scroll back for a reasonable price. This is something belonging to a person other than myself."

The household people assented and left. Not long afterward one of them, named Li Sheng, returned and said, "I have just found out exactly what happened. While you were drinking with your friends, this thing was stolen by a member of the White Coin gang and afterward sold to manager Liu of the Old Studio Antique Shop. He bought it for thirty ounces of silver. He had been befriended by people at the estate of Prime Minister Chin, to whom the scroll has been sold for five hundred ounces of silver. It has been hung in an upper story of the five-story Great Pavilion in the flower garden to protect the estate from demons and calamities."

When Li Guoyuan heard this, he realized how bad the situation was.

"If it were only still in the antique shop, I could still have spent a little more money and bought it back, but I have neither the power nor the connections with powerful friends necessary to deal with these people."

Just as he was hesitating about what to do next, someone knocked at the gate outside. When he sent a man to see who was there, it turned out to be none other then Li Chunshan's young son, Little Crab Apple. He said, "Just now after you left, we heard that tomorrow a ceremony will be conducted at the shrine in the home of official Du's family. My father asked me to bring back the prince's tally with the five thunders and the eight trigrams to have it ready to be used in the ceremony tomorrow."

Li Guoyuan said, "You may go back now and tell your father that, when I started to hang the scroll, I found a small tear in it. I sent it to the shop of a scroll mounter to have it repaired. In a little while it will be returned. You need not come for it."

After Little Crab Apple had gone, just when Li Guoyuan was driven to the point of absolute despair by his anxiety, one of the household people announced that a Zhao Yuanwai had come. Li Guoyuan went out and saw that it was Zhao Wenhui. The two men were intimate friends, and Li Guoyuan immediately raised his clasped hands in greeting, saying, "I have been looking forward to seeing you, Elder Brother."

Zhao Wenhui said, "I came today to invite you, dear brother, to visit the City God Hill and afterward to have a drink and something to eat at the Riverview Restaurant on Heavenly Pearl Street. We can see the sights together and have a view of the river from the restaurant."

But Li Guoyuan interrupted him, saying, "Elder Brother, today I cannot go with you. I have the most distressing business. Please come in and sit down."

When they went into the library, Li Guoyuan related all the details concerning the loss of the prince's tally scroll.

Zhao Yuanwai immediately said, "Do not worry! I can help you with this affair. There is a senior monk named Ji Gong at the Monastery of the Soul's Retreat in the West Lake area. He is a Buddha living in this world. You and I will go to him and beg the venerable monk to help. He can get back the prince's tally, and he can cure the illness of your wife, whom I consider my sister. He truly communicates with the divine. He knows by intuition, and his power through his mastery of Buddha's law is unlimited."

Li Guoyuan thought to himself, "I have heard his name, but up to now I have not seen the man. If he should come back with us, I must invite him to eat, so I will have to take some silver along." Going out with Zhao

Wenhui, Li Guoyuan bought forty cash worth of tea leaves, so that including the change from the tea leaves he had exactly ten ounces of silver and three hundred and sixty cash with him.

As they walked on, they found themselves on the three-mile-long causeway with six bridges and with willow trees and peach trees one after the other. We speak of spring nights on the Su Embankment. Why is it so named? The great Su Dongbo wrote a famous poem about the adornment of the causeway with trees, and how during the third spring after they were planted, the peach and willow trees seemed to contend with each other to be the more beautiful. In the center of the lake was the spring that was the lake's heart. Looking south one could see the Barrier Mountain and the pagoda on Thunder Peak. On the hillside to the north were forests and tranquil plum orchards. Looking far away to the west one could see the tomb of Yueh Fei, the legendary hero of the Song Dynasty. There, too, was the grave mound of Su Xiaoxiao, a beautiful and talented woman who was famous for flouting convention.

Just as the two men came to the Cold Spring Pavilion, they heard someone in the middle of the crowd of people shouting out: "Li Guoyuan, Li Guoyuan, you do not need to go to the West Lake Monastery of the Soul's Retreat to find Ji Gong. Give me the ten ounces of silver that you are carrying and keep the three hundred and sixty cash."

When Zhao Wenhui heard this he said, "My dear brother, the saintly monk is able to see the future through his intuition, and he is here waiting for you and me."

As they pressed their way through the crowd and looked, they saw Ji Gong's clothing, but the man wearing it was not Ji Gong. Zhao Wenhui went over and grasped him with his hands, saying, "You good-for-nothing Daoist, you have done something bad to Ji Gong and you are trying to profit from his affairs."

The old Daoist said, "I certainly have not harmed Ji Gong, but he has eaten up everything we have until we are all, master and apprentices, almost without a scrap of clothing. He gave me these sentences and told me to come here and say them."

Zhao Wenhui said, "Where is Ji Gong? Take us to see him."

The old Daoist then took them to the Shrine of Three Virtues. When Zhao Wenhui saw the shrine, he noticed how poor the place looked, with almost nothing except the bare floor and walls. There were half-clad apprentices lounging about, and Ji Gong was sitting in a chair with his naked back toward the visitors.

Wenhui said, "Teacher who is above me, Zhao Wenhui, your follower, presents his respects." He then suggested to Li Guoyuan that he also should pay the proper courtesies to the holy monk.

Even though at first the monk looked like nothing more than a beggar, to save Zhao Yuanwai's face Li Guoyuan could not do otherwise than go forward to offer a ceremonial greeting. He bowed his head while he raised his clasped hands respectfully.

The monk asked, "What business brings you here?"

Zhao Wenhui quickly explained about the loss of the prince's tally scroll with the five thunders and the eight trigrams.

Ji Gong said, "Do not worry," and had the old Daoist take off the ragged clothes. Ji Gong then put them on. He asked Li Guoyuan to hand over his silver, and Ji Gong gave it to the Daoist to redeem the pawned articles. The monk then left the Shrine of the Three Virtues with the two men and went to the home of Li Guoyuan.

The monk said, "First I will cure the illness of your wife, and after that I will get back the prince's tally. But there is one thing: to cure your wife, I must take hold of her and go round and round with her."

When Li Guoyuan heard this, he was half speechless, but Zhao Wenhui said, "Dear brother, you need not be suspicious. Ji Gong is a Buddha living on earth. He would certainly do no wrong. If he were an improper person, of course, I would not have asked him to come here."

Li Guoyuan said, "Well, then, that's it," and led Ji Gong to a courtyard containing a pleasant house facing south. When they arrived, the door was locked. Li Guoyuan's wife unlocked it from the inside. The serving girls and women had fled sometime previously from that part of the estate, fearing they would be struck by the insane woman. When the door opened and the wife saw the ragged monk outside, she ran straight at him.

The monk ran from her out into the courtyard. In the center was a large wide-mouthed jar for goldfish. Ji Gong ran round and round the jar, shouting, "This is terrible! If she catches me, it will be my life," while the insane woman ran after him.

After a while, the wife tripped over a basket and fell. Immediately she coughed up some mucus. At the same time her understanding returned to her and she asked, "How did I get here?"

As soon as she fell, one of the braver women ran forward and helped her up. The monk, meanwhile, took a piece of medicine, and after he had had someone bring some water, he dissolved the medicine and gave it to Li Guoyuan's wife to drink.

Now, this illness of hers had originated with a confusion in the chambers of her heart. It was through the effect of certain affairs upon her that she had been brought to an extreme pitch of anxiety. She had a younger brother named Lin Tingyo. He had already squandered part of the property of his parents in the company of some bad characters with whom he had made friends.

One day he came to his older sister, asking that she lend him several hundred ounces of silver to go into business. Since he was her own flesh and blood, it was natural she would be sympathetic to him. She deceived her husband about her brother's reliability and persuaded him to lend her brother the silver. In a short time he had wasted it all running with his friends who, in truth, were no better than a pack of foxes or dogs. Then he came back another day and asked her to lend him an ounce of silver for ready money, and she gave it to him. Some days after that, while Li Guoyuan's wife was sitting in a flower garden at her home, her brother suddenly appeared dressed in clothing so shabby, it was not fit for him to wear. He seemed like a different person, unkempt and ragged. The sight was such a shock to her that she nearly choked to death. This was what had brought on her sickness. When the congestion in her throat was relieved, she immediately recovered.

Li Guoyuan was extremely grateful to the monk and invited him into the library, where wine had been prepared. Just as they were about to drink, one of the household people came in and said that Little Crab Apple was again at the gate demanding the prince's tally scroll. Li Guoyuan went out with the rest and told him that it would be sent to him later.

Li Guoyuan then turned and said to Ji Gong, "Teacher, what are we going to do?"

The monk said, "I will hire the Wei Tuo from our temple to get the scroll back."

Li Guoyuan said, "Teacher, the Wei Tuo from your temple is a clay image—how can it steal things?

Ji Gong replied, "It can. That Wei Tuo of ours is always taking on such trivial business for people, but you cannot ask him to go and do something for nothing. You two wait here and drink your wine. I will go now and have a drink when I get back." The monk stood up, and left.

After the two men had seen him out and returned, Li Guoyuan said, "Brother Zhao, do you think what we heard the monk say is true or false?"

"I don't know whether it is genuine or not. Previously, when we were at the home of 'Half a City' Zhou, Ji Gong was carrying the Wei Tuo at the time he chased the goblin away. Now we are at a second crisis. Perhaps the talk about the Wei Tuo is true."

After the two men had had some wine, they waited for Ji Gong until past lamp-lighting time. Then they began to get anxious, fearing that the city gates would be closed, shutting him outside the city walls.

Just as they were speaking of this, they saw Ji Gong come in, and they said, "Our teacher has returned to us."

Ji Gong said, "I'm so angry I could die!"

Zhao Wenhui asked, "With whom is our teacher angry?"

Ji Gong replied, "With the Wei Tuo of our temple. He is really hateful. Ordinarily when I go out, he says, 'If you have any business, let me take care of it for you.' Today when I came back, he just glanced at me and turned away. He turned his face completely away and would not speak to me. I just laughed and said, 'I have some business for you, old Wei.' He asked what the business was, and I mentioned that I wanted him to go to Prime Minister Chin's estate and steal back the five thunders, eight tri-gram scroll from an upstairs room in the flower garden pavilion. I asked him how much he wanted to be paid to do it. Right away he put his price way up."

Li Guoyuan and Zhao Wenhui both asked at once: "How much did he want?"

The monk replied, "He wanted five strings of cash. I offered him five hundred cash."

Li Guoyuan said, "Five strings of cash is not so much."

The monk said, "That was his first price. That did not mean anything. He actually wanted two strings of cash, and he would not go for anything less. I said, 'Now you have come down a little. If you will take off a bit more, I will increase from the five hundred cash I offered. It is not very much cash either way, now.' He still said he would not go for less.

"After that the bargaining broke up and we parted. I left that temple and went to the Big Buddha temple, and there I bumped into its Wei Tuo. He asked me where I was going. I said, 'I have some business for you. Will you do it or not?' He asked what it was. I replied that it was to go and do something. He asked, 'Haven't you talked to the Wei Tuo in your own temple about it?' I explained that our Wei Tuo wanted too much money. The Big Buddha temple Wei Tuo wanted three strings of cash, and again I said I would give five hundred cash. Without blinking an eye he said, 'I also will not come down on my price. If I do it for less, I will offend the other Wei Tuo.' I said that if I spent more, it would be wrong, too. Because of this, we also parted."

When Li Guoyuan heard that all of this had been fruitless, he asked what should be done.

The monk said, "Well, I kept on going until I came to the Purple Bamboo Forest. In the temple there, the Wei Tuo was so hungry that he was pounding on the entry screen in the gateway. He called to me as soon as he caught sight of me. As soon as I mentioned business, he said he wanted to do it. He said he would be here in just a little while, and he accepted my first offer as payment."

Li Guoyuan asked, "When will he be here?"

The monk replied, "As soon as we have finished eating. Have the table set in the courtyard. As soon as I call, he will come."

Li Guoyuan busily set about getting dinner out of the way, calling upon the household people to prepare whatever was needed and serve it in the courtyard.

The monk said, "There is no need to panic. In a twinkling of an eye, the stars will all be out, and at that time I will invite the Wei Tuo join us."

At last the monk called out, "I am here, the monk Ji Dian from the West Lake Monastery of the Soul's Retreat."

The Wei Tuo had still not arrived, but after a little while they heard a shout that seemed to come from the air above.

"I am here—the spirit has come."

CHAPTER 6

Zhao Bin attempts to visit the Great Pavilion; a fearless hero is sent upon a horrible errand

Not like a warrior in armor astride a valiant steed.
Not riding through the flames.
We contest for fame and wealth in the tiny space
    between the antennae of a snail
In the flash of a moment—less than a spark of light—
    we live this light
Whether rich or poor—let us just seek happiness
If you can't laugh out loud, you're an idiot.

WHEN Ji Gong had lighted the incense and called out his invitation to Wei Tuo, the monk was still following heavenly principles. He had summoned neither heavenly spirits nor infernal demons, and there was nothing supernatural involved. He who replied, therefore, was not the true and genuine Wei Tuo. He was, in fact, Zhao Bin, a hero of the kind that could startle heaven and move earth.

Zhao Bin's father, Zhao Jijou, who was also called Majestic Bright Moon, had been a man of Jenjiang, the provincial capital in Tanyang prefecture. Over the five main roads to the north, south, east, and west from this central area he had a reputation as the most important bodyguard and escort for travelers. His wife was from the Mei family, and they had only one son, Zhao Bin.

At that time, the country had truly fallen upon evil times. The roads were lonely and dangerous. These conditions were fortunate for the father, who was much in demand. The experienced man taught his profession to two followers and his son. The first of these followers was Fang Yangming, an awe-inspiring man from the Jade Mountain country in Jiangsi. The second was Yin Shixiong, who had previously been an employee of an escort group in the East Road.

When Zhao Jijou fell sick, he called his wife and said, "After I am dead, whatever you do, do not let Zhao Bin work as an escort. He is too proud and headstrong for such work. Let me then carry my reputation into the afterworld." With this as his last cry, he died.

When mother and son had finished with the funeral ceremonies, the two passed their days as best they could. The little property the father had left them was sufficient for their daily needs. Zhao Bin liked to amuse himself and made several friends in the neighborhood. One of them was Jin Yuanliang, nicknamed "The Fiery Father Who Flies Through the Air." There was another named Ma Zhaoshiang, whom people called "The God of Pestilence." The two were both men of the Green Forest, and understood Zhao Bin rather well.

One day while the three were together eating a meal, Jin Yuanliang said, "Dear brother Zhao, do you know what we do for a living?"

Zhao Bin replied, "No, I do not know what trade my elder brothers follow."

Jin Yuanliang said, "We are both robbers, but we are not those licentious robbers who break into houses and mistreat women. We take from the rich and give to the poor. We kill vicious and oppressive officials and cut down the ringleaders of crime who bribe them. We do away with cruelty and restore good practices. We concern ourselves with the inequalities that we find everywhere. This is what is meant by a hero who fights for right. Dear brother, it is because we think highly of your abilities that we would like you to enter into a partnership with us. I have here a suit of clothing to give you. It is made especially for going out at night with us."

As Jin Yuanliang spoke, he handed over a package to Zhao Bin. When Zhao Bin opened it, he saw that it contained a complete set of black clothing. From this day on Zhao Bin frequently went out with these two men during the night, robbing the rich and giving to the poor.

One day Zhao Bin left the bundle of clothing at home, and his mother opened it. She immediately realized that it was the kind of clothing that was worn by robbers when they went out in the darkness. Her eyes opened wide at what she saw.

Just at this time Zhao Bin came into the house. As soon as his mother saw him, she became furiously angry, saying, "Zhao Bin, your father was a hero among the armed escorts. You have cheapened his memory by daring to become a robber. A good son you are! You have killed me and may you also die quickly!"

Zhao Bin said, "Mother, do not be angry. If you do not want me to, I will not be a robber."

His mother said, "Burn this clothing and break your sword."

Then she thought to herself that they could no longer live in their present home and that the friendships he had made would have to be broken. If not, she feared that he would be captured. She thought of the mother of Mencius, the philosopher second only to Confucius, she who three times, once, then again, and yet again moved with her son Mencius to a new home, so that he might grow up a worthy person. Zhao Bin's mother wished to follow that example. As quickly as she could, she sold their household possessions and changed their money into fine gold and silver. Together with Zhao Bin she came to Linan. Here they rented a place in the fourth lane past the Green Bamboo Nunnery, in the home of a fruit seller named Wang Xing.

Still Zhao Bin had no occupation to which he could turn. After a while, Wang Xing's mother, known as Old Mother Wang, spoke to his mother, saying, "Madame Zhao, why not ask your son to sell fruit? He feels sad sitting around the house, and he eats a mountain of food."

Zhao Bin's mother replied, "He is still young with no experience and no understanding."

But Old Mother Wang countered: "You can ask him to go with my son to the wholesale fruit market. There, he can buy a little fruit and take it to sell elsewhere for a profit. In that way he can practice and see how it goes."

Zhao Bin's mother thought that this would be a good idea. When she discussed it with Zhao Bin, he wanted to try it.

The following day, taking two strings of cash, he went with Wang Xing to the fruit market and bought fresh fruit from the north. Wang Xing said to him: "You bought this fruit quite cheaply. Fifty per cent of your price must be profit. When you earn two strings of cash, you buy again. Think about this when you sell."

After Zhao Bin had had something to eat at home, he left, carrying the fruit in a small wicker case. Yet when he saw people, he did not have the courage to hawk his produce. He walked through several lanes, but everyone who saw him thought that he was taking a gift from one house to another instead of trying to sell something. Of course, no one bought anything. When Zhao Bin came to Phoenix Hill Street, he saw on the north side of the street a great gateway with a large wooden tablet above. It appeared to be the home of a national official of high rank.

Zhao Bin put his case on the ground and sat down beside the gate. Just as he was sitting there looking at his fruit and feeling unenthusiastic, he saw a *yuanwai* come out to say goodbye to some guests who were leaving. He was a tall, bearded man with piercing eyes named Zheng Xiong, nicknamed the "King of Heaven with the Iron Face." He belonged to a family in which there had been many generations of officials. He himself was a high military official, well known for his integrity in office and in private life, and for his delight in good works.

After having said goodbye to his guests, he noticed Zhao Bin sitting dejectedly beside the gate. Zheng Xiong, who enjoyed speaking to people, asked him, "My friend, what are you doing here?" Zhao Bin explained that he was selling fruit, that he had bought it for two strings of cash, and that he wanted to sell it for four strings.

Zheng Xiong called a servant and had him empty the case of fruit into a large bowl and bring four strings of cash to give the young man. Zheng Xiong questioned him, and Zhao Bin explained that it was his first attempt at buying and selling.

The next day he went to the market with Wang Xing and again with two strings of cash bought some northern fresh fruit.

After returning home and having something to eat, he took the case of fruit and without going elsewhere went straight to the Zheng mansion on Phoenix Hill Street. He put down the case, sat down, and waited until noon. When Zheng Yuanwai started to leave the house, Zhao Bin said, "Don't go. I have brought you some fresh fruit."

Zheng Xiong asked, "Who told you to bring it?"

Zhao Bin said, "Take it inside. I did not bring it to sell."

Zheng Xiong said, "That is your wish, but not my wish. I would prefer simply to give you two strings of cash every day. How would that work?"

Zhao Bin replied, "Good!"

When Zheng Xiong heard this, he was amused and said, "How easily you gave up the idea of becoming a merchant. I will take them today, but tomorrow when you come, do not bring any more." Then he told the servant to give Zhao Bin four strings of cash for the fruit, and Zheng Xiong and Zhao Bin went their separate ways.

Zhao Bin took the money home and from that time became more skilled in buying and selling. Sometimes he lost money and at other times he made up his losses. Occasionally he saw Zheng Yuanwai.

One day, Zhao Bin was at the West Lake looking at the girls passing over the causeway when a gang of toughs attacked him. The gang had nearly killed him when Ji Gong rescued him and saved his life. From then on Zhao Bin recognized Ji Gong as his teacher.

Now when Ji Gong had left the home of Li Guoyuan, he met Zhao Bin as he was selling fruit. The monk said, "Zhao Bin, come and have a drink of wine with me." Zhao Bin went with the monk to a wine shop for a few drinks.

The monk said, "Today you will take on the role of Wei Tuo for me."

Zhao Bin asked, "How will I act as Wei Tuo?"

Ji Gong explained how Li Guoyuan had lost the prince's tally scroll and how it had found its way into the upper room of a pavilion in the flower garden of the prime minister's estate. Ji Gong then asked Zhao Bin to steal it unseen and unheard and get it back to the home of Li Guoyuan while pretending to be Wei Tuo.

Zhao Bin said, "But I do not know Li Guoyuan."

The monk said, "I will take you there."

After they had finished eating and drinking, he gave Zhao Bin the money he had received from Li Guoyuan and took him to the gate of the Li family home.

The monk said, "Come tonight," and then gave him some further instructions.

Zhao Bin nodded his head. Then he went home and told his mother: "My teacher, Ji Gong, wants me to act as Wei Tuo tonight."

His mother asked, "What is acting as a Wei Tuo?"

Zhao Bin replied, "My teacher wants me to go to the prime minister's estate and find a five-thunder, eight-trigram scroll for someone while pretending to be a Wei Tuo."

His mother knew that Ji Gong was a good man. If it had been anyone but Ji Gong, she would not have let Zhao Bin venture out at night.

Zhao Bin changed his clothing and took a large knife used for chopping vegetables. When it grew dark, he climbed out over the wall, telling his mother to keep the gate fastened. He then went over the rooftops to the Li home and waited there above in the darkness. When he heard Ji Gong say that Wei Tuo had not yet arrived, Zhao Bin waited for a short time and then answered: "I am here! The spirit has come!"

The monk said, "Old Wei, go to the upper room of the pavilion in the flower garden of the prime minister's estate. Get the prince's tally scroll and bring it here."

Zhao Bin said, "I will obey!" Then he turned and dashed nimbly off across the roofs.

He quickly arrived at the neighborhood of the prime minister's estate and hastened on to the flower garden. When he looked around, he saw that the garden was very large. He could not immediately identify the pavilion for which he was looking. There was a little pavilion over the water, a pagoda in a miniature forest, flowers for the four seasons, and foliage for the eight festivals. He leapt down and began to search about until he came to the northeast corner of the garden, where there was a small courtyard. The largest building there was a house of three sections on the north side. To the east and west were two smaller matching buildings.

In a room of the north building, the light of a lamp shone dimly, and the shadows of people passed across the paper windows. Zhao Bin moved closer. From outside he moistened the paper of the window with the tip of his tongue and made a small hole. When he looked inside, he saw along one wall a bed and on the north side a square table with two chairs. A sharp-edged saber hung on that wall. There was a candle in the lantern on the table.

Two men sat in the chairs facing each other and drinking tea. The man on the east side was at least sixty years old. The skin of his face had a sickly pallor. His two eyebrows were like spear points and his eyes like a pair of triangles. His hair was as white as a white flower. On his head he wore a blue kerchief, and around his body a blue silk robe with a pattern of seal characters.

The man to the west was about thirty. He wore a dark green cloth hat and a black silk jacket. Around his waist was tightly tied a wide silk sash, while over his shoulders was carelessly thrown a dark cloak of the kind commonly called a hero's cloak.

Zhao Bin could hear the older man saying, "Now, my brave young man, I have sheltered and taken care of you well. If you perform the business that I have asked you to do and if you really do it properly, I will give you a hundred ounces of silver. You may take it to the faraway places of heaven and the edges of the seas, where you will be beyond men's powers to try you for taking a man's life." As he spoke, the older man reached into his clothing, took out two packages of silver, and placed them on the table. It was truly silver of the finest quality.

The younger man said, "I have learned so much from your kindness, venerable sir. You have granted me favors often when it would have been rude to refuse and embarrassing to accept. They have been such that now it would be a sin to refuse your request."

The older one said, "Young man, carrying out an order is worth much more than being respectful."

Zhao Bin then saw the younger man take the silver and place it inside the front of the upper part of his jacket. The man then reached out and took down the saber hanging on the wall, saying, "Venerable sir, whatever you hear moving outside, I say one thousand times ten thousand times, pay no attention. In a little while a man's head will come to see you." With this he went out of the building.

Zhao Bin quickly concealed himself and watched where the young man went. Zhao followed him, thinking to himself: "He must be going somewhere to kill a man. I will go along and watch!" He observed the man walk west through two courtyards, until on the west side there was a screen decorated with wooden placards covered with characters. Following the man through the gate beyond the screen, Zhao Bin saw a flickering light in a building of three parts to the north. There was a sound, as if someone were reading aloud to himself from a book. After he saw the man holding the saber go into the building, Zhao Bin made a hole in the paper window and saw a square table and two chairs. Seated in one of the chairs was a refined and studious-looking young man, while nearby was an old manservant.

The man who had just come in struck the table with the saber and said, "Whoever is the master, quickly speak for yourself. I have come here to put an end to your life."

The young gentleman, who had been intimidated by the sight of the armed intruder, prostrated himself on the floor together with the servant, and spoke: "Spare our lives, good man! Since you ask, let me tell you why I am here."

As he heard this, Zhao Bin began to burn with anger at the would-be assassin. He grasped his vegetable chopper and was about to burst into the room and intervene.

CHAPTER 7

Reunited heroes rescue a studious young man;
Han Dianyuan reforms his ways with Ji Gong's help

Life in a thatched hut beside a mountain stream,
Watching the years pass,
Counting the reds and whites of blossoming peach and pear trees,
Seeing the green shoots in the fields,
Lying at night on a bamboo bed listening to the rain,
Seeing streaks of light on paper windows
As sun breaks through the clouds,
Such are the simple joys of those
Free from the lust for wealth and power.

ZHAO Bin, in the darkness, saw the man with the sword enter the building where he was about to kill the two men, master and servant. The horrified young gentleman, trembling with fear, knelt on the floor and begged: "Great sir, forgive me. Hold your peals of thunder and tolerate my slow report to you." The old servant was also kneeling.

Then Zhao Bin heard the man with the sword say to them, "Who are you two, master and servant, and what have you been doing? Speak quickly!"

The old servant replied: "Since you ask, sir, the young master of our house is named Xiu Zhibing. His original home was in Chienan province. His father's name was Xiu Changuei. The father was on good terms with Han Dianyuan, the then-chief military officer. He is here now in the prime minister's flower garden, acting as superintendent of the estate. Han Dianyuan has a daughter of the same age as our young master. Her father suggested that he should give her to be the wife of our young master. The arrangement was made when they were very young. Later, our old master died. Shortly after that the buildings of our estate burned, leaving hardly a tile intact. Then I came here with our young master.

"When we came here to live as poor relations, Han Dianyuan saw that the clothing we wore was in tatters, and he regretted the marriage agreement. Han Dianyuan hates poverty and loves only wealth. It is now clear why he kept the two of us here, telling the young master to go on with his studies in this flower garden. Who would have thought that he would have sent you here to kill us?"

When the man with the saber heard this, he said, "So that is how it all came about. I truly did not know." At the same time he took out the hundred ounces of silver, saying to the young master, "I will give this to you. Take it quickly and escape with your lives! Find a safe place where you can study diligently. When you are older, you may become famous. You cannot wait here, for fear that he will try again to harm you."

Outside, when Zhao Bin heard this, he said, "This business was well taken care of. He is a man of character." He was so pleased that he forgot he was eavesdropping and spoke the words aloud.

When the man with the sword heard someone speak outside, he leapt out through the doorway, sword in hand. Seeing Zhao Bin, he struck at him, but Zhao Bin parried the blow with his vegetable chopper. The two faced one another, each probing and searching for an opening in the other's defense. Zhao Bin had a strange feeling, as he said to himself, "How is it that his manner of handling a sword is the same as mine?"

The other had similar feelings, for he quickly moved out of reach and, with his sword still at the ready, called out: "Slowly! Do not move until you tell me your name, where you live, with whom you have practiced sword fighting, and for what reason you have come here."

Zhao Bin said, "I am named Zhao Bin. People have nicknamed me the Helping Hand. You ought to know that I am dangerous. You need not try to find out whether I will kill you."

When the other man heard this, he quickly threw down his sword, saying, "All this time it was one who was the same as a dear brother. This is like taking water to the Dragon King temple, people of the same household not recognizing each other!"

"Who are you?" Zhao Bin asked.

The other man replied, "I am surnamed Yin—my personal name is Shixiong. Dear brother, you have forgotten your elder brother."

Zhao Bin thought to himself, "When I was eight or nine years old, Yin Shixiong came to work for my father. That was several years more than ten years ago." He put down his vegetable chopper and greeted him in a more polite manner, and the two exchanged news of what had happened since they had parted.

Yin Shixiong said, "After I stopped acting as an armed escort on the east road, I worked for your father until his death. Then I heard that my teacher's wife and my dear brother had moved to the capital. I thought I would seek you out, but until now I was unsuccessful. While staying at the Thrice Lucky Inn, I fell sick with an ulcer on my leg. At the inn, I met the former chief military officer, Han Dianyuan, who is living in the flower garden and is the superintendent of this estate. He is also the owner of the Thrice Lucky Inn. He looked after me during my illness and brought me here, where I stayed until I recovered. Today he gave me a hundred ounces of silver and asked me to kill a person whom he hates. I came here and asked—and only then did I understand what it was all about. Dear brother, you came at just the right time."

Zhao Bin then explained about the other affair, ending, "Tonight I am carrying out the orders of Ji Gong. I came here to get the five-thunders, eight-trigram prince's tally scroll."

Yin Shixiong said, "It was lucky that you met me tonight. If you had not, you would not have been able to get the scroll. First, help me to get Xiu Zhibing and the old servant safely away—then I will help you."

The two then went into the room and told Xiu Zhibing to leave quickly, taking the hundred ounces of silver for traveling expenses. Xiu Zhibing asked Yin Shixiong's name. The old servant kowtowed to Yin, thanking him for his kindness.

The servant then rapidly prepared the young master's lute and a small chest of books to take with them. "Yin, kind sir," he asked, "where shall we go on such a dark night as this? Here in the capital the watchmen are very numerous and investigate everyone they find out at night. If you simply tell us to go, how will we manage?"

Yin Shixiong thought this sounded reasonable and said, "Zhao Bin, if you have a place where they could safely stay for the night, tomorrow an inn can be found for them."

Zhao Bin replied, "Brother Yin, would you remain here for a short time, and would you, young master, and your servant come with me?"

He then took the two out through the corner gate of the flower garden. Zhao Bin was thinking of taking the two men to his own home, but they had not gone very far past the gate when he saw a man standing before him. It was Ji Gong. As soon as Zhao Bin saw him he said, "Ah, Teacher, you have come. Very good!" and explained about the two people with him.

Ji Gong said, "Good, I came about this very business. I was in the library drinking at Li Guoyuan's house, and I told him that I was going to pay my respects to you and came here. You go quickly now and carry out what we talked about—I will take care of these two."

Hearing this, Xiu Zhibing immediately raised his clasped hands in respect to Ji Gong, who then took them away to the home of Li Guoyuan.

Telling the servant to leave their baggage in the courtyard, Ji Gong took the two into the library. Zhao Wenhui and Li Guoyuan were drinking wine. When they saw Ji Gong bring in the studious-looking young gentleman with his servant, they quickly rose to their feet. "Teacher, where have you been that you have returned with these two people?" they asked.

The monk explained the affairs of Xiu Zhibing. When he was sure that Li Guoyuan understood, the monk asked, "Could you give them a few rooms here, where the young man can continue his studies? If there should be any problem, I would be responsible."

Li Guoyuan could see that Xiu Zhibing was extremely refined and intelligent. He agreed at once to the monk's request and asked everyone to sit down and drink with him.

At the third watch they heard a sound outside, and a voice. "I am the spirit and I have come. Senior Monk Ji Gong, who is above others, I have brought the five-thunder, eight-trigram prince's tally scroll."

Ji Gong quickly went out and saw Zhao Bin and Yin Shixiong on the roof.

Earlier that evening, after handing over Xiu Zhibing to Ji Gong, Zhao Bin had returned to the flower garden. As soon as he met Yin Shixiong, they immediately hurried over to the five-story pavilion. This pavilion had twenty-five rooms, all of spacious proportions. It was entirely covered inside, with paper folded into pleats for extra warmth and comfort. In the center of the building outside was a hanging balcony. Yin Shixiong climbed up and went into the adjoining room.

There on a table he saw a small hardwood box. Opening it, he saw that inside was the actual prince's tally. On it were the characters "five thunders" surrounded by the eight sets of trigrams, each consisting of three whole and or broken parallel lines in various combinations, as they were used for divination.

Zhao Bin said, "We have finished, brother. Let us go together."

Yin Shixiong replied, "After we leave, things will be in chaos here."

Zhao Bin asked, "What do you mean?"

"Think about it," Yin Shixiong said. "The person who bought the scroll is the prime minister of this present dynasty. If he loses this treasured piece, would he not go to the local officials? Would not the local officials carry out extensive investigations to get to the bottom of it? Could the great numbers of suspects escape from being brought in to be questioned, and perhaps from being beaten to death?"

So saying, he took out fire-making implements and set fire to one of the paper-covered window lattices. As the two men fled from the estate over the roofs, they could see the light from a great fire behind them.

It was like a golden serpent leaping wildly with a trail of sparks. Then the fierce power of the blazing flames broke through everywhere. The fire followed the winds like waves. There was a sound of "Hu! Hu!" as if a monster were breathing within the concealing smoke, while a red glow illuminated heaven and earth.

Well before this, the two men had sped away over the walls of nearby estates. Using their skills, they flew over the houses until they reached the rooftop of the Li home, where Zhao Bin called out: "I am here. The spirit has come!"

Ji Gong came out and, reaching up, took the scroll from Zhao Bin and handed up to him a yellow bag. In it were five hundred cash, an incense burner filled with rice, and five bowls filled with small cakes. Such a gift was indeed appropriate for a temple image.

The monk said, "Take it, venerable Wei Tuo. This contains the material thanks of this household."

Up above, Zhao Bin took it and called out, "I, the spirit, am leaving." Then, with Yin Shixiong, he went home to his mother.

Now Ji Gong took the five-thunder, eight-trigram prince's tally scroll inside. When it was unrolled, it was seen to be the correct one. Li Guoyuan quickly sent it by a trusted servant to give it to Li Chunshan.

Li Guoyuan and his guests sat drinking and talking through the rest of the night. When morning came, Ji Gong took his leave. Li Guoyuan wanted to give him gold or silver, but Ji Gong said, "If you want to thank me, let our relationship simply continue as it is now. As a monk, I will appreciate your care in helping Xiu Zhibing to go on with his studies."

Li Guoyuan agreed and Ji Gong left.

As he walked straight along on his way, he saw a man standing in front of him. The man, who seemed to be an attendant, said, "Where is Ji Gong going?"

The monk asked, "Who are you?"

The attendant replied, "The man who owns our inn has been given forty strokes with the bamboo, and he has wounds from the beating. I hear that you, sir, have the pill of the immortals containing a subtle medicine. I beg you to cure him."

The monk asked, "Who is the owner of your inn?"

The attendant replied. "The man who founded the Thrice Lucky Inn is Han Dianyuan. He was the superintendent of the prime minister's estate. Because last night the great pavilion in the flower garden was lost in a fire, the prime minister was very angry. He said that Han Dianyuan had neglected his duty. Han Dianyuan was given forty strokes with the big bamboo and is now suffering from pain."

When the monk heard this, he went with the man to the Thrice Lucky Inn. As soon as he entered the cashier's room, he saw Han Dianyuan, who was lying down and groaning continuously. Several friendly waiters were standing around him, advising and trying to comfort him. When they saw the monk come in, they said, "Success! The honorable teacher indeed has the pill of the immortals made from subtle medicine. The great teacher is especially compassionate."

The monk laughed and pointed at the suffering man. "Even with subtle medicine it is difficult to heal an illness that is a punishment for a person's own evil acts. Heaven above quickly requites merciless men."

These words struck Han Dianyuan to the core. He thought to himself: "This monk knows things that others do not. During the night I sent Yin Shixiong to kill Xiu Zhibing, to whom my daughter has long been promised. I did not see Yin Shixiong return, but the young man and his servant went away. Then for no reason the great pavilion was lost in a fire." He thought about it and then asked, "Holy monk, could Your Reverence save me? I repent."

The monk replied, "I will take care of you and cure your sickness. Will you give your daughter in marriage to Xiu Zhibing, or not?"

Han Dianyuan answered, "If I can be better, I will gladly ask Xiu Zhibing to return and give him my daughter. I will have no more evil thoughts. I have been driven out of the prime minister's estate. I now do not dare to let evil rule my heart. If I were to let evil into my heart again, I fear that heaven and earth would destroy me."

The monk gave him some medicine that immediately relieved his pain. The monk then told him to go to the home of Li Guoyuan to receive back Xiu Zhibing as the husband-to-be of his daughter. Han Dianyuan bowed his head in assent.

CHAPTER 8

A false order from the prime minister commands that the Great Pagoda be pulled down; the vagabond saint manifests his powers to punish the evil lower officials

NOW, from that day when Ji Gong had left the Monastery of the Soul's Retreat, he had been staying sometimes at the home of Su Beishan, and sometimes at the home of Zhao Wenhui. Today he had been playing chess in the home of Su Beishan with Su Yuanwai. Suddenly Ji Gong moved a chess piece that committed him to the attack. At the same moment, Ji Gong's thoughts turned to the temple, and by the light of his intuition he knew what was taking place there.

At once he slapped his hand on the table three times and said, "Su Beishan, I cannot remain here in your home. I must go immediately. Prime Minister Qin has sent people to demolish the Great Memorial Pagoda in my temple. I am going to fight with this Prime Minister Qin."

Su Beishan said, "Saintly monk, you cannot. It is he who is the prime minister. He ranks with the most glorious nobles. My teacher is a man who has left the world. How can you provoke the wrath of such a powerful man?"

Ji Gong did not give Su Beishan any further explanation, but simply stood up to leave. Su Beishan went with him to the mansion gate and watched as he walked off into the distance. Ji Gong walked straight out through the Qiantang gate and along the Su Embankment, singing to himself.

> Those who live a century
> Since the ancient times are few,
> First a child, then faltering age,
> In between not too much time.
> There is sadness; there are cares.
> Though our nation brims with wealth,
> This dynasty's governed ill.

> Though officials gain much gold,
> Few have wisdom, none are brave.
> Once disturbed, their hair turns white.
> Autumn's moon will soon grow dim;
> Autumn's flowers quickly fade;
> Time for flowers passes soon.
> Bring the wine jar round once more
> And forget the dusty tombs,
> 'Til the grass turns green again.

The monk was still singing when he came to the mountain gate. The moment that Guang Liang saw him, the superintendent said, "Brother teacher, thank heaven that you are here! Such a calamity! It is as if the sky has fallen on our temple!"

After Ji Gong had asked for the details about which he already knew, he said, "No matter what the calamity, even if the heavens fall, Brother Teacher, it does not matter. Leave it all to me, Mad Ji! But this pagoda is something we cannot give them. Do you think that I would fail the body of monks in this temple?"

Guang Liang said, "But, Brother Teacher, you must not provoke these men to anger. They are the four great managers of the prime minister's estate. He has sent them here to take down the Great Memorial Pagoda and use the materials from it to restore his lofty pavilion."

Ji Gong said, "Ah! He is the prime minister of the present reign, and he wants to destroy the Great Memorial Pagoda, so it must be destroyed! Then after another two days pass, the commander of the capital's palace garrison will order us to have the Great Treasure Hall taken down, and we will let him destroy that! And there will be still more! Again, after another two days, a letter will come from Linan prefecture, saying that its officials want us to take down the two halls to the east and west! Again we will have to let them be destroyed! After still another two days, a letter will come from Qiantang prefecture, or some other prefecture, saying that its officials want to take down the storage building for sutras, and we will have to let them destroy it! And there will be still more! I raised the money for the Great Memorial Pagoda, and I cannot give it to them to take down!"

Hearing this talk, the superintendent thought in his heart, "Ji Gong was never right for us in the past. This situation may be our chance to get rid of him." Thus, even now, the superintendent was still trying to take advantage of the situation to injure Ji Gong. Then Superintendent Guang Liang said, "Brother Teacher, do you dare to ask them not to take down the Great Memorial Pagoda? The four honorable great managers are now sitting in the large meditation hall. You may go to look for them, but I fear that you will make trouble that you cannot control."

Ji Gong gave a cold little laugh saying, "Brother Teacher, I do not want you to concern yourself with this matter." Having spoken, he walked quickly toward the large meditation hall.

The courtyard that he entered was shut in on three sides by buildings. A dozen or more low-ranking officials were standing about in the courtyard, and the four honorable managers were just then drinking tea in the best building on the north side. When the low-ranking officials saw the poor monk with clothing so badly torn and ragged, they quickly stopped him saying, "Who is this?"

Ji Gong said, "It is I."

The lower officials asked, "Who are you? The various great people are now here talking. What is a poor monk like you doing by coming here? To what temple do you belong?"

Ji Gong replied, "I belong to a nun's convent."

When the lower officials heard his reply, they admonished him, saying, "That is no kind of language to use. You are a monk. What are you doing in a nun's convent? Men and women mixed together!"

Ji Gong said, "You do not understand. The old nun in the convent died, and the young nun has run off with somebody. I am staying at that temple as the caretaker. I have heard it said that all you honorable great people have come asking about large pieces of timber. In large temple where I come from we have accumulated a great pile of timber, a pile like a mountain, truly large and truly bulky, like these long beams that hold up the roof. If a man squats down at this end and another man squats down at the other end, the pile is so big that the man at this end cannot see the man at the other end."

The low-ranking officers said, "What a big pile of timber that must be!"

The monk went on with another rush of words, repeating himself. "That big pile of beams in our temple, with a man squatting down at one end and the other man squatting down at the other end, and the man on this end unable to see the man at the other end!"

Again the low-ranking officers said in unison, "What a big pile of timber that must be!"

The monk rattled on, repeating, "The pillars and rafters under the roof in our temple are piled so high that the man squatting at this end cannot see the man squatting at that end, and the one at that end cannot see the man at this end."

When the low-ranking officials heard this, they all laughed and asked, "What do you expect to do about these timbers, Monk? Do you want to sell them? Do you want to give them to our great man?"

The monk replied, "I do not want to sell anything to the great man. I would only like the great man to give me some money to fix my pants."

Inside the large meditation hall, Qin An had heard all this conversation very clearly. Deciding that it was some kind of trickery, he had someone call the monk inside. One of the low ranking officials said, "Monk, our great man has called you. When you see our great man, be polite. None of your fox and monkey antics!"

The monk did not respond, but strode over to the hall, pushed aside the bamboo curtain, and entered. When the four men (Qin An, Qin Sheng, Qin Zhi, and Qin Ming) saw that it was this miserably poor monk, Qin An asked, "Monk, does your temple actually have some timbers?"

Ji Gong blinked his eyes and asked, "Where did you four honorable people come from?"

They answered, "We have been sent from Prime Minister Qin's residence. The great man has given an order that the Great Memorial Pagoda be torn down and the materials used to repair the large, many-storied pavilion in the prime minister's flower garden."

Ji Gong said, "You four honorable people have been ordered to come and take down the Memorial Pagoda by the great person of your houses."

The four men exclaimed, "How could there be a great person in our houses!"

Ji Gong said, "The fact that you have no idea about how to perform your duties can be blamed upon your never having had any great person in any of your houses. When you return, tell that great man of yours that I, the monk, have said the following. From start to finish, the matter of his drawing a salary depends upon the fact that, at the beginning, the three imperial boards arranged to have such an official. They expected that he would harmonize the yin and the yang, settle matters in the way that they ought to be settled, and be himself deserving of his own share of happiness. He has no reason to pull down the property of Buddha. You return and tell him that I, the old man, say that it is not permitted."

Hearing these words of Ji Gong, how could these several honorable managers not be enraged by them and not become more reckless?

Qin An said, "All right! You ignorant monk! First of all I will beat you!"

With his arms flailing, he came at Ji Gong and attempted to land a blow.

Ji Gong stepped to one side, saying, "If you want to fight, let us go outside."

Qin An straightened up and walked outside after the monk. There, Qin An told his people, "Beat this monk for me!"

The low-ranking officials all came at him together, fists swinging, each trying to get in a blow at the monk's face or legs. There were sounds of unceasing groans, in the midst of which they heard a voice say, "Do not strike! It is I!"

The low officials cried out, "Of course it is you that we are beating. You had no business to come running in among us, asking to get yourself killed. You really are too old to be putting dirt on your own head!"

While they were still beating him, they heard Qin Sheng, who had come out and was standing there beside them, say: "Stop beating him. I heard a sound that was not right. Let me look, before you beat him any more."

Oh, it was dreadful! Suddenly Qin Sheng and the others realized that the monk was standing off to the east observing them. Naturally, he was laughing. Looking down, they saw the chief manager, Qin An, disheveled and bruised. The people gathered round him and said, "Manager, how did you happen to get beaten, sir?"

Qin An said, "You were all getting even with me for some private grudges you had. I told you to beat the monk, but you beat me. I said, 'It is I!' and you all said that it was I that you were beating. All right, all right, all right!"

The other two, Qin Zhi and Qin Ming, came out to look. They saw that Qin An's injuries seemed rather serious, and Qin Sheng said, "This certainly is the result of some witchcraft of that monk. Every one of you beat him for me."

When the low officials heard this, they all went toward the monk, their eyes glaring and their expressions most forbidding.

The monk said, "How nice! How nice! A quiet man may ride, but a quiet horse is ridden." Then he said under his breath the six sacred words: "Om Ma Ni Pad Me Hum! I command!"

His words were frightening enough to make them all fall silent. Then they all became angry with each other. Chang Sheng looked at Li Lu and said, "Every time I look at you, my fury rises. I have long wanted to beat you, you subservient dog's head."

Li Lu said, "Good! Let us face off and see who stays up and who goes down!"

Over on the other side of the courtyard things were much the same. Jia and Yi were battling in one place; elsewhere, Tzu and Zhou were fighting to the death; eighteen people were beating each other in nine pairs.

Qin Sheng looked at the battered and bruised Qin An and said, "I am always angry when I look at you. You asked the people to beat you up. If you are angry at me, come over and I will give you a good one." At once the two struck out at each other.

Ji Gong was standing watching one man and asked him, "Why are you hitting that man?"

The man looked and said, "Something is wrong. I am not the right adversary for him."

Ji Gong said, "Let me help you with a suggestion. Hit him a few more times, then exchange him for someone else."

The monk watched them go on fighting. One hit the other a slanting blow and then almost bit off his ear. The other, enraged, then bit off a piece of the first one's nose. They were all fighting wildly with each other.

The superintendent of the monks came over, looked and said, "Dao Ji, you have created a great disturbance. You have put these honorable managers of Prime Minister Qin through more than beasts could bear. Is this right? Are you not ready to release them from your spell?"

Ji Gong replied, "Brother Teacher, if you had not asked me, I might have let this band of robbers kill each other, one by one. Today I will spare them." Then he said, "Stop fighting, everyone!"

Naturally at this command they all came to their senses, each one blaming the other. One said, "Sheng, my brother in arms! You and I have had such a long friendship! Why did you beat me so cruelly?"

His friend Sheng replied, "How should I know? Look at my ear—you bit off a piece!"

The other retorted, "Don't talk about it! Wasn't that a piece of my nose that you just spat out?"

All of the others had recovered their wits, including Qin An, who seemed in no serious danger after all. "Which temple does that crazy monk come from?" Qin An asked the superintendent. "You had better not let him get away. In a little while, if that crazy monk is not available, I will ask you for someone in his place!"

The managers and their men mounted their horses and then left the Monastery of the Soul's Retreat. All along the road they whipped their steeds. The shaken men were unwilling to slow down until they had passed through the Qiantang gate and reached the prime minister's estate. There they dismounted. Then they saw coming out of the mansion gate a fellow worker who looked at them and asked, "How did you come to return like this?"

Qin An told the whole story from beginning to end. Then the man advised him: "When you see the prime minister, do not tell him the exact details of what has happened; instead, let him take responsibility for finding this monk who brought you ill luck and seems to be the ringleader of the temple."

When Qin An came to the library, Prime Minister Qin was there reading. As soon as he lifted his head, he said, "You four men were sent to the Monastery of the Soul's Retreat to borrow some timbers. Why did you come back looking like this?"

Qin An replied, "We were just carrying out your orders, sir, and had reached the Monastery of the Soul's Retreat beyond the West Lake to borrow the timbers. All the monks in the temple were glad to lend the lumber, except one crazy monk. He not only would not lend it to us, but he beat and insulted us. I beg the prime minister to make a ruling concerning this matter."

When Prime Minister Qin heard Qin An's explanation, he said, "So! In addition to everything else, the Monastery of the Soul's Retreat has produced a crazy monk. How does he dare to beat the people of my household? It really is a pity!"

He then used his brush to write a warrant that was sent to the capital's garrison, ordering that five hundred soldiers under the command of two senior officers be provided to maintain order in the area. These officers were to surround the Monastery of the Soul's Retreat and to bring back Ji Gong in irons.

CHAPTER 9

Soldiers surround the Monastery of the Soul's Retreat and bring back the mad monk in fetters; Ji Gong's games with the village headmen end with a drunken entrance into the prime minister's estate

Smoke in the distance slowly ascends
Through mists and driving rain,
A stillness by a knowing master hand.
The unwearied eye sweeps over
Hills and streams a thousand *li*.
Each day we thank the painter for his gift.

THE garrison commander complied as soon as he received the order to send five hundred soldiers to surround the Monastery of the Soul's Retreat and to arrest Ji Gong, and detailed two senior officials to command the men. In addition, officials of Linan prefecture detailed eight village headmen, and officials of other prefectures appointed another eight. All of them were dispatched as if they were on a military mission.

When they all arrived at the Monastery of the Soul's Retreat, the officers and soldiers surrounded the temple. The headmen then entered and asked the master of the temple where the crazy monk had gone. The old master of the temple said that he did not know. The headmen were as hard as steel. They immediately placed the master of the temple, senior monk Yuan Kong, in irons, saying: "Monk, your bravery is no little thing. You dared to have the great managers of Prime Minister Qin's estate beaten!"

Then the attendant who served the master of the temple came and beseeched them to show mercy and not keep the old monk in irons. But the headmen simply put fetters on the attendant. The temple receptionist who kept the record of guests also pleaded with them, and he was treated in the same manner. Altogether, including the master of the temple and the superintendent of monks, seven monks were manacled and taken away to Prime Minister Qin's estate.

When the headmen went to report, Prime Minister Qin immediately set up court in a summerhouse in the flower garden. Up to seventy people of his household stood outside in attendance. Those who had been sent on the mission came forward and gave their report, saying that they had brought back the master of the temple and other monks. They talked a bit more, and then the prime minister ordered that the monks appear before him. The headmen relayed the order to the soldiers, who brought the monks forward. The master of the temple was given a seat within the summerhouse, while the other monks were kept waiting outside on their knees.

Inside the summerhouse, the prime minister watched from behind a bamboo curtain, where he could see them clearly, but they could not see him. The prime minister asked, "Who among you several monks is the mad Buddhist priest? Speak your name!"

Each of the monks said his own name. The master of the temple said, "I am called Yuan Kong. I am the master of the temple."

One said, "I am Guang Liang, the superintendent of monks."

Another said, "I am the one who keeps the record of the guests."

While another said, "I am the master's attendant, Sung Duan."

And still another, "I am the head caretaker of the mausoleum."

As Prime Minister Qin heard these statements, he said, "Then the insane monk is not among you! I sent the people to bring in the mad monk because of his having beaten my managers."

Guang Liang said, "I beg to inform the Great One. Ji Dian, the crazy monk of our temple, was originally a disciple of our temple master, Yuan Kong. When the honorable managers came, Ji Dian used his magical arts to cause the great managers to be beaten. We had no way of preventing what happened. I beg the Great One to be compassionate toward us and find us innocent."

When Prime Minister Qin heard this statement, he ordered some of the estate people to go with the prefectural headmen to capture the mad monk. Later, when a few of the Qiantang headmen were searching inside the temple, they came to the place where the Great Memorial Pagoda was to be torn down. There, they saw the mad monk pointing and directing the workmen as he viewed the destruction that had occurred at the Great Memorial Pagoda.

Now, when these tile workers, carpenters, and laborers had heard that there had been an official order from Prime Minister Qin to demolish the Great Memorial Pagoda and to repair the prime minister's great multistoried pavilion, who among them would dare to disobey? Among them, however, were some good people who thought: "It is not an easy matter to build a temple. Who knows how much work is needed and how many contributions are required for the construction of such a high edifice? It would be a great misdeed to tear this down in one day, and I do not want to do such a thing. If I used my iron tools and broke one of the better tiles, that would amount to two hundred cash. I will not do it!"

Just then Ji Gong, who was off at one side, pointed with his hand, and the workmen simply dropped to the ground from wherever they were on the arch. Even though some of them were seven or eight yards above the ground, they all landed safely on their feet. As they fell, they thought to themselves, "How fortunate that we had not begun to destroy the arch! We might have fallen to our deaths. It was very dangerous!" They stood looking at one another and saying, "This will be something to talk about for some time to come!"

However, there were others who were actually starting to demolish the structure. They were those who had thought from the first, "To demolish this one and reconstruct the other will be two months' work. Then the temple will require workmen to build another memorial pagoda, and that will be another couple of months' work. That will be almost half a year's work altogether." Just as they began the demolition, Ji Gong pointed at them. They fell to the ground with their legs drawn up on some three-cornered rocks and were injured. Those rascals crawled home on all fours and lost half a year's work while they recovered.

Ji Gong was just beginning to direct the first group of tile workers, carpenters, and laborers in the work of repair when the prime minister's headmen appeared with thunderous shouts, brandishing their weapons of tempered steel. "All right, you monk, there," said one, "you have caused all this turmoil and you are still here busily pointing and directing things." They then put Ji Gong in irons.

The monk raised his head and looked about at the eight headmen: Big Zhou, Wang the second, Jang the third, Li the fourth, Sun the fifth, Liu the sixth, Keng the seventh, and Ma the eighth. They all pulled at him. So Ji Gong asked, "How great a disaster did I cause?"

Headman Zhou replied, "That is difficult to tell, and why should I? When you arrive at the prime minister's residence, you will know and be happy."

The monk said, "If you ask me to go like that, I will not go."

Headman Zhou said, "Are you still trying to waste our time?"

The monk simply sat down on the ground. Under his breath he said, "Amitabha, Om Ma Ni Pad Me Hum."

Headman Zhou took his sword and tried to strike the monk, but was unable to do so. He called Wang the second to come to his aid. Wang the second pulled at Ji Gong with all his might, but could not move him. Wang the second said, "All the rest of you come here and help—don't just stand there watching!"

They all tried. Chang the third, Li the fourth, Sun the fifth, Liu the sixth, Keng the seventh, and Ma the eighth all came and tried with all their might to make him move. But the monk was like a mountain of stone.

They all said, "This is very strange!" Then they heard behind them a man laughing at them. Headman Zhou turned his head and saw two of the headmen from another prefecture. One was named Tian Laibao, the other Wan Hengshan. These two were responsible to the same officer as the others. They were stout fellows and longtime friends of Headman Zhou. When they saw that Zhou and the others were unable to move the monk, one of them laughed and said: "All you fellows can do is eat. You have no business trying to quell disturbances with the rest of the headmen. Today something happens and you are not paying attention."

When headman Zhou heard this, he said, "First of all, you two should not be so ready with your talk. If you two want to pull the monk up and along, we are willing to let you do it."

Tian Laibao said, "If I cannot pull the monk up, I will drop the family name of Tian."

Wan Hengshan said, "If I am unable to get the monk up and going, I will no longer eat my meals in the six-family village. Now, if you will just step aside…"

The others stepped back. They saw the two hitch up their pants, tighten their belts, and straighten their hats and clothing. Then the two stepped forward a few paces and fell on their knees before the monk, saying, "Respected sir, please stop distressing these people. Just look at them. If you will not go, the prime minister will be angry with them. He will talk to our boss, who will have to do something. We will then all be disciplined and discharged. The old and young in our homes will go hungry. I beg you, respected sir, to show compassion."

Hearing this, the monk smiled coldly and replied, "If you two had asked in this way before, I would have gone long ago. Headman Tian, what is your honorable name?"

When Headman Tian heard this question, he said, "You know my name is Tian. Why do you ask?"

The monk said, "Your name was not mentioned before."

Headman Tian said, "My personal name is Laibao."

Again the monk spoke: "Headman Wan, what is your honorable name?"

Wan Hengshan said, "Teacher, do not be annoyed with us. Have mercy, have mercy upon us. Let us go with them."

The monk said, "Go then. Go!"

Then Tian Laibao said, "Headman Zhou, now that the worst of this business is over, I beg to leave you."

"You can go now," said Headman Zhou, coming over to take Tian's place.

By this time they had led the monk out of the Monastery of the Soul's Retreat and had covered two *li* (roughly two-thirds of a mile) along the shore of the West Lake and the Su Embankment. In this area there were many wine shops. The monk stopped in front of the gate of one wine shop, sat down on the ground, and would not go on.

Headman Zhou asked, "Teacher, why don't we go on? Do you want a drink?"

The monk replied, "Perhaps I do not want a drink, but I want to ask you something. In this sort of business you adapt yourself. If you are on a mountain, you eat what is on the mountain. If you are near water, you drink the water. If you are among yellow trees, you wear yellow clothing. If there be not many, there may be few. If it be not large, it may be small. Now, if there are friends of mine who see me being taken to the prime minister's residence, how will you handle that? In this business I feel that you must spend a few cash on the monk. If not, I cannot calmly and peacefully go along with you."

When Headman Zhou heard this, he thought to himself, "I have been in this business for so many years, but this is the first time that anyone involved in a court action has asked me for money." Headman Zhou then said, "Teacher, you are a person who has left the world. What do you want to do with the money you are asking for?"

The monk replied, "I must drink wine. If I am not befuddled, I cannot go on."

Headman Zhou said, "It is possible to drink wine. How many pots of wine does Teacher usually drink?" The monk asked for twenty pots. The wine shop sent out the wine. The monk pretended that his neck was that of a bottle and declaimed as he drank:

Restraint!
In drinking keeps the temper mild,
From lechery, brings long life.
Property thus accumulates,
And families are kept from strife.

In the twinkling of an eye, the monk had finished the wine. Headman Zhou had just the number of cash in his pocket needed to pay for the wine, not one more and not one less. As he noticed this, he said, "Teacher, if you had drunk another pot, my money would not have been enough, and if you had drunk one pot less, I would have had a few cash left over."

The monk said, "Headman Zhou, when you got up this morning, wasn't it your wife who gave you that money?"

"That is so," he replied.

The monk said, "That is the money that I gave your wife last night."

Headman Zhou said, "Teacher, do not joke. Let us go on quickly." And he led the monk on for about two *li* more.

The monk said, "Headman Zhou, you change over and let someone else lead me."

Headman Zhou asked, "What for?"

The monk replied, "You do not have enough money. Change to another man."

Headman Zhou called upon Headman Wang to lead. As he started off with the monk he said, "Teacher, keep going."

The monk said, "I will not go. Do you know why Headman Zhou is not leading me?" Headman Wang did not know, so Ji Gong continued: "In order to lead this monk, he had to spend some money on him."

Headman Wang said, "What does the teacher want to do with money?"

The monk said, "Drink wine!"

Headman Wang said, "Drink then, Teacher."

The monk said, "Give me ten pots of wine."

"Right!" said Headman Wang. "I brought only four hundred cash, just enough. I have no more."

Ji Gong drank the ten pots of wine. He wanted to be drunk when he reached the prime minister's estate. Wang led the monk for another two *li*.

The monk then said, "Headman Wang, you, too, must change places with someone else. Another person must lead me."

Headman Wang said, "Teacher, you are not being reasonable. When Headman Wang led you from the Monastery of the Soul's Retreat, that was two *li*, and then you drank wine. When you finished drinking, you again went two *li*. After four *li* you changed leaders. Then you would not go. Before you would move another step, you had to drink some wine. Now you have gone only two *li*. Why do you want to change leaders again?"

The monk explained, "Headman Zhou gave me twenty pots of wine. You are worth ten pots of wine."

"I will not argue with you," said Headman Wang. "Headman Zhang, you come and lead."

Headman Zhang said, "Teacher, if you want to drink, just go ahead and drink. Here we are in front of the Inn of the Drunken Immortal. I have credit here—drink your fill."

The monk said, "Give me thirty pots of wine."

When Zhang the third heard this, he opened his mouth, sticking out his tongue in astonishment, and said: "Teacher, old man, how much wine do you drink in one day?"

The monk answered, "I really do not drink very much. In the morning when I get up, I drink two catties. After I eat breakfast, I drink another two catties. After I eat the evening meal, I drink two more catties. If I get up in the night, I do not drink."

"Then you just go to bed after the evening meal?" asked Zhang the third.

"I jump into the wine jar and soak myself," said the monk. "If I do not soak myself, I cannot satisfy my habitual thirst."

He then drank the thirty pints given him by Zhang the third. There was a pause in the conversation after all this explanation, and the eight headmen also had a drink.

When they arrived at the gate of Prime Minister Qin's residence, the servants, who thought that the prime minister should be given a little time until his anger had cooled, detained them.

Headman Zhou announced, "We are here, we are here!" and led Ji Gong into the residence. He looked around at the awe-inspiring surroundings.

> Along the winding corridors were cases
> Made to contain the great man's curios.
> Within were pairs of hollow white jade vessels
> Carved in the shape of Chinese unicorns.
> Beside the door of the great hall, a man-made grotto,
> Crafted of curious stones from distant places,
> Enclosed beneath the vault of its most spacious cavern

A chair with wheels, a chair of great antiquity,
Encrusted everywhere with precious coral.
In such a chair an emperor might ride
Or a noble's mother pushed by her filial son behind,
For it was clearly made for ceremony.
Embowering, but not concealing it, there was
A standing screen of pierced and sculptured lacquer
In color and brightness like the wings of kingfishers.
Closely crowded everywhere among the fine embroideries
Gleamed treasures from ancient ruined dynasties,
Like jewels spread out upon the richest tapestry,
Gifts from the palace of the emperor
Proclaiming Chin to be that reign's prime minister.

Headman Zhou led Ji Gong into the interior. There, Headman Zhou would make his report, and there the *lohan* would exercise the arts of Buddha and make manifest their powers.

As Ji Gong was led further into the residence by Headman Zhou, he saw that the old master of the temple, together with the superintendent, the attendant, and some others were standing along the veranda. When the monk arrived in front of the summerhouse, he did not kneel as the others had. Prime Minister Qin looked out at him through the bamboo blind and now realized that he was only a poor, ragged Buddhist priest.

Prime Minister Qin slapped the table before him loudly as he spoke. "You have a lot of gall for a crazy monk! I sent my household people to the temple to borrow some large timbers in a friendly way, not acting as if they were carrying out official duties. But you dared to use your demonic arts and beat my managers. Tell me the truth!"

The monk then wanted to explain how the managers had wanted to tear down the Great Memorial Pagoda, and how he had told them not to, and how the fight had started—but of these things he did not speak. Instead the monk said, "Oh great man, you still ask me! You hold the office of prime minister established by the three great councils, an office in which one should promote goodness, perform virtuous deeds, and bring about general prosperity. Now, without reason, you tear down and destroy buildings on Buddhist land—the more I think of it, the more my anger as a monk rises. Let the great man have me thrown down and given forty strokes of the bamboo and then ask again!"

When Prime Minister Qin heard these words, he broke into a rage and said, "What a brave, crazy priest! How do you dare to criticize a great minister? Come! You two from the left and right there, seize this crazy monk and throw him to the ground. Give him a good forty strokes for me."

Now these bamboo clubs used in punishments at the home of the prime minister were more terrible than those used anywhere else, because the hollow parts of the bamboo were filled with water. No matter how strong a man might be, forty strokes would break skin and bones. When Ji Gong heard the order given to beat him and the two men were about to begin, he pulled himself loose from their grasp. He leapt between the old temple master and the superintendent of the monks and stood among the other monks.

Three of the household people came over and thrust out their arms to grasp Ji Gong and throw him down upon the ground saying, "Very good, monk! You think you can hide from us and that will be the end of it."

One held his head down and one held his feet. The monk's head was to the west. The man with the bamboo stood at the south so that the prime minister could witness the punishment. The man raised the bamboo and administered forty strokes. The monk said not a word. After the three had finished, they stepped aside.

When the prime minister looked, he shouted, "You dog heads! I told you to beat the crazy monk! Why did you beat the superintendent?"

The three looked and felt a bit odd. Just now they had been sure that they were holding the mad monk. How could he have changed into Superintendent Guang Liang?

Guang Liang was now able to say, "Ai ya! You have killed me!" Up to this moment his mouth had been covered and he had been unable to speak during the forty blows. There was broken skin, wounded flesh, and much blood!

CHAPTER 10

Prime Minister Qin sees a ghostly spirit in a dream; Ji Gong comes by night to exercise the arts of Buddha

Only from the most extravagant hopes in the most simple heart,
May the profoundest changes come to pass.
The serenity of moonlit mountain peaks
May be reflected on the storm-tossed sea;
The frightened boatman sees and calmly steers his craft.
Such is the peace reflected from within the Buddhist's heart.

PRIME Minister Qin summoned a new set of executioners, saying, "Give this crazy monk forty heavy strokes for me. Now, my good mad priest, if I do not have you beaten, I swear that you need not call me a man."

So three executioners came before the summerhouse. One seized Ji Gong and said, "This time, monk, we will not beat the wrong one."

Ji Gong said, "You have me. I will go."

The three men shouted, "Are you trying to waste our time? Get down!"

Ji Gong asked, "Do you monks make bedding in that shop of yours?" pretending he thought that their bamboo staves were used to beat cotton into floss.

The executioners replied, "Don't pretend that you don't know what's going on. We are going to beat you more than cotton is beaten in a cotton-floss shop!"

They forced Ji Gong down. One of them sat astride Ji Gong's head and shoulders while grasping his ears, and another sat astride his legs. The third man uncovered the back of Ji Gong's body and raised the bamboo. Prime Minister Qin called out, "Strike! Strike! Strike!"

The executioner brought the bamboo down with great force, but missed Ji Gong by more than a foot. Not only that, but the bamboo hit the executioner who was astride Ji Gong's head and shoulders squarely in the back with a resounding thwack, and knocked him three or four paces away.

Holding his back with both hands, the fellow yelled, "Ai yah! Ai yah! You're trying to kill me. Good, good, good! When you wanted me to lend you two hundred cash, I didn't, and you have been holding a grudge against me ever since."

Prime Minister Qin was extremely angry. He told the three men to stand back and ordered another three to come forward, saying, "Give this crazy priest eighty strokes for me. If I do not beat you, you crazy monk, I swear that I will no longer be an official."

Ji Gong countered, "I swear that if you do not get this business over with, I will no longer be a monk."

As the new executioners came up, one said, "Let me sit astride his head and shoulders, Qin Shun can hold down his legs, and you take the bamboo. But do not let the bamboo miss the mark."

So they stretched out Ji Gong. Then the bamboo came down with a blow, but right in the middle of the back of the one holding Ji Gong's legs and knocked him forward.

Inside the summerhouse, as the prime minister watched, he understood. The first time, the executioners had mistakenly beaten the superintendent of the monks. The second time, the man holding Ji Gong's head and shoulders had been struck. This time, the man holding Ji Gong's legs was hit. These surely were examples of the magical arts arising from the monk's heretical practices. He therefore instructed some of his household servants to go and get a large hanging scroll from the great hall. He thought that the writing on the scroll, which affirmed that he was indeed the prime minister of the present reign, would overawe the monk and vanquish his magic.

The prime minister stepped down out of the summerhouse and advanced. Lying there on the ground, Ji Gong looked up and opened his eyes. The anger of Prime Minister Qin was so clearly shown on his face that it frightened nearly everyone who saw him. When he shouted, "Strike! Strike! Strike!" this time, who dared to hinder him? The next group of evil-looking executioners came forward. One of them raised the bamboo and brought it down with great force, but it flew out of his hands and hit the prime minister. The man was frightened out of his wits by his carelessness.

When the prime minister saw how things were going, he was in a towering rage. Bending his back, he picked up the bamboo stave and looked at it, intending the beat the monk himself. Suddenly he heard a clamor from the inner apartments. Prime Minister Qin was greatly surprised. It had long been the rule in his household that other than the prime minister himself, there should be no men in the inner apartments. Only the old women and maids could enter. Boys over three feet tall could go in only if they were called on urgent business.

Today as he heard the outcry, he was startled to see one of the old women come running and hear her call, "Oh, Great One, it is terrible! The Great One's chamber is on fire!"

Hearing this, the prime minister exclaimed, "I know it is probably one more of this monk's magic tricks." Hurriedly he called for twenty of his men to lock the monk in an empty room, saying, "At the third watch I will examine the monk." Pointing at Ji Gong he said, "Crazy monk, if you burn the prime minister's residence until there is not a tile left, I will still take you through the military barracks gate. There I will give you eighty strokes—and perhaps that will relieve the hatred I feel for you in my breast." He sent him off with the twenty men, telling them to guard the monk well.

Then, saying, "I must go to the inner apartments and see what is happening," Prime Minister Qin took several dozen people with him. There he saw his wife standing in a courtyard frightened and trembling, while the women and maids were busily putting out the fire. He asked her where the fire had originated.

She replied, "Sparks flew out of the incense burner and set fire to the paper on the lattice windows."

Prime Minister Qin gave orders that everyone should work to put the fire out. He himself carried out the incense burner and threw it on the ground. One of the serving women anxiously picked it up but found that it was undamaged. Made of unrefined gold, the heavy incense burner, even if it had been broken, would still have been a treasure, because according to the old saying, "Gold is gold!"

When Prime Minister Qin saw that the fire had been put out, he and his wife went inside. She asked, "Why did the Great One become so angry?"

He then told her how the mad monk had used his magic arts to beat the estate managers; how he, the prime minister, had ordered soldiers to surround the Monastery of the Soul's Retreat; and how the soldiers and headmen had brought back the monk in irons. "When I was about to punish him by beating, the inner apartments caught fire. I now have a number of monks locked up in vacant rooms, and at the third watch I intend to beat that insane monk."

When his wife heard this, she said, "Does the great man need to contend with these ignorant people?" Just as she said these words, a serving woman announced that the evening meal was prepared, and invited the prime minister to partake of it in another room.

Prime Minister Qin said, "We will just have it in here." A slave girl brought cups and chopsticks, but the prime minister was still too full of his pent-up anger to eat. He drank two small cups of wine and then withdrew from the table. For a while he read a book, but soon put out the light. He seemed to see several roads leading forward, but could not tell where they went. He yielded to his weariness for a while and then drifted toward sleep. Now, with his arm for a pillow, all things began to become indistinct and fade. As he was sinking into a deeper sleep, he heard footsteps.

> A deep foggy draft getting colder and colder,
> A sound like the wind in a forest so lonely,
> A forest in autumn when leaves lose their color,
> Then a hoarse, ugly cry like a stricken cow's bellow
> And something or someone was pulled through the door.
> Then he saw through the mist as the fog began clearing,
> Moving close there beside him a vision from hell,
> With a soul still in suffering whose face was familiar
> And a hideous goblin repulsive and fierce.
> Qin Kuei's only wish was to shun them and flee.

As Prime Minister Qin looked, he saw a huge, unearthly being come into the room from the courtyard. His face was like black smoke. He wore a dark blue or black satin cap like a soldier's, divided into six sections by seams, and a short padded jacket of dark cloth. A mesh pocket or string bag was fastened at his waist. Beneath the jacket was a garment with long, dark-red sleeves. Above his large eyes were rounded eyebrows. In his hand he carried a blazing and smoking pitchfork.

Close behind him entered another tall figure clothed all in white, wearing a hat two feet in height. The skin of his face was a sickly, transparent purple, revealing black beneath. In his hand he held a knotty wooden club from which tears fell as if the knots were eyes.

The two stood before the prime minister. Behind them another figure entered. On his head was a kerchief tied with the ends turned up and toward each other in the shape of a Chinese scepter. His robe was embroidered satin and his shoes were those of an official. His face was white and square in shape. In his hands he carried a writing brush and tablet.

One more figure appeared. On his head he wore a soft blue kerchief wound and tied into a turban, while on his body was a robe decorated with medallions of flowers in five colors against a dark-blue background. On his feet he wore soft, dark cloth slippers. His skin was a light, sickly purple in color, his eyebrows heavy and long, shading his widely spaced eyes. His hands were manacled and his ankles in fetters. With his hands he dragged the long chains with which he was bound and the heavy lock that fastened them together. He had a dry, emaciated look. His tangled hair was tied in a loose knot and his beard was like trampled grass.

Prime Minister Qin gazed at him and exclaimed, "Alas!" Yes, it was his adoptive father and patron, Qin Guai, returning home as a baleful ghost! Behind him followed a small demon with a kerchief of glazed material tied about its head. Green clay seemed to cover its face, and above its two protruding golden eyes were pointed vermilion eyebrows. Its body seemed to be painted with lacquer, and around its waist was tied an apron of tiger skin. In its hands it held a huge cudgel studded with wolves' teeth, which he held close behind the back of Qin Guai.

"My old father!" exclaimed Prime Minister Qin. "I thought that you would have been in heaven long ago. Who would have thought that you could still be suffering in the underworld! Why don't you go ahead and return now? Tomorrow your child will definitely invite high-ranking Daoists and Buddhists to raise you from suffering, that you may quickly ascend to heaven."

Qin Guai answered: "Son, for your father's sake, while you are yet in the world of light occupying your high position, return to the path of virtue before father and son-in-law both go down in the stormy sea. When men inspire hatred, heaven above is angry. Now I am punished in the black depths of hell, suffering every imaginable misery. From there I was ordered by the grand secretary of the Buddhist disciples in heaven to come home to you in this terrible form, to admonish you and to dissuade you from your evil course. You are the embodiment of the prime minister's office. You must do good deeds, promote the prosperity of all, and be virtuous. You not only failed to do good deeds, but you wanted to destroy a Buddhist building, a monstrous sin of the deepest kind. Because you tried to destroy the Great Memorial Pagoda in the Monastery of the Soul's Retreat and locked up the monks, I want you to listen to my wholesome advice. Release the monks quickly; then restore the Great Memorial Pagoda completely."

Just as the ghost had spoken to this point, the huge demon with the pitchfork said, "Brothers, take him away." There was a tremendous roar as the demon shook his flaming iron pitchfork. Qin Guai fell to the ground, was pulled to his feet, and then left with the others.

Prime Minister Qin called to him: "Father, wait! Your child has something more to say!"

But the demons paid no attention simply saying, "Lead on."

The prime minister was starting forward to grasp him when he suddenly heard the sound of a bell and opened his eyes.

CHAPTER 11

Zhao Bin stealthily visits the estate of Prime Minister Qin; the guiltless Wang Xing is mercilessly punished

In winter, to remember spring's not far away,
We pile the willow twigs in the roof's frost,
But wine is given to us that we may drink,
And grieve for sons and grandsons we have lost.

ONCE Prime Minister Qin had his eyes open, he realized that the dream about the demons leading his adoptive father had all come from things that existed only in his imagination. He threw the candle down upon the floor. At that moment a serving woman who was on night duty came into the room and picked up the candle before it could go out. His wife, who was inside the curtained bed, also awoke and asked, "Why is the Great One so disturbed at such trifles?"

Prime Minister Qin replied, "Just now I was reading a book and I had a sudden shock. I fell asleep and entered the land of dreams. There, I saw my old adoptive father and patron returning home as a frightful ghost, chained hand and foot, under the escort of several demon guards. He explained to me my sins in the world of light. I am planning now to stop the work of destruction at the Great Memorial Pagoda and to release all the monks. What do you think, wife?"

When his wife heard this, she laughed and replied, "Great One, you are a true man of books. How can you still believe in such heresies as supernatural powers and disorderly spirits?"

When Prime Minister Qin heard these words from his wife, he again suppressed his heart's natural goodness. He asked the serving woman what time it was.

She replied, "Just now the third drum sounded."

Prime Minister Qin said, "Pass on my order that in the third watch I will be at the outer library to conduct a close interrogation of the mad monk. I must punish him severely."

Just as he spoke these words, they noticed that the candle lantern in the room was making a sound like heavy breathing, and that the flame of the candle had become a foot high. Prime Minister Qin gasped. When he rashly commanded the candle flame to come back to its usual height, the flame did diminish, but it flared up again and continued moving to and fro like a weaver's shuttle. The stub of the candle was no larger than a date stone. The room was filled with a green light. After this had happened three times, Prime Minister Qin took down the precious family heirloom sword and pointed it at the candle. Suddenly, the candle began to produce two flames. Prime Minister Qin took another sword and the two flames became four. As the prime minister made slash after slash with his swords, the whole room was filled with the light of candle flames circling and whirling round and round.

Next he heard his wife cry out, "Great One! A demon with a huge head is standing outside the gate. Its head can be seen right up above the screen!"

The serving woman said, "But this is terrible. There is a demon squatting under the table and gnashing its long, ugly teeth! Look quickly by the bamboo blind there! That is one of our local demons. It is actually nodding its head."

Prime Minister Qin asked his wife to sound the gong calling the household people so that they might come and do battle with the demons. His wife and the serving woman went outside to call for help. The household people outside rushed in upon hearing that demons were bedeviling the inner courtyard and came to a stop in front of the prime minister. As they arrived, they heard a terrible scream. One demon seemed to be wounded and its head was bleeding. The men cried out at the awful sight. One of them shouted, "Honorable Prime Minister, there is a spirit wearing a cangue. It is incredible." People everywhere had always said that no one had ever seen a ghost wearing a cangue, one of those cumbersome wooden collars worn as a punishment, yet now one had appeared.

"Look, Honorable Prime Minister," another cried. "There is the spirit of someone who has hanged himself. How dreadful!"

"Honorable Prime Minister, there is a demon with no head!" called still another. "There are also other mischievous spirits."

Now all these things that seemed to be happening were creations of Ji Gong's Buddhist arts. At the time that Prime Minister Qin had instructed those twenty household people to confine and guard Ji Gong and the other monks, Qin Sheng had talked with the others gathered on the veranda watching the proceedings. "This business in which we are involved is not a matter for our amusement. Since yesterday I have not slept. Today, again we have this unfortunate business. Let me make a suggestion. Each of us should contribute two hundred cash to buy wine and several kinds of dishes to sustain all of us through the night. At the third watch the honorable prime minister will be sitting officially in the library to question the mad monk closely and severely. We then must not delay or mismanage this business. What do you all think about this?"

Everyone said, "Good, good, good. Let us do just that." Each of them handed in four small strings of cash. One of them took charge of the purchase of food and wine, and all helped as much as necessary.

As the first watch neared, one of them said, "Let us drink." And everyone joined in, eating and drinking.

Then Ji Gong said, "Honorable sirs, be compassionate, be compassionate. Won't you give this poor monk a small cup of wine?"

Qin Sheng replied, "Monks are not supposed to drink wine. Why do you ask us to give it to you?"

Ji Gong answered, "Wine drowns my wicked thoughts, the fifth among forbidden things."

"But wouldn't drinking also be a forbidden thing?" Qin Sheng countered.

The monk laughed. "Ah, ha! The honorable manager knows a part, but not the rest. The rest includes many advantages. Heaven has the winey stars, earth its wine-y springs. Man has his wine-y divinity, and wine encompasses ten thousand things. Confucius said, 'Wine is the way, but follow it reverently.'"

Qin Sheng said, "Since you know all these things, I will, after all, give you a cup of wine to drink." Then he filled a cup to the brim and gave it to the monk.

As he took it, Ji Gong said, "Good! Good! Good! Though the day may have been long, with wine the evening is like the morning of a day of rest and great affairs are but recreation after wine." After he had finished drinking that cup he said, "Honorable sirs, give me another cup of wine to drink."

Qin Sheng said, "I just gave you a cup of wine and you ask for more! Truly, you have no sense of self-respect."

Ji Gong said, "If you do not give me another cup of wine, it is because you do not have as much as a cup of kindness toward others."

Qin Sheng filled another cup to the brim for him. The monk drank it and said, "Come! Give me one cup more. Make it three cups."

Qin Sheng replied, "I have no more. It is not that I would not give it to you. Ask someone else."

Ji Gong gave a great laugh, "Ha, ha! I can drink myself." He took the wine cup in his hand and said, "Om! I command. Come, come, come!"

Then the others saw the cup fill with wine. The monk drank several cups of wine in succession and put the cup down. When the household people guarding the monk decided that they, too, would like another cup, they went one after another to the wine jug and tipped it, but nothing came out. They all began to say that the one who went to buy the food and wine had kept some of the money. Again they all looked at the jug, but it was indeed empty.

Qin Sheng did not say a word, all talk ceased, and a spirit of sadness settled over them all. Soon they slept, lying this way and that wherever they were. Then they were all transformed temporarily into ghosts and demons and instructed in their roles by Ji Gong.

As soon as the monk had seen that everyone was sleeping throughout the house, he removed his locks and chains and went toward the inner apartments to bestow just retribution. First, however, he looked for those evil servants who had been swaggering about, doing cruel deeds, while depending on their influence with the prime minister for their power. Ji Gong sought them out and gave each one a pinch.

Then he saw a man on the roof of a building to the north side, over the place where the prime minister was sleeping. He was holding in his hand a large knife with which he intended to kill Prime Minister Qin, who hated Ji Gong so much. Looking closely, Ji Gong saw that it was none other than Zhao Bin, the young fruit merchant. He had a string bag fastened at his waist to use in case he decided to carry something away. This was the same Zhao Bin who had helped Ji Gong to restore to its rightful owner the magnificent five-thunder, eight-trigram prince's tally scroll.

On that occasion, while Zhao Bin had been inside the prime minister's estate pretending that he was the Wei Tuo, Zhao Bin had met Yin Shixiong, who had once worked with Zhao Bin's father as an armed escort. The two had returned together to Zhao Bin's mother. Yin Shixiong had stayed a couple of days and then taken his leave.

Zhao Bin was only a small merchant and was not saving any money for the future. His poor old mother talked to him seriously about taking care of himself and his future. From then on, he became less careless and indolent.

On the morning of the day that Ji Gong was arrested, Zhao Bin had been at the West Lake selling fresh fruit when he saw a large number of soldiers surrounding the Monastery of the Soul's Retreat. He saw someone he recognized and went over to ask what was happening. Then he learned about how Ji Gong had beaten the managers and how Prime Minister Qin had sent the soldiers to surround the monastery, seize Ji Gong, and bring him back. He also heard that Ji Gong no doubt would be beaten to death.

When he heard all this, Zhao Bin was terribly shocked. He thought to himself, "Ji Gong was kind enough to save my own life, and now the reverend gentleman is in deep trouble. How can I not save him? My mother does not want me to go out at night! I have it. I will deceive her. I will wait until she is asleep. Then I will take that big vegetable chopping knife and go to find Prime Minister Qin at his estate, where I will kill him. Thus I will avenge my teacher, the senior monk Ji Gong."

He slowly returned home. There his mother asked, "Why did you not sell the rest of your fruit today?"

Zhao Bin answered, "Today I did not feel well."

The old lady said, "If, indeed, your body does not seem well, you had best rest at home."

After the evening meal, as Zhao Bin and his mother were about to go to their beds, they suddenly heard someone knocking at the gate. When Zhao Bin heard it, he felt quite unhappy. He thought to himself, "My mother was just about to go to sleep and then someone knocks at the gate."

When he went out to look, it was Old Lady Wang from across the way. As soon as she saw him, she said, "Zhao Bin, I have to trouble you about something. Early this morning when my son, Wang Xing, went out, he spread his carpet and arranged the fruit he was selling on the ground near the prime minister's gate. At exactly noon a man came here, riding in a small sedan chair. He said that my son had just been stricken with cholera, and he took my daughter-in-law away with him. I have not seen either my son or his wife since, and I am very worried. May I trouble you to go and ask about them?"

Zhao Bin immediately agreed to go. He had always done such things with a willing heart. He told his mother, changed his clothes, and took the large vegetable chopping knife with him. When he left, he went straight to the neighborhood of the Qin estate. By this time it was already late. He saw that Wang Xing's carpet with the fruit spread on it had not yet been taken away. He also saw that a guard named Guo Four was there keeping

watch over it. As soon as Zhao Bin saw that the guard was someone he
knew, he asked, "Headman Guo, where did my dear brother Wang go?"

Guo Four replied, "Ah, it is you, Zhao Bin. You ask about Wang Xing.
Do not mention it. Today at mid-morning the second master, the prime
minister's son, called to him to come in. Wang Xing sold him some fruit
amounting to a good deal of money. I was told to keep watch here. I had
other things to do, and when he did not come out, I went in and asked
about him. Everyone I saw told me not to ask, and no one knew anything."

Zhao Bin himself did not understand what could have happened to
Wang Xing, or what it was all about. After leaving Guo Four, he asked in
many places without learning anything. It was very dark and now at the
second watch. He quickly went again to the estate of Prime Minister Qin
and climbed stealthily over the roofs. Looking down from a rooftop, he
was surprised to see in the courtyard below, lit by flickering candlelight,
those household people who truly resembled a troop of demons. Trembling with fear and very cautious, Zhao Bin leaped from roof to roof and
hurried off to the west.

Arriving at a distant flower garden, Zhao Bin stopped, looked east
and west, and then said to himself, "This flower garden is not part of the
prime minister's mansion. Whose home is it?"

When he had looked about for some time, he saw that at the northeast corner there was a courtyard where he could see a twinkling light.
He jumped down and moved in for a closer look. He saw that the flower
garden was surrounded by the saplings of cassia trees. When he went
through the gate, he saw before his eyes a short section of an ornamental
wall that closed off the view to anyone standing in the gateway. In the
center of the wall there was a design like a chessboard done in gray plaster. Beyond, to the north, was a building of three sections on a high platform with appropriate lower buildings on the east and west, each with
three sections. A bamboo curtain was hanging in the door of the north
building, and because of the light it was possible to see quite clearly into
the room from the outside. He could see a square table inside. On the
table was some fruit, hot and cold dishes with meat and fish, and the best
quality strong wine. It was a most finely set table.

Zhao Bin thought to himself, "It would suit me just right to have such
a meal prepared for me to eat and drink my fill, before going to kill that
beastly person."

He took a couple of steps forward. Just then he began to feel quite differently and said to himself, "Zhao Bin, you are too simple-minded. What

if there is someone in the room and you simply walk in? How could you avoid being seen? That would be most inconvenient. I will have to find a small stone with which to try to find out whether anyone is there." He searched about in the courtyard until he found some small stones, and threw one against the lattice. It was an oft-repeated saying among the brotherhood of the Greenwood that, if one threw stones in this way and the sound was heard, there would be a reply. More importantly, if there was a guard dog it would bark, and the one who had thrown the stone would swiftly depart.

Zhao Bin threw the stone, but there was no apparent movement within. Feeling satisfied that there was no one there, he walked forward. Not until he was on the first step did he hear someone say, "Ai yah! Big Brother has come. Quick, come and save us!"

Zhao Bin was greatly surprised. As he looked about carefully, he saw Wang Xing and his wife hanging upside down from a beam. Both were covered with blood.

CHAPTER 12

Qin Da practices a cruel deception;
Qin Da seeks to separate a faithful couple

> A thousand ounces of the yellowest gold
> Would not suffice to buy that little body.
> It is her love that made her rouge besmeared
> And left a puzzle in the library.

ZHAO Bin could hardly help but be terribly shocked at the sight of his friend Wang Xing and Wang Xing's wife both hanging there from a beam, certainly injured. How could they have been so mistreated?

Now this was the flower garden of Qin Da, the second noble son of Prime Minister Qin. Ordinarily, Qin Da made no attempt to behave in ways proper to his position. He took advantage of the fact that his father was prime minister. Since Qin Da's elder brother had died some time earlier, Qin Da was now the only remaining son. He was quite unrestrained in his vicious behavior. Under his patronage he had a considerable number of hired thugs, whom he had gathered and trained. Frequently they went out robbing, plundering, and taking young wives and girls by force. Then the ruffians treated them without mercy. Qin Da even permitted his uncontrolled thugs to kill these unfortunate females. If anyone came to the prefectural offices to complain, the guards would not accept their petitions. They all knew that Qin Da was the noble son of Prime Minister Qin. Because of this, they gave Qin Da the nickname of "Demon of Doom."

On this particular day he had been reading a book in the flower garden. When he read, he never looked at proper books. They were always licentious books with perverted viewpoints. The one he had been reading was *The Emperor Tang Minghuang Vows to Make Yang Gueifei His Favorite Concubine*. He had just reached a very satisfying place when he slapped the table in astonishment.

There beside him was one of his household servants, Qin Yu, who commonly was most eager to do any service for him. "Which good part has pleased the honorable young master so much?" Qin Yu asked.

"Do you know, it is not surprising that one of the Tang-dynasty poems tells how the emperor's wife frankly expressed her opinions, how she openly rode her horse through the palace gates, and how she made it the fashion to use delicately applied adornments and to complain about impurities in the rouge and other cosmetics," said Qin Da. "This Yang Gueifei was certainly a fine woman!"

"Honorable young master, did you see these things yourself?" asked Qin Yu.

"This toady is always showing how addle-brained he is by his talk," Qin Da said. "That was the Tang Dynasty. This is the Song Dynasty. How could I have seen these things with my own eyes?"

"But there is one person now before the eyes of men who is more beautiful than Yang Gueifei," said Qin Yu. "Truly she is one of the few beneath heaven. There is not another such in the world. Since the time when I was born, I have seen only one such beautiful woman. She is neither tall nor short, fat nor thin, with eyebrows and eyes and everything else of great beauty."

Qin Da was not a good person at all. When he heard these words, his eyes became fixed and staring and he quickly spoke up. "Qin Yu, where did you see her?"

Qin Yu replied, "At the gate of our estate there is a man named Wang Xing, who has spread his carpet and displayed there the fruit that he sells. He lives in the city. One day this small person, myself, went to buy two chairs of hard yellow cedar. I wanted to hire someone to take them to my home for me, but there was no suitable person around. I therefore went to the home of Wang Xing to ask him to carry them. Just as I knocked, his wife was leaving the house. When this small person saw her, he knew beyond any doubt that hers was a very rare beauty. She was at the highest level among beautiful women. Since the day that I saw her, I have wanted to tell the young master about her, but there was no suitable time. She is just right for you."

"Impossible!" Qin Da said, "I would like to have her, indeed, but it is not an easy matter. Can I simply say that someone in Wang Xing's home belongs to me? Do you know of any way to drop this beautiful woman into my hands? I would certainly give you much silver for your efforts."

Qin Yu replied, "If the young master wants this beautiful woman, it is not difficult. If you can spend two hundred ounces of silver, this toady has a suitable plan that will ensure this beautiful woman will be in your hands today. If only you, young master, will give me the two hundred ounces of silver, I will put my plan into operation for you."

Qin Da said, "Go to my treasury, get the silver, and bring it here."

When the two hundred ounces of silver was in his hands, Qin Yu came close to Qin Da and told him his plan. When Qin Da heard it, he laughed loudly, "Ha, ha! You just go and call him."

After that, Qin Da simply followed Qin Yu's plan. Without any further words, Qin Yu went outside to look and saw that Wang Xing had just finished arranging his produce. "Our young master has asked me to come and call you," said Qin Yu.

Wang Xing quickly asked Guo Four to watch his fruit for him and went inside with Qin Yu. Wang Xing was smiling and thinking that he would probably sell enough fruit to earn several ounces of silver. It must have seemed to him that the young master wished to buy the best-quality fruit. They hurried on until they came to a palatial studio in a flower garden. There, Wang Xing saw that the Demon of Doom, Qin Da, was just sitting down on the veranda with several of his attendants standing on either side of him.

Wang Xing immediately went forward and said, "The small person whom the honorable young master has called is here. What may I do?"

Qin Da asked, "Wang Xing, what people do you have at home and how old are you? Speak the truth!"

Wang Xing did not know what this was all about, but promptly replied, "Since the honorable young master asks, in my home there are only this insignificant person, who is twenty-two years old; my mother, who is fifty; and my wife of nineteen. There are only three of us at home."

When Qin Da heard this, the rascal gave a wild laugh and said, "Wang Xing, I have heard it said that your wife is not bad-looking. I will give you two hundred ounces of silver for her and you may get another. Bring your wife here and give her to me."

Hearing these words, Wang Xing felt a cold chill, and he thought to himself: "If I refuse, they will beat me to death." So, trying to guess the thoughts in Qin Da's mind, Wang Xing said, "Honorable young master, you are above me, and I, beneath, beg for your kindness. My wife is nothing but someone who takes care of my old mother. After my mother dies, I will send my wife to the honorable young master, but I would not dare to accept the two hundred ounces of silver you offer."

When Qin Da heard the words of Wang Xing, he was about to say, "Go! Be off with you!"

But Qin Yu came to him and said, "Honorable young master, do not listen to this kind of talk. This is clearly just a pretense. His mother is just now fifty and will probably live another thirty years. Then he will send his wife to you to take care of in her old age."

Upon hearing this, Qin Da suddenly became very angry and cried out, "You dog head, you dare try to deceive the one who is master of your household, and to his very face! You are being quite vexatious. Come, my men, seize him, tie him, and hang him up for me!"

Qin Da's wicked thugs tied Wang Xing and hung him up. Qin Da then said, "Qin Yu, what do you suggest? Suppose you trick his wife into coming here. I will have her look at him to get her consent to stay with me."

Qin Yu rolled his eyes. This was just as he had planned. He went outside and, calling three of the other rogues together, instructed them in several sentences. They then hired a sedan chair and two of the three men carried it. The third went with them to Wang Xing's home and knocked at the gate. Wang Xing's mother came out of the house immediately and asked, "Who is there at the gate?"

The third man then said, "Old lady, you do not know me. My name is Zhang. There is a little problem at Prime Minister Qin's flower garden. I am a good friend of Elder Brother Wang. Early today, just as Elder Brother came and spread out his fruit, he fell down flat; froth began to come from his mouth, and he lost his understanding of things. We carried him into the flower garden and asked a doctor to look at him. The doctor said that Brother Wang's illness is extremely serious. The doctor wants to speak to a near relative of Wang before treating him. Elder Brother Wang said that I should bring his wife."

The old lady said, "Perhaps it would be good for me to go to see him."

The man said, "Old lady, at your age if you go to see him, you might be quite shocked. Also, leaving the young wife here at home alone might not be fitting."

The old woman replied, "What, then, is best?" She went back into her house to talk the matter over with her daughter-in-law, Wu Shi.

Wu Shi was a person who understood about three-fourths of what she heard. When she heard that her husband was ill, her heart was in turmoil. She quickly changed her clothing, saying, "Your daughter will go and see." Outside, she said a few polite words to the waiting people and got into the sedan chair.

At Prime Minister Qin's estate she was taken into the flower garden. The sedan chair was put down. When the curtain of the chair was pulled up, she looked out and saw the young master sitting under the roof of the high veranda. Qin Da had dressed with especial care for his meeting with Wu Shi. The kerchief on his head was shaped into the form of a regal scepter from which hung a number of gaudy streamers. His loose robe was embroidered with flowers and bordered with gold. He sat with his feet propped up, showing the white soles of his shoes. The bulbous chin of his repulsive face was thrust out at her. His cruel eyes staring at her made him seem like the image of an evil demon that had somehow come to life.

After Wu Shi had looked at him she asked, "Young master, who are you? Why have you tied up my husband?"

One of the men who was standing at Qin Da's side said, "This is our young master, no less than the honorable son of Prime Minister Qin. Are you not going to bow your head to him?"

Before Wu Shi could reply, she heard Qin Da say, "Do not be afraid, young woman. I am truly very kind and gentle. To my surprise, this dog head, Wang Xing, is not willing to agree with me. I wanted so much to see the lovely face of the young woman, yourself, admired by the entire city—in fact, by the entire nation. I thought of your being with Wang Xing, where you had no choice but to drink his crude tea, eat his tasteless rice, and wear garments made from the coarsest cloth. Therefore, I called him in to discuss this matter with him. I thought that I would give him two hundred ounces of silver to take another wife. Was this not killing two birds with one stone and the best possible arrangement for both of you? After all, he would not need two hundred ounces of silver to buy a wife, and he would still be a little rich. To spare him punishment I had you brought here to see me. I have here with me a person who understands me very well. He has also discussed this matter with your husband, who was extremely unwilling to agree with me. Because of this, I had him tied up."

When Wu Shi heard this speech, she raised her long, beautiful eyebrows and gave Qin Da an angry look from her almond-shaped eyes. Then she said, "Young master, take my advice. Forget this idea and let us, husband and wife, go before it is too late. You are indeed the son of the prime minister of the present reign, and you are living in the house of this high government official. Your house is filled with charming concubines. Why must you take such actions against us? Young masters should be benevolent, help others in need, and maintain their own virtue. If such actions as yours become known to the imperial censors, even great ones may be ruined."

Wang Xing also spoke up from where he was tied up. "Honorable young master, when I was selling fruit at the gate of your estate, I did no wrong to you. Be merciful and release us both, husband and wife."

When Qin Da heard these words, they made him very angry. He ordered two of his rogues to hang the husband and wife up together. His underlings then did so, striking the husband and wife with their bamboo staves. Wang Xing and Wu Shi were terrified, but called out that they would die before they would submit to Qin Da's demands.

By this time it was already evening, and Qin Da called for wine, saying that he would have them beaten later. Suddenly, from the eastern courtyard of the estate came the cry that demons were creating a disturbance. Qin Da sent his people to inquire. They in turn sent word back to him that he should come and look. Upon hearing this, Qin Da sent the rest of his household ahead, and then he followed. Everyone wanted to have a look at the demons. As a result, no one was left behind with the two prisoners.

Wang Xing and his wife were both bruised and sore, but Wang Xing said, "Wife, you have suffered a terrible wrong for my sake."

Wu Shi answered, "Even though we two should be killed, our ghosts will return here to accuse this young princeling to his face."

Just as they said this, they saw that someone was approaching outside. It was Zhao Bin.

Wang Xing, startled to see him arriving as if in answer to their need, exclaimed, "Ai yah! Elder Brother Zhao has come to save us!"

As soon as Zhao Bin saw that they were injured, he started to release Wang Xing and get him down, so that they could both release Wu Shi. However, he found that the knots that held Wang Xing were very tightly tied. Zhao Bin was becoming quite anxious when he was suddenly seized from behind. He struggled to escape the grip, but he could not move. It was hard to believe that anyone could be so strong. The one who held him was as solid as Mount Taishan—the man had a grip like steel.

CHAPTER 13

Wang Xing and his family leave Linan forever; Qin Da is stricken by a strange illness that Ji Gong is asked to cure

Though rich or poor may fall in their estate
And meet with unimaginable woe,
The virtuous greet each trial with fortitude and pride,
Defying even death to bring their spirits low.
Most evil springs from weakness in the soul.
Errors lead on to ever-deeper sin.
Before the remedy the illness comes
To open the heart to virtue once again.

WHO would have thought that, when Zhao Bin was able to turn his head, he would see that the man who held him was senior monk Ji Gong?

Zhao Bin said, "Teacher, let me go. I was afraid that the prime minister had harmed you. I am surprised to see my teacher here!"

Ji Gong released him and said, "As soon as you have set those two free, come into the other room. I have something I need to say to you."

Zhao Bin untied Wang Xing and his wife. Ji Gong took out some medicine which, when applied to the wounds that the two had received, cured them rapidly. The monk then went into the next room and began to eat and drink with great relish.

Zhao Bin said, "So this table full of food was prepared for my teacher in the first place."

"Zhao Bin, go to the north section of the room on the west side," said Ji Gong. "There, you will see four chests. In the third chest there is a small case filled with gold weighing one hundred ounces, and six envelopes containing white silver weighing three hundred ounces. Bring them to me."

Zhao Bin went there at once. Naturally, it was just as Ji Gong had said, and Zhao Bin returned with the gold and silver.

Ji Gong then asked Wang Xing, "Where did your family originally live?"

Wang Xing replied, "I came here from Yuhang prefecture."

Ji Gong said, "Wang Xing, take this gold and silver with you. Tomorrow you must hire a boat and go back to Yuhang prefecture with your wife and mother. Give all the old and broken things in your home to Zhao Bin. When you reach your former home, use the gold and silver that you have to buy land and go into business. There will be enough to support you and your family."

When Wang Xing heard this, he immediately knelt before Ji Gong, saying, "I kowtow to the *lohan* Buddha."

Ji Gong said, "Zhao Bin, you shall go with them and see that they get back safely."

Zhao Bin asked, "Teacher, will you yourself not need someone? I had at first been thinking that I would kill the prime minister and avenge you, sir."

Ji Gong replied, "Do not ask how, but I have my own ways. After three days you will receive news of me."

Zhao Bin bowed his head in assent. Just as the three were about to leave, they heard some people talking a little distance away. Someone said, "Come with me, young fellows, and see whether Wang Xing's wife will yield to me or not." Several voices replied, "Yes."

By lantern light, the second young master, Qin Da, with several of his thugs could be seen coming back from the prime minister's courtyards. When Qin Da had heard that hobgoblins were creating a disturbance in the western buildings, he went to pay his respects to the prime minister. Prime Minister Qin had a deep love for his son and, fearing that he would be frightened, would not permit him to enter. Instead, the prime minister told Qin Da to go back to his own flower-garden courtyard and take care of himself. Therefore, Qin Da had come back, bringing his people with him. Just as he reached the flower-garden, he remembered Wang Xing's wife. "Young fellows," Qin Da said, "go and see whether Wang Xing's wife is ready to submit to me or not. If not, as I live, I will have her beaten to death!"

When Zhao Bin heard this, it was a horrible shock to him. He whispered, "Teacher, this is terrible! We will have to hide somewhere inside!"

Ji Gong said, "Do not worry." Pointing outward with his hand, he recited the six true words, "Om Ma Ni Pad Me Hum."

Qin Da was suddenly struck to the ground by a cold chill. His household people all rushed to help him. Taking advantage of the confusion, Zhao Bin led Wang Xing and his wife out of the flower garden by a corner gate. Once they were through that, he quickly saw them home.

Early the next morning, following Ji Gong's suggestion, Wang Xing gave his family's furniture and household things to Zhao Bin. Then, together with his wife and mother, he went away secretly by boat, far beyond the reach of Qin Da and his evil hirelings.

Now, after Ji Gong had seen Zhao Bin and his family leave the prime minister's estate, the monk finished his dinner and went back to the empty room in the eastern part of the estate. Meanwhile, Qin Da was still in the flower garden, where he had fallen flat. He was nearly out of his head with terror as his people helped him to his room.

"Ai yah! How hot it is!" Qin Da exclaimed. Qin Yu removed his hat.

Qin Da still said, "Hot!" His people than took off his robe.

He again said, "Hot!" They quickly took off his shirt.

He repeated, "Hot!" Qin Yu pulled off Qin Da's boots and stockings.

Once more Qin Da said, "Hot!" Qin Yu removed Qin Da's underclothes.

When Qin Da said "Hot!" again, Qin Yu started fanning him.

Even though the servants were fanning him, Qin Da was still hot. Qin Yu called upon the others to hurry and bring in two large blocks of ice. At once they brought in large perforated ice chests to cool the air. Then Qin Da said he was cold, and they took them out.

Qin Da now said, "Cold!" They pulled his pants on.

Once again he said, "Cold!" They put his stockings and boots on.

When he said, "Cold!" again, they put his robe on. With his robe on, he was still cold, so they put his hat on. After his hat was on, he still felt cold, so they spread two quilts over him. Qin Yu called for a fire, and a brazier of hot coals was brought in.

Then Qin Da called out that he was hot. They took out the fire, but he was still hot. Then they took off his clothing again. In short, he was hot and cold four or five times in all.

At this time it was not yet daybreak. Qin Da suddenly said that his head itched severely. "Quickly, someone, scratch it for me!"

Qin Yu came to him and began to scratch with his hand. To his surprise, the more he scratched, the larger Qin Da's head became. In just a quarter of an hour it became as big as a basket used to measure a peck of grain. Qin Yu was terrified and did not dare to scratch any more. Everyone was standing around with eyes and mouth wide open. As soon as it grew light at dawn, Qin Yu said, "Quickly, send word to the east residence."

When the news was brought to the east section of the estate, Prime Minister Qin was neither attending the morning audience at the palace, nor had he gone to ask for a leave of absence. He had been disturbed for more than half the night by hobgoblins, and he had not had an opportunity to question the monk. At daybreak he was trying to get some rest when a servant came in to report that the young master was sick. When the prime minister heard this, he was filled with paternal concern. Taking some people with him, he went at once to Qin Da's pavilion in the flower garden.

Prime Minister Qin entered the room where Qin Da was lying on a brick platform bed. He was tossing and turning about with his head swollen to the size of a peck measure. The prime minister said in an exasperated tone, "You slaves are truly infuriating. With the young master as seriously ill as this, why did you not notify me at once?"

Qin Yu replied, "The honorable prime minister does not understand. Last night when the young master returned from the east residence, he was struck with a chill. When we brought him into the room, he said he was hot. When he was disrobed, he said he was cold. When he had his clothes back on, he was hot again. This happened several times. After that, he said his head itched. This slave scratched his head. The more I scratched, the bigger his head grew. This illness came on in a very strange way."

Prime Minister Qin immediately instructed his people to invite a famous doctor to come to diagnose and treat Qin Da's illness. The servants said that within the walls of Linan there were two such famous doctors. One was named Tang Wanfang. The other was Li Huaiqun. The household people quickly reached the home of the latter and asked him to accompany them.

When Li Huaiqun heard that the call was from the prime minister's estate, he could hardly fail to go. Led by the household people, he quickly arrived at the prime minister's gate. The prime minister felt as if his heart were on fire. He hastily asked the doctor in. As the prime minister did so, he noticed the doctor's square cap, blue gown, and generally austere and remarkably dignified appearance and expression.

The doctor was taken at once to see Qin Da. Tea was served as the doctor felt the patient's pulse. Li Huaiqun felt alarmed at seeing that the young man's head was so big. There were, however, no other signs of a physical illness. After the doctor had observed Qin Da for some time, he could not discover any reason for the trouble with the patient's head. Truly, Li Huaiqun had no medical remedy for Qin Da's condition. He said, "My scanty learning is such that the prime minister should ask someone greater. I truly cannot cure your son."

The prime minister asked, "How can I know what greater one to consult? Doctor Li, you must know some gentleman that you can recommend."

Li Huaiqun thought to himself, "If I cannot cure him, Brother Tang Wanfang cannot cure him either, and what he cannot cure I cannot cure. Beyond the two of us who is there that I could recommend?" After thinking he said, "Honorable Prime Minister, I truly have no one whom I can recommend."

As soon as Prime Minister Qin heard this, he was genuinely upset and said heatedly, "Since you cannot cure my son and there is no one whom you can recommend, you may forget about the possibility of leaving my estate today!"

Hearing this, Li Huaiqun was concerned only about the power that would soon crush him. Suddenly he thought, "Why do I not recommend Ji Gong?" As he thought this, he spoke: "If you wish to cure the young master, there is only one person I can name. That is the drunken Ji Dian, but his appearance is most untidy. I fear that the prime minister would take offense at him."

"What would that matter, if only he can cure my child?" Prime Minister Qin countered.

"But he is a monk," said Li Huaiqun.

"I do not care whether he is a monk," Prime Minister Qin said, "if only he can make the sick well. Quickly, say his name again, please!"

"It is Ji Dian of the Monastery of the Soul's Retreat at the West Lake," said Li Huaiqun.

When Prime Minister Qin heard this, he said, "Ah, so it is he. The mad monk is locked up in my east courtyard."

The moment Li Huaiqun was told by the prime minister that he had locked up Ji Gong, Li Huaiqun suddenly understood the cause of Qin Da's mysterious illness. "There was something strange about his head swelling up with no other symptoms. That was it!" he said to himself.

Prime Minister Qin immediately sent one of his household people to summon the mad monk. "If he can cure my son's illness, I will pardon his crimes and let him go back to the monastery."

The household people hurried to the east courtyards. When they arrived, all the monks stood up. A household person said to Ji Gong, "Monk, your luck has turned."

Ji Gong said, "For a big cooking fire, one must waste a little firewood."

The man then said, "Our prime minister has called you to cure the young master's illness. If you can do it, he will release you to go back to the monastery."

The monk said, "Your master had me locked up. If he sends an order for me to come, I will be there. If he asks me as a monk to cure illness, you must say that I said I am in disgrace."

The household person said, "Good. I will take your message back to the prime minister."

The men returned and, when they saw the prime minister, the household person reported: "Honorable Prime Minister, we have returned. I told the monk that the chief minister called upon him to cure illness. He replied that, if there is an order for him to come, he will be here. If, however, he is called upon to cure illness, he is in disgrace."

The prime minister did not understand Ji Gong's message and asked Li Huaiqun what the monk meant by "in disgrace." Li Huaiqun half concealed a smile, saying, "This expression is really a kind of jest. If the prime minister wishes to have Ji Gong cure the illness, the prime minister might add the word 'invite' to the message."

The prime minister, still concerned for his child, said, "Good. You people go and say that I invite him to come and cure this illness."

The household people immediately thought, "The monk is really in luck," and hurried to the east courtyard. Upon seeing the monk, they said, "Really, monk, you are putting on airs. Our prime minister told us to come and say that you are invited to cure illness."

The monk said, "The position your prime minister holds is one conferred upon him by the three councils. Ordinarily, as monk I actually should not be exchanging visits with him. If he associates with Buddhist monks and Daoist priests and the imperial censors learn of it, you will all be censured."

The household people hearing Ji Gong said, "Good, monk. You put it well. We will go and report for you to our great one." When they arrived at the west flower garden, they said, "Honorable Prime Minister, we return and report. We went and saw the monk there, and we slaves said that the Great One had invited him to cure illness. The monk said that the Great One's position was conferred upon him by the three councils. He also said that he did not commonly visit back and forth with the Great One and that, if the great one associated with Buddhists and Daoists and the imperial censors heard of it, the Great One would be censured."

When the prime minister heard these words, he broke into a rage: "That monk has a lot of gall!" he said.

Li Huaiqun interposed, "Honorable Prime Minister, do not lose your temper. If he wants to get the monk to cure the young master's illness, the Great One must go himself."

The prime minister looked at his son tossing on his bed. There was nothing else to do. "Dr. Li," he asked, "will you go with me to see what the monk is like?"

"Certainly!" Li Huaiqun replied, and went with Prime Minister Qin to the empty rooms of the east section courtyards.

There, the prime minister made a coughing sound. He informed the doctor, "Clearing my throat tells my people that I am coming and that they must all be on their best behavior."

Of course, hearing the sound, all the household people quickly stood up respectfully and said, "The Great One has come."

Ji Gong asked, "Did I hear a dog bark?"

Everyone quickly admonished him. "Do not talk nonsense! The Great One has come." Then they saw Prime Minister Qin and Li Huaiqun enter and come before Ji Gong.

"Because my little child has become afflicted with a strange illness," began Prime Minister Qin, "I, the chief minister, have come especially to invite you to cure his sickness."

The monk said, "But I was brought here in chains and locked up by the Great One. I was by no means invited here to cure sickness."

When Prime Minister Qin heard this, he again became furious and angrily exclaimed, "Very well!"

Li Huaiqun realized that things were going badly and at once intervened. "Great One, be patient and try to quell the thunder of your anger. Allow me to go forward and invite Ji Gong to come."

Prime Minister Qin stepped back and saw Dr. Li go forward to speak to Ji Gong.

CHAPTER 14

A *subtle medicine is used to play a joke upon the prime minister's household; a talent for matching couplets amazes the prime minister*

As hastening travelers in boats with slackening speed
May, with unreasonable force,
Curse at the river's sluggish flow,
Men in their journey through this toilsome world
May have perception
Injured and impaired.
So in most melancholy times,
If entering despair usurps the better mind,
It may not be unwise to turn aside
And briefly leave material things behind.

UPON coming face to face with Ji Gong, Li Huaiqun said, "Teacher, we have been separated for too long a time. I offer you most courteous greetings. Today the young master Qin has developed a strange tumescent illness. I recommended you, sir, as one who could cure the young master's sickness. Whatever there may be wrong in this matter, please see that I, your younger brother, am partly to blame."

Ji Gong said, "All right. If you want me to cure someone, take all these locks and chains off me!"

Li Huaiqun looked at them and said, "Very well. Qin, Great One, will you please, sir, have someone release the saintly monk from these steel fetters?"

Prime Minister Qin immediately had the locks and chains removed.

Li Huaiqun asked, "Teacher, do you have anything else to say? Will you not go now?"

The monk said, "The master of the monastery, my teacher who is like my father, is here, and my brother teachers are all here suffering punishment. How could I have the heart to go to cure sickness for someone?"

Prime Minister Qin, upon hearing Ji Gong's statement, immediately ordered that all the other monks should be set free to return to the temple. After all the monks had departed, Li Huaiqun said, "Teacher, there is nothing more for which you need to ask. Why do you not go to the young master now?"

Ji Gong said, "Dr. Li, soldiers have surrounded the Monastery of the Soul's Retreat and they are tearing down the Great Memorial Pagoda within the walls of the temple grounds. How could I be willing to go to cure sickness while these terrible things are going on?"

Prime Minister Qin knew that the monk wanted the soldiers withdrawn from the temple, and there was nothing he could do but agree. He hastily sent his official order to recall the soldiers who were dismantling the memorial pagoda, as well as the soldiers surrounding the temple.

Li Huaiqun said, "Saintly monk, there is now nothing more that you can desire. Now go."

The monk said, "I will go." He stood up. "Do good works, promote the general prosperity, and be virtuous. Do evil, and you will meet strange misfortunes. I, the poor monk, now advance to meet a swarm of evils. I only fear that they may be difficult to understand." He was laughing and talking as if to himself.

The listening prime minister said, "The monk is getting off too lightly—if he really makes my son well again, I will still tear down his memorial pagoda. If I do not, I will be the laughingstock of everyone. He will have beaten up my deputies but not been punished, and I will have had him locked up, but not punished. Once he has cured my son's illness, I will then go ahead and tear down his pagoda."

Behind, Ji Gong heard him and laughed loudly: "Ha ha! Good, good! Goodness indeed! I will sing one of my little monk's songs for the great one to hear."

> In his hat, in his hat,
> In his black official hat
> And uncomfortable gown,
> He's the first among all men,
> Among merely mortal men,
> Most disliked among all men,
> Among merely mortal men.
>
> From his hat, from his hat,
> From his high official hat
> There are streamers that hang down.

Left and right, two great leaves
Dance and shake on their stems
Made of wires.
And the gems on the leaves
Left and right in the light
Gleam like fires.

And the men who see them shake,
Cringe and quake to his face,
But they would like to take his place.
Though the mind may range free
Over land, over sea,
It is hard to read men's hearts.

Though the kingfisher's feathers
Often decorate a hat,
Does the bird think of that?
Does the pig ever think
What a feast men will make
Of its fat?

He has risen like a bird
In the sky,
But his home is on the ground.
And of those who rise so high,
Very few look around.
Very few look back.
Very few look down.

While the monk was singing his country mountain song, the prime minister was unconsciously nodding his head in time with the tune. When the song was finished, he said to himself, "The monk knows; he knows." The prime minister realized that somehow, the ragged monk understood his problems. Together they came to Qin Da's library in the west flower garden and heard Qin Da there coughing ceaselessly.

When the monk came into the room he said, "Oh, what a big head indeed! This is terrible!"

As Li Huaiqun heard the monk's words, the doctor had a shock and said to himself, "After taking all this trouble to invite the monk here, if he cannot cure the prime minister's son, I am done for."

The prime minister was also shocked, and at once asked, "Can you cure him or not?"

The monk replied, "There is nothing to worry about. I can cure even the biggest heads. This illness has a special name—it is called the big jar head. The head, you see, looks like a big jar." After saying this, the monk felt about inside his pockets and then said, "Oh, but this is terrible! I have lost the medicine!"

"What medicine?" Prime Minister Qin asked.

The monk replied, "The medicine that cures the big jar head!"

When the prime minister heard this, he was quite taken aback and asked, "Is it possible that you knew, when you came to my estate, that my son would be stricken with the big jar head disease?"

The monk replied, "No, it is not, but there is a certain Wang Yuanwai whose son has this same illness. Anyone who gets this disease is not a virtuous person. He is one who goes outside of the home and does bad things, seizing young girls and women by force and so on. Then this illness appears. Wang Yuanwai's son had offended heaven and earth and came down with this big jar head sickness. I was invited to cure him. I was carrying the medicine with me and was just about to go when I was seized by the prime minister's men and put in chains. At the time when I was brought into the prime minister's mansion, I felt in my pocket and it was there. Will the prime minister direct some of his people to search and find it?"

Everyone called, "Monk, your medicine, was it a pill or a powder? Tell us and we will go and look for it."

"It is a pill in the shape of a bead as big as a grain of rice. It is the color of a banana peel, and it is not wrapped in paper," Ji Gong replied.

Each one said, "I will go!"

"Great One," said the monk, "this illness of your son could take a turn for the worse. This is only the lesser third stage. If it becomes a really big jar head, there may be no way to treat it."

"Then what must we do?" the prime minister asked.

The monk answered, "I must eat and satisfy my appetite. If I try to cure him without satisfying my appetite, the more I try to cure him, the worse he may become."

As soon as the prime minister heard this, fearing that his son would go into the worst stage of big jar head, he directed his people to set up three tables of wine and food in the large reception room. He then asked the monk to come into the hall to eat and drink and, afterward, as soon as he had finished, to cure the sickness. Li Huaiqun came up the steps into the room with the monk. The monk, seeing the three tables, did not stand on ceremony, but immediately sat down at the head in the place of honor.

The prime minister was a little unhappy at seeing this, and thought to himself, "There is something unusual about this monk. He sat down at the place of honor as if there were no such rank as prime minister." But there was nothing the prime minister could do. He sat down on one side of the seat of honor and invited Li Huaiqun to sit on the east side.

After the third round of drinks, the monk said, "Great One, this is melancholy stuff, like solitary drinking. There is no point in it!"

Prime Minister Qin asked, "What would you like to do to avoid this spiritless drinking? I rely upon you."

The monk replied, "Riddles, forfeits, matching words, and defining words are all ways to relieve melancholy and tedium."

The prime minister asked, "Are you able to recognize written characters, monk?"

Ji Gong replied, "Oh, though I would not dare to say that I recognize written characters, I do know one or two."

"If we were to do forfeits," said Prime Minister Qin, "would you like to forfeit by drinking or would you rather risk something else?"

The monk answered, "I do not want to wager drinks. If the Great One will give a sentence to be matched and I then match it, I will win ten thousand ounces of silver from the great man. If I cannot match it, I will lose ten thousand ounces of silver. The Great One is wondering how I, a poor monk, could afford to lose ten thousand ounces of silver. Does not the Great One wish to tear down the Great Memorial Pagoda of mine? If I lose, I will give the memorial pagoda to the Great One."

When the prime minister heard this, he was delighted and said, "I will first try out your literary style. If you truly are a man of learning, then I will make wagers with you. I will first give you two words to match."

The monk said, "Speak, Great One."

"'Secluded study,'" said Prime Minister Qin.

The monk said, "I will match it with the words 'thatched cottage.'"

The prime minister nodded and said, "'Open window.'"

The monk said, "'Closed door.'"

Prime Minister Qin said, "'Read books.'"

The monk said, "'Write words.'"

The prime minister said, "You have lost, monk. My six words together make a sentence: 'The window of the secluded study is open while the books are being read.' Your 'thatched cottage closed door write words' is not a sentence."

The monk countered, "Those six of words of mine together also make a sentence: 'The thatched cottage door was closed when the words were written.' Prime Minister, you have just lost the seat of your britches."

Prime Minister Qin exclaimed, "Do not fool around, monk! I will now give you some words by splitting up the characters. If you match them, I will have lost ten thousand ounces of silver to you."

The monk said, "That is also all right."

The prime minister said, "The character for 'ripe' and the character for 'finally' together make the character for 'intoxicated.' The character for 'eye' and the character for 'drop' together make the character for 'sleep.' My sentences are: 'The poet Li Taibo sleeps on the mountainside, holding his arms around a large jar of wine. He is not aware that he is asleep and he is not aware that he is rather drunk.'"

The monk drank a cup of wine and, laughing loudly, said, "Ha, ha! This is a good one to match. The character for 'moon' and the character for 'increase' together make the character for 'extend.' The character for 'moon' and the character for 'half' together make the character for 'fat.' My sentences are: 'Madame Qin walks around the courtyard, holding her arms around her large stomach. She is not aware of how far it extends, and she is not aware that she is rather fat.'"

As the prime minister heard this, he shook his finger at the monk saying, "Do not make jokes, monk!" He thought to himself: "This monk is really mischievous. I will give him another set of words to match and let him know that Prime Minister Qin is a learned and elegantly literary man." He searched his mind for something with an ornamental style, but with a hidden pearl of meaning. Then he asked, "How was it that, when the original Buddha released all other beings from bondage, he seemed to do just the opposite with the monks? Was that not a blunder?"

The monk replied, "Ah, Great One, that is really very good, but my mediocre talents are very shallow."

Prime Minister Qin said, "Match it and I will have lost another ten thousand ounces of silver. If you cannot match it, I will tear down your memorial pagoda."

The monk said, "Good," and after drinking a cup of wine, continued. "I will give you a match. It is just as it is when the Son of Heaven takes up the jade lock and chain and places them about the neck of a great minister and commissions him as the prime minister. Again I have won ten thousand ounces of silver."

Prime Minister Qin thought, "It is just as I expected. The monk is full of talent. I cannot win by matching words with him." Then he said aloud,

"Let us not match words any more. Let us try forfeits."

The monk said, "If it is to be forfeits, we will do forfeits. The Great One has said it, so the Great One may start."

The prime minister said, "I want to talk about two men of ancient times and two things. These two men were both quite fat. Their occupations were the same, but they had different opportunities. Therefore, in the picture, which we may now imagine, one is moving and one is still. If you also can describe such an imaginary picture, you will be the winner, and if you cannot, you will be the loser."

The monk said, "Tell me more about your imaginary picture first, Great One."

Prime Minister Qin said, "Monk, you must listen carefully. In the distance we see a tall shrine; in the foreground we see a water buffalo. Lu Dongbin is drunk and is sleeping in the Yueh Yang shrine. Sun Binjia is stealing a ride on the water buffalo."

The monk said, "In the distance we see a hut; in the foreground we see a fish. Zhang Fei reflects in his hut; Ching De hangs up a fish by its heels."

The prime minister said, "Monk, you have lost ten thousand ounces of silver. As for Zhang Fei reflecting in his hut, you may even say that Zhang Fei reflects in his hut three times over. But Ching De hangs up a fish by its heels! Where do fish have legs?"

The monk answered, "A fish may have all four legs if it is a griddle fish, and that is what we call the green turtle."

Indeed, there was in that very room a griddle shaped like a turtle, with four legs and a turtle's head and tail, commonly used over open fires; the green turtle had taken its nickname from such griddles. The prime minister was left with no further argument and again he admitted that the monk had won another ten thousand ounces of silver. Then he thought to himself, "I must still think of a way to triumph over him."

Going outside, he said to the servant Qin An, "Take a gift presentation box and put into it some chilled gelatinous rice cakes. Then wait outside. The monk will be asked to guess what is in the box. If he guesses that the box has nothing in it, take the box of rice cakes and bring it in. If he guesses that the box has something in it, then you bring in the empty box." Qin An nodded in assent.

The prime minister went back inside and said, "Monk, I have been wondering for a long time whether you could predict the past and the future. Therefore I have just sent a man to get a box, about which you may make a guess. Guess whether the box has anything inside or not. If you guess correctly, I will have lost another ten thousand ounces of silver. If you guess incorrectly, I will tear down your memorial pagoda."

The monk said, "Great One, you are becoming too reckless."

Prime Minister Qin said, "I am not taking reckless chances at all. I want to test your abilities."

The monk drank a cup of wine as if to maintain his composure before saying, "The intentions of the great Qin are of the highest, and this method is remarkably ingenious. To begin with, there was an empty presentation box with nothing in it." After these words, the monk drew a long audible sigh. Hearing the monk say that the box was empty, Qin An quickly picked up the box with the cold rice cakes and brought it in. Just as he came into the room, the monk went on speaking: "That which was put inside is cold gelatinous rice cakes." When Qin An heard the monk's words, he was astonished. The monk had guessed correctly after all.

Prime Minister Qin suddenly thought to himself, "It is getting late. You had better stop the matching games and go to cure your son." Having decided, the prime minister said aloud, "Monk, if you have had enough to eat and drink, what about curing my son's illness?"

The monk replied, "I have already eaten and drunk sufficiently. Ai ya! Have your people found the medicine?"

The household people answered, "We have been crawling around on our hands and knees until our noses are all black and dirty, but we have not found it."

The monk reached in and took something out of his pocket, saying, "I do have a little medicine here, and if I add a couple of things to it, that will do."

Prime Minister Qin went over to look, but the characters on the paper packet were written in a scrawl that he could not read. When the little packet was opened, there was something white inside.

When Dr. Li Huaiqun looked at it, he recognized it as a piece of bread like that which they had just been eating and which he had just seen the monk rolling between his thumb and finger. "What is this?" he asked.

The monk replied, "It is called the essence of Buddhist wisdom."

"What else is needed?" asked the prime minister.

The monk answered, "One ounce of cinnabar, four ounces of white flour, a small box, boiling water to make an infusion, and a brush."

Prime Minister Qin ordered that the materials should be prepared immediately. The household people went to do so and in a short time returned to say that all was in readiness. The monk put down his cup and chopsticks and followed the prime minister toward the library. Ji Gong was now about to cure the big jar head disease with his Buddhist arts.

CHAPTER 15

Changed beyond recognition, an honored monk returns to the Monastery of the Soul's Retreat; Ji Gong's money is stolen by a bold ruffian

A S Ji Gong entered the library in the flower garden together with the prime minister and Dr. Li Huaiqun, the monk first saw Qin Yu, one of the household people. He was holding a box of flour paste mixed with the cinnabar. There was a brush inside the box.

The monk reached out and took the brush, saying, "Whatever the Great One wishes may be done." Then he began writing on Qin Da's head. Wherever the reddish brown paste adhered, the swelling immediately subsided, and the young man's head went back to normal. At the same time, Qin Da's illness left him completely.

The monk said, "This illness sometimes recurs. It is necessary to rest carefully. I will now prescribe some directions for you to follow, which I will write down on paper. If the illness comes back, simply read what I have written. Follow my directions and all will be well."

The prime minister realized that this was an example of the monk's subtle arts. He invited Ji Gong into the great hall at the front of the estate.

Li Huaiqun said, "I will not be able to accompany you, and now will take my leave. There are still several families who have invited me to cure sickness, so I should go." The prime minister sent some people to see him out.

Ji Gong talked with the prime minister in the library. There was a true meeting of minds as they discussed a wide variety of subjects. The monk's answers to the prime minister's questions came gushing out like a stream.

The prime minister was so delighted he exclaimed, "Oh, that I might leap out of the red dust of this world to study and cultivate my mind in some ancient temple. I would not ask about the rise and fall of nations or whether our country was prosperous or not, but chant the sutras and respect the name of Buddha. That would be happiness indeed! Though I am a high officer in the present reign, to live in the company of a ruler every day is like living with a tiger. Granted that there may have been some reigns during which this was not so, there is now not only the danger one must face, but also the danger hanging over one's family to fear."

The monk asked, "Great One, where do such words come from? The Great One's office, fixed by the three councils, is that of prime minister. You are beneath one man in the nation, but above all others. With your vital talents you assist in carrying out the emperor's plans, examining all other officials and keeping the populace peaceful."

"Ai ya, monk," said the prime minister. "Say no more about the present reign. The three councils had no such reign as this in mind. As soon as the words are mentioned, I realize that in my heart I am apprehensive. There is a common saying: 'A great office attracts danger, a great tree attracts the wind, and great power attracts scandal.' Ever since I came into office, I have been as if in the shadow of dreadful wings. In doing the sovereign's business, though I am prudent in all things, outside people are fond of saying all sorts of ugly things about me. How can I ever have repose and contentment such as yours, without anxieties or sorrows? There is a popular saying that expresses it well: 'In the darkness, the general in armor crosses the frontier. At the cold fifth watch, the court official awaits the signal for the audience. In the mountain temple the sun is high, but the monk has yet to rise. He knows in his wisdom that leisure is better than fame.'" The prime minister continued, "I am thinking of asking you to be a monk in my stead, as a substitute for myself, but I do not know how you may feel about this."

Ji Gong said, "Great One, of course, I would be willing, but a monk such as I would never dare to ask for such an honor."

Just as he said this, a servant came in from outside to report. "The honorable young master's illness has returned, and his head is as big as it was before."

The monk said, "There is no need for me to go to the young master. Just tell him to open my prescription. If he carries out my directions, he will be all right by himself. If, however, he fails to follow the directions, he will get worse each time an attack comes on."

Now after his illness had been relieved, Qin Da had remembered Wang Xing's wife and asked his servant, "Where is my pretty lady?"

"Lost!" answered Qin Yu.

Qin Da shouted, "You worthless thing! You dared to let the pretty lady get away. That will never do!" As his temper rose, his head again swelled.

Qin Yu was sent at once from the west courtyard to notify the prime minister. Having heard what the monk said, Qin Yu came back to inform Qin Da. "Honorable young master, just now the monk said that you should look at what the prescription tells you to do. Do it and your illness will pass without further help from him."

Qin Da said, "Bring the prescription quickly and I will look at it." The man hurriedly brought it to him—Qin Da opened it. On the paper was written:

> The illness of the body is known to the body itself.
> The heart has the cure for the sickness of the heart.
> When the heart is correct, the body will be at peace.
> When the heart is out of control, the sickness will be
>   out of control.

As soon as Qin Da read it, he said to himself: "Ai ya, this illness of mine is entirely brought on by myself. I abducted other men's wives and did bad things. From now I will turn my bad behavior to good and this sickness of mine will be well." Just as his thoughts had reached this point, his head made a sound, "Hu, hu, hu!"—and then became its normal size again.

The household quickly went to the east courtyard to report, "Prime Minister, the honorable young master was cured as soon as he read the monk's prescription."

The prime minister said, "Very good. You slaves must take good care of the young master." They promised to do so and left.

Just then the people of the eastern household came from the inner courtyard to report. "Madame Qin has developed a painful semicircular dragon headache."

The prime minister said, "I understand." Then he asked Ji Gong, "Saintly monk, can you can cure an encircling dragon headache?"

The monk replied, "Madame must have said the wrong thing in some way. If that is not the case, it is not an illness I can cure. I will go and see."

Prime Minister Qin said, "There was nothing in particular that my wife said ... but there was! Last night, just before the demons troubled us, I had a dream in which my old patron came back to visit me and urged me to improve my ways. When I awoke, I wanted to stop the people from tearing down the memorial pagoda and to release all the monks. Then my wife said that it all came from my own mind and stopped me from doing the right thing. A little while later, the demons came."

Prime Minister Qin went with the monk to the raised building in the inner courtyard of the east section, where they heard the sound of continual coughing.

The monk said, "Do not be alarmed, lady—I am here. Everything will soon be all right." After saying this, he made a gesture toward the center of the room. Immediately she recovered completely.

The monk asked, "Great One, does she seem well to you?"

The prime minister replied, "Very well, very well."

The monk explained. "I scratched the offending spirit and one scratch was enough. However, even though it was driven out, it is still lurking about. Did you notice how that dog lying there barked twice? If the spirit can complete a circle, it causes death."

The prime minister said, "If a mistaken sentence can cause an encircling dragon headache, that is very dangerous. After this, I will be more careful and prudent in my duties at court."

Prime Minister Qin then went with Ji Gong into the library. After they had sat down, the prime minister gave a servant orders to have food and wine prepared and brought in for them. They passed the evening pleasantly. At about the third watch, they heard a great wind rising outside.

The prime minister said, "This is not good. It was at this same hour last night that the demons came to trouble us."

Ji Gong said, "The Great One need not be anxious. I will go and exorcise this demon for you, and I will bring an end to it at the same time. Whatever happens, pay no attention."

The monk went outside and was heard to say, "Good demon, good demon, you may devour me at the risk of your own existence."

Inside the room, the prime minister, hearing this, was most uneasy. After waiting until it was fully light in the morning, the great one went outside to look. There he saw the monk lying motionless on the ground. The prime minister called the servants to help revive the monk and assist him inside, where they seated him in a chair.

The prime minister said, "I am going to get a change of clothing in here for you and then have you escorted back to the monastery."

Prime Minister Qin called upon the household people to buy monk's clothing, shoes, and stockings. They acknowledged the order and before long brought back three sets of monk's clothes, which were all of the finest quality. One set was made of yellow silk embroidered with white clouds, the second of white silk embroidered with flowers, and the third of patterned blue silk. The three sets, complete with shoes and stockings, had cost 120 ounces of silver.

The prime minister sent the library boy with Ji Gong while he bathed and changed his clothing. After Ji Gong had washed his face and changed his clothes for the first time in a long while, he returned to the library and sat down. Prime Minister Qin paid him the silver that the monk had won from him. Then the prime minister told one of the household people to prepare the horse which he himself, the prime minister, was in the habit of riding, with all the usual trappings and attendants, so that the monk might be sent back to the monastery in honor.

The monk said, "I am sorry that our affinity was so shallow, that we met so late, and that we had to separate so soon. Today, as our hands part, we do not know in what year we may meet again."

The prime minister said, "Whenever you wish to come, Monk, simply come. We will not be separated by a thousand mountains and ten thousand waters. Whenever I am free from my duties, I would like to stroll about with you."

Ji Gong said, "If I, a monk, were to come often to your door to see the Great One, where would I get the money to pay all of the gatekeepers' fees?"

The prime minister gave directions that the gatekeepers should be called in, and in a short time over a dozen of the household people were standing outside the library door. The great one said, "Ji Gong is my officially appointed substitute and friend. Whenever he comes, even though I may be busy, do not detain him and inform me at once."

All together they said, "Yes, yes. Your slaves hear your orders."

Ji Gong said, "I, the monk, would like to give these men a few cash each, if the Great One pleases."

The prime minister knew that with the thousands of ounces of silver that Ji Gong had won, he had more than enough to spare. After thinking that it would be well for the monk to build up his reputation, the prime minister said, "That is for you to judge, Monk."

Ji Gong said, "To each of these under officials I will give one hundred cash."

Prime Minister Qin said, "Oh, give them a few ounces more, Monk. I will add it to yours."

Ji Gong said, "I would have given them each a hundred cash today, and tomorrow I would not have given them any. Then, when I did come, that hundred cash would have taken care of their speaking with me. If this is not to be, then when I do not come, each day will be counted as one day. For each man, during each month, three strings of cash can be added to the regular wages, and the Great One may be my substitute."

The prime minister said, "So be it. And now, monk, I will say good-bye." Prime Minister Qin sent twenty men as an escort for Ji Gong, saying to them, "Convey my official orders. Those at every Buddhist temple must kneel in receiving him as a guest and kneel in bidding him farewell, for he is none other than my official substitute, whom I have sent back in honor to his temple."

The household people all promised to obey. Outside, the horse had been made ready. The monk took his leave from Prime Minister Qin, left the residence, and mounted the horse. The household people whipped up the horse and led it off. Ahead walked others carrying placards, manacles, staves, gongs, flags, umbrellas, and fans to drive back those who might hinder Ji Gong's passage. On the streets they saw crowds of noisy people all wanting to see the monk whom the prime minister had named as his substitute. When the monk on his horse reached the Monastery of the Soul's Retreat, bells were rung and drums beaten to call the monks together.

The monk first called the superintendent of the temple to come forward saying, "Take the silver I have behind me and weigh out twenty piles of fifty ounces each. Then weigh out one hundred piles of ten ounces each." The superintendent did so.

Ji Gong said, "All estate managers who brought me here, you are to carry out my official orders!"

The estate managers said, "Yes! Though we do not yet know what orders the saintly monk is about to give, we will obey."

Ji Gong said, "You monks of this temple, listen carefully. I, Ji Gong, am none other than the monk appointed to serve as the honorable Prime Minister Qin's substitute. Today I have returned to the temple in honor. This saintly monk wishes to join with the rest of you monks in advancing money to buy drinks. Those who have money and will not share will forthwith be taken to the yamen to be punished."

The people from the prime minister's household listened carefully. The monks heard his words and thought, "We will give nothing."

Again Ji Gong spoke. "All estate managers, come closer. Once more carry out my orders. By and by I will not have any money, and I will come to ask these monks to advance me a little. Furthermore, if there is no one in the rooms and I steal a little something, they must not talk about it and they may not look at me and say that I steal. If they disobey, push the temple gate open and destroy them at once."

At this, the estate managers all began to laugh and could only make indistinct replies in agreement. Hearing all this, the monks thought to themselves: "He has turned the temple upside down." They felt great displeasure in their hearts. Although they dared to feel angry, they dared not put their anger into words.

Ji Gong then distributed the silver: fifty ounces to each of the estate managers and ten ounces to each of the hundred men who had walked ahead of him to clear the way. Each of them knew no bounds to his joy, and finally each went his separate way from the temple.

The monk took off his new clothing and put on his ragged monk's gown as usual. Then, taking the new clothing that he had wrapped in the square of cloth that had contained his old things, he strolled away from the monastery.

As he was about to pass through the Qiantang gate, he saw a pawnshop just outside the gate. The monk went in, put the bundle on the counter, and pressed his arms down firmly upon it, as if he thought that someone might try to take his bundle away from him.

When the proprietor looked up, he saw a poor monk dressed all in rags who had brought with him a number of garments, all quite new. He also noticed that the monk had looked out through the bamboo blind to the east and west, as if there might be someone following him, and that he seemed a little frightened. The proprietor of the pawnshop asked sharply, "Monk, how did you get these clothes of yours? Now tell the truth!"

Ji Gong replied, "Proprietor, just see how much they can be pawned for, and I will pawn them for that much. If not, wrap them up and I will take them somewhere else to pawn."

The second proprietor came up beside his partner and said to him, "You should never fail to open your eyes. You did not recognize him. Is this not the honorable great teacher who came out of the city through the gate just now riding a horse, and who is the prime minister's substitute as a monk?" Then he turned to Ji Gong and asked, "For how much money does the honorable great teacher wish to pawn the garments?"

Ji Gong answered, "Let me pawn them for 150 strings of cash."

The second proprietor inquired, "Does the monk wish silver or paper notes?"

The monk replied, "I would like cash—and please keep the pawn ticket with your records."

The proprietor called a man to take the money to the door. Ji Gong then called out, "Who will come to carry money?"

A great, sturdy, ruffian-like fellow came up and said, "Monk, I will carry your money."

Ji Gong said, "You are a scoundrel. I do not want you to carry it." The monk then called to several poor people, one to carry three strings, another to carry two strings, and so on, dividing the money among a large crowd until there were only five strings left. Ji Gong then said, "Call that big fellow to carry them." The sturdy fellow picked up the five strings and immediately ran off. The monk did not run after him.

The other people queried, "Monk, where shall we carry the money?"

The monk replied, "Where you wish," and the people scattered. The monk then started walking along the alley into which the sturdy fellow had fled.

CHAPTER 16

Spring Fragrance meets a saintly monk in a house of prostitution; Zhao Wenhui sees a poem and feels pity for the writer

The flowers opened on a butterfly-filled branch
And, scattered by butterflies, they fell.
Ah! They are soiled and faded blossoms now
And butterflies wear only threadbare rags.

IN the alley, Ji Gong went up to the big, sturdy fellow and took hold of him with his hand saying, "A good thing you are! You won't give good fortune a chance. If you had stood still for one moment, I would have given you those five strings of cash, but you wanted to rob and run, and that will not do. Your entire destiny is worth only five hundred cash. If you take these five strings of cash and run, I will haul you into the Qiantang prefecture court."

When the great fellow heard this, he was frightened, and tearing himself away with great force, raced off. The monk said, "Follow!"

In his haste, the fellow was not paying much attention to where he was going. Just as he came to the mouth of the alley, he ran smack into a porcelain peddler and broke seventeen porcelain bowls. Together with two broken poles, the damages came to four and a half strings of cash. There was nothing the big fellow could do except pay. He was left with five hundred cash and the no longer surprising knowledge that he was actually not worth much, just as the monk had said.

The monk, having gotten rid of all his money, continued on his way until he saw coming toward him two familiar *yuanwai*. One was Zhao Wenhui; the other was Su Beishan. As soon as they saw Ji Gong, they came up and greeted him respectfully. Su Beishan asked, "How did your affair with the law turn out, Teacher? We heard that the prime minister had locked up our teacher and we were all most uneasy. Today I was going with Wenhui to the Monastery of the Soul's Retreat to inquire about you."

Ji Gong replied, "My affair with the law is over and Prime Minister Qin did not harm me." Then he told the two about what had happened at the prime minister's estate.

After listening, Su Beishan said, "Today, perhaps you might have a drink."

Ji Gong said, "I was just thinking about having something to drink. Where would you two like to go now?"

Su Beishan said, "We have heard some gossip among the servants to the effect that a girl from an official family has fallen into the hands of the keeper of a house of prostitution. We would like to go and take a look."

The monk said, "Good, I also will go and take a look."

Zhao Wenhui said, "Teacher, it would not be fitting for you, sir, to visit a harlot's house. You are a person who has left the world, teaching and studying the mysteries of Chan. If you go to such a place, how can you keep people from laughing at you?"

The monk replied, "To a conjurer, nothing is impossible! You two and I, the three of us, will simply go."

Su Beishan laughed loudly. The three walked on until they saw an alley running from east to west. On a wall at the entrance to the alley was a board on which was written FRAGRANT FLOWER LANE. They entered, and at the second gate on the north side they saw a lantern hanging high above their heads. On the gate were written the words of the following couplet:

> At the first watch, what joy with the exchange of fans and wine cups.
> At the third cockcrow, the parting with largesse scattered as in an
>   empty field.

After the monk had finished looking at the words, the three men walked in. As soon as they went in, the gatekeeper said, "Ah! the honorable venerable Zhao and venerable Su. The two *yuanwai* have arrived."

The monk raised his head and looked about. Facing the gate was a high wall that screened the courtyard beyond from view. A huge, round pottery fish tank filled with large-leaved blooming lotus plants was placed before the screen wall. On the wall four lines of verse were written.

> Though there are fairies in the underworld,
>   the upper world has none.
> And those beneath depend upon the help of those on high.
> So we must lead into our chambers, night after night, new guests.
> And change our bridegrooms as the stars, when seasons pass,
>   move in the sky.

The three men went on into the courtyard beyond and were seated.
The monk could see that the courtyard was paved with tiles. On the north
side was a large raised building of five sections with a veranda in front
and another courtyard behind. On the east and west sides of the main
courtyard were matching buildings, each having three sections. In the
east and west walls were matching open gates through which other courtyards could be seen. High above the main courtyard was an awning made
of split bamboo mats spread over a framework of bamboo poles to keep
out the sun. Upon the veranda pillars of the main north building, a pair
of verses was written:

> Before the pavilion of songs and dances
> Are planted many flowers and lovely trees.
> From within the pool of white lotus
> A compelling fragrance unceasingly arises.

The large characters of the inscription had been regilded in recent
days. The three men sitting in the courtyard saw a maidservant come out
of the north building, and she asked, "Venerable Su and Venerable Zhao,
why are you two being so quiet today, there under that big bamboo awning?"

The three men entered the main building and saw against the north
wall a long, handsome table of flowering pear wood. In front of it was a
smaller square table of the kind called an "eight immortals table," because
it was just possible for eight people to sit at it, two on each side. At one
side of the room was a long settee. On the center of the pear-wood table
was a crystal globe with goldfish-like dragons with phoenix tails. On the
east side of the table was a fruit dish filled with many kinds of fruit. On
the west side was displayed a bronze mirror on a stand. Above the table
hung a scroll painting of a mountain, and beside this painting was a portrait of a woman showing only her head and shoulders. At the bottom of
the portrait was the artist's title: A Pitiful Flower. On the edge of the
portrait someone had scribbled:

> Each part must be as lovely in such a winsome maid.
> The artist painted only half; then at the waist he stayed.
> How hateful that the colors could not find a clever brush
> That might persuade the artist to add what's not portrayed.

At either side of the two pictures, the landscape and the portrait, there
was one of a pair of hanging scrolls of calligraphy. On them was written:

One who has known the heart understands
Fulfillment is to revel in every intimacy without distaste.

Zhao Wenhui, who was a connoisseur of calligraphy, looked closely at the scrolls and nodded his head. "Undoubtedly they were written by a dissolute person of great talent," he thought.

When the three men had seated themselves, the old brothel keeper asked, "What wind has blown the venerable masters this way today? It has been a long time since you two *yuanwai* have been here."

Su Beishan replied, "We have heard that you have a beautiful person as a new guest. Would you call her out that we may see her?"

The brothel keeper answered, "In my courtyard, all of the guests are newly arrived. I will call them out for you venerable masters to have a look." Having said this, she called out in a commanding tone: "See guests!"

Then they heard outside ripples of agreeable coquettish laughter that sounded refined, yet dissipated. In came four pretty young prostitutes, neatly washed and combed and brilliantly dressed. Each had moth-like eyebrows and lightly powdered and rouged cheeks. They stood before Zhao Wenhui and Su Beishan and asked their names. When they saw that the poor monk was also sitting there, they covered their mouths and giggled.

Ji Gong said, "Good! Good! Su Beishan, how do these maidens look to you?"

Su Beishan replied, "Very good."

The monk exclaimed, "These women all look good to you! I see a pretty whitened face that is simply carried on a skeleton and made to look beautiful with a little rouge. It is all killing people for profit!" So saying, he picked up a writing brush from the table and wrote on a sheet of white paper.

> A girl within the harlot's house,
> Night after night with a new husband,
> There in the wilderness that is her chamber,
> Her white wrists pillow to a thousand men,
> Vermilion lips ten thousand men have tasted.
> Her clothes, the delicacy of her behavior
> Simply assist the falseness of her feelings.
> Those tender, sympathetic tears of hers are shed

Because she's brought in new,
Thrown out when old.
Who knows how soon?

Zhao Wenhui and Su Beishan looked at what the monk had written and laughed, "Ha, ha!"

Then they heard the old procuress speaking. "Are the venerable gentlemen prepared to choose whom they will have to serve them?" Pointing to each in turn, she pronounced their names, "Orchid Fragrance, Autumn Cassia, Fragrant Lotus, and Little Plum."

Su Beishan said, "None of these is the guest that has newly come into your home. We have heard that she is also a girl from an official family. Our reason for coming to this house of fragrances was to visit her."

The procuress knew that these two men were heads of the wealthiest families in Linan, so she immediately spoke out. "The venerable gentleman need not speak of the newly bought person. That finishes it! Speaking of that newly bought one is most difficult for me. To begin with, people who eat the food of this establishment will no longer do so as soon as they begin to grow old. I had a girl called Naughty Flower. When she was told to eat, she would eat a mountain of food. The great man, Wang Shangshen, bought her to be his concubine, and I managed to make a few hundred ounces of silver.

"And then I bought another. She was from Qinling. Her father had been the magistrate of a department there and her mother had died very early. Because his work was criticized at the capital, they came here and were staying at an inn. Her father, named Yin Mingzhuan, wanted to find a place to live. Unexpectedly a confidence man cheated him out of several thousand ounces of silver. Then, after all that, he was not able to find work. He was very distressed. For three months he was sick at the inn. Father and daughter used up what money he had left and he died in debt. His daughter, Spring Fragrance, was sold into prostitution, and I used 350 ounces of silver to buy her.

"As soon as Spring Fragrance came here and saw that I kept a house of prostitution, she became very upset and wanted to commit suicide. I talked with her and spent altogether one hundred ounces of silver making inquiries about the circumstances of her sale. Everyone said to go back to the creditors. They said that she had been sold as a concubine and that it made no difference whether or not she had been sold into a house of prostitution. Again Spring Fragrance wanted to die, but I reasoned with her. I explained how difficult it would be for me to lose 350 ounces and what a grievous thing it would be to me if she died.

"Then she was better and said she would live here with me temporarily, simply accepting my house as a place of refuge. She said that, if I met someone who understood verses or music, he might redeem her. Of course, she would not want to leave me with less money than I had paid for her. She wrote some pieces with her own hand, and a friend of mine suggested that I might show the paper to some refined merchant or member of the gentry."

Su Beishan said, "Bring it and show it to us."

The procuress brought a paper and unrolled it. When the two *yuan-wai* saw it, they were startled. On it was written:

> To whom may I describe my endless griefs and fears?
> Only one glad to share another's sorrows.
> My words are not for ordinary ears,
> Each line is written with a thousand tears.

When Ji Gong and the others had finished looking, they asked: "In which courtyard is the girl called Spring Fragrance? We want to see this person."

The procuress answered, "The eastern courtyard is where my girls live. The three venerable gentlemen may come with me."

Su Beishan and the others stood up and left the principal building. Going east, they passed through three gates. The courtyard they entered was somewhat neglected in appearance. There were buildings on three sides. The main building had a veranda in front and a small extension at the back. The men lifted up the bamboo blind over the center door in the main building and entered. On the north wall opposite the door they saw a series of four plaques.

On the first was pictured a girl standing in a gateway. Five or six young men had stopped and were staring at the girl. Above the girl was an inscription:

> Her youthful phoenix curls wound round and round,
> The wedge-shaped comb thrust through them white as silver.
> How many passing men have looked and paused
> And stood and suffered as they watched?

On the second plaque was pictured a seated girl combing her hair and a young man who seemed about to leave her. The girl was looking at him as if she were reluctant to let him go. The picture was extremely expressive. The inscription on this second plaque read:

> Love that's predestined should exist past death.
> So how can two such mutual lovers part?
> The spirit prints its picture on the flesh.
> Each knows what now is in the other's heart.

The third plaque showed a girl and a young man in a bedroom. They were holding hands. They were walking toward the bed and seemed about to get into it. On this picture were also four lines of characters.

> Desire now like two orchid branches meeting
> With flowers yet to open to the air.
> The delicate beauty, feeling the wind and rain of love,
> Now calls upon her master in her need.

On the fourth plaque was a picture of a bed with a canopy of mosquito netting. Within, a young man and a girl could dimly be seen in a loving embrace. Written above again were four lines of characters.

> Joined now and all made right, the male and female phoenix
> Ascend the many-colored clouds of spring.
> She turns her head; the golden hairpin falls
> And moth-like eyebrows hide in clouds of hair.

Flanking these plaques were two hanging scrolls of calligraphy on which was written:

> The house where a dozen hairpins are hoarded
> Welcomes three thousand guests with pearl-embroidered shoes.

The two *yuanwai* observed these unusual decorations as they went in and sat down. The building was divided into three rooms by two paper-covered lattice walls. Through the door into the east section a canopied bed could be seen. The arrangement was the same on the west side. On the east wall of the center room was a scroll depicting a picture of a Chinese junk with the god of wealth and honor aboard. On the scroll was written two sentences taken from the *Four Books* of Confucian classics.

> If a man has wealth and rank his actions should proclaim them.
> The scholar who is poor and lowly should act as becomes one
> poor and lowly.

On either side of this scroll was a scroll of calligraphy with the words:

> **Confucius commended the enjoyment of music.**
> **He remained silent about sensual pleasures.**

The old procuress went inside the east room and was heard to say, "Miss, just now I have brought the venerable Zhao Yuanwai and Su Yuanwai to visit you. They have long wished to meet someone of your outstanding talents."

Then the visitors heard a charming but sad voice inside say, "Why, if these two venerable gentlemen have come to inquire about me, please take your slave out to see them." Then, using her hand to lift the bamboo curtain, the girl came out into the center room.

CHAPTER 17

A young woman in distress is escorted to the Bright Purity Nunnery; driven by poverty, Gao Guoqin returns to his native place

> Now I put down my lute and raise my glass.
> The wind is rising, while the waning moon
> Brings on the month of autumn frosts.
> Our song is like that sad song that we sang
> In leaving Zhengdingfu so long ago.
> Though fate may tear the two apart,
> It cannot break the tie that binds their hearts.

THE three men—Zhao Wenhui, Su Beishan, and Ji Gong, who were sitting in the outer room—looked up as the bamboo curtain was lifted. They saw a gentle and beautiful girl, about eighteen or nineteen years of age, coming out of the east room. Her hair was neatly combed and dressed into a dragon coil. She was wearing simple white mourning clothes.

As soon as Su Beishan saw her, he knew that she was a girl from a good family. He asked her to tell the circumstances of her coming to the house of prostitution. With a most melancholy air, the girl explained from beginning to end the details of how she had sold herself in order to obtain money to bury her father, and how afterward she had been treacherously resold to the old procuress.

The two *yuanwai* were exceedingly touched by her story. Zhao Yuanwai asked, "Spring Fragrance, are you able to compose poetry?"

Spring Fragrance replied, "I have had some acquaintance with the classical style and a general understanding of some of it."

Zhao Yuanwai said, "If that is so, perhaps you could write a couple of impromptu verses of the kind that influences the reader's feelings, so that I may read them." Zhao Yuanwai had suspected after reading the first poem that she might not have written it herself. Therefore he wished to test her knowledge of the classical style.

Spring Fragrance, however, did not ask whether that was the case. Taking a brush in her hand, she wrote a poetic sketch of a wandering musician who played the *piba*, or Chinese lute.

> She learned of harlots from the village girls
> And carelessly let virtue slip away.
> She hates the old songs now, that once they used to sing,
> And in her mirror looks for white hairs among the black.
> She thinks of home but knows there's no one there,
> While tears fall, dampening her rouge.
> In towns and hamlets that she passes through,
> Wherever men are gathered with their wine,
> She lifts her *piba*, strikes its strings
> And with the music tells her tale.

When she had finished writing, she handed the verse to Su Yuanwai and Zhao Yuanwai to read. They and Ji Gong praised it. Su Beishan said, "How sad it is that a person with such talent as Spring Fragrance should have fallen into the hands of a procuress!"

"Grievous indeed, and lamentable!" added Zhao Wenhui.

Meanwhile, they saw that Spring Fragrance, drawing a deep sigh, had again been writing, using as a reference the classical story of a great beauty who, though of obscure origins, had married an emperor. Spring Fragrance had constructed some verses with quite a different theme, but had included in her version some of the vocabulary of the famous tale.

> The business of spoiling flesh and bones
> Is a precarious and melancholy trade.
> And for the girls, a school where most will fail.
> To one, there comes a high official of the court
> Still in his robes of richest silk.
> Told just today he is disgraced and must resign,
> He comes to see a prostitute in his despair.
> But this she does not know.
> She goes to meet him on her lily feet,
> And he finds solace in her arms.
> The polished surface of her mirror shows
> That fabled beauty of most ancient times.
> She dreams of swaying empires by his side.
> 'Tis spring. The rains have made
> The world a sea of mud.

> They marry and she learns the truth.
> Position and salary both are gone,
> And destitution lies not far ahead.

After Ji Gong and the others had taken the poem and read it, all three exclaimed, "Good!"

Zhao Wenhui said, "Come, come! I also will write a poem!" The old procuress brought him the writing set. Without stopping to think it over, Zhao Wenhui took the brush and wrote with a flourish:

> How in this house of lust and shame
> Can hearts like ours so fill with joy,
> Having now found Spring Fragrance here
> And heard her tale of misery?
> Her purity, her firm resolve
> She kept despite men's treachery.
> And though she had to wait for us,
> We've waited long for such as she.

Su Beishan was eager to show off his ability to write verses. What he wrote was:

> Ranking with ivory and precious gems,
> Among the luxuries our trade with Indochina brings,
> Are feathers of the brilliant kingfisher
> The magic alchemy of this bird's small body
> Converts the iridescence of the fishes' scales
> Into a gleaming blue like nothing else.
> The fish are dazzled thus and made unwary
> Of this swift bird's most cruel and fatal beak.
> Our artisans affix bits of these blue kingfisher feathers
> To delicate gold and silver leaves and flowers.
> Such ornaments may beautify a residence of wealth,
> But chiefly they are used for crownlike hats
> Which lords and ladies sometimes wear
> And others fortunate enough to own them, too.
> Our young wastrels love kingfisher hats
> With shoulder-touching tassels on each side.
> In gowns of soft and brilliant silks
> That hide the various cruelties within their hearts.
> Masters and victims, too, of every vice,

> They come with loud and strident laughter,
> Dazzling the slaves of the procuress,
> Soon to be soiled and faded flowers.
> But our Spring Fragrance now has seen
> And heard in twice these thirty days
> More than enough of all these vicious follies.

Ji Gong said, "I also have a line or two," and he recited, "Today, we have indeed opened our hearts to one another."

Spring Fragrance, upon hearing this, broke in, "Teacher, you sir, who spend each day improving yourself, what would you have me do?"

Ji Gong said, "Quickly, quickly open this net in which we are caught, and let this poor monk tie his broken-down sandals so that he can be on his way." As they all heard this, they laughed together. Then the monk said, "You two *yuanwai* now have a chance to do a truly virtuous deed."

Su Beishan then asked, "Spring Fragrance, do you want to marry someone—what would you really like to do?"

Spring Fragrance answered, "If it were possible for some good person to save me from this fiery pit, I would like to ask whether I could become a novice in a nunnery. My ancestors would be grateful to you back through three generations."

Su Yuanwai asked, "Procuress, what price do you want for this body?"

The procuress replied, "I spent over 350 ounces of silver for her. That does not include the fact that she has been in my house these two months with daily food and clothing."

Su Beishan said, "Easily managed."

Zhao Wenhui said, "Brother Su, let me take care of this matter. I will give five hundred ounces of silver to set her free from here. We will escort her to the old nun, Shining Truth, of the Bright Purity Nunnery at City God Mountain, and ask her to take care of Spring Fragrance."

He then instructed a man from his household to bring five hundred ounces of silver immediately and give it to the procuress. He also told him to engage a sedan chair to take Spring Fragrance to the nunnery. As soon as Spring Fragrance heard this, she quickly kowtowed to the three men and begged them to escort her there safely.

Ji Gong said, "Very good. We three will go now and wait for you. Zhao Ming, one of Zhao Wenhui's household people, and some others will go with the sedan chairs."

Ji Gong and the other two left the courtyards of the procuress and went straight toward City God Mountain. Ji Gong said spontaneously,

"Fate will be kind to those who do good, but heaven will not favor those who do evil. This poor monk now goes forward to reverse the errors of stupidity. I only fear that the person I now seek will not be able to control his agitation."

Just as Ji Gong said this, he heard someone in front of them calling, "Ji Gong, you have come! I have been to the Monastery of the Soul's Retreat three times and did not see you, but now today you have come! Something very distressing has happened at the Bright Purity Nunnery, and the old nun, Shining Truth, says that you are the only one who can help."

Saying this, the person speaking ran forward and with bowed head knelt before Ji Gong. The monk judged him to be a man of about sixty years of age. He was wearing a cape of earthen-gray crane feathers, a robe tied at the waist with a sash, and white cloud design slippers. His face was pleasant and honest.

Now, what this person had come about was as follows. At City God Mountain there was another old nun called Pure Chastity. She had a niece named Lu Shi, called Simple Chastity, who was married to a certain Gao Guoqin. Originally they had lived inside the south gate of the walled city in Yuhang prefecture on Scholars' Street. Gao Guoqin was from a wealthy family, but he knew only about books and nothing about managing money. As a result, after his parents died, shortly they had neither a roof over their heads nor a foot of land upon which to stand. Then the day came when they had neither a stick of wood nor a grain of rice.

At that time his wife, Lu Shi said, "It simply will not do to sit here until we die. There is a good everyday saying: 'When trees are moved from one place to another, they may die. When people move in the same way, they may live.' Why should we not go quickly to Linan? I have an aunt there who lives at City God Mountain. We can go there and find a place for you to study for your degree. First of all, we can get by from day to day. Secondly, you will be able to apply yourself, so that, when the year for the examination comes, you will have a chance to show your understanding of learning and you will be successful. How do you feel about this, my husband?"

Gao Guoqin responded, "This is the only thing that you and I can do. Let us go. There is no other way."

The husband and wife then sold their old and worn furniture and a few odds and ends. Then, after counting up what they had made, they set out. On the same day they arrived at City God Mountain.

When the old nun, Pure Chastity, saw them, her heart was moved to pity. Looking about the temple, she chose a small building of three sections and told them they could live there. The wife, Lu Shi, was able to help by doing some needlework. Gao Guoqin was roused to great efforts in his studies in the temple. Husband and wife were quite contented during the first month.

One day, however, an unpleasant incident occurred. Shining Truth had a novice, named Wise by Nature, who was older than the rest of the novices. She could see that Gao Guoqin came from a wealthy and talented family, that both elegance and substance were combined in him, and that he was full of learning. Altogether she deemed him a refined young degree student, handsome and upright.

The two studied in the same hall in the temple and often had loud and spirited arguments. She would challenge him in the classical style and he would reply in the same manner. One day, when the two were alone together in the hall, Wise by Nature took a writing brush and wrote a stanza of poetry that she handed to Gao Guoqin. He took it and read:

> Here in this other world of nuns all robed in white
> I do not ask for Nirvana's selfless bliss
> Nor immortality achieved by Daoist arts
> But only a little of the water
> In which the willow twigs have soaked
> Scattered between us as a charm
> That there the lotus with the double stem may bloom,
> A love fulfilled and shared in mutual delight.

When Gao Guoqin read this poem and realized its meaning, the color of his face changed. "Little teacher," he said, "this is unnecessary. Ours is the fate into which people are born upon this earth. A short time of happiness for a man and woman may spoil their good names for their entire lives and leave a foul reputation for all time. Even their ancestors might be held up to ridicule. Moreover, this is a blessed place of the Buddhist faith. How can one do wicked and disgraceful things here?"

When Wise by Nature heard these words, her face and even her ears turned red, and finally she left the hall. From this time on, whenever Wise by Nature saw Gao Guoqin, she was obviously ashamed and quickly went away. Gao Guoqin, for his part, felt that the nunnery was no longer a suitable place to live. Then he asked Pure Chastity to find him and his wife a couple of rooms below the mountain, saying, "My wife and I should move down from the mountain. It is not proper for us to live in a nunnery."

There was nothing else that the old nun could do. She then found a building of three sections with a separate gate and a small private courtyard. It was a house belonging to Zhou Yuanwai, also called Zhou Bancheng. He asked the old nun the name of the prospective tenant.

The old nun replied, "It is one of my relatives who came from Suhang prefecture and is now living in the temple. It is my niece and her husband. There are just the two. This nephew-in-law of mine is surnamed Gao; his personal name is Guoqin. He is a studious person. Because it is not convenient for him to stay in the temple, they are looking for a place to live."

Zhou Bancheng said, "Tomorrow bring Gao Guoqin and I will see him."

The old nun therefore brought Guoqin to see the landlord the next day. Zhou Yuanwai saw that Gao Guoqin was an upright person, studious and refined. Immediately Zhou Yuanwai thought that he would like to help Gao Guoqin. However, Zhou Yuanwai feared that his help would not be accepted. He therefore spoke in a way that he himself considered to be rather abrupt. Nevertheless, he told his servant that, if Gao Guoqin missed any payments, he should not be pressed for the money. Such were Zhou Yuanwai's feelings of commiseration for those in distress.

So it was that husband and wife moved down from the mountain and Gao Guoqin began to cast horoscopes for a living. If he earned one hundred cash, they would spend it for food, and if he earned two hundred cash, they would spend that on food. Thus they got by from day to day, although they were still in poverty. Without realizing it, they came to owe six months' back rent. Yet they had not been asked for it.

Then something unfortunate happened. The landlord's man who was responsible for collecting the rent asked for a leave of absence. He explained his duties to the individual taking his place, but this substitute did not understand the fine details. When he was examining the records, he realized that there was unpaid rent owed by Gao Guoqin. The substitute said to himself, "I must visit him."

When this household man arrived at Gao Guoqin's gate and knocked, Gao Guoqin's wife, Lu Shi, who was inside, called out: "Who is at the gate?"

The man replied, "It is a man of the Zhou household who has come to collect the rent."

Lu Shi said, "My husband is not at home. When he comes back, I will tell him."

The household man said, "If he is not at home, is the money also not at home? A whole six months and nothing at home? You live on another man's property and you are in over your heads with nothing to stand on. You don't give money, you put off and put off some more. Now it is finished."

Lu Shi said, "Wait until my husband returns—he will send you the money."

The household man said, "Do not send it. We are going to fix this outside gate. You can lend us this gate for a while." The household man then had the gate opening into the street carried away.

That night when Gao Guoqin came back, he saw that there was no street gate and asked his wife Lu Shi about it. Lu Shi said, "The landlord sent for his rent money and his household man carried the gate away."

When Gao Guoqin heard this, he lost his temper and said angrily, "Zhou Bancheng has a great deal of gall! How dare he take the gate? I will go to the Qiantang prefecture court and make a complaint against him."

Lu Shi countered, "Oh, sir, we have no money, and so we have no argument. For six months we have not paid any rent. If we made any accusation, it would be considered unreasonable."

Just as the two were talking, they noticed the old nun, Pure Chastity, coming. She could see that they were troubled about something. When the old nun inquired, Lu Shi described the entire affair concerning the rent collector and the gate.

The old nun said, "You should not be living outside; you really must come back to my temple. It is so difficult to make money elsewhere. And you, sir, to be writing horoscopes for a living! Nowadays nobody wants a genuine horoscope. You could sell three imitation horoscopes in a day, but a genuine horoscope you couldn't sell once in three days. People wouldn't want it! You are too good a person to be doing this, sir! You don't need to be on the outside."

The old nun told Lu Shi to sweep up and then took the couple back to the temple, despite the fact that Gao Guoqin felt a great sense of unease about returning. At the nunnery she gave them their old quarters in which to live. As for the six months' rent owed to Zhou Bancheng, she considered that to be incense money.

CHAPTER 18

Gao Guoqin goes to visit a friend, leaving some verses as a message to his wife; Ji Gong is begged to foretell the absent husband's fate

The scholar was young, unrecognized, and not yet wed.
A painted lady called to him and offered tea.
In her secluded courtyard far within
She trod upon a flower where none could see.

WHEN Gao Guoqin came a second time to City God Mountain, he stayed in the room to which he and his wife Lu Shi had returned and did not go into the hall to study. One evening, however, as he was sitting with Lu Shi, he said, "Wife, tomorrow I wish to go to visit a friend."

Lu Shi said, "Sir, I still have two hundred cash that my aunt gave me to buy needles and thread. Tomorrow, when you leave, take the money to use for tea and cakes." When she had finished speaking, she brought the money to him.

As Gao Guoqin held it in his hand, he was filled with shame, and said, "Do not be anxious, wife."

When Lu Shi was sleeping peacefully, Guoqin sat staring abstractedly, a prey to gloomy fancies, cut off from heaven with no resources on earth. His heart was filled with sorrow. He took a writing brush, wrote a note on three slips of paper, and placed them under the inkstone. He wanted with all his heart to wake his wife, but he feared that she would be troubled if he did so. He hardened his heart, then stood up and went outside.

There was attached to the nunnery a man whose work included taking care of the incense burners. His surname was Feng, and he was called Feng Xun. He asked, when he saw Gao Guoqin come out, "Why has Gao Guoqin risen so early?"

Guoqin said, "Would you open the gate, old gentleman? I am going down the mountain to visit a friend."

Feng Xun opened the gate and Gao Guoqin hurriedly went down City God Mountain and on into the distance.

When Lu Shi awoke and did not see her husband, she involuntarily experienced a terrible shock. She quickly went outside and began searching for him until she heard Feng Xun say, "Ah, Gao Guoqin left early this morning."

Lu Shi immediately went back inside and started to look around. Then she saw the three slips of paper. On the first he had written:

> Time seems to limp along in rags,
> Each day almost beyond enduring.
> We came into this nunnery
> As I held back my burning shame.
> Though kindness of the family
> Has led us here through Buddha's gate,
> I could not stay while all about
> Men mocked my wretchedness.

Lu Shi read this verse. She understood it to mean that he was so poor that he could not take care of a family, and that he was leaving the nunnery because he could not bear men's ridicule. Then she read the second verse:

> I now leave for some far-off place.
> My chances to return are few
> And whether I shall live or die
> Is something that I do not know.
> The possibility is scant
> That we may ever meet again.
> Yet fate ordained that we be born
> And also ruled we two be wed.

Thus Lu Shi learned that her husband was leaving for a distant place from which he might not return, that he did not know whether he would live or die, and that everything was in the hands of fate. Finally, she read the third verse:

> As I put down my writing brush
> Abandoning my classic books
> The worst is that I understand
> I only have myself to blame.

My dearest wife may understand
These few poor words I leave behind.
I now entrust her dear sweet self
To those who gave her shelter here.
While I take with me as I go
The memory of her lovely eyes.

When Lu Shi had finished reading this third verse, she began to scream with pain as if she were being torn into pieces. Hearing her, the old nun came and asked, "Why are you in such distress, niece?"

Lu Shi, saying that she felt almost certain that her husband would die, showed her aunt the three verses left by Gao Guoqin.

The old nun said, "You need not be so disturbed, child. I have an idea. There is now at the Monastery of the Soul's Retreat at the West Lake a monk called Ji Gong. He is a true living Buddha, able to foretell the destinies of others. He knows about things that have not yet happened. I will send Feng Xun, the man who takes care of the incense burners, to the Monastery of the Soul's Retreat to invite Ji Gong to come here. He will use his powers to tell where your husband went and where he is now. Then we will send someone there to ask him to come back."

Lu Shi said, "If that is so, quickly send the man to invite Ji Gong here."

The abbess sent Feng Xun down to find Ji Gong. The first time that Feng Xun visited the Monastery of the Soul's Retreat, Ji Gong was not there. The second time that Feng Xun went to ask for Ji Gong, the monastery was surrounded by soldiers. The third time that Feng Xun went, he heard that Ji Gong had been taken away in fetters by order of Prime Minister Qin. Therefore things were delayed for several days. At last, Feng Xun was successful when he again went down the mountain in search of the monk. Feng Xun saw the revered *lohan* just as he was coming up the mountain with Zhao Wenhui and Su Beishan.

Feng Xun quickly ran forward and prostrated himself at Ji Gong's feet, saying, "Teacher, you did come! I have been to the monastery over and over asking for you, sir, several times. And today, sir, what about the things I have heard—and where are you going now?"

Ji Gong replied, "I am going to your temple to see the old nun. We are presenting her with a person who is going to leave the world."

Feng Xun said, "Good, good, good. Our abbess, just now, wants to ask your help in an urgent matter."

Zhao Wenhui and Su Beishan asked, "What is the matter at the temple?"

Feng Xun then described in detail the affair of Gao Guoqin from beginning to end as they all hurried on to the temple. Feng Xun led the way.

When they entered the nunnery, they went to the west courtyard. This courtyard had buildings on three sides—the east, the west, and the north. Each of the buildings was divided into three sections. Feng Xun went with the rest into the north building. Zhou Yuanwai noticed that the room that they had entered was extremely neat and clean. Against the north wall was a long, high table on which were many volumes of the classics. In front of this table was a square "eight immortals" table with chairs on either side. Ji Gong sat down at the head of the table, Zhao Wenhui sat at the foot, and Su Beishan sat at the side. Looking about, they saw a pair of hanging scrolls with calligraphy. There was another scroll in the center on which a large peach was painted, and on which there was also some writing:

> Could I but leave the quest for wealth and fame,
> I'd build my thatched hut close against a hill
> With half an acre reflected in a pool,
> Some willow trees and stalks of green bamboo.
> There on a warm spring day I'd entertain a guest
> And sit half drunk with him in the sun.
> At night, in the red circle of the lamp,
> I'd visit in books the mind's most distant realms.
> Thus would I cultivate true purity of heart
> Secluded from the world and petty cares.

On the pair of matching scrolls of calligraphy, the following two sentences were written:

> Though painted by artists for a thousand years,
>   the mountain has not changed.
> Its waterfalls have given life to countless ancient poems.

At the bottom of each of the three scrolls was the signature of Gao Guoqin.

Su Beishan looked at them and said, "Saintly monk, you can see that Gao Guoqin is a man of natural talent. Everything that Feng Xun said about him is certainly right. See the quality of the calligraphy in these two scrolls. Please, saintly monk, show compassion for him and bring him back. I will help him find a place to study and carry him through until the time of the examination. I will also bestow silver upon him and help him to succeed afterward."

The monk said, "Good! This is added evidence of the *yuanwai's* merit."

As they were talking thus, the old nun came in, leading her niece. She approached the old monk and greeted him reverently saying, "I beg the *lohan* to be compassionate. This is my niece, Lu Shi, called Simple Chastity. I speak for her because her husband, Gao Guoqin, left her in my care here at the nunnery. Today it is already several days since he left. I beg the holy monk to show his mercy and use his powers to foretell what is about to happen."

The monk said, "That is easy. However, we have just rescued a person, the daughter of a well-known family, who fell into the hands of a procuress. It is the young lady's desire to leave the world. We thought we could bring her to this nunnery of yours. Please receive her as your follower."

The old nun said, "Whatever Teacher directs will be done."

Zhao Wenhui said, "In a little while I will send my gift of three hundred ounces of silver to the nunnery to continue the burning of incense."

The old nun thanked Zhou Yuanwai and again begged the monk for his prediction concerning the whereabouts of Gao Guoqin.

Ji Gong sent forth the light from the innermost part of his being. Then the monk cried out, "Ai yah! It is finished! It is finished!"

When Lu Shi heard this, she was so frightened that her face changed color. She begged, "Holy monk! Have mercy! Save him! Save him!" Having uttered these words, she began to weep piteously and continued to implore the monk's help.

"What time is it just now?" the monk asked.

"The sun is just past the midpoint," answered Feng Xun.

Ji Gong said, "This man has now traveled 180 *li*. When it is time for the sun to set, his life will be in danger."

Su Beishan offered, "I will do anything I can to help."

"Then select someone from your household to go with me," Ji Gong instructed him. "I will also need two hundred silver pieces for traveling expenses."

Su Beishan said, "Su Lu, go quickly to a money shop and get the two hundred silver pieces. Then go with the saintly monk to find Gao Guoqin."

The old nun said, "Feng Xun, you also shall go with Ji Gong."

Lu Shi, meanwhile, was bowing in respect and gratitude to Ji Gong, who said, "Zhao Wenhui and Su Beishan, you will see that Spring Fragrance is brought safely here to become a nun. Then you may leave."

The two *yuanwai* agreed to do so. Su Lu returned, bringing the silver. Then Ji Gong left the Bright Purity Nunnery with Su Lu and Feng Xun. When they reached the foot of City God Mountain, Ji Gong suddenly stopped. Then he took three steps forward and next went back three steps.

Su Lu said, "Teacher, we must travel 180 *li* before dark. If you continue in this way, you will not be able to cover eight *li*. If you will change your way of walking, it will be easier."

The monk replied, "It is not difficult to change my way of walking." With this remark, he began taking three steps forward and two steps backward.

Feng Xun secretly realized that this was a kind of joke and said, "Teacher, at this rate you will be back where we started before dark, but what good will that do?"

Ji Gong countered, "If I go quickly, will you be able to keep up with me?"

The two said they could. Then left, right! Left, right! Ji Gong was off and running on ahead. In the twinkling of an eye he was out of sight. The two men quickly ran after him for two or three *li*. They were both soaked with perspiration.

One of them said, "When we reach those woods, let us rest."

Just as the two entered the woods, the monk said, "Oh, come now, a little further."

"We have not had any rest at all, and you reached here earlier," the two protested.

The monk said, "Perhaps I did doze for a few moments. Do those legs belong to you two?"

The two answered, "They are fastened to our bodies. If they are not ours, whose are they?"

The monk replied, "Well, in that case, they probably do belong to you two. I will recite one of my incantations and then they will be able to move again."

Feng Xun said, "Good! Good! Do recite one of your incantations."

When the monk saw that the two men were standing firmly on their feet, he said under his breath, "Om Ma Ni Pad Me Hum, I command!"

Quite beyond control of the two men, their legs rapidly carried them forward as if they were flying. Su Lu could only call out, "Teacher, there are nothing but trees ahead of us. If we hit one, we will die!"

The monk said, "Never mind. It is all safely in my hands. When you get there, you will not hit anything."

Naturally, as they came to the woods, the two simply passed between the trees. After they had passed through the woods and as they still ran on, they saw a man coming out of a village carrying a bowl in his hand. Ji Gong took one look at him.

Now this man was an unruly son. His surname was Wu, and he was called by the personal name Yun. In his home there was only his old widowed mother. On this day they had had meat dumplings for their noon meal. His mother had prepared them well, but when this Wu Yun had looked at the table, he saw that she had not bought the vinegar to go with them. Then he became angry, saying, "The older you get, the more mixed up you get. Where is there a family that eats meat dumplings without vinegar? You are useless and I resent it!" His mother said nothing. He walked out still angry, carrying a bowl to get some vinegar. It was then that he was seen by Ji Gong.

Ji Gong had known from the beginning all about what had happened. For this reason he made a slight pointing motion with his hand toward Wu Yun. As a result, Wu Yun joined Feng Xun and Su Lu and started running alongside them.

Involuntarily Wu Yun called out, "I am not going this way! What kind of business is this? My legs have gone mad!"

Then there was a great sound in the ears of the three men, like the howling of the wind as it drives the clouds across the sky. Ahead of them they saw light reflected on a river. Su Lu then called out, "Holy monk, stop making me run! A river is up ahead. If we fall in, we will die."

The monk said, "Do not worry. Just use a little effort and we will pass over it."

When they came to the river, it seemed as though they were flying as they crossed it. Su Lu thought to himself, "When we reach the other bank, I will manage to catch hold of one of those trees." As soon as this thought came into his mind, he selected a tree. Su Lu quickly grasped it with ease and fell to the ground. Feng Xun also fell to the ground, and the man who had gone out to buy vinegar fell as well.

The monk came to them and said, "You may all get up now."

The three said they were not able to stand. The monk took a piece of medicine from his pocket, divided it into three pieces, and gave one piece to each of the men to eat. The three then realized that their bodies were capable of movement and they could stand without difficulty. Wu Yun was amazed that they had traveled so far.

Just at that moment another man approached them, and Su Lu asked, "May I inquire what place this is?"

The man replied, "This is small Liu village. Where are you people going?"

Su Lu answered, "We have come from Linan City and we are going to Yuhang prefecture."

The man said, "You have gone past it! From here it is twenty *li* back to Yuhang prefecture."

When Wu Yun heard this, he said, "Ai yah! I broke the bowl I brought to carry home the vinegar! I never ate the meat dumplings, either! Because of the river, I will have to go two hundred *li* to get back."

The monk said, "I will take you back."

Wu Yun said, "Do not take me back. I can hardly stand. We are at the northern frontier. How am I going to get back?"

It took him two days and two nights to get home. From that time forward, whenever he saw a monk, he would run away from him. Wu Yun's heart was forever filled with fear of the poor ragged monk.

Su Lu asked, "Will we get to Yuhang prefecture today, and will we find Gao Guoqin?"

Ji Gong answered, "That is exactly right."

Then Ji Gong, Su Lu, and Feng Xun continued on their way.

CHAPTER 19

The searchers find the impoverished scholar; the desperate Gao Guoqin returns to familiar scenes

WHEN Ji Gong, accompanied by Su Lu and Feng Xun, arrived outside the South Gate of Yuhang prefecture, he saw an inn on the east side. The monk nodded toward it, saying, "Su Lu and Feng Xun, you two and I will go in, drink a cup of wine, eat, and rest. After that, we will go on." The two men agreed and went into the restaurant. There, they asked for several different sorts of dishes.

Su Lu said, "Saintly monk, finally we are here with you in Yuhang prefecture, but where is Gao Guoqin now? Can you bring him here? How would it be for the four of us to eat and drink together?"

The monk replied, "First, we will drink a little wine, and after that we will go to look for him." Having traveled so far, the three men talked a little more as they finished their wine. Then they paid for the food and wine, left the inn, and went into the town through the South Gate. As they came to the first crossroads, they turned east. On the north side of the road they saw the yamen, the official residence of the magistrate, and the offices of the prefecture. The monk quickened his step and started to hurry inside.

Su Lu asked, "Teacher, where are you going?"

The monk answered, "You two men wait here. I am going in to look for someone."

As the monk came to the great gate, he heard someone who seemed to be a person of authority in the yamen shout, "No one may fail to confess! Gao Guoqin will now have the instruments of torture applied to the right and left legs. Then he will be brought forward for interrogation." When Ji Gong heard this, he felt a chill of terror in sympathy.

Now, on the day that Gao Guoqin came down from City God Mountain, he had thought to himself that if he were to depart for some other place, he still would not have any relatives to turn to nor any place where he could seek shelter. Then he thought, "Why not go back to Yuhang prefecture?" He took passage on a boat, paying the fare with half of the money given him by his wife. With the remaining one hundred cash he bought something to eat. Therefore, by the time he reached Yuhang prefecture he had used up his two hundred cash.

"This time," he thought, "I have come once more to my old haunts, and once more I am without resources. First of all, I have no relatives here; secondly, I have no close friends. I can think of nothing to do." He considered going back to the old house, but wondered what good it would do. "If I had a few relatives, they might cheer me up, or if I had some friends that I knew very well, I could talk things over with them." His situation really seemed to illustrate the old saying—that truly, whether in busy towns or lonely hills, the best connections are those with relatives and true friends.

Gao Guoqin was a courageous person, but he did not feel that he could live by begging, even from friends and relatives. The more he thought, the closer he came to the idea that the best thing he could do was to end his problems with death.

When he came to the river outside the wall at the South Gate, intending to jump into the river and die, he stood looking out over the water at the many boats coming and going. He was thinking to himself, "Dead! Dead! Once dead and it will be finished. Everything will come to an end. There is a time to be born and a place to die, and this is the place where I will cut short my life."

Just as he was about to jump down, he heard someone behind him say, "Friend, whatever you do, do not jump! I have come."

Gao Guoqin turned his head and saw a rather tall, slender man with a narrow waist and broad shoulders. He had a blue kerchief tied around his head and wore matching blue close-fitting pants and jacket with no cuffs at the wrist. Over his shoulders he wore a short crane's-feather cloak with round purple markings, in the center of which were red dots. His eyebrows arched over lively and kind eyes. His nose was strong, straight, and a little pointed, but not unpleasantly so. The still-youthful features of his rather narrow face were well in proportion to one another. He seemed to be somewhat more than twenty years old.

The man continued, saying, "Sir, you are certainly an educated and intelligent man. Why should you be thinking of ending it all?"

Gao Guoqin replied, "You need not ask me, friend. There is nothing else I can do in the world. I simply must die."

The man asked, "Sir, what is your difficulty and why should we not talk about it?"

Gao Guoqin could see that the man was sincere, and asked him, "What is your honorable surname and your personal name?"

The man answered, "My name is Wang and my personal name is Chengbi, and I live in this vicinity. Along these riverbanks I am a kind of manager or shipping agent. I employ people to load and unload all of the merchandise that is purchased on account for others. And now, sir, why is it that you are thinking about death?"

Gao Guoqin said, "I am also a native of this place, Brother Wang. I lived within the South Gate. My name is Gao Guoqin. I took my wife to the city of Linan to seek help from her relative. We lived in a nunnery there. I thought of myself as a man who was in the world, and yet neither able to serve his prince and benefit the people, nor to protect his wife and rear children. It seemed an empty life on earth. Because of this, I thought that death was better than life."

"Brother," said Wang Chengbi, "your brilliant mind has deceived itself. How can you value your life so lightly? First, come into a restaurant with me and have a little wine. After that I will think of something for you. You need not have such foolish ideas. When people die, they do not come back to life."

Gao Guoqin then went with Wang Chengbi into a wine shop. Wang asked for wine and several dishes. After they had finished drinking and eating together, Wang Chengbi said, "Just now I have no money and no immediate way to get any, but if we wait until late in the afternoon, then some money will come into my hands. Today you can go and help to pull the tow rope of a barge."

Gao Guoqin said, "My hands do not have that kind of strength. How can I pull the tow rope of a barge?"

"Sir, you don't want to talk like that," said Wang Chengbi. "People can do what they try to do. You must remember two sentences of the ancients: 'The perfect man can be great, or he can be small;' and 'The hero may retreat in order to advance.' Go and pull the barge today. Wait until I have the money in my hands. Then I will give you a few ounces of silver to send to your home. Afterward, I will ask some friend to help you start a school. How does that appeal to you?"

Gao Guoqin first thought, "Since this man whom I have just met offers to help me, and since he urges me to do this work, I cannot be too obstinate and unreasonable." Having thought thus, he said, "Friend, since you show so much concern for me, I will listen like a younger brother and go to pull the barge."

"Good!' said Wang Chengbi. And standing up, he led Gao Guoqin to the riverbank. There, he saw a barge that had just been loaded with cargo and was about to depart. Wang Chengbi called out, "Barge master! I have a friend here. I want him to help pull the tow rope. Take good care of him, barge master, and when you reach your destination, make sure you bring him back. Otherwise, though, do not bother about him."

The barge master replied, "Yes, indeed. Since this concerns young Master Wang, we will certainly not treat your friend badly."

Gao Guoqin stood waiting with the rest of the tow rope gang. As the barge was pushed off at the barge master's order, everyone picked up the tow rope. Gao Guoqin understood nothing about such things, but the rest were all used to pulling. One of the men showed him how to grasp the rope, and they all moved off. As the other people were shouting out in unison to keep time, Gao Guoqin thought of the classic doctrine of moderation. To mark his own steps, he recited the lines concerning the adaptability of the superior man to each situation in which he finds himself. All the rest began laughing loudly to hear someone reciting the classics while pulling the tow rope of a barge.

When they reached the wealthy man's wharf, which was their destination, the barge was unloaded. Afterward, Gao Guoqin was so exhausted that he could not leave the barge with the rest of the men and so slept on the deck. The next day, the barge was loaded with other goods and began the return journey. Again Gao Guoqin pulled with the rest. When they reached Yuhang prefecture and arrived at the pier, Gao Guoqin saw Wang Chengbi standing there and quickly went to him.

"Sir, this time we are indeed fortunate!" said Wang Chengbi, "I have been waiting for you here. We brothers must have been fated to meet from our previous lives. Today I signed an agreement for thirty-five loads. First, come with me and have some tea and meat pastries. Afterward, you can go into town and change some notes for me. Tomorrow you will go to take some silver home—but, today, buy some wine and meat. We will feast and enjoy ourselves together."

Gao Guoqin said, "Good! Good! Brother Wang, I thank you from the bottom of my heart for treating me so kindly so soon after our having met."

Wang Chengbi said, "You and I are simply brothers now. You don't need to be polite. At first sight it was as if we had always known each other."

Gao Guoqin thought to himself, "This friend is no doubt truly sincere." By the time he had finished drinking tea and eating several meat pastries with Wang Chengbi, it was growing late. Wang Chengbi gave the notes that were to be exchanged to Gao Guoqin. He was to go into the walled town and exchange them for silver. Wang also gave him a bottle to be filled with wine when he bought the wine and the meat.

Gao Guoqin went into the town with the notes that he exchanged for fifty ounces of silver. He then bought the wine and the meat and immediately started to return to Wang Chengbi, since the town gates were about to close. Guoqin was just hurrying through the gates when he saw a man coming from the opposite direction. He was running so hard that he seemed to be flying on the most pressing business. In fact, he ran straight into Gao Guoqin, and quickly said, "Do not be angry, sir. I was in too great a hurry because I have important business to take care of. It was my fault entirely." All this the man said with folded hands and many bows. Then he quickly hurried on in through the gates.

Gao Guoqin was a refined and scholarly person, and, even though the running man had struck him, he thought to himself, "He is not a man without heart. What harm was there in his actions?" Just as Guoqin was continuing on his way, he felt with his hand in his pocket to make sure he hadn't dropped any of the silver. But not a trace of it was there. He thought, "Surely I could not have dropped all the silver when I was struck!" Shocked, he stood with staring eyes and mouth stupidly dropped open. The man who had seemed to be in such a hurry was actually a daylight robber. Earlier, he had seen Gao Guoqin change the notes. With a thief's true cunning, he had intentionally run into Gao Guoqin, taking the silver and making off with it.

The more Gao Guoqin thought about this matter, the worse it seemed. "What can I say when I see Wang Chengbi? It is worse than if I had died. Yesterday I was about to die and did not—and in these two days my troubles have grown worse. Now it is as if the King of Hell has condemned me to the third hell. What horrors may await one who dares to go down to the fifth hell?"

Thinking thus to himself, he again came to the river that flowed past the town. And again he intended to drown himself. Then he called out to himself: "Gao Guoqin! Gao Guoqin! There is no way by which you can ever arrive at a decent life. I did not think that I had come here to die!"

Just as he was speaking aloud to himself in his sorrow, he heard someone ask, "Is that my dear brother, Gao Guoqin, who is speaking? I have looked everywhere for you but did not find you. I did not expect to meet you here today." As he spoke, the man approached and craned his neck to get a better view. Looking at the man, Gao Guoqin did not recognize him. He seemed a little familiar, but Gao Guoqin could not remember him, and therefore asked, "Are you not mistaken, sir?"

The man replied, "Elder Brother, do you not even remember the one who was the same as your little brother? I am Li Seming."

When Gao Guoqin heard this, he said, "Ai yah! So it is you!" When younger, Li Seming was part of a poor family. He and his widowed mother had lived in a house near the Gao household. Gao Guoqin's family had all been generous and had often helped the Lis when they were in need. Later, Li Seming had studied in the Gao home. When his mother died, the Gao family paid for her burial.

Gao Guoqin had then asked Li Seming whether he wanted to study for a government post or whether he wanted to become a merchant. Li Seming said, "If I had personal resources, I might like to study for a government career. Since I have no money, how can I hope to pursue such studies? Therefore, I would like to work in a shop."

Gao Guoqin said, "That also may be good." He then arranged with a grain shop in town to take Li Seming as an apprentice to learn the grain trade. Guoqin also provided him with a set of clothing, since it was the custom for an apprentice to bring with him a working wardrobe of his own.

Li Seming was diligent in his work, did not make any really careless mistakes, and took to the trade. After the three full years of his apprenticeship were completed, the proprietor evaluated Seming's work. The proprietor, having grown very fond of the young man and realizing that he was an excellent worker, made him a member of his family and opened a separate branch shop for him in Chengjiang. This venture became very profitable. The proprietor had no son and only one daughter, whom he gave to Li Seming in marriage. The proprietor then retired, giving the young people the entire property. Afterward, the old man and his wife died, and Li Seming managed the whole business.

He had often thought to himself, "If it had not been for the kindness shown to me that year by Gao Guoqin, where would I be today?" And so he took his family and some of their personal belongings and returned to the home of his late father-in-law. He intended to find Gao Guoqin and express his gratitude. However, when he reached Yuhang prefecture, there was no one who could tell him where the Gao family had gone. All said simply that the Gaos had become impoverished and gone away. Li Seming felt very bad. He bought a house outside the West Gate and opened still another grain shop outside the South Gate. On this day he was returning home when he happened to meet Gao Guoqin.

Both men were overjoyed at their meeting and sad to think of their long separation. Each explained what had happened to him since they had last seen each other. Gao Guoqin said, "Dear brother, if I had not lost that money, we two would not have met."

Li Seming said, "First of all, come home with me. We still have much to tell each other." The two started off together, but before they had gone very far Gao Guoqin struck something with his foot. Bending down, he picked up the object.

CHAPTER 20

When sympathetic friends meet, kindness is repaid with kindness; resentment cherished in the heart of an inferior man brings grievous injury

AS Gao Guoqin examined the object he had picked up, he saw that it was a bundle containing two rolls of fabric. When he opened the bundle, he and Li Seming could see by the bright moonlight that the edges of the cloth were marked with a name, the Ever-Flourishing Silk Shop. Li Seming said, "The name on those two rolls is not that of one of our Yuhang prefecture firms. We have two silk shops in Yuhang, both called Ever Following Heaven's Guidance. I do not know where the Ever-Flourishing Silk Shop can be."

Gao Guoqin said, "We will stand here and wait. If someone comes who says that he has lost his silk, we will give it to him. If this were lost by someone who had been sent on an errand by his master, the matter could be most serious for him."

The two men stood there for quite a long time, but did not see anyone come looking for the silk. Li Seming then said, "It is now quite late. Let us go back to my house and wait until tomorrow. If we find anyone who is looking for the silk and describes it, we will consider the matter ended. If no one comes, we will put up notices about the two rolls. This action will show that we did not want to hide them."

Gao Guoqin said, "First, I must go to inform Wang Chengbi about my situation. He gave me some notes that I was to change into silver, a small part of which I was to use to buy some things. He wanted me to come back and drink some wine with him. It was because I lost the silver that I was thinking of committing suicide. If I do not go back now, I fear that he will suspect me of stealing."

Li Seming countered, "First come home with me, brother, and then I will send one of my household servants to him with a message. Then tomorrow you may take me to meet him."

As they talked, they continued on their way until they reached the home of Li Seming at the West Gate. The front gate was not completely closed. They pushed it open and entered.

Before they reached the second gate, which closed off the inner courtyard, Gao Guoqin could see a light shining through the window lattice of a house with three sections on the west side of the outer courtyard. Gao Guoqin said, "It is very late now. Tomorrow I will go within, but tonight let us just sit in that room and talk."

Li Seming said, "Those three sections are rented out. I really do not bother about rent money, because I am often away from home and I need to have someone live there to keep an eye on the outer gate." Gao Guoqin nodded. They went on to the second gate and knocked.

A serving woman opened the gate from inside, saying, "Ah, the master has returned."

Li Seming said, "Go in and tell your mistress that my kind friend Gao Guoqin has come."

The old woman went in. Before long they heard a voice say, "Please enter." The two men then walked through the inner courtyard and into the principal house.

After Li's wife, Ho Shi, had politely come to greet their guest, Li Seming told the old serving woman, "Have several kinds of dishes prepared. We two brotherly friends will go to eat in the east building."

The two then went there to sit and under the lamplight opened the rolled up fabric to look at it. Li Seming said, "These two rolls are a real treasure. I simply do not know where the Ever-Flourishing Silk Shop is located. Tomorrow we will post notices, and if anyone answers and tells a satisfactory story, we will give him the silk. If no one claims it, why not use it to make two long gowns—one for you and one for me?"

Gao Guoqin answered, "Yes, but tomorrow, dear friend, you will go with me to see Wang Chengbi. If he had not saved me, I would already have been beneath the Nine Yellow Springs. He is a friend who truly seems to be sincere and straightforward, a prince of a man who treated me from the first as if he had always known me. I feel very grateful to him. Good friends are not easy to find."

Li Seming said, "Good. Tomorrow I will go with you to meet that friend of yours." After the two had finished drinking and talking together, they slept peacefully in the east room.

The next morning the two men awoke and were drinking tea together when they heard someone shout: "Li Seming! Do you have a man named

Gao Guoqin staying with you?" The shouts from the outer courtyard continued. The two men stood up, went outside, and opened the gate to see who was calling. There stood two headmen with four underlings, all wearing dark kerchiefs and dark clothing, with uniform jackets. Each wore a leather belt and boots and carried a wooden staff with an iron tip. One of the heads was named Qin Lushou. The other, Dong Shichang, asked, "Friend, you are named Gao, are you not, and is your personal name not Guoqin?"

Gao Guoqin replied, "That is not wrong. Why do you two ask?"

Dong Shichang immediately took iron fetters and locked them upon the wrists of Gao Guoqin. Li Seming started to protest, and he was locked in irons as well.

One of the heads said, "We will now enter the inner courtyard and search for stolen property." Searching everywhere, they soon brought out the two rolls of silk.

Li Seming asked the two men, "Headmen, why have you manacled us?"

Headman Qin answered, "We have here a warrant by which the highest official of the prefecture urgently dispatched us to arrest you, but we two have no reason to mistreat you, nor would we dare to mistreat anyone who is arrested. We take no pleasure in mistreating people. Whatever you may have done, you yourselves know. Therefore, why should you ask us?"

The headmen said to the underlings, "Take them away with as little talk as possible. When you get to the yamen, you will all understand." The men were taken away quickly, along with the two bolts of silk. When the party reached the prefecture yamen, Gao Guoqin and Li Seming were taken inside.

At this time everyone was waiting for the magistrate, who was away on official business and had not yet returned. After they all had waited until the sun was approaching the horizon in the west, the magistrate came into the yamen and took his seat upon the bench.

There were three classes of underlings who stood during court and served by assisting in carrying out the magistrate's court functions and by maintaining a sense of orderliness. First were the robust and vigorous fellows who acted as bailiffs, either serving summonses or as guards, or performed other similar tasks in which they might have to overawe the accused. Second were the ugly fellows who acted as jailers or executioners, beating the prisoners with bamboo and applying other tortures. Third were the quick fellows who acted as constables and detectives, serving warrants and uncovering hidden criminal activities.

The magistrate's surname was Wu and his personal name was Daoguei. He had entered into government life through the competitive public examinations. As soon as he had begun his duties, he had kept away from anything questionable, as if he were a saintly immortal. No taint of improper influence had ever touched his sleeves. He loved the common people as if they were his children. He truly went through his life neglecting nothing, and his gate was never closed at night to anyone who had a complaint.

This evening he took his seat in the court and prepared to take up the business at hand. He began at once with the case of the armed attack upon the Ever-Following Heaven's Guidance Silk Shop, during which the owner had been wounded with a knife and fifty bolts of silk had been stolen, together with a thousand ounces of silver. Now the alleged head of the robbers, Gao Guoqin, with his accomplice, Li Seming, had been captured.

The bailiffs immediately brought the two men before the bench. They knelt and identified themselves.

"Gao Guoqin, bachelor degree graduate, kowtows to his lordship above!"

"Li Seming, an insignificant person, kowtows to his lordship above."

The magistrate looked down and saw Gao Guoqin, polished and gentlemanly with upright deportment and extreme politeness, whose clear and regular features and facial aspect had no suggestion of baleful criminality. Then the magistrate shot a question at him. "You slave, Gao Guoqin, when you and the rest committed the armed robbery at the Ever-flourishing Silk Shop, how many men did you have with you and where did you take your loot? Explain in detail!"

Upon hearing this, Gao Guoqin replied, "Revered as my father above, this student is a man of books and knows nothing about the Ever-Flourishing Silk Shop, nor any armed robbery."

The magistrate struck the desk and gave a look that frightened the entire yamen, saying, "Ha! Seize him for interrogation! Though not one in ten thousand wishes to confess at first, after interrogation they all do! Drag him here and beat him for me."

Gao Guoqin said, "Do not be angry, good father. This graduate speaks sincerely. About the robbery of the silk shop and the wounding of the proprietor, I truly know nothing. If you beat me during the examination, it will only be to make me say something that is not true and about which I know nothing."

The magistrate said, "As I see it, you are a base-hearted person with a long experience in crime, and you certainly stole from the silk shop. If you do not understand why I believe so, then why were these two bolts of silk in your possession?"

Gao Guoqin answered, "Yesterday evening this graduate was outside the southwest corner of the wall and I found the silk. I had intended to put up notices about it today in order to find the owner and return it to them. It had never occurred to me that we would be brought here. This is a true account of what happened."

When the magistrate heard this, he took the two bolts of silk into his hands to examine them. At the same time he ordered that Wang Hai, the proprietor of the Ever-Following Heaven's Guidance Silk Shop, be brought into court. Before long a man was seen coming in from the outside. He was about fifty years of age with a broad round face. He seemed to be a worthy, simple, and straightforward person. He knelt and kowtowed. The magistrate had one of the court underlings take the two bolts of silk down to Wang Hai, saying, "Look and see if these were something usually sold by your shop. If so, were they taken from your shop by the robbers? In a matter of such importance we cannot be careless."

Wang Hai took the rolls, and after looking at them said, "Your worship, these two bolts of silk are very clearly among those taken by the robbers."

When the magistrate heard this, he asked, "How do you know that they were stolen by the robbers? What evidence is there of the fact? Explain."

Wang Hai said, "To reply to your worship about the proof, in my store the goods on the shelves are only marked with the words EVER-FLOUR-ISHING SILK SHOP. They do not have the imprint of our own shop seal. If someone comes to us to buy silk, at the time of the purchase we stamp the goods with our seal. The words on this seal are A REASONABLE PROFIT, with characters formed in the ornamental style. This silk is not stamped with our seal. Because of this fact, I know that the bolts were taken, and not purchased, by the robbers."

The magistrate prepared to come down from the bench. Gao Guoqin knelt again as he realized the meaning of what had been said. The magistrate asked, "Gao Guoqin, did you hear that?" Then the magistrate commanded, "Have the instruments of torture affixed to Gao Guoqin, and afterward we will question him again."

Gao Guoqin said, "Truly, your worship, this graduate found the silk. The robbers took it, and perhaps they lost it and I found it. What proof does the magistrate have that I am the robber? Can't this be investigated?"

When the magistrate heard this, he suddenly became very angry. Frightening everyone in the yamen, he shouted, "You low creature! It is clear that you are a habitual criminal. How do you dare to attempt such deception in this district? You still say that the prefecture is treating you wrongfully. Attendants, left and right! Have the eyewitness brought forward."

When Gao Guoqin heard that there was an eyewitness, he was so frightened that his face changed color. Then he saw the attendants leading a man forward from one side of the courtroom. When Gao Guoqin looked at him, however, he did not recognize him, but saw only a man somewhat over twenty years old with a dark blue kerchief on his head. The man was wearing a short, dark cloth jacket over a dark-blue shirt and pants, a white sash and dark shoes. He had a grayish face with darker touches, eyebrows like the spurs of a fighting cock, and a pair of eyes like the bottoms of teacups. His nose and lips were thin, his forehead and face were narrow, and his rather large chin slanted back into emptiness.

Li Seming recognized him as soon as he saw him. He was the man who lived in the three-sectioned building in the outer courtyard of Li's home. He was supposed to watch the outer gate. His name was Leng Er. The neighbors called him Leng, and nicknamed him "the Unwatchful." He usually attempted to borrow money without returning it. His heart was filled with vengeful thoughts. Leng was a person who lived from day to day. He could not take care of his wife, who went out to work for other people. He spent his days at home spinning schemes and plans and nursing his hatred for Li Seming, who would no longer lend him money.

On the evening of the day that Li Seming brought Gao Guoqin home, Leng was there sitting in his room, vexed and melancholy, when he heard the voice of Li Seming's wife inviting someone to come in. Unwatchful Leng thought, "Li Seming does not ordinarily invite friends home. Perhaps there is some business afoot." He peeked out, saw Gao Guoqin with Li Seming, and heard Li Seming say Gao Guoqin's name. Leng went to the inner gate and stood listening. He heard Li Seming say that the two bolts of silk they had picked up came from the Ever-Flourishing Silk Shop, and that, if no one claimed them, "we two could make two gowns from them." Leng, as he was listening, recalled that a short time before, there had been an armed robbery at the Ever-Following Heaven's Guidance Silk Shop and that the case had not yet been solved.

"Tomorrow," Leng decided, "I will go to the yamen and I will make this crime stick to Li Seming like plaster is stuck to a sore. I will simply say that he is a receiver of stolen goods. He really deserves to be hated, getting so rich. I went to him to borrow a few strings of cash and he would not lend them to me. I will let him know how dangerous I am, and if I want to borrow money again, he will not dare to refuse to lend it to me."

In this frame of mind, early the next morning Leng went to the district offices and asked who the headman was. Someone said that it was Qin Lingshou and that it was his watch. Leng went in to see him and asked, "Headman Qin, about the case of the armed robbery at the silk shop—do you have anything on the investigation?"

Headman Qin replied, "We haven't."

Leng said, "Li Seming, the landlord in our courtyard, has received a quantity of stolen goods. Yesterday the head of a band of robbers, Gao Guoqin, stayed at Li Seming's house. The two men were negotiating all through the night. I clearly heard Li Seming say, 'Bring it here and I will send you word.'"

When Headman Qin heard this, he said, "Very good. I will take you to see our magistrate," and sent someone with a message to the magistrate. The magistrate immediately went into the courtroom and sent for Leng to come and talk with him.

Leng went in and knelt saying, "Your Worship, this insignificant person lives in the house of Li Seming. I often see him greeting and talking to evil-looking people as they go in and out of his house. Last evening Gao Guoqin, the head of a band of robbers, was in the house talking about the armed robbery at the Ever-flourishing Silk Shop and the stabbing of the proprietor. I have nothing against my landlord, but I feared that, if I did not report this matter to Your Worship, I would be guilty of letting the robbers escape."

The magistrate then ordered, first, that Leng should be taken out of the courtroom. The magistrate further ordered that Qin Lingshou and Dong Shichang should immediately go to bring back Gao Guoqin and Li Seming in irons. After these two were in court and the magistrate called for the eyewitness, the constables were then to bring Leng forward.

CHAPTER 21

The virtuous magistrate investigates a strange case;
Ji Gong follows the robbers to Yin Family Ford

WHEN Leng Er was brought forward to give his testimony, the magistrate asked, "Leng Er, you have said that Gao Guoqin committed the armed robbery. Now we have Gao Guoqin before us. Do you recognize him?"

Leng replied, "I recognize him. In answer to Your Worship, he was with Li Seming, talking while this small person listened."

Gao Guoqin interrupted saying, "Your Worship, I say to you as to my father, I, the graduate, do not recognize him."

Li Seming went forward half a pace on his knees, saying, "Your Worship, this Leng came to live in my house. He has never paid me any rent, but he was always borrowing money from me. Because he had failed to pay me back several times, when he wanted to borrow still more, I would not lend him anything. Then he began to hate me, and now he is simply trying to injure a good person. I beg your worship over and over to be compassionate."

The magistrate said, "Good. I will have you flogged, flogged until who is who becomes clear. When I punish someone, there is no doubt. When my people seize someone for questioning, they never fail to get a confession. Have Gao Guoqin and Li Seming both punished, and then we will interrogate them again."

The yamen functionaries to the left and right acknowledged the order with one voice. Just as they were about to apply the torture, suddenly a violent gust of wind, truly frightening in its severity, tore through the courtroom. Two people standing face to face could not even see each other. In a short time the wind ceased. When His Worship looked at the top of his desk, there was a sheet of paper bearing two words, GRIEVOUS WRONG!

His Worship did not know who could have written them, but it was his conjecture that there had to be a good reason for the message. He therefore ordered that for the present the two, Gao Guoqin and Li Seming, should simply be detained in custody and not tortured. He also ordered that Leng Er should be detained as well. With that, the magistrate left the court.

Now, the great wind had been no less than the arrival of Ji Gong. He had simply pointed and raised this strange wind that had temporarily blinded everyone in the courtroom while he wrote the two words, GRIEVOUS WRONG! and left them on the magistrate's desk. Ji Gong then left the yamen. Taking with him his two companions, Feng Xun and Su Lu, Ji Gong went out through the west gate of the town. He said nothing, however, about stopping for the night, and went on toward the west for perhaps two *li*. He then halted and said, "Now we have gone two *li*. Wait! Where did this silver come from?"

Ji Gong was pointing at a bag, and the two men, Su Lu and Feng Xun, picked it up at once. Su Lu thrust his hand into the bag and immediately clutched a handful of silver. When the two asked where it had come from, Ji Gong answered, "This must be the silver for which Gao Guoqin exchanged the notes before his meeting with the thief, when the silver was stolen. This is what was left over after Gao Guoqin purchased the meat and wine. We will now select a convenient place to stay."

When the three had finished speaking, they went west until they came to a market town at a river crossing called called the Yin Family Ford. From there they went south for a short distance until they saw on the east side of the road a grayish-white wall on which was written "The Old Meng Family Inn—Fodder for Your Horse and Safety for Your Merchandise."

Ji Gong stood in front of the inn gate and called out, "Open the gate!"

Inside, someone asked, "What for?"

Ji Gong replied, "To stay at the inn. Quickly! Open the gate!"

Inside, the voice said, "No rooms. All full."

Ji Gong insisted, "We want a single room. Anything will do."

Inside, the voice said, "We do not have one."

Ji Gong countered, "We have much silver. We cannot go on. What shall we do?" Inside, these words were understood.

Now this inn was indeed the old Meng family inn, and the manager of the inn was Meng Sixiong, known as Fearless Fourth. His partner was called Tiger Li. There were two porters, one named Liu, the other Li. They had long been accustomed to killing people. If there was a solitary trader with much baggage or with a great deal of clothing, they would immediately give him the drugged wine containing a powder known as the "Mongolian Sweat," which would render him helpless and ready to be killed. The raised building at the north side of the inn courtyard was completely undermined with tunnels. This inn never did business in the ordinary way, since the proprietor was interested only in murder and robbery.

When the porter heard the people outside the gate mention silver, he quickly went to the gate, looked out, and saw three men carrying what looked like a good deal of silver. Then he went at once to the manager's office and said, "Proprietor, outside there are two men who have come with a monk. They are carrying much silver with them and they want to pass the night at the inn."

Meng Sixiong said, "Why have you not invited them inside?"

The porter replied, "I had already told them that there was no room."

Meng Sixiong said, "Let me teach you a few sentences. You are just to say, 'Our manager said that he fears that, carrying such a great weight of silver and being quite tired, you might meet some robbers who would lighten your load and come down heavily upon your very lives. Our manager likes to do good deeds most of all. He has found you three a room and invites you to stay.'"

The porter understood, turned about, and went to open the gate. There he saw the three men still standing in the gateway. The porter said, "You three gentlemen have not left."

Ji Gong said, "Your manager listened to you. He has found us a room and wants us to stay there. He is afraid that we might lose the silver if we go on. Is that not so?"

The porter replied, "Quite right."

"Good," said Ji Gong, "Lead the way."

The porter went ahead. Ji Gong and the others took a great step over the high threshold of the inn and saw before their faces a masonry screen. To the east was the manager's office, to the west the kitchen. The screen shut off the view of the courtyard from the gate. On the east side of the courtyard there was a building housing a sitting room; there was also a similar building on the west side of the courtyard. Straight to the north was the best building—it was on a raised platform.

The monk stopped and stood still in the middle of the courtyard, saying, "What is this odor in your courtyard?"

The porter asked, "What odor?"

The monk replied, "It has a slight smell of robbers."

The porter said, "Do not make us laugh, monk. You will be staying in the north building."

The monk said, "Good. The upper building is cool and open on all sides."

The porter said, "It is only that way because the lattice windows have not been repapered recently—but go inside."

The monk entered the north building and went on into the west chamber with Su Lu and Feng Xun. As they looked about, they saw that against the north wall was a brick platform bed. Beneath the window was a square "eight immortals" table with two chairs. Because Feng Xun and Su Lu were tired, they sat down in the chairs to rest. The porter first brought water for them to wash their hands and faces. Afterward he brought tea and poured it, asking, "What would you three like to eat?"

The monk replied, "You can cook up whatever you like—a proper choice of four dishes with two pots of wine besides."

Su Lu and Feng Xun protested, "But we two will not drink because we want to go to sleep."

Ji Gong said, "You may not drink, but I will."

The porter went out of the door and called, "Prepare four dishes and two pots of dry white liquor, the Forgetful Sea brand."

"Porter, come back here!" said the monk.

"What do you want?" the porter asked.

The monk said, "You said I wanted two pots of dry white liquor, the Forgetful Sea brand."

When the porter heard, he was quite surprised and thought to himself, "This priest is terrible. He must be in the know. Otherwise, how would he be able to speak the black language of the rivers and marshes?" The porter then asked, "Monk, what do you mean by Forgetful Sea brand?"

"Are you going to answer properly or not?" Ji Gong asked. "If not, I will slap your face!"

The porter asked, "How am I not answering properly?"

The monk replied, "Just now you said 'Forgetful Sea brand.' And you still ask me! I ask you again. What is meant by Forgetful Sea brand?"

The porter thought it over. "He is right. After all, was that not what I said? Perhaps that is why the monk asked me." Then the porter said aloud, "Just now I said to have the Forgetful Sea brand prepared because I wanted to give you the better wine."

The monk said, "I myself said I wanted the better wine. Why do you not go ahead and get it?"

The porter went outside and brought the wine. The monk then took the cover off the wine pots and peered into the wine, first with one eye and then with the other. The porter asked, "What are you looking at, monk?"

The monk answered, "I am looking to see how much there is. What is your honorable surname, Porter Liu?"

The porter replied, "You know my name is Liu. Why do you ask?"

The monk said, "I can see you probably are a very friendly sort of person. We seemed to know each other at first sight. Come on, we will drink a cup of wine together."

The porter said, "I cannot do that. I do not drink even a little wine. Even the smell of wine makes me drunk and then I do not know what is going on."

The monk urged, "You can drink a little, just one cup."

The porter said, "No, I cannot. If our proprietor knew that I drank with a guest, he would send me away immediately."

The monk said, "You will not drink my wine and now you make me suspicious. It seems that something has been put into the wine. If you will not drink, I will not drink either."

The porter said, "Drink your wine, monk. That is not for me. If our proprietor knew, there would be trouble. It is not the custom in our business."

The monk countered, "It will not matter if you drink a mouthful of wine—such a little thing."

The porter picked up one of the wine pots, saying, "I will take this pot of wine and heat it again. It is probably cold by now."

The porter took the wine pot to the proprietor and said, "Proprietor, this monk is very strange. I took the wine to him and he wanted me to drink. I would not drink and then he would not drink. First I will change this pot for one without the drug, and if he asks me to drink, I will drink from that."

The proprietor gave him a pot of good wine and the porter took it to the upper room, where he said, "Monk, even though this small inn does not have such a custom, if you still ask me to drink, then I will drink."

The monk said, "You have heated the wine."

The porter said, "I heated it for you, monk."

The monk, pretending to appreciate the porter's trouble, took the good wine and quickly drank all of it. Then he handed the pot of drugged wine to the porter, saying, "You drink this one."

The porter quickly went outside.

The monk said, "If you will not drink, I will not drink either. For one to drink alone is too boring." The monk ate several dishes of food and had the table cleared. Then he shut the doors and went to sleep.

The porter went to the proprietor's room and reported, "Proprietor, among those three, it is the monk who gives the orders. Later, when we make our move, be careful of him."

Tiger Li, Meng's partner, told him, "Never mind. Later call Porter Li to come with a big knife. You yourself, rest now. I will not need you." Porter Liu bowed his head to show that he understood.

When the night was past the third watch, Porter Li, taking his big knife with him, went to the north building. He pushed a small stick between the door and the frame to trip the latch. This door opened into the center hall. He entered, and lifting a trapdoor, went down into an underground passage. When he reached the trapdoor under the monk's room, however, he could not open it. "Strange!" the porter thought.

He returned and came up through the first trapdoor. Then he made a small hole in the paper covering the wooden lattice separating the west chamber from the hall. He could see that the three men seemed to be sleeping soundly and he heard them snoring. He tried to open the door by which he had originally entered the hall, but could not. Again he tried the door, but it resisted all his efforts.

In another room to the west that was empty, there was also a trapdoor that led into a passage connected to the one where he had just been. He planned to get into the sleepers' room through that part of the tunnel. He moved a table in the second west room, lifted the trapdoor, and went down again into the underground passages; but as he went forward, he suddenly found that he could go no further—nor could he go back. It was as if something had stopped and held him where he was.

The proprietor, Fearless Fourth, and Tiger Li waited in the office for a long time. Not knowing whether Porter Li's plan had succeeded, they told Porter Liu to go and look around. Porter Liu took a knife and, when he reached the north building, saw that the door was closed. He could not tell where Porter Li had gone. Porter Liu then hurried to the east of the north building, where there was a small building with a single room that also had an underground passage that linked with the west rooms. When he reached the east room, he moved a table and rolled up the silk hanging behind it, thinking to go through the underground passage. When he entered it, however, he found that for some reason he, too, could not go forward, nor could he leave the passage.

Again Tiger Li and Fearless Fourth Meng waited and waited. Seeing that neither Porter Li nor Porter Liu had returned, the two became impatient. They each took a knife and went to the north building. There, they noticed the closed door. They still did not know where the two porters had gone. Tiger Li forced the door open with a knife and the two entered the center hall, where they stopped and listened carefully.

In the room to the west, the noise of snoring was like thunder. Tiger Li lifted the bamboo blind in the west room doorway with the point of his knife. He went into the room and looked around. He saw the monk lying with his head pointing south and his neck stretched out. Tiger Li pulled up the curtain in front of the platform bed and saw the other two men asleep and unaware of what anyone was doing.

"You three deserve the death that you are about to die," Tiger Li thought to himself. He stepped forward and lifted the knife, intending to kill the monk, then saw the monk show his teeth as his face burst into a broad grin. Tiger Li was so frightened that he turned and was about to flee. Then, however, he saw that the monk was sleeping normally again. Tiger Li thought to himself, "The monk must have been dreaming. How was it that just as I was about to kill him, he grinned at me?" After a time, Tiger Li recovered from his fright and again stepped forward. He lifted the knife and started to bring it down. The monk pointed and touched the man with his magical power. Tiger Li was unable to move.

Fearless Fourth Meng waited outside the door of the room for a long time. He could see that Tiger Li had not brought the knife down. Fearless Fourth became more and more anxious. Suddenly, he dashed into the room, holding his knife in his outstretched hand.

CHAPTER 22

The capture of the robbers solves the strange case; a plan for systematic charity is put into action

A S Meng, the Fearless Fourth, was just about to kill Ji Gong, the *lohan* rolled over, rose into a crouching position, and pointed. As he did so, he uttered the six true words, "Om Ma Ni Pad Me Hum. I command!" Thus, by arresting the movement of their spirits, he fixed the robbers in their places. Then, with one kick the monk awakened Su Lu, and with another he awoke Feng Xun, who immediately cried out, "Ai yah! There are robbers who are going to kill us!"

The monk stood up as if he were about to run outside. When Su Lu and Feng Xun looked more closely, they saw that Meng and Tiger Li, who were each holding a sharp blade, were standing motionless. Su Lu and Feng Xun at once jumped down from the brick platform bed and ran outside, where they stood in the courtyard and raised the cry: "Robbers! Murderers! Help! Save us!"

Just then, the guard soldiers on their rounds heard some people in the inn shouting that there were robbers. Now, the reason why Lieutenant Liu Guobin was patrolling with these twenty soldiers was that in the street just ahead, there had recently been an armed robbery at the Ever-Following Heaven's Guidance Silk Shop. The owner had been wounded by a knife, fifty bolts of silk had been stolen, and a thousand ounces of silver had been taken. However, the case had not yet been closed.

That morning, hearing someone call out that there were robbers, Lieutenant Liu Guobin quickly ordered the soldiers to go up a ladder onto the buildings and jump down into the courtyard. Having done so, they opened the gate, and Lieutenant Liu came in and put Su Lu in irons.

Su Lu said, "Do not lock me up, honorable gentlemen. I am not the robber. The robbers are in the room. There are three of us. There is an old man named Feng Xun and a monk, Ji Gong. We came from Linan looking for someone. Last night we stayed at the inn and robbers wanted to kill us. It was because of this that we were shouting."

The officer in charge of the soldiers said, "Good. If we have not fallen into a snare, as we did before, we will not begin by locking you up. On our last watch we went into the courtyard of the Ever-Following Heaven's Guidance Silk Shop to chase the robbers because people were shouting. We suspected that someone at the shop was a thief when we went in to look. We locked up everyone in the shop, the robbers escaped, and our efforts led nowhere. This time we will not make the same blunder."

Su Lu said, "First, go into the room and look at the robbers. Find my friends and the two porters." When the soldiers went and looked in the north building, they found Meng, the Fearless Fourth, and Tiger Li. They also found the trapdoors and the porters, Big Liu and Li the Second, inside the tunnels. The soldiers took possession of the four robbers' knives and then locked the four in irons.

Coming out, the soldiers looked everywhere but did not see the other two men. Just as the soldiers began to worry, they heard a moaning sound under the horse trough. Looking closer, they saw that it was a man. In fact, it was Feng Xun, lying on his belly underneath. When he crawled out and was questioned, his story was the same as that of Su Lu. The soldiers first released Su Lu and then began to search for the monk.

All the soldiers helped Su Lu and Feng Xun to search for the monk, but after looking in each room, they still had not found him. Finally they came to the privy, where they heard the sound of snoring. When they looked inside, there was the monk, leaning against the wall, sleeping.

Feng Xun went over and pushed him, saying, "Ji Gong, are you still sleeping? The soldiers have come with an officer and captured the robbers."

The monk opened his eyes and said, "This is terrible! Robbers! Save us!"

Su Lu said, "If there are robbers, why are you sleeping?"

Ji Gong answered, "It is because of the robbers bothering us that I am still sleepy."

The soldiers said, "Go into the north building and collect your things." When the three returned to their room and looked, all the silver that they had found had turned into a pile of stones. Su Lu asked the monk how the silver could change into stones, but Ji Gong only laughed without answering.

The soldiers took the three to the yamen's guardhouse. There they questioned Feng Xun, who told them the entire story of what had happened. Lieutenant Liu Guobin asked the robbers for their names and completed his records. Then the soldiers took the robbers, together with the travelers, including Ji Gong, to the Yuhang prefecture yamen.

Meanwhile, the Yuhang magistrate had been sorely troubled about the case involving Gao Guoqin, because no further clues to the cause of the crime had been found. Then he saw the guard from the Yin Family Ford village arrive in connection with this very case.

First, Ji Gong was told to go forward. When the magistrate saw the poor, disreputable-looking monk standing there, his worship asked him to explain where he had come from, what he was doing, and why he did not kneel before a magistrate.

Ji Gong laughed loudly and said, "Your Worship, I am the monk, Ji Dian, from the Monastery of the Soul's Retreat at the West Lake."

> To a temple high up on the City God Mountain
> I traveled to offer my simple respects
> But abruptly was sent on an errand most urgent,
> To find a poor stray that we feared had been lost.
> Gao Guoqin is the one that I seek here in Yuhang,
> The same one who protests he is falsely accused.

Upon hearing this, the magistrate said, "Ah! It is Ji Gong. Your disciple did not know. Someone bring a seat for him!"

The monk sat and told the story of his stay at the inn. Su Lu and Feng Xun kowtowed to the magistrate and then stood to one side. When the magistrate had heard Ji Gong's entire story, he ordered that the robbers be brought in. The attendants complied.

First, Meng, the Fearless Fourth, was brought forward. He knelt and touched the floor with his forehead. The magistrate said, "You are called Meng, the Fearless Fourth. Did you open the inn?"

The robber answered, "I did."

Then the magistrate asked, "Why have you murdered people? Why did you make your inn a den of robbers? How many years altogether has this gone on? How many men altogether have you killed? Explain in detail."

Meng answered, "In reply to your worship, this insignificant person's work is business and certainly not killing people. Yesterday evening, however, robbers entered my little inn, and just as I was chasing them with a knife, I encountered the soldiers of the night watch with their officer. They mistook me for robber."

The magistrate said, "You may step down now."

He then called the officer of the guard soldiers and asked about the circumstances in which the prisoners were taken. The officer gave a short description of the events. The magistrate then ordered that Tiger Li be brought before him and that the prisoners should be kept apart from one another. When Tiger Li was brought forward, he knelt. Looking at the man, his worship saw an evil countenance without the slightest hint of anything good, a man somewhat above thirty years old, with a dark yellow face and dark yellow flesh, short eyebrows, and round eyes.

Looking intently at the prisoner, the magistrate said, "Tiger Li, just now Meng, the Fearless Fourth, made a full confession. Will you also tell the truth?"

Tiger Li thought, "If Meng has told the truth, there is no reason why I should hide it myself." Then he said, "Your worship, since Meng has told all, this insignificant person will tell all as well. We two were from the same street in Yin Family Ford village. We had been good friends since we were very young. At the time we opened this inn we were partners. As of this year we have been open for more than ten years.

"Each time a guest traveling on business came with many bags and bedding rolls, he would be given several drinks of drugged wine. After he become unconscious, we would kill him and take his valuables. Altogether we killed thirty or forty men.

"This year, on the twenty-sixth of last month, three men came to our inn from Penglai Island in Shandong. They were all friends of the Greenwood. At their head was a sinister man named Zhou Tienming. His two followers were named Lang Guei and Wang Lien. Our downfall came from the recklessness of Lang Guei. The three wanted to buy some silk. Their wrangling over the price at the Ever-Following Heaven's Guidance Silk Shop turned into a fight. That night, they invited the four of us from the inn to go with them to rob the shop. We stole fifty bolts of silk and one thousand ounces of silver. One of our gang used a knife to slit the throat of the watchman. When we returned from the robbery, the leader of the other gang left in anger with his two followers, because he was unwilling to divide the plunder evenly.

"Then last night the monk came to the inn with two men and we saw a great deal of silver. I therefore sent the porter to kill them. I did not imagine that the officer and his men would arrest us. This is how it happened. This insignificant person certainly would not dare to give false witness."

When the magistrate had heard and understood this account, he had the two porters brought forward. As soon as he questioned Big Liu and Li the Second, they each made a complete confession. When Meng, the Fearless Fourth, was confronted with the other three confessions, he, too, confessed all.

Gao Guoqin, Li Seming, and their accuser, Leng Er, were then brought before the court and the secretary read the testimony concerning the robbery of the Ever-Following Heaven's Guidance Silk Shop that clearly had nothing to do with Gao Guoqin or Li Seming. The magistrate then ordered that the first two should be released.

Gao Guoqin had stepped to the back of the courtroom and was standing about, when he saw Feng Xun approach. "I have not seen you for a long time." Feng Xun said, "I have been looking everywhere for you!"

Gao Guoqin greeted him and then described to him the different things that had happened. Meanwhile, they could see that Leng Er was before the court being given forty strokes with the bamboo and later being fastened into the cangue, a flat wooden collar as big as a cart wheel that he would have to wear with a notice attached to warn the public against committing offenses similar to his. Meng, the Fearless Fourth, was also given forty strokes with the bamboo. Then, along with Tiger Li and the two porters, Meng was fastened into fetters and sent to prison.

Ji Gong, seeing that the case was finished, at once stood up and thanked the magistrate. When Li Seming saw Gao Guoqin and learned all that had happened, he said, "First, let me invite you, my honorable friend, and Ji Gong to my home. You may then go on your way tomorrow."

Ji Gong said, "That will be good," and walked on with them. Then he asked, "Who was it that stole the silver you had received for the notes given to you by Wang Chengbi?"

Gao Guoqin replied, "Your disciple does not know. Perhaps the saintly monk knows."

The monk laughed loudly and said, "Come with me and I will look around!" Then he pointed with his finger. They saw a man coming out of Li Seming's courtyard. He was about twenty years old, with a light-skinned face, short eyebrows, fleshless jowls, and hair done up into a knot shaped like a bullock's heart. He was wearing a dark, short jacket with a dark-blue shirt beneath, dark pants, white stockings, and black shoes. His eyes were like those of a chicken looking this way and that through a bamboo fence.

Li Seming immediately recognized him as Sha Itiao, the younger brother of Leng Er's wife. He had long roamed the streets of the city, robbing and stealing. He was a daylight robber, and there was nothing evil that he would not do. On the day that Gao Guoqin had changed the notes at the money shop, this man had seen him. Sha Itiao, with his thief's cunning, had pretended to be coming in through the town wall in order to run into Gao Guoqin and take the silver. After that, Sha Itiao had spent the next two nights in a gambling den, where he had lost the stolen silver.

Today he had come to borrow money from Leng Er. Only then did Sha Itiao learn that Leng Er had gone to court as a witness. Sha Itiao was just leaving when he met Ji Gong, who was leading the others and pointing a finger at him.

Sha Itiao said, "Gentlemen, if you will wait and see, the time has come for me to repay my debts." With that he raised his hand and struck his own cheek several times. He then ran to the riverside and leapt into the water. For a moment he rose to the surface, singing a song, and then died. When the local official learned of the drowning, he conducted an inquest. Later he wrote that the matter was ended and that a nameless person had been buried.

Li Seming invited the company into his home for a feast as an excuse to detain Ji Gong. Gao Guoqin said, "Dear brother Li, go outside the South Gate and find Wang Chengbi. Tell him the entire story of my affairs and thank him for me."

Li Seming said, "Tomorrow I will go."

He was host to Ji Gong that night. The next day when it was light, Ji Gong left Yuhang prefecture, taking Gao Guoqin, Su Lu, and Feng Xun with him. They hurried off along the highway to Linan.

On this day, as they went onward, they reached a market. There they saw through the crowds of merchants and their customers a great gate to the east, on the north side of the road. Just beyond the gate was a high wooden platform of the kind used in performing Buddhist or Daoist rites. It was about thirty-six feet high. On it was a ceremonial chair and a table adorned with ribbons of five colors and with various things spread out upon it.

Ji Gong looked, and as the light of his intuition swept over the scene, he said indignantly, "Well! Well! Since I, a monk, now encounter this affair, how can I just put my hands in my sleeves and look on when such things exist? But wait! I must do what I will do in a particular way!"

Now, this market town was called the Yunlan Market, and the home to the north of the road was that of a man surnamed Liang with the personal name Wanzang. His family possessions were beyond number. He had one child, a boy named Liang Shiyuan. The old *yuanwai* liked to treat people well, and especially enjoyed having roads and bridges repaired at his own expense. He helped both Buddhists and Daoists. He would shore up and restore temples and shrines, and he paid for the printing of the texts of sutras.

But then an unfortunate thing happened. A Daoist priest who lived in the vicinity came to him and asked for one hundred ounces of silver, saying that it was needed to repair a shrine. The *yuanwai* gave him the money, and the Daoist left. Afterward, the old *yuanwai* was visiting a friend in West Street and just happened to see the Daoist priest coming out of a gambling den. When the old *yuanwai* returned home, he said to his household people, "I gave the Daoist priest money and all he wanted it for was to go and play cards! I will hand out no more money!"

One of the household, named Liang Xiude, said to the *yuanwai*, "The *yuanwai* is a person who likes to do good deeds. We may indeed have made mistakes. Over these past years, rice has continued to be as dear as pearls. Why not set up a rice-porridge kitchen to help the poor in the neighborhood? Doubtless that would be a good thing. I do not know what you may think about this idea."

When the *yuanwai* Liang Wanzang heard this suggestion, he was most happy. He immediately notified the proper local official, asking him to choose a day for the Liang household to begin the distribution of the rice porridge. Early each morning, the old *yuanwai* would go outside his gate with the people who prepared the rice porridge. As each person ate a portion, the *yuanwai* would give him one hundred cash and with kind words encourage him to work in the fields.

For more than half a year, Liang Yuanwai had been outside his gate each morning overseeing the distribution of rice porridge. Three days before the arrival of Ji Gong, the *yuanwai*'s young son, Liang Shiyuan, had been idly standing outside the gate while the porridge was being distributed. Now it was nearly noon and he was by himself, intently observing the people who passed, when he saw a Daoist priest approaching from the west. He was about fifty years old, wearing a dark Daoist hat and robe, white socks, and dark shoes. He carried a precious ceremonial sword on his back and a fly whisk in his hand. The skin of his face was like transparent gold paper with darkness showing through. His eyebrows were heavy and his eyes large. Trailing locks of hair and a beard covered the lower part of his face. As soon as he saw Liang Shiyuan, the Daoist priest's evil plans began to take shape. Today he was truly a demon of a man!

CHAPTER 23

In the market town of Yunlan, an evil Daoist brings forth a supernatural manifestation; the benevolent Liang Wanzang suffers a calamity

THE Daoist stopped and faced the boy, saying, "May the blessings of the Unlimited Being be upon you. I, a poor Daoist, have strolled over the three hidden hills of Fuzhou and wearily climbed the five sacred mountains. I study and investigate the Dao and the spirits. I can read a person's fortune in his face and I can cure misfortune. When I look at the young master's face with its regular features, I can tell that it is certainly that of a future graduate honored by admission to the Hanlin College of Literature."

As soon as he heard these words, Liang Shiyuan quickly bowed and greeted the Daoist ceremoniously saying, "May I ask the Master Daoist's honorable name and inquire as to which famous mountain or in what sacred grotto I may search for you to improve myself? I would like to receive your instruction."

The Daoist replied, "This poor Daoist is only about five *li* away, straight to the north. I became a Daoist priest at the Xiang Yun Temple on Wuxian mountain. My surname is Chang and I am called Miaoyu. I am especially skilled at reading faces."

Liang Shiyuan said, "Daoist Master, since you are good at reading faces, may I respectfully beg you to demonstrate?"

When the Daoist heard this request, the evil that was in the center of his heart grew stronger. Now, the reason that he had come to the Liang household gate thus was as follows. When he had returned from his ramble over the three hidden hills and once more saw the surrounding wall and the hall of his Daoist shrine, he said to his acolyte Liu Miaotong, "Do you not know how to go out and beg for the shrine? You have simply been staying here at home and eating!"

Liu Miaotong said, "I cannot get anything by begging. Nowadays, the good Liang Yuanwai no longer gives in the way that he used to do. He has been distributing rice porridge at his home. I heard all about it from Ching Jingyi, one of the poor people in this area who is a Daoist believer. He told me all about the scandal as something just between ourselves.

"Some time ago, one of our honorable Daoist priests received a donation of one hundred ounces of pure silver from the good Liang Yuanwai. The Daoist said he would use it to repair the shrine. Afterward, instead of repairing the shrine, he spent the entire hundred ounces of pure silver in a gambling house, and he was seen coming out of the place by Liang Yuanwai. Because of this incident, the old *yuanwai* no longer gives to Buddhist monks or Daoist priests. How can I still go there and beg?"

When Chang Miaoyu heard this story he said, "If I cannot get a contribution from the good man Liang, I will kowtow to you! Tomorrow I will go to his gate."

It was because of that conversation that he had come here and now stood face to face with the boy. When he saw the young Liang Shiyuan standing outside the gate, the Daoist drew his eyebrows down in thought, as a plan arose in his heart. By the time that the young master asked him to demonstrate his powers, Chang Miaoyu already was eager to use the five demon needles and the seven arrows piercing the throat to work an evil transformation.

Chang Miaoyu took the hand of the young master and said, "Young master, your face is one of the best. I can see by your eyebrows and bright, clear eyes that you were born into a family that esteems poetry, books, and music. You had no lowly or careless men as ancestors. They were like jade among ordinary stones, like the crimson cinnamon among flowers.

"But even among those candidates already with their first degree and preparing for their second degree about the round pond in the imperial college, the star of officialdom has not yet fallen. And when it falls, is it to be, or is it not to be? Will they succeed, or will they not succeed? One may be as a bird that soars among the clouds but falls among thorny brambles. One may be as the greedy fish that swallows the fisherman's hook. Yet near as that fish is to the wide waters, it will never again reach the place where the three rivers join. How can it ever shed its skin and be transformed into a dragon? Young master, if you will explain clearly the eight characters for the astrological signs at the time of your birth, I will carefully prepare a horoscope for you."

Liang Shiyuan explained the eight characters for the signs at the time of his birth. The evil Daoist memorized them, and then secretly twisted his fingers together and muttered a spell. Suddenly, without warning, he struck the boy with his open hand. Before the boy had time to recover from the shock, out of the three divisions of the boy's soul the Daoist summoned forth one of them. Out of the seven divisions of the boy's soul the Daoist also summoned two. The frightened Liang Shiyuan turned and fell senseless to the ground.

The Daoist himself returned to the shrine and told his acolyte to take some dry straw and make a figure of a man. Then the Daoist took a vermilion brush and wrote upon the completed figure the characters for the boy's eight signs. Using seven new needles, he thrust each into the heart of the straw man.

Liu Miaotong, the acolyte, was a guileless person, and when he saw this kind of behavior, he asked who was going to be killed. Chang Maioyu said, "You had better not talk nonsense! I am not doing this to kill anyone. I am going to get much silver from Liang Wanzang."

From this day forward, he went daily through the Yunlan market town and past the old *yuanwai*'s gate.

Now, after the Daoist had left the Liang family gate, one of the household people came out, saw the young master lying outside the gate, and quickly called a fellow servant. Together they carried the boy to the main house in the inner courtyard. When Liang Yuanwai heard what had happened, he was frightened almost out of his mind. He was sixty years old and had only this one child. If something fatal were to happen to him, there would be no second chance! Liang Yuanwai immediately sent people to invite the most famous doctors to come to cure his child. But when the gentlemen who had been invited came, they all said that some part of the boy's soul had been lost and that taking medicine would not help.

In his distress, the old *yuanwai* prayed to the spirits in heaven, asking them to allow this supernatural illness to pass. However, two days went by with no change. On the morning of the third day, the charitable-hearted Liang was standing at his gateway watching the people coming to get the rice porridge. There were not a few. It was a dismal sight to see so many in need, and he himself was troubled and sad. Then he saw coming from the south a woman with three little ones running before her. They seemed to be about ten, eleven, and twelve years old. Two more little ones about seven and eight followed behind her. She also carried on her back a boy of three or four years, and in her arms another not more than a year or two old. When Liang Yuanwai saw her, he said, "Ai ya! This woman had brought all her children with her. Someone ask her to come here."

A household person went to her and said, "Madame, the *yuanwai* of our household invites you to speak with him."

The woman approached and slowly put down the two small children. She bowed her head in greeting and said, "May I offer the *yuanwai* three times nine great good fortune, great long life, and many children, boys and girls, and good fortune and long life extending on and on."

Liang Yuanwai asked, "These boys, are they all yours?"

The woman answered, "My name is Jou. My husband has been away on his business for a long time. With so many mouths to feed and a year of near famine, I come here to receive some of the rice porridge. It makes it possible for my family to live."

Liang Yuanwai instructed one of his household to take ten strings of cash and give them to the children. The woman prostrated herself before the *yuanwai*, thanking him again. Then, taking the money, she and the children departed.

The old *yuanwai* thought to himself, "That woman I saw just now, although she is poor, has seven boys. If they all grow up, it will be great good fortune for her. While I have great wealth, my only child now is so sick with this strange illness. Perhaps it is the fate that heaven ordains for me, that I should become childless. Although I have begged the spirits in heaven in my distress, it is all in vain."

Just as he was searching back and forth in his mind for something that might help, he saw a Daoist priest coming from the west wearing a dark robe. He had a face the color of rusty iron and a beard covering the lower part of his face. The beard hung down over his chest in flowing strands and mixed with the long locks of hair that escaped from the coil partially hidden by his hat. On his back he had a precious sword.

He was speaking as he approached. "May the blessings of the Limitless Being be upon you. This poor Daoist has wandered over the three hidden hills and wearily climbed the five sacred mountains, but never have I seen a household so troubled by such a baleful influence. This home has been invaded by five noxious flying demons, with their dreadful powers. They have searched out your little one and bound his body with their evil cords."

As soon as Liang Yuanwai heard the Daoist's words, he quickly went up to him and said, "Please, saintly master, enter. Five flying poisonous evil spirits have indeed invaded my family's home. I beg the saintly master to break their evil spell."

The Daoist priest listened and then said, "The *yuanwai* must take me inside his household to examine the true state of affairs carefully."

Liang Wanzang took the Daoist inside. When they arrived at the inner courtyard, the Daoist looked around everywhere. Afterward he followed the *yuanwai* into the library, where he said, "Tomorrow, the *yuanwai* must have a ceremonial platform thirty-six feet high constructed inside the great gate. On it must be prepared an eight immortals table and a high-backed chair. Also, prepare some long-life incense, the five offerings, a sheet of yellow paper, an inkstone, a writing brush, a piece of white orchid root, a packet of vermilion, a piece of coriander root, a bowl of clear water, and a dish filled with the five grains. On the front of the platform prepare hangings with the five colors—blue, yellow, red, white, and black, to represent metal, wood, water, fire, and earth. Prepare five hundred ounces of silver. I will spend some of your wealth, but this invasion of your household will be over. I will first drive out those five demons and afterward I will cure your son."

When the *yuanwai* heard the Daoist's final words, his heart was filled with joy. He quickly directed his household people to serve tea, saying, "I have not previously been instructed by the honorable Daoist master. May I ask: what is your honorable age? What you are called? And on which famous mountain in what sacred grotto may I seek you?"

The Daoist priest replied, "Perhaps the *yuanwai* has forgotten, but I have often come here to the *yuanwai*. My surname is Chang and my personal name is Miaoyu. I am only five *li* north from this village. I am the resident Daoist at the Fortunate Cloud Shrine on Five Spirits Hill."

Hearing the Daoist's answer the *yuanwai* said, "Ah, we have been neighbors all along. I truly have been neglectful. I will quickly direct that you be properly served."

The Daoist waved his hand several times in a modestly protesting manner, saying, "The *yuanwai* must not feel distress. I will trouble you again another day. Now I must go back to the shrine to prepare the necessary things. Tomorrow I will gladly come to get rid of those evil influences." Having said this, the Daoist stood and took his leave. The *yuanwai* himself accompanied him outside and said farewell with folded hands respectfully raised.

After the Daoist priest had gone, the *yuanwai* immediately directed his household people to erect the high platform inside the great gate and to prepare all the things that would be needed. All of the household people were running about in busy confusion half the day, and by the end of the day all things had been prepared. Everyone then went silently to his rest and that night all was quiet.

The next day they all rose early. With their hearts filled with simple piety they waited respectfully for the Daoist to come. At noon the Daoist priest had not yet arrived, but a Buddhist monk appeared. Of course, it was Ji Gong leading Gao Guoqin, Su Lu, and Feng Xun on their return to the capital from Yuhang prefecture. As they were passing through, the monk had stared in wide-eyed surprise at the ceremonial platform inside the great gate and rising high above it.

The *lohan* quickly understood what was happening and said to himself, "What evil thing has been brought into being here! How dare anyone let loose those uncanny spells to do monstrous things!"

He then instructed the three men, Gao Guoqin, Su Lu, and Feng Xun, to wait for him. Then with long strides Ji Gong hurried up to the great gate. There he saw several of the Liang household people standing in the gateway. He greeted them, saying, "Good day, gentlemen. This monk is just passing through and since early this morning has had nothing to eat. I came to this worthy place to beg for a meal."

The people said to him, "You came too late, monk. You see us standing here at the gate. We are not a group of scholars talking together. Originally our *yuanwai*, who is a good man, loved to give alms to Buddhists monks and Daoist priests. But now, whether Buddhist or Daoist, our *yuanwai* gives nothing. If you had come early to ask, you could have had some of the rice porridge, but you came late. Come tomorrow."

The monk said, "I have not eaten since morning. Have mercy upon me."

An old manager of the household sitting off at one side particularly liked to do good works, and it seemed to him that the monk's speech was both strange and piteous. He stood and came to the monk, saying, "Monk, I have not felt well this morning and I still have a bowl of rice from which I have not eaten anything. I will go and get it for you."

So saying, he went inside, brought the bowl out and was about to give it to the monk. However, as the old man loosened his hold on the bowl, the monk suddenly pulled back his hand. The bowl and its contents fell to the ground. The bowl smashed and the contents scattered.

The old manager said, "You monk! I brought this to you out of the goodness of my heart. Why did you break my bowl?"

The monk gave a loud laugh and said, "You asked me, a monk, to eat this leftover rice!"

The old manager said, "If you will not eat leftover rice, what will you eat?"

The monk replied, "I wish to eat all the things that go with wine, such as fresh fruit, cold cooked meats, and sliced dried fruit, and plenty of hot chicken, fish, duck, and pork dishes. Then invite me to sit at the head of the table alone and have your *yuanwai* wait upon me. Then I will eat."

When the household people heard this speech, their anger rose to a fever pitch and they cried out, "You miserable pauper of a monk! Your mouth is full of nonsense! Our *yuanwai* wait upon you! You are dreaming! You would have to break the world out of its orbit first!"

The monk said, "We will see whether your words amount to anything or not. If I do not receive a meal of this sort, I will beg your pardon." Then he threw back his head and shouted, "I came to beg for alms." After that he called out, "Sou! Sou!" as if he were driving birds away from a planted field. He had lifted his hands and was clawing at his mouth. At the same time he was pushing his way through the gathering at the gate. All of the people were covering their mouths and laughing.

The monk called out three times at close intervals, one after the other. Then someone inside was heard to ask in a commanding voice, "What is that uproar out there?" Out came an impressive *yuanwai*. He wore a soft kerchief-like hat of the kind called a philosopher's cap. Standing out on each side at the back were two small stiff silken leaves that seemed almost to be growing from twigs. He was dressed in a robe of precious blue silk with a short cape of downy crane's feathers. The soles of his shoes curved up over the toes in the style common among officials. His face was like the autumn moon, serious and calm, with kindly eyebrows and friendly eyes. At his chin was a tuft of white beard.

CHAPTER 24

Ji Gong hampers the defrauding of the Liang family; the merciful one amuses himself at Chang Maioyu's expense

A S Ji Gong saw Liang Yuanwai coming out and heard him asking about the clamor, the monk went over and greeted him respectfully. Then he said, "Since the *yuanwai* asks, the one responsible is myself, the monk. I was passing this way and I had long wanted to meet you because of your goodness to others. However, as soon as I saw this mansion I knew that it was plagued by the five flying evil spirits and that someone in this house was certainly ill as a result. I would like to cleanse the house, chase out the demons, and cure the sickness. As soon as I arrived at the door, these several household people first asked me for a gate gift. I said that I had not come to ask a favor from the *yuanwai* and asked why there should be a reason to bring a gate gift. It was because of this matter that the argument arose."

Now, even if Liang Wanzang had heard the phrase Ji Gong had been shouting, the *yuanwai* might have misunderstood it, since the literal meaning of the words Ji Gong used was "I come to change karma." These were also the same words that monks used when they came to beg for food.

As soon as Liang Yuanwai heard Ji Gong's side of the story he said, "You slaves! I do not know what corrupt practices have been going on at the gate!"

The house people said, "Yuanwai, it is not true. He came here and said he wanted a meal," and then they recited all that had happened.

The *yuanwai* paid no attention to them, but addressed the monk instead. "Where is the monk's precious pagoda?"

The monk replied, "I am at the Monastery of the Soul's Retreat at the West Lake outside the Hangzhou walls. My name is Dao Ji. The name "Mad Monk" is wrongfully applied to me as well."

Liang Yuanwai looked closely at him for the first time. Hearing him speak in this way, the *yuanwai* half believed and half doubted as he said, "Since you are the famous Ji Gong, please be compassionate. Come with me."

Ji Gong went with the *yuanwai* straight into the east section of the main house. There he saw lying on the brick platform bed the young master, Liang Shiyuan, in a deep sleep from which he could not be wakened. On either side were a number of old women and household people who were taking care of him. Seeing him, Liang Yuanwai quickly cried out, "Oh my son, Liang Shiyuan, awaken!" He continued to call out several times, but it could be seen that Liang Shiyuan was still fast asleep and knew nothing of what was happening. He did not even nod his head.

Ji Gong said, "The *yuanwai* need not be alarmed. I will have the boy speak a couple of sentences and eat a little food. In a short time we will quickly see some improvement."

The old *yuanwai* was so overjoyed that he said, "Then, if this be possible, saintly monk, have compassion! Do have compassion!"

The *lohan*, master of so many things, raised his head and took off his hat. Then, while he had some people raise Liang Shiyuan up a bit, Ji Gong slowly fitted his monk's hat on the boy's head. Under his breath Ji Gong repeated the true, sacred words: "Om Ma Ni Pad Me Hum. I command!"

Everyone watching saw Liang Shiyuan slowly open his eyes. He coughed once and said, "Someone come and bring me a little water to drink."

As soon as the old *yuanwai* saw this change, he was so happy that he kept saying, "Good! Good!" over and over again.

The monk said, "For this labor of mine I only ask if perhaps you will give me a meal."

Liang Yuanwai asked, "Saintly monk, where do such words come from? Do not say a meal! Indeed, I will constantly give alms to you. It could not be otherwise!"

The monk said, "That is really unnecessary."

The *yuanwai* said, "Saintly monk, what would you like to eat? I will have the servants prepare it."

The monk said, "Call your manager and I will tell him." The household people called the cook and the monk said, "Go and prepare sliced dried fruit, fresh fruit, cold cooked meats and everything to go with wine, as well as some hot dishes. I will eat just here in the outer room."

The cook answered, "This is a house of wealth and honor. We are always ready to prepare every sort of dish." The household people prepared a table and chair, and in a little while the cook brought forth the various dishes. The *yuanwai* invited the monk to be seated in the place of honor and have some wine. The old *yuanwai* waited upon him, seeing that he had some of each dish and keeping his wine cup full.

However, the old *yuanwai* was thinking to himself, "That hat of the monk's is really a fine thing and no mistake, stronger than any pill made from the most unusual medicine. I will ask him how much he wants for it and keep the hat to give to my boy to wear."

The *yuanwai* could hear Liang Shiyuan inside the inner room talking. "I would like some water with sugar syrup in it, and I want to eat something."

The *yuanwai* was so happy that he said, "The subtle arts of the saintly monk are naturally effective in curing sickness."

The monk said, "Yuanwai, what do you think about this hat of mine?"

The *yuanwai* answered, "Good!"

The monk said, "Good is good, but I have been thinking of something I might do—sell it."

The *yuanwai* heard the monk's words and his heart filled with joy as he said, "Monk, if you want to sell it, how much do you want for it? I would like to keep it."

Ji Gong replied, "It would be easy for you to buy it and keep it. Take your furniture, your business, your house, and your lands and give them all to me. Then I will give you my hat."

When the old *yuanwai* heard the price, he shook his head and said, "I cannot afford it!" The household people then removed the dishes and the monk sat drinking wine while the *yuanwai* poured.

The monk said, "Yuanwai, would you call the manager who has charge of the gatekeepers? I want to speak to him." The *yuanwai* directed a household person to go and call him.

In a little while the man arrived, saying, "What would the *yuanwai* like me to do?"

The monk said, "Just a little while ago I said that I wanted to eat a special meal with fresh fruit, cold cooked meats, and sliced dried fruits, and have your *yuanwai* wait upon me. You may see that I did not speak incorrectly. I wanted to remind you."

The manager of the gatekeepers simply said, "Yes."

The monk said, "Yuanwai, if you will forgive me, I still have three companions outside waiting for me and they have had nothing to eat or drink." The *yuanwai* immediately sent a household person, Liang Fu, to invite them to come into the room and to have food and wine prepared for them.

Liang Fu thought to himself, "The monk has his followers and doubt-less not one of them has anything decent to wear. Whoever is among his followers must be even more poverty-stricken than he is." It was with such thoughts in his mind that he went out and called to them. "Who came with the poor monk?"

Gao Guoqin replied, "I did."

When Liang Fu looked, he saw a man who seemed to be a scholar, apparently very refined and meticulously correct in his attire.

The household man asked, "Where are the other two?"

Su Lu and Feng Xun approached, saying, "We also came with the monk. Looking at them, Liang Fu thought these two were even more prosper-ous. Of course, Su Lu was one of Su Beishan's household and he dressed very well.

Liang Fu thought to himself, "The monk has money to dress his reti-nue in this way." He quickly asked the three in, had a table prepared with food and wine, and invited them to eat. Inside, meanwhile, the *yuanwai* was drinking wine with the monk and talking about a wide range of sub-jects. Just as the conversation was becoming particularly interesting, one of the *yuanwai*'s people came in, went up to the *yuanwai*'s ear and spoke as if he did not care to let the monk hear his report.

As it turned out, the news itself that the Daoist had arrived did not matter. However, Liang Yuanwai was troubled. He wanted to stay and talk with the monk, but he feared that the Daoist priest would find fault with the monk's being there. Liang Yuanwai wanted to welcome the Daoist and entertain him but feared that the monk would find fault. The old *yuan-wai* was in difficulty, but was not at fault. He simply could not entertain both the monk and the Daoist at the same time. Of course, the old *yuan-wai* would have been grateful to anyone who could cure his son's illness.

Just as the *yuanwai* was wavering in his heart, the monk spoke, "Yuan-wai, perhaps some relative has arrived. You need not apologize."

This remark brought the *yuanwai* to his senses, and he said, "That is right."

The monk said, "It is important that you go and feast your relative. To a large degree we are no longer strangers. Perhaps it is your wife's younger sister." Liang Wanzang was not in a position to take offense at Ji Gong's half-innocent remark that could also mean, "Perhaps you have a little concubine waiting for you."

The *yuanwai* laughed and began to stand up. He directed his people to pour wine for the saintly monk, saying, "I will return and drink some wine with the saintly monk." Having said this, he stood up and went out of the room.

Then he hurried to the outer library located inside a small courtyard with verandas on all four sides. A single house on the west side of the courtyard was used for the library. The old *yuanwai* went in and saw that the Daoist had already entered and seated himself. The household people were offering him tea. When Liang Yuanwai saw the Daoist, he quickly greeted him politely with raised, folded hands and said, "The master of spirits has arrived and I was not here to welcome him. I hope that I have not offended him."

The Daoist priest said, "What are you saying? You know that you must not say such things."

The *yuanwai* quickly instructed that wine be brought and asked, "Does the Daoist priest eat ordinary or vegetarian food?"

Chang Miaoyu answered, "Ordinary or vegetarian, both are fine." The household people prepared a feast, placed cups and dishes on the table, and brought food and drink. The old *yuanwai* sat beside the Daoist and poured wine for him while they chatted about various things.

Liang Yuanwai said, "Spirit master, I would like to ask you about a man of whom you perhaps know."

The Daoist said, "If he is famous, I would know about him. If not, I might not."

Liang Yuanwai said, "At the Monastery of the Soul's Retreat there is an honorable Ji Gong. Perhaps you know of him."

There was a movement in the heart of the Daoist priest. "If I say that Ji Gong has abilities, no glory will shine upon me," he thought. Therefore, the Daoist said, "Yuanwai, the one you mention is that wine-soaked, insane monk, the mad Ji. I really do not know into what class he falls, but there is nothing there into which you can sink your teeth. In other words, he is undistinguished."

He had not finished speaking when they heard someone in the court-yard reply. "The good Daoist with his frowsy hair! How unpleasant for a person to be talked about by him!" They saw the bamboo curtain rise and Ji Gong appeared from outside.

At the sight of Ji Gong, the old *yuanwai* thought to himself that all those household people were really hateful in having failed to observe his wishes. In his mind he rehearsed reproachful things to say to them. "I asked you to keep the monk company while he ate and drank. Why did you let him go?" As for the Daoist, it was as if his words had been driven back between his teeth. It was most embarrassing.

Now, while the monk had been inside drinking wine with the household people in attendance, he for no apparent reason stood up and went into the inner section. He then removed his monk's cap from Liang Shiyuan's head. Liang Shiyuan had been sitting up talking and laughing, but when the monk removed his cap, Liang Shiyuan fell back unconscious again on the bed. It was as if his soul had left his body once more and he could not be awakened.

The household people said, "Monk, why did you remove the cap from his head?"

The monk said, "How much time does it take to prepare a festive table?"

The household people said, "Good. Trade the cap for food and drink! We will do it without having our *yuanwai* give the order. We will give you another tableful and you can give the cap to the young master in exchange!"

The monk said, "I am not hungry now. Wait until I am hungry again." So saying, the monk walked outside.

The household people asked, "Where are you going, monk?"

He replied, "I am going to the privy."

The people said, "We will go and show you the way."

The monk said, "That will not do. If anyone is with me, I cannot pay my respects."

The household people did not dare to go with him. The monk hurried to the west with long strides and arrived in the courtyard just in time to catch the Daoist speaking badly of him to the *yuanwai*.

The monk had lifted the bamboo curtain just as he said, "frowsy-haired Daoist."

Chang Miaoyu was just about to reply when Ji Gong pointed and said, "Yüüü!" making a sound like a deer bleating. "There is a Daoist priest in this room. You must not be offended, Yuanwai. I did not curse you. I cursed that Daoist!"

Liang Yuanwai, to whom Ji Gong had spoken, quickly stood up and said, "Saintly monk, please sit down and, Master of Spirits, please sit down. Let me introduce each of you to the other."

Ji Gong said, "Yuanwai, do not make us know each other." After saying this, the monk sat down. One of the household people put another cup on the table and the monk poured wine and drank.

The Daoist still did not recognize him. The Daoist only saw that the monk was intolerably shabby as he sat there drinking, and so the Daoist asked, "Where is your temple, monk?"

Ji Gong turned up his eyes as he answered. "Since you want to know, I am just that wine-soaked, crazy, mad monk from the Monastery of the Soul's Retreat at the West Lake, the Ji Gong for whom you could not find a classification, the one who has nothing into which one can sink one's teeth." As the Daoist listened, he had some uneasy feelings in his heart. The monk then said, "Daoist priest Chang, what is your honorable surname?"

The Daoist replied, "Monk, you are an artless person. You know my name is Chang and yet you still ask me my honorable name."

The monk said, "Let me ask you about a person that perhaps you know."

The Daoist asked, "Which one?"

The monk replied, "One of my pupils is named Hua Chingfeng. Perhaps you know him."

When the Daoist heard this name, his anger knew no bounds, as he said to himself, "He said my teacher is like a grandson to him. Wait until I cut off his existence!" After thinking, he said, "Monk, your mouth is full of nonsense. You just wait. This hermit will settle your account!" The Daoist, meanwhile, was a making a sign with his fingers inside his hand as he muttered a spell. He wanted to have a contest with Ji Gong. It would be a match of power and skill.

CHAPTER 25

By his uncanny arts, the vicious Daoist strives to harm Ji Gong; the Spirit Master and the Chan master duel with magic spells

AS the exchange between Ji Gong and the evil Daoist became more heated, the Daoist said, "Monk, I will now direct three particular words at you and I dare you to reply with three of your own."

Ji Gong said, "Say your words slowly and I will not be afraid to say six in return. Say them!"

The Daoist began to speak his three words, muttering them under his breath. Suddenly, the Daoist's wine cup on the table gave a jump as if it had been commanded to do so. Just at that time the monk was drinking from his cup of wine, but abruptly he turned and fell to the floor.

Liang Yuanwai was shocked at the sight, saying, "Teacher of the laws, what is this?"

The Daoist said, "Since you wish to know, I simply used one of my minor arts to cause him to fall to the floor. If I leave this wine cup sitting here for a day, the monk will lie there for a day. If I pick up the wine cup or give him a certain medicine, he will be able to revive." But when he'd finished speaking these words, the monk stood up. Looking at the monk, the surprised Daoist said, "I have not picked up the wine cup and you simply stood up!"

The monk said, "Come, you still have not given me the medicine. I will lie down again and let you continue."

The Daoist said, "Monk, do you dare to tell me the eight characters that represent the exact date and time of your birth?"

The monk said, "I have no objection to that. I will just tell you." After explaining that he had born in such and such a year, in such and such a month, on such and such a day and so forth, he ended by saying, "I have told you all. What about it?"

The Daoist began at once reciting a spell under his breath. Then, while repeating the name of a particular spirit he was calling upon, he struck Ji

Gong upon the crown of his head. Hurriedly the Daoist finished saying the spell and stood up. "Yuanwai, after I go, you must quickly find a way to release the monk. Otherwise, when the cock cries once, the monk will die. You will then be involved with the courts."

Liang Yuanwai looked at Ji Gong. It seemed as if the monk's soul had fled, as if he were beyond awakening and knew nothing of human affairs.

The old Daoist had gone out of the library and was leaving the mansion. The *yuanwai* quickly ran after him, pleading, "Spirit Master, go slowly. Let me take upon myself any misdeed committed by the monk."

The Daoist, however, would not answer the *yuanwai*, but instead returned to the Fortunate Cloud Temple on the Five Spirits Hill.

Going in, he called out to his acolyte, Liu Miaotong, "Quickly tie up a straw man for me."

"And whom are you going to harm this time?" asked Liu Miaotong.

Chang Miaoyu answered, "This time I am not trying to harm someone for no reason at all. I am doing harm because when I tried to obtain money from Liang Yuanwai, the monk Ji Dian dared to play tricks on me. I desire to harm Ji Gong secretly, to take vengeance and give vent to my anger."

Liu Miaotong did not dare to oppose him, but quickly bound up a straw man using dry straw and brought it in to Chang Miaoyu. The evil Daoist then sent Liu Miaotong to make other objects from dry straw.

Meanwhile, the Daoist ate dinner. Afterward he himself took an "eight immortals" table and placed it in the courtyard before the principal hall. He brought out an incense burner, the five kinds of grain, and the other necessary things. When they were all properly arranged, he took the two straw men and placed one of them on each side of the other objects on the table. The wicked Daoist went back inside and waited there until the stars came out.

Then he again went outside and first took off his Daoist hat. Next he took the cord from around his head that held the strip of cloth binding his hair. After doing these things, he let down his hair. He drew his precious sword from its scabbard, lit the incense burner, and addressed the three pure ones of the Daoist trinity, the rulers of the heavens of the upper air.

The ruler of the highest heaven was sometimes called Yu Huang Shangdi, the Pearly Emperor, who ruled heaven and earth and was supposed to keep in his records the names of eight hundred lesser divinities and almost countless immortals. He was also called Tian Bao, the Treasure of Heaven, and was said to be the source of all truth.

The ruler of the second heaven was said by some to be Ling Bao, the custodian of the sacred books, the timekeeper of eternity and inspirer of emperors and philosophers. Others said that the second ruler was Pangu, who was supposed to have come out of chaos and created the universe. Finally, Pangu grew so large that his head became the mountains, his arms and legs turned into the four quarters of the earth, and the lice upon his body became the human beings on earth.

The ruler of the third or lowest heaven of the Daoists was Lao Tzu, the transcendental philosopher who had lived in the sixth century B.C. It was he, it is believed, who first taught the mystical system of Daoism and incorporated in it the ancient myths of the Chinese people.

The Daoist prayed, "Oh pure ones, protect your disciple. I want to injure Ji Dian. If I am able to obtain the silver from Liang Yuanwai, I will burn incense and provide new clothing for your images. I promise to keep this vow."

When he had finished speaking, he first used the tip of his sword to uncover a bowl of water on the "eight immortals" table. He took some of the five grains—hemp, millet, rice, wheat, and pulse—which had been prepared with sugar and he scattered them. He ground the cinnabar into fine grains and mixed them with other things to make ink, tore the yellow paper into strips, and wrote three spells upon them. He again took the sword and, with its tip, picked up the strips with the charms written on them. He fed the strips into the fire, and the flames burned higher and higher.

Then he began speaking his Daoist formula: "With the first charm a great wind will arise. With the second charm the soul of Ji Gong will be captured and brought here. With the third charm I will cut off Ji Gong's existence. When a man dies, he becomes a disembodied spirit. When a disembodied spirit dies, it becomes a hungry ghost." Just as he was growing confident that he would get his wish, he became aware of a draft of cold air against his back. The Daoist took his sword and prepared to slash out. He dodged to the side and, lifting his head, saw that the one who had just come was apparently a hero of the Greenwood.

Taking a more careful look by the light of the lantern, the Daoist could see that the person was wearing an open-mesh cap made of horsehair. His hair, in which a flower had been carefully arranged, was pulled to one side and tied with a short, thin silken cord. He was wearing a set of close-fitting garments fastened by many buttons, closely set at regular intervals. The tops of his thick-soled boots were of blue material embroidered with flowers. His face was as clear as white jade and his eyes were like bright starts. His features all had a look of refinement. In his hand he had a sharp knife, with which he seemed to be intending to chop the Daoist.

Chang Miaoyu stepped aside and pointed with his hand while reciting a spell followed by a command. The man at once turned himself around and fell to the ground. The Daoist went to him and was about to kill him with his treasured sword.

Then from inside the room he heard his acolyte's voice. "Teacher, you must not kill him! He is my friend." Running out into the courtyard, the acolyte helped the young man up.

Now this young man who had just arrived was originally from the Tanyang prefecture of Zhejiang. His surname was Chen and his personal name was Liang. His home was in what was called the Chen family village, which was also a small military post. His parents had both died when he was very young and until he grew into manhood he had lived with his father's younger brother and his wife. Chen Liang also had a sister named Jade Plum. His father's brother, Chen Guangqin, kept a shop that sold white cloth.

Chen Liang loved to practice fighting with his fists, with his feet, and with the quarterstaff. He constantly practiced with other men about the military post, learning new strategies in the art of fighting. Later he became acquainted with a local man named Lei Ming, nicknamed "The Dark Wind-Driven Cloud." The two became as close as flesh and bone.

It was Lei Ming who led Chen Liang into the company of the men of the Greenwood. In Yushan prefecture in Jiangsu province, there was a guarantor named Yang Ming, nicknamed the Fierce Commander of the Marauding Spirits. These spirits were a band of chivalrous men who loved to remedy the inequities that they encountered. They would kill avaricious men and tyrants and gladly made friends with every heroic fellow who shared their sentiments. After Chen Liang had entered the company of the men of the Greenwood, he went to stay with these brave men, who were called the thirty-six bold fellows of Yushan prefecture. Among them were all sorts of men.

One day, everyone came with gifts to congratulate the mother of their leader, Yang Ming, on her birthday. But when Chen Liang arrived, he brought nothing. Lei Ming said to him: "Dear brother, you should have brought something as a gift to show your respect for filial piety. Furthermore, in the eyes of the others, it will look well if you honor the mother of our senior member."

Chen Liang said, "I have a present different from any of the others, and I will bring it in a short time."

It was then the beginning of the fourth month. At the third watch that night, Chen Liang stole a dish of large fresh peaches and brought the fruit as his gift. Everyone said that, since fresh peaches were usually not yet ripe, it was very strange for him to be able to find ten such peaches. Truly it could not have been easy. After this incident, he was nicknamed "The White Monkey with the Supernatural Hands."

That same year, Chen Liang went home to inquire about his uncle's health. When he arrived, his sister, Jade Plum, joined with his uncle in saying, "Chen Liang, you cannot belong to the Greenwood and still come to the Chen household. Although it is said that there were no officials among our ancestors, there were those who knew poetry and propriety. In joining this barbarous Greenwood association and becoming an outlaw, you not only bring dishonor upon your ancestors and relatives, but upon your neighbors as well. As long as there are officials, you cannot evade the law! One day as a robber could bring your life to an end. Parents who are robbers bring forth children who also are robbers. We urge you to look back and begin your life anew. Besides, the family business needs your help."

Chen Liang said not a word, but enough had been said already. The next day he did not take his leave from the family, although he still wished to go away from home. He realized that there was something else he could do. He thought to himself, "This time when I leave, it will be to go to the capital. There, I will seek out some famous Buddhist or Daoist with the intention of leaving the world and learning to be a monk. Thus I will put an end to all my past sins. There are no parents to hold me back and no wife to hinder me."

By evening he had reached the Yunlan market town. After dark, he changed into his black thief's suit of darkness. He entered a home with a large gate and took a quantity of silver in order to have something to spend during the rest of his journey. It was then getting late and he decided to visit his friend, the acolyte, Liu Miaotong, at the Fortunate Cloud Shrine.

When he came to the front of the shrine, he did not knock at the gate. Instead he climbed up and crossed over the roofs to look around. In front of the main hall was a table. Before it stood the Daoist priest with his hair let down in disorder. His blackened face gave him an especially baleful air. He held the precious sword in his hand and was in the act of performing a ceremonial rite.

Chen Liang did not recognize him, and thought to himself, "This is definitely being done to harm my brother, Liu Miaotong. The Daoist is calling up a demon to do evil to him. Truly the Daoist is detestable. He will not escape death once my anger is unleashed." With these thoughts in mind, Chen Liang leapt down with his knife poised. But before he could chop at the Daoist, the priest pointed and shook the sleeve of his robe at Chen Liang and caused him to fall to the ground.

Chen Liang was about to close his eyes and wait for death. Then he saw Liu Miaotong come out of the main hall and heard him say, "Teacher, this is my friend—blame me but do not kill him."

The Daoist priest replied, "Well! So you are bringing in someone from outside and planning to kill me so that you will have this shrine to yourself."

Chen Liang contradicted him saying, "No! I was very clumsy and stupid on this occasion. I did not know that you two were teacher and acolyte. I thought that you were going to kill Liu Miaotong so that you could get the shrine." Chen Liang explained his mistake as Liu Miaotong introduced him to the priest.

After the two friends had gone inside the main hall, Chen Liang asked, "What is the master Daoist doing with his arts?"

Liu Miaotong said, "Dear brother, each day I waited for you early and late, thinking that you would come, but you did not come. Now you have come here today! The priest is going to kill senior monk Ji Gong of the Monastery of the Soul's Retreat. Furthermore, the priest has taken three parts of another person's soul and seven parts of his senses. I have heard it said that Ji Gong is a virtuous person, but I fear that he will not be able to prevent the Daoist from taking his soul."

When Chen Liang heard what Liu Miaotong had to say, he thought to himself, "I was just trying to meet some famous Daoists or Buddhists with the idea of leaving the world myself. I did not expect to encounter anything like that which I have seen and heard about tonight. Now I will watch and see whose powers are stronger."

Just as these thoughts were going through Chen Liang's mind, the two friends heard the Daoist outside beginning to cast another spell as he said, "The soul of the mad monk Ji has not yet arrived. What is it waiting for?" He then began once more to take the papers with the spells and burn them. The flames flared higher as he threw in the strips of papers.

Then the two friends saw a furious wind arise from the northwest. It was a wind that killed trees in the forest. The river and the trees resounded and mountainous waves arose on the sea. It seemed as though the heavens were filled with ten thousand angry demons throwing rocks that went flying into the air, endangering the lives of men.

When the wind had passed, there was the sound of straw sandals slowly padding along, "Left, right, left, right." The sound did not last long, and then they saw standing before the table a poor, ragged monk.

CHAPTER 26

The duel between the Spirit Master and the Chan master continues; the powers of the Chan master are observed by Chen Liang

CHANG Miaoyu became furious when he saw that, instead of Ji Gong's soul materializing, Ji Gong himself had appeared in the flesh. "Wrong-headed, obstinate monk," he shouted, "I summoned your soul! What are you doing here?"

Now, when the Daoist had left the Liang home, Liang Yuanwai was unable to catch up with him. Liang Yuanwai simply thought that Ji Gong was dead, but when the *yuanwai* returned to the library, he saw Ji Gong sitting in a chair drinking wine. Liang Yuanwai was overjoyed at the sight and cried out, "Saintly monk! Oh, dear sir, you have not died after all! The old Daoist said that he had drawn the soul out of your body."

"Do you think that he could ever draw out my soul!" Ji Gong exclaimed. "One thing is certain, however—he has surely drawn the soul out of your son's body. Tonight I will go to find that Daoist."

The old *yuanwai* said, "Oh no! There is no need for that. Any person who has left the world and still commits such wickedness sooner or later will suffer the vengeance of heaven. The saintly monk need not go to find him. As I see it, we should merely let him go away."

Ji Gong did not answer, but continued to drink his wine. When it was evening, he said, "I will go outside for a bit and perform a charitable act. A little later I will return."

The old *yuanwai* believed him, but when Ji Gong left the Liang mansion, he hurried straight toward Five Spirits Hill. Arriving at the Shrine of the Fortunate Cloud, he saw the Daoist just beginning to work his arts. When Chen Liang appeared, Ji Gong perceived everything quite clearly. He saw the Daoist once more write the charms and begin his incantations. This time, Ji Gong came with the wind to the front of the table. From the way that the Daoist spoke, it was evident that he had been taken by surprise. He had cast his hook to catch the soul and had brought in the person instead! Ji Gong had most certainly awakened from the Dao-ist's spell.

The Daoist realized as a result of what had happened that Ji Gong's skills were formidable, but the Daoist's deep anger gave him confidence. Thrusting with his precious sword at Ji Gong, the Daoist said, "Crazy monk! If I take money from Liang Wanzang, what is that to you? You are spoiling my great venture for no reason. You are indeed a heavy burden to me! You must know that, though you succeeded in coming here today, there is danger in coming before my sacrificial table. You had better kow-tow to me and call me your ancestor three times over. Hermits of your sort have one special power. They cannot be killed by supernatural fire. If this were not so, I would already have cut off your existence."

Ji Gong retorted, "You demonic Daoist! You are here calling up ghosts to do wickedness. There is no reason for you to do evil things to Liang Wanzang and you dare to treat me with disrespect. The more I speak of it, the angrier I become!" Without a word of warning, he slapped the Dao-ist on the cheek. The Daoist's face grew red with anger. He seemed about to explode with fury. He aimed his sword at Ji Gong's head.

There before the great hall the two used all their arts. The Daoist was unable to touch Ji Gong with his deadly thrusts. The monk moved with him, twisting and turning in every direction. The mouth of the frustrated Daoist opened and closed as he alternately ground his teeth and screeched out obscene curses. He dodged to one side and pulled out the first of his treasured objects from his bag. After reciting a spell and a command, he threw the treasure at Ji Gong. A white, nearly transparent object shot through the air.

The *lohan* perceived this strange white thing that seemed to be half suspended, half pushing its way through the air and making a rushing sound as it moved. Ji Gong recognized the object as the stone called the whirling pearl of delusion, which could be as small as a hen's egg or grow to be several yards in diameter. Although when small it could be carried in a bag, it could also bring about broken heads and flowing blood. Ji Gong, the Chan master, simply pointed with his hand and recited the six true words, "Om Ma Ni Pad Me Hum." The stone wavered, grew smaller, and came to rest in Ji Gong's pocket.

The Daoist, upon seeing that Ji Gong had destroyed the power of this treasure of delusion, was so angry that the three spirits of his body in his head, belly, and feet were all wildly moving about. The seven apertures of his eyes, ears, nose, and mouth were fairly smoking. Again, he reached into his bag and took out something. The Daoist stood with his back toward the exact north. Shaking his sword to and fro, he recited a spell while holding the thing in his hand. From the spell came a strange wind that pulled at the hair and struck terror into the bones. Ji Gong opened his eyes wide and saw a striped Mongolian tiger shaking its head and lashing its tail.

The tiger rushed straight at Ji Gong. As the *lohan* looked at it, the tiger did seem quite fearsome. Its large head, round ears, and slender tail would have been the despair of an artist. The cowherd would have lost his courage at the sight. The soul of the lonely woodcutter would have melted in terror at the sound of its roar. Even the bravest of men would have trembled at seeing its stripes.

Ji Gong merely laughed loudly as he saw it. "You, son of a concubine, born into this world as punishment for your parents' misdeeds," he said to the Daoist, "you use these kinds of tricks to show off your skills to me. Really? You would try to sell water at the riverbank!" As the monk spoke, he pointed, and the tiger quickly changed and became visible in its original form, a paper tiger.

The Daoist, upon seeing that two of his favorite charms had been brought to naught, felt his anger reach its very limits. He said, "Good monk, you are a very brave man indeed, but I want you to know that a hermit such as I can still be very dangerous." He put his hand down into his bag and drew out a magic cord. He held it in his hand, saying, "A man may have no desire to harm a tiger, but the tiger may have every intention of harming the man. Originally I had no desire to harm you. The present situation is something you brought upon yourself. You have asked for death many times over, but now you may stop complaining about being alive, for today I will kill you. This cord is stronger than anything else, more powerful than any uncanny supernatural thing in reducing things to their original elements."

With its ends joined, the cord would enclose a portion of the primordial Yin, a region of cold, darkness, dampness, and utter silence that contrasted with the warm, life-giving qualities of Yang. The monk looked at it and said, "Very bad," several times. He heard the Daoist recite a spell and saw him throw the cord down. It coiled into a circle and gave off a golden light as it moved rapidly toward the monk. The monk cried over and over again: "Ai yah! Save me! This is terrible!" The brilliant circle passed around the monk three times as he continued his cries.

Chang Miaoyu laughed a great laugh, saying, "Originally I thought that you had some great supernatural powers, monk. Now it is clear that all the time you were one of those who know nothing at all. Now you await the moment when I terminate your existence." As the Daoist said these words, he raised his sword, intending to cut the monk's head into two pieces. He had raised the sword as confidently as an official might raise a seal to affix its mark.

Then the Daoist saw the monk looking at him intently. The Daoist could not utter a sound, nor could he bring down his sword. He thought to himself, "Strange! Why is it that my treasured sword will not chop the monk?" He brandished it in the air back and forth several times, but he still could not bring it down.

It seemed to the Daoist that he had been awakened by the sound of a crash. He felt a movement of his heart. "Perhaps this is all an illusion." As he thought, he looked around carefully. The terrible cord enclosing the cold essence of Yin had settled upon the rim of his hot stone incense burner and blended into it. He looked for the monk, but there was no sign of him.

Just as the Daoist was peering about everywhere, the monk, who was behind him, gave him a slap. The Daoist turned his head. Driven on by his fury, he shouted out, "Stupid monk, you are causing me to die from my anger. Tonight there are no two ways open for me as far as you are concerned—one of us must die." Thrusting out his hand, the Daoist took some of the burning incense sticks from the incense burner and carried them to the front of the great hall, where there was a pile of grass faggots. He mouthed one of his spells and lighted one of the bundles. With the flaming grass in his outstretched hand, he rushed at Ji Gong. After the failure of his three strong charms, the Daoist had ceased to rely upon the use of his poisonous supernatural arts alone. He was about to burn the monk to death with fire.

As the Daoist resumed his spells, the fire reached out toward Ji Gong. He pointed at it and, as he said, "Om Ma Ni Pad Me Hum. I command!" the fire rushed back at the Daoist. His beard caught fire, then his long hair and his clothing. He turned and ran inside the great hall of the shrine. There, the fire from his burning hair and clothing ignited the hangings, and in an instant the place had become an inferno. As the raging fire burned out of control, the flesh and bones of the Daoist were turned into ashes, along with all the things in the great hall of the Shrine of the Fortunate Cloud.

The monk paid no attention to all this. He at once picked up the straw man that the Daoist had used to represent Liang Shiyuan and pulled out the seven needles that had held the boy's soul inside. Not stopping to think whether the Daoist's apprentice, Liu Miaotong, was alive or dead, the monk departed from Five Spirits Hill.

During this time, Chen Liang had been watching everything intently from within a side building. This was on the east side of the shrine courtyard, where he had gone to get a closer look at what was happening. He had left Liu Miaotong in the great hall. As Chen Liang saw that the fire was spreading to this side building as well, he kicked out the lattice window, jumped through the opening, and fled close behind Ji Gong. Matching his own pace to that of the monk, Chen Liang followed the monk into Yunlan market town. He saw the monk hurry up to the gate of the mansion belonging to Liang Yuanwai.

One of the household people was standing in the gateway. Seeing the monk return, the man said, "Saintly monk, where have you been? Our *yuanwai* has been waiting for you most impatiently."

The monk said, "Good," and hurried inside.

When Ji Gong reached the library, Liang Yuanwai immediately asked, "Holy monk, where have you been, dear sir?"

The monk replied, "I have found your child's soul for you, and now I have brought it back." Ji Gong then went on to Liang Shiyuan's room. There he saw the unconscious boy still lying motionless. Ji Gong at once prepared some medicine and gave it to him. In a short time Liang Shiyuan was able to move again.

The old *yuanwai* had food and wine prepared in the outer room. Ji Gong and Liang Yuanwai sat until they had drunk two or three cups together. Then Ji Gong asked, "Has the *yuanwai* been troubled by burglars in recent times?"

Liang Yuanwai answered, "Recently I have had no trouble with them. The good burglars know that I am a charitable person and they will not steal from me. The riffraff among the thieves cannot gain entrance to my houses and courtyards."

Ji Gong said, "Good. I will mention the names of some of the good burglars. You may recognize them."

Liang Yuanwai said, "I do not know who any of them are."

Now, for some time Chen Liang had secretly been on the roof just above them, eavesdropping. When he heard that several robbers were going to be mentioned, he felt disturbed, because he did not know which group Ji Gong was going to discuss. Then he heard Ji Gong say, "There is one named Lucky Willow who walks on snow without leaving a trace. Perhaps you know him."

Liang Yuanwai said, "I do not know him."

Ji Gong said, "This person's name is Trackless Walker in the Snow. When he goes over the snow, he leaves no footprints. Quite strange!"

Liang Yuanwai said, "Indeed, it is very strange for a person to walk over snow-covered ground and not leave footprints."

Ji Gong said, "He really does walk over the snow-covered ground leaving no footprints, but only because he wipes them away with a broom as he goes."

When Liang Yuanwai heard this explanation, he laughed. The monk continued. "There is one who goes out over the water, gracefully floating across. This man can walk on water and not fall in."

Liang Yuanwai said, "In the whole world there can hardly be another with such an ability. But this is truly strange. I have never seen anything such as this."

Ji Gong said, "That is not considered strange, because this was at a time when the water was frozen."

The *yuanwai* said, "In the winter I can do that, too."

Ji Gong said, "Liang Shiyuan is well now. Tomorrow I must hurry on back to Linan."

Liang Yuanwai said, "Saintly monk, you need not be in such haste. I would so like to have my teacher stay for a few days. I wish to show you how much I appreciate you saving my only child's life."

Ji Gong replied, "Call one of your household people." Liang Fu came and Ji Gong whispered several words in his ear. Liang Fu then went out.

Chen Liang had crept down over the roof, toward the eaves of the house, and was still secretly watching and listening. He had heard what Ji Gong had said earlier. The two men who had been mentioned were Chen Liang's friends. He thought to himself: "Ji Gong is a person who has left the world! How does he come to know the business of our Greenwood?" Just as he was thinking these thoughts, he saw that the house had been surrounded. Liang Fu had called together the gatekeepers, the watchmen, escorts, and others—twenty-four in all. Each of them had a weapon in his hand. They were calling to each other to seize the man on the roof.

Chen Liang was frightened out of his usual confidence. "So that was what Ji Gong had been talking about when he whispered to the household man. Ji Gong had sent him to get people to capture me!" Chen Liang stood up on the roof, and, raising his knife in his hand, cried, "Make a way for me to pass through. I did not come to steal. You must let me go, or I will kill whoever tries to stop me. Keep out of my way!" Turning, he jumped down from the roof. As Chen Liang landed on his feet, Ji Gong had just started out through the door.

CHAPTER 27

Ji Gong takes pity upon the Daoist acolyte; Chen Liang makes a stealthy entrance into the mansion of Su Beishan

BY the time that Ji Gong had gone out through the door, Chen Liang was already dashing away. The monk followed him to the edge of town. Chen Liang had run so fast that he had left those following him far behind.

In the gray early-morning light Ji Gong could see that the Shrine of the Fortunate Cloud had collapsed. Its tiles were scattered, and nothing was left. Not a foot of unburned wood or an unbroken tile remained. Around the ruins of the shrine were countless people who had been fighting to save the shrine from the fire. To the west, a dozen or so men were gathered in a circle. Ji Gong went closer to look. There he saw Liu Miaotong badly burned, with blisters covering his body. There seemed hardly a place untouched. He appeared to be at the point of death.

As he looked at the young man, Ji Gong's heart was moved to pity. Approaching him, Ji Gong asked, "How is it with you, young Daoist?"

Liu Miaotong recognized Ji Gong and said, "I did no evil against you, saintly monk. It was my brother and teacher, whose behavior has been punished by heaven. I beg you, Teacher, be merciful and save me!"

The monk laughed loudly saying, "Since you know that he deserved his fate, you must have known that he was doing unpardonable acts. Come! I will give you some medicine."

A local official then spoke up. "Indeed, you may not! Monk, do not interfere. If you give him medicine, it may not be the proper remedy, and then his condition will be worse than before."

Liu Miaotong said, "It does not matter. If I take it and die, the monk cannot be blamed. It will be my fate."

The other bystanders said, "Since he wants to take it, why prevent him?"

Ji Gong asked one of them to bring a bowl of warm water in which to dissolve the medicine, and then gave it to Liu Miaotong. The young man drank, and before long he felt his stomach rumble. Then the blisters opened and the poisonous liquid in them drained away. He ceased to be in pain.

One of the bystanders said, "That is good medicine!"

Standing behind Ji Gong was another who said, "It is true. He really is a holy man, and that is a most unusual medicine!"

Ji Gong turned his head and saw a tall young man with a slender waist. On his head was an embroidered blue cap made from six triangular sections and topped with a colorful ornament. He was wearing a white silk jacket and a belt with a yellow goose-feather design over close-fitting garments of blue. His face was as pale as white jade. His eyebrows were high, full, and aristocratic looking, arched over his bright eyes. His features were handsome and pleasant.

As Ji Gong turned and saw him, the monk spat at him. Immediately the man ran, with Ji Gong after him. It was the same young man, Chen Liang, who had been on the roof. He had changed his clothing in order to come and find out whether his friend Liu Miaotong was alive or dead. Chen Liang had arrived on the scene just in time to see Ji Gong give the young Daoist some medicine. As Chen Liang said, "He really is a holy man," the monk had turned and spat at him. Chen Liang then fled, with the monk in pursuit.

As he ran, Chen Liang thought to himself, "Even though I may be a robber, he has not tried to catch me, so why should I run? I will ask the monk why he is following me. With this thought, he stopped and saw that the monk had also stopped.

"Why are you chasing me, monk?" Chen Liang asked.

The monk, in turn, asked, "Why are you running?"

As he heard this question, Chen Liang laughed and said, "I know that you, sir, are a famous Buddhist monk. Will you take me for your disciple? I will leave the world to follow you."

Ji Gong shook his head again and again, saying, "You are a criminal. Could you leave the world to follow me? We who leave the world speak of following the three rules of right conduct and observing the five prohibitions. The rules are those of Buddha, the laws, and the monks. The five prohibitions order us to abstain from killing, wantonness, stealing, eating meat, and drinking wine. If you were to leave the world, how could you reform in all these ways?"

Chen Liang replied, "I have no father or mother to guide me, no wife or child for whom I must be responsible. I would like to pay for my sins. I am able to do all that Teacher has just said."

Ji Gong said, "If you really can do these things, go to Linan and wait for me. After I have finished my present business, we will meet again in Linan."

When Chen Liang heard these words, he asked, "Teacher, you tell me to wait for you in Linan, but Linan is a big city. Where would you have me wait for you, sir?"

Ji Gong thought for a long time and answered, "I will see you in Linan under the bed."

Chen Liang thought, "Under the Bed must be the name of a place in Linan." He bade farewell to Ji Gong saying, "Teacher, I will go now and wait for you in Linan."

Ji Gong said, "Go on ahead," and Chen Liang took his leave. He did not go back to the Fortunate Cloud Shrine and his friend, Liu Miaotong, but hurried along the road. He did not stop to eat or rest overnight, so that he arrived in Linan that same day.

This was the first time that Chen Liang had been to see the capital, with its crowds of people and bustling activity. He found an inn where he could stay on India Street at the Qiantang Gate. The next day he went out, intending to visit the West Lake. As he walked along the shore, he saw the Cold Spring Pavilion on the island. Standing on the Su Embankment and looking in all directions, he still could not see the farthest limits of the lake.

From there he walked quickly on to the Monastery of the Soul's Retreat, where he saw two monks sitting in charge of the mountain gate. Chen Liang went up to them and asked, "May I inquire of you two respected teachers whether senior monk Ji Gong has returned to the temple?"

The monks at the gate answered, "He is not in the temple, and it is usual for him to be away most of the time. Perhaps he may return in eight or ten days, or perhaps he may be away for three months. He has no fixed times to come and go."

Chen Liang turned away and went back toward Linan. On the way, he continued to inquire of people he met where there was a place called Under the Bed. Though he met a great many people, none of them knew. Sore at heart, he decided to find a restaurant where he could eat and ask among the waiters.

On the north side of India Street he saw a place called Harmony with Heaven, with a large sign shaped like a wine pot hanging outside. A waiter immediately led him to a table upstairs near a window. Chen Liang sat down. When the waiter brought the menu, Chen Liang chose several dishes. While he sat enjoying the food and drink, he called a waiter over.

"What else would you like?" the waiter asked.

"Nothing to eat, but I would like to ask about a place," replied Chen Liang.

"Please do," said the waiter. "I know every place, large and small, in Linan."

"Is there a place here in Linan called Under the Bed?"

The waiter shook his head several times and said, "There is no such place."

After that Chen Liang did not ask anyone else. He began to feel a bit depressed. He thought to himself, "Ji Gong could not simply have been playing a joke on me, but how can I find out whether there is such a place?"

At the same time that he was becoming quite disappointed, there was a rather loud, continuous noise in the street below. Looking out, Chen Liang saw a crowd of people accompanying a sedan chair. From inside the chair he could hear sounds of weeping. The people seemed to be moving from east to west. As he stood up to look, he saw another man coming, all covered with blood and surrounded by several noisy people. Chen Liang could not hear what they were saying, and so he asked the waiter, "What has been going on? Who was the man who was beaten, and who was beating him?"

"You are not from around here or you would understand," said the waiter. "This is a very hateful business. That person you saw who was beaten was a sworn brother of our proprietor. One of the others is Han Wenzheng, who has a little money-changing business. Because he owed two hundred ounces of silver to Su Beishan, they came and took his daughter away, even though Han Wenzheng asked them to wait until he could sell a piece of property. When he went to get her, he was beaten. Another man named Wang the Third tried to stop them and he was beaten as well. They came here to see our proprietor. This Su Beishan is one of the gentry and the richest man in the neighborhood. If he were anyone else, he would be punished. He lives on an estate on the north side of Fourth Street in the Green Bamboo Nunnery area. There is a big gate with four dragon-claw locust trees outside."

Chen Liang listened while he finished eating. Then he paid the bill, went downstairs, and left. He entered the Green Bamboo Nunnery area and looked everywhere until he found the place. Then he went to a teahouse and sat with a cup of tea, thinking to himself, "That such things should happen in the capital city! Tonight I will go there and kill Su Beishan and his family to let everyone know that such people cannot escape heaven's fury!" Having made his decision, he waited until it grew dark.

Then he found a fairly deserted place and changed into his suit of darkness. His daytime clothing he made into a small bundle and tied it to his waist. Going up onto to the roofs of the Su estate, he roamed about until he had explored the entire place. There was a large flower garden to the south with a small lake and a terraced rocky hill overlooking it. On top of the hill was a pavilion. There was no sound in that area, and that clearly was not the family center.

To the east there was a long building that he judged to be the library or reception hall. Going north at the center, he saw a large courtyard with verandas on three sides, surrounded by many small courtyards and gardens and linked together by many pleasant winding walkways covered with tiled roofs. This was certainly the family area. To the west, one court-yard surely contained the master bedroom. It was deserted, though nearly everywhere else there were sounds of conversation and movement.

In the western courtyard, the north building stood on a stone plat-form with a marble railing. Chen Liang dropped down from the roof and made a hole in the paper window. Inside were elegant furnishings of all kinds. There was a large wooden bed like a small room, enclosed on three sides with finely carved lattice work and hung with colorfully embroi-dered silk. He slipped inside and waited. In a little while he heard the sound of people coming, and he hid himself under the bed.

CHAPTER 28

Malicious talk about the Su family gives rise to a deadly plan; Su Beishan meets old Han in a wine shop

JUST as Su Beishan's wife, Zhao Shi, was talking in her room with the womenfolk, they heard a cry from outside. Looking out, they saw flames leaping up toward the sky. The fire was in the pile of wooden stands for flowerpots, and its light made all the apricot and quince trees visible. As the women hurriedly assembled outside, they were able to put out the fires on their first attempt.

Now Chen Liang, the White Monkey, had started this fire in order to draw the women out of the house. As soon as he saw everyone come out, he came down from the roof, crept around to the front of the building while keeping out of sight, and entered the house. There, he saw everything was in the best of taste. On the walls were a number of scrolls, some by famous calligraphers, one pair with peach blossoms; other scrolls showed landscapes or figures painted in fine detail with great sensitivity and imagination. Opposite the door there was a large, elaborate bed with posts and canopy fashioned from polished bamboo. It was completely enclosed by curtains. About the room were chairs and tables, upon some of which were arranged antique ornaments and useful objects.

As Chen Liang was taking note of his surroundings, he heard someone say, "No doubt that fire resulted from the mischief of those two children, Little Fu and Little Lu. They were probably playing with fire."

Realizing that everyone was coming back into the house, Chen Liang thought to himself: "How am I going to get out of sight before they all come in again?" As quick as thought, he pulled the lower curtains apart and wriggled under the bed.

When everyone was back inside, no one had any idea that someone was hiding in the room, and they again sat down. Then they heard footsteps and a voice outside.

Autumn Fragrance immediately asked, "Who is there?"

From outside came the answer, "It is De Fu, one of the household men."

"On what business?" Autumn Fragrance asked.

"The household *yuanwai* has returned with a monk," De Fu replied. "The monk will not be seated in the library, nor in the guest hall. He wants to be seated in our lady's chamber. Our *yuanwai* has said that we should at once ask Madame to withdraw."

As Su Beishan's wife heard this, she immediately asked the maids to put things in order, thinking as she did so, "This is very wrong of the *yuanwai*! There is a guest hall outside, as well as the library. Why must he invite the monk to come and sit in a bedchamber?"

Just as she was thinking these thoughts, another serving man, De Lu, came in and said, "Madame, go quickly; the *yuanwai* is about to come in with the monk!"

Su Beishan's wife left the room at once. The maids were not yet finished putting things away when they heard the *yuanwai* speaking outside. "Teacher, please enter my home. Treat it as your own. Do not feel any restrictions—you may come to sit in any room you choose."

Chen Liang, hidden under the bed, thought to himself, "Any monk that he invites into his home cannot be a good one. This monk must be some sort of procurer."

Outside Ji Gong laughed and said, "No, I am not a good monk. I am afraid I have kept you waiting a long time. I had promised to see you soon!"

The surprised Su Beishan thought, "Good heavens! The monk simply came here to meet someone in my wife's room." But aloud he said, "Teacher, you must have had too much to drink."

The monk said, "I am not drunk," and quickly went into the room.

Chen Liang, hearing the monk's voice, was shocked. "It is none other than Senior Monk Ji Gong from the West Lake Monastery of the Soul's Retreat! How did he happen to come here?" Chen Liang wondered.

Now, after Ji Gong had said goodbye to Chen Liang near Five Spirits Hill, the Chan master had returned to the home of Liang Yuanwai in the market town of Yunlan.

Upon seeing Ji Gong, the old man said: "Teacher! You have returned! I have been very worried ever since you went off late last night pursuing that robber and we did not see you again. I sent some of my people to look for you. Where did you go, sir?"

Ji Gong replied, "I went to Five Spirits Hill to see the fire at the Fortunate Cloud Shrine. It has collapsed and there is not a single tile left undamaged, nor a piece of wood unburned."

Liang Yuanwai directed the servants to prepare wine. After it had been served, the *yuanwai* raised his cup to the monk and then asked, "Teacher, yesterday when you came, who were the people you brought with you?"

Ji Gong explained from start to finish about how the old nun at City God Mountain had asked him to go to Yuhang prefecture to search for Gao Guoqin, and how he had brought Su Lu and Feng Xun with him to help find Gao Guoqin and bring him back to Linan. He also explained all that had happened there at the Yunlan market town and the Fortunate Cloud Shrine.

Liang Yuanwai exclaimed: "So you really came to find Gao Guoqin! I know who he is! He came from a good family. When his father was alive, he used to come to visit me here at Yunlan. I had no idea that they had fallen into poverty!"

Then he had one of the servants call Gao Guoqin and ask him to come in. In a little while, Gao Guoqin appeared. Liang Yuanwai asked him to sit down and said, "Gao Guoqin, you must know something about your family's past affairs."

Gao Guoqin said, "I do know a little."

Liang Yuanwai said, "Your father's name was Gao Wenhua. He was the most gifted graduate in Yuhang prefecture, and was well known and admired here in Yunlan market town. I was the best graduate in Yunlan. You were very young then—it was more than ten years ago. Afterward, when your father died, you were still very young and I did not hear from you of his death. It was because of these facts that we became separated. I never thought, during all these years in which I did not see you, that you might have become poor. Just now I heard this holy monk say your name, and only then did I know that you were here."

When Gao Guoqin heard the *yuanwai*'s words, he remembered his mother speaking of these things when he was a child. Quickly he rose to his feet and raised his hands in a polite greeting, saying, "So this is the one who is like my old uncle. Your young nephew offers his compliments. I have heard my late mother speak your name. Because we became so poor, I have not been able to keep in touch with friends, and I have not been able to pay my respects to my uncle."

Liang Yuanwai replied, "You have in this house one who will be like a younger brother to you. My son, Liang Shiyuan, is just beginning his studies and needs someone to direct him. You need not return to Yuhang prefecture. I will have your family brought here. You may study with your little brother, and if you both work hard, after the examinations you two may be fellow graduates."

Ji Gong then spoke. "Liang Yuanwai, as a monk I beg for a donation."

Liang Yuanwai answered, "Let the saintly monk speak and it will be attended to."

Ji Gong said, "You should use several hundred ounces of silver to buy Five Spirits Hill, the place where the Fortunate Cloud Shrine burned. You should also bring the Daoist novice, Liu Miaotong, here. Give him five hundred ounces of silver and then send him to the shrine at Fortunate Heaven Mountain. Build a small nunnery on Five Spirits Hill that will be called the Fresh Cloud Nunnery. Ask the old nun who is the aunt of Gao Guoqin's wife to live in it. Gao Guoqin and his wife may live there with her. This is all I, the monk, will ask of you. If it had not been thus, the Daoist Chang Miaoyu would have made you give him many thousands of ounces of silver."

Liang Yuan Wai said, "That is so. I will follow my teacher's commands."

He then immediately sent some of his people to find Liu Miaotong and bring him to the house. By this time, Liu Miaotong had quite recovered from the pain of the injuries he had received in the fire. When he arrived, Liang Yuanwai gave him the five hundred ounces of silver. Liu Miaotong thanked the *yuanwai* for his kindness, accepted the silver, and took his leave. From there Liu Miaotong, following the *yuanwai*'s instructions, went by himself to the Daoist Monastery in the Clouds, on Fortunate Heaven Mountain. Liang Yuanwai urged Gao Guoqin to remain with him, keeping Feng Xun as well, and sent his own people to City God Mountain to invite the old nun and her niece, Gao Guoqin's wife, to join them.

Ji Gong went on his way with Su Lu, stopping to eat when hungry and drinking when thirsty. They started at dawn each morning and found a place to stay each night until they reached Linan. There, they saw ahead of them the West Lake, and to the east a wine shop.

The monk said, "Su Lu, let us have a cup of wine here before we go on." Su Lu nodded his head in agreement.

As soon as they went into the wine shop, they saw Su Beishan, accompanied by Su Sheng, just having a drink. Seeing Ji Gong enter, Su Beishan immediately stood up and said, "Teacher, dear sir, you have returned! You must have had many hardships on your way. Were you able to find Gao Guoqin and bring him back? And where did Feng Xun go?"

Ji Gong then told the story of finding Gao Guoqin and about the other events from start to finish.

Su Beishan said, "So that is how it was. Our teacher has been to a great deal of trouble. Please sit with us and have some wine."

Ji Gong and Su Yuanwai had just sat down when suddenly an old man entered who seemed to be an old retainer. His hair was silvery white. As he walked, he leaned on a tall old-man's staff. His manner was agitated, and he raised his staff and shook it at Su Yuanwai. Then the old man seized Su Beishan and began to beat him with the staff.

Su Beishan quickly pulled away and stepped aside out of reach. Shaken and pale, he said, "Han, old fellow, you and I have known each other for many years and there has never been anything wrong between us. Why should you beat me with your staff today? You have no grudge against me. What is the reason for this?"

The old man replied, "Su Beishan, from today until my death, I reject you. I myself no longer want to live, and my son has already gone to the Chientang prefecture court to make a complaint against you. I will hang myself in front of your gate so that my ghost will haunt you. This is my dying declaration!"

Su Lu and Su Sheng quickly took hold of the old man, who, as they could see, was beside himself in his agitation. Su Beishan still did not understand the cause. His two household people helped the old man to sit down on a bench. Su Beishan said, "Han, old fellow, whatever the affair is that has made you turn against me, explain it to me and I will listen."

The old man simply sat there, hesitating, for some time. Then with a long sigh he began to speak: "Su Beishan, just because my son owed you two hundred ounces of silver, he had to shut down his business. He was trying to sell the building to pay you back your money. You were asked to wait until he could sell it. You not only would not wait, but you sent rowdies with clubs. They seized my daughter and took her away. They beat my son. Do you think that because you hold a note for some money that it gives you the right to take a person's life? My family, the Hans, have been in business for generations. How could you take away my daughter for no reason?"

When Su Beishan heard this he said, "My dear old friend! This is utterly wrong. Truly, I knew nothing about this. Although there must be something behind this, it cannot have been any of my people. You may ask anyone how I could do such a thing that offends heaven and all the rules of proper conduct. Who was it that came to you and asked for money?"

The old man said, "It clearly was one of your household people. At that time when you lent us the money, he was the one who brought the money." Su Beishan thought for some time, but could not remember who it was.

Ji Gong laughed and said, "Su Beishan, do not let this upset you. I will take you to find this person. First, send someone to call back old Han's son. It will not be necessary for him to lodge a complaint at Chientang prefecture."

It did not take long for Su Sheng to summon Han Wenzheng. As soon as he saw Su Beishan, the young man's face flushed as he angrily exclaimed, "It is all over between us! I want nothing more to do with you!"

Su Beishan said, "Dear younger brother, we are friends! I had never intended that you should be asked for the two hundred ounces of silver that I lent you. Whoever did the kidnapping has made it seem that I am to blame."

Han Wenzheng replied, "It was certainly one of your people who stole my sister away and had me beaten. I will surely make an accusation against you if you do not confess."

Su Beishan said, "Oh, no, this is not true. Ji Gong is here now, and I beg this honorable monk to manage this affair for us."

Ji Gong said, "You two must not quarrel. In a little while you will all understand everything clearly. Come with me."

When the bill for the wine had been paid, Ji Gong led Su Beishan and the two Hans, father and son, out of the wine shop. Going south, they came to a lane, where they entered. Soon they reached the gate of a house where Ji Gong knocked and called out, "We have brought some money for the manager of the Su family finances."

CHAPTER 29

Ji Gong makes it possible to distinguish true from false; the Chan master meets a hero under the bed

SOON after Ji Gong had called out, a man came out who had the appearance of a steward or accountant. Seeing him, Han Wenzheng immediately said, "There is no mistake. He is the man who came and demanded money from us, and afterward took away my sister."

Su Beishan also recognized him. He was the one who had been called Su Fu. Su Beishan at once told Su Lu and Su Sheng to seize him. Now, this Su Fu had come from Chinhua prefecture many years ago, when for ten ounces of silver his father, a refugee, had sold him to be a servant in the Su family. After he came into the household of Su Yuanwai, the boy had served in the library and Su Beishan's late father had been fond of him. Su Fu himself soon demonstrated that he knew very well how money was accumulated, and eventually was promoted to the position of steward. As he grew older, he had only one bad trait. Su Fu particularly liked to drink, and when he was drunk, he became recklessly bold and presumptuous, with the blind courage of a drunkard. He would sit at the gate, and, paying no attention to who it was, send a stream of curses at anyone he saw.

One day, a number of his fellow workers and friends tried to reason with him, saying, "Su Fu, you cannot go on creating such a disturbance. You are always cursing people. If the *yuanwai* were to hear you, you would be out on your own."

Su Fu, made bold by the wine, blustered: "Let me tell you all, don't talk about the *yuanwai*. I would cut him up into pieces and I would dare to hit the emperor. I would slap the emperor in the face, even if he had me chopped up. The *yuanwai* is only a man. Let him hear. What does he dare to do to me?"

Just as Su Fu started to say these words, Su Beishan returned home and heard Su Fu shouting and swearing inside the gateway. Su Beishan thought to himself, "This Su Fu is something that no law under heaven can control. This behavior and mad talk of his is too bad for other people to hear." He covered his ears to shut out the sound. However, he had already heard what Su Fu had said, and he became extremely angry. Going inside, he directed that Su Fu be brought before him. In a little while some men brought Su Fu in.

Su Beishan said, "Su Fu, you have often been like this outside, talking about me, making threats and saying ridiculous things. As soon as you drink, you begin to make trouble. I have warned you before—now, seeing that is your nature, it has become too difficult to bear. I should send you to the yamen to be beaten, but kindness is the way in this house. I cannot have an injury done to anyone. However, if you cannot behave as a human being, I must do my duty. I will not ask for the fifty ounces of silver to release you. I will throw that paper contract into the fire." He then told the other houshold people, "Get him out of here quickly! See that he takes all his things with him, and never let him enter my gate again!"

Su Fu had several chests full of clothes, and he also had more than two hundred ounces of silver. After he left the Su household, he stayed for a while at an inn. He had money in his hand—he was still young and carefree with nothing to do. He spent his days in pleasure and he made a friend. The friend was surnamed Yu, with Tong as his personal name. He was nicknamed "the Goldfish." He lived in Lane Number Three, where he and his wife passed their days. Outside it was often said that he was a kind of go-between, bringing people together, and that he even took men into his own house. He pretended to know nothing of such things, masquerading as a good man.

Yu Tong saw that Su Fu was a young man who had money. He took Su Fu into his family and made him his sworn brother. Su Fu then lived with the Yu family for over a year. He also spent all his money. When Yu Tong saw that Su Fu had no more money, Yu Tong wanted Su Fu to leave. Su Fu was always wrangling, quarreling, and starting arguments with Yu Tong. The wife of the Goldfish, Ma Shi, secretly spoke to Su Fu, saying: "You must find a way to get some money into your hands. If you cannot think of a plan, Yu Tong says that he doesn't want you to live here. He says that you have no money and that you are simply a non-paying boarder. He cannot take care of you."

When Su Fu heard this, he was distraught. His money was all spent and he had no plans. Suddenly he remembered that Han Wenzheng had opened a shop. Su Fu thought, "At that time Han Wenzheng borrowed two hundred ounces of silver from our *yuanwai*. I was the one who took it to him. I will go and find him and ask him for it." On this very day, Su Fu called on Han Wenzheng, who tried to sell the shop to pay back the silver. He had no idea that Su Beishan had driven Su Fu out of the estate.

Later that day the Goldfish said to Su Fu, "If you really think that you can get the money from Han Wenzheng, perhaps I have a good idea. The eldest son of Headman Lo of Purification Street is offering two or three hundred ounces of silver to buy a concubine. Do you think it is a good idea to wait until Han Wenzheng sells the shop? Do you know how many days it will take before it goes?"

When Su Fu heard this, he spoke out: "Give me some men to go with me and I will go tomorrow. If he does not give me the money, I will take the daughter away by force." Yu Tong assembled some lawless scoundrels, twenty or more, all completely unscrupulous. Su Fu took Yu Tong, and even Yu Tong's wife, and together they went to Han Wenzheng to demand the money.

When Han Wenzheng came out and saw them, he said, "Manager Su, I already told you to ask the *yuanwai* of your house to wait until I had the money to pay. Why do you come again?"

Su Fu replied, "The *yuanwai* of my house said he could not wait in this way. If you do not give us the money, the *yuanwai* ordered us to take your younger sister away. Then he will not ask you for the money."

After Su Fu said this, Ma Shi took some men inside and brought out Han Wenzheng's sister, put her into a sedan chair, and carried her off. When Han Wenzheng tried to detain them, several of the men beat him. When the old man tried to stop them, they gave the old man a good measure also. Then the next door neighbor came out, and seeing that things were not right, tried to interfere. The men then beat the neighbor as well.

They carried the girl back to Yu Tong's home. Ma Shi then sent someone off to Lo's home, asking for four hundred ounces of silver. The eldest son of the Lo family said, "By and by I will go to Yu Tong's home and look at the girl. After that we can do some bargaining."

Yu Tong and Su Fu were at home, waiting for the eldest son of the Lo family to come for his inspection. Outside, Ji Gong called at the gate. Su Fu thought it was someone who had come from the Lo family and quickly went out to look. Of course, it was Su Yuanwai with old Han, his son Han Wenzheng, and Ji Gong. When Su Beishan saw Su Fu, Su Beishan was naturally very angry. He called upon Su Lu and Su Sheng to seize him. When Yu Tong came out and tried to detain them, Su Beishan ordered him to be seized as well. To the guards in the area, whom he had already summoned, he said, "Do not let these two men go."

In that place Su Beishan was regarded almost as if he were a supernatural hero, and so the guards immediately took Su Fu and Yu Tong into their care. At the same time, Han Wenzheng went inside to look for his sister and saw that she had fallen forward and was supporting herself on her forearms. She had been bound so tightly that, having fallen, if she were not quickly untied, she would be in danger of dying. Han Wenzheng entered the room and released her. Then he took her outside and called for a sedan chair, telling his father to go home with her.

At this time the lamps were already being lighted. Su Beishan asked, "Teacher, as to Su Fu and these other rascals, should we have them sent to the guardhouse for the night, or should we send them to the Chientang yamen?"

Ji Gong said, "That will not be necessary. For the time being, have the two men taken to your home. I have my own methods. In addition, I have something else to do."

Su Beishan, who trusted Ji Gong completely, ordered Su Lu and the others to convey the two men to his home. When they all arrived at Su Yuanwai's home, the evening was already past the first watch. Telling his men to guard Su Fu and Yu Tong well, Su Beishan invited Ji Gong to come inside to the library.

Ji Gong replied, "Tonight I will not sit in that room."

Su Beishan asked, "In which room would you like to sit, Teacher?"

Ji Gong answered, "I wish to sit in your bedroom."

When Su Beishan heard this, he said, "Teacher, when you come into my home, it is the same as if it were your own. You may sit in whatever room you like." He then called upon servant De Fu to hurry with a message to Madame Su, telling her to leave the room. The lady quickly departed.

As the monk started to enter the room with Su Beishan, Ji Gong stopped in the doorway and asked, "Has he come to meet me?"

Su Beishan asked, "Teacher, did you arrange to meet someone?"

Ji Gong answered, "We meet because we did not truly part." After these remarks, Su Yuanwai, with Ji Gong, as well as Han Wenzheng, who also had been invited, came into the room together.

When Chen Liang heard that it was Ji Gong, the young robber parted the bed curtains and saw the monk enter. In the room there was a square "eight immortals" table with two chairs flanking it. Ji Gong sat down in the chair at the head of the table and Han Wenzheng sat opposite. Su Beishan asked, "Teacher, will you first drink wine or will you first drink tea?"

Ji Gong answered, "First, we will hold court. Have Su Fu brought here."

The *yuanwai* ordered one of the household persons: "Bring Su Fu to me."

Ji Gong said, "Su Fu, tonight you must speak the truth to me. Who planned the kidnapping? If you speak the truth, I, as a monk, will be merciful to you. If you do not speak the truth, I will send you to court to be punished."

Hearing these words, Su Fu understood that Ji Gong went beyond all others in his forgiveness and mercy. He therefore did not dare to lie to the monk and began: "It was suggested by the man in whose house I live. When I was staying at an inn, the Goldfish, Yu Tong, took me to live in his house. As long as I had good clothing and silver, he helped me. When the money was gone, he wanted to send me away. His wife told me that because I had no money, he did not want me to live in his home. In my miserable poverty, I thought of the time when Han Wenzheng had borrowed two hundred ounces of silver from my master—it was sent to him by me. I thought if I could get it, I could use that for a while. I did not imagine that he could not pay. When Yu Tong learned of this, he suggested that I seize the younger sister and sell her to young master Lo of Purification Street. The debt would be exchanged for a person. I did not think that my old master would learn about it and bring me here. Truly, this is what happened."

After listening Ji Gong said, "Come some of you people, take him and put him in front of the bed. Have him kneel close up against the bed."

Chen Liang, under the bed, had heard and understood quite clearly. Silently he said to himself, "Ai yah! I have been wrong in this matter. In reality this *yuanwai*, Su Beishan, is a good person. In everything that was done, this servant of his was pretending to carry out his orders. Luckily, Ji Gong appeared. If not, I probably would have killed some good people by mistake."

Outside the curtains of the bed, Ji Gong pointed at Su Fu and said, "I want you to remember his face. Tomorrow you may pay him back for the fact that for no reason you were going to take your knife and kill someone. You have a great deal of gall, but now you realize you were wrong."

Su Beishan, who had been listening, asked, "Teacher, to whom is it that you are speaking?"

Ji Gong said, "You do not know, but do not say any more." Then to the others he commanded, "Now, fellows, bring Yu Tong in here."

The household people brought in Yu Tong, who knelt before Ji Gong. The monk pointed at him and said, "Yu Tong, you scoundrel, you became very daring indeed! You did not think that the things you did would be found out by me! Now, if you speak the truth this time, I will show mercy and not have you executed. If you do not, I will send you to be punished."

Yu Tong said, "Listen, everyone, I am not to blame for what happened. Actually it was Su Fu who wanted to get the money owing to his employer. I had nothing to do with it."

The monk commented, "Even though it was Su Fu who wanted to collect the money, did you not give him some other idea?"

Yu Tong thought to himself: "In this matter I cannot avoid speaking. If I tell the truth and beg the monk to forgive me, perhaps he will release me." After thinking it over he said, "Saintly monk, you need not ask me further. I was to blame in this matter. It was all because Su Fu was living in my house, and he thought of going to Han Wenzheng for the money. When Han Wenzheng did not give it, Su Fu and I talked the matter over and decided to kidnap someone from the family in place of money."

The monk nodded his head as he said, "Have him kneel up against the bed. Did you hear me?"

Chen Liang's heart began to pound as he thought, "That was intended for me to hear."

The monk said, "But it was not simply for you to hear."

Chen Liang thought, "Ji Gong must know that I am in here!"

The monk laughed and said, "That is certain. If I did not know, I would not be here. I want you to remember these two men well so that tomorrow you may repay them."

Su Beishan exclaimed, "Teacher, who is it you are speaking with?"

The monk answered. "Do not worry about it."

Su Beishan then directed that wine should be served. When it was ready, he said, "Han Wenzheng, let us go on with our business connection as before, and may we always remember the ties of friendship that bind us together. I have always tried to behave as a man should. You probably know this. How could I do something that offends against heaven and all the rules of propriety?"

Han Wenzheng said, "You are also most compassionate. Let us allow bygones to be bygones."

Su Beishan said, "Pour a cup of wine for the saintly monk."

The monk said, "To pour wine is no small thing. But I can detect that there is an odor here."

Su Beishan asked, "What odor?"

The monk answered, "The smell of robbers."

Su Beishan asked, "Where is there the smell of robbers?"

The monk replied, "Under the bed."

CHAPTER 30

Master and monkey enter the Monastery of the Soul's Retreat for the first time

WHEN Ji Gong told Su Beishan that there was a robber under the bed, Su Beishan immediately called some household people. They came, bringing a rope and wooden staves that they thrust under the bed a number of times without touching anything that moved.

At this time, the already frightened Chen Liang had leaped up onto the canopy of the bed concealed by the hangings in the rear. He did this in less time than it takes to draw a breath.

While the men were thrusting their staves under the bed without touching anything, Chen Liang, believing that he had safely hidden from them, was thinking to himself, "Teacher is playing with me, but if those people catch me, what should I do?"

Then he heard the household people say, "There is no robber under this bed, Teacher. If there were, we would have brought him out with our staves."

The monk said, "How can there not be any robber? Bring lights and examine the bed carefully. Or you four men can overturn the bed. Then see if there is not someone there. If I say there is a robber, there must be one!"

Su Beishan called in more household men to turn the bed upside down. The other men entered the room, and as the four men started to tip the bed, Chen Liang, who was no longer able to conceal himself, leapt down, brandishing his knife and giving everyone a fright. The household men came at him with their wooden staves and Chen Liang's knife was knocked from his hand. In his terror, Chen Liang made one great leap, broke out of the circle of men and dashed outside, leaving his knife behind. After him the men came, shouting, "Catch the robber!" But Chen Liang was already on the roofs.

He dared not linger before reaching a deserted area. First, he changed from his close-fitting black suit of darkness and waited in secret until the sky became light. Then he returned to the outside of the Su family mansion, where he saw the great gate open and Su Fu come out. Su Fu was speaking to himself. "The *yuanwai* does not want me anymore. What can I do?"

While Su Fu was feeling sorry for himself, he saw Chen Liang approaching, saying, "Stand where you are and do not move! I am going to give you a beating." With that, Chen Liang seized him with one hand and began striking him with the other. After he had beaten the miscreant into begging for his life, Chen Liang began to feel somewhat happier.

Then two men came by who were on their way to the vegetable market. Seeing what looked like a fight, the passersby came up and said, "Stop fighting, you two. How did you get into a quarrel so early in the morning? Do not hit him any more."

Chen Liang retorted, "When one has done enough of a good thing, it is time to stop. Since you ask me, this is the time to end it."

The two passersby saw that they had been successful in ending the beating. Looking again, they recognized Su Fu, and asked, "Is this not the manager of the Su household? How did you two get into a fight?"

Su Fu replied, "I do not know either. I do not know this gentleman. When I left the house this morning, this man against whom I had committed no offense or given any grievance called upon me to stop. I do not know why he beat me."

The two men said, "Go now, Master Su."

Su Fu was afraid to leave, feeling that his punishment was not complete. Yet uneasily he moved along.

He had just left when Yu Tong came out of the gate. Su Beishan had wanted to send the two kidnappers to the yamen to be punished, but Ji Gong had said, "It is not necessary. The two men will suffer enough. They only need to understand that, if they continue in their ways, they will be punished even more severely."

Su Beishan said, "Since our teacher has spoken up for you two, we will let you go after daybreak." He then instructed his men to release the two after daybreak.

Yu Tong had just been released and gone out through the gate when Chen Liang saw him and became furious, saying to himself: "You thing! If it were not for you, I would not now be in disgrace."

He quickly went up to Yu Tong. With no explanation, Chen Liang immediately began to beat and kick the man, not stopping until he had beaten Yu severely. Then, after being urged by other passersby to stop, he refrained, simply saying, "It is finished."

Yu Tong went on his way, not knowing what to make of his beating.

Chen Liang stood there. Not very long afterward, he saw Ji Gong come out, carrying Chen Liang's knife. Su Beishan had said to Ji Gong, "Please, teacher. Have breakfast here and then go. Why must you go back to the temple so early?"

Ji Gong replied, "I must go back to the temple right now. Somehow I feel uneasy. It has been half a year since I last returned." With these words, he went on his way.

He had not gone far when Chen Liang, seeing that there was no one else in sight, wanted to go up to him and ask for his knife. Still, he was afraid to do so. Then he heard Ji Gong say, "You really have a lot of gall! You want to ask me for the knife. If you approach me, I will take this knife and kill you!"

From Ji Gong's appearance, Chen Liang could not tell whether this was Ji Gong's intention or not, but from the sound of his voice Chen Liang guessed that Ji Gong might not mean it.

Chen Liang wondered, "Would he kill me for no reason in this place where so many people live close together? It is hard to tell the false from the true."

Then he heard Ji Gong say, "Perhaps I can sell the knife. I will sell it to anyone who wants it." He saw a man whose business it was to buy antique paintings and other antique articles.

Hearing Ji Gong's words, the man came up to him to examine the knife and then asked, "Teacher, how much will you sell it for, sir? I will buy it."

The monk replied, "Give me enough for two pots of wine and you may take it away."

"Teacher," the man asked, "what price will you ask for each pot?"

The monk answered, "I drink wine at ten ounces of silver a pot."

The man laughed and walked away.

They had now reached the Cold Spring Pavilion at West Lake. Chen Liang came and knelt at Ji Gong's feet, saying, "Teacher, I became confused and made a mistake. Will you take pity on me, sir?"

Ji Gong said, "Get up and I will give you back your knife. Come with me to the temple." Chen Liang agreed and followed behind him. When they reached the mountain gate of the temple, they saw two monks acting as gatemen there. Ji Gong said, "Brother teachers, I have taken a disciple. How does he look to you two?"

Jing Ming looked at him and said several times, "Great happiness, great happiness! Welcome, Brother Teacher."

Ji Gong said, "I must also introduce him to you. Chen Liang, you must come and kowtow to your teacher uncles."

The monk in charge of the gate said, "We do not deserve this."

Ji Gong retorted, "You need not be polite. If he kowtows, you should accept his obeisance. And how much money will you give to your nephew disciple?"

The two replied, "We have nothing. Where would we get money? You must not joke!"

Ji Gong took Chen Liang through the mountain gate of the temple. Just inside Ji Gong saw the superintendent of the monks, who happened to be standing there. Ji Gong said, "Chen Liang, come and make a kowtow to the master of the monks."

Guang Liang, the superintendent, said, "Do not kowtow. I have no money!"

Ji Gong took Chen Liang on into the room of the master of the temple, where he respectfully greeted the old temple master. Afterward Ji Gong went to the Great Treasure Hall, where he first worshipped the Buddha's image. He then struck the bell summoning the monks to assemble. To them he said, "Brother teachers and younger brother teachers, I have taken a disciple. You must all look after him. But there is one condition, Chen Liang. You are my disciple. If I want to drink, you must get the wine for me. If I want to eat meat, you must purchase it for me."

Chen Liang assented, "Yes, the disciple must serve his teacher!"

Ji Gong continued, "What if you have no money?"

Chen Liang answered, "Whether your disciple has money or not, he knows a place to find it."

The monk said, "You need not go to find it! If you steal it within the temple, these are all your uncle teachers and your master teachers, and if they see you, they dare not speak of it!" Looking around, Ji Gong asked them, "Have I spoken correctly about this matter or not?"

The assembled monks all laughed when they heard him and said, "Good! First you teach him to steal. What kind of a teacher—and what kind of a disciple!" The monks did not dare to oppose Ji Gong because of his powerful connection with the prime minister, but Chen Liang knew nothing of all that had gone before.

From this day forward, Chen Liang bought wine and meat and served them to Ji Gong. Although both were forbidden to monks, nothing was said against Ji Gong. After he had spent all the money he had, Chen Liang pawned his clothing. After a couple of weeks, there was nothing left that he could pawn, and there came a day when there truly was no money. Chen Liang thought to himself, "Tonight I must go out and steal some money." He got out the bundle containing his suit of darkness, intending to go out from the monastery.

At the third watch he looked to see that Ji Gong was sleeping. Then Chen Liang rose, took the bundle with his thief's clothing, and was about to leave when he heard Ji Gong speak. "I told you not to steal here in the monastery and you did not listen to me! Well, then. First, I will get the hair off your head and then I will be able to manage you!"

Ji Gong got up and went into the kitchen. There he said, "Kitchen workers, give me a pot of boiling water."

The kitchen monks asked, "What are you going to do with the hot water in the middle of the night?"

Ji Gong replied, "I am going to shave the hair off my disciple's head."

While the water was being heated, other monks, hearing the sound of loud talking, had come to the kitchen. One of them said, "Even in the middle of the night you do these crazy things!"

Chen Liang did not dare to move, but some of the monks, out of good or malicious intentions, pulled him out of the room, saying, "Go quickly! Run! He is mad!" Now Chen Liang could move.

Once away from the monastery, he put on his suit of darkness and stole some forty or fifty ounces of silver. When it was morning, he redeemed all of his pawned clothing. Then he found a small restaurant. Going in, he chose a seat near the back door and ordered four dishes and drank a mouthful of wine. He was thinking to himself: "When I first had the idea of leaving the world, I did not imagine it would be so much trouble. I thought that Ji Gong was a monk who had great abilities and who followed the way of Dao. He would not cut off my hair when we first went into the monastery. Perhaps it was not my fate to leave the world."

He was sitting thus filled with melancholy regret when he heard a voice outside. "Good! A wine shop! I would like to get drunk and have a rest. As the ancients said, 'Men are born that they may drink and forget that they must die.'" With these words the speaker entered—and it was indeed Senior Monk Ji Gong.

CHAPTER 31

Ji Gong is recalled to Linan; Cloud Dragon Hua looks into a sedan chair and sees a victim

THE story goes that for some time Ji Gong had been at leisure in the Zhao home in Kunshan prefecture. He had completely cured the old lady's eyes and repeatedly he had asked to leave. However, he was urged to stay by the second Zhao Yuanwai, prefect of Kunshan and younger brother to the first Zhao Yuanwai, high protector of Linan, the Southern Sung capital. In the library each day, the second Zhao Yuanwai and Ji Gong talked of poetry and essays. Ji Gong was eloquent, and the Second Yuanwai looked upon him with increasing respect, saying, "How hateful it will be not to see Ji Gong. I must see you again soon, and the letters must be long."

Without realizing it, Ji Gong had passed a hundred days there. On the hundredth day someone came in, bringing two headmen from the high protector of Linan. They stood before Ji Gong and greeted him respectfully. "Holy monk, during these days while you have been away from Linan, there has been mischief that has offended heaven and appalled earth. We two are here especially to invite you, sir, to come."

When the monk asked the two headmen what had happened, the two explained all from beginning to end. A major riverene robber from Four Rivers had come to everyone's attention. His surname was Hua and his personal name was Jong, but he was called Yun Long ("Cloud Dragon"). He was also nicknamed "the Robber Rat of the Universe." He had fallen into the Greenwood when he was eighteen, and for a long time he had been among the followers of the sinister ghost, Reng Tian Shou.

They all lived in the farming country at Jen Mountain, where there were leopards. They had many friendly connections, but there were only five intimates who were actually members of the Greenwood, whom people called the Five Ghosts. Among them were the Kaifeng Ghost, Li Zhaoming; the Cockcrow Ghost, Chuan Deliang; the Tangled Hair Ghost, Yun Fang; and the Black Wind Ghost, Jang Ying. People who knew of them spoke of the five ghosts that made up the Long Dragon. Because the gang leader who had protected and sheltered them moved away from Four Rivers and they had no place to go, the ghosts scattered, four of them finding other relatives and friends. As for Cloud Dragon, he was accused of nine cases of rape and murder. Local officials had dispatched deputies to search for signs of him and to bring him back at once.

As soon as Cloud Dragon realized that he could not long remain there, he left Four Rivers. When he reached Yushan prefecture in Kiangsi province, he heard people say that there was a prominent official named Yang Ming in charge of armed escorts for travelers and merchants. People spoke of him as one who could quell disorders in every direction. Yang Ming was a brave man himself, and he liked to form friendships with men who were talented, intelligent, and courageous.

At Ruyi Village in the Phoenix Mountain Range area, Cloud Dragon went to pay his respects. In response to Yun Long's request, the household servant went inside to announce him. As soon as Yang Ming heard who it was, knowing that Cloud Dragon was a dissolute thief who some said had committed rape, he told the servant that he would not see him. The servant went outside and said, "Our master is not at home."

There was nothing else Cloud Dragon could do, so he went away. After several days someone mentioned that Yang Ming was at home. Again Cloud Dragon went to visit him, but was not admitted. Altogether Cloud Dragon went three times to see Yang Ming, and on this third occasion Yang Ming invited him in to talk.

Hua Yun Long was by nature a person who could converse easily. He saw that Yang Ming was tall with a slender waist, that he wore a blue silk kerchief tied around the knot of hair at the base of his head with a golden ornament in the shape of two dragons contending for a jewel, an embroidered blue silk robe, a sash with the male and female phoenix, and brocade slippers. His head was erect and his features pleasant. His beard divided into three parts as it fell toward his chest.

Cloud Dragon was filled with both admiration and envy as he said, "This younger brother has heard of Older Brother's great name and deeply longed to see you. Now it is my great good fortune to meet you—truly good fortune enough for three lives."

Yang Ming replied, "As ignorant as I am, what can I do to serve you? I am honored by your refined attention and surprised that we have not met before."

And so the two made several polite remarks.

Then Cloud Dragon went on. "I am but a guest in a place strange to me, young and knowing nothing. Perhaps Elder Brother could advise me."

Yang Ming was pleased that Cloud Dragon could make polite conversation, and detained him in the great hall to eat and drink. During the meal, Yang Ming remarked that it had been said that while Cloud Dragon was in Four Rivers he had been involved in a case of flower plucking. Hua Yun Long regretted what he had done. Yang Ming wished to turn him from his vicious ways. He might play among the flowers but he was not to pluck them. Hua Yun Long was willing to follow Yang Ming's advice.

Thereupon Yang Ming sent out invitations. Altogether there were thirty-six brave men who came, including the young Chen Liang, who had hoped to become a follower of Ji Gong, with his friend Lei Ming. They all welcomed Cloud Dragon and congratulated him upon his rehabilitation. After they had drunk wine with blood to show their brotherhood, they departed.

Hua Yun Long remained at Yang Ming's home. When he had nothing to do, he sometimes visited the town with Yang Ming. He learned to throw the javelin and studied the art of sword fighting. And so he passed three years there, until one day he felt a desire to go to the capital, Linan. Yang Ming gave him one hundred ounces of silver for traveling expenses, cautioned him against getting into trouble, and urged him to return soon safely.

Cloud Dragon left Ruyi Village and journeyed alone, sleeping during the day and traveling by night, eating when hungry and drinking when thirsty, until he reached Linan. He first stopped outside the Qiantang Gate. In the street he saw crowds of people and a great number of storefronts. On the north side of the road he saw an inn named the Riverfront Tower. The piece of red cloth hanging by its corner showed it to be a wine shop, while the teapot sign announced food. On either side of the door were carved characters that read: THE DRUNKARD'S UNIVERSE EXPANDS, WHILE IN THE WINE POT TIME EXTENDS.

Hua Yun Long thought that he would have a couple of cups of wine, and quickly entered. At first sight, he noticed that upstairs and downstairs were both busy. He went upstairs and found a table. Turning his head to the east, he saw seated beneath a window a man wearing a six-sided embroidered, and a dark-blue jacket with arrows on the sleeves, and a wide leather belt. The man's eyes were rather strange and a narrow beard hung from his chin. He was sitting alone holding a cup of wine. Cloud Dragon recognized him and immediately went over to his table, saying,

"I have not seen Elder Brother since we parted in Four Rivers, and never expected to meet here. Are you well?"

The man laughed and replied, "So it is my dear younger brother Hua. We indeed have come a thousand leagues to meet."

Now this man was surnamed Wang, with the personal name of Tong. His nickname was "the Monkey with Iron Legs." He had been, in fact, one of the chief robbers back in Four Rivers, and he had been a sworn brother of Cloud Dragon back in the Greenwood. The two had met many times before, and today, meeting in this way, each wanted to tell whatever had happened since they parted.

The two sat down together and again ordered wine and food. As they drank, Wang Tong asked, "Second Brother, since you and I parted in Four Rivers, where, dear brother, have you been preserving your body and what did you come here for today?"

Cloud Dragon told the whole story from beginning to end of how he had met Yang Ming in Jiangsi and about the thirty-six friends who had assembled to congratulate him upon his reform from vicious habits. Then he asked, "Did Elder Brother come here to see the sights, or are you about some business?"

"I came here because of a person against whom I have a grudge," Wang Tong replied. "An elder brother in the provincial capital needed money and signed a note. Later, because he could not pay two hundred ounces of silver, this dog of an official threw my elder brother in jail, where he died. At that time I was not at home, and only learned about it when I returned. I went to find that dog of an official and avenge my brother's wrong. Not knowing where the dog was to be found, I have just come here to Linan and have not yet found an inn. You and I can stay at the same place."

"Good!" said Cloud Dragon. "I also have just arrived."

As the two men were speaking, they heard a coughing sound from the stairway and a man came up carrying a wicker basket of fruit. He was about forty years old. He was wearing a blue kerchief on his head and a padded jacket and pants. His skin was yellow. His eyebrows were thin, and a small bird-beak of nose marked the center of his round face.

He wanted to drink some wine. After looking around the room, he quickly came up to Cloud Dragon's table, put down his wicker basket, and said as he bowed toward the floor, "Ah, so, it is my two masters. This small person presents his respects."

When Hua looked at him, he said, "Let me guess who this is. It is Liu

Chang." Liu Chang had been born in Four Rivers and for a very long time had associated with the men of the Greenwood as a dishwasher or servant. When it became known that he was connected to their affairs, he had run away to Linan and had become a peddler. Now he knelt in front of the two robbers.

"Get up, Liu Chang," said Wang Tong. "What are you doing here? Where do you live and where are the fashionable and busy spots? Tell us and we will listen. We two have just arrived and are not acquainted with the people or places."

"Then my two masters should go sightseeing at West Lake," Liu Chang answered. "The three great avenues in town have every kind of merchant and shop. The West Lake has its ten famous views and the best hill of worship under heaven. All of these are busy and crowded places. Come with me, and in the evening you need not stay at an inn. I have a small building where you may stay."

Upon hearing this, Cloud Dragon was very pleased. Liu Chang sat down and ate and drank with them. When the three had finished their meal, Wang Tong paid the bill and they went downstairs and out of the restaurant. In the street as they walked to City God Hill, the crowds of people seemed endless. The woods were beautiful and many people were walking to and fro under the trees. As they went on, they saw approaching them a sedan chair. In it was sitting a young woman with a face as lovely and delicate as a flower. No snowy heron in all its beauty could have compared with her. No jewels could have been compared to her eyes.

To Cloud Dragon she seemed hardly to be an earthly being. He followed the sedan chair back to the Qiantang Gate. He saw the sedan chair enter the Bird and Bamboo Nunnery. Looking back, he saw Wang Tang and Liu Chang, who had been walking behind him. When they had reached a place where there were no people, he asked Liu Chang, "Do you know where this woman comes from?"

Liu Chang said, "Master, you must not think about her. That is the daughter of Shao Tongpan. She was to be given to Son Taokang in marriage, but before she left the family's gate the son of the Son family died. As soon as he died, the daughter of the Shao family went to pay her respects to the parents of the dead young man. Then she said, 'I do not bear your son's name, but our betrothal has made us the same as man and wife. Open the coffin and I will look at him.' The Son family had someone open the coffin. Immediately, the girl cut off her hair. Although both the boy's parents and her own have urged her against doing so, she is taking her hair to the Bird and Bamboo Nunnery and is going to become a nun. This is the young woman that you have just seen. Since the second master asked, I have to tell you that you must think of someone else. I am afraid this one cannot be for you."

When Cloud Dragon heard, his heart leaped. He decided that, when night came, he would go to the nunnery and pluck that heavenly flower.

CHAPTER 32

The Robber Rat creeps into the nunnery; Prime Minister Qin reads the robber's message

WHEN Cloud Dragon heard what Liu Chang said, he did not say anything in return. The three ate dinner that evening and went to Liu Chang's house outside the Qiantang Gate. When the drum sounded the first watch of the night, Cloud Dragon lay awake until he saw that Wang and Liu Chang were sleeping. Then Cloud Dragon got up and opened a bundle. He took out his black close-fitting thief's garments, changed, packed his other light-colored clothing into the bag, and using the cords inside the bag fastened it to his back. Then he slipped his broad-sword into its flat leather sheath and tied it to his waist. He left the house and fastened the door. Looking up, he saw a sky full of stars and a great bridge of moonlight. With one leap, he was on the wall and then out of the court-yard. There were no watchmen to be seen.

Arriving at the nunnery, he went up onto the roof. Looking about, he saw a great temple hall, three stories high. Just east of it was a corner gate and a courtyard. Continuing over the roofs he saw that the eastern court-yard had a one-story building of three sections to the north, and similar buildings to the east and west. On the south side there was a wall. In the courtyard there was a pine tree and a few bamboo. There was a flickering light in the north building and the sound of low voices chanting a sutra. He leaped down in front of the northern building.

Making a small hole in the paper window, he looked in and saw a brick platform bed along the opposite wall. On the bed was a small table with a candle. There were four nuns of fourteen or fifteen years old. One was holding a sutra and reading while the rest followed. At the east end of the room was a long table piled high with sutras. In front of it was a smaller square table with an armchair at each side. In one of them sat a nun, about sixty years old with a kind face, listening to the young nuns chant.

Hua Yun Long looked for a while. The young woman who had cut off her hair and brought it to the nunnery was nowhere in sight. He turned and crept to the eastern building. Outside the window there, he again

made a hole in the paper and looked within. Again he saw a brick platform bed with a small table, upon which was a candle. There beside it sat
the young woman he had seen that day sitting in the sedan chair. She was
in the middle of reading a sutra by the light of the candle. When Cloud
Dragon saw her, he pushed the door open and entered the room.

As she was reading, Shao Shi was frightened to see a man dressed all
in black carrying a sword entering the room. Immediately she asked,
"Who are you and why do you enter a quiet Buddhist place at night in
this manner? Answer me!"

Cloud Dragon replied, "Young lady, today I saw you passing the City
God Hill in your sedan chair. I saw that you were very beautiful. I followed
you here. This is why I have come here tonight to find you. If you are willing, for a little while we will just exchange the wine cups of marriage."

The young woman blushed as she said, "Leave this place at once or I
will call out and summon our teacher, who will send you to the yamen.
Then it will be too late to simply regret what you have done."

Hearing her, Cloud Dragon Hua asked angrily, "Will you do what I
wish, or not? If you will not, then look at this!" He drew his sword from
its scabbard.

At the sight, the young woman who would die to defend her chastity
called out, "Help! Murder! Save me!"

When he heard her, Cloud Dragon feared that someone would come.
He stepped forward and grasped her shortened hair, raised his sword, and
with one slash killed her. It was sad to see the young woman return to the
red dust just as she was saying a prayer, but Cloud Dragon was happy.
Now that he had killed her, he felt satisfied.

Outside the old nun was saying, "Who is there that comes among us
to make trouble?" As she opened the door and entered, Cloud Dragon
became anxious. He struck her once with a sword upon her head, and as
she turned, again in her face. She said only, "Ah! Ah!" and fell to the
ground. Cloud Dragon took advantage of that moment to leap into the
courtyard and haul himself up onto the roof. He then returned to Liu
Chang's by his earlier route.

Liu Chang had just awakened. "Where have you been, Second Master
Hua?" he asked.

Cloud Dragon did not try to hide the truth, but told all the details of
his flower-plucking affair. As soon as he started to speak, Wang Tong
awoke, and understanding what had happened, remarked, "Younger
Brother has only just arrived and already he has performed this terrible

act. I fear that you will not be able to remain here long."

At this Cloud Dragon chuckled. "It's nothing to worry about. It gives our local headmen something to do. I would like to hear what people are saying."

After this Wang Tong and Liu Chang arose. The sky was growing light.

"Liu Chang," Cloud Dragon said, "You go and do your buying and selling. Do not go sightseeing with us. You have your business to do."

Liu Chang agreed, and Wang Tong went with Cloud Dragon toward the Qiantang Gate. The street was already crowded. They could hear snatches of talk about the murder at the Bird and Bamboo Nunnery. Wang Tong said, "Younger Brother, let us find a quiet and pleasant place to drink a little wine. Let us not do our sightseeing here."

The two men quickly hastened through the Qiantang Gate into the city. Here also the streets were crowded. On the north side of Phoenix Hill Street there was a place called the Tai Shan Tower. It was a large restaurant selling wine and food. Deciding to eat and drink there, the two quickly went in. Seeing that the place was crowded, they went upstairs. At one table there was a man seated alone. His complexion was like bronze powder. He wore a blue head kerchief and a long blue robe. His eyes and other features had an evil and ugly look. There were four or five servants about. It did not seem like an ordinary place of business.

They sat down for some time, but no one came to wait on them. After a while, they heard the man with the bronze complexion, who seemed to be the manager, ask: "Just now as I was coming upstairs, what was that I heard you waiters talking about?"

One of them replied, "Don't even mention it! Why don't you eat your bowl of rice or look out the window at the crowd! Well! You must know that outside the Qiantang Gate there is a Bird and Bamboo Nunnery. Yesterday morning the chaste widow of a young son cut off her hair and took it there. Last night a dirty robber killed her! He also seriously wounded the old nun and in a little while she died. Don't you think that strange?"

Then they heard the manager with the coppery complexion say, "That robber is truly hateful. It is too bad that a licentious outlaw should kill such a virtuous person. No doubt he was the sort of villain who had something foul done to him and he wanted to do the same thing to someone else."

Cloud Dragon was so angry that his eyes were sending out sparks. Yet it did not seem to be a good time to speak out. But his anger was rising within him. He stamped loudly on the floor with one foot, saying loudly,

"Have you no eyes? When two masters have been waiting for half the day, why do you not come to our table?"

One of the waiters looked over and retorted: "You needn't shout. If you came here to find fault, ask around to find out who opened this business. Let me tell you. Since this business was opened, there has been more than one who was beaten up here. In fact, scores of people have been beaten up. And after they were beaten, we took one of our cards and sent it with each of them to the local yamen. I tell you this in a nice way. Do not criticize."

When Hua Yun Long heard this, his eyes flashed as he said, "We two masters do not care who opened this place. If you turn your head away from me, I will burn your place down. Call the owner and I will have a talk with him. Even though he has three heads growing from his neck or six arms sprouting from his shoulders, I will turn up his eyes for good."

Now the owner of this restaurant, Qin An, originally had been one of Prime Minister Qin's managers. His nephew, Qin La, a very powerful and feared individual, operated it. The second floor of the restaurant was not intended to serve guests, but it was purposely used as a place in which disagreements would lead to fights. The prime minister's manager would then handle the case and large sums of money would be extorted from the victims. A number of officials were involved in this profitable scheme.

Today, as Cloud Dragon spoke up, Qin La came from behind the counter and said, "What kind of a person is he that dares to come here to make trouble? Come, fellows, beat him up, and when you have finished, take my card and send him to the district court."

At this Hua's anger rose still higher and he drew his broadsword. Qin La, thrusting his head forward as he spoke, asked, "Do you dare to kill someone? What are you doing with that sword? You will be cut to pieces if you depend upon that for power!"

"Killing you would be no more than turning over a bedbug," said Cloud Dragon. He raised his hand and brought down the heavy sword. Qin La's head left his body.

One frightened waiter screamed, "My mother! My mother!" and ran down the stairs several steps at a time, while gurgling sounds came from the back of his throat.

Soon people were arriving at the local guardhouse and saying, "Two men came upstairs in our restaurant and killed the manager."

The guards shouted, "Seize them," but when they went upstairs there was no one there. Cloud Dragon and Wang Tong had escaped by jumping out of the window. They were now standing in the midst of the crowd watching the excitement.

The restaurant was full of men. Some were saying, "The outlaws have run away." Others were saying, "Never mind—the outlaws will not get far. In our headquarters there are four headmen named Chai Yuanlo, She Jengying, Lei Siyuan, and Ma Anjye. These four are accustomed to catching famous outlaws. For this type of criminal, they only need three or four days to catch them." Cloud Dragon, standing among the listeners, heard this. He understood and remembered.

He and Wang Tong sought out a quiet place and went into a private room in a wine shop. When they had sat down, Wang Tong remarked, "My dear younger brother, you have been unbelievably unruly. Yesterday you arrived here, last night you killed someone, and today you killed another."

"Let me tell you, Elder Brother," replied Cloud Dragon, "that since I am here, I want to do several things that will startle heaven and earth, but the restaurant manager was looking for someone to kill him. Just now I heard people saying that there were several unusually able detectives. I would like to make them feel very disturbed. Tonight I'm going to Prime Minister Qin's estate to take a head from the neck of a person very much liked by the prime minister of this reign, Qin! I am going to reside in Linan City for six months. I intend to see what kind of a person will come to capture me."

Wang Tong asked him, "Dear brother, are you really as brave as that?"

"Did you imagine I spoke without thinking?" responded Cloud Dragon.

"Then," said Wang Tong, "Your brother will go with you. We have had many cups of wine together."

Stirred even more by Wang Tong's words, Cloud Dragon's excitement was raised to a feverish state. After they had finished eating and drinking, the two went quietly to a place opposite the Qin residence. After surveying the road, they found a quiet wine shop where they remained talking intimately until evening. When it was dark enough to offer concealment, they then went to a deserted spot and changed into their close-fitting black thieves' clothing and packed their clothing into the bags.

At Prime Minister Qin's residence, they pulled themselves up onto the wall. They dashed over the roofs, leaping from one to the other as if they were simply running over level ground. When they reached the inner apartments of Prime Minister Qin's estate, they searched about until they saw a light in the north building of a rear courtyard. They thought to themselves, "These are the inner apartments of the estate, and that most probably is the room of the prime minister."

Looking inside, they saw two serving maids on night duty. They were about fourteen or fifteen years old. There was a candle burning on the table. The two men leaped onto the roof above. They then took out some incense containing a sleeping drug, lit it, and held it so that the smoke would go inside. In a little while the two maids had fallen into a drugged sleep.

Cloud Dragon then entered the central section of the building. He reasoned that this must be where the prime minister actually lived, and felt certain that this was the prime minister's wife's bedroom. There in front of him he saw a jade bracelet and nearby a pair of cleverly carved, delicate white-jade pendants. Hanging in midair, half a lifetime's work, they had been part of the imperial tribute from a foreign country, but the prime minister had kept them for himself. Hua asked, "Wang, do you want these?"

"No," said Wang Tong, " I do not want them—you take them."

Turning his head, Cloud Dragon saw a lady's hatbox. Inside there were precious pendants lying on top of a coronet tipped with pearls. He gathered all these things together and took them with him. Going into the outer room, he saw a writing brush on a table.

He picked it up and wrote two lines of verse on the wall. Then he joined Wang Tong outside and the two left as they had come.

Early in the morning Prime Minister Qin arose. When he came into the building, he saw that the two serving maids were sleeping and found they could not be awakened. Going into the next room, he saw that the contents of the hatbox and the pendants were missing. He immediately called out for people to help his wife's serving maids. As soon as he noticed the wall, he realized from the words that had been written upon it that this was the work of a robber.

CHAPTER 33

The Great Protector is called to investigate;
Ji Gong catches one of three

THE prime minister saw written on the wall the lines of verse written by the robber:

> In heaven can be seen a hero from the outer universe.
> A sword obedient to his every wish hangs at his side.
> The crafty river rat off with his rich haul
> May suddenly change into a glancing ray of light,
> A dragon dancing in the clouds or sporting in the
>   waves of the four seas.
> The minister blessed by the emperor and helped by
>   spirits divine
> Must be disturbed to find his little treasures gone.

Cloud Dragon had left clues of his name throughout the verse, because the character for "change" is pronounced "hua" and Yun Long means Cloud Dragon. He had also inserted his nickname, "Robber Rat of the Universe." In the following lines that he added below the verse, the outlaw had openly revealed his identity.

> A wound opens in your back!
> It is Hua Yun Long behind you with his dagger.
> If Prime Minister Qin would find his ghostly visitor,
> He must send the Great Protector of Linan after him.

When Prime Minister Chin had read these words, he immediately called for someone to get the special folded paper needed to submit a memorial to the throne. Afterward he sent a message to the Great Protector's yamen, asking the Great Protector of Linan to come to the estate. In a little while the Great Protector, Zhao Fengshan, arrived and was ushered into the library. "Since Prime Minister Qin has summoned me, what are your instructions to me?" he asked.

"I have invited the Great Protector to my home to investigate the robbery here last night in which jewels were taken, including two fine white-jade pendants that were family heirlooms, thirteen other precious pendants, and a crownlike hat topped with pearls. The robber left behind two verses."

As the Great Protector learned the details about the theft, he began to feel a terrible fear and said, "I will send people everywhere to investigate, but there are great crowds of people in the city and it will be very easy to hide. With your kind permission, as soon as I return, I will send out people to quickly find and arrest the outlaw."

Prime Minister Qin said, "I will give the Great Protector a limit of three days to capture the robber and recover my treasured heirlooms."

The Great Protector could say nothing and only follow instructions. He made a copy of the words that the outlaw had written and took it away with him. Back at the yamen, he sent people to call together all his officers in Qiantang, as well as officers from the Subdued Tiger Temple region.

When all had hurriedly assembled at the Great Protector's yamen, Zhao Fengshan said, "Now Prime Minister Qin has lost some jade pendants and a pearl coronet. He called me and gave me three days to catch the robber. I returned here at once. The officers must immediately send out the men in their special jurisdictions to investigate, arrest the robber, and bring him back to either prefectural yamen. The person who accomplishes this will be rewarded with twelve hundred ounces of pure silver. We must be quick and clever, for we cannot tell where this outlaw has gone into hiding, and I fear that the prime minister will insist upon his three-day limit."

The officers returned and each sent out his men at once. How could they find and arrest this robber in three days? The Qiantang prefect, Liu Tenying, was originally from Liangpang, and he treated people very fairly. From his yamen he sent out some twenty-eight detectives to investigate and carry out the wishes of Great Protector Zhao. The Renhe yamen sent Tian Laibao and Wan Hengshan to find out what they could along the roads leading from the capital. Everyone had visions of the reward in his heart, but after three days there was not a sign of the robber.

When the prime minister saw the Great Protector, he gave the Great Protector another three-day limit. Then the limit was extended again. One after another, the lower yamens were reporting that they had not found a shadow, not a trace. All of them were begging for the forbearance of the higher yamen. Again and again the prime minister was persuaded to extend the limit another three days, until, before they knew it, two months had passed without their catching the robber.

Finally, when the Great Protector again went to beg the prime minister for another extension, the prime minister said: "I originally gave you three days to do this task. All sorts of people have been begging that I extend the time limit, until it has turned out to be two months! You still have not captured the robber. This is now a case of neglect of your duty to make an arrest. Tomorrow I will consider that the three days I gave you have come to an end!"

"May the prime minister show an exceptional kindness," pleaded the Great Protector. "Even now a messenger that I sent to ask Senior Monk Ji Gong of the Monastery of the Soul's Retreat is on his way. If he will only come here to help us in catching the robbers involved, it will be as easy as turning the palm of your hand, and will require no more strength than that needed to blow the ash off the end of a hair."

"The monk that you mention is none other than the one designated as my second self. He is also called Ji Dian!" the prime minister exclaimed. "I have just been thinking about him now. Where is he?"

"Ji Gong is now at my younger brother's home," answered Zhao Fengshan. "He has just cured my old aunt's eye trouble. I have already sent some people there to invite him to come to us."

"If I can see Ji Gong's face, I will give you a few more days. Ask him to come to see me as quickly as possible," said the prime minister.

The Great Protector could only say, "Yes, yes, yes!" to this order. Back at the yamen, he ordered that Chai Yuanlo and She Jenying take traveling expenses sufficient to journey to his brother's home and invite Ji Gong to come to Linan.

On the day that the men arrived at Zhao Fengming's gate, they asked a servant to go in and report their arrival. Ji Gong was in the library talking with Zhao Fengming as the servant announced, "Chai Yuanlo and She Jenying, two headmen from the yamen of the Great Protector of Linan, wish to see you."

Ji Gong said, "Ask them to come in."

The servant brought the two headmen into the library. Chai Yuanlo and She Jenying bowed to Ji Gong and afterward to Zhao Fengming. Then they stood to one side and described the events at Linan from beginning to end.

Ji Gong listened carefully and then said, "As a monk, I must take care of this business." Then he politely started to take his leave of the Second Yuanwai.

Zhao Fengming protested and asked, "Why not go tomorrow, Teacher? Why must there be such haste?"

The monk replied, "When I have a duty to perform, I cannot wait."

Zhao Fengming then had wine served and said goodbye to the monk.

Ji Gong left the younger brother's home with the two headmen and went off along the Yangguon Highway. On the way they stopped to eat and drink, sleeping in inns at night and traveling by day. When they were about thirty *li* from Linan, Ji Gong asked the two, "Headman Chai and Headman She, do you men wish to capture the robber who stole the jewels or not?"

Headman Chai asked, "How could we not wish to do that?"

"If you really want to catch the robber," Ji Gong told them, "hasten on to Qiantang Gate. Just outside the covered way, through the wall at the inner gate, a man dressed in dark clothing will be standing. You two must catch him and hold him. This is your robber, and when you take him to the yamen, the reward of twelve hundred ounces of silver will be yours."

Then we will go on ahead," the two men answered. Their hearts were filled with joy, thinking that they had such a good thing, and they hurried on their way. As soon as they reached the covered way through the wall at Qiantang Gate, naturally a man in dark-colored clothing was standing there. He was staring straight toward the east.

At the sight, She Jenying overflowed with happiness as he said, "Elder Brother Chai, we will have accomplished the greatest success of our lives when this is over and we get the reward at the yamen. The three of us will divide it equally." With that he pulled out his chain and locks with a great rattling and clanking, and put the man in irons.

She Jenying then said to the man, "My friend, we may now take your case to court. You yourself must know what you have done."

The man was shocked, and turning his head, asked, "Why are you two putting these locks and chains on me? Who has accused me?"

Looking at him more closely, She Jenying and Chao Yuanlo were dumbfounded when they recognized him as the manager of the charcoal business at the Qiantang Gate. As he again asked why he had been put in chains, the two headmen were unable to say anything.

At this moment, the monk arrived and asked, "Did you catch him?"

Headman Chai said, "You told us to arrest the man wearing dark clothing, and this is the man."

The man asked, "Monk, why have you arrested me?"

"I bought your charcoal and it was no good. It was all cinders! You don't sell good charcoal!" Ji Gong retorted.

When Headman Chai heard this, he realized that things were not as they should be. "Teacher, this man is not the jewel thief!" he exclaimed.

"He is not. I was just giving him a scare," the monk explained.

At that remark, Chai quickly unlocked the man's chains saying, "Teacher, this is not something to play games with, to lock a man up for no reason. Fortunately he is mild tempered. Otherwise we would have had to answer for this."

"Well, perhaps I did deceive you," the monk said. "You were too quick for me. The thief had not arrived yet. Come along with me. That man won't dare to say anything."

The monk led the two headmen on through the wall, and before they had gone very far he said, "Headman Chai, take a look. Business is coming," and he pointed with his finger in a way not to draw attention.

Headman Chai was an old hand at detecting, and he looked at once where the monk was pointing with his finger. Approaching them from the opposite direction was a man glancing to right and left as he walked. He was carrying a bundle in his hand. Observing his head, Chai noticed that the man had all the marks of a person of dubious character. Going up to him, the two men stopped him saying, "Friend, go no further. You are a lawbreaker."

When the man heard this, he threw back his head, dashed off, and turned into a side lane to the south with the two headmen running after him. The man was extremely fleet of foot. The two headmen went into the lane after him. The monk was also running. As the man came to a cross lane, he turned east, and again into another lane, where he went north. But when the headmen came to the cross lane, they turned west.

When the robber came running out of the north end of the lane, the monk was waiting for him, and asked, "Where are you running to, my good robber?" Pointing at him, the monk stopped him with his hypnotic power. Then the monk called out, "I have him! Come and take him from me!"

Some local guards from nearby came up and said, "Monk, this is a robber. Hand him over to us."

"Hand him over to you?" the monk questioned. "That will set your mind at rest, but not mine."

Just then headmen Chai and She arrived on the scene and said, "Teacher, you may let go of him now and we will lock him up."

The guardsmen recognized them and said, "Headman Chai, you may hand him over to us." Headman Chai could see that they were of the local guard, but not knowing their names, asked for them.

"I am named Kuai," one said, "and this is guardsman Ai with me."

"Then you two may take the man to Prime Minister Qin's residence and there hand him over to the prime minister." The two guardsmen agreed, and leading the chained man, came to the gate of the residence. All of the gatekeepers recognized Ji Gong, and, after greeting him politely, went in to announce him.

The prime minister was in the guest hall with two of Qiantang's prefects and Great Protector Zhao, talking about city affairs. The servant entered and said, "Prime Minister, the monk Ji Gong of the Monastery of the Soul's Retreat and two headmen from the Great Protector's yamen are bringing with them a robber. They are at the gate and beg to see you."

The prime minister directed the servant to invite Ji Gong to enter.

The household person went to the gate and said, "Our prime minister said that the saintly monk is invited to enter as he is, and that he is respectfully awaited in the guest hall."

The *lohan* hurried in, and the Great Protector welcomed him and thanked him for curing his aunt's eye trouble. When Ji Gong came into the room and sat down, the two Qiantang prefects did not know who he was and saw only a poor, ragged monk being welcomed by the Great Protector and the prime minister. "What power can he have?" they wondered. They saw Ji Gong and the prime minister sitting side by side with no suggestion of precedence and chatting in a familiar manner.

Then the monk said, "I hurried here because I had helped to capture a robber."

When the prime minister heard that, he was overjoyed and directed the household people: "Bring the robber here to me."

"Yes, Prime Minister," the attendants replied. Outside they said, "The prime minister has ordered that the robber be brought in for examination and be made to kneel before him in the guest hall."

When the robber was brought in, the prime minister immediately asked, "Who is this kneeling here? Identify yourself by name. Where did you sell the jewels you stole from me?"

CHAPTER 34

The Chicken Thief tells his story;
Tian Laibao sells his clothes

WHEN the prime minister asked the man's name and where he had sold the stolen jewels, the man replied, "This small person's name is Liu. I am called Liu the Second, a Four Rivers man who makes his living as a peddler. All because today I wanted to return home for a visit, I was walking along the main street, and for some reason I do not understand, these officers brought me here. As for the pearl coronet, I know nothing."

When the prime minister heard this, he said to Ji Gong, "He's only a peddler, holy monk."

The monk smiled slightly as he spoke. "The Great One is not an interrogator in criminal cases. May the Great Protector Zhao ask about the business. I am sure that he will understand."

Prime Minister Qin assented. "So be it. Come, Great Protector, you may interrogate in this case."

Zhao Fengshan immediately went outside under the broad eaves of the guest hall, asked for a table and a chair, in which he sat down, and had the robber brought before him. Then he said, "You say you are a peddler. Bring whatever things he was carrying and show them to me."

In a moment the man's cloth bundle and his knife were brought and shown to the Great Protector. "What do you use this knife for?" he asked.

"That is for protection on the road," Liu the Second replied.

"And what kind of things do you peddle?" the Great Protector continued.

"I have been selling fresh fruit for a living," the man answered.

As the man was being questioned, he saw the monk approach and heard him say, "I ask you, what is in this little bundle of yours?"

Liu the Second replied, "They are items of personal use."

The monk had the cloth-wrapped bundle opened. Two sets of garments and two pair of new socks fell out. The monk commented, "You are a peddler and you wear new socks!"

Hearing this, the Great Protector said to himself, "What kind of talk is this?" but thought it best not to speak.

Liu the Second was saying, "In answer to Your Worship, I had some money and bought some socks. That was not a violation."

The monk was feeling inside the socks and brought out a little package. When it was opened, they saw a huge pearl. The monk then asked, "You buy new socks and that is no violation, but what about this pearl? Where did it come from?"

Liu the Second was so frightened that his color changed as he replied, "In answer to Your Worship, the pearl is one that I stole."

Prime Minister Qin heard and realized that the great pearl was from the very top of the phoenix coronet. He asked a servant to bring it to him for close examination. Of course, there was no mistake. "Holy monk," he said, "This pearl is from my lost phoenix coronet."

Hearing this, the Great Protector became very angry. "You creature! If I do not beat you, you probably never will tell the truth!"

An order was given to one of the underlings to bring some of the bamboo staves at the residence and beat him.

Just as they were about to stretch him out for the beating, the frightened Liu the Second began to speak. "I will tell the truth. This small person's name is Liu and my personal name is Chang. My nickname is 'the Chicken Thief.' I used to be a servant to the men of the Greenwood in Four Rivers Road, until I came here. The pearl is not one I stole. This morning there was a great thief from Four Rivers named Cloud Dragon, nicknamed 'the Robber Rat of the Universe,' together with 'the Iron Monkey,' Wang Tong. These two first had attacked the nun and afterward killed a man in a restaurant. Then they came to Prime Minister Qin's residence and stole the jade pendants and the phoenix coronet. A long time ago I used to work for the two of them. Today they gave this pearl to me and told me to go back to Four Rivers. They said that I could sell the pearl for four or five hundred ounces of silver. The money would have been enough to live on and to open a small business. Today I was just going to the Qiantang Gate. Unexpectedly, the two detectives arrested me. This is a true account of what happened, without a single false statement."

"Where do Cloud Dragon and Wang Tong live now?" The Great Protector asked. "You must know."

"They used to live at the Happy and Glorious Inn, but they have moved. I do not know where they are now," Liu Chang answered.

"Great Protector," said Ji Gong, "Fasten the fetters on him and send him to the Qiantang yamen. This case is considered broken open. The prime minister will want to reward the captors."

The prime minister sent a household person for fifty silver pieces, and the two headmen and the two local Qiantang guards were each given two ounces of silver. Chai Yuanlo and She Chenying thanked the prime minister and took Liu Chang away with them.

"Saintly monk," the prime minister queried, "Where is Cloud Dragon? I beg the teacher's help in taking him and I thank you for what you have already done."

"I can try to find out where he may be by divination," said Ji Gong.

The prime minister welcomed the idea. "Very good."

"Do you have an ancient eight-legged bronze vessel?" asked the monk. "I will try it with that."

The prime minister sent a household person to get an ancient eight-legged vessel from a cabinet. Shortly afterward, a servant brought the vessel and gave it to Ji Gong. The monk placed it on a table and chanted some indistinct words. When he had finished, he lifted the vessel into the air. "Where is the prefect from the Jenhe district?" the monk asked.

"Outside," the prime minister replied. "Have the prefect from the Jenhe district come here quickly," he commanded.

"Honorable prefect," the monk said, "you have under your command a headman named Tian Laibao. Summon him for me."

The face of the prefect turned white with fear. He had no idea what this was about. "That is right," he said, "there is one with that name."

Ji Gong said, "Call him for me."

The prefect did not know what was going on in Ji Gong's mind. His own mind was in turmoil. He wondered whether Tian Laibao might have hidden the thief who stole the coronet and other jewels. Quickly he sent someone off to summon Tian Laibao.

At this time Tian Laibao was talking with Wan Hengshan in the guardroom. In came a servant who said, "Tian Laibao, something dreadful! The case of the jewel thief has been broken open. They have caught a thief called Liu Chang and they have sent out word to catch the two jewel thieves. One is the Robber Rat of the Universe, Cloud Dragon, and the other is the Iron Monkey, Wang Tong. Prime Minister Qin asked Ji Gong of the Monastery of the Soul's Retreat to do a divination to find out where these two robbers have gone. Ji Gong performed the ritual for a long time and he didn't say anything. Then he called our prefect and said: 'I have something to say to you.' It frightened the prefect so and he didn't know what it was all about. Then he sent me to call you to come at once."

Tian Laibao heaved a long sigh and said, "That is terrible! Dear brother Wan, we have been friends for a long time. Now I must go—I have an old mother at home who is like your own aunt, with no one to look after her. Take good care of her."

When Wan Hengshan heard these words, he could not imagine the reason for them, and remonstrated: "Elder Brother Tian, where do such words come from?"

"You need not ask," replied Tian Laibao. "In a little while you will know." He stood up and went out with the messenger toward the prime minister's residence.

At the residence, the messenger went in and reported that he had brought Tian Laibao. Ji Gong directed that he should be shown in. As he entered, he first bowed to Prime Minister Qin, then to Ji Gong, and finally to everyone else. Then he stood to one side.

The monk approached him and said, "Come with me, Tian Laibao." Taking him by the sleeve, he pulled him into another room and said, "Take off that hat with the feather and tassel on top."

Tian Laibao thought, "He wants me to have my head unprotected."

The monk next said, "Now take off that stiff leather belt, your jacket, your blue cloth shirt, and your boots."

When he heard that, Tian Laibao said, "You are asking me to take off all my clothes. What are you going to do?"

The monk said, "I have a good reason for asking you to take them off. Let me ask you. How much is this hat worth?"

"Probably I bought it for two strings of cash," replied Tian Laibao.

"Not much," commented the monk. "How much are all the rest of these clothes worth?"

"They might come to two strings, five hundred cash," answered Tian Laibao. "That includes the jacket, shirt, belt, and boots."

The monk nodded his head a couple of times. Then he called one of the prime minister's household servants and told him to bring two hundred silver coins. The household person knew that Ji Gong was the prime minister's monk, designated as a second self. The servant dared not ask any questions. Soon he was back with the coins, which he gave to Ji Gong. The monk received them with his cupped hands and in turn gave them to Tian Laibao, who accepted them. The monk said, "Take them and go."

Tian Laibao still did not understand what this was all about, but he took the silver and left the prime minister's residence. Just as he was leaving, he saw Wan Hengshan standing at the gate. Wan Hengshan saw that Tian Laibao had no hat, jacket, belt, or boots—nothing but a pair of unlined pants. Wan Hengshan quickly spoke up. "Brother Tian! Where have your clothes gone? When I heard what you said a little while ago, I was worried and followed you here. Where did your clothes go?"

"I sold my clothes," Tian Laibao answered.

"How much did you sell them for?" Wan Hengshan asked.

"Two hundred silver pieces," Tian Laibao replied, and went on to tell Wan what had just happened.

"Ask if he wants any more. I have an extra set," urged Wan Hengshan.

"I couldn't go back in there," said Tian Laibao.

"Elder Brother Tian, a little while ago your language sounded so mournful," protested Wan Hengshan. "You were asking me to look after your old mother as if she were my aunt. What was that all about?"

"You are being very reckless," said Tian Laibao. "You must forget everything that passed between us today. Don't you remember the time when the soldiers surrounded the Monastery of the Soul's Retreat? We had to put fetters on Ji Gong. Were not you and I the ones that brought Ji Gong to the Prime Minister's residence? I fear that he remembers us and still bears a grudge!"

Only then did Wan Hengshan understand. Silently, the two returned to their barracks, carrying the silver with them.

During this same time the prime minister had seen that the monk had taken Tian Laibao's clothing and given him two hundred silver coins. The prime minister did not know what the monk had in mind. Just as he was about to ask, the monk spoke. "Where did the Great Protector go?"

"He is outside," replied the prime minister.

"Ask him to come in," Ji Gong said.

"Did you call me, Teacher?" asked the Great Protector Zhao. "What may I do?"

"You may take off your plumed hat, your jacket, your belt with the jade sections, and your boots," Ji Gong told him.

The prime minister was thinking, "Not bad. He bought that set of clothing for two hundred silver pieces and exchanged it for a set worth two thousand. One can see what kind of man the monk is!"

"Do not play jokes on me," the Great Protector said. "I am not Tian Laibao. He is a headman."

"Take them off," repeated the monk. "There is a good reason." There was nothing that the Great Protector could do but take off his clothing. "Now," said the monk, "I ask you, the Great Protector, to put on this set of clothing. Can you guess why?"

"Your disciple does not know," answered the Great Protector.

"Well, Great Protector," said Ji Gong, "just put on Tian Laibao's plumed hat, his jacket, his stiff leather belt, and his boots. Do you remember the lines of verse that the jewel thief wrote on the wall? At the end there was a line in which he said to send the Great Protector after him. Now I will send you to catch the robber."

"How could I take him myself?" asked the Great Protector. "I have detectives to carry out this work."

"I will help you to catch him," said the monk. "Bring four men with you—Chai Yuanlo, She Jenying, Lei Siyuan, and Ma Anjie. Tonight, between the third and the fifth watch, I intend to catch the robber." Then, turning to the prime minister, he said, "Do not sleep tonight, Prime Minister, between the third and fifth watch. I will bring the robber here. You will want to interrogate him about the jewels." The prime minister nodded.

That night, with the Great Protector and the four headmen, the monk left the prime minister's residence and hurried off down the street. To the Great Protector it seemed as though they had walked all around the inside of the city walls.

At the end of the second watch Great Protector Zhao asked: "Teacher, where are we actually going? I truly cannot walk much further."

"We are here!" said the monk.

They had arrived at the mouth of an alley called Rui Lane. To the west was a night watchman's mat shed. Near the wall a yellow porcelain bowl held a flickering candle that cast gloomy shadows over the inside of the shed. The watchman was sleeping, using his rattle for a pillow. The monk slowly crept inside, and, picking up half a brick, gently pulled the rattle out from under the watchman's head while he slipped the brick under instead. The watchman was still asleep. The monk told the others that the watchman had said the great man was down for the night. Headmen Chai and She came into the shed and called the watchman, who got up and took the half brick outside.

The monk asked, "What watch is it? The watchman is going to mark the hour with that half brick!" Suddenly the sleepy watchman realized what he was holding and became frightened. The monk said, "Don't be afraid," and then whispered in his ear. The watchman nodded and the monk gave him back his rattle.

The monk led the five men on to a big gate not far away and said, "If we catch the jewel thief now, we will find him in this house."

CHAPTER 35

Yang Zaitian has his fortune told; jealousy brings failure to four headmen

AS the monk stood outside the big gate in Rui Lane, he gave instructions to the four headmen. "Headman Chai and Headman She, you two stand at the north side of the crack between the two gates. Headman Lei and Headman Ma, you two will stand at the south side of the crack between the two gates."

"And what will you do, Teacher?" they asked.

"You will block the gate. I will get inside, and when I blow, I will blow the robber out through the crack." The four headmen did not dare to question his word. They could only follow the monk's instructions. He then stepped forward and slapped the gate, calling out, "Come and open the gate! Come and open the gate!" Then he beat on the gate several times.

Inside there were two young gentlemen just trying to get to sleep in their room. When they heard someone calling at the gate, one said to the other, "Go out and look through the gates." The second young gentleman was extremely timid. He lit a candle, trimmed the wick to make it brighter, went to the gate, and was just about to open it and look out when he felt a cold blast of wind. It also blew out the candle. The frightened young gentleman turned his head and ran back. Inside the room, the other young man asked, "What was it?"

"A black monster made a thunderous howling wind blow," he answered.

As the two were talking thus, they again heard a shout, "Open the gate! Open the gate!" The two frightened young fellows did not dare to go out.

Just at this point the master came out. Now, the master of this house was surnamed Yang and his personal name was Zaitian. He had previously been at the capital of Four Rivers province as the governor. Because his mother had died, he had returned home here to go into a period of mourning. When he heard the thunderous clamor at the gate, he told the library boy to light a lantern, go out, and have a servant open the gate. There they saw several headmen in uniform standing in the gateway. At that time Ji Gong had stepped back into the shadows.

Great Protector Zhao saw the gate open and a man come out wearing a simple cap of rough material and a long blue outer garment. His features were regular and pleasant. Three strands from his black beard reached his chest. Protector Zhao recognized him at once and quickly stepped forward, saying, "Why, it is Elder Brother. You are not asleep yet."

Yang Zaitian gave a grunt of disapproval. "What person is this that dares to call out that he is my younger brother?"

Protector Zhao said, "I am your younger brother, Zhao Fengshan. No doubt you did not know me." The two men had been fellow students as children and had remained close friends throughout their lives. At night, seeing Protector Zhao dressed as he was, the master had not recognized him.

Hearing Protector Zhao speak this time, Yang Zaitian said, "Dear brother, let me take you into the guest hall. Why are you dressed in this way? Is it possible that you have lost your official title and been demoted? Tell me about your situation, and I will make sure that it is corrected."

"Elder Brother," said Zhao Fengshan, "you do not understand. It is all because the wife of Prime Minister Chin had her phoenix coronet and other jewels stolen. Senior Monk Ji Gong of the Monastery of the Soul's Retreat captured one robber named Liu Cheng. Interrogating him, we learned about two more robbers named Cloud Dragon and Wang Tong. Because of this, I changed my clothes and came here to catch the robbers."

Yang Zaitian heaved an audible sigh of reproval. "Dear younger brother, indeed! You and I are educated people. How could you be led into believing such things? This business of strange powers and unruly spirits is the sort of thing that monks' stories cause the populace to believe."

"Do not act like this, Elder Brother," said Protector Zhao. "Ji Gong came with me to help solve the case!"

At this point Ji Gong stepped forward and said, "Protector Zhao, can we not go in and sit down?"

"I must hear what news my elder brother has," said Protector Zhao. "Let these men wait outside."

Yang Zaitian said, "Please do come in."

The two friends went on inside, with the monk following behind. In the courtyard a large building of three sections had a pair of smaller matching buildings, one on the east and one on the west. The monk looked all about as he went in and sat himself down in the seat of honor.

Yang Zaitian was quite displeased at seeing this, and said to himself, "From the emperor down to the common people, each man has his proper place. This ragged fellow does not even care about his own person." But although he was unhappy about the monk, Yang Zaitian did not want to say anything aloud, and went and sat down.

Protector Zhao said, "I have forgotten to introduce you two."

"Do not introduce us. I already know," retorted Yang Zaitian. He then instructed a servant to bring tea.

"Don't pour tea for me," said the monk. "Pour wine!"

Yang Zaitian purposely acted as if he had not heard, and was asking Protector Zhao about Liu Chang, how they caught the robber, and the robber's origin.

Again the monk said, "Pour wine!"

Protector Zhao and Yang Zaitian went on talking until the monk had asked for wine more than ten times.

Finally, Protector Zhao could stand it no longer and said, "Elder Brother, I am a little hungry. Do you have anything to eat that could be prepared?"

"I heard the monk say something also," said Yang Zaitian, "but because there is not much around in my poor home, I hesitated to offer it—but if my dear brother is hungry, come! Let us have something." With a word from Yang Zaitian, food and wine appeared.

The monk immediately picked up the wine pot and said, "We are like old friends at first sight. Away with ceremony!" Then he drank three bowls of wine, one after the other, without so much as a toast.

Yang Zaitian decided to test the monk and said, "Monk, with your powers of goodness can you tell about things past and things yet to come? I have something I would like to ask you. I have forgotten my birthday and can remember neither the year or the month. I beg you to calculate it for me."

The monk said, "That is easy. You were born in such and such a year and such and such a month and this year you are fifty-eight years old."

When Yang Zaitian heard this, he knew at once that the monk was right, but it was not his nature to believe in anything supernatural, even though the monk had given the correct answer. Again he asked, "Monk, can you tell by looking at my face what I should best do?"

The monk replied, "You had best not make a nuisance of yourself."

Yang Zaitian said, "I ask you this as a scholar and a gentleman. Simply speak the truth as you see it."

Ji Gong answered, "Your aura is not good, Great One. There are shadows and your eyes grow dim. At the third watch your head will fall, severed at the neck!"

Hearing this, Yang Zaitian asked, "What proof do you have that I will die at the third hour?"

"Even now," said Ji Gong, "one of your household people has admitted a robber who is your enemy and who comes to kill you."

"Which of my household people is this?" asked Yang Zaitian.

"I can tell that as soon as I see him," answered the monk.

Yang Zaitian immediately ordered all the people in the household to assemble. In this home there were twenty-seven male household members and nine old women and young serving maids. The men all gathered outside the library, all standing together. As soon as the monk looked at them, he laid his hands upon one of the men, thirty-five or thirty-six years old with handsome features.

"What is your name?" asked the monk.

"I am called Yang Liangsheng." He was indeed an honest and loyal person, a son of the old master, Yang Shun.

Ji Gong said, "You have let a robber in this house from outside, and tonight he has come to kill the master of the house."

Yang Liangsheng's face fell as he heard this and he protested, "What proof of this have you, monk? You are simply slandering me. I have always received every kindness from the head of our household. How could I do such a thing against all the rules of propriety? You are saying this with no evidence whatsoever!"

"Do not become angry," said Ji Gong. "This morning, when you were sweeping the gate, was there not a man who looked into the gate? You asked him who he was looking for. He asked you whether this home was that of former District Magistrate Yang in the capital of Four Rivers. You answered, 'Yes.' Is that not right?"

Yang Liangsheng thought for a moment after hearing the monk's words, and then said, "You are right, that did happen this morning. However, I did not let any robber into the house to kill the master."

"As soon as you told him that the master had been the district magistrate of the capital of Four Rivers and that his name was Yang, you opened the door of the house to your master's enemy. Tonight, without your knowledge, he came seeking revenge."

Yang Zaitian had half believed and half disbelieved. Now, as he listened to the monk questioning Yang Liangshang, he realized that this was not simply slander, and he was afraid. "Saintly monk," he said, "What should be done about this?"

"Magistrate Yang need not worry. It was simply because the robber came here that we came! Call the four headmen that we brought with us. I have some instructions for them." Yang Zaitian immediately sent someone to call the four headmen inside. "Headman Chai and Headman She, stand under the eaves of the house on the east side of the door," said Ji Gong. "Headman Lei and Headman Ma, you two stand under the eaves at the west side of the door. Wait until after the third watch. The robber will come over the roofs from the east. Wait until he leaps down in front of the door. You four men will then come at him with your weapons. Surround and capture him. Magistrate Yang will reward you."

The four stepped outside and separated into pairs. Lei Siyuan then said, "Brother Ma, we serve in the same yamen as Chai and She, but today those two got fifty ounces of silver. They should have turned over even shares to you and me as a matter of course. Not only did they not share with us, but they never even said a word about it. Tonight when the robber comes, they will approach him, but we will not. If they arrest the robber, let them go in and get the reward. If they cannot make the arrest, then you and I will arrest him and we two will share the reward equally, and not share it with those two."

"That is reasonable," said Ma Anjie. "We will do just as you say." The two followed their secret plan, and without their realizing it the third watch came with no movement seen.

On the other side, Chai and She had also been speaking softly. "The night has almost passed, but how is it that we have seen no robber? Could it be that Ji Gong did not foresee this? If the robber does not appear, what will happen to Ji Gong?"

The two had just finished speaking when they heard the sound of something striking, as an exploratory pebble fell into the courtyard. Then a tall man dressed in the dark clothing of a thief leaped down from the roof above. Chai Yuanlo and She Jengying sprang forward, shouting: "Stop, outlaw! We two have been waiting for you. Tonight you say goodbye to heaven and hello to hell," as they pointed their swords at him.

The robber laughed a cold laugh and said, "Good, Yang Zaitian, you have a guard. You may be guarded for a year, but sooner or later I or my brother will come to take your head!" Then he drew his sword and came at Chai and She as if to kill them then and there.

The two headmen found that the robber's swordsmanship was extraordinary. They truly could not take him; their swords could not reach him, nor could they afford to put down their guard. Both were covered with sweat. They could not see any movement from Lei Siyuan or Ma Anjie. Headman Chai was hard pressed and called out, "Ji Gong, come out! We two cannot manage it."

From inside the room Ji Gong answered, "I am coming," and rushed out.

The outlaw lost his confidence and retreated, saying, "Tonight I will not kill you two after all, but we will meet another day." Then with a flying leap he was on the roof.

Chai and She said, "No good, our robber has escaped!"

Ji Gong had been saying something under his breath. He pointed and spoke the six true words, "Om Ma Ni Pad Me Hum!" and the robber fell from the roof into the courtyard. Chai and She quickly went forward, laid hands upon him, held him down, and took his sword.

When he was brought into the room, Yang Zaitian looked at him, and noticing his heroic figure, asked, "Outlaw, I have never done you any wrong and so you should not hate me now. Why did you come to kill me and what is your name? Speak!"

The robber looked at him in amusement for some time. Then he lifted his head and exclaimed, "I hate you! I hate you! There is no more to say. It was predestined."

Yang Zaitian again asked, "Why do you hate me enough to kill me? Quickly answer me! If you do not, I will have you beaten."

The outlaw said, "Do not beat me. I will talk." Then he told how his brother had been imprisoned for an unpaid note and had died in prison, and how he had come to Linan to avenge his brother's death.

CHAPTER 36

The prime minister questions a false dragon;
Chai and She find a hanging man

IN the library when Yang Zaitian asked the assassin's name, the outlaw replied, "My name is Hua and I am called Cloud Dragon. My nickname is Robber Rat of the Universe, and I am, indeed, from Four Rivers."

"Do not ask further, Elder Brother," Protector Zhao said. "I will have him taken to the residence of Prime Minister Qin and follow the prime minister's instructions."

Yang Zaitian went over to Ji Gong and thanked him. "If it were not for the help of the saintly monk, I would now be beneath the Yellow Springs. From now on I will never dare to doubt the words of Buddhist and Daoist monks."

There was a knock at the library door and a gatekeeper entered to report that the men had come from the yamen of the Great Protector. A moment later Zhao Fu and Zhao Lu came in, bringing a parcel of clothing. Protector Zhao at once changed into his usual attire. "Who knew that I was here and sent for my things?" he asked as he dressed.

"It was the watchman at the entrance of Rui Lane," Zhao Fu replied. "He came at Ji Gong's orders. He brought the news very early and told us to bring the clothing to the home of Yang Zaitian."

When he heard this, Protector Zhao understood for the first time what had been happening. After he had finished dressing, he asked Ji Gong whether he wished to return on horseback or in a sedan chair.

Ji Gong said, "Protector, why don't you go to see that the robber is locked up. I will follow after you." Yang Zaitian came out to the gate to see everyone off. The protector then said farewell. The four headmen— Chai Yuanlo, She Jengying, Lei Siyuan, and Ma Anjie—transferred the prisoner under guard to the estate of Prime Minister Qin, and word was sent on that they had arrived.

The night before, after the monk had left with the Great Protector, Prime Minister Qin had waited in the library until after the fourth watch. When he failed to see the monk return, he began to feel tired and went to sleep in his clothes on the *kang* in the library. In a little while it grew light. He rose, drank some tea, and ate some pastries. Then one of the household people came in to report: "Protector Zhao is now at the gate, bringing with him some headmen who are guarding an outlaw they captured. They await your pleasure."

Prime Minister Qin said, "First invite the Great Protector in; after a little while bring the robber before me."

The household person went out and said, "The prime minister has invited Great Protector Zhao to come within."

When he arrived in the library, Great Protector Zhao explained in detail the events that had occurred at Rui Lane, including the capture of the robber, praising Ji Gong for his part in the capture.

Prime Minister Qin immediately asked that the outlaw be led in. When the robber was brought before him, the prime minister noticed that in his black thief's clothing this robber was much more impressive than Liu Chang had been.

Angrily the prime minister addressed the prisoner: "What is your surname and your personal name? Where do you come from and what did you do with the pearl coronet and the jade pendants? Speak the truth and save your flesh from much pain!"

The outlaw kneeling before him said, "You need not apply the extreme questioning, Great One. I am a man of Four Rivers called Cloud Dragon. I did steal the jades and the pearl coronet."

"Where did you sell them?" Prime Minister Qin asked.

"I sold them to a traveling merchant whose name I do not know for thirteen ounces of silver, which I spent wastefully eating and drinking."

When Prime Minister Qin heard these words, he became very angry and shouted, "You took my family heirlooms and wasted them like that!" In his fury he was about to strike the robber.

Just then a servant entered with a message: "Ji Gong, the Chan master, has arrived. The prime minister ordered that he be invited in."

Now, why had Ji Gong arrived so late? It was because when he left Yang Zaitian's house, he walked through Rui Lane into the main street and saw a man with a wicker case of fruit, who immediately bowed and addressed him: "Teacher, my old friend, how have you been?"

Ji Gong stepped forward at once and took him by the hand. It was Zhao Bin, a young peddler who had been helped by Ji Gong several times and who in return had helped Ji Gong. "Come with me, my disciple," said the monk. "I have something to say to you."

Zhao Bin answered, "I have just been to the wholesale market today to buy fruit that I was going to peddle. What is it, Teacher?"

"Come with me to a wine shop for a cup of wine," Ji Gong said. Zhao Bin nodded his head. At the wine shop, Ji Gong ordered two pots of wine and then said, "Zhao Bin, there is a darkness in the space between your eyebrows and your color is poor. I will give you eight golden ingots if you will take them home, buy food, and rest for one hundred days until you are well. Then go back to business."

Zhao Bin thanked the saintly monk and paid for the wine. Then the two left the wine shop together. Ji Gong then hurried on to the prime minister's residence. When he reached the gate, a household person announced him and returned to say, "Prime Minister Qin invites you inside."

Inside, the monk saw the prime minister in the midst of questioning the robber. Ji Gong asked, "Is everything clear now after the great man's questioning?"

"Yes, it is all clear now," said Prime Minister Qin. "He is called Cloud Dragon Hua. He stole my jade pendants and the phoenix coronet and sold them to some unknown person. My two great treasure are simply lost!"

Ji Gong looked at the outlaw and said, "A robber named Cloud Dragon! You should be ashamed of yourself. A person like you, without even a name of your own! You say your name is Hua. Well, that is indeed a rich name."

The outlaw rolled his eyes upward towards Ji Gong and said, "Monk, you are truly my match as an enemy. I was thinking that if I used the name of Brother Hua it would close the case, since I would die anyway for my crimes. I never imagined that a monk would recognize me."

The prime minister asked, "What is the meaning of this? What is your surname and what are you called? Explain!"

"My name is Wang Tong," said the robber. "I am truly from Four Rivers, and my home was in the capital. My younger brother at home was a book publisher. Because he failed to pay a note for two hundred ounces of silver, he was thrown into prison by a dishonest, venal official and died there. At that time I was roaming around away from home and only learned what had happened when I returned. When I found out how my younger brother had died, I decided to take vengeance upon the grasping magistrate, Yang Zaitian. I was surprised to find that the magistrate had returned home to mourn his late mother. This is why I came to Linan.

"I met Cloud Dragon here in a wine shop. He was also from Four Rivers and we had been friends in the Greenwood. After we two met, we stayed in the home of Liu Chang. Walking on City God Hill, we saw a young woman who had cut off her hair and was taking it to a nunnery, wishing to become a nun. Cloud Dragon desired her at first sight. That night he went to the Bird and Bamboo Nunnery, intending to pluck the flower of her virtue. Unexpectedly, he failed to seduce the young lady and so he killed her after wounding the old nun. When he returned to the house and told me what he had done, I warned him that he had made a mistake.

"The next day we two went to the Qin Hill Restaurant to drink wine. Because of an argument, he killed the ruffian Qin Lo with one chop of his sword. Then I went with him to a wine shop to drink. I advised him that he could not behave in this wild manner without being arrested. Was he not concerned about losing his own life, I asked. He said that my gall was too small and therefore I lacked courage. He wanted to do something that would shock heaven and earth. He even wanted to kill the prime minister. Again I urged him not to do such a thing.

"During the night, we two came to the prime minister's estate. Inside he stole the curiously carved white-jade pendants, thirteen other jewels, and the phoenix coronet. He also wrote the verses on the wall. All of those things he did by himself, alone."

As he spoke, a secretary wrote down the outlaw's confession. After the secretary had finished, he gave it to the prime minister to read. Prime Minister Qin looked it over and for the first time understood everything clearly.

"Wang Tong," he asked, "where is Cloud Dragon Hua now? You must know. If you speak the truth, I will treat you lightly. If you do not speak the truth, you will be beaten severely."

"The great man need not become angry," answered Wang Tong. "Until recently I stayed together with Cloud Dragon in the same place, but we did not sleep in an inn. Sometimes we hid in the flower garden of the house of some wealthy man. We heard yesterday afternoon that Liu Chang had confessed to a crime, so Cloud Dragon no longer dared to stay in Linan. We talked it over and came to a decision. He was to go to the Happy and Comfortable Inn in the Thousand Family Village and wait for me there, not leaving until he saw me. I was to meet him there and together we would go back to Four Rivers."

Prime Minister Qin heard and understood. Then he asked Ji Gong, "How should this business be handled?"

Ji Gong replied, "The Great One should send people to take him."

"But how can the people I have under me catch such a robber as this?" the prime minister asked. "Please, Teacher, manifest your kindness and wisdom once more."

Ji Gong said, "I can go and catch him. If we succeed, we will get the reward, and if we fail, we may be punished. The Great One should give two hundred ounces of silver to Chai Yuanlo and She Jengying as traveling expenses. If the two succeed in this business of catching the criminal, give them two hundred more ounces of silver for their work. The Great One should also prepare a warrant saying that I am taking these two men to catch the robber. But first send Wang Tong in fetters to the Qiantang yamen to be locked up. Do not misuse him, but when Cloud Dragon Hua is captured, have the two brought into the hall of justice to be tried at the same time."

Prime Minister Qin agreed. "That is well." He immediately ordered the Protector to return to his yamen and prepare a warrant, and then the prime minister wrote a few words with his own hand.

The monk then spoke to the two headmen. "Headman Chai and Headman She, you will be going with the monk to work on this case, but do not wear your official uniforms. Change into something like the clothes country people wear outside the city. We must be able to deceive the eye."

The two headmen nodded in agreement and went back with the Protector to the yamen. There, the Protector completed the warrant while headmen Chai and She purchased two suits of silvery gray-white clothing. They also bought gowns with square-cut, apronlike panels front and back; rather long jackets all in the same color, fastened with bone buttons, and two pairs of shoes to match the clothing. When they had changed, they packed their uniforms into bags. Then, bringing the warrant with them, they returned to the prime minister's residence.

While Ji Gong finished eating breakfast, he talked with the two headmen about his plans. Prime Minister Qin said, "Teacher, when you get to the Thousand Family Village, if you capture this outlaw, you will not only get the reward of twelve hundred ounces of silver but it will be a very happy thing indeed."

Ji Gong left through the gate with the two headmen. The peach trees were red in bloom, the willow trees were green, and the weather was fine—in the fields the grass had a fresh color. Ji Gong began to sing:

> Suffering and sighing men will ask when they may leave
>   this dusty world.

Do your work with cheerful grace; in all things be tolerant;
Throw away vexatious cares and send old hatreds far away.
Gentlemen, let's think a bit about which of the faiths has
    the greatest age.
Heroes upon whom our state depends journeying over
    the desolate plain
A thousand years of careless sin, you may atone yet if
    you choose.
If your load may seem too great, do a good deed now
    and then.
It will lighten your load, though still bound by
    karma's chains.

After the monk had finished his mountain song, he suddenly exclaimed: "Quick, you two headmen, hurry! Cloud Dragon Hua is about to hang himself there in that wood just ahead. If he dies, we cannot take him in to claim our reward."

The two men, Chai and She, responded and fairly made their bodies fly, dashing on five or six *li* very quickly. Ahead, they saw a man just in the act of hanging himself. Chai Yuanlo said, "This is terrible. If the robber hangs himself, we will lose the twelve hundred ounces of silver and it will do no good to ask for it."

As they entered the woods, they saw the man was already hanging. Chai Yuanlo ran forward and grasped the man by his legs, lifting him into the air.

CHAPTER 37

Juan Yoting sleeps at the roadside;
Ji Gong waits in the inn

AS Chai Yuanlo lifted the hanging man, She Jengying came just after and said: "Elder Brother, you have caught Cloud Dragon Hua."

Chai Yuanlo lifted the man's head, and looking at him, said, "This is Cloud Dragon Hua's grandfather!"

"What!" exclaimed She Jengying. "How is that?"

"Look," replied Chai Yuanlo, "the hair of this man is all white. At his age he would be no flower plucker, but he might be the flower plucker's father."

The two supported the old man and unfastened the rope from around his neck. One beat him around the waist, while the other called out, "Wake up, old man!"

After some time the old man slowly began to breathe, his eyes opened, and he looked around. Suddenly, he broke into a rage, shouting, "Two little juniors! You stopped along the way to do something that was none of your business."

Headman Chai waited until the old man had stopped cursing them and then replied, "You really are not being reasonable, old man. If we two were hanging ourselves and you saw us, would you not have done something? Who would not try to save another person from dying? Don't think that we are ordinary people because we are wearing these clothes. We are in fact officials from the Grand Protector's yamen, and it is our business to see that wrongs are righted. Why should a person as old as you want to do this? Was it because of money? Was it because someone was mistreating you? Tell us the details. As to whether your two rescuers should have rescued you or not, we are not concerned. I ask you to tell us the truth about the whole matter."

The old man drew a deep, sighing breath and said, "Just now I was somewhat excited and I wronged you very much, but there was no other reason why I should have cursed you. I think that if I were to tell you the details of my affairs, it would not be something that concerned you. In any case, I must die. You are only forcing me do it another time."

Headman Chai said, "You must tell us why you are seeking death. Perhaps we two can help you, and perhaps not. You can see that our clothes are those of country gentlemen—but I am not boasting when I say that there is not very much about which we may not concern ourselves."

"Then since you ask," said the old man, "please sit down, the two of you, and I will explain. I am from Ruhua Village in the Fuxing district. My name is Juan and I am called Yoting. The head of our household is named Feng and called Wentai. He was formerly a county magistrate in one of the Anwei river counties. He was an honest official who was above suspicion and who treated the people like his children. He became ill while he was still in office, and without his salary he became penniless before he died. I returned to our native village with his wife, son, and daughter, together with his corpse in a coffin.

"The daughter was promised in marriage to the son of an official in Linan City. His mother was related to a member of a powerful official named Chu in the department of civil personnel. The late magistrate's widow wanted to meet her daughter-in-law with proper ceremony, but she lacked the money to purchase the bride's trousseau to accompany her daughter. She told me to go to the official residence at Suhang, where her maternal uncle was an official, and ask him to lend her two hundred ounces of silver so that she could take her daughter to be married.

"When I reached there and saw her uncle, he became very angry upon hearing that the magistrate had died. 'Why,' he asked, 'had the granddaughter not been sent to me instead of her being a burden to the poor widow in these bitter days?' The uncle then gave me six hundred ounces of silver: five hundred to pay for the trousseau and escorting the bride; and one hundred to pay for the expenses of my journey. Thinking of my own age and weakness, I feared that the six hundred ounces would be too heavy for me to carry, and so I exchanged the silver for twelve gold ingots and sewed them into a strip of cloth that I could wear fastened around my waist. As I traveled, I found that the days were hot but that the nights were cool. When I reached these woods, I had a stomachache so painful that I could not go on.

"Just at that time, a man of about twenty years old came by, carrying a length of rope in his hand. He asked me why I was sitting there under the tree and I told him it was because my stomach ached and was very painful. He gave me two pills to relieve the pain. I felt some sort of movement as I went to sleep. Afterward I awoke and looked around. There was no sign of the man. The rope lay on the ground and the strip of cloth with the twelve gold ingots that I had around my waist was gone.

"Now think, you two gentlemen, if I returned and saw the lady of our household, how would I be treated? She was already very disturbed because she had no money for her daughter's marriage. If I went back to the uncle and told him what had happened, he would not believe me. I thought about first one and then the other. There was no door in front and no road behind but, if I died, I would not have to worry about it all. Even though you two had good intentions in saving me, I still will have to die. It is just dying a second time."

When the two headmen, Chai and She, heard this story, they realized that this was one of Ji Gong's clever tricks. "He has tricked us into rescuing this man, and where is Cloud Dragon Hua?" Chai thought. "Why should we not hand the problem over to Ji Gong?" Then he said aloud, "Having heard your story, I still say that you should not die. In a moment a poor monk will come along from the south. Stop him and ask for the silver you need. If he will not give you any silver, do not let him go. He will think of some way out for you."

Just as Chai Yuanlo was speaking, a poor monk came in sight from the north strolling along in a slightly crooked and confused way. It was Ji Gong. As he walked, he was half saying and half singing to himself: "You say I am simply mad. There are those who have studied the mad Ji disease, but they had to give the poor monk a pot of wine."

"Teacher," said Chai Yuanlo, "you must come here quickly."

Juan Yoting was looking at this poor monk with his clothing in tatters as he came to them and asked, "Who is this, you two?"

Chai and She then told him the whole story. The monk asked them, "Did you say you have six hundred ounces of silver?"

"No!" replied Chai and She.

"If you do not have six hundred ounces of silver," asked the monk, "how are you going to help this man? Is this not a waste of time? How much silver do you two have?"

"We have only these two hundred ounces of silver," answered Chai and She. "We have nothing else anywhere."

Juan Yoting listened to the three men talking and said to himself: "I lost the silver. Why should I trouble them about it?" Then he said to them, "You three need not concern yourselves about this."

"How can we not be concerned?" asked the monk. "I have heard these two explain and now I understand. Come, I will help you to hang yourself."

"Teacher," Chai Yuanlo exclaimed, "What kind of talk is this? You told us to come and save him. How can you not care about this now? You must think of a way to help him!"

The monk said, "Well, if that is the way things are, Juan Yoting, you should come with us. When we approach the Thousand Family Village, you will see a man who will call out to us. That is your fortune."

"So be it," responded Juan Yoting.

The three men with Ji Gong walked on out of the woods, straight toward the Thousand Family Village. When there were still about four or five *li* to go, the monk walked on ahead, singing:

> Though I may seem strange to you,
> You do not seem strange to me.
> I am like the rest of you,
> I am bound by karma's chains.
>
> Though my chains may seem more light,
> I know every link by name.
> If I'm mad, perhaps I am
> Driven mad by karma's chains.
>
> Fortune smiles or fortune frowns.
> If the bargaining goes wrong
> And you sell yourself as well,
> Then you add to karma's chains.
>
> If your burden seems too great,
> Do a good deed now and then.
> You will find your burden light
> Though still bound by karma's chains.
>
> *Lohans* high in heaven above,
> Each one must come back to earth.
> If they must be born again,
> They are bound by karma's chains.
>
> Dragons rolling in the clouds,
> Monsters in the foaming sea,
> Every creature that exists
> Still is bound by karma's chains.

As he sang, the monk walked steadily onward, until suddenly, from the edge of the Thousand Family Village, a man shouted in a loud voice: "Saintly senior monk! You have come! I have been searching for you, as a thirsty man in a desert searches for a spring."

Slightly behind the man followed another. The two ran to Ji Gong and fell on their knees before him. As soon as the two headmen saw them, they recognized them. The one who had been ahead was tall, with three widely spaced markings on his shoulders. On his head he wore a red turban of fine silk, with a rosette made of a ribbon with five colors to indicate his rank. His jacket was marked with the broad arrowheads of the travelers' guards. His face was white as snow, with fine narrow eyebrows and large eyes. His cheeks and forehead were lined by exposure to the weather.

The one who had followed wore a blue embroidered head kerchief and a blue embroidered jacket with a stiff leather belt. His skin was light golden in color. His heavy eyebrows hung over open and alert eyes, and from his chin hung three strands of a beard. This was Chen Xiao, nicknamed "the Man with the Beautiful Whiskers." The first one was Yang Meng, nicknamed "the Pale Spirit." The two were officers in the travelers' guards.

They had been journeying toward Chuzhou prefecture. The man who had hired them, Wang Jong, was staying at the Happy and Comfortable Inn when he developed a severe case of dysentery. They immediately requested that a doctor see him. The doctor gave him medicine. There were many foods that he could not eat. Day by day his condition grew worse. He lay in bed weeping while remembering his old father and mother, who were themselves ill. He had no relatives with him and he had thirty thousand ounces of silver in his possession. He feared that if he lost his appetite completely and could no longer take nourishment, he would die and be like the ghost of a wrongfully executed man haunting a village, or the lonely spirit of an orphan in a strange land.

Yang Meng and Chen Xiao were honest, kind people. Seeing the man so severely ill and knowing that he was concerned about his parents, the two wanted to find someone to cure his illness as quickly as possible. But there were no skilled doctors in the Thousand Family Village. The two went to the Monastery of the Soul's Retreat to ask about Ji Gong, but when they inquired at the temple, they heard that he was not there. Asking further, they heard that Ji Gong had been requested to go to Pishan prefecture. There was nothing more that they could do except to leave a message at the temple and return.

They waited for two days with no sign of Ji Gong, and were becoming discouraged. That day they went out for a walk and suddenly heard the voice of Ji Gong. Yang Meng let out a great shout and the two ran forward to greet him.

"Where did you two come from?" asked the monk.

Chen Xiao then told about the young man who was ill in the inn and about how they had gone to look for Ji Gong at the temple. "We could not find you and we could not leave again. We beg you, Teacher, demonstrate your kindness."

Ji Gong nodded his head and said, "Please, you two, stand up!"

Headmen Chai and She also recognized them and Chai asked, "Where did you two officers come from?"

At this point, Chen Xiao noticed the two headmen and burst out laughing. "Why are you dressed like that?' he asked.

"We have come out secretly to solve a case," replied Headman Chai.

They all entered the village with Ji Gong. The street ran from north to south, and on the east and west sides of the street were shops and other places of business. On the west side there was a restaurant. The monk stopped and would go no further. There were four different ideas among members of the party. Headman Chai and Headman She wanted to solve the case and arrest Cloud Dragon Hua. Juan Yoting wanted to cry out, "Do not ask these two men for my lost six hundred ounces of silver." The two armed travelers' guards were thinking that they would like Ji Gong to cure their employer, Wang Jong, as soon as possible. But the monk was looking toward the restaurant and thinking about drinking wine. He said, "Now, everyone, we will go in and drink a little wine." Although the rest were unwilling, at the same time they found it difficult to refuse.

Together the five men with the monk all went into the restaurant. Ji Gong observed that it was a two-story establishment. His heart leaped, and he said, "If we are to catch Cloud Dragon Hua, we must wait for him here."

CHAPTER 38

Ji Gong finds a private room;
Cloud Dragon Hua meets an opponent

AS Ji Gong entered the wine shop, the manager noticed that Ji Gong's clothing was that of a very poor monk and did not welcome him with a greeting. Yang Meng, Chen Xiao, and the rest of the five went in, and the manager quickly came forward and said, "Come in, gentlemen, and be seated."

Ji Gong stood outside and said, "Manager, I am also here."

The manager said, "Monk, you are welcome. Please come in and sit down," and so the six went in.

When they reached the rear hall, a waiter came over to them and said, "You six men go upstairs. That is still part of the same establishment."

"Do you have private rooms?" the monk asked.

The waiter answered, "We only have one private room. Just now three gentlemen entered it and called for food and wine. You six go upstairs."

The monk did not go upstairs, but said, "I will not go upstairs. How will it be if I go into the private room and make those three go out?"

"You cannot do that," said the waiter.

When the monk pulled aside the curtain and stepped inside the private room, he saw three men drinking together. They were newly sworn brothers, and the eldest had invited the two younger brothers for drinks. They were in the midst of a private talk when they saw a monk enter who said, "You three drinking here—the wine will be at my expense, and please order several kinds of dishes."

Two of the men stood up. The elder brother supposed that the monk was a friend of the other two, and the two newly sworn thought that the elder brother knew him. All together the three said, "The monk need not pay the check. Have some food and wine with us."

The monk said, "Please, please, go ahead," and backed out of the room.

The elder brother asked, "What temple does the monk come from, my two brothers?"

The two replied, "We do not know. Is he not our elder brother's friend?"

"No, he is not," the elder brother answered. They all laughed and sat down to drink again. But as they sat down, they all immediately stood up with an exclamation.

The elder brother said, "Just as I sat down, something pierced my backside."

The others said, "Quickly, call the waiter and we will change to a table outside."

When the waiter had moved them to another place and Ji Gong saw the three men come out, the others went in. Once they were seated they ordered food and wine. After they had drunk several of the small cups, they heard someone speaking with a rather musical voice. The words were clearly and quite loudly spoken, but they did not convey any meaning.

"Reasonable and sincere, gnaw scatter cave. Reasonable and sincere, cave seek monkey." When the person speaking had finished, three robbers entered the wine shop.

Now among these three was Cloud Dragon Hua. When he had parted from Wang Tong and left Linan City, they had agreed to meet at the Happy and Comfortable Inn. Cloud Dragon Hua said that he would not leave until they saw each other. While he was at the Happy and Comfortable Inn, everyone thought that he was one of the many travelers' armed escorts. During those days he had stayed in one of the best rooms in an inner courtyard. But on the evening before, his spirit had begun to feel uneasy, as if someone had seized him by the hair or was catching hold of his flesh. He called a servant of the inn and asked to have his bill prepared, saying, "I am going to leave now. If a Four Rivers man named Wang Tong comes to find me, tell him I have already left and will meet him at his home." The servant said he would, and Cloud Dragon Hua went out through the inn gate. It was then in the middle of the first watch. He walked outside the village. There was a bright, unclouded moon and the sky was filled with stars.

When he had walked about five or six *li*, he came to a grove of trees, and from among them a man leaped out saying:

> From the very time that I was born,
> I was a stupid lad.
> I loved to learn of knives and clubs
> But was not inclined toward books.

I roamed and grew wise
In the ways of the world
Not harming the little folk.

Where the ripples and waves
Of the rivers and lakes
Meet their borders of rushes and grass,

Whenever I meet with
Another good fellow,
I beg for his good will.

But greedy officials
And other such men
I make it a point to kill.

How can the emperor's laws apply
To this little inch I occupy?

When he had finished these sentences, he drew his sword and said, "Ha! He who approaches on the road will now put down his passage money in gold or silver if you are not prepared to die!"

Cloud Dragon Hua replied, "You are the Reasonable One."

His opponent laughed and said, "Ha ha! I am called many names. I am also called the Helpful One."

Cloud Dragon Hua queried, "Are you not one of the Greenwood fellows called Reasonable?"

The man said, "I do not understand," and, as he spoke, he advanced with a sword, making several thrusts as if to kill the other.

Cloud Dragon Hua noticed the man's height, the kingfisher blue turban and scarf hiding a part of his bluish face, his sandy hair, and his closely clipped red beard. There was an odor of wine about him and his face was as ugly as that of the statue of the god of pestilence. Altogether he looked ferocious and savage.

Cloud Dragon Hua was not aware that the man had returned his sword to his scabbard until he said, "Why, it is Brother Hua. Where did you come from, and why are you out upon the road in the night?"

Cloud Dragon Hua looking at him closely said, "So it has been Brother Lei all along! Words can hardly express my pleasure." Cloud Dragon then told the whole story of what had taken place when he left Jiangsi and went to Linan. However, he did not mention the matter of how he had tried to pluck the flower at the nunnery and what happened there.

Now the man who had approached Cloud Dragon Hua in the woods was called Lei Ming. He originally came from the walled Dragon Well Village in the Tanyang district. He was a close friend of Chen Liang, one of the heroes of the Greenwood who had recently hoped to become a novice instructed by Ji Gong. The two, Lei Ming and Chen Liang, had parted company more than a year earlier without having seen each other since. Lei Ming had gone to the Chen family village looking for Chen Liang a short time earlier. The family had told him that Chen Liang had gone to the capital, Linan. Lei Ming became worried about Chen Liang and decided to go to Linan to find him. He was about halfway there when he saw a man in dark clothing approaching and he purposely leaped out of the woods to surprise him. When the two recognized each other, they politely exchanged greetings.

"Lei Ming," Cloud Dragon Hua asked, "did you compose those lines that you spoke just now by yourself?"

"No," answered Lei Ming. "They were composed by our elder brother, Yang Ming. Brother Hua, when you were in Linan did you see Chen Liang? I was just going there to look for him."

"I did not get to see Chen Liang," said Hua Yun Long, "but, if I may say, you should not go to Linan. Since I killed a man in the Qin Hill Restaurant and stole the pearl coronet from the residence of Prime Minister Qin, if you go there, I am afraid that someone would notice you and arrest you. That would be very inconvenient."

Lei Ming said, "Don't worry. Nothing will happen to me when I get to Linan, and in case I lose my way I ask you, Elder Brother, to do one more thing. Go with me to Linan. We will look for him for one month. Then I will go back to Jiangsi with you without further delay."

Cloud Dragon was not a person unprepared for a challenge. When he heard Lei Ming's proposal, he was excited and said, "Well, so we will! Brother Lei, we will go together!"

The two walked on for a short distance talking until they saw someone coming toward them. They blocked the road, and then they saw it was none other than the White Monkey, Chen Liang himself.

Now at the time that Ji Gong had boiled the water in the monastery kitchen and had been about to shave Chen Liang's head with the big vegetable chopping knife, Chen Liang had become frightened and run away. Afterward, he had found a quiet inn and stayed there. He had learned about all the things that Cloud Dragon Hua had done: the capture of the Chicken Thief, Liu Chang, and the fact that Ji Gong had been dispatched to solve the case. Chen Liang was looking for Hua with a message urging him to leave the province. Chen Liang did not expect to meet Lei Ming and Cloud Dragon Hua on the road at all, let alone together.

The three greeted each other and sat down where they were on the ground, exchanging their stories until it grew light. Chen Liang said, "Why not go on to the Thousand Family Village to refresh ourselves, eat something, and discuss our plans, and then go on?"

Cloud Dragon Hua nodded. "The three of us can go to the Thousand Family Village, bathe, eat some pastries, and drink tea."

When it was just about noon, the three decided to drink some wine and went to the Meeting Heroes Inn. Cloud Dragon Hua said, "Brother Lei and Brother Chen, be careful and watch out for any monkey catchers," using the outlaw language of the river and marshes. Ji Gong heard him speak but did not come out of the private room. Upstairs, the three saw that the place was clean and ordered several kinds of dishes with hot wine, saying, "Just let it be good and don't worry about the price."

Immediately, the waiter went down to tell the manager, and in a short time food and drink were prepared. The three enjoyed themselves eating and drinking. There seemed to be just the right amount of wine and conversation.

Lei Ming remarked to Cloud Dragon Hua, "There is no need to go if there are no detectives from Linan. That is the end of it. If they come, I will recognize them. If one comes, I will take care of him; if two come, I will take care of the pair of them."

Chen Liang heard this and said, "Second brother, do not be careless. Even now Senior Monk Ji Gong with two detectives is coming to take Hua Yun Long. That Ji Gong's supernatural powers exceed anything known before."

Lei Ming laughed loudly at this. "You may be afraid of a monk, old Chen, but I am not afraid of any monk. As to whether those three people can take Cloud Dragon Hua, I am not boasting when I say that two hundred officers and men could not take him."

"Brother," said Chen Liang, "you do not understand. I will tell you. That Ji Gong's powers of understanding and his invisible arts are beyond normal limits. If he points with his hand, no one can move."

Lei Ming pounded on the table with his hand and cried out, "Old Chen, you are killing me! Let's not get excited. If this monk does not come, that is the end of it. If he comes, I will kill him. If he does not come, I will go the Monastery of the Soul's Retreat and find him and kill him. That will end what I feel about him."

Chen Liang replied, "The sooner you stop talking like this, the better. Do not talk as if this is nothing. Even while you are speaking, Ji Gong may decide to come looking for you, and if he comes, we cannot escape."

"Drink your wine, my two friends," said Cloud Dragon Hua. "Even though we are alone up here, if anyone heard you, it would be inconvenient. We must be careful when we talk."

"Brother Hua," Lei Ming said, "Brother Chen is afraid of monks and their invisible arts. I am not afraid of monks."

Just as he said this, someone downstairs let out an exclamation and said: "Well my good robbers, I am the monk that came to take Cloud Dragon Hua, but today I will take all of you. Not one of you will escape!"

Now the monk had been in the private room sitting with Yang Meng and Chen Xiao, together with the two headmen and Juan Yoting. Just as they were eating and drinking, they heard a voice speaking in the black language of the Greenwood. The monk knew that the person speaking was Cloud Dragon Hua, the man they were looking for. The monk then left the private room saying to Yang Meng and the rest, "I am going out to the convenience." When he reached the foot of the stairs, he heard Lei Ming's boast. The monk answered and started up the stairs to catch the Robber Rat of the Universe, Cloud Dragon Hua.

CHAPTER 39

Ji Gong introduces two followers;
Lei Ming brings wine to the forest

AT the time when Ji Gong answered from downstairs, Cloud Dragon was like a person haunted by some experience from his past. His courage humbled, he leaped from a window and escaped. When Chen Liang heard, he said, "You see how it is, brother. I told you not to talk. You see, he has come."

Lei Ming seized his sword and hurried to the door at the top of the stairs. Looking down, he saw the monk in his unsuitable ragged and torn garments, with two inches of hair on his unshaven head and his face oily and dusty. Lei Ming raised his sword, thinking that when the monk came up the stairs, he would cleave the monk's head from his shoulders. Ji Gong had raised his head and as he saw Lei Ming, the monk pointed and recited the six true words, "Om Ma Ni Pad Me Hum." With his hypnotic powers, the monk stopped Lei Ming so that he was motionless. Ji Gong then came up the stairs, passing by the side of Lei Ming.

When Chen Liang saw him, he asked, "Teacher, how have you been?"

The monk inquired, "Liang, my child, are you well?"

Chen Liang replied, "Your disciple has waited a long time. Come and have a drink of wine, Teacher."

The monk came to him and sat down. Chen Liang poured him a cup of wine—the monk picked it up and drank. Chen Liang came closer and said, "Teacher, manifest your mercy and loosen your power. If someone sees, how will it be?" The monk nodded.

Just as this was happening, they heard sounds from downstairs. "Aiee yah! Gu lo lo. Hwaaa! La! La! Yang dong! Yang dong!" It was the waiter bringing the tray with the dishes. He had been thinking, "Those three gentlemen upstairs are men of wealth and influence. If I serve them well, I will get a large tip." Just as he started up the stairs carrying the tray, he lifted his head to look and saw the man with the blue face and red hair holding a sword high in the air as if he wanted to kill him. As the waiter took fright, his arms and legs grew weak. The tray fell and he turned and made his way uncertainly downstairs.

Upstairs, Chen Liang heard and again begged Ji Gong to loosen his power: "Teacher, quickly remove your hypnotic spell. Do not let people see this. It is not proper."

Accordingly, the monk released Lei Ming, who came and sat down at the table as if nothing had happened. Inwardly Lei Ming was shocked and frightened. "Don't worry, Teacher," said Chen Liang. "My brother is a coarse, unrefined person, but he would not dare to do anything improper to our teacher."

The monk said, "I know that also."

While they were speaking, the waiter came upstairs, and going to Lei Ming, said, "Oh sir, I have wronged you. When I saw you with the sword, I was frightened. I dropped the tray and ruined the food."

"Never mind," Lei Ming said. "In a little while I will come down and pay for it anyway, so that you will not lose anything. It was because I thought I heard an enemy of mine speaking below that I drew my sword and started downstairs. I did not hate you. Just let us keep this between ourselves."

Looking again at the monk, Lei Ming saw that he seemed to be only paying attention to Chen Liang as they talked and did not look over his way. Without warning, he again drew his sword and came at the monk as if he were about to kill him. The monk pointed and again stopped Lei Ming so that he was motionless. The monk then slapped the table and laughed loudly. "My good robber, you really want to kill the monk!" Then he called downstairs. "Will the two headmen come quickly and take the robber? There is a robber upstairs."

Below, in the private dining room, everyone heard. Chai Yuanlo and She Jenying said, "You two travelers' guards can assist us. There is a robber upstairs."

The two headmen took their iron-tipped staves and dashed out of the room toward the stairs. Chen Xiao had no sword, only an axe handle with an iron socket into which an axe could be fitted. Yang Meng was also without a sword, but looking around as he came out, he saw a length of water pipe that the manager was holding. Yang Meng seized it from him and rushed to the stairs. Other guests had crowded around the foot of the stairs in a disorderly fashion. When the two headmen came upstairs with Chen Xiao and Yang Meng, they saw the monk sitting down between a handsome, refined-looking young man and another man with a bluish face, red hair, and staring eyes, who was holding a sword. The waiter stood beside them. Otherwise there was no one else.

Headman Chai asked, "Holy monk, where is the robber?"

The monk replied, "As soon as I called, the robber fled. These are my two followers. Let me introduce them to you." Pointing toward Chen Liang, he said, "This is my son Liang."

Headman Chai politely said, "Master Liang."

Chen Liang said, "My surname is Chen."

Headman Chai corrected himself, "Oh, then it is Master Chen Liang."

The monk then pointed to Lei Ming, saying, "This is also my follower, my son Ming."

At this time Lei Ming was also able to move, but his heart was pounding. The two headmen approached him and said, "Master Ming."

Lei Ming said, "My surname is Lei."

"Ah, Master Lei Ming," the two headmen said.

The monk then introduced the two headmen by name and told them, "You four men may now go down and wait for me in the private room." There was nothing else the four could do.

As they came down, the manager took Yang Meng aside, saying, "I did not provoke you, sir, but when you took that pipe away from me with your flying somersault, you knocked my tooth out."

Chen Xiao immediately apologized on his friend's behalf with a great many words, then the four went into the private dining room and sat down.

When Lei Ming saw the four men go back downstairs, he replaced his sword in his scabbard, thinking, "This monk is hard to provoke. I will never manage it openly. I must think of some secret plan to take his life." Then he stood up and started downstairs. Below, he asked the waiter: "How much is our bill? Include the food and wine for the private room and add in the dishes you broke. How much will it be altogether?"

The waiter went to the office and added up the bill. Lei Ming took out some silver and paid. Then he requested a bottle of wine and asked the waiter to wrap up a pair of roast chickens, saying, "In a little while we will take them away with us."

Again the waiter went to the office. This time he asked for a bottle that he filled with wine. He wrapped up the roast chickens and gave them to Lei Ming as well. Lei Ming took out of his pocket a packet of the powder called Mongolian sweat and poured it into the wine.

Now Lei Ming had not prepared this Mongolian sweat drug. After he had left Zhenjiang prefecture and while he was on the road, he met a man named Liu Feng. Liu Feng had once been a servant to the men of the Greenwood, and he had served both Chen Liang and Lei Ming, but had been dismissed because he constantly gambled, bullied other servants, and acted as if he were a law unto himself. More than two years had passed since Lei Ming and Liu Feng had seen each other.

On this day when he met Lei Ming, Liu Feng was wearing fine new clothes and riding a horse. As soon as he saw Lei Ming, he got down from his horse and greeted Lei Ming respectfully. Lei Ming asked Liu Feng, "Where have you been all this time, and what have you been doing?"

"I have opened a thug's inn," replied Liu Feng. "When a solitary traveler with much baggage comes to us, I simply kill him. I have just been to the Compassionate Cloud Shrine and bought ten ounces of the Mongolian sweat powder." He explained that in Mongolia the drug was actually used in minute quantities to cause sweating and cure fever. A slightly larger dose could cause a long period of unconsciousness. More would cause death.

"And how many people could your ten ounces of Mongolian sweat powder kill?" asked Lei Ming.

"It is enough to kill a hundred men," answered Liu Feng.

"Take it out and let me look at it," said Lei Ming.

Liu Feng took out a small bag from his pocket and handed it to Lei Ming.

Lei Ming said, "Look! Someone is coming." As soon as Liu Feng turned his head, with one thrust of his knife Lei Ming finished him off. Then he took the corpse and disposed of it under the surface of a mountain stream. He then made off with the drug.

Lei Ming now took some of this drug and put it into the wine bottle. He then immediately went upstairs and said to Ji Gong, "Teacher, I think you could teach me something that is not clear to me, but there are now too many people upstairs for us to talk conveniently. Could the teacher come with us to a place where there are no people about so that we could talk in detail?"

Chen Liang called for someone to come and add up the bill, but Ji Gong said, "Never mind. Someone has already paid. Let us go."

The three went downstairs and the monk said to Lei Ming, "After you get those things, we will leave."

Lei Ming agreed, and carrying the wine bottle and the roasted chickens, they left the restaurant. They walked straight north until they arrived at a place about one or two *li* outside the entrance to the village. Ahead was a grove of pine trees with a clearing, in the center of which there was a stone table. As the three reached the table, Lei Ming put down the bottle and said, "I asked you here to instruct me, sir, and for no other reason. I would like to ask you about one thing. You are a monk who has left the world and you do not need to concern yourself with the world's business. Although it is said that Cloud Dragon Hua is an outlaw and that he stole from the prime minister's residence, still he did not go to your temple and take any of the hangings or the five vessels from the surrounding altars. Then why must you concern yourself with him, Teacher?'

Ji Gong replied, "You have not put it correctly. Speaking as a monk, if he had not gone into a Buddhist temple, then I would not be coming to take him—if he had not gone into one of our temples and done the most unendurable things."

Chen Liang said, "Teacher, he has not really gone into one of your temples."

The monk answered, "Not into one of my temples, but he has gone into a nunnery and destroyed the peace of a quiet Buddhist place—therefore I will take him."

"You need not mention those idle tales, teacher," said Lei Ming. "There is some wine here among the things I have prepared. Won't you just have a drink?"

The monk picked up the bottle and set it down again. Lei Ming unwrapped the roasted chicken, saying, "Please, Teacher, eat something."

Ji Gong said, "I cannot drink this wine. If the host will not eat, the guest will not drink. Chen Liang, you drink first."

Chen Liang picked up the bottle and was about to drink. Lei Ming reached out and snatched it away. "That was prepared for our teacher—don't be greedy," he said.

Chen Liang did not understand the reason why, but he said, "Then drink, Teacher."

Ji Gong lifted up the bottle and said, "Chen Liang, you are my follower. I am your teacher. Teacher and follower are like father and son. If someone killed me, what would you do?"

"I would avenge you," answered Chen Liang.

The monk asked, "Is what you said true?"

"Of course!" said Chen Liang.

The monk went on speaking until Chen Liang said, "Teacher goes on about his worries too much. Do not worry. If anyone were to injure you, of course I would avenge you."

"So you would," said Ji Gong. He picked up the wine bottle and waved it back and forth as if toasting the other two. He then took a dozen or so swallows, and turning about, fell to the ground.

Lei Ming laughed a great laugh.

CHAPTER 40

Lei Ming hears his victim's voice;
an innkeeper waits at the inn gate

LOOKING at Ji Gong as he lay senseless on the ground from drinking the drugged wine, Lei Ming was laughing as he said, "Monk, I thought that you were a living spirit who knew about things that had not yet happened. Yet I have quickly brought you under control."

"What kind of thing is this, Second Brother?" asked Chen Liang.

"Third Brother," replied Lei Ming, "it is because I have paralyzed him with the Mongolian sweat drug that I put into the wine. Now I will tie him up and place him beside the road. When he wakes up, I will insult and shame him and see what he says to me."

Hearing this, Chen Liang said, "You are wrong. He is my teacher. You should not do this."

Lei Ming did not answer, but picked up the monk and simply started walking toward the east. Chen Liang naturally thought that Lei Ming was taking the monk to place him at the roadside. Could Chen Liang have imagined that when Lei Ming arrived at the east bank of the mountain torrent, he would cast the monk down into the rushing water, turn, and walk rapidly to the west?

Chen Liang, who had been following and trying to keep up with Lei Ming, saw him throw the monk into the water. Chen Liang was shocked by Lei Ming's action, but then he saw the monk rise out of the water and fall halfway back. The monk's teeth were chattering loudly. Frightened by the sight and sound, Chen Liang fled. To Lei Ming he said, "Second Brother, you are wrong to do this. Your mischief will make trouble for us. Ji Gong is in touch with all the spirits and his arts are unlimited. Do you want to suffer retribution?"

"Don't talk nonsense, Third Brother," Lei Ming replied. "I paralyzed him with the Mongolian sweat powder."

They were just approaching a small hill. When they started to climb it, they heard a mournful voice saying, "I did wrongfully! They told me not to approach the King of Hell, but to see the Dragon King of the Four

Seas. The Dragon King was not at home. The night river patrol said that I was too dirty and threw me out. The big temples would not take me and the little temple would not let me stay. It is miserable to be dead. I am just waiting for the man who killed me to come by. Then I will tear him apart and kill him. The wrong done to me binds us two together as opposites, like yang and yin."

Lei Ming and Chen Liang turned their heads and saw Ji Gong behind them. Frightened out of their wits, they turned and ran to the south. Behind them they could hear the monk following them. Left! Right! Left! Right! If they ran faster, the monk followed faster. If they went more slowly, the monk went more slowly.

After five or six *li* over somewhat firm ground, Lei Ming and Chen Liang found that they could hardly hear the sound of the straw sandals. Then Lei Ming said, "Third Brother, when we get under those trees ahead, let us stop and rest."

Just as they reached the trees, they heard the monk say, "Ah! Come, you two!"

When the two saw that it was Ji Gong ahead, they wheeled about in their fright and ran in the opposite direction, with the monk following. With great difficulty they felt that they were leaving him behind, but then they saw him. The monk was standing on top of the mound that they had left before. Sarcastically he said, "And you have just arrived!"

Lei Ming and Chen Liang turned about and ran in the other direction, thinking to themselves: "Strange! How did the monk get ahead of us?"

Again the two ran into the woods and the monk was there ahead of them, saying, "Just arrived."

Altogether they ran first one way and then the other six times. Then Lei Ming said, "Stop running over the same ground. Let's turn off and go to the southwest." And so they followed a road that went in a southwesterly direction. It was difficult to keep ahead of the sound of those straw sandals. Truly the two had run until they were quite weary.

Then they saw a grove of trees and Lei Ming said, "Let's climb up into one of those trees, Third Brother, and rest awhile out of the way."

And so while Lei Ming was still speaking, they began to scramble up into a tree; but when they were halfway up the tree, they saw the monk already up in the tree and heard him talking to them. "I've been watching you running all over the place." He pointed at them and kept them motionless with his hypnotic spell as he climbed down. On the ground, he looked up at them. "You good for nothings! I will neither beat you nor curse you. I'll get some big grubs to come and bite you."

The monk recited a spell, and immediately the ground beneath the trees was covered with huge green grubs. The monk took off his hat and said, "I'll send these grubs away. Liang, my friend, you watch for me." Then he walked off to the east.

Now, back in the restaurant, the two headmen, together with Yang Meng, Chen Xiao, and Juan Yoting, had been waiting all this time in the private dining room without seeing Ji Gong come downstairs. At length, they all went upstairs to look for him, but there was no one there. "Waiter," called Headman Chai, "where did our monk go?"

"He left long ago," replied the waiter, "and the gentleman named Lei paid the bill for all of you that were there in the private room with the monk."

When he heard that, Headman Chai turned to Yang Meng and Chen Xiao and asked, "Would you two escort officers go with me to the Happy and Comfortable Inn to make an arrest?" Yang Meng and Chen Xiao nodded in agreement and said they would.

Together, the five including Juan Yoting left the restaurant and went straight on to the Happy and Comfortable Inn.

When they arrived at the gate, Headman Chai went to the office and inquired: "Greetings. Do you have a gentleman named Hua living here?"

"We did," said the manager, "but he left yesterday."

"Oh! Dreadful!" said Chai Yuanlo upon hearing this. "He just left."

"Never mind," said Chen Xiao. "Ji Gong's divine range of perceptions is very wide and his supernatural acts are limitless. To capture such an outlaw one needs more than ordinary powers to succeed. Why not come with us to the Heaven Rising Inn and look things over, then decide what to do?"

The two headmen had nothing else they could do, and so with Juan Yoting went on to the Heaven Rising Inn. There they saw the escort officers' guest, Wang Jong, lying in bed moaning and sighing unceasingly. Chen Xiao said to him, "You may expect great happiness!"

"Huh!" said Wang Jong. "I'm the most miserable of men, about to die and become a ghost! How could I ever be happy!"

"I am bringing the monk Ji Gong from the Monastery of the Soul's Retreat. His powers are very wide, particularly in medicine. In a short time he will be here."

By chance this conversation was overheard by one of the waiters. The proprietor of this inn had a bad back that was extremely painful. The waiter told the proprietor, "If you go and stand at the gate, in a little while you will see a monk. Kowtow to him and beg him to cure your illness. That is the *lohan* Ji Gong. His skill is very famous."

The proprietor naturally went to the gate and waited, hat in hand. As luck would have it, a monk came walking by. The proprietor got down on his hands and knees and knocked his forehead on the ground, saying, "Save me, holy monk." Then he looked up and saw that it was the second monk of the nearby temple. "Why am I kowtowing to you?" the proprietor exclaimed.

"I don't know why you're doing it," answered the second monk. "Why are you?"

"I was waiting for Ji Gong," said the proprietor.

The second monk walked off. In a little while a poor monk came along. As he came nearer he said, "Greetings! Is there an empty room in this inn? I will be staying at an inn."

The proprietor could see that this monk did not amount to much, and so he said, "Monk, this inn is one of the great inns!"

"But as I came walking up the road, I noticed that this inn of yours was smaller than the others," said the monk.

In his anger, the proprietor turned his back and pointedly ignored the ragged monk and would say no more to him. Unexpectedly the monk, without a word of warning, gave him a blow with his fist, knocking him to the ground. Several of the servants saw the blow and were about to attack the monk. But at that moment Yang Meng and Chen Xiao came out, crying, "A thousand! Ten thousand times do not hit the monk! Why should you?"

The proprietor was lying on the ground, moaning, "Ah ah, ah ah. That is a bad monk. He has killed me. Don't pay attention to those two guests. Hit him!"

"Indeed, do not hit him," said Chen Xiao. "Explain clearly what happened." The proprietor explained all that had gone before. "This monk is Ji Gong," said Chen Xiao.

"If he is really Ji Gong, just help me up and we will forget about what happened."

"Don't forget what happened," said the monk. "Your bad back is cured." Ji Gong pointed at him and said the six true words, "Om Ma Ni Pad Me Hum." Immediately all the proprietor's pain disappeared.

The proprietor and all the servants at the inn kowtowed to the monk and ushered him inside with a great welcoming shout.

In the great suite of the north building, Ji Gong was led into the chamber where the invalid lay motionless in bed. The sick man, Wang Jong, upon seeing Ji Gong enter, said, "Holy monk, my illness has taken a turn for the worse. I cannot greet you with proper ceremony. Be compassionate, holy monk, and take pity upon me."

"This will be easily managed," said the monk. He told the waiter to bring half a bowl of cold water and half a bowl of boiling water. The monk then broke a piece of medicine into small pieces, dropped them into the boiling water, and let it dissolve. Then he mixed the hot water with the cold water and gave it to the invalid to drink.

Before long, the blood began to flow normally through the young man's arms and legs and the color returned to his cheeks. In the outer room of the suite Ji Gong sat down to rest. Juan Yoting and the escorts who were with the young man came and sat beside Ji Gong. Taking a number of gold coins, Chen Xiao attempted to slip them quietly into Ji Gong's pocket, but the monk called out, "Headmen Chai and She! Here is enough to make up the six hundred ounces of silver lost by that man whose life you saved. This is a great relief to me."

Juan Yoting protested, "I did not want to put you all to so much trouble, and I did not want to worry the monk!"

The young man who had been so sick heard them talking and called Headman Chai to him for an explanation. Chai explained everything that had happened. "Then let me add something to the money you gave to Juan Yoting," the young man said and took out six hundred ounces of silver to give to him.

Juan Yoting thanked him sincerely and was about to take the money when Ji Gong protested. "You have had the money you lost returned. You do not need another six hundred. However, I can see that you are a worthy person, and I will give you these two hundred in silver." This was, in fact, the last of the remaining funds which Ji Gong and his two headmen had for expenses.

The two headmen could only take to the road with the monk. On the west side of town they came to a restaurant. Noise of great activity could be heard coming from the kitchen and every seat seemed to be taken. The monk ran inside and the two headmen followed him straight through to the dining area in the rear, where they found seats.

CHAPTER 41

A Phoenix Hill yuanwai *reaches Country Hill Inn; a rough robber meets his match*

W HEN Ji Gong had finished eating and drinking and did not have the money to pay the check, the manager was not in the least agreeable, but just as things were becoming unpleasant, two men entered. The first was very tall, with shoulders three times as broad as those of ordinary men. He was wearing a scholar's kerchief over the knot of hair at the back of his head. The silk material of his robe was brocaded in an arrow pattern and drawn in by a silk sash of a contrasting hue. His complexion was a bright gold, his nose prominent, his eyes lively and piercing and the corners of his mouth square. This was none other than the *yuanwai* who lived in the Phoenix Hill section of Linan city, who was called the Iron-faced Celestial Warrior because of his unblemished record as a public official.

Several followers accompanied him. Just behind him was an elegant young man with a military bearing named Ma Jun. The two men were from the same province, and the younger, who was devoted to his parents, had come to Linan because he had heard that the eyesight of his friend's mother had been helped. "How did that monk cure the old lady's eyes?" he asked. The *yuanwai* told him the whole story about Ji Gong.

"If this monk from the Monastery of the Soul's Retreat can cure eye problems, would you go with me to ask him to cure the eyes of my own mother?" he asked. The *yuanwai* agreed, and the two men went to the Monastery of the Soul's Retreat to inquire, but found that Ji Gong was not there. They heard that he had gone to the province of the Great Protector for some reason, and after making several more inquiries without success, Ma Jun was thinking of returning home.

"Let me go back with you," said the *yuanwai*. After they had purchased a considerable number of things in the city to take with them, they set out. A light rain was falling as they were journeying along the road. Seeing an inn before them, the *yuanwai* said, "Why not stop for some refreshment?"

Just as they entered the door, they heard voices, and as the *yuanwai* looked he recognized Ji Gong. Going up to him he asked, "My teacher, how have you been?"

The two headmen Chai and She, seeing the *yuanwai,* asked, "What brings the great one here?"

The *yuanwai,* recognizing them in return, asked, "What are you two headmen doing dressed like this?"

"We are on a secret mission," explained Chai and She.

The *yuanwai* again turned to Ji Gong and asked, "How is my teacher?"

"Ah! Ah!" said the monk, "they are annoying me to my very death."

"Who dares to annoy you?" asked the *yuanwai.*

The monk pointed to the waiter. The frightened waiter ran from the room. "Before you get excited, you must ask why they are annoying him," said Chai and She.

"My teacher, why are they annoying you?" asked the *yuanwai.*

"After I had finished eating," replied the monk, "they wouldn't let me go. They care only about money."

At that the *yuanwai* began to laugh, "If people have their things eaten, who doesn't want money in return? That is not considered to be annoying. Whatever it was, I will pay it. But Teacher, why don't you carry money with you when you go out?"

"But I did take money," said the monk. "I had two hundred ounces of silver."

"Yes," broke in Chai, "and he gave all that two hundred ounces away. There is not a cash left."

"Teacher," said the *yuanwai,* "If you have no money, you must not simply sit down and eat. This time you were lucky. But what would have happened if I had not arrived?"

"If you had not been about to arrive, I would not have eaten," replied the monk. The *yuanwai* thought for a moment and realized that he was probably right. He paid the bill and ordered more food for the party.

While they were all sitting there with Chai and She, two more men entered. The first was a studious and refined young man in the simple attire of a bachelor graduate. The one who followed was in blue traveling clothes. He had a pale face with somewhat squinting, snakelike eyes and a crooked mouth. He had a lean, rough look. Ji Gong, upon looking at him, decided at once that he was not a good man.

Now the young man who had entered first was named Gao Guangrui, and was from the Youlong district. He was the heir of a family that had a famous money exchange outside the north gate at Youlong. The family was wealthy, and marriages had been arranged so that he had three wives, with the understanding that whoever first gave birth to a son would become the first-ranking wife. His uncle was a prosperous dry-goods merchant in Linan, and for some time he had been with his uncle, learning the business. But on this day he had asked to go home.

His uncle said, "If you leave, you need not come back."

"It is not my intention to leave you and return home for good," said Gao Guangrui, "but last night I had a frightening dream. In my dream I saw my mother dead. Let me go home and see her and I will return." His uncle gave Gao Guangrui ten ounces of silver for expenses in addition to the several tens of ounces he already had intended to take.

Upon reaching the Village of the Thousand Gates, he stopped to eat in a restaurant where an old man came over to him, saying, "Great sir, grant me a few cash that will let me eat a little something."

Gao Guangrui was moved to pity as he looked at him and said, "You may eat your fill of meat and the rest, old fellow, and I will pay the bill."

The old man ate and was about to leave, but Gao Guangrui opened his purse and gave him a silver coin. Afterward, he paid the bill and was ready to leave the restaurant when a man wearing a a complete suit of dark-blue traveling clothes approached, saying, "What is the guest's honorable name?"

Gao Guangrui answered, "I am from the Youlong district and my name is Gao."

"My name is Wang," said the man, "Wang Gui. I am from Youlong as well. We are fellows in our district origins. However, when you gave some silver to that fellow just now, I could see that he was not an honest man. He is a member of a gang of mountain robbers. He saw that you have silver. Later he will lie in wait for you along the road. Not only will you lose your silver, he will also want your life. Let us walk together, you and I."

Gao Guangrui had never really been on his own before, and hearing this, he became frightened, so he went on his way with Wang Gui. When they had reached the Country Hill Inn, a light rain had begun to fall. Wang Gui said, "Well, my friend, let us have something to eat and then go on."

As the two entered, the monk knew with one look that Wang Gui was not a reliable person. Ji Gong stared straight at him, and as a result all the rest turned and looked. "Brother," said Wang Gui, "let us go somewhere else for refreshments." The two left and went on their way.

When they reached a wooded area where no one could be seen on any side, Wang Gui suddenly said, "You stop here."

"To do what?" asked Gao Guangrui.

"This is your old lady's home," said Wang Gui. "Now listen to your old man! What do I do? My surname is Wang and my personal name is Gui, but I am called the Spirit of the Green Sprout. When the sprout is short, I am not on the road. When the sprout is long, I am on the great highway doing business. You may now give me your silver and all your clothing, and then I will kill you!"

As Gao Guangrui listened, his face turned pale from fright. "Elder Brother Wang," he said, "you and I are fellow district men. I will give you the silver. Let me keep my life."

The Spirit of the Green Sprout, Wang Gui, laughed loudly. "You may forget that idea. For as many years as I have done this business, I have never left a living mouth to speak. If I spare your life today, tomorrow you will point your finger at me and you will want my life. You would point your finger and say, 'You are the highway robber who did those things to me.' Now! Do as I say and hand me your clothing as you take it off, one piece at a time. If not, I will kill you all the more quickly with this knife. Clothing also brings in a little money. Then thrust your head out for me to kill you. If not, I will simply stab you anywhere."

Hearing this, Gao Guangrui began to tremble violently. Almost speechless with fear, he began to beg. "Good sir, I am giving you my money," he said as he handed it over. "I will give you all my clothing. Just let me keep my pants. Just let me keep my life. I wish the best for you, sir."

Wang Gui laughed his cold laugh as he listened. "There is no need to talk so much, little fellow," he said. "I never leave a living voice."

Gao Guangrui, seeing that his pleas were useless, suddenly found his anger rising. Picking up a rock, he was about to hit the robber with it. Wang Gui laughed loudly. "Your gall must be as big as the world if you dare to stir up the ground in front of the almighty. Now you will feel the teeth inside the tiger's lips." With that he moved in with his scimitar for the kill.

But just then he heard a voice speaking words with a special meaning to men of the Greenwood. The voice came from among the trees just to the west of where he was standing. "The pieces fit together, and now it is fitting that you should yield to me!"

Wang Gui turned his head to look and saw two men coming toward him. The foremost had bright red hair and the lower part of his face had been colored blue. It was none other than Lei Ming, and the person with him was Chen Liang.

The evening before, Lei Ming had experienced the force of Ji Gong's hypnotic power. Later the two had been running back and forth through the woods, fleeing Ji Gong and hearing his voice again and again, first behind them, then just before them. After this night of terrors, they had slept through the day, sinking upon the ground to rest. Upon wakening, they had looked out of the woods and had seen two men coming along the road.

"Look at those two men, my brother. They seem to be an unlikely pair. One is a scholarly, refined young gentleman and the other has the face of a robber with the body of a ruffian. There must be a reason for this."

Then Lei Ming and Chen Liang had watched until just after the point where the road entered the woods, when Wang Gui called out, "Stop." They noticed Gao Guangrui's confusion and fear. They had heard every word that was spoken and understood completely.

As the two friends stepped out of the woods, the Spirit of the Green Sprout, Wang Gui, recognized their faces and was shocked with fright. "I know, of course, your honorable names," he said. "You are my young uncle, Borne by the Wind, Lei Ming, and this gentleman is the famous White Monkey, Chen Liang."

As the two heard these words, they opened their eyes wide and raised their eyebrows. "I will knock the ball back to you," said Chen Liang. "You might be his little uncle, but he is your grandfather!"

"My great-grandchildren," answered Wang Gui insultingly, but half under his breath. Chen Liang gripped his knife. "You are my great-grandparents," said Wang Gui, suddenly becoming respectful. "I said my grandparents."

"We heard very clearly the first time just now," said Lei Ming. "Hand over that silver." Wang Gui handed him the silver that he had taken from Gao Guangrui. "Give me the rest of the silver you have hidden there in your clothing," said Lei Ming. Wang Gui took it out as he was asked. "And now take off your clothing."

"Dear grandfather, how can this be?" asked Wang Gui, suddenly pleading. "We are all pieces of the same puzzle. We all fit together!"

"But your mother was a dog!" cried Lei Ming. With one slash of his knife he completely cut off one of Wang Gui's ears.

"Someone else is coming, grandfathers," cried Wang Gui. The two friends turned their heads, and though they saw no one, they felt a chill.

CHAPTER 42

Two heroes are almost killed in the Dong Family Hotel; the Chan monk brings retribution to robbers

JUST when Lei Ming and Chen Liang were about to kill the robber Wang Gui, he had pointed and said someone was coming. Then, as the two turned their heads to look, he ran into the woods, with the two running after him.

"Run, you slippery scoundrel," they shouted. "You thought we were no better than you."

At a little distance away there was a swift-running creek that was quite deep and about nine feet wide. Wang Gui jumped into the water and swam to the other side. Lei Ming and Chen Liang thought of following him, but Chen Liang said, "That's enough of him," and they turned back.

Gao Guangrui, the young man whom they had saved, came up to them saying, "If it had not been for you two great sirs, I would certainly have lost my life at the hands of that robber."

"What is your name, who are you, and why were you traveling along the highway with such a ruffian?" asked Chen Liang.

"My name is Gao Guangrui. I had stopped at a restaurant in the Village of a Thousand Gates…" and so he went on to tell the whole story.

"We are not men of the Greenwood," Chen Liang told him. "We are giving you back these thirty ounces of silver." With that he handed the young man his silver.

Gao Guangrui could not praise their kindness enough. "You two saved my life. I live just in the next village, Youlong. We have a famous money exchange. Please come and see me there, or at my uncle's in Linan."

The two then drew aside. Chen Liang, who was especially warm-hearted, said, "Let us watch him until he is safely home. We are not in a hurry. Later, we will find a place, somewhere to pass the night." So they followed Gao Guangrui until they saw him reach home.

By this time they were beginning to feel hungry and a light rain was falling. At last Chen Liang said, "We must find an inn where we can eat and sleep. It is getting late."

"Just ahead there is an inn where I once stayed," Lei Ming responded. "It is the Dong Family Inn. They are very friendly. About a year ago I stayed there while I was sick and the manager, a man named Dong, was most helpful. But I do not know whether that old man is still there or whether the manager has changed."

Chen Liang agreed. "We will stay at this Dong Family Inn."

When they came to the next village, one street ran from north to south. "This is it," said Lei Ming.

On the east side of the street they entered the gate of an inn. Facing them was a large standing screen of masonry that completely blocked the view from the gateway. Going around the screen they found themselves in a large courtyard. The main building, a large one-story structure with a veranda, was on their left to the north. There were two smaller buildings at right angles to it, on the east and west.

On the veranda a small table was set, and on it was a gauze lantern. A man was sitting at the table eating and drinking. As he saw Lei Ming and Chen Liang enter, he extinguished the light with a single motion of his hand. Lei Ming and Chen Liang did not pay any attention to this and did not see who it was. The waiter called to them to come into the building on the east side and seated them.

Now this inn was no longer the same Dong Family Inn that it had once been. This was because the old manager had died and the two young managers who succeeded him had no interest in the business. They spent most of their time with a certain Wang Gui, drinking and gambling. One day Wang Gui said, "You two young managers should entrust the business to me. Every year I could give you several strings of cash for doing nothing."

This Wang Gui was an unmarried man and unsociable by nature. He gathered about him several men of the Greenwood as waiters and men of all work. Whenever there were solitary travelers with valuable luggage, they would murder them. The group was already becoming wealthy with their ill-gotten gains.

Wang Gui liked to brag to the others about his exploits and spoke of himself as a famous member of the Greenwood, but this was mostly empty talk. No one really knew anything about his abilities. Tonight he had returned with his clothing soaked and an ear gone. Indeed, the bleeding could not be entirely stopped. One of the waiters who loved to joke asked: "How come there's an ear missing and the clothes are all wet?"

"I was in a restaurant, eating," said Wang Gui, "when a fight broke out. In the confusion a fellow with a knife cut off my ear. The man with me ran after him and the fellow jumped into the river. I went in after him, but he escaped and I got my clothing wet. A number of people helped me out of the water, so I had to stand drinks all around. Some of them will probably be here tomorrow to see how I am doing and wish me well. Give me some dry clothes and something in the way of hot food to put inside me."

The waiters believed him and did not inquire further. They brought him a change of clothes and made him two dishes of food. Wang Gui was sitting at the table drinking, and the more he thought, the more he regretted his adventure. "It was lucky that I made two flying leaps—otherwise Lei Ming and Chen Liang would have killed me."

Just as these thoughts were going through his head, he heard voices outside. He thought of telling the waiter to bar the door, but the man was already inviting the two guests inside. When he saw them, he almost took to his heels again. He put the lantern out and went quickly into the north building. Once inside, his heart was still beating wildly as he wondered whether the two had gone into the east building or whether they were still in the courtyard.

After a while he called one of his helpers inside. "Did you recognize the two men who just arrived?" he asked.

"No," the waiter replied, "I didn't."

"One of them is called Borne by the Wind, Lei Ming," Wang Gui explained. "The other, the one with the light complexion, is the White Monkey, Chen Liang."

"The names are famous among us," said the waiter. "We must treat them well and not ask them to pay the bill when they leave."

"Let me tell you," said Wang Gui, "These two men are my enemies."

"What could you have against them?" asked the waiter.

"Today I was traveling from the Village of a Thousand Gates with a merchant. I was coming through the woods with him. Just as I was about to make my move, Lei Ming and Chen Liang came up and said, 'How are you, Uncle Wang?' I asked, 'What are you to rascals up to?' They answered, 'Just looking things over.' I did not say anything, and then they both came at me and wouldn't stop. They cheated me out of the money I would have gotten, and I not only lost the money, but they made me lose an ear. Now we will kill them and it will serve them right. I will have my revenge. You can divide whatever silver there is. I don't want it."

"That's it, then," the waiter said.

Wang Gui whispered in his ear. "Do this and such and so forth."

The waiter nodded his head.

When he arrived at the east building, the waiter asked, "What will you two men eat?"

"What do you have here?" asked Chen Liang.

"We have fried bean curd, boiled bean curd, and dried bean curd."

"We don't eat bean curd. Do you have anything else?" asked Chen Liang.

"Nothing," replied the waiter. "Our manager took everything to somebody's wedding, including most of the help. He even lent them the cooking utensils. We can roast two chickens with some cabbage. We have no little wine pots to warm the wine. We have wine in two-catty bottles."

"Then we will have a two-catty bottle and a pair of roast chickens," directed Chen Liang.

After they had waited a while, the waiter brought everything in. Lei Ming and Chen Liang each drank a few mouthfuls of wine. Then Chen Liang said, "Not good. Brother, why am I becoming confused?"

"I'm beginning to feel the same way," said Lei Ming.

Suddenly Chen Liang cried out, "It fits! We have fallen into the cave of the ear." Then he and Lei Ming both turned and fell to the ground.

"Master," the waiter called out to Wang Gui, "these two are finished."

At this time, Chen Liang was still able to hear, and recognizing the answering voice of the spirit of the Green Sprout, Wang Gui, he knew that he had not long to live. The waiter watched them for a little while and then went to talk to Wang Gui.

"Somewhere about them they have a purse with thirty ounces of silver that I had taken from the merchant. There is another with five ounces that they took from me. Whatever they have, I don't want it. That is for you waiters."

The waiter was not especially eager to kill them. Whether they had gone against the Greenwood or not, the two men were famous. "First Wang Gui was talking about revenge and now he is talking about money," he thought. But the waiter did not dare to say what he was thinking.

Prepared to do the deed or not, the waiter took the knife and went out of the north building to kill Lei Ming and Chen Liang, but just as he approached the east building, he heard someone knocking at the gate and saying, "Open the gate! Open the gate! I came here to sleep."

Wang Gui, hearing the noise, called to the servant: "You had better find out who that is—but don't let him see me."

The waiter went to the crack in the gate and called, "Who is it?"

The voice outside repeated, "I came here to sleep."

"We don't have any empty chambers," the waiter said.

"If you don't have any in the north building, one of the side buildings will do," the voice outside insisted.

"There's nothing in the side buildings either," said the waiter.

Then from outside the voice said, "If the side buildings are full, let me sleep in the shed."

The waiter opened the gate a little and looked out. There was a monk. Now, the one who had just arrived was Ji Gong. He had been at the little inn with the two headmen. When they had finished eating and drinking, one of them said, "This is a convenient place, teacher. Let us all stay here overnight and go on in the morning."

"Good," said Ji Gong. They made arrangements to stay and went to bed. At the second watch, the monk woke them up and said, "Get up and we'll go catch Cloud Dragon. He's out in the woods."

"Is this really true?" they asked.

"It is true," said the monk.

The two got up and left the inn with the monk. It was raining and still very dark. After a while one of the two headmen asked, "Teacher, where is Cloud Dragon?"

"I don't know," answered the monk.

"That's not what you said before," said Headman Chai.

"I called you out to stroll about in this rainy scene," the monk said. "The rain comes down from up above and underfoot it is all mud. At such a time it would be nice to be sleeping in bed, wouldn't it?"

The two headmen, Chai and She, could hardly control themselves, but they did not speak. The monk went on with them until they arrived at the Dong Family Inn. The monk asked them to make a bundle with their outer clothing, into which he put some stones to make it larger in appearance. Then he knocked at the gate.

When the waiter said there was no room, the monk persisted. "I don't want to go elsewhere. I have some valuables here and I am afraid to be out on the road. I'm afraid I will lose them. I'm begging you to let me stay the night."

When the waiter opened the door a little and saw him, he exclaimed, "You're a monk! What is this talk of valuables?"

"I'm carrying them secretly," said the monk.

"What's that you're carrying?" asked the waiter.

"Crystal, cat's eyes, agates, and all sorts of semi-precious stones and little antique jewels in curious shapes," the monk answered.

When the waiter heard that, he went in and told Wang Gui. "Outside there is a monk who is secretly carrying a pack with valuable little treasures of all sorts. Shall we get rich this time? It may be worth tens of thousands and we will each have seven or eight thousand as a share."

"That's good then," said Wang Gui, "but first lock the door of the east building. Bring the monk into the north building."

And so the waiter went and opened the door to the monk who had come to aid Lei Ming and Chen Liang.

CHAPTER 43

Wang Gui prepares his revenge; three friends meet in New Moon Village

WHEN the waiter had locked the east building and finally opened the gate, he saw that the monk had two men with him and that the three were carrying the bundle among them. "Give us a hand with this bundle," said the monk.

The waiter tried to lift it but failed. "Help, you two," said the monk to the headmen, and between them they carried it to the north building.

"This must be something valuable," said the waiter to himself. "I don't know how the three of them carried it."

As they came into the room the monk asked, "And what is Waiter Ji's name?"

"You know my name is Ji. Why do you ask?" asked the waiter in return.

"I looked at you and you were the sort of person who would be named Ji. I just guessed at it."

"And what would the great teacher like to eat?" asked the waiter.

"What do you have?" the monk asked.

"Whatever you like," replied the waiter.

"I like fried bean curd, boiled bean curd, dried bean curd, and bean-curd shreds," said the monk. "You said there was a party and everything was taken there, even the cooking utensils—but as you said, you do have two chickens that aren't cooked yet. Isn't that right?"

"Strange," thought the waiter. "That's what I said to the other two fellows just now." Then he asked the monk how he knew.

"I heard you say it," said the monk.

"No," said the waiter. "I said we have whatever you want."

"Bring some wine and some freshly brewed tea," ordered the monk.

The waiter called out to the kitchen, "Three pots of the Forgetful Sea brand."

"Right, the Forgetful Sea brand," the monk repeated. "Three pots."

The waiter was shocked. "Did the monk understand?" he wondered. "Why did you repeat the name Forgetful Sea, Monk?" asked the waiter.

"Why do you go on asking questions back and forth?" asked the monk. "But I will ask you, what is this Forgetful Sea brand?"

The waiter thought the question over and replied. "No, I told him not to forget to see if we had some good brand."

"I do want some good wine," said the monk.

The waiter brought some food with the wine and tea. The monk looked at the wine for some time and then said, "Waiter, you have a drink."

"I don't drink," the waiter said.

"Well, you two go ahead and drink it, Chai and She," said the monk. The three drank and immediately fell down senseless.

The waiter then went and told Wang Gui that the three were all down. "Good!" exclaimed Wang Gui. "First, I will take my revenge and kill Lei Ming and Chen Liang, and afterward we will all get rich."

They took knives and went toward the east building. When they arrived there, Wang Gui could not find the door. "Waiter, why can't I find the door?"

"I can't find the way to the door either. This is strange," answered the waiter.

Wang Gui was becoming impatient. "Let us go first into the north building and kill the monk we have there." The two men with the servants and other waiters then went to the north building.

"I will do it," said the servant. With that he went into the western section of the building. As soon as the man lifted the knife, the monk showed his teeth in a grin that frightened the servant. He stood there unable to move. Wang Gui looked in from the outside and saw the servant with the knife uplifted, but not using it to kill the monk.

Wang Gui's anger rose. "I told you to kill him," he exclaimed. "You have your knife but you're too afraid to use it!" Then Wang Gui went inside with a knife to kill the monk himself. Just as he raised his knife, the monk pointed with his finger and used his hypnotic power to paralyze Wang Gui.

"You are a good thing!" said the monk sarcastically. "You wanted to kill the monk, did you? I want you to realize my power." With that he pointed again, and the waiters and servants standing outside were all unable to move.

The monk then went to the east building to revive Lei Ming and Chen Liang. Putting a piece of medicine in some boiling water, he gave some to each of them, and in a little while both were revived. When he opened his eyes and saw Ji Gong standing there, Lei Ming quickly knelt and kowtowed. "Your disciple knew nothing," he said. "I tried to kill you. Not only did you not take revenge, but also you came to rescue me with your great kindness. I wish to do penance."

"There will be no penance," the monk said, "but there are two head-men with me that someone poisoned with Mongolian mandrake. They are both in the north building. I will give you two pieces of medicine and you two may go ahead and revive them. If they ask you any questions, tell them…" —and the monk whispered something to the two.

The monk then went back into the north building and pretended to go to sleep. Chen Liang and Lei Meng went in and revived headmen Chai and She. The two headmen opened their eyes and one said, "Oh, so Master Lei and Master Chen are here. Where did you come from?"

"We came from the Village of a Thousand Gates. We came here to spend the night at the inn. When no one answered our knock, we climbed in over the wall. We could see that the people of the inn were planning to kill you, so we quieted them down and came to your rescue."

When Headman Chai and Headman She saw that Ji Gong was still sleeping, they became quite angry. Headman Chai said, "This monk is now learning about pickpocketing, so he brought us here to this den of robbers. If it weren't for you two, we would have lost our lives. You two had better get some more medicine ready and save this monk. After that, ask him about all this."

Chen Liang said,"There's no more medicine."

"It's in my shoe, idiot," said the monk. "Shake it out and put some of it between my lips. I'm not done for."

Lei Ming and the rest began to laugh. Just then, the whole inn seemed to be in flames. A fire had started in the kitchen while it was unattended and was spreading to the other buildings.

"Get those men out of here," ordered the monk. They got the dazed robbers out into the street and left them with their wrists bound under the guard of the two headmen. Ji Gong called, "Save me! Save me!"

Chen Liang and Lei Ming dashed back in and saw the monk standing in the flames. "I'm all right, but you will have to carry me," he told them.

Lei Ming got the monk on his back and Chen Liang helped hold up his feet, but the gate was now blocked by burning and falling timber. "We will have to go over the wall," said Chen Liang.

With great difficulty they managed to get the monk up on a corner shed and lower him down from the wall. Once on the ground he said, "I seem to be all right now. Headman Chai and Headman She can take those robbers to the local yamen. They have the authority and will be believed. We three had better get out of here or someone may think we started the fire."

After they had walked for some time, Chen Liang pulled at Lei Ming's sleeve and the two fell back behind the monk. "Should we be walking with our teacher, or should we be walking separately?" asked Chen Liang.

"What difference would it make?' asked Lei Ming.

"Brother, have you no eyes?" countered Chen Liang. "Why do you think he has been traveling with those two headmen? You are stronger than I am and more skillful with weapons. Yet you don't seem to think about what's going on. I think that the monk has brought those two headmen to help him take Cloud Dragon Hua. If we go with Teacher, then when we meet Cloud Dragon, shall we help Teacher to take him, or shall we help our brother Hua if he moves against our teacher?"

Lei Ming thought about the matter. "Right. What shall we do?"

"We must help him find Cloud Dragon, but then we must tell Cloud Dragon that the monk is trying to take him. That way we cannot go wrong," said Chen Liang.

"Good!" said Lei Ming. "Your ideas are always clearer than mine. This is the right idea."

Having finished their discusion, they caught up with Ji Gong. "Have you two talked everything over?" asked the monk.

"We haved decided to help our teacher find Cloud Dragon Hua," said Chen Liang.

"Right," the monk said, "and when you see this Hua, you will tell him that I want to catch him and that he had better be off quickly. Then you two will not be in the wrong. Isn't that right?"

"No, that isn't right," contradicted Chen Liang. "We will help him, but we must tell you." Having said that, the two started to leave.

"But where shall we meet?" asked the monk.

"Wherever our teacher says," answered Chen Liang.

"Let us meet in Longyou in the New Moon Village," the monk told them. Then he went off to meet the two headmen by himself.

Chen Liang began to think about the monk's having chosen New Moon Village. He thought to himself: "That's no good. There are some friends of the Greenwood in New Moon Village. Cloud Dragon is likely to be there." He told his fears to Lei Ming.

But it was getting late and Longyou was still ten miles away. They stopped at an inn along the way and the next morning they arrived at

New Moon Village. Approaching them from the opposite direction was a rather elegantly dressed young man wearing a cap with six sections. They immediately recognized the pale complexion and the heavy eyebrows and lashes that made one notice his lively, mocking eyes hinting at the desperate schemes running through the brain behind them. From one hand there dangled a bundle of freshly cut Chinese celery cabbage, and from the other a still slightly struggling fish. It was none other than Cloud Dragon Hua.

CHAPTER 44

Cloud Dragon Hua goes to New Moon Village; Black Tiger teaches at the ruined temple

NOW, the reason why Lei Ming and Chen Liang saw Cloud Dragon Hua coming toward them as they entered the New Moon Village was as follows. In New Moon Village there was an older man with a chivalrous reputation named Ma Yuanzhang, nicknamed the Far-Traveling Bachelor. There was a special tradition in his family by which unusual martial-art skills had been passed down from generation to generation. Although ordinarily he never accepted any pupils, he did have two nephews to whom he had passed on some of his skills. One of them was named Ma Jing, nicknamed "the Black Tiger" because of his dark face. The other was named Ma Zeng, nicknamed "the Sea Dragon." The two also carried on the family tradition of skill in the martial arts.

The old warrior had been making forays out into the vast region of lakes, rivers, and streams surrounding New Moon Village and far beyond for a good number of decades. At those times he never associated with other men of the Greenwood. He had two male servants, one called Tan Hualong and the other called Zhou Lan, who was also known as Little White Tiger. None of the other people in the area knew that the two men, as well as their families, were members of the Greenwood.

Ma Yuanzhang, the uncle, owned a small private temple where he behaved as if he had left the world, dressing in monk's clothing when he was at home and reading books about Buddhism. He had never had any Buddhist instruction, and, of course, had no monk's certificate. In fact, he really knew almost nothing about the essence of Buddhism. It was all part of his disguise. Every year he would go away for long periods of time, telling one of his two servants to take care of the temple. During the months that he was absent, the two nephews, Ma Jing and Ma Zeng, would be in charge of all the family business.

On these trips he would travel for hundreds of miles, each time to a different destination. There, he would set himself up as merchant, buying and selling goods. At the same time he would rob the homes of wealthy people in that area. When he had accumulated a certain amount of money and other valuables, he would close up his shop, and then, riding a mule and leading a donkey, return home. All the neighbors would learn that he was back from his travels.

The nephew Ma Jing was also quite skilled in the martial arts, and he had made friends with a local man named Li Ping to whom he had taught karate. Li Ping's friends soon started calling him the Red Panther. Li Ping's younger brother was named Li An. Li Ping lived outside New Moon Village, where he kept a tavern for a living. It was the custom that out of the thirty-five men of the Greenwood in the area, a dozen or so gathered at Li Ping's wine shop to drink and practice the martial arts. These men were all vagabonds, foxes pretending to be tigers, loitering about, with nothing bad that they would not hesitate to do. They all had nicknames such as "the Roaming Fox," "the Bushy-Tailed Fox," "the Black Ferret," "the Inquisitive Badger," and so forth.

Outside New Moon Village there was an abandoned Daoist temple. There in its courtyard they would practice using swords and quarterstaves. They recognized Li Ping as their teacher. While other people practiced to make themselves strong and healthy, these people sharpened their abilities to polish the luster of their quarterstaves that they needed for performing their misdeeds.

Li Ping was willing to teach them so that he could sell more wine. All of these bullies were so poor that, when they ate elsewhere, they would not pay the bill. When they drank at Li Ping's, however, no one dared to leave without paying.

Li Ping spent a good deal of time practicing feats of strength, sometimes with the spear. After a time there was one among the group, who was nicknamed "the General," who asked: "In this area of ours, who would you say is the most famous?"

"To tell the truth," the others answered, "The Black Tiger, Ma Jing, is the best."

The General asked, "Then why shouldn't we invite the great Black Tiger Ma to come out here and practice with us?"

"Well said," the rest thought, and so, after more discussion, they came to a decision. Early the next morning, they went to Black Tiger Ma's gate, knocked, and handed the servant a fancy red-and-white card with their names.

The servant went in, and as soon as Black Tiger Ma saw the card, he came out. Everyone spoke at once. "An early good morning to you, Ma Jing!"

"And why have you all come to see me?" Ma Jing asked.

"We have long heard of the great Black Tiger's fame," they cried, "and have come to invite you to visit us, as a great favor, at our practicing ground at the temple of the Three Worthies, and teach us the martial arts."

Black Tiger Ma looked at them and thought to himself: "If I associate with you scoundrels, it will drag my family down into the dust." He could not say that because they were all local residents, so instead he said, "It was kind of you to come, but my old mother is not well and I am not able to leave her. Please wait until she is better, and then I certainly must visit you."

Everyone was very disappointed and criticized the General for making a suggestion that exposed them to embarrassment. "Don't criticize me yet," said the General. "If I don't get Li Ping to ask him out, you can stop calling me the General! You can call me the Toy Soldier! How is that?"

"Very well then," they all agreed. Just then Li Ping arrived at the ruined temple.

"Teacher Li Ping," said the General, "I guess there is someone who is ashamed to say they know you."

"Who is ashamed to say they know me?" asked Li Ping, the Red Panther.

"It's Ma Jing," said the General.

"You're talking nonsense," said Li Ping. "I know him very well as a friend, as well as my own hand or foot. We see each other constantly. He would never be ashamed to say he knows me."

"Li, my good sir," said the General, "don't say that. You are always saying that Ma Jing, the Black Tiger, is a good friend of yours, but today, when I met Ma Jing and I mentioned your name and said that he no doubt knew you, he stopped and thought for quite a while. I said, 'Li Ping of New Moon Village.' He said, 'Oh, yes, I know of him, but there is no friendship between us.'"

Upon hearing this Li Ping became quite angry. "I tell you we know each other intimately! There is nothing false about our friendship!"

"My most respected sir," said the General, "if you two are really such good friends, perhaps you might get him to come here and give us a demonstration of his skill in martial arts. I would certainly believe you then."

"What does that amount to?" replied Li Ping. "I'll ask him and see. If he won't come, that's it."

"Very well then," said the General.

Li Ping was upset and angry. He went straight to Ma Jing's house and walked inside without knocking. "Where did you come from, dear brother?" asked Ma Jing, upon seeing him.

"Elder Brother," asked Li Ping, "is it true that there is no friendship between us? Did you tell that fellow we call the General that there is nothing between us?" Li Ping repeated what the General had said.

"Dear brother," said Black Tiger, "He was trying to upset you. You mustn't listen to such talk."

"Then would you go with me tomorrow and tell him that to his face?" asked Li Ping.

"Yes, tomorrow I will go with you," Black Tiger Ma answered him.

The next day Li Ping met Black Tiger and together they went to the ruined Temple of the Three Worthies. As soon as the others saw Black Tiger Ma, they were overjoyed. They were saying, "We had hoped you might come." One was pouring tea; another was running off to buy pastries. They showed him the things they used in their exercises and had him sit in the seat of honor.

One of them, named Hu, nicknamed "the Blackhearted Fox," said to him, "Ma Jing, let me give you a demonstration." He then took the heavy iron cutlass and went through several exercises, after which he asked Black Tiger to criticize his performance. Black Tiger made a number of comments, and then another man took a spear and went through the appropriate movements. Ma Jing praised the man's abilities, which pleased him very much.

So it went on until each of the group had performed, except Li Ping himself. As Ma Jing had watched, he had thought to himself, "The sword is not treated like a sword; the spear is not treated like a spear. There is no force behind either." Then he turned and said to Li Ping, "Why don't you go through the exercises and let them watch?"

Then Li Ping began moving in the true style with his body and weapon in the correct positions, making no mistakes and smoothly going through all the classic sequences. Everyone felt completely satisfied and all in unison uttered an exclamation of approval. Afterward they turned to Ma Jing. "We have heard that you excel at brandishing a pair of double-ended maces. Please let us see an example of your skill."

"Well, I will give them an eye-opener," he thought, and taking the two maces he said, "Stand clear of the road from here to the gate."

Then he began a whirlwind of movements so fast that the eye could hardly follow them. Everyone was amazed and delighted. There was loud applause at the end. In the silence that followed it, a voice spoke from outside the gate. "Well performed!" Ma Jing turned to see who it was and a look of fright passed over his face.

CHAPTER 45

Ma Yuanzhang warns his nephew;
Ma Jing asks a favor

WHAT Ma Jing saw in the gateway of the ruined temple was a tall, elderly monk with a round face like a full moon. He was dressed in a dark-saffron-colored robe, and a rosary with 108 beads hung from his neck. Ma Jing quickly put down the pair of maces and ran out through the gateway, saying, "Excuse me, everybody."

"Where are you going, Ma Jing?" they cried.

Li Ping remarked, "How unfortunate. That was Ma Jing's uncle."

Now the old monk was in reality the robber known to respectable people as the Far-Traveling Bachelor, Ma Yuanzhang. He had just returned home from one of his long absences. When he had asked where his nephew Ma Jing was, Ma Jing's wife said that he had been invited to a martial-arts practice. Hearing that, Ma Yuanzhang was furious. "A good boy he is! We members of the Ma family have lived here all these years and none of the people around here know that we are members of the Greenwood. Perhaps he was afraid that others might not know about us, shaking things in the air like that! I will go and find him!"

And it was because of this that the old monk arrived at the gateway of the ruined temple. At first he thought that he would go inside and call his nephew, but with all those people present it did not seem convenient, and so he called from outside with a cold laugh in his voice. As soon as Ma Jing saw him, he hurried outside and fell down in a kowtow, knocking his head on the ground before his uncle.

Ma Yuanzhang turned about and walked quickly home. Upon arriving he said to his nephew, "Ma Jing, you really don't care about yourself, do you? After all these years that we have lived here in New Moon Village without people knowing that we are members of the Greenwood, you go out and make a display of yourself, doing martial arts for everyone to see!"

"Uncle, you don't know the whole story. It was because one of them was making my friend, Li Ping, lose face." And so he told the story from beginning to end.

Ma Yuanzhang's anger evaporated as if he were coming out of a bad dream. "I understand, but don't associate with them any more."

Ma Jing agreed. The two had a drink of wine together and Ma Yuanzhang said, "Tomorrow I am going off again. While I am gone, if the people who watch my temple need money, give them a little silver." Again Ma Jing agreed. The next day Ma Yuanzhang went away.

After two or three weeks, Ma Jing noticed while taking care of his mother that the old lady seemed to be getting a little worse, and thought to himself, "Perhaps it might help her if she had some fresh mountain bamboo shoots to eat—and besides, we are a little short of ready money. We also need to think about giving some silver to the people who take care of the temple. I think I will leave here for a while to do some selling. I can make some money and also bring back some fresh bamboo shoots. I can ask Li Ping to watch over things while I am gone."

After he had thought it over, he went to Li Ping's wine shop. He knocked and Li Ping immediately came out and asked him to come back into the office. There he saw Li Ping's brother, Li An, lying in bed, making no sound or movement.

"Your brother is not well!" exclaimed Ma Jing.

"No, his illness is getting more serious," replied Li Ping. "We have invited several doctors to see him, but they have not helped."

"You must find someone with greater skills and help him to recover soon! I came to see you today because I must ask a favor. I am thinking of leaving for a while and my old mother is at home sick. My wife will have no one to turn to. After I have gone, would you go in the morning and evening, before and after the shop is open, and look in on them? If they are short of money, give them a little. After I return, I will repay you."

"Of course, I will," said Li Ping. "We are intimate friends. Don't think about repaying me. You need not worry about it. I will carry out your wishes. Where are you thinking of going and when are you leaving?"

"I will leave tomorrow," replied Ma Jing.

"If you leave tomorrow, then I will go on the day after tomorrow to see that everything is all right, and I will give them money every day as they need it. Just tell your wife to let me know what she needs. If you are gone three or even five months, do not be concerned."

"Very good," said Ma Jing. "Then I will say good night." He returned and told his wife, He Shi: "When I come back I will repay any money that my friend Li Ping gives you. Just keep a record of everything. Until I return, just borrow anything you need from Li Ping and I will repay that, too. I will probably be gone only two months. If anyone asks where I've gone, just say I went to collect the rents." He Shi nodded her head. The next day Ma Jing got up and left.

But Li Ping, after one day, thought to himself: "Ma Jing put his trust in me. I must go and see that all is well." Leaving one of his servants to watch his shop, he took two ounces of silver and went out. Ma Jing's house was directly to the east. Coming out of Ma Jing's gate, he saw a woman, and looking at her from a little distance, he recognized He Shi, Ma Jing's wife. She was dressed in a flowered robe and was wearing jewelry. He thought to himself, "Whenever I have been in the house, everything has been very plain and his wife never went beyond the gate. Yet today, just after Ma Jing has left, she goes out dressed like that. I had better go and ask about the old lady's health."

But just as he was about to go up to the gate, he heard someone calling his name: "Li Ping, sir! Li Ping, sir!" He turned and saw one of the shop apprentices.

"What is it?" Li Ping asked.

"Someone is in the shop asking for you."

Li Ping went back to the shop and found that it was a man named Yang Wanian, the proprietor of a clothing store on East Street.

When he saw Li Ping, he said, "Oh, Li Ping, sir, I have been waiting for you for some time. At the time when I first started in business, the building was rented from you through a guarantor who acted as the middleman, and now he has rented the property to another man who wants to take possession. If you give the lease to another man, he can open up the same business where I started up with my shop. The guarantor who acted as your middleman must give me a chance to renew my lease. Otherwise I will bring a lawsuit against him."

Li Ping said, "Brother Yang, do not get excited. Just tend to your store and let me find this middleman. I will talk to with him. There are ways of handling such affairs." Li Ping immediately went off, found the middleman, and came to an agreement, but the affair was time-consuming. By the time he was finished it was already late. "Tomorrow then I will go to the Ma family home," he decided.

The next day he again took some money and instructed his clerk, saying, "Watch the business carefully. I must visit the Ma family." But when he got to the crossroads, he again saw the two leaves of the great gate open and Ma Jing's wife in her finery and jewels stepping out. Li Ping quickened his step. Again she turned toward the eastern part of the village. Li

Ping hurried after her, thinking to ask her about things, but she was going so rapidly that he could not catch up. As she disappeared into the distance, Li Ping thought to himself, "Well, I will ask the old lady where she has gone."

But just as he approached the gate of Ma Jing's house and was about to knock, a little apprentice came running and calling his name, "Li Ping, sir! Li Ping, sir! This time it is terrible! There is a drunken man in the shop hitting another man. Come quickly! The man's head is bleeding and we don't know whether he is alive or dead. One of the officers has come from the yamen. You must come back at once!"

Of course, there was nothing he could do but return. Naturally it turned out to be two drunken men fighting. They had exchanged insults and blows. Everyone was trying to help and the man from the yamen had a lot of questions before he would leave. Then things had to be put right in the shop.

By that time it was already late in the afternoon, but Li Ping started back to the Ma residence with the money. He left the wine shop and when he was at the crossroads, he again saw He Shi entering the east section of the village. "Strange," he thought, "that she should spend all this time away from home just when Ma Jing is absent." He could not help thinking terrible thoughts. "A man never knows what his wife or his children may do." He did not want to talk with her and hear her say things he might not believe. He let out a deep sigh. "I wish that Ma Jing were not my friend."

There was only one road by which she could return. "I will wait here until she appears and see what time she returns." He waited until late at night. At the second watch she had still failed to reappear. At last Li Ping returned to his shop and never went to the home of Ma Jing again.

Before Ma Jing realized it, two months had flown by since his departure. He had accomplished all he had hoped to do. It was as if he had met the fairy Fortune herself, killed her protecting dragon, and stripped off its precious skin. Now he was returning satisfied, laden with gold and jewels that he had stolen. He had bought a number of things back, and like his uncle, rode a mule and led a donkey with a pack behind.

When he reached his home at New Moon Village, he lifted off the pack and went in to see his mother, whose illness had grown worse while he was gone. As soon as his wife He Shi saw him, she prepared some tea and pastries. "Wife," asked Ma Jing, "how much money did Li Ping lend you while I was away and how many times did he visit you altogether?"

"A great friend you made with him," she said. "After you were gone, he did not come a single time, nor send any money. I managed to get a few ounces of silver by pawning things, and I don't know how many times he has eaten a meal here in the days before you left. He must be the kind who forgets all his friends have done for him."

As Ma Jing heard this, he could feel his anger building up inside. After he had finished eating, he took several presents, saying, "I am going to pay a social call on Li Ping and see what he has to say."

He went out through the big gate and went to Li Ping's wine shop at the west end of the block. As soon as he was inside, Ma Jing asked a servant, "Is your proprietor at home?"

"Yes," said the servant. Ma went straight into the back room.

As soon as Li Ping saw him, he quickly bid him welcome. Ma Jing was not without a certain dignity, and he could conceal his emotions. He smiled and began to talk pleasantly. "I have brought you a few things from my trip, dear brother, all things I know you like to eat."

"And how is my elder brother?" asked Li Ping. "Please have a seat." He took the things and the two sat down together. Li Ping was silent for a long time, while Ma Jing looked at him.

Finally Ma Jing asked, "And how is business?"

"About ready to shut down," said Li Ping.

"And how is my younger brother, Li Ping?" asked Ma Jing.

"About ready to die," responded Li Ping.

"Does Younger Brother have something to say that is difficult to put into words?" asked Ma Jing. "Tell me and I will listen."

Slowly, and with great reluctance, Li Ping told him the whole story. As Ma Jing listened, he felt a shock as if an explosion had blown a door open. He left the shop hardly able to make his way home.

CHAPTER 46

Ma Jing waits in the darkness;
a dragon hides behind a scroll

NOW, when Li Ping saw Ma Jing, Li Ping was unable to speak. He just sat looking at him for a long time and thought, "If I don't speak, I will lose his friendship, and if I do, it will be most difficult to open my mouth."

And then Ma Jing had said, "Whatever you have to say, just say it. Don't hold it in."

So Li Ping told what had happened from beginning to end. How he had taken the silver and started toward Ma Jing's home only to see Ma Jing's wife in strange finery leave her house and go east, how he'd run after her and was called back. Then of the second and third day, when the same thing happened.

Then Ma Jing had laughed, "Ha! Ha! Today I came thinking to bring our friendship to its end. I don't know how to say it. Whether this is true or not I cannot say, but I am leaving now."

He stood up, and when he reached home he said nothing. Two days passed. Then he told his wife, He Shi, "I must go to see a wealthy man. Please watch the house. Perhaps I will be gone a couple of months." He took a great knife, said goodbye to his mother, and left home.

To the south, a little more than a mile away, there was another village that had some shops. On the south side of the road that ran through it there was an inn. Ma Jing went in. Everyone knew him. Several people spoke up and asked why he was idling about. Ma Jing said, "Find me a room. My house is full of relatives and friends and I can't stay there."

"Yes," said the servant. "We will give you our largest room."

When Ma Jing went into his room, he ordered food and drink. His heart was sad indeed. After he had drunk several pots of wine, he called the servant and told him to take the tray. Then he lay down and slept. After a while he awoke and ate a bit, all the while thinking, "Cheating! A robber must find an unfaithful wife and an unfaithful wife must wed a robber! When I am away, she must go out again to meet whomever it is.

I will take my knife and go to wait at the entrance to the east section—and, if I meet him, I will kill him with one slash of my knife." And so he returned and waited at New Moon Village.

He waited until the third watch but saw no one. He went up to the door of his house and looked. It was tightly closed. He leapt up to the rooftop and stealthily listened everywhere. There was no movement that he could detect. Then he returned to the hotel and called for someone to open the gate. When he reached his room in the hotel, he lay down and slept until daybreak. Then he had a drink and slept again.

When it was dark again, he took the knife and returned to the entrance to the east section of his village. At the second watch he heard a man and woman talking and laughing. He moved closer. It was not his wife's voice. "Go now, quickly," he heard the woman say. "Last night I would have liked to ask you, but it was a women's party and all the wives would have liked to see you, since it was very dull."

"They're all doing it," thought Ma Jing. Then he hid himself behind some trees near his house. Some time passed. Then he heard the footsteps of a single person walking very quickly, with a light step that almost flew. He could see someone of about thirty, who perhaps had a pale face. The man went up to Ma Jing's gate and stopped. He looked for some time and it seemed that he wanted to knock at the gate, but was afraid or did not dare to. Ma Jing watched in the darkness. Then he saw the man walking back and forth and heard him saying to himself, "Ah! Ah! I would like to knock but I'm afraid that Brother Ma may not be at home. As dark as it is, I can't see any pebble to throw."

When Ma Jing heard the man's voice, he realized that it was someone with whom he was familiar and he went up closer to see. It was the River Rat, Cloud Dragon Hua. "Second Brother," said Ma Jing, "where did you come from?"

Cloud Dragon bowed to him and immediately fell to asking him, "But what are you doing out here in the dark, Brother Ma?"

"I was waiting for someone," said Ma Jing. "Let us go inside and sit." The two leapt up and over the wall. Inside the courtyard Ma Jing opened the door of the east room. His wife, He Shi, heard them and got up and made tea for them. Ma Jing sat down with Hua Yun Long and again asked about where he had been.

Cloud Dragon Hua told all about what he had done in the city of Linan, with one exception. He did not tell about how he had attempted to abduct a beautiful young nun from the nunnery, nor about how he had killed her with his knife when she refused to submit to him.

"You may feel secure here, Brother Hua," said Ma Jing. "No one will come here with a search warrant, and even if they should, I already have a walled cellar prepared for just such a situation. And I must tell you that I know the district magistrate and other local officials. They absolutely cannot come here. No one here knows that I am a member of the Greenwood."

"Very good," said Cloud Dragon and he thanked Ma Jing.

When day broke, the warming sun came forth. While the two were sitting down with tea and morning refreshments, there was a sudden clamor outside and the confused sound of many voices. Cloud Dragon was terrified, and turned pale with fright.

"Don't be afraid," said Ma Jing. "I will go out and see about it." As he opened the gate and looked out, he saw standing there fifty or sixty people. They included everyone from the families of the more well-to-do inhabitants of the area in and about New Moon Village.

"Respected sir, how are you?" asked one. "We need you because of a certain problem. The question has nothing to do with you, but we have not been able to settle it. It concerns some certificates for duty paid upon imported mules and donkeys about to be sold in the local horse market. We have a legal contest that seems about to turn into an actual fight between these people. We have tried but failed to settle the question. Everyone here knows you and we think that you can settle our dispute."

"Very well," replied Ma. "I ask you all to come in and sit down, even though the place is small and inconvenient. We will talk for two days, and if we are unable to come to an agreement, you can all leave and that will be it. Now I must go briefly to the inner courtyard and talk with my family."

In the inner courtyard he said to Cloud Dragon, "While I am busy helping these people to come to an agreement, someone has to take care of things here." He gave Hua two ounces of silver and a large vegetable basket. "We will need fish, a couple of chickens, vegetables, and other things. I depend upon your kind help to go to the market. Just bring the things back and give them to my wife. Later, in a little while, I will come back and have a drink and something good to eat with you."

"Of course," said Cloud Dragon. So he took the basket and went out into the market. He was just about to carry some things back when he saw Lei Ming and Chen Liang walking quickly toward him.

Seeing him, Lei Ming was surprised. "Brother Hua, why have you not quickly fled?"

"The senior monk of the Monastery of the Soul's Retreat, Ji Gong, is behind us, coming to arrest you," added Chen Liang.

"Dear brothers," said Cloud Dragon, "How have you been since we parted in the Village of a Thousand Gates, and how do you know that Ji Gong is coming to take me?"

The two explained all that had happened and finally that Ji Gong was bringing two headmen with him. "He is following close behind us and he mentioned New Moon Village. He must have known that you would be here."

As Cloud Dragon listened, he began to feel worried. He thought of throwing away the market basket and running, but just then he saw Ma Jing coming. The three went up to him and saluted him respectfully. Ma Jing welcomed them. "Why don't you come into the house instead of standing here in the street talking?"

Again Lei Ming and Chen Liang told their story. "Never mind," Ma Jing said. "It's nothing to worry about. Why don't my brothers Lei and Chen and Second Brother Hua all come with me?" And so the four went straight into Ma Jing's home. Ma Jing took the things to the kitchen and they went to sit in the east room.

Cloud Dragon turned to Ma Jing and said, "I have still not paid my respects to your old mother. Would you take me to see her?"

"May we also?" asked Lei Ming and Chen Liang.

"The old lady really is not very well," replied Ma Jing. "Perhaps it is better not to disturb her. Why don't you three rest and in a little while we will have something to eat and drink." Then he asked Lei Ming and Chen Liang to tell their story in detail.

As he listened, he began to laugh loudly. "My dear brothers! Do you simply believe that a monk with two headmen can capture Brother Hua here? Even if he had two hundred officers and soldiers, they could not take him. No one would dare to come in here. If he doesn't come, that's it. If he comes, I will take him first and take his life from him."

"Don't say such things, Elder Brother," said Lei Ming. "You don't know the powers of Senior Monk Ji Gong. If you just say a word, he can foretell the future. If you try to run out the front gate, he will be there at the front gate; if you try to run out the back gate, he will be waiting there for you. If you go east, he will be in the east, and if you go west, there he will be. There is no place where you can run that you will not be seized by him."

When Ma Jing heard these words, he struck the table with his fist and shouted, "Stop that insane behavior and calm yourselves. If he does come, look!" and he pointed at a scroll hanging on the east wall. "If I roll up the scroll and open the door in the wall behind it, there is a cellar inside where you can hide," he said.

These words had hardly been spoken when they heard someone outside knock on the door and say, "Is Cloud Dragon Hua in there? If he is, tell him to come out and see me, the monk."

When Lei Ming and Chen Liang heard these words, their faces turned pale and one said, "See, Elder Brother Ma, the monk has come."

Ma Jing simply rolled up the scroll and said, "You three go in there. I will take care of things myself." There was nothing the three could do except go down into the cellar. Ma Jing rolled the scroll down and went outside to look around.

Now, where did Ji Gong come from? After the two headmen had turned the people from the assassins' inn over to the local yamen, the monk met the two and went on here and there until they were very hungry. Then they saw a small inn. The monk went in. Headman Chai said, "If the monk eats, we will eat, too," so they also went inside. After they had eaten, the monk got up and walked out. He was gone for a long time. Headman Chai turned to the other headman and said, "Well, She, old fellow, we have eaten and the monk has gone, leaving us with no money to pay the bill. Let us leave now." They could see the waiter coming with the bill. Just as they were about to walk out, suddenly there was the monk. "Very good! You walk out and leave us to pay the bill," they said.

"You two come with me," said Ji Gong. "There is money to be made in the dark."

CHAPTER 47

Ji Gong cracks an egg; Ma Jing has an unwelcome visitor

WHEN Ji Gong and the two headmen, Chai and She, were eating together in the little wine shop, the headmen had finished before the monk. She got up first and said he was leaving. Chai started to follow him. "So you two are leaving me stuck with the table," said the monk.

"You did that to us last time," said Chai. "This is just setting things up the other way around. There is no money and we are leaving," and so the two went out.

The waiter, who had overheard the conversation, noticed that the two men had left, and carefully watched the monk. As luck would have it, someone holding a bowl of mushroom soup bumped into a man coming in from outside. Crash! Splash! The bowl was broken and the soup spilled on the newcomer.

One shouted, "You have spilled my soup!"

The other shouted, "You have soaked my clothing!"

Hot words soon led to blows and the place was in uproar. While the waiter was watching what was happening, the monk left and met the two headmen outside in the village street.

"Well done," said the monk. "You went off and left me."

"Just as you did with us," said Headman Chai.

"Right," said the monk, "so now we're even."

"But how did you get out?" they asked.

"I had the owner charge the bill to my account," answered the monk.

"So they knew you," said Chai, "and let you charge it."

"Never mind about that," said Ji Gong. "However, I have an idea. I will hide, and if you find me, I will give you breakfast tomorrow morning. If you cannot find me, then you can give me breakfast."

"Not a bad idea," commented Chai. So the monk hid, but the two men could not find him, because in the dark he slipped away to New Moon Village. When morning came, the monk went up to Li Ping's wineshop. The waiter was just opening the blinds.

The monk quickly walked in and noticed that there were six tables, on each of which there were four small dishes. One dish was filled with eggs, one with slices of dried bean curd, one with large boiled beans, and one with dried melon seeds. He chose a table and sat down, took a boiled egg, and cracked the shell against the table. Then he called for the owner.

The waiter came and said, "Monk, you're up bright and early, cracking eggs and calling for the owner. Are you looking for trouble?"

"What do you charge for eggs this big?" asked the monk.

"Eggs this big sell for several cash," replied the waiter.

"I asked how many cash for these eggs," said the monk.

"Six cash apiece," said the waiter.

"And how much for each slice of dried bean curd?"

"Three cash each," the waiter replied.

"And this plate of boiled beans? You could probably sell that for a whole string of cash. Cooking them must be a lot of work for you," said Ji Gong.

"Monk, you are very kindhearted," said the waiter, "but when we boil the beans, the skin comes off automatically."

"Oh, we're automatic, are we?" said the monk.

"Monk, don't joke about being automatic," said the waiter.

"I was only talking about the beans," said the monk. "Bring me a pot of tea." The waiter brought the tea and the monk ate and drank. Then he asked for the check. The waiter made out a check for 256 cash. "Write it on my account," said the monk.

"You came in here bright and early and knew all along that when you were finished eating, you wouldn't have the money to pay the check. That won't do, monk," said the waiter.

"You simply write it up. How is it that you can't do that?" asked the monk.

While the two men were arguing, Li Ping came in from the back room and asked, "Waiter, what's going on?"

"He ate and drank and won't pay," the waiter explained.

"You don't carry any money, monk, and you just sit down and eat and drink?" asked Li Ping.

"I am waiting here at this wine shop for someone—someone you know very well. He asked me to come here and have something while I waited. If not, I wouldn't have eaten or drunk anything. I've waited for him for a long time and he has not arrived. This is why I have not paid."

"When did you make this appointment?" asked Li Ping.

"Last year," said the monk.

"And where was this appointment made?" Li Ping queried further.

"Along the road," answered the monk.

"And what was the name of the person who made this appointment?" Li Ping continued with his questioning.

"I have forgotten," answered the monk.

Li Ping had been thinking that if the monk mentioned the name of a person who was well known, he would not have to ask the monk for money but could just let him go. Now, however, he said, "You're talking nonsense, monk."

"No, I'm not talking nonsense because I can cure all sorts of illnesses, both internal and external. It doesn't matter whether the person who is ill is male or female, old or young, I can cure everything. This person asked me to cure an illness, but I have forgotten his name."

When Li Ping heard that the monk could cure illnesses, he thought of his younger brother, Li An, whose sickness had reached a critical stage. Li Ping said to himself, "If this monk could cure my brother, wouldn't that be wonderful!" Aloud, Li Ping said, "Since you can cure illnesses, can you cure my younger brother, who is very ill?"

The monk said, "I can."

"If you can really cure him," said Li Ping, "not only will I not ask you to pay your bill, but I will buy you a new set of clothes."

"You're very kind," said the monk.

Li Ping led the monk into the back room. At one glance, the monk took in the condition of Li An lying on the brick platform bed. His breathing could not be heard. His face was like white paper, with not a trace of color. His eyes were open, his nose moist, and his ears dry. Li An was still a tender youth. Li Ping had been trying to take care of him, and that was why he had brought him to his wine shop. Unexpectedly, Li An's illness had grown worse. As the monk looked at him, Li Ping asked, "Can you cure him, monk?"

"I can cure him, replied the monk. "I have some medicine here." With that, the monk took out a large pill.

"What medicine is that?" asked Li Ping.

"This is called the stiff legs and staring eyes pill," replied Ji Gong.

"It is not a pleasant name," said Li Ping.

"If a person takes this medicine, it cures the stiff legs and staring eyes, but let me tell you, this is not like ordinary medicine. It cures all sort of sicknesses, and that is why it has this strange name," the monk explained.

The monk took the pill and crushed it and mixed it with water. "No! No!" said Li An as he watched, but the monk pointed at him, and as he opened his mouth wide, the monk poured the mixture down his throat.

In a short time the boy felt some movement in his stomach and then experienced a feeling of energy as the blood coursed through his veins. His color returned. He felt as if he were on a high mountaintop with a fresh breeze blowing. "Good medicine! It is like the pill of immortality!" Li An exclaimed. He sat up and he was thirsty. After he drank, he wanted food.

Li Ping's heart was filled with happiness at seeing this change. "Teacher," he said, "this is wonderful medicine, in spite of its strange name."

"It is also called the pill that calls to life, because even if the soul has almost left the body, this pill will call it back again," the monk explained. "Your younger brother was near death, but he has been called back to life."

"That is true," said Li Ping. "But Teacher, since you can cure sicknesses, I must tell you that the mother of my closest friend, Ma Jing, is also very ill. Could you cure her as well?"

I could—it is really nothing," said the monk. "It is just that unless they ask, I can do nothing. If I went, they might not let me in. That would be very embarrassing."

"If it were not that his home is the same as mine, I would not ask. Don't worry about a thing. I will go with you." As the two left the wine shop, Li Ping asked, "Where did you become a monk, Teacher?"

"I became a monk at the Monastery of the Soul's Retreat. The first character of my name is Dao and the second is Ji. They also call me Mad Ji," the monk told Li Ping. And so they walked on, talking, until they reached Ma Jing's gate.

"I will call someone to the gate," said Li Ping.

But the monk said, "I will call." Then he shouted, "Is Cloud Dragon Hua in there?"

"Teacher, what is that you said just now?" asked Li Ping.

"Never mind," said Ji Gong.

After a little while, Ma Jing opened the gate and said, "Dear brother, did you call someone to open the gate?"

"It was not I," replied Li Ping. "It was the honorable monk. We came together. This is the famous Chan teacher Ji from the Monastery of the Soul's Retreat, who has just cured my younger brother. I came with him to introduce him so that he could cure your mother."

"Dear brother," said Ma Jing, "you came at an unfortunate time. I am just sitting down with some friends. Could you ask the monk to wait until I call and invite him?"

"I was right, wasn't I?" said the monk. "I came at the wrong time. Am I to be asked in or not?"

"Elder Brother," exclaimed Li Ping, "you're acting foolishly! What friends could you have that would prevent you from seeing me and getting the old lady cured? Why are you hiding from people? You cannot trifle with your mother's illness! If it had not been that Ji Gong cured my younger brother, I would not have come!"

But Ma Jing kept saying, "Come another day."

Li Ping became impatient, and taking the monk with him, simply walked inside. The two men had long been the kind of friends who simply entered each other's door without knocking. Therefore, Ma Jing could not very well prevent Li Ping from doing that now, so he simply followed along behind.

The monk went straight to the east building and sat down. Ma Jing instantly beckoned to the monk, saying, "Teacher, let us go and sit in the north building."

"Why won't you let me sit here in the east building?" the monk asked.

"There are guests," Ma Jing replied.

"Oh, your three little friends. Well, there is one that won't be able to run away while we're in here," said the monk.

Li Ping did not understand. He was thinking, "This is the library. Why doesn't Ma Jing want the monk here?" He could see no one and felt uneasy.

The three men then went to the north building and Li Ping said, "If you are going to perform the cure now, I will go back to my shop. Later, please come to my place and we will have some refreshments together."

"Go ahead," said the monk.

After Li Ping had gone, the monk took out a piece of medicine and asked for boiling water in which to dissolve it and also cold water to cool it. He then gave the mixture to the old lady to drink. In a short time, the old lady began to feel energy in her body. She sat up and asked, "Son, how is it that after having been so sick and unable to move for these many months, now I suddenly feel well?"

"Mother," Ma Jing explained, "you did not know that here we have Ji Gong from the Monastery of the Soul's Retreat who has given you a strange and wonderful medicine."

As soon as the old lady heard that this was Ji Gong, she recalled that Ji Gong liked meat pastries: "My son, you must kowtow to Ji Gong and then take him into the east room and give him some tea and meat pastries."

Ma Jing approached Ji Gong and said, "Teacher, my mother wants me to kowtow to you and also offer you some refreshment. Let us go outside, then."

"Good," said Ji Gong, and the two went to the east room.

CHAPTER 48

Ji Gong asks for a scroll; Ma Jing kills a temple guardian

MA Jing had, indeed, been very happy to see Ji Gong cure his mother. As she had recommended, he immediately kowtowed, falling to his knees and knocking his head against the floor. After what his mother had said, there was nothing he could do except invite the monk into the east room library.

As the monk followed Ma Jing into the east building, he saw at once that the table was set with four places. "Who was here drinking wine?" he asked.

"I was," answered Ma Jing.

"If you were drinking here alone, why are there four wine cups?" asked the monk.

"I was drinking from each of them in turn," said Ma Jing. Then he quickly had the dishes removed and two places set instead in front of the monk and himself.

"May I ask your honorable name?" queried the monk.

"I am called Ma Jing," he replied.

"May I ask you about someone you might know?" asked the monk.

"Who is that?" asked Ma Jing.

"I have a pupil named Ma Yuanzhang. Do you know him?" asked the monk.

Ma Jing was thinking, "This monk is really hateful, saying my uncle is his pupil. This is an insult." He looked the monk straight in the eye and said aloud, "I do not know a Ma Yuanzhang."

"I cured your mother's illness and how do you thank me?" asked the monk.

"How much did that medicine cost?" asked Ma Jing. "How much gold and silver? You tell me. I must give you what you ask."

"I really don't want any money, but I truly love scrolls," replied the monk.

"If you like scrolls," said Ma Jing, "I have many. Please come with me and make your selection."

"I really don't want any other," said the monk. "I just want this one hanging here on the wall."

"You may have it," said Ma Jing. "A little later, when you are leaving, I will give it to you to take away."

"I said I want it because I just want it now," said the monk, and standing up he moved forward as if to take it.

Ma Jing quickly stepped in between the monk and the picture. "Teacher, the wall is very dirty. If you disturb the picture, how can we eat? But after we have eaten, we will discuss it."

"This, too, is possible, but I will not leave this room, and I will see that not one of them escapes," the monk insisted. At this time, Lei Ming and Chen Liang, together with Cloud Dragon, were there in the cellar behind the picture on the wall. They heard and very clearly understood what Ji Gong meant. The three of them began to shake with fear.

"This monk is uncontrollable," thought Ma Jing. "If I kill him with one slash of my knife, then to satisfy my young brother Li Ping I will have to erect a pagoda in recognition of him curing my mother's illness, and every year I will have to burn incense and paper money there in his memory." He moved toward the center of the room, secretly fingering his long knife. He thought he would get the monk drunk on wine. He poured a cup and waited.

The monk raised his cup and said, "You're waiting until you get me drunk, aren't you? It will be easier to manage things then." Then he sat there for a long while and began to hum with a mournful, moaning sound. By this time the day was drawing to a close.

"Why are you making that moaning sound, monk?" asked Ma Jing.

"I am getting bored with this place and would like to leave," answered the monk. Together they walked out of the room and through the gate. It was getting dark. As they walked, the monk was asking, "Ma Jing, what do you think of that medicine?"

"Good," said Ma Jing.

"Ma Jing, can you guess how much that medicine cost?" asked the monk.

"How much was it?" countered Ma Jing.

"Ma Jing, would you have guessed that that medicine cost only one cash each for a pill?" asked the monk.

"That's very cheap," commented Ma Jing.

"Cheap or not, I don't think I will come again," the monk said. "People are not good-hearted any more. I cured your mother and you are think-ing of killing me. Then you will build a pagoda in my memory and offer incense and burn paper money to my spirit."

As Ma Jing listened, he thought, "This is a very strange monk." Then, as they came to the entrance to the east section, the monk sat down on a stone. Ma Jing stepped behind his back and leaned over him with knife in hand, ready to kill him. Suddenly the monk pointed with his finger and Ma Jing was unable to move. He stood still with the knife upraised in his hand.

"Help! He's going to kill me! I'm a monk!" Ji Gong shouted.

Along the street there were many shops, and their doors began to open. People were coming out of them with lights. Ma Jing was frightened as he thought, "If people see me standing here unable to move with the knife in my upraised hand, they will question me—what shall I say to them?"

At that point the monk used his Buddhist arts so that they both became invisible. People walked by them but saw nothing. "I was in the wrong," said Ma Jing, "and yet you would not let people see me."

"You took your knife to me," said the monk, "but you paid no atten-tion to your wife's lover."

"I didn't know where he was," said Ma Jing.

"Come with me and I will show you," said the monk. Ma Jing followed the monk until they came to the Temple of the God of Wealth. "He is in this temple," the monk told Ma Jing.

"Let me knock at the gate," said Ma Jing.

But the monk said, "You won't catch people committing adultery by knocking at gates. You go over the wall."

"I can go over the wall," said Ma Jing, "but how will you manage?"

"I can go over walls, too," the monk assured him.

Ma Jing took a great leap to the top of the wall and looked down. There was Ji Gong on the inside. "How did you get in here?" Ma Jing asked.

"I leapt over the wall," the monk replied.

"Show me," said Ma Jing. "I would like to see how Teacher does it."

Ji Gong was up on the wall with one leap. Then he chanted, "I com-mand by the word Om," and disappeared. Once more he chanted, "I com-mand by the word Om," and he became visible again.

"These magic tricks are not bad," said Ma Jing to himself. "Tomorrow, perhaps I can learn them."

Again the monk said, "Come with me." Around the corner of the building they saw before them a two-story hall. At the corner was a gate leading into another large courtyard filled with pines and bamboo. At the back of this courtyard was a three-story building.

At the top floor they could see a light. Shadows moved over the paper-covered latticed windows. Stealthily they climbed upstairs to the third-story veranda. Ma Jing made a tiny hole in the paper window-covering to look inside. The building faced south, and on the north side, opposite the windows, he could see a long, raised brick platform that was used as a bed. On the brick platform was a low table, and on the table was a paper lantern with a candle inside. Directly opposite him, seated on the platform, was none other than his wife. She was dressed in brightly colored, richly embroidered silk garments. He looked again. It could be no one else but his He Shi.

On either side were sitting two monks. One was a large man with dark reddish features wearing a loose saffron-colored robe and white shoes. Ma Jing recognized him as a ruffian known as Tan, "the Striped Wolf." The other man was smaller and dressed in a brown monk's robe. It was Zhou Lan, nicknamed "the White Tiger." They were the two men hired to take care of the little private temple in his uncle's absence.

Then he heard Tan speaking. "Why are you concerned, Sister? We both heard that Ma Jing would not return tonight. You don't have to leave now. We were just thinking of having some tea and something to eat. We were pleasantly surprised to see you tonight."

"No, I really can't stay," Ma Jing heard his wife say. "The monk Ji Gong called at our house and cured the old lady of her illness. Ma Jing has been entertaining him in the east room. I told the household people that I was going to see my aunt, and so I was able to come here briefly. I knew you'd be missing me. Well, if I don't go back tonight, I can go in the morning and say that I stayed overnight with my aunt. Let's have something to eat. I haven't had anything."

Ma Jing grew more and more angry as he looked. "What is a husband to do if his wife is not true to him and his children pay no attention to him? Behaving in this disgraceful way!" Suddenly he gripped his knife and burst into the room. His arm rose and fell. He had killed the man named Tan. The other man threw himself through the latticed window. His wife stood up and quickly ran out through the door. Ma Jing followed after her. In the courtyard she turned and he saw her touch her face with her hand. A huge mouth opened with teeth nearly a foot long. Ma Jing was stunned with terror.

"You dare to interfere with me!" she screamed. Out of her mouth came a black jet of smoke that struck Ma Jing, making him fall to the ground more dead than alive.

Now this creature was not He Shi, Ma Jing's wife, at all. He Shi could never have sent forth that black smoke. It was a fox spirit that had copied her features to appear as a physical being. She was one of a group of fox spirits that haunted the Jade Mountains. She had come looking for human companionship, and she had grown attached to He Shi in the following way.

Long before He Shi had married Ma Jing, she had been a girl named He Qin, and a family member had given her an old Daoist cap that she liked to put on and play at being a sorceress. On one occasion, she had been at a wedding in a house where the groom's younger brother had been ill for some time. Another girl said to her, "Why don't you get your Daoist cap and see if you have any luck at curing him?"

He Qin laughingly agreed to try. "Perhaps I can get my spirit to come to me and help."

"Don't you need a table, the five grains, and things like that?" her girlfriend asked.

"No. I will just put the cap on, lie down, and ask my friendly spirit to come to me. Then I will ask her to cure the boy." At this time there was a great wind that rattled the doors and the windows. Immediately afterward, several things in the room moved mysteriously, as if an unseen person were in the room.

He Qin was not frightened at all. She described the boy's illness and asked the spirit to help her. Oddly enough, the boy got well and He Qin was rewarded with a present of money. For a while she left the Daoist cap at her friend's home, but as objects continued to move about, she was asked to take it back.

After she married Ma Jing, her husband was angered when mysterious things happened, and the fox spirit in turn came to dislike Ma Jing. While Ma Jing was away from home for two months doing his thievery disguised as a businessman, the fox spirit decided to come down from the Jade Mountains in her fox-like body. From that body she was able to transform herself into other material forms, in this case into a likeness of He Shi, the one person she knew well enough to duplicate. Her purpose in taking the form of He Shi was certainly not to cause trouble for Ma Jing's wife, to whom she was greatly attached, but to use her mischief as a fox spirit to damage the relationship between Ma Jing and his close friend Li Ping.

The two monks in the temple were not actually monks, but two unprincipled ruffians who had been dressing in monk's robes while staying in the empty Temple of the God of Wealth. They had been persuading people to give them undeserved gifts and doing other bad things as well.

They had picked up a little monkish lore from Ma Yuanzhang, who, of course, pretended to be a monk, but it was all simply a masquerade to cover their devilry. They both admired Ma Jing's wife and hoped that she might respond in kind, but their compliments had just the opposite effect. The one named Tan had been particularly troublesome, and Ma Jing's wife had asked her husband to tell them to keep away from her because of their behavior. The fox spirit had thought that it would be amusing to pay the two men a visit. It was at that point that Ma Jing had burst into the room with his knife.

CHAPTER 49

The fox spirit hears a story; Ma Jing receives the monk's instructions

WHEN Ma Jing ran after the fox spirit thinking that she was his wife, she had suddenly turned and, as she showed her teeth, shouted: "I am going to eat you!"

And so she would have done, had not Ji Gong confronted her, saying, "You are not going to eat people. Why don't we talk things over? We might get along well together."

"You shameless monk! What do you mean? I will simply eat you also," she said. With that she sent forth another blast of smoke at Ji Gong.

The monk only laughed and said, "Fox Spirit, if you like monks, let me tell you a story. There was once a famous monk who went up into the mountains and lived as a hermit. Because of his abstinence from everything worldly, the natural order of things was affected and no rain fell. The villagers who needed the rain for their crops therefore asked a certain woman named Water Lily to go up and persuade the monk to make, rain. They promised her 200 ounces of silver.

"'If I am to try to do this,' she said, 'you must first give me fine clothing, a sedan chair, and attendants so that he will think I am a great lady and pay attention to me.'

"All this was done. When she reached the mountaintop, she saw the monk sitting in meditation with his eyes closed. 'Old monk,' she cried, 'have pity on me. My stomach aches terribly, and it will only stop if some skillful gentleman rubs it.'

"The monk opened his mouth and chanted, 'O Mi To Fu, Holy Buddha! Don't talk nonsense, young lady. Men and women should not touch each other carelessly. Moreover, I have left the world and have come up to the mountaintop for undisturbed meditation, abstaining from eating flesh or drinking wine. I can see also that the young lady comes from a family of high pedigree. It would all be most unseemly.'

"At this point the woman called Water Lily laughed, and going up to the monk, seized his robe at the shoulders, pulling it away from his chest.

Again she said, 'Pity me.' The monk could not help but smell the fragrance of powder and perfume. He saw that she was indeed beautiful to look upon. Men are, after all, not made of grass and wood. Suddenly he threw his arms around her in an embrace, and immediately rain began to fall. Water Lily returned to the village and collected her reward."

The fox spirit laughed when Ji Gong had finished his story. "You are a naughty monk. Perhaps we would make a good pair," she said, smiling enticingly at the monk.

But Ji Gong said, "I said we were kindred spirits because we both like to make friends with human beings. I know that you are fond of Ma Jing's wife, but she is a good woman and would not want you to do harm to anyone. As long as you continue to help her and do not eat people or do other mischievous and malicious things, I will let you go."

"Foolish monk," the fox spirit said, "How can you imagine that you can tell me what to do and what not to do? What powers do you have, and where do they come from?"

"For one thing, I was born into a human body to people who had prayed for a son," he replied. "I do not occupy the dead body of an animal that was found while it was still warm from the life that had just left it. I came into this world to help a few people from making foolish mistakes, to ease their pains and sorrows, and to prevent some of the greater evils from occurring. The spirits of darkness will always cause trouble for mankind, but as long as people live upon this earth, those dark spirits can never extinguish the spirits of light."

At these words, the enraged fox spirit let out a roar and started toward the monk, but Ji Gong raised his hand and said, "I am not like that monk meditating on the mountain. I did my meditating some time ago. If you approach too closely, you will never again be able to use that fox's body and transform it into the likeness of a human being!"

A short time afterward, when Ma Jing had been revived by Ji Gong, the robber saw the dead body of the fox lying stiff and motionless. The fiend that had been about to eat him was nowhere to be seen. He realized that Ji Gong had saved his life, and he knelt to perform the kowtow.

"Ma Jing," the monk said, "your wife is a good woman. That woman you saw in the temple was not your wife, but a fox spirit. You must treat your mother and your wife kindly and not criticize your wife if a ghostly spirit comes to visit her. Tomorrow, when people find the body of the man you killed and the body of the fox, they will come to you for advice. Tell them to gather a great quantity of dry yellow reeds and place the bodies upon the pile. Then they are to burn the bodies until there is nothing left. The fox will never harm you again.

"But before the fox is burned, you must call your friend Li Ping and explain that the thing he saw was not your wife but a fox spirit. Bring him here and show him the fox and he will understand. Your friendship with him will be completely repaired. Now I must ask you to deliver Cloud Dragon Hua into my hands."

"I will treat my mother and my wife better than before," Ma Jing said, "but I cannot betray a friend."

"I did not think you could," said the monk. "Though you may be his friend, he is not yours. Sooner or later he may bring sorrow to you and your family. You must tell him to leave, and those two young men who are with him, too. I can take him into custody whenever I am ready."

CHAPTER 50

Ma Jing parts from his guests;
Ji Gong lends his robe

MA Jing went into his house and told the three who were still hiding in the cellar that they would have to leave the house. Cloud Dragon Hua left immediately and fled directly south, while Lei Ming and Chen Liang left later. As Cloud Dragon ran, he couldn't see or hear the monk following behind. They passed over low hills and through little valleys, into a place where there was no sign of people or dwelling places. It was in the first light of morning that Cloud Dragon began to catch sight of the monk ahead, and yet still see him following behind. "I no longer know whether I am chasing the monk or the monk is chasing me," he thought. He remembered the story of how the monk had appeared wherever the two men had fled in the forest.

At length, while passing over a small stone bridge, he saw the monk peeping out from underneath an arch. Hua was upon him in a flash. With several swift stabs the monk was dead, but it was not Ji Gong that Cloud Dragon Hua had killed. The monk was the White Tiger, the false monk who had escaped from Ma Jing by crashing through the latticed window of the temple. His masquerade was over.

Cloud Dragon Hua left the road and ran through the meadows, swamps, and thorny thickets, until looking back he no longer saw Ji Gong behind him. "At last," he thought, "I have given him the slip."

Now, when Ji Gong had ceased chasing Cloud Dragon Hua, he turned off on a side road. After walking for a while, he came upon a crowd of people all looking toward the center. Ji Gong pushed into the crowd and saw that they were looking at a young man lying beside the road. He was stark naked, without a stitch of clothing on or near him.

The people were asking questions. One asked, "What kind of a business is this?"

The young man said only, "Wa."

Another asked, "Where do you come from?"

The young man said only, "Wa."

A third asked, "What is your name?"

Again the answer was the same: "Wa."

"He is trying to ask for some water," exclaimed Ji Gong.

"Where is there some water?"

One of the people pointed to a well nearby and said, "But the water is too far down to reach, and no one has a bucket and rope."

Seeing that no one was going to help, Ji Gong walked over to the well and promptly disappeared.

"The monk has fallen into the well!" someone cried. When they approached the well, they saw that the monk was holding on to the well curb with his hands. He had dropped his oily hat into the water and was grasping it with his feet. Then he pulled himself up as he managed to keep some water in his hat. Once out of the well, he gave a drink of water to the young man, who, then able to speak, exclaimed, "Cursed monk!"

The onlookers immediately began to reproach him. "How can you curse this monk who has just gone to so much trouble to get you a drink of water—and in his own hat, too!"

"You do not understand," said the young man. "My name is Jiang and my personal name is Wenkui. I live outside the north gate of Youlong in the Jiang family hamlet. I am a graduate with a bachelor's degree. Recently, being short of money, I went to the house of my aunt in Linan and was returning with two hundred ounces of silver.

"The day was hot and I had walked a long distance when I suddenly felt a terrible pain in my stomach and sat down here. Shortly, a tall monk dressed in a saffron robe came by. His head was shaven and he wore a rosary with 108 beads around his neck. He asked me what was the matter, and I told him about the pain in my stomach. He then gave me a black pill. When I said 'cursed monk' just now, I meant not this monk here but that one, for immediately after taking the medicine, I was unable to move. I could see him taking the two hundred ounces of silver out of my pack, and after that I knew nothing until I awoke with people looking at me and all my clothes gone."

"Someone give him something to wear," said Ji Gong. But no one would give him anything. The monk then put his ragged robe around the young man, which left Ji Gong in an even more disgraceful-looking costume, all full of holes. The two then walked away, leaving the unhelpful crowd behind.

After a while the two came to an inn. Ji Gong led the young man inside. The waiter, upon seeing them, took them for a couple of beggars, but he let them sit down and brought the food that Ji Gong ordered. The young man looked at the food and said, "I won't eat."

"How is that? Why won't you eat?" asked the monk.

"I will not eat food for which I cannot pay," said the young man.

"Eat up and talk about it later," admonished the monk. "If they want to beat us, we'll be selling a couple of blows for the meal. If we are lightly beaten, that's it. If we're severely beaten and injured, they will have to take care of us until we're better."

The waiter who was listening had by now realized that this man was a monk, and thought it most amusing that the monk would be willing to be beaten for a meal. However, just then two men walked in and one said loudly, "Oh there you are, Monk."

CHAPTER 51

Ji Gong writes a strange order; Chen Liang observes Cloud Dragon Hua's companions

A S these two men entered the inn, the waiter noticed that they were dressed just alike, in gray trimmed with white. They were, in fact, the two headmen, Chai and She. Since Ji Gong had left them and gone off in the midst of a game of hide-and-seek, they had wandered throughout the night searching for him. The next day they reached the New Moon Village without any money between them. They were hungry, and all that day they had walked about the village without seeing Ji Gong, who was actually sitting in Ma Jing's east room eating pastries. That night they had missed him when he was on the way to the temple and encountering the fox spirit. After that, they had failed to see him when he had chased Cloud Dragon Hua out of the village during the night. Hour by hour they were getting hungrier and hungrier. At last they saw the monk walking with the young man who was wearing the monk's cloak just as the two turned in to the inn.

When they saw Ji Gong, they immediately began to complain. "Good!" exclaimed Chai. "You are here eating and we have been two nights and a long day without anything to eat."

"Why didn't you eat?" asked Ji Gong.

"We had no money," said Chai.

"We had no money," repeated She.

The listening waiter said to himself, "Another two without money."

Then the monk again asked the headmen, "If you're hungry, why don't you eat?" Chai and She sat down and began to eat ravenously.

Going to the manager, the waiter said, "First, we have a monk and a young man dressed only in a monk's ragged cloak. Then we have two men dressed just alike in gray who say that they haven't eaten for two nights and a day. Probably none of the four have any money!"

"Wait until they have finished eating and then we'll talk about it," the manager said.

Just then they heard someone talking outside the door. One of them said, "Well, well! Let's go in and have something before we go on our way."

Two men came in dressed in the latest fashion, with short jackets and everything made of expensive strong silk material. One had hair that was dyed red, with clothing in colors that matched his hair. The other was dressed all in white except for occasional touches of color. They were Lei Ming, nicknamed "the Wind Borne," and "the White Monkey," Chen Liang. They had stayed at Ma Jing's a bit longer than Cloud Dragon Hua, but not as long as Ma Jing had asked them to stay. Chen Liang had explained to Ma Jing, "We have business elsewhere, but we will stay until dawn and then say goodbye."

"At least have some breakfast," Ma Jing urged.

"We really are urgently pressed," said Lei Ming. They parted in the friendliest manner possible. At the inn they immediately went into the back dining room, and there they saw Ji Gong with Chai, She and a young man in Ji Gong's cloak. Both went at once and bowed reverently to Ji Gong.

The proprietor, seeing how well the two men were dressed, now followed their example and went to the table. Though he decided to bow reverently to the monk, he thought that the whole business was very strange.

"Teacher," asked Lei Ming, "where did you come from, and why are you half dressed? Who is this person to whom you have given your monk's robe?"

Ji Gong told the whole story of what had happened to the young man. When Lei Ming and Chen Liang clearly understood, the monk said, "Chen Liang, would you take Jiang Wenkui to a tailor's and buy him a set of scholar's clothing appropriate to his bachelor's degree? He will need shoes and a cap as well."

Chen Liang nodded in assent. At the shop he was able to buy everything needed, including the proper white socks. When Jiang had put them all on, they came back and returned the monk's robe, and then they all sat down together, calling for more food and wine.

"Do either of you have enough money to replace what Jiang here has lost?" Ji Gong asked his two young friends.

"I have four ingots of gold," said Chen Liang. "If I gave him two ingots, I would still have two ingots left. Each ingot can be changed for fifty ounces of silver."

"And I have fifty ounces of silver I can give him," said Lei Ming. They took out their money and gave it to Jiang Wenkui.

"I was already in your debt, and now with this, how can I thank you enough?" said Jiang Wenkui.

"Oh, it is nothing, really," responded Lei Ming. "Within the four seas all men are brothers!"

Then they all sat eating and drinking for a while until Lei Ming and Chen Liang drew Ji Gong away to another table out of earshot. "What are you up to?" asked the monk.

"Teacher," said Chen Liang, "have mercy on us. How can we show our faces if you take Cloud Dragon prisoner? We beg you not to take him."

"Not take Cloud Dragon?" said the monk. "That can be easily managed. Chen Liang, go out and get a large sheet of paper and an envelope. Then go to the cashier here and borrow a writing brush and ink."

Chen Liang did not know what the monk wanted to write, but he got the paper and other things and brought them to the monk. Ji Gong turned his back to them and wrote for a long time. Then he put the paper in the envelope and sealed it. Then he drew a picture of a wine shop sign on the envelope.

"I am giving you this envelope to take with you," he said. "After you have escorted Jiang Wenkui to his home outside the north gate of You-long, go into town through the north gate, and on the west side you will see a wine shop with this sign. Enter the shop and go upstairs. Sit down at a table there and read this letter of mine. If Cloud Dragon Hua does not commit the deed mentioned in the letter tonight, I will not capture him."

Lei Ming and Chen Liang had no idea what was in the monk's letter, but they nodded their heads in agreement. "I have asked you to escort Jiang Wenkui safely to his home. If he does not reach his home safely, all is over between us and I will then certainly have your lives!" admonished the monk.

"Yes," the two replied.

"Remember," the monk went on, "if you do not escort Jiang Wenkui properly, if you do not go through the north gate, if you do not go to the wine shop known as the Meeting Place of the Immortals, it will be all over between us. The monk will be through with you! Then, if you do not go straight upstairs, find a table against the wall, and then open the letter, I will be through with you and will want your lives! Then have a meal, and after you have eaten, pay the bill and leave. That is it."

Lei Ming and Chen Liang listened. Both agreed that everything must be done from the beginning to end in the exact order and manner that Ji Gong had described. They finished eating and paid the bill.

Ji Gong turned to the young graduate and said, "Jiang Wenkui, I am sending these two men to go with you as far as your home. Now leave with them."

Jiang Wenkui knelt and kowtowed to Ji Gong. The three young men said goodbye to the monk. It was only ninety *li* to Youlong, and before they realized it, they had arrived.

"Now that we are almost at my home, won't you come in and sit for a while?" asked Jiang Wenkui.

"No, we have other things we must do," said Chen Liang. "Why don't you just go in? Jiang Wenkui begged the two to stop, but they could not be persuaded. Again he thanked them and they parted.

Lei Ming and Chen Liang passed through the north gate into the town and walked along the street looking for the wine shop. Of course, in a moment they recognized the Meeting Place of the Immortals with the famous quotation from the poet Li Po, in which he declared that he could not go aboard the emperor's barge because he had become a spirit imprisoned in a jug of wine.

As they entered the restaurant, they saw great cooking ranges on both sides. They passed into the back, where there were crowds of people, and saw a stairway against the rear wall. Upstairs there was a somewhat similar arrangement so that they again had to pass the cooking ranges in order to go forward. At last they found a table against the wall.

Just then, they heard loud voices as three men entered the floor below from outside. One of the voices they recognized as belonging to Cloud Dragon Hua. Chen Liang went partway downstairs and peeped around a corner. It was indeed Cloud Dragon Hua, with two men who seemed particularly rough. Returning to the table, he told Lei Ming, "Brother Hua has two evil-looking men with him."

"Pay no attention," said Lei Ming. "We should be reading our teacher's letter to see what he says."

Chen Liang was shocked at what he read, and exclaimed, "Brother! Look at this! This is terrible!"

"But I cannot read," said Lei Ming. "What would I look at? Read it to me."

Chen Liang replied, "Teacher's letter is in eight lines. Listen while I read what it says."

> **High-minded heroes ever prevail.**
> **To save Cloud Dragon as you have begged**
> **Tonight in Youlong at the third watch**
> **Find Zhao Towers within the north gate.**
> **Thoughts of seizing a lovely maid**

Fill a wicked robber's head.
If by Cloud Dragon the deed's not done,
Tomorrow to Hangzhou I'll be gone.'

After Chen Liang had looked at the letter for a while, he said, "Brother, our teacher is saying that Cloud Dragon is going to the Zhao Family Towers to abduct a girl. And the monk also says that if Cloud Dragon doesn't accomplish this act tonight, then he will not arrest him. Whether this is true or false, he is telling us to keep a secret watch and prevent it from happening. Let us ask how to find the Zhao Towers."

"That's right," said Lei Ming. The two then ordered four dishes. When they had finished eating and drinking, they paid the bill and left. By that time Cloud Dragon and his friends had left, and therefore did not see Chen Liang and Lei Ming. Outside the restaurant they headed north until they saw coming toward them an old man with white hair.

Chen Liang went up to him, saluted him respectfully, and then asked, "Where are the Zhao Towers? Could you please tell us and point them out to us?"

"You ask about the Zhao Towers," replied the old man. "This insignificant person is now more than seventy. I have lived here all my life and know every alley, but I have never seen a place called Zhao Towers. Ai yah! But there is a wealthy man named Zhao. People call him the good Zhao Yuanwai, and there is a building with a second story within his place."

When Chen Liang heard this, he knew that the Zhao family home must be the place they were looking for, and said, "Of course. Someone asked us to take a letter there. They said it was in Youlong and that it had a tower. That meant it was the home of wealthy people. Now I understand."

"If you want to find the Zhao family home," said the old man, "go north until you see a store that sells flour and meal, continue walking north, and go into the next alley on the east. At the east end you will see a large tree and a great gate. There is the Zhao family home."

Chen Liang clearly understood, and decided to go there at night to protect the home against the evil plan of Cloud Dragon Hua.

CHAPTER 52

A thief sees the Spirit of the Night;
Chen Liang surveys the Zhao Tower

LATER that night, Chen Liang and Lei Ming waited outside Zhao Towers. But just as they were whispering together, they heard a tiny bit of earth fall from the top of the courtyard wall. Next, they saw the top of a ladder appear. Finally a very small man appeared at the top and descended into the courtyard. Now this man was named Qian, a well-known petty burglar.

Now Chen Liang watched as Qian went into a house on the north side of the street. Peering through a crack in the gate, Chen Liang saw Qian carrying a flexible centipede ladder inside the north building. Chen Liang dropped down into the courtyard. The building on the north side had three sections. The burglar went into the east section and lit a lamp.

Chen Liang went to the latticed window and made a small hole in the paper. Looking inside, he saw that a brick platform bed was opposite the window. On the bed there was a small table and a pile of cotton quilts. Below in front was a square table and a stool with a money drawer. The burglar sat down on the brick bed and took out the purse. He was clearly very happy when he opened it, talking to himself and taking out one piece of silver after another and saying, "With this I will build a house, with this I will buy land, with this I will go into business," and so on. After talking to himself in this fashion for some time, he put the silver back in the purse and put it in the money drawer, from which he took out one hundred cash. Getting down a wine jug that he had hidden among the rafters, Qian went off through the front gate to get some wine, humming and singing first a verse of a song and then a poem in his happiness, which he could hardly find ways to express.

Arriving at the liquor store, he said, "Draw me a bottle of wine, Manager Wang." Now, the manager of the liquor store was from the province called the Western Mountains, and so he was known as "Old West." Some time before this, Qian had gone to get some wine at a time when Old

West's shop was closed. Qian went to a neighboring place and bought a jug of wine there, and then said, "Write it up." Qian had actually brought two jugs with him, one empty and one filled with water. He kept the one filled with water under his coat. The storekeeper filled the empty jug and handed it to Qian, who secretly put it under his coat and took out the jug filled with water. When he asked for credit, the storekeeper refused, and Qian said, "Pour it back, then." But Qian had really handed back the jug filled with water. The storekeeper poured the water into his wine jar and Qian gained a jug of wine for nothing.

The next time, Qian did the same thing with Old West. Afterward, some other customers complained that there was water in the wine. This evening Qian again asked for credit, and when it was refused, handed back a jug, saying, "Pour it back then." But Old West came around the counter and soon discovered the extra jug that Qian was carrying.

Old West said, "Qian, you're trying to cheat me."

"I handed you the money first," Qian replied. There was a row and Qian received a few blows. Old West, however, poured out the water and filled the jug with wine, so Qian returned satisfied. As he entered his gate, however, Chen Liang seized him by the back of the neck with his fingers.

Now, when Qian had gone out to get the wine, Chen Liang went into the room, and opening the money drawer, took out the silver and also nine strings of cash that Qian had been saving from his burglaries. Chen Liang overturned the table and went outside to wait. When Qian came back with his wine, Chen Liang seized him, bound him, and then gagged him. Then he held up the knife and said, "If you cry out, I will have your life." The burglar did not dare to make a sound. As he left, Chen Liang said, "I am the Spirit of the Night and I watch out for good and evil deeds. You stole, and I have punished you."

Qian looked around when Chen Liang was gone and saw the overturned table and the empty money drawer. He was upset, but he could not move or make very much noise.

In a little while the night watchmen came by, striking the hour on their little wooden gong. "It's dark in the alley," said one.

"Don't frighten me," said the other. "I'm not very brave."

Then they heard a sound. "What was that?" asked one.

"A ghost," replied the other. Then they looked through the open gate and saw Qian calling out as best he could through his nose and trying to attract attention. The two watchmen soon released him.

"How did you get tied up?" asked one of the night watchmen.

"I have seen the Spirit of the Night," answered Qian. He showed them the overturned table and the empty money drawer. "I want to report a robbery," he said, but he did not say how much money was gone.

Meanwhile, Chen Liang had returned to the Liu family home. He placed the silver on one side of the dead body and the nine strings of cash on the other side. He removed the paper with the descriptions of young gentlemen from the tablet and went outside. There he picked up a piece of broken pottery and dashed it against the ground. At the sound, the young wife awakened, rose, and lit the lamp. She saw the silver and the strings of cash and realized that the paper was gone.

Outside, Chen Liang called out, "Tomorrow do not burn incense to us again, nor make such mistakes in the future. We are not gods. We are leaving you forever." Then he and Lei Ming went on their way.

At the Zhao household there was still no sound of humans to be heard and no suspicious animal cries, but a dim light could be seen through the paper windows. Looking down into other courtyards, they saw one window more brightly lit and heard the sound of the *piba* guitar and the Mongolian violin. Someone was singing. A voice said, "It's getting late. We must go to bed." People were walking through the courtyards here and there and saying good night. The watchers on the roof saw three young women cross a courtyard together, laughing and talking, and go toward a building, evidently their chamber for the night. They were indeed very beautiful.

"Those are the ones we must guard," said Chen Liang to Lei Ming.

The three young women were going up a stairway into the second story of the large flower-viewing pavilion. This was clearly the tower that Ji Gong had mentioned in his order to them. "There has been a family birthday party, no doubt," continued Chen Liang. Behind the three young women were two more who appeared to be serving maids, and then another not more then eighteen or nineteen. She was more beautiful than anyone they had ever seen. She seemed almost like a jade statue or an immortal spirit. Then followed a lovely girl of about sixteen and two more serving maids. After everyone was inside, the watchers could hear sounds of conversation and singing. Then all was silent and the lights were dimmed.

From a distant courtyard in the Zhao family estate came the sound of the wooden gong as Chen Liang and Lei Ming heard the watchers strike three times for the third watch.

CHAPTER 53

Seeing lovely ladies arouses wicked thoughts; three outlaws plan an abduction

A S Chen Liang and Lei Ming watched and waited, Chen Liang whispered, "You have seen these beautiful young ladies. It would not surprise me if Cloud Dragon Hua would try to kidnap one." Then they saw away to the east three black shadows that seemed to be flying across the rooftops. "Brother," Chen Liang said, "You see those three. The one in the center is Cloud Dragon Hua; the one in the front is from Four Rivers; the other I do not know."

"I know the one at the back," said Lei Ming. "He is called the Flying White Lotus Master." As Chen Liang and Lei Ming spoke, the three arrived at the rooftop on the east side of the courtyard.

Now, after Cloud Dragon Hua had left the home of Ma Jing, he had been followed by Ji Gong throughout the night. So Cloud Dragon Hua returned to Youlong town and at the north gate met two men. One had a somewhat military appearance, and the other looked more like a young gentleman. They were both actually famous Four Rivers robbers who had long been friends and associates in crime with Cloud Dragon Hua. Seeing him today, the two went forward and greeted him. "Brother Hua," said one, "how are you and what brings you here today?"

"Dear brothers," said Cloud Dragon Hua, "today I hardly dare show my face to the world."

"How can you say such a thing?" asked the one who was called Han Xiu.

"Since we parted in Four Rivers," explained Hua, "I've been doing all sorts of things. I've been all over the Phoenix Hill section of the capital. I stole the Phoenix Coronet from Prime Minister Qin, killed a couple of women in a nunnery, and also killed a man in a restaurant." And so from beginning to end he told his story to the two men.

"Well, good!" exclaimed Han Xiu. "All these things our good brother has been doing to startle heaven and shake up the earth in the capital are certainly extraordinary! Where will you be going now?"

"I have no particular place in mind," replied Cloud Dragon Hua.

"Are you able to work with drugged incense?" asked Han Xiu.

"To do what?" queried Cloud Dragon Hua.

"Let me talk to you, brother," said Han Xiu. "We have been here in the Grand Hotel at the crossroads for about ten days with nothing to do, just amusing ourselves. There is a wealthy man named Zhao who lives on Xing Liu Street. The estate has a flower garden with a two-story building. One day, we looked through a hole in the window and saw three beautiful young women, truly the prettiest on earth.

"We two had none of that drugged incense, and so we could not abduct them. There are too many people there to do it any other way. We have been thinking about them ever since we saw them that day, but there was nothing we could do. If we had not met you, we would have given up the idea. If you have any of the incense that makes people sleep, we could do something together about these lovely young women."

As Cloud Dragon Hua heard this, his wicked heart was stirred. "Easily managed," he said, "but first let us have a few drinks together." They then went back inside the town to the Meeting Place of the Immortals Inn, ordered food and drink, and happily began to develop their plot. When the three had eaten and drunk to their satisfaction, the waiter added up the amount. The three called for their bill, paid it, and left. When they had first arrived, Chen Liang had seen Cloud Dragon Hua with the other two, but they did not know that Chen Liang and Lei Ming were upstairs.

As the three men left the restaurant, Han Xiu said, "Brother Hua, come back with us to our hotel. There is no need for you to wait in the street."

"Good," said Hua.

They went together to the Grand Hotel at the street corner, where the servant greeted them. "Ah, the two gentlemen have returned."

"We met a friend," said Han Xiu, "and so we shall not be leaving for another few days. Would you open up the room?" The servant assented and brought them a pot of tea. The three were all a little drunk.

"Since there is nothing to do now, we might as well have a nap," said Cloud Dragon. The three lay down and slept until after dark. Then they called for food and drink. All three joined in eating a light supper.

At the first watch Han Xiu said, "Shall we go now?"

"You two are in a great hurry," said Cloud Dragon Hua. "Where do people go this early? Everybody is still awake and we would be caught. How would that be? If you want to go kidnapping, the third watch is the time. Not many people are on the street. People will be sleeping and the sleep-producing incense will do its work."

The two robbers were so impatient that they could hardly keep still. All three were ready to leave at the third watch. They changed into their suits of darkness and left the room. Everyone in the hotel was asleep and so they went over the wall and on their way, flying over the rooftops.

Arriving at the flower garden, they saw that all was quiet. All seemed deserted. There was no sound of people talking, no barking dogs. One of them threw a pebble and they listened for a response. Then the three robbers immediately approached the pavilion and came to the outside of the windows. Cloud Dragon Hua took out six rolls of material and the three put the drugging incense in place. Cloud Dragon took out a device called the buzzard's beak and the buzzard's ribs. He placed the beak in a small hole that he had made in the paper window. The beak was attached to the ribs, which unfolded to make a tube or duct. This he attached to a small box. As soon as the incense was properly lighted, he put out the flame, but the incense continued to smoke. Placed in the box, the smoke and fumes went through the duct and the buzzard's beak into the room. It was an operation that required a little time and patience. Soon the people inside would be unconscious and know nothing.

All this time Chen Liang and Lei Ming were lying on the roof just above, watching and wondering what would happen and what they should do.

Han Xiu peeped in through a hole he had made in the window and whispered, "Look, Brother Hua, aren't they beautiful?"

"Of course they're beautiful," whispered Cloud Dragon. "We will each take one and we needn't fight about them."

"That would be all right—I like them all," whispered Han Xiu.

"I think the simplest thing to do would be to draw lots for them," whispered Cloud Dragon, "after we get them away from here. Then we will have no problems."

"That's good, too," said Han Xiu. "Any of the three would be all right with me."

While the three robbers were filled with excitement at the thought of the success of their plan, the two young men on the roof were growing more and more angry and indignant. Chen Liang was thinking of raising the alarm, but Lei Ming could restrain himself no longer and leapt down among the three men below. Cloud Dragon Hua was still kneeling, tending the poisonous buzzard. Lei Ming struck him a blow to the side of the head and knocked him over. Then he turned and struck Han Xiu and knocked him down as well. But both men were back on their feet in an instant.

Chen Liang could see that the odds of the three older and stronger men against the two of them were hopeless. He stood up on the rooftop and shouted, "Robbers in the flower garden! Come now quickly, everyone, or it will be too late!" As the watchmen began to pound their hollow wooden gongs in another part of the estate, others, waking and thinking it might be a fire, began to beat upon pans and to seize buckets of water. Most, however, came with weapons, knives, clubs, and even heavy soup ladles and pokers.

The three robbers fled over the wall and onto the roofs away to the south, abandoning their buzzard box.

Lei Ming joined Chen Liang, and the two went speedily over the rooftops to the west until they were well away from the clamor. Then they changed into their ordinary clothes. "Brother," said Chen Liang, "after this, you and I can stop worrying about whether Ji Gong takes Cloud Dragon or not."

"Right!" said Lei Ming, "just never mind about him. Those three are really detestable villains with no sense of right and wrong, the kind of people that should be beheaded."

The two rested until morning. As day broke and the red sun appeared in the east, Chen Liang said, "Let us go and find our teacher."

They started walking slowly forward, talking together. Ahead they saw two men coming toward them, one of whom said to them, "You should see all the excitement just outside the east gate. Some men bought a coffin and were just about to take it away when a ragged monk appeared. The monk asked whether they were going to store clothes in the coffin or keep money in it. Someone said that they would do neither, but instead put a corpse in it. Then the monk wanted to get in the coffin and try it out. They didn't want him to try it out. Then the monk kicked the coffin and broke it up. Then there was a fight. You should take a look."

"Brother," said Chen Liang, "the monk must be Ji Gong. Let's go and see."

When the two arrived at the east gate and looked, naturally they saw Ji Gong. Now, after Ji Gong had sent Lei Ming and Chen Liang off with the young graduate Jiang Wenkui, he left the restaurant with the two headmen, Chai and She. "Teacher," said Headman Chai, "some time ago you said that if we came to the Village of a Thousand Gates, we would catch Cloud Dragon Hua. Yet how are things now?"

"Just come with me to Youlong and prepare to take Cloud Dragon Hua," said the monk.

The two headmen then walked with Ji Gong to the north gate of You-long. It was already dark, so they found a place to stay the night. They ordered dinner, ate and drank, and asked for quilts.

Before they went to sleep, Chai asked, "Teacher, what about money for food and lodging tomorrow?"

"There's nothing to worry about," replied the monk. "It's all on me." They slept until the fourth watch. Then the monk awoke and looked around. Out in the courtyard he slapped the window and said, "Headman Chai and Headman She, I will see you in Longyou. I don't have the money for our food and lodging, and I don't care. I'm off!"

Having finished speaking, the monk leapt over the wall of the inn and walked to the east gate. There he waited until the sun came up and he saw four men carrying a coffin, with an old man walking behind. The monk went up to them and stopped them, saying, "Where are you taking this?"

"Into town," answered one of the men.

"Is this coffin meant to store clothing inside, or keep money in?" queried the monk.

The owner of the shop that sold coffins was nearby. "Monk, you are crazy!" he exclaimed. "Where do people buy coffins to store their clothes? This is to put a dead person in."

"If it's for a dead person, then a live person should get in and see if it's the right length," said the monk. "Put it down and I'll get in and try it out."

"We don't want you to try it out," said the shop owner.

The monk gave the coffin a kick and broke it into several pieces. The shop owner was in a rage, and called upon his apprentices to beat the monk.

CHAPTER 54

Ji Gong foretells misfortune; Cloud Dragon Hua wounds two friends

WHEN Ji Gong kicked the coffin and it fell to pieces, the owner of the coffin shop was furious and ordered his assistants to beat Ji Gong. But why had Ji Gong done this? It was because the shop owner was only interested in property and not community. His idea was to let the buyers watch out for themselves. The old man who came to buy the coffin was a neighbor of the Lius, the same one who had gone out with the young wife to beg. Since she had no one else to help her, she had given the forty ounces of silver that she had received from Lei Ming and Chen Liang to the old man, who had then gone to buy the coffin on her behalf. When he reached the shop at the east gate and saw this coffin—which was five or six feet long and quite big enough for the dead woman—he bought it, not realizing that the wood was completely rotten and simply held together by the paint that covered it. Indeed, the price was only fifteen ounces of silver. The shopkeeper had said that it was very good quality and had offered to deliver it. The old man handed the money over, and the shopkeeper told four of his assistants to deliver it. Who would have thought that, as soon as they set out, a ragged monk would appear and ask to try it out—and then, when the shopkeeper refused to allow him to do so, would kick the coffin to pieces? The old neighbor, Li, said, "I won't take it."

But the shopkeeper already had the fifteen ounces of silver in his hand and did not intend to give it up. After all, the monk had kicked the coffin apart. The shopkeeper was angry at the monk, and the four assistants were about to attack him as the shopkeeper had ordered. But the monk pointed and said the six true words, "Om Ma Ni Pad Me Hum!" The four shop assistants who had been carrying the coffin promptly seized the shopkeeper and began to beat him, thinking him to be Ji Gong as the result of the monk's spell.

The shopkeeper cried, "Don't beat me! It's me!"

"Of course it's you," said one of the assistants. "Who did you think we were beating? Why do you interfere with our business?"

"I am owner Wang," the shopkeeper said. Then the four assistants slowly began to come to themselves and saw that they had been beating their employer, and again turned toward the monk.

At this time, however, Lei Ming and Chen Liang stepped forward, demanding, "What is this all about?"

The shopkeeper, seeing that they were dressed like young gentlemen, said, "Oh sirs, this has nothing to do with you. My quarrel is with the monk."

At the same time, the old man named Li, who had bought the coffin, recognized the two from the day before and approached them.

"Why did all this happen?" Chen Liang asked him.

Old man Li told the whole story and ended by saying, "It was because I was too old to manage things well."

Ji Gong took out some medicine and said to him, "When you go back to the Lius, tell the young man to apply this to the ulcer and his leg will heal."

"Who is this monk?" asked the old man.

"He is Ji Gong, the senior monk at the Monastery of the Soul's Retreat," said Chen Liang. Then he turned and told the shopkeeper, "You were in the wrong. You should not be in the business of cheating people. You must give this man something better than rotten wood for the money. Otherwise I will leave my card with you."

The shopkeeper, not knowing how important Chen Liang might be, promptly brought out a sound coffin and sent it off to the Liu family. The young man recovered. The old woman received a proper burial and the family further spread the fame of Ji Gong.

But when Ji Gong saw Chen Liang and Lei Ming, he asked, "Where have you two been?"

"Don't ask," replied Chen Liang, "but neither of us cares about Cloud Dragon any more."

"Good," said Ji Gong. "Let us go and have something to eat."

They walked through the gate into town and found a restaurant, where they went into the rear hall and sat down. After they had had some refreshments, the monk sat looking at them and let out a long sigh.

"Why this sigh, teacher," asked Chen Liang.

"I sighed because something strange is going to happen. What time is it?" he asked.

"It is still early in the morning," answered Lei Ming.

"At noon you two may die," said the monk.

Chen Liang knew that Ji Gong could foretell the future, and he was startled. "Teacher, since you know that we will be in mortal danger, can we do anything to avoid certain death?"

"If you two are to escape your fate," the monk replied, "at exactly noon you must be outside the limits of the Youlong district. Then you may be out of harm's way."

Chen Liang did not know how great an area the district of Youlong covered. "How large is Youlong district?" he asked a waiter.

"If you go west, it is about ten miles. If you go east, it is more than eighteen miles. To the north or south it is twenty-six miles," answered the waiter.

Chen Liang decided to go west. "Teacher," he said, "We fly for our lives."

"Go, then," said Ji Gong. "Whatever you do, when noon comes, be far away."

"Yes," they said. They paid the bill, left the restaurant, and went straight west. But just as they passed out through the west gate, Lei Ming called out, "Second brother, I truly cannot go on. I had no sleep last night and I cannot keep my eyes open. My feet will not move."

"We must go quickly, brother," urged Chen Liang. "We must believe what Teacher told us."

And so they went on until they saw before them a large wood. Then Lei Ming said again, "I cannot go on."

"If you don't go," said Chen Liang, "perhaps we will lose our lives."

"There is no one here. Let me rest." As he said that, Lei Ming simply sat down on the ground, leaned against a tree, and went to sleep. Chen Liang was uneasy. He sat down beside him but did not dare to sleep. It was not long before he saw a man coming from the south. It was Cloud Dragon Hua.

Now, after Cloud Dragon Hua had run from the Zhao Towers, the three robbers had returned to the hotel. Cloud Dragon Hua was secretly feeling angry with Han Xiu and Yun Fei and said, "If it were not for you two, I would not have put myself in danger."

"Don't be angry with us," said Yun Fei. "You evidently wanted to go. Now we two are going to Lin An. You can go where you like." In the morning, Yun Fei and Han Xiu arose early and left.

Cloud Dragon Hua was vexed and in low spirits. He went out and ambled about. Just as he came to the woods and saw Chen Liang and Lei Ming, his heart seemed to move. He thought to himself, "Last night at the Zhao family estate the one who attacked me looked like Lei Ming. Perhaps it was he."

Chen Liang was clever. He immediately stood up and said, "Brother Hua, how are you? Where do you come from, and why haven't you gone safely away yet?"

"And where do you two come from?" asked Cloud Dragon Hua.

"We came from New Moon Village," answered Chen Liang.

While they were speaking, Lei Ming awoke and said, "Greetings, Brother Hua. Congratulations. I wish you happiness."

"And where would my happiness come from?" asked Hua.

Lei Ming was hot-blooded and unable to carry on the deception. "You were at the Zhao home to get a wife," he replied. "Isn't that great happiness?"

"How did you know that?" asked Cloud Dragon Hua.

"If the people who were there didn't know, who would know?" replied Lei Ming.

"Good," said Cloud Dragon. "Last night you were the rascal who raised his hand against me! Why did you do it?"

Because your mother was a dog!" shouted Lei Ming. "You called me a rascal—I'll take my knife and run you through!" and he drew out his dagger and stabbed at the other.

Cloud Dragon Hua took out his own dagger and engaged in combat. Chen Liang, seeing that the two were about to kill each other, called out, "Brother Hua! Brother Lei! Don't fight over two or three words. We are all brothers of the Greenwood. If we kill each other, people will laugh at us." But Lei Ming would not listen, and kept stabbing again and again without being able to get a thrust home. Cloud Dragon Hua's art was more than equal to Lei Ming's strength. The two were covered with sweat. Chen Liang drew his knife and said, "Lei Ming! Step back!" and then said, "Brother Hua! You also step back! We are brothers sworn to eternal friendship, and we are supposed to help each other. Brother Hua, go your own way!"

But Lei Ming's anger had not yet begun to cool and again he started toward Cloud Dragon Hua. Again Chen Liang urged them to behave as brothers, and at length Lei Ming's anger began to cool.

Cloud Dragon Hua also seemed willing to stop. "Good! Good!" he said. "Now listen to me. Lei Ming was the one who first raised his hand against me, and you two are the ones in the wrong." Then he turned and began to run, and Lei Ming followed him. Cloud Dragon suddenly turned and shouted, "Poisoned dart coming!" Lei Ming saw him throw a miniature spear with an iron point. Lei Ming tried to avoid it, but it struck him in his left armpit. Instantly he turned and fell to the ground in great pain. He realized that the dart was indeed poisoned, as his whole body began to tremble and weaken.

Chen Liang ran to him and asked, "What is the matter, brother?"

"I am finished," said Lei Ming. "I have been poisoned by his dart. In twelve hours I will be dead. Go away. When you reach the Jade Mountain district, go to the Phoenix Cliff and ask how to find Yang Ming. Then tell Yang that Brother Cloud Dragon Hua has killed me with a poisoned dart. Ask him to call a meeting of the brothers of the Greenwood and tell them to punish Cloud Dragon Hua. In that way my death will be avenged."

Meanwhile, Cloud Dragon Hua stood not far away listening to Lei Ming, and thought to himself, "If that happens, I am finished." He then threw a second poisoned dart, which struck Chen Liang in the back.

Chen Liang laughed and called out, "Hua, you have finished me. All the Greenwood knows that where Lei Ming was, Chen Liang could also be found. While we lived, we were like one person, and when we are dead, we will be like one corpse." At that point he ceased to speak. He and Lei Ming could only utter sounds of pain.

Cloud Dragon Hua, looking at them, thought to himself, "For a little while they were like younger brothers to me. The least that I can do is stop their suffering." With that thought in mind, he drew his dagger and prepared to end their lives.

CHAPTER 55

Cloud Dragon makes a false accusation;
Yang Ming is wounded by a poisoned dart

JUST as Hua Yun Long approached the two young men he had poisoned with a knife in his hand, he heard a voice behind him say, "Dear Brother Hua, who are those men you are about to kill?" He turned his head and saw approaching him a tall, handsome man of middle age who nevertheless seemed much younger. He was slender, muscular, and filled with energy. His bright eyes especially gave him a look of compassionate intelligence. He was dressed in clothing appropriate to a man of action, rugged clothing made from fine quality silk. This was none other than Yang Ming, a man respected by men of the Greenwood throughout the region for his character, kindness, and generosity.

Cloud Dragon was thinking to himself, "This is most inconvenient. I had not wanted to be connected with their deaths." Aloud he said, "I had to use the poisoned darts to defend myself. Now I am thinking of ending their suffering."

"But when I described the poisoned darts to you, I never thought that you would use such things. It is wrong to use such weapons on another human being." Yang Ming stepped forward to look at the two men. "Who are they?" he asked.

Then, as Yang Ming recognized them, Cloud Dragon said, "Lei Ming is, in fact, a desperate robber who stole the pearl coronet from the house of the prime minister. He killed a man in a restaurant in Linan because he became angry with him. Lei Ming also tried to abduct a young nun from a nunnery outside Linan. When she resisted, he killed her. This other fellow, Chen Liang, is his accomplice. They don't deserve to live."

Yang Ming had walked forward and was looking at Chen Liang and Lei Ming. Cloud Dragon Hua was behind Yang Ming, who suddenly felt the sharp iron head of a dart enter his upper arm. Cloud Dragon had thrown it. Yang Ming fell to the ground.

There was another man with Yang Ming whom Cloud Dragon Hua had not noticed, an old man named Kang Deyuan. He now stepped forward and said, "If you are going to kill him, please kill me as well. My wife died long ago, and the daughter who had been my only happiness for many years has been taken from me. I no longer wish to live. This kind gentleman said that he might be able to find her and told me to come along with him. Now there is no hope for me, and I am ready to die with him. If you kill me, there will be no witness to your crimes."

For a moment Cloud Dragon Hua was ready to do as Kang Deyuan wished, but then he hesitated. Killing the old man seemed disgusting to him. Just then he heard a soft rustling sound, like a continued sighing, as though someone were brushing the grass with his straw sandals and his cloak. It was Ji Gong.

CHAPTER 56

Ji Gong surprises an outlaw in the forest; headmen meet the holy monk in a wine shop

"GOOD, Cloud Dragon Hua," the monk said. "Where have you been?" The poisoner looked as if he would like to flee in his terror.

Now, where had Ji Gong been? After he had risen halfway through the night and left the inn, the two headmen, Chai and She, did not dare to go back to sleep. They were afraid of what might happen the next morning when they would have to pay the bill, because they had no money. Therefore, they also got up and climbed over the courtyard wall. Arriving at New Moon Village in the morning, they entered the town and noticed a teahouse nearby. They walked in and saw a number of local headmen sitting and drinking tea. "We are trying to find a monk," said Chai. "Have any of you seen him?"

"His case just passed the magistrate's desk this morning," one of the local headmen said.

"What for?" asked Chai.

"Isn't that the monk who was secretly married?" asked the headman.

"No," replied Chai. "The one I'm asking about is a poor monk in rags."

Then another headman spoke up. "Just now I heard that outside the east gate there was a poor monk who stopped some people carrying a coffin. Why don't you go there and look?"

The two, Chai and She, hurried to the area outside the east gate and looked, but Ji Gong had left. They went back and forth, looking in restaurants everywhere, but with no success. Finally, in a small wine shop that also sold food, they found him.

"Good enough, you're here," said Headman Chai. "You ran off during the middle of the night. We two men don't deserve this kind of punishment. Explain yourself."

"Just sit down, you two," said the monk. The two sat down and the monk called for food and drink. When it was brought, the two hungry men fell to eating. After a few moments, the monk stood up and said, "Excuse me," and walked out.

He passed through a door on the west side of the wine shop and went straight out. A little later he was walking along a towpath on a narrow strip of ground between a stream and a canal. Coming from the opposite direction was a mule with a young woman riding on it its back. A man was leading the mule. He was an ugly-looking man with a head shaped like a rabbit's, and eyes like a snake's. This man was Kang Cheng, and the woman was Kang Deyuan's daughter. The evil-hearted rascal had decided to sell his niece for several hundred ounces of silver and use the money to buy a wife for himself.

That morning while his uncle was away, Kang Cheng had tied the mule in the alley near her father's shop and then told the girl that her father wanted her to wait for him there. Then he simply picked her up and seated her upon the mule. She was afraid to get down by herself, and he had walked off along the towpath leading the mule. The girl was unwilling to go, but her uncle said, "Your father is waiting further along."

Of course, Ji Gong knew all this and stood still in the middle of the towpath, blocking the way.

"Go back, monk," said Kang Cheng.

"You go back," countered the monk.

"We've a mule here," said Kang Cheng.

"I'm a man here," said the monk.

"Haven't you noticed that we have a guest of the hall here?" asked Kang Cheng. Now the homes of wealthy Chinese often had a large room, called the guest hall or library, in a separate courtyard to the east. To the west, the first courtyard usually included the servants' quarters, while the family lived in a courtyard further back to the north, and sometimes even further to the west from there. Guests of the hall were usually not invited into the family's quarters, and sometimes the guests included women from outside who filled the men's wine cups and made themselves pleasant company.

Kang Cheng thought that he would impress the monk by saying that they were going to a wealthy home, but the monk replied, "I myself have been the guest of great officials."

"But we cannot turn around," said Kang Cheng.

"And I will not turn around," said Ji Gong.

"Monk," cried Kang Cheng, "you are detestable!"

"And you are really something!' said Ji Gong. Then he pointed and said, "O Mi To Fu! I command!" and Kang Cheng was paralyzed.

The monk then walked off, leading the mule with the young woman still on its back. When he came to the wooded area and saw Cloud Dragon Hua, he stopped the mule, walked up, and started to speak.

The moment Cloud Dragon Hua saw Ji Gong, he turned and ran, with the monk following him. At this time Lei Ming and Chen Liang were still conscious and able to speak. When Yang Ming asked them why Cloud Dragon had poisoned them with the iron-headed darts, Chen Liang said, "When I was at Linan and wanted to become a monk, Ji Gong was going to accept me as his disciple. They even had water ready to shave my head, but then I ran away. Later I heard that because Cloud Dragon Hua had stolen the pearl coronet from the prime minister, killed a man in a restaurant, and murdered a nun, Ji Gong had been sent to arrest him. We begged Ji Gong not to arrest Cloud Dragon Hua. The monk promised not to do so if we prevented Cloud Dragon from abducting the girls from the Zhao Towers. That was why Cloud Dragon was angry at us." But now Chen Liang was no longer able to go on talking because of the pain from his poisoned wound.

Yang Ming, after hearing Chen Liang's story, exclaimed, "Oh, Cloud Dragon, after some of the things you have done, even if you had not poisoned me, our friendship would be at an end!"

The old man, Kang Deyuan, had been listening, and now asked Yang Ming, "How do you feel, sir?"

"I'm finished," said Yang Ming. "I cannot go on."

"You must not die," urged Lei Ming. "It does not matter if we two die. Neither of us has a father or a mother, nor a wife and children. When we die, we die, and that is all. Everything will be over for us. But you still have an old white-haired mother, a wife, and a young child. What will become of them?"

As Lei Ming said these words, they touched Yang Ming's heart and he was filled with regret. Lei Ming was in agony and Yang Ming's suffering was even greater than before. Chen Liang and Lei Ming were both unconscious now, but Yang Ming's eyes were still open and he was still able to speak. In the distance among the trees the monk became visible. He walked in an odd way, as if he were lost and did not know where he was. Yang Ming called to the old man, "Go to the monk and see if he is all right."

Kang Deyuan went to meet the monk, and taking him by the hand, led him to where Yang Ming and the two men were lying on the ground. "How is it with you, monk?" asked Yang Ming. "Were you also poisoned by one of Hua Yun Long's darts?"

"No, but I wish I were dying instead of you three people," said the monk. "I feel that I am a worthless creature who has no reason to live, and yet I see others dying, while I am still forced to live and despise myself."

"Tell me," said Yang Ming, "why you wish to die. You are still much younger than I am."

"When I first became a monk and was given my monk's certificate," Ji Gong related, "my teacher, who lived in poverty wearing rags not much better than these I wear today, gave me two ounces of silver and told me to go and buy two complete sets of monk's clothing, one for each of us, so that he could present me to the other monks. I took the money, went off, and never went back. I spent the money on food. I had thought that some day I might return, but I have never had as much as two ounces of silver since that time. My ingratitude has been a reproach to me ever since that day. Now, seeing you three about to die, I feel that I should have died instead."

"Come now," said Yang Ming, "even though I must die, there is no reason for you to feel as you do. I still have a few ounces of silver here. Take it, buy two sets of monk's clothing, and go back to your teacher." With these words he handed the monk the silver in his pocket.

The monk looked at it and said, "But this silver is all broken up into little pieces—the silver I had was much better looking." Then he turned and started to walk off.

Yang Ming could not help thinking, "I did a good deed and this is the thanks I get. This monk is not a very nice person."

Just then the monk turned back to him, and looking at his clothing remarked, "There is one other favor that you could do for me. Those clothes you are wearing are not going to be of much use to you when you are dead. If you would give them to me, I could sell them for a little money and save their being wasted."

At that, Yang Ming could not restrain his feelings. "What kind of a monk are you?" he exclaimed. "You have no decent human feelings!"

"Good! Good!" said Ji Gong. "You are not dead after all!"

Ji Gong then placed a piece of medicine in the mouth of Chen Liang, who awakened and said, "Holy monk, you have saved my life."

But the monk scolded him saying, "I asked you two to go beyond the limits of Youlong district and you failed to do so. As a result, Cloud Dragon Hua poisoned you. As your teacher, I must say a prayer for you after you are dead."

"Save us, teacher," begged Chen Liang.

"I will try, but it is not certain that the medicine will save you," the monk said. Then he put a piece of medicine in Lei Ming's mouth, and in a little while the two were as before.

"Please save our brother Yang Ming, too," Lei Ming asked.

The monk then gave a piece of the medicine to Yang Ming as well. When Yang Ming was able to stand again, Lei Ming told him, "This is the senior monk, Ji Gong, from the Monastery of the Soul's Retreat." Yang Ming knelt and performed the kowtow to Ji Gong.

"Lei Ming," said Ji Gong, "go along the towpath a little way until you see a man standing in a trance. Throw him in the water, and when he comes out of his trance, tell him that he must go a hundred *li* from here and never return. If he ever comes back or bothers his uncle or his cousin, I will have him severely beaten."

Yang Ming then asked Ji Gong, "Holy monk, is there some way that you might help Kang Deyuan to find his lost daughter again?"

"Do not worry," said Ji Gong to the old man. "Your daughter is just outside these woods." The monk clapped his hands and the mule came walking into the woods, with the old man's daughter on its back.

"You have given me back my daughter!" cried the old man.

"But I have sent your nephew far away," said the monk.

"Why?" the old man asked.

Otherwise he would try to harm you again," replied Ji Gong.

Kang Deyuan thanked Ji Gong again and walked away, leading the mule with his daughter on its back. Then Ji Gong asked Yang Ming, Chen Liang, and Lei Ming to go with him, and they went northward.

CHAPTER 57

The warrant for Cloud Dragon Hua is stolen; the holy monk lies for a banquet

AHEAD, passing through the intersection on the way to the town, was a crowd of officers and men with several local headmen at the front, leading Ji Gong's headmen Chai and She in chains. How could such a thing have happened?

Now, after the monk had gone over the wall and left the inn, there was a terrible scream. Chai and She awoke and saw that Ji Gong was gone. They called the waiter and looked everywhere about the courtyard, but Ji Gong was not to be seen. The waiter went from door to door, asking each guest if he had seen Ji Gong. At the north building there was no answer. "Where could he have gone?" asked the waiter. "The gate is locked."

The two headmen went back to their room. "Let us see if we still have the warrant for Hua Yun Long's arrest made out by the Lord Protector," said Chai. In the pack they found the oiled paper envelope. With the passing of days it had become a little the worse for wear at the corners. Inside was the warrant with the Lord Protector's seal still intact, although badly stained with water that had leaked through the cracked oiled paper.

"At least that is still safe," said Headmen She, and the two went outside again. A little later they saw a dark figure slip out of their door and swiftly disappear. They gave chase, but the dark figure vanished without a trace.

"Let us go back in and see if we have lost anything," said Chai. To their horror, the warrant was gone. As they rushed outside, they saw the waiter standing near the front office with a lantern in his hand.

"Come and see what has happened," She shouted to the waiter.

"What is it?" the waiter asked.

"We have lost something important," answered Chai.

"No wonder," said the waiter. "Three of you come here and only two of you are left. Now you say you have lost something as if it were our fault. Ask anyone if it is not true that our place hasn't been open for a year and a half—and even though jokers like this are always coming around, our business has always been reputable."

Headman Chai was frantic and the waiter was becoming abusive. Now the manager came out. Before becoming proprietor of this inn, Yang Guodong had been in charge of all the headmen in Longyou. He was a man of substance and there was no one who did not know him. When he asked what the matter was, the waiter explained. "Three people came together to the inn, including a monk. We don't know where he has gone, and these two men say that they have lost something."

The proprietor, upon hearing this, immediately said, "Good! It must be that the monk has taken something away. They are trying to defraud us. Waiter, go and ask all our other guests staying here whether they have lost anything. If anything has been lost, we will ask these two men for it."

The waiter then shouted out, "All guests staying in this inn, look and see if you have lost anything." Lights began to show in all the rooms, and every occupant said that nothing was missing. When he went to ask at the north room, no one answered.

"The teacher in the north chamber did not say whether he had lost anything or not, though I asked several times," said the waiter. "There is no reply from inside the room." The waiter pushed the door to the room, and it swung open. Then he lifted the bamboo curtain hanging in the doorway and stepped inside. There was a lamp burning in the room, and looking around he saw something by its light that made him make a long, low sound like that of a deer bleating. The terrified young waiter turned and ran outside.

Everyone asked, "What is it?"

The waiter was unable to speak for a long time. Then he exclaimed, "Oh, mother! I was frightened to death!"

Everyone crowded into the room to look, and saw the headless form of the fierce-looking monk half-sitting, half-reclining in the chair, with his head close by on the floor.

"Don't let those two men escape!" directed the proprietor as he sent word to the magistrate's yamen. "It must be that poor monk who came with them who cut off the head from the monk in here."

"That's right!" everyone agreed. They quickly went to the east chamber and seized Chai and She.

"That poor, ragged monk killed the other monk and then ran away. You two must know something! We must go to the magistrate, and there must be no delay," said the proprietor.

Headmen Chai and She did not know what was going on, so what could they say? Everyone was shouting and the proprietor was saying,

"Don't let these two go! In a little while we will give them over to the guard."

Soon the officers, soldiers, and headmen arrived. "You are going to the magistrate's yamen," said Headman Liu as he fastened chains upon their wrists and ankles.

"Why are you locking us in chains?" asked Chai.

"There is to be no talking now," said Headman Liu. "Whatever you have to say can be said when you reach the audience chamber."

Headmen Chai and She had been frantic because they had lost the warrant, and now they were accused of murder. They secretly hated Ji Gong in their hearts. As day broke, the officers and men of the guard left the hotel, with the headmen leading Chai and She at the head of the procession as it moved toward the magistrate's yamen. At the intersection Ji Gong, who was coming from the opposite direction, met them.

"Well, you two," he said. "After all, foggy day bright dawn, still need flower handle to pick calabash. No hurry when picked throw to the winds, tear apart still alive, call winds to cave. Make you two stop floating. I will have to go to the magistrate."

When Headmen Chai and She heard this, they simply stared at him.

Now, what were these apparently meaningless phrases that Ji Gong had just spoken to Chai and She? They were actually the black language of the Yangtze River. "Foggy day" meant "during the night"; "Need flower handle to pick calabash" meant "Take knife and cut off monk's head"; "No hurry when picked throw to winds, tear apart still alive, call winds to cave" meant "Don't run away—let the officers take you."

Headman Chai asked, "Good monk, who taught you to talk like that?"

"Wasn't that the way you two taught me?" countered the monk.

The listening officers said, "Teacher is a friend of theirs."

People were saying, "Go to the magistrate."

Ji Gong said, "I'll go! A friend is a friend."

At that time a young servant at the yamen who had been carrying a handcuff and chain stepped up and snapped the handcuff on Ji Gong's wrist. Then, as he started leading the monk along, this little yamen servant said, "The monk is really quite friendly."

"Well, so you have me," said Ji Gong to him. "Would it be too much to ask you to treat me to something on the way?"

At that request, this servant, who had only recently started work said, "Go on! That would be getting too friendly for me. If I gave you a drink, I would never get rid of you."

"You stingy little thing!" exclaimed the monk. "I was giving you a chance to establish your reputation and you missed it! I'm not going to the yamen with you!" Then he pulled the chain out of the young fellow's hand and leaped onto a wall, and then up on the roof of a house beside the road.

Headman Liu, seeing this, slapped the young servant's face and said, "You went too far and you're delaying things." The young servant did not dare reply.

"Teacher, please come down and have some refreshment," called Headman Liu. "I will invite you."

"I have no quarrel with you," replied the monk and crawled down. "What is your honorable name, Headman Liu?"

"You're a man with feelings to call me Headman Liu and then to ask my honorable name," said the headman.

"Well, where are we going, since you're inviting me?" asked the monk.

"Just opposite the Longyou yamen," answered headman Liu. "There is a large restaurant that has everything, whatever you want to eat or drink, and I'm not stingy. I have an account there, though I haven't a cash in my pocket."

"That's it, then," said the monk. And so as they went along toward the yamen, there on the south side of the street was a restaurant called the Inn of the Three Virtues. The monk and everyone else went inside and sat down in the hall to the rear.

"Now, monk, you're a good friend, so you won't make us waste a lot of time. You can describe all these cases later on," said Liu.

"I will describe all," said the monk, "and hold nothing back."

"About that case outside the south gate—that's yours, isn't?" asked Headman Liu.

"That's mine," said the monk.

"And that case outside the north gate at the famous money-changer's gate. That is also yours," said Liu.

"That's mine," said the monk. "Whatever needs to be said, let's say it after we eat."

"Also good," said Liu. "Afterward, when we have finished eating and get to the guardroom, you can tell the whole story and we can write it down. That will be it."

"Let's eat first," said the monk. "Waiter, come here." Headmen Chai and She knew that the monk was not doing things in good faith, and only wanted to eat a meal at someone else's expense.

The waiter came and asked, "What will Teacher have?"

"What can you bring us?" asked the monk.

"Right now we have pastries," replied the waiter, "as well as everything to make a banquet."

"Fill up the table with one of your best banquets," said the monk. In a little while the table was covered with tasty-looking dishes. The wine was heated. There were cold dishes and hot ones. The table could hold nothing more.

"Headman Chai and Headman She, you two are not eating!" the monk exclaimed. "You see I am eating!" And indeed he was.

Headman Liu was thinking that the monk caused one to think. With all these capital crimes behind him and the punishment that surely must lie before him, the monk could still eat until he was completely satisfied.

When the waiter was called to calculate the bill, altogether it came to ten ounces of silver and four coins. "Put it on my account," said Headman Liu. Then they left with the monk, together with Chai and She.

Arriving at the guardroom at the yamen, Liu asked, "Monk, now tell us: what about the case at Scholar Gao's flower garden outside the south gate, when the Daoist went to exorcise the demon. What became of the Daoist's missing head?"

"I don't know," replied Ji Gong.

"Now, monk, this is not right," said Headman Liu. "Just a little while ago you said that you were involved in the case outside the south gate. You said you did it and now how can you not know about it?"

"I said that outside the south gate I stole a little chicken," answered the monk, "but I didn't kill anyone. I'm not brave enough for that."

"And outside the north gate, that senseless killing. Torn apart as a fox or wildcat might do. That was yours, wasn't it?" asked Headman Liu.

"No," replied the monk. "Outside the north gate I stole—I've forgotten whether it was a fox or a wildcat—and went off with it. I did nothing more."

"That's not it at all!" exclaimed Headman Liu. "I never asked you about stealing anything. That case at the Yang family hotel outside the east gate, when the monk's head was cut off. That was you!"

"I know nothing about that," said the monk.

"Afterward, when the magistrate comes to the hall, you will be persuaded to speak and then you will remember! That's all!" exclaimed Headman Liu.

"I really do not know," said the monk. "It cannot be helped."

After that exchange, all of the yamen headmen were angry and would not speak to the monk. Someone went in and notified the magistrate that the prisoners were at the yamen. He gave orders to prepare to hold court. He also ordered that the monk should be brought before him and wondered what he would say.

CHAPTER 58

The Longyou headmen have three cases;
Ji Gong goes to the Inn of the Two Dragons

SHORTLY after Ji Gong was brought into court, the magistrate entered and sat down at the bench. Looking down, he saw the ragged monk before him and said, "You, monk, when you saw the district magistrate, why did you not kneel?"

"Honorable sir," replied Ji Gong, "Officials have rank among themselves. Some are more honorable than others. Buddhists also have their places, and some are more respected than others. I do not fail to observe national laws, but those do not concern Buddhist rules, and it is to those I pay homage."

When the magistrate heard this, he said, "And you, monk, what are you called, and from what temple did you receive your certificate?"

"Since Your Honor wishes to know," answered the monk, "I am the monk Ji Dian from the Monastery of the Soul's Retreat."

The magistrate knew that the name of Ji Dian was famous and very highly regarded. He thought to himself, "Ji Gong is the monk that Prime Minister Qin asked to act as a substitute for himself. How could he be someone like that?" And the magistrate felt disbelief. Then he said, "If you are Ji Gong, you must know the details of the murder of the monk in the Yang family hotel outside the east gate."

In fact, I do not know," said Ji Gong.

The magistrate continued by asking, "If you are the monk Ji Dian from the Monastery of the Soul's Retreat, why have you come here?"

"Since Your Honor asks," responded the ragged monk, "I came at Prime Minister Qin's order with two headmen from Linan City. We came in relation to a case and brought with us a warrant signed and sealed by the Grand Protector appointed by the emperor to arrest the outlaw Cloud Dragon Hua."

The magistrate then ordered the two headmen, Chai and She, to be brought forward in the court.

As soon as the two were brought into the hall, Headman Chai said, "Your Honor above, here below Chai Yuanlo and She Jenying both pay their respects."

"Are you two the headmen from the city of Linan?"

"Yes," answered Chai. "We are sent from the yamen of the Grand Protector."

"If indeed you were sent on a case, you must have a warrant that you can let me see," said the magistrate.

"Since you ask about the warrant," intervened Ji Gong, "it was stolen last night in the hotel."

As soon as the magistrate heard this, he became furiously angry. "There was no such document!" he exclaimed. "The truth will be forced out of you. No one escapes the law. Give the monk forty blows with the bamboo. When you have beaten him, we will ask for the same information again."

The local headmen standing at the side of the courtroom made a sound of agreement and stepped forward, intending to hold Ji Gong down so that he could be beaten. Just when matters had reached this point, there was a shout from outside the hall. "A thousand times, ten thousand times! Don't beat the monk! I am coming!" Into the hall rushed Yin Shixiong, who had uttered these words. "Your Honor," cried the man, "A thousand times, ten thousand times, we must not beat the monk! I know he is Ji Gong from the Monastery of the Soul's Retreat."

"Yin Shixiong," queried the magistrate, "how do you know he is Ji Gong?"

"I was at the prime minister's estate," the man answered, "when the five-thunder eight-trigram scroll was stolen. And I saw him there talking with the prime minister."

Now how was it that Yin Shixiong was there in the yamen? He had been promoted because of his abilities as a headman in Linan. Then, when the chief headman in Longyou had retired to become an innkeeper, Yin Shixiong was sent to Longyou to take his place. When he had heard that Ji Gong was at the court, Headman Yin wanted to see what he looked like again. When he heard the magistrate give the order to beat the monk, Yin was horrified and had rushed into the audience hall to prevent it.

The magistrate had no reason to doubt his chief headman's word. He immediately stepped down from behind the bench and approached Ji Gong saying, "Holy monk, a thousand times, ten thousand times, please do not take offense. Your disciple simply did not understand. Please come and sit beside me."

"Of course you did not," said the monk. "Why should you even speak of such a thing?"

The magistrate was bowing and saying, "Of course, I have heard of the famous Ji Gong and of your goodness and kindness. Now we are having so much trouble here in Longyou with all these cases and no suspect in any of the three. I must beg the holy monk to look into the past and future in order to help us."

"There is no need for fortune-telling," said the monk. "However, if Your Honor will briefly provide me with the treasures of literature, that is, a writing brush and some ink, I will write something for you. How will that be?"

The moment the magistrate heard this, he quickly put paper, a writing brush, and ink before the monk. Ji Gong turned his back upon the magistrate, and after writing for some time, folded the paper and said, "Now, Your Honor, please keep this paper with you. Wait until you have visited the Yang Family Inn outside the east gate. Then afterward, when your sedan chair has been set down at the crossroads, unfold the paper and read what I have written. You will understand about all three cases. But please don't unfold the paper too early. If you do, it may not be possible to solve the cases."

The magistrate nodded. He looked at the folded paper. On the outside was drawn a picture of a cracked earthenware jar mended with seven rivets. This was the monk's special mark. The magistrate put the paper safely in his wallet.

"Your Honor," asked the monk, "would you send the two headmen, Yang Guodong and Yin Shixiong, with me to help me solve these two cases and let my headmen rest here at the yamen?" The magistrate assented and told Yang Guodong and Yin Shixiong to go with the monk. The two agreed and left the hall with Ji Gong.

As they left the yamen, Yin Shixiong asked, "Is the holy monk well?"

"Well?" replied the monk, "Not sick!"

Then Yin Shixiong spoke to the other headman, asking, "Brother Yang, didn't I hear that your sister-in-law is unwell?"

"That's right," replied Yang Guodong.

"Brother Yang," said Yin, "if you kowtow to Ji Gong and ask him, he may give you a miraculous pill that you can take to her. There is no illness that he cannot cure."

Upon hearing this, Yang Guodong immediately began to bow and said, "Holy monk, show your kindness by giving me a little medicine for her."

"Don't get in a hurry," said the monk. "There probably is some medicine that will help her, but let us first take care of these cases."

"Where are we going, Teacher?" asked Yin Shixiong

"To Five Tombstones," answered the monk. Then, as the two men watched, he took three steps forward and two back.

"Holy monk," said Yin Shixiong, "if you walk that way, when will you ever get there? Could we go a little more quickly?"

"If I go quickly, will you two be able to keep up?" asked the monk.

"We can keep up," said Yang Guodong.

The monk then kicked up his heels, and like the flash of a shooting star was gone. The two headmen sped after him but still saw no trace of the monk. "Quickly onward as fast as we can, then," the two thought, and so shortly arrived at Five Tombstones.

The monk was hiding in an alley. Waiting until they were almost there, he stepped out and began slowly walking ahead of them. Soon they saw a wine shop on the west side of the street. The owner's name was Hai. He had a habit of adding up the bill for each patron. As soon as he saw how much it was, he would add a flourish at the bottom of the bill with his brush. His flourish looked like a total price higher than the actual one, and many people would simply pay it. If they protested, he would simply say that his flourish was just that, an ornamental ending and nothing more. If the guest did not look carefully, he would have paid a little more than he should have.

The monk quickly slipped inside unseen by the two headmen and said, "Greetings. The owner's name is Hai, isn't it?"

"My name is Hai," said the owner. "What about it?"

Aren't you the sworn brother of the headman Yang Guodong?" asked the monk.

"That's right," replied the wineshop owner.

"Yang Guodong's sister-in-law is dead," said the monk. "Did you know that?"

The owner was shocked and disturbed when he heard this. He dropped his writing brush, which made a big zero on the paper. He looked at it and tore up the check. Then he asked, "Monk, how do you know this?"

"Early this morning, Headman Yang came to my temple to talk about services for the third day after death. He wanted five monks to perform the service and seven monks to conduct the soul over the bridge, past the demons. I said that there should be seven people to perform the service and eleven to take the soul over the bridge, and we should end up by singing operatic songs."

"You must be very busy in the temple," said the wine shop proprietor.

"Extremely busy," said the monk, "but Headman Yang asked me to tell you about the death as soon as I could, and that's why I'm here."

"I'm obliged to you, Teacher," the owner said. "Please come in and sit down and have a cup of tea or wine."

"Good," said the monk. "I was just thinking of a cup of wine."

The owner called a waiter, who brought two small jugs of wine. The owner was saying, "Of course, I must go to the funeral, but first I must go to the bakery and order a tableful of fragrant cakes at my own expense."

"Since we all are on such good terms with Yang Guodong, we must all send our respects on a banner eight feet long in four gold characters," the waiter urged.

"Yes, indeed!" the others chimed in.

After the monk had drunk the wine, he only said, "I am leaving."

As he departed, everyone called out, "You have put yourself to too much trouble for us." In fact, he had given this momentous and totally false news for no other reason than to make them give him two small pots of wine.

While Ji Gong was drinking in the wine shop, the two headmen, Yang and Yin, had gone back toward the yamen, thinking that they were unlikely to find the monk again. The monk, meanwhile, went slowly onward until he came to an intersection where he stopped and looked about. On the south side was an inn called the Mansion House. The air rang with the sound of the chopping block. Dishes of all sorts were being rushed to and fro. There seemed to be no place left to sit down. It was packed with guests.

Across the road on the north side was another inn called the Inn of the Two Dragons. Inside there was not a single customer. The manager sat dozing and the waiters sat with melancholy looks on their faces. The stove was empty and cold. The rolling pins were still. The monk strode inside and asked, "Waiter, why is it so peaceful in here?"

"Don't mention it, teacher," said the waiter. "When our previous manager was alive, the business in this place was considered number one in the whole Longyou district. Who didn't know the Two Dragons! But now that our old manager has left this earth, the assistant manager is just not up to it. Really, it is as if business is something that depends upon people. As soon as he put his hand to it, business became bad. Some of our people left and opened the Mansion House across the way. Even though it is true that people say 'Many boats do not block the river,' over there each day is better than the one before, and here each day is worse than the one before. Last night we sold a little over eight hundred cash worth, enough so that we could eat. Today, nothing! I was an apprentice in this room. I thought, well, if they sell a hundred and twenty dishes, we could still sell a hundred. I want to do it, but there is nothing I can do."

The monk laughed loudly and asked, "Do you want to make more or not?"

"How could I not want to!" exclaimed the waiter.

"If you want to, I have a way," the ragged monk told him.

And now the *lohan* would use his Buddhist arts there in the Inn of the Two Dragons to catch the guilty parties in the three unsolved crimes.

CHAPTER 59

A waiter's story moves the monk to pity;
Ji Gong sees two unwholesome men

NOW, when Ji Gong had come into the Inn of the Two Dragons and heard the sad story told by the waiter, he had asked, "Do you want to make more money or not?"

The waiter had replied, "I do want to make more money, but look, we have nothing with which to work. There are a few pounds of meat and about ten pounds of flour, a pair of little chickens and not much wine, either. We're just sitting here with nothing. How can we make much money?"

"Never mind," said the ragged monk. "Do you have water?"

"There is a small well in the back," said the waiter.

"If there is water, we will have wine," said the monk. "You just draw the water and use it for wine. I guarantee that no one will dislike it. Then you can sell it for hundreds of strings of cash. You just get the manager to keep his abacus going and start the fire in the stove. I will ask for two pots of wine. You sing the order out and have them repeat it with a shout after you. Then there will be guests. Keep the kitchen busy. It will be best if everything seems to be in a turmoil."

The waiter had become so bitterly poor that he eagerly fell in with the monk's plan. He told the manager to keep the abacus busy, he had the fire started up and the rolling pin ready.

Then the ragged monk said, "Let's have two pots of wine."

The waiter sang out, "White wine, two pots!" The manager and all the rest echoed the cry. Just as the waiter brought the two pots of wine to the monk, some guests walked in from outside. When the waiter looked, he recognized Manager Chen from across the road.

Now, Manager Chen was known to have a strong dislike for people who drank wine, and if any of the waiters had a drink and he knew about it, he would no longer want them to work in his restaurant. But today he had just finished eating and was standing in the doorway of the Mansion

House when suddenly he crossed the street, went in, and asked for two pots of wine.

The waiter knew that Manager Chen did not drink, and therefore asked him, "Manager Chen, how is it that today you are asking for wine?"

Manager Chen looked at him and said, "I want a drink. What's it to you?" The waiter, a little embarrassed, brought him the wine. Manager Chen dimly realized what was happening. He thought to himself, "I don't drink. What has made me want to have some wine?" But then he thought, "Well, as long as I do want it, I might as well find out what their wine tastes like."

Other people who did not normally like to drink were drinking that day. One man came in carrying a bowl of turnip blossoms in sesame oil that he had bought for three cash. He had gone out to buy something, and when he reached the gate of the Two Dragons, he came in and sat down. He asked for two jugs of wine, and when the waiter brought them, he suddenly remembered, "We were just about to eat at home. What made me come in here?"

Another man came in carrying a piece of bean curd in a bowl that his wife needed to fix dinner. He was unwilling to come in, and sat down near the door. When the waiter brought his wine, he remembered that his wife was waiting for the tofu and said, "What am I doing drinking wine?"

The other said, "I did not come of my own will, either. I have a bowl of turnip blossoms. Put down your bowl of bean curd and let's sit together to drink our wine."

Groups of three to five people were coming in together. One old man, however, came in alone and sat down with five packages of food. He started putting a package at each place as he spoke out loud to himself: "Old Two, one package for you; Old Three, one for you; Old Four, one for you; Old Five, one for you." And then he said to the waiter, "Bring ten pots of wine and six platters of food. Now, you four, ask for whatever you want."

The waiter looked and saw one person and wondered what was happening, but, as it turned out, the old man was one of five sworn brothers. He had invited the rest to the Mansion House, but when he was drawn to the Inn of the Two Dragons, he expected to find his brothers there. As soon as it was understood, the others were called from across the street.

In a little while there was hardly a vacant place and the waiters were as busy as could be. But as the number of customers increased, the amount of wine in the wine cistern became low. "When there is no wine, draw some water," the waiter remembered the monk had said, so the waiter went back to the well and came back with a pail of water, which he poured into the wine cistern. It diluted the wine, but the waiter served it to the guests anyway. Almost at once he was called back. "Oh, now I'm in for it. They know it's water," thought the waiter.

But the guest only said, "This wine is changed."

"Perhaps I made a mistake," the waiter said.

"But this wine is much better than the wine you served before," the man said. "If you served this all the time, I would be here every day."

"Strange!" the waiter thought. "I gave him water and he praised it." Some guests were leaving, but other customers filled their places. It was like old times.

Then two men entered. The first had a head shaped like a rabbit's, always a bad sign, and eyes shaped like triangles. His face was pale and, though not unhealthy, was somehow unwholesome in appearance. The other had the same rabbity head. His complexion was darker and his appearance was more threatening than the other's. Neither man wore a cap or hat, but they were dressed in well-made clothing.

As soon as the two entered, several people called a greeting, but the two hardly responded. They sat down at a table next to the one where Ji Gong was sitting, but behind his back. From their behavior it seemed clear that the two simply wanted to quietly finish their conversation. The waiter, however, had no choice. He went up to their table, wiped it with a cloth, and asked, "What would you like to eat?" They ordered two pots of wine and two plates of food.

The monk turned his head and spoke to them. "Did you two just arrive?" They did not hear him and did not answer. The monk slapped the table and said, "I, the monk, spoke to you in a friendly fashion. You can ignore me if you want to, but I will call you a couple of pigs in a friendly fashion, and if you still ignore me, call you vermin, lice, and a few other things."

The two did not realize that the monk was speaking to them and again did not reply, although all the other customers knew that the monk was cursing these two men. The other customers wondered if those two had something to be ashamed of. Everyone was now looking at the two. The monk continued to call them names until one of them said to the other, "I'm going to ask him who he's cursing," and started to get up.

"Sit down," the other said.

The monk proceeded to link their ancestry to every despised and disgusting beast in the lower regions of Chinese mythology. "Go ask your parents if it isn't true!" he temporarily concluded.

One of the men said, "Don't talk nonsense!" and started to rise.

The other remonstrated, "You don't know him. Don't speak to him!" and the first man sat down again.

"I am speaking to you!" said the ragged monk.

At this the two men stood up and one asked, "Monk, who is it that you are cursing?" They were becoming angry.

The monk repeated everything he had said, adding, "You think you can ignore me because I'm poor and you don't like my ragged clothing."

At this the two men, who had been growing warm with anger, became reasonable again. One said, "Look, monk, if you even know who we are, just say our names and we'll see if what you're saying applies to us."

The monk turned to the first man and said, "You are called 'the High-Flying Buzzard' and your name is Zhang Fu. You're the third of three children. There are two people in your family now, yourself and your partner in crime, a woman with a pale face like yours. You are now twenty-five years old."

Then turning to the second man he said, "You are called 'the Street Rat' and your name is Li Lu. You are the fourth child of your parents. There are also two of you now, and your, partner in crime is a woman with a dark complexion like yours. I know everything—how many tables and chairs each of you have, how many quilts and pillows. I know all! All!"

At that the two men were ready to fight. The monk said, "Fight! If you want to fight, let's go out in the street. Let's not disturb the business of the restaurant." The two men, Zhang Fu and Li Lu, left the Inn of the Two Dragons and walked outside with the monk.

Zhang Fu and Li Lu each tried to catch hold of the monk but the monk always seemed to be circling around them both. Twist and turn, snatch and grab, they could not catch him. Then the infuriated Zhang Fu managed to punch the monk on the back of the head at the base of the skull. It was like hitting a piece of soft tofu. Blood began to flow.

The monk said, "But you hit me!" He turned and fell. His legs kicked a few times and his lips twitched. Then the life seemed to leave him and the monk's body was still.

Zhang Fu was shocked. "What a weak old drunkard's head!" he thought. "I hit his head and it simply smashed."

"Well," said one of the local officers who had seen the men fighting with the monk and now approached the men, "you have killed the monk. Don't argue with us. Just come to the yamen. Then you may tell us all about it." As he spoke, the other officers were locking the two in cuffs and chains.

Just as they were about to take the two men away, the officers heard the sound of an approaching group and a voice calling out, "Make way for the magistrate's sedan chair!" Then the magistrate came into view. He was on his way back to the yamen from examining the scene at the Yang's hotel.

Now, when the magistrate had earlier reached the Yang family's hotel outside the east gate to examine the corpse of the monk who had been beheaded, he had brought with him several interrogators and attendants. The local officers had already prepared fifty pints of spirits for washing their hands after touching the corpse, and had asked for a roll of new matting with which to wrap the corpse and a new pan for hand washing. The local official's name was Gan. He had rushed there early and said, "Now, everybody, close your eyes when the examination is over. I, because of my position, must have my little something—the remaining spirits."

These underlings whose duty it was to examine the body and call out any marks or wounds they saw replied: "Very well, we will use only half a pint." The underlings made their report to Gan, who prepared the death certificate for the magistrate to sign. The murder weapon, however, was nowhere to be found.

When the magistrate arrived, he called for the manager of the inn to appear and asked him, "Do you know who killed this monk?"

"Sir, it happened last night at the third watch, but I do not know who killed him."

How many days had he stayed here?" continued the magistrate with his questioning. "And how many were staying with him?"

He lived here by himself for twenty-three days," the manager replied.

"How many servants have you, and who among them had trouble with the monk?" were the magistrates next questions.

"There are eight servants," the manager answered, "and none of them had any trouble with the monk."

As the magistrate made ready to leave the inn in his sedan chair, the underlings asked Gan: "How was it? Was everything all right?"

"If you like noodles," Gan said, "you may each go across the street and have two bowls. I will be over to keep count and pay the bill."

"We had hoped there might be a few coins," said the underlings. "Who would have thought of noodles? Anyway, we don't feel much like eating right now. There is other work we have to do, so we'll talk about it later."

The magistrate then entered his sedan chair and started back with his retinue to the yamen. They had just reached the crossroads, when an officer approached his chair saying, "Sir, I must report to you that a monk has just been killed in a fight."

"Which monk is that?" asked the magistrate.

"A poor, ragged monk," replied the officer, "and we already have two suspects."

The magistrate ordered his chair to be put down and to have the suspects brought before him. Zhang Fu and Li Lu were immediately led before the magistrate for questioning. Who would have expected still another case of murder?

CHAPTER 60

Two scoundrels accuse each other; Ji Gong teaches strange table manners

WHEN the magistrate looked at the two suspects, Zhang Fu and Li Lu, he said, "You two men, what are your family and personal names and what are you called?"

The first one replied, "This small person is named Zhang Fu, and he is called the High-Flying Buzzard."

The other answered, "This small person's name is Li Lu, and he is called the Street Rat."

"Which of you two men killed the ragged monk?" asked the magistrate.

"It was Zhang Fu who killed the monk," said Li Lu. "I was trying to stop him."

"It was Li Lu who killed that monk!" protested Zhang Fu.

"Who actually killed him? You two scoundrels!" exclaimed the magistrate.

"If Your Honor doesn't believe me, look at the blood on Zhang Fu's hand," pointed out Li Lu. "There is no blood on my hand."

The magistrate at once ordered an officer to make an examination. Of course, there was blood on Zhang Fu's hand. "Zhang Fu, it is very clear that you killed the monk. Do you still deny it?"

"Yes, Your Honor," replied Zhang Fu. "I killed the monk—but outside the north gate at the entrance to the Gao family money changers, the murder of Liu Er Hun was committed by Li Lu." As soon as the magistrate heard this, he suddenly remembered something.

Now, strangely enough, when the monk had insulted these two men at the table, he talked about their each having a woman who was his partner in crime. To begin with, Zhang Fu and Li Lu were riffraff who pretended to be more respectable than they actually were. They would loiter around together sometimes, but each of them usually acted separately. One of them would find a younger man who came from a well-to-do family, but who spent his time idling around town away from his home.

The older man would then gradually make friends with him, treating him to meals and drinks, lending him small amounts of money, and finally bringing him to his house and making him feel like a member of the family. After a while the wealthy young man would be supporting Zhang Fu or Li Lu and buying expensive presents for the woman who was his partner. Zhang Fu or Li Lu would encourage the younger man's every weakness and let him drink himself to death or ruin himself gambling. When his money was gone, Zhang Fu or Li Lu would turn him out and find another victim. The two were not seen as breaking any law, but their conduct was low and despicable.

Li Lu, however, had finally come upon a spoiled young man named Liu Er Hun who had been given a few hundred ounces of silver by his family and told not to return. After Li Lu and his female partner had helped Liu Er Hun to use up his silver, they tried to turn Liu Er Hun out, but he refused to go, saying, "I spent my money with you—now you can take care of me. I have nowhere to go. You can't send me away. I will simply eat and drink with you."

In his heart Li Lu had come to hate Liu Er Hun. He mentioned his feeling to his friend Zhang Fu while the two were having a pot of wine in a restaurant. "Brother Zhang, look at this fellow Liu Er Hun. He's drinking and eating me out of my own house. I can't get rid of him. It's really hateful! I'm thinking about taking him out and getting him drunk and then killing him. Could you help me with this matter? Afterward, sometime I could do you a favor in return."

"Well, let's do it," said Zhang. The two planned what to do. The next day they took Liu Er Hun out drinking. Li Lu was secretly carrying a long knife. The two friends kept handing the young man drinks until he lost control and no longer knew what was happening. When he was thoroughly drunk, Zhang Fu and Li Lu led him out of the wine shop.

At the second watch that night, they led the drunken Liu Er Hun to the gate of the Gao family money changers. Li Lu had been holding a grudge against this money-changing shop for a long time because he felt he had once been shortchanged there. He thought that it would be good revenge to leave a dead body there, particularly one that was mysteriously headless. Zhang Fu told the story in detail from beginning to end, and finished by saying, "But it was Li Lu who ended the man's life with one slash of his knife."

Once the magistrate understood what had occurred, he turned to Li Lu and asked, "Just how did you kill Liu Er Hun?"

Hesitantly, half swallowing his words, Li Lu recited the details. "But it was Zhang Fu's idea," he maintained throughout his recital. "He helped me kill him."

"You two miserable scoundrels!" the magistrate said to them. Then he called to his men and ordered, "Take these two away and keep them in custody. We will now perform an examination of the body of Liu the monk."

Just as he was about to give the order to the attendants who would make the examination of the corpse, the magistrate suddenly thought about the note that Ji Gong had folded up and given to him. "The monk told me that, when I returned from outside the east gate, after my sedan chair was put down at the crossroads, I should read it," the magistrate thought to himself. "I think that now I should look at the monk's writing."

When the magistrate unfolded the paper, he read these words:

> Today this poor monk must die.
> Your Honor should first hold an examination of my body.
> Order your underlings to look at the wound.
> Do not put my body in the grave.

The magistrate secretly bowed his head. "Undoubtedly," he thought, "Ji Gong had second sight and could foretell the future." He told his attendants not to remove the monk's clothing or greatly disturb the body, but simply to examine at the wound.

When the attendants thoroughly understood his order, they responded, "Yes, Your Honor." Then they looked and reported: "There is a wound between two and three inches long that caused death. There was a great loss of blood."

The magistrate nodded his head and ordered the death certificate prepared. He then told his men to procure a new roll of matting with which to wrap the body and called the local official as a witness. He repeated his order that Zhang Fu and Li Lu be kept in custody.

The local official then had the body covered with the matting. Outside, he saw the watchman running toward him and asked what was the matter.

"The dead man just smiled at me!" exclaimed the watchman.

"Nonsense!" retorted the local official. "After someone is dead, he can't smile. There must be something wrong with your eyes. I will look myself."

The official went to look. Just as he lifted a corner of the matting, the monk rolled over. Then he sat up, touched his head with his hand, and said, "Ah, ha!'" He stood up and ran away to the south, with the official chasing after him shouting, "Hey, stop the corpse!"

Hearing that a dead man was walking, who wouldn't run the other way? The people all feared that if they were touched by a dead man they would die.

The monk went straight to the south gate, passed through it, and then turned east. Just as he came to the corner of the city wall and turned north, he saw a man walking in front of him. The man was quite short. He wore a matching cap and jacket of dark brown with gold markings. As Ji Gong passed him, he noticed that the man's face had an evil appearance and that he had dark, thick hair growing from his ears. Ji Gong thought, "If I am to solve the other two murder cases, this is the man I must deal with." Then he started talking aloud to himself. "This place is not like other places. If a person wanted to get something to eat, he would be wise to observe where others go."

At the same time, a thought formed itself in the other man's brain. "I must follow him and do whatever he does."

They went on northward to the cluster of buildings outside the east gate. There, the monk entered a wine shop on the north side of the street. The short man followed him. Ji Gong found a chair, sat down, and stamped with one foot as he called out, "Come, you rascal. Bring a pot of wine."

The short man thought to himself, "This must be the local custom. If I want anything, I had better do the same as he does, so he also stamped and called out, "Come, you rascal. Bring me a pot of wine."

The waiter thought it amusing. He did not dare speak to the short man, but he did say to the monk, "Teacher, do not shout out 'you rascal' like that."

The monk said, "Well, I guess I was wrong, but do bring the wine, and if you have any of those pancakes filled with meat and vegetables, bring me one of those, too."

"Strange," thought the waiter, "we call them stuffed biscuits." And he started back to the kitchen.

Just then the short man called him and said, "I will have one of those filled pancakes with my wine, too."

The pancakes or biscuits, each about two and a half inches across and three-quarters of an inch thick, arrived on a saucer just a little larger than necessary. They were fried to a rich, dark golden brown, and the combined odor of pork, green vegetables, and seasoning was tantalizing. When Ji Gong received his stuffed pancake, he said, "There's only one way to eat these things." He thrust a single chopstick through the round of flat filled bread and bit off half at one bite. The juices from the filling ran down his chin in a way that was unpleasant to see. The short man watched and copied the monk's actions.

The monk ordered more pancakes until he had eaten ten. The short man followed suit. Each of them then had ten saucers on his table. Ji Gong carefully stacked the saucers and stood up. He picked up the saucers and held the stack in his right hand, low and almost level with his knees. He was facing the short man, looking him straight in the eye. The short man was doing the same thing. Suddenly the monk threw the saucers, striking the man in the face and covering him not only with the juices that had run out of the filling, but also the soy sauce and vinegar that Ji Gong had added to the saucers while eating. Before the other man had a chance to throw his stack of saucers, the monk ran out of the restaurant. The short man chased after him, clutching the saucers and hoping to get close enough to the monk to throw them effectively.

CHAPTER 61

A reformed robber meets a false monk;
Xu Za meets the Painted Lame Man

NOW, when Ji Gong threw the saucers at the short man, the man was furious and wanted to fight, but the monk ran with the short man chasing him, and the waiter chased them both. The waiter saw their flight as a way of cheating the restaurant—two people finished eating, threw the dishes at each other, and pretended to fight, all to avoid paying. So he ran after them, shouting, "Don't go off, you two, pay up! Twenty pots of wine, twenty stuffed biscuits! You have to pay!"

The monk never turned his head. He ran through the east gate into town and continued west. The short man was following closely behind and calling out, "You monk, for no reason you threw those saucers at me! Do you think you can get away from me now? You can't escape me! You can run to heaven or to hell, into the earth or into water, but I'll catch you!"

The monk ran on calling out, "Oh dear, we're having a fight. Let's go to the yamen." Meanwhile, he ran on until he reached the crossroads where he supposedly had been lying dead under the matting. There he encountered Yang Guodong and Yin Shixiong coming from the south. These two headmen had also been chasing the monk.

When they reached Five Tombstones without catching up to him, Yang said, "Let's go back." The two started back. When they came to the south gate, the local official saw them and asked, "Headmen Yin and Yang, did you see the dead body?"

"Where is there a dead body?" asked Yin Shixiong.

"It was my duty to cover the dead body of a poor monk," replied the local official.

"Was that at your place?" asked Yin Shixiong. "We haven't been to the crossroads yet. How did you come to see him?"

"No," answered the local official. "The dead man ran off through the south gate."

"Who was this dead man?" queried Yin Shixiong.

The local official then told them the story of how Zhang Fu and Li Lu had killed the monk, and of how the magistrate held an inquest and left a man to watch the dead man, and finally of how the dead monk had ran off.

When Yang Guodong heard the tale, he exclaimed: "That's terrible! Ji Gong killed!"

"You don't know the extent of Ji Gong's powers," said Yin Shixiong. "He could not have died. Let's go back."

At this time the local official went back with them. They had just reached the crossroads when they saw the monk come running from the east. When the local official saw him, he said, "The dead man is coming."

Yin Shixiong And Yang Guodong went up to the monk and Yin asked, "What's the matter, Teacher?"

The monk replied, "This is terrible. We're going to have to go to the yamen. Just don't let that short fellow that's chasing me get away!"

Yang Goudong stopped the short man. "Don't move," said Yin Shixiong. "If you are having a quarrel with the monk, we will go to the yamen."

"Good!" said the short man. "We do have a quarrel." Yin Shixiong then locked hand and leg cuffs, with chains attached, on the short man.

"It was the monk who attacked me," protested the short man. "Why don't you put the chains on him? You can't have me locked in chains."

"The magistrate has given us orders that when ordinary folks and monks fight, we should put cuffs and chains on the ordinary folks but not on the monks," explained Yin Shixiong. "Let's go!"

But just as they were about to leave the intersection, the waiter came up and exclaimed, "Don't go!"

Yang Guodong recognized him and asked, "Waiter Liu! What's this?"

"This person ate ten stuffed biscuits and drank ten jugs of wine, and the monk did the same. Then they fought and broke twenty saucers and never paid. They just ran off!"

"Just go back and write it on my account," said Yang Guodong. "Whatever it is, I will pay it."

"Well, since you say so, I'll go back." The waiter turned on his heel and left.

"Let's go on to the yamen," said the monk.

The local official then asked, "Yang Guodong, would you tell the magistrate for me that the teacher is alive? Then I will not go to the yamen."

"That's all right," said Yang Guodong.

He led the short man along and everybody went north, but before they had gone very far, Manager Hai came running out. "Yang, sir, you have been a great trouble to me," he said.

"How have I troubled you?" Headman Yang asked.

"Wasn't your sister-in-law supposed to be dead?" asked the manager.

"Who told you that?" asked the headman.

The manager pointed with his finger. "That teacher brought me a message from you."

"Teacher," asked Headman Yang, "How did you come to take a message for me?"

"I was playing a joke on him because he makes these deceptive flourishes on his checks."

When he heard that Ji Gong had played a joke on him, Manager Hai exclaimed, "A good monk you are! You tricked me for no reason at all! I bought all these cakes that I haven't sent yet. You can pay me for all this!"

"So you are out of pocket a little, my friend Hai," said Yang Guodong. "This monk is no stranger to us all. Look to me for the money you are owed."

"Teacher," asked Yin Shixiong, "why did you say that someone was dead? Originally we had been talking about someone being sick."

"A curse always brings good luck, you know," said the monk. "She should be in fine shape for the next ten years. Who knows—she may never die."

"Teacher, manifest your mercy!" pleaded Yang Guodong. "Give me a piece of medicine for her!" The monk nodded, took out a piece of medicine, and handed it to him.

"Which temple does this monk come from?" asked the short man.

"You ask about the monk!" said Yin Shixiong. "I will tell you. If you ever go to law with him, you will lose your case and that will be an honor! This is Ji Dian from the Monastery of the Soul's Retreat."

The short man made a gasping sound. "If he is Ji Dian, I will drop my complaint." And without saying anything further, he held out his wrists for them to take off the handcuffs.

"Don't let him go," ordered the monk. "He is involved in both of the two unsolved murder cases at Longyou."

In fact, the short man was named Xu Za, and he was nicknamed "the Little Sprite." He had been a river pirate on the Yangtze. He had once lived at Four Rivers Road in Linan and had already been charged with two previous murders. But how were these two latest murders linked to him?

Now, the Daoist priest who had been called to do an exorcism in the flower garden was murdered there. He was named She Qiushuang. The Daoist had been a member of the Greenwood before he became a Daoist and left the world to enter the Three Purities Shrine outside the south gate. While there, he had come into possession of a sorcerer's book titled *The Precious Record of the Dark Spirits*. It contained information on such subjects as the art of refining elixirs, ways of calling up wind or rain, making soldiers from beans, moving mountains to the sea, keeping the five demons under control, changing stones to gods, capturing goblins, and causing spirits to do one's bidding.

One day, a man dressed in monk's clothing came to see him. In fact, he was not a monk at all, but one of the outlaws known as "the Five Demons of Four Rivers Road." He was named Li Daoming and nicknamed "the Devil from Kaifeng." He had been friends with the Daoist a long time ago. Then they had been in the habit of visiting back and forth. As soon as they saw each other, they began warmly talking of the good times they had had and what they had done since they last had met.

"Dear Brother Li," asked She Qiushuang, "where have you been?"

"I came from Four Rivers," replied Li Daoming. "The Greenwood is all closed out there. The others have all been driven away. I have no place to go." The Daoist let Li Daoming live at the Three Purities Shrine. Li noticed that the Daoist seemed to be studying from morning to night, and so he asked, "What is it that you are doing all this time?"

"I have obtained a sorcerer's book that describes all sorts of magic arts," answered the Daoist.

"Daoist brother," said Li Daoming, "Teach me how to practice some of them."

"You could never practice these arts," said the Daoist. "If you tried, you would be disappointed a thousand times."

"He simply does not want to teach me," thought Li Daoming. Secretly he began to hate the Daoist priest.

One day the Gao family asked the Daoist to exorcise a goblin in their flower garden. Li Daoming knew about the request. While the Daoist priest, using the sorcerer's book, was performing the exorcism at a table in the garden, Li Daoming came up behind him under cover of darkness and killed him with one thrust of his knife.

Once Li Daoming had the sorcerer's book in his hand, the supposed monk never went back to the shrine. Instead he went to the Yang family's hotel, named the Thriving Fortune Inn, where everyone thought he was a Buddhist monk. There, whenever he had nothing else to do, he studied the book early and late. One day he was standing at the entrance to the Thriving Fortune Inn when he saw coming from the east the man named

Xu Za, the Little Sprite. Although Li Daoming was dressed in monk's cloth-ing, Xu Za immediately recognized him. He approached him and bowed.

"Brother Xu Za," asked Li Daoming, "where did you come from?"

"I am going to Linan to look around," answered Xu Za. "My friends at the Greenwood in Four Rivers are all scattered, and I have nowhere to go." Li Daoming invited him into his hotel room to talk.

Xu Za asked, "What are you doing while you are staying here?"

"I have got my hands on a divine book from which I am learning," replied Li Daoming.

"Can you use it to teach me?" queried Xu Za.

"If you want to learn from it, you can try," replied Li Dao Ming, "but first we must have the cloth cover from a young dead girl's spirit tablet. Then we will be able to see and hear from great distances."

Xu Za was a simple person and believed what Li Daoming had said. For some time he went about, asking where he might find the cloth cover from a young dead girl's spirit tablet. He asked several people, but they could tell him nothing. One day, however, while he was walking in the woods near town, he met a man who limped, pretending that he was lame. He recognized the short man at once. "Brother Xu," the man exclaimed, "what are you doing here?!"

The limping man was named Ping Yuanzhi and nicknamed "the Painted Lame Man." He was one of the most famous robbers from the Four Rivers. He had gotten his nickname because he only pretended to be lame during the day to make people think that he would be unable to go over the rooftops at night. Xu Za told him about his search for the cloth cover from a young dead girl's spirit tablet and about the book of magic.

"Brother Xu, you are a simpleton!" exclaimed Ping Yuanzhi. "Li Dao-ming is playing a joke on you. Tonight I will go with you to the hotel. Why don't you kill Li Daoming and take the book?'

"Good!" said Xu Za. Ping had a grudge against Li, and was using Xu as a "borrowed knife" to kill Li. The two talked the proposed deed over.

After they'd had a meal at a wine shop, they waited until the second watch. After they reached the hotel by going over the roofs, Ping stayed on the roof to watch while Xu went down and entered the north cham-ber. Li Daoming was sleeping in a chair, with his head resting on a table. Xu let his heavy knife fall and grasped the book.

Just then he heard someone shout, "Murder!" Xu Za was startled, but he remained in the north chamber. It was Ji Gong who had shouted, "Mur-der!" when he awoke from sleep. Ping remained hidden, still on the roof.

Next Ji Gong was heard to say, "I am going out into the courtyard." That was when Ji Gong went outside, climbed over the wall, and went off to the Daoist abbey.

After a while the two listening robbers heard Headman Chai ask She, "Is the warrant safe?" Ping did not know what the warrant was, but he could see Chai and She back inside and heard them getting something out of their pack. Xu Za came out of the north chamber and left with the sorcerer's book.

Ping waited until Chai and She again came out to look for Ji Gong. Then Ping came down and went into the east room, where he found the warrant lying on the brick sleeping platform. He thrust it inside his jacket. Although Chai and She saw him come out of the door, they were unable to stop him before he was up and away over the roofs.

When they were well away, Ping asked Xu Za. "How did it go?"

"Well, I have the sorcerer's book," answered Xu Za, "but where shall we go now?"

"Let's go to the Kaihua district," said Ping Yuanzhi. "At the Iron Buddha Temple there is a master outlaw who is a heaven-sent elder brother to us. He has sent invitations to men of the Greenwood, especially those among us who have been exposed. There are dozens of our Greenwood friends from Four Rivers Road there in his temple. He wants to make it a place of refuge, where we can all hide our faces behind our rice bowls. If we go there, it is like a hole in the ground. So let us go to the Kaihua district."

Xu Za replied, "We might as well!"

The two went off, following the highway, until they came to a man they recognized as a friend.

CHAPTER 62

Xu Za describes the Iron Buddha Temple; the Daoist gives Ji Gong medicine

THERE on the highway passing through the forest, the short man, Xu Za, with the sorcerer's book that had caused the murder of both the Daoist and the imposter monk, walked with the false lame man, Ping Yuanzhi, who now had the warrant for Cloud Dragon Hua's arrest. Approaching them from the opposite direction was none other than the Water Rat, Cloud Dragon Hua. Xu Za and Ping Yuanzhi quickened their pace and bowed to the other.

Then Ping said, "Brother Hua, let me tell you something that will make you feel easier. I have brought the warrant for your arrest."

"Is this true?" asked Cloud Dragon Hua. Ping Yuanzhi then told him the story of how Li Daoming had been killed when Xu Za took the sorcerer's book and about how the two headmen had kept the warrant in the hotel.

When Cloud Dragon Hua understood everything, he asked, "Where are you two going now?"

"To the Kaihua district," responded Ping Yuanzhi. "Why not come with us? There is a master outlaw named Jiang Tianrui at the Iron Buddha Temple who has invited all of the men of the Greenwood to come there. A great many of our friends have gone there to hide out in safety. Let the three of us go together."

"Indeed, yes!" said Cloud Dragon.

The three went on their way and that very day came to the Iron Buddha Temple in Kaihua. Looking around outside, they saw a great crowd of people packed together. Someone said, "The spirit of the Iron Buddha spits the words of men out of its mouth."

The three outlaws walked straight ahead and on into the back of the temple. There, they saw Jiang Tianrui, who was using his title, "the Golden Eye of Buddha."

The three bowed to him and Ping Yuanzhi asked, "Brother Jiang, where are all your friends?"

"All of our friends have gone off on business along four different roads, except for a few whom I will call out and introduce to you." There was much bowing and scraping and exchanging of greetings. Then Jiang asked, "Where did you three come from?"

Cloud Dragon Hua and Xu Za each told his story. Then Jiang said, "Brother Xu, let me see that book you obtained, whatever it was." Xu Za took out the book and handed it to Jiang. He looked at it and then said, "Brother Xu, this book is not something you could use. I will keep it here."

Xu Za was not very pleased and thought to himself, "That is my property, and I have not yet begun to tire of it. I didn't offer to give it to him and he just kept it." This turn of events was infuriating and he did not like it at all, but he could not object. He could not anger Jiang Tianrui, and so kept silent.

At that time Cloud Dragon Hua spoke up. "I want to leave," he stated.

"Why?" asked Jiang Tianrui.

"I am uneasy," replied Cloud Dragon Hua. "I am afraid that Ji Gong will come looking for me and he will gather everyone else up at once. No one will escape."

"Friends," said Jiang when he heard Cloud Dragon's statement, "who will go to Longyou, find the monk Ji Dian, kill him, and bring back his head? Who can do it and relieve Brother Hua?"

"I will go!" volunteered Xu Za. However, he was thinking to himself: "If I do not waste any time when I get to Longyou, find Ji Gong and behead him, very well. If I do waste my time, fail in that attempt, and get caught myself, I will draw everyone here out and not one person will get away." He had offered to go out of hatred and resentment over his lost book.

"Good!" said Jiang Tianrui. "Xu Za, I wish you luck in your attempt!"

Xu Za then left Kaihua. That same day he arrived at the southeast corner of the wall at Longyou, where he happened to run into Ji Gong. As soon as Xu Za heard the monk saying, as if to himself, "Longyou is not like other places. You have to know what to do in a restaurant, or no matter how much you spend, they will laugh at you."

Xu Za, especially since he was rather stupid, followed Ji Gong into a restaurant. There, the monk intentionally picked a fight with Xu Za and ran off down the street into town. Then the monk told the headmen to lock Xu Za in chains. When he tried to escape, the monk pointed at him and prevented him from getting away.

When they reached the yamen, headman Yang Guodong went in and reported, "Ji Gong is not dead. He has just captured an outlaw."

The magistrate was in the midst of interrogating Jiang Fu and Li Lu and preparing their confessions. When he heard that Ji Gong was not dead, he immediately prepared to receive him. Ji Gong had the two head-men, Yin Shixiong and Yang Guodong, bring the outlaw into the audi-ence hall. When the magistrate saw them, he said, "Holy monk, please be seated. What is the name of the robber there?"

Xu Za was not at all unwilling to speak: "In reply to Your Honor, my name is Xu Za and I am called the Little Sprite. The monk who was beheaded in the Yang family's hotel outside East Gate was really an out-law named Li Daoming, known as the Kaifeng Demon. I killed him. Since he had taken the life of She Qiushuang, that lets me off the matter. It's no business of mine."

"Nonsense!" stated the magistrate. "You killed the monk at the hotel. We have your confession and you stole the warrant."

"I did not steal the warrant," countered Xu Za. "That was stolen by the painted lame man, Ping Yuanzhi. He and Cloud Dragon Hua are both living at the Iron Buddha Temple in Kaihua. That temple has many more men of the Greenwood living there."

When the magistrate heard this, he did not ask anything further, but ordered that Xu Za be put in prison and kept in chains. Then the magis-trate said, "Saintly monk, I ask once more for your help. Will you take my headmen and capture these outlaws?"

"I can do it," replied the monk. "If Your Honor will prepare a warrant, I will take Yang Guodong, Yin Shixiong, Chai Yuanlo, and She Chenying and go." The magistrate prepared the warrant and handed it to Yang Guodong. The monk took the four men, and leaving the yamen went straight to the highway. As the monk walked, he sang:

> Come south, turn north, east or west.
> Come south, turn north, east or west.
> I see lives that pass are void.
> Heaven is void.
> Earth is void.
> Men are dimly seen therein.
> Sun is void.
> Moon is void.
> Come, come; go, go. What is done?
> Fields are void.
> Soil is void.
> Change your master; still it's void.

> Gold is void.
> Silver is void.
> Once dead, what's it in your hand?
> Wives are void.
> Children are void.
> Who meets at the Yellow Springs?
> Titles void.
> Knowledge void.
> Pains that are infinite, alas
> From the morning to the eve.
> Man's life is like that of the bee.
> When all the flowers have been searched,
> When the honey all is made.
> Think of it carefully. You will see
> That it was only in your mind.

The monk had just finished singing his song when they heard a sound behind them. "Oh, Limitless One!"

The monk said, "Ai yah! O Mi To Fu!" They turned their heads and saw that a Daoist had come up alongside them. On his head was a kerchief with nine folds. He wore a copper-colored robe and elegant white-soled shoes. His face was like the autumn moon in the third quarter. He was about seventy years old, with hair like snow. He had a frosty white beard on his chin that he had combed down over his breast with a silver comb that was attached to his sash. He was the very picture of a Daoist saint.

With him were two Daoist novices of about fifteen or sixteen. They were both handsome, with hair pulled into a knot on each side of the head. They were dressed in the blue gowns of novices with matching collars in a darker color. Each wore white shoes with a cloud design on the toes. One of the boys carried a precious sword and the other a parasol.

As he walked, the Daoist chanted:

> A cave in the mountains,
> A dark and gloomy place,
> With begging bowl in hand
> Is better than a palace
> With jade and jasper towers
> And locks of gold and silver.
> Unaware of springtime
> Of summer or of fall
> To follow up a mountain stream

> With clouds and moon
> For company
> Is pure happiness.

"Oh, Limitless One!" the Daoist said as he passed. The monk turned and looked at him. Before the Daoist had gone very far, the monk said loudly, "Ai yah! My legs and back hurt so that I can't walk!"

"What is it, Teacher?" asked Headman Yang.

"I'm going to die! I can't go on!" the monk exclaimed.

Yin Shixiong, who also did not understand the monk's temperament, came over and asked, "What's the matter, Teacher?"

"My heart is about to stop. I have a bitter taste in my mouth and my eyes are getting dim," answered the monk.

"Right!" said Headman Chai. "And your speech is all mixed up!" Chai and his fellow headman She ignored the monk. The monk sat down beside the road and began to moan and groan.

"Oh, Limitless One!' said the Daoist as he turned back. "This monk is a fellow traveler. We are brothers in leaving the world!"

Yin Shixiong said, "We all set off together!"

"The monk's illness seems to have gotten worse," noted the Daoist, "and as a hermit, I do have medicine."

"Venerable Daoist," said Headman Chai, "don't pay any attention to him. Go along! As soon as you give him any medicine, he will die!"

"The medicine I have is good!" argued the Daoist. "If a person takes one dose, he can live a year. If he takes two doses, he will live two years. If he takes three, he will live six years. And if he takes nine, he will live twelve years more. I will guarantee that the monk will not die."

"I told you, but you would not listen," said Chai. "Go ahead and give it to him." The Daoist prepared to administer the medicine. It looked like a cherry and was red as fire. It had a strong odor. The Daoist gave Ji Gong the first dose.

The monk swallowed it and shouted, "My stomach is on fire!"

"Is it or isn't it?" asked Chai.

The Daoist gave Ji Gong a second dose. "My stomach is bursting!" cried the monk.

Again the Daoist prepared the medicine and gave Ji Gong a third dose. "My heart is on fire and my liver is all in pieces!" moaned the monk.

The Daoist gave him nine pills altogether and the monk swallowed them. "Not good!" groaned the monk. "I am going to die!" Having said this, the monk gave one cry and nothing more. His legs kicked and all his breath seemed to go out through his lips. He appeared to be dead.

CHAPTER 63

The Daoist and the monk exchange medicines;
the ragged monk smells the odor of robbers

HEADMAN Chai looked at Ji Gong and said, "Reverend Daoist, look and see whether he is not dead. I told you not to give him anything, but you did."

The old Daoist turned pale with fright and said, "Oh, Limitless One! Very strange! Very strange!"

"And don't be saying, 'Oh, Limitless One,'" said Chai. "You made him die, but I can make him live!"

"Headman Chai," asked Yin Shixiong, "how can you cure him and make him live again?"

"Headman She," said Chai, "you might as well drink the last bit of wine in the jug. There's no point in saving it for Teacher now that he's gone."

"I'll do that right away," said She. Before he had finished speaking, the monk rolled over and sat up.

"Where is that wine?" he asked. "It's just what I need."

"You all saw this, didn't you?" asked Chai.

The monk got to his feet, saying, "Well, my good Daoist, those pills you gave me almost cost me my life. Don't try to get away now." Going over to the Daoist, Ji Gong took hold of his sleeve.

Now this Daoist was none other than the former pupil and protegé of the venerable Great Sage of the East, Fang Tai, from the famous shrine in the Tiandai mountains. Outside the northeast gate of the Kaihua district town there was a monastery called the North Rising, and in the shrine there was a Daoist named Chen Xuanliang, who had also been a pupil of the venerable Fang. Daoist Chen was in the shrine, pursuing his search for virtue and honor, when he became aware of a strong blast of demonic energy rising up toward heaven. Immediately he thought to himself, "Since I am nearby, why should these demons be permitted to do these evil things? I will go and find the source of this demonic evil and eradicate it so that the world can be saved from disruption."

So saying, he took his precious sword and went directly north, searching until he found the Iron Buddha Temple. He arrived just as the Iron Buddha was spitting out human speech from its mouth: "To all virtuous men and pious women who come seeking medicine, I, the Buddha, am here to help all living beings. Each of you should bring one string of cash so that your combined efforts may help to repair the temple. Each of you will receive a package of medicine to take home and relieve your family's illness."

Chen Xuanliang perceived that the evil influences were coming from inside this Iron Buddha. He could hear people who were burning incense saying, "There is an epidemic of illness going around here. As soon as people help the Iron Buddha, they get well."

Daoist Chen thought, "There is some kind of poisonous influence coming from this demon. I must put an end to it." Therefore he drew his precious sword and began an exorcism. Unexpectedly a black jet of vapor came forth from the lips of the iron image and Chen fell helpless to the ground. He was unable to move.

Word of the Daoist's presence had already been carried to Jiang, the Golden Eye of Buddha, who thought to himself, "This Chen Xuanliang, with no orders from anyone else and for no reason at all, has come here to interfere with my affairs. Why shouldn't I have him brought back here and finish him off? The sooner I get him out of the way, the better."

But just as he was about to send someone out for the Daoist, one of his men came back and reported, "Some of the magistrate's people who came to burn incense saw the Daoist and took him away to the yamen."

"Very well," Jiang said, "let the magistrate handle him."

When the magistrate questioned Chen Xuanliang at the yamen, the magistrate realized that Daoist Chen was a good person. "There are demonic influences doing strange things at the Iron Buddha Temple," said Chen Xuanliang when he awakened from his stupor. "I thought that I might exorcise them, but I did not realize the power that they have and the ability that they had to attack me. I am not sure whether the effects of their attack may be fatal."

"Since you now know that there are demonic influences, what is to be done?" asked the magistrate.

"I will ask my teacher to come," replied the Daoist. "He will expel the goblin."

"That is a good idea," said the magistrate, and sent some of his men to escort the Daoist back to the shrine in a sedan chair.

On the way back, the Daoist was thinking, "If I ask my teacher, the Great Sage of the East, to come, I fear that the journey may be too much for him." So he sent two of his novices to the Three Purities Shrine at Longyou to ask his brother Daoist, Ma Xuantong, to come instead. He also told the two novices, "Ask the teacher to bring me some of the Nine Lives pills. Go swiftly on your way and return quickly."

The two novices were off. They found Ma Xuantong and asked him to come. They were already half way back to their master with the Daoist Ma when they met Ji Gong. Daoist Ma had never seen Ji Gong. When he heard him singing, he thought, "That poor monk's words show that he understands about trying to be virtuous and honorable." When he saw that the monk was sick and could not go on, the Daoist, out of the goodness of his heart, gave him all the pills that he had brought with him. Then the monk appeared to die and was revived by Headman Chai.

When the monk caught hold of the Daoist's sleeve, Headman Yin Shixiong protested. "Teacher, you should be grateful to the venerable Daoist for giving you the medicine—now you are well again."

The monk released the Daoist's sleeve and queried, "This Daoist gave me medicine?"

"That's right," said the Daoist. "From what temple does the venerable monk come?"

"The Monastery of the Soul's Retreat at the West Lake. The upper character of my name is Dao and the lower character is Ji. The person commonly known by the name Ji Dian, 'Mad Ji,' is myself. And what is Daoist Ma's name?"

"You know that my surname is Ma," said the Daoist, "and you still ask me my honorable name?"

"And isn't your personal name Xuantong?" asked the monk.

"Yes," replied the Daoist. "I am called Xuantong."

"And where are you going?" asked the monk.

"To the North Rising Shrine at Kaihua," replied the Daoist.

"I am also going to the North Rising Shrine," said the monk. "May we go together?"

"Good," said the Daoist.

"I hear that you Daoists are able to travel like the wind," said the monk. "Will you take me along with you?"

"I can," said the Daoist. "Just shut your eyes and be sure that you don't open them." The Daoist arranged the monk's position. Then there was the sound of a great wind as they moved through the air.

About halfway there the monk opened his eyes and cried, "Stop! Stop! This is terrible. Stop, honorable Daoist!"

The Daoist stopped, and then, since he was in hurry, went on his way without bothering to look to see where the monk had fallen. When the Daoist arrived at Kaihua, there at the doorway of the North Rising Shrine, he saw that someone was sitting asleep on the doorstep. The person got up and said, "Ah! You have arrived!"

"I came as quickly as I could. I'm quite out of breath," said the Daoist, secretly thinking, "This is very strange! This monk must have some special abilities. Otherwise how did he get here before me?"

Ma Xuantong knocked at the shrine gate. A little Daoist novice answered. As he opened the gate, he greeted the Daoist and said, "Teacher has come, but where are the two novices?"

"Those two are coming behind me and will be here soon," answered Daoist Ma. "Monk, please come in and sit down."

Ji Gong went inside with him. Looking around, he saw that the great hall was on the north side. To the east and west were two accompanying buildings, each of three sections. The little Daoist novice opened the door of the eastern one and the monk and Daoist entered. Directly opposite the door was an "eight immortals" table about three feet square, with an armchair on each side. At the left end of the room to the north the resident Daoist, Chen Xuanliang, was lying motionless on the brick platform bed.

As soon as Chen Xuanliang saw the two enter, he said, "Ah, you have arrived, my brother Daoist, and who is this honorable monk?"

"This is Ji Gong from the Monastery of the Soul's Retreat," answered Ma Xuantong.

"And did you bring the Nine Lives pills?" asked Daoist Chen. "I am still suffering from the effects of that demon's breath."

"I did bring the pills," replied Daoist Ma, "but on the way I met this honorable monk who was ill, and I gave them to him."

"And I recovered," said the monk. "Perhaps some medicine that I have will help my Daoist brother." He took the medicine out and gave it to Daoist Chen, who took it and shortly recovered.

"Good medicine," said Chen, "very good medicine! I feel well and even young again."

"We are your disciples," said Ma Xuantong. Both of them bowed and thanked Ji Gong.

"Oh, that is nothing," said Ji Gong, "but this room has a strange odor. I feel as if there were smoke in my nostrils."

"What kind of odor is it?" asked Chen Xuanliang.

"It is the smell of robbers," answered Ji Gong.

The two Daoists were amazed to hear this. Now there were actually two outlaws under the brick platform bed hidden in the fire chamber, but this fact was unknown to the Daoists. When the magistrate of Kaihua, who had gone to the Iron Buddha Temple, had taken the Daoist Chen to the yamen for creating a disturbance, Golden Eye Jiang had first thought that the Daoist would be punished. When the Daoist was sent back to this shrine, the word quickly reached Jiang. "He will certainly ask his teacher at Tiandai Mountain to help," Golden Eye reasoned. "If I don't act quickly now, it will be worse later. I have a great business here which he may destroy." He therefore sent the two outlaws to murder Daoist Chen.

At the shrine they managed to enter and conceal themselves under the brick bed in the fire chamber, but when they heard that the other Daoist was coming, they decided to wait and kill them both.

CHAPTER 64

Ji Gong sends a gift of pickled eggs; the Painted Lame Man walks into a trap

AS the two outlaws emerged from the fire chamber under the brick platform bed and collected themselves, they drew their swords and prepared to attack Ji Gong, but the monk simply pointed his finger and paralyzed them. At the same time, the bamboo blind hanging at the door was lifted and the four headmen and two Daoist novices burst into the room. The four headmen were indeed Chai Yuanlo, She Jengying, Yang Guodong, and Yin Shixiong.

Now, a short time before, the four headmen and the two Daoist novices had been walking along the road. The Daoist Ma Xuantong had flown off, taking Ji Gong with him and leaving the six others behind.

"Tell us," said Headman Chai, "from which shrine do you novices come?"

"We are from the Kaihua district North Rising Shrine," said one of the novices.

"And is the Daoist who was here just now your teacher?" asked Chai.

"No, he is not our teacher, but our teacher's elder brother," the same novice answered.

"Well, since our monk has gone with your teacher's elder brother to your temple," said Chai, "let us go together."

"I'm afraid," said the novice, "that your four headmen will not be able to keep up with us. We are going to walk on air."

"We four headmen can almost fly over the ground," said Chai. "If you two will only go a little slower, we will go faster so that we can go together."

"Very well," agreed the novice. And the six of them followed the road and quickly arrived at the North Rising Shrine. "Here we are," said the novice. "Just wait till I knock at the gate."

"Don't bother with that," said Chai. "I will go in and open it." And as he spoke, Chai and She both leapt over the wall. They had seized this opportunity to show off their skills to the other two headmen, as if to say, "We were sent to capture the great outlaw Hua Yun Long and are not without some special abilities."

The novices hardly expected the local headmen, Yang Guodong and Yin Shixiong, to be able to jump over the wall just as well as they did. Without actually saying so in words, their actions implied that they, though only local headmen, were not completely without skill. After this bit of unspoken rivalry among the four headmen, they opened the gate. The two novices entered, closed the gate, and with the four headmen got into the room just as Ji Gong brought the two outlaws to a standstill.

"Teacher," asked Headman Chai, "which of these is Cloud Dragon Hua?"

"We have no Cloud Dragon Hua," replied the monk.

"Then," asked Chai, "which of them is the robber who stole the warrant?"

"Nor do we have the thief who stole the warrant," answered the monk. "But first, put these two in chains. Even though they're not the ones we want most, don't let them escape."

Chai and the others fastened cuffs and chains on the two outlaws and Yin Shixiong asked the two novices to get some refreshments. The four headmen then politely greeted their Daoist hosts and all sat down to eat and drink.

"Now, my Daoist friends," said Ji Gong, "while it is still light, we should get these outlaws to the magistrate's yamen and send him word that I am going to exorcise the Iron Buddha Temple. Tell the commander of the guards also. But, my Daoist friends, we cannot do any of this openly. If we let the word out, not only will the outlaws get away, but you two Daoists will be in danger of their revenge and may lose your lives."

"But how can this be managed, teacher?" asked Headman Yin Shixiong.

"Wrap these two outlaws in quilts so they will not be recognized and say that the shrine is sending a present to His Honor, the magistrate."

The Daoists agreed. It was now midday. When the bound and gagged outlaws had been made into unrecognizable bales, four strong porters were called in. They picked up one of the bales and asked, "What's this?" The Daoists said nothing.

"Pickled eggs," said Ji Gong.

"We never saw pickled eggs packed like this," commented one of the porters.

"Never mind that," said the monk. "Just carry them carefully." The two Daoists then went off with the porters to the Magistrate's yamen.

"Headman Chai," said the monk, "you four men first go to the guard office nearest the Iron Buddha Temple and say that I will be there soon."

The four headmen went quickly to the guard office and reported. The supervisor of the guard, named Liu Guoshen, immediately invited the four headmen inside. When asked about their mission, Headman Chai said that they were working on a case with Ji Gong.

"Ah," said Supervisor Liu, "so the saintly monk is coming here to solve a case. But why is he not here yet?"

"He will be here presently," said Chai.

In a short time Ji Gong did arrive at the gate. "I would like to ask a favor of the manager," said the ragged monk.

The officer who heard this said, "There is no manager here, Teacher. This is a yamen."

"If there is no one to manage the yamen, what do you have?" asked the monk.

"We have an honorable supervisor," replied the officer.

"Is he your uncle?" asked the ragged monk.

"Are you asking for a beating?" countered the officer.

"Just tell your old gentleman that the old man is here," said the monk.

"Who are you, monk?" asked the officer.

"Oh, I am Mad Ji from the Monastery of the Soul's Retreat," replied the monk.

At once someone was sent inside to announce him. Soon Supervisor Liu came out, and hurrying over to him, said, "Ah! the saintly monk has arrived! Please come inside and sit down."

"After you," the monk said. Together they went into the library, where the four headmen were waiting. As soon as the monk came in and sat down, tea was served.

"Honorable Supervisor Liu," the monk began, "would you send someone to the Iron Buddha Temple and ask the chief monk to come here. Explain that there is a rich man who lives very nearby who wishes to make some repairs to the temple and who would like to ask how much in silver the repairs would cost. I would like to get the thief who stole the warrant and question him. Afterward I will go and exorcise the temple."

Supervisor Liu nodded his head in answer. Then he immediately sent some underlings to the Iron Buddha Temple with his card and an invitation to the monk there.

Now it happened that Golden Eye Jiang had only Cloud Dragon Hua and the Painted Lame Man with him, plus two other men. The two men Jiang had sent to kill the Daoist had not yet returned, and all the other friends of the Greenwood who had been staying at the temple had gone off on their business. Therefore, altogether there were just five men at the temple at noon.

Meanwhile, at a little hamlet to the west some knowledgeable people had been talking with other well-to-do gentry there about what was happening in the eight hundred or more villages in Kaihua. Household after household was coming down with a strange illness that not even the most famous doctor was able to cure. The only thing that helped was to go to the Iron Buddha Temple. There had to be some reason for this. In seeking help from the Iron Buddha, a poor family had to give a string of cash, but a wealthier family had to give an ounce of silver. Perhaps, people said, if they could talk with the chief monk at the temple and arrange to repair the temple with a substantial fund collected from the wealthy families, this epidemic might cease? After talking it over, the people in the hamlet sent some people with an invitation to the chief monk at the Iron Buddha Temple.

Golden Eye Jiang and Cloud Dragon Hua hurried off to the little west hamlet. They had just left when the men arrived with an invitation from the supervisor of the guard, saying that there was a rich man who wanted to discuss repairs to the temple with a monk from the temple. The Painted Lame Man, Ping Yuanzhi, said, "I will go."

When he arrived at the guard office with the men sent by the guard supervisor, he was shown into the library. "Ah, the monk has arrived," said Supervisor Liu. The false monk, Ping Yuanzhi, went up to him and greeted him politely. Ji Gong at this time was behind the lattice in the east section of the library, while the four headmen were waiting behind the partition in the west section. Supervisor Liu, asking Ping Yuanzhi to sit down, said, "What is the monk's honorable name?"

The Painted Lame Man replied, "At home I was named Ping. My Buddhist name is Yuanzhi."

"And how many years has it been since you left the world?" queried Liu.

"I am really halfway along the road because of an accident in which I injured my leg," answered the Painted Lame Man.

"Just now there is a man who desires to repair a temple," said Supervisor Liu. "Your temple is greatly in need of repair. How much will be needed?"

Ping, the Painted Lame Man, was only an outlaw who knew nothing about repairing temples. There was not much that he could say.

"You seem unable to say very much about the subject. Let me introduce you to another monk," said the supervisor. "Saintly monk, will you come out now?"

As soon as Ji Gong came into the room, he exclaimed, "You rascal, Ping Yuanzhi! How dare you steal our warrant? I have had my eye on you!"

Ping Yuanzhi was shocked, and started to stand up to run outside. Ji Gong pointed and the outlaw was unable to move. The monk then reached inside the robber's clothing, taking out the warrant for Cloud Dragon Hua. The monk handed it to Headman Chai, saying, "Take it, Headman Chai, and look it over." Naturally it was the same as before. "Your honor," said the monk, "first call your officers and have them keep this outlaw locked up in your yamen. Now I am going to the Iron Buddha Temple to exorcise the evil spirit. Keep this outlaw in chains, Your Honor." Supervisor Liu had his guard officers lock up the robber until the time that he would be called for in the examination room.

The four headmen left the guard station and went off with Ji Gong. When they reached the temple, they noticed first that the crowd in the temple gateway was so thick that people could hardly move. There were people selling food to the temple visitors, and other vendors with all sorts of goods for sale. Inside the temple, as well as outside, throngs of worshippers were packed together, coming and going. Countless good men and pious women were there to burn incense and to beg for medicine to cure their illness.

The door of the main gate and the two smaller gates on each side were all open wide. Inside there was a flagstaff with two flags flying. Above the entrance was a signboard, into which were carved the words: THE IRON BUDDHA TEMPLE, ESTABLISHED BY IMPERIAL COMMAND. The monk with his four headmen went in through the gate on the east side. Straight to the north was the great hall with five sections, and to the east and west were two accompanying buildings, each with five sections.

On the east side of the great hall were four green panels of a high wooden screen-like wall. Two of these panels were open and two closed. They entered the second courtyard. The central hall here was five stories high. There were more than one hundred sections in the temple.

The Iron Buddha was within this main hall. A great cloud of smoke from burning incense poured out of the doors. "O Mi To Fu. Goodness!" It would be here that the *lohan* would use his Buddhist arts to exorcise the demon spirit within this great temple.

CHAPTER 65

The Iron Buddha falls from the altar;
Sorcerer Hua has a strange visitor

AS Ji Gong entered the Iron Buddha Temple with his four headmen, he perceived in that great hall an almost overpowering demonic essence that seemed to rise up to heaven like a cloud of smoke. Looking around, he noticed a table on the east side and a man with an account book who received only silver. On the west side there was a similar table and a man with an account book where only strings of cash were taken.

Then he saw a woman burning incense. She was about twenty years old with hair that was oiled until it shone like a mirror. Her face was powdered and her clothing was not that expected of a respectable woman. "Buddha above," she was saying, "the little wife, Yao Shi, asks on behalf of a sick relative that you manifest your kindness and give me a little medicine to cure her, and I will worship and burn incense to you."

Then a voice speaking human speech issued from the mouth of the Iron Buddha. "Yao Shi, did you bring a string of cash that you are able to give Buddha?"

"I have brought it," she replied.

"If you have indeed brought the string of cash," the Iron Buddha said, "hand it over at the table and you will receive a package of good medicine. Take it back to your house and all will be well."

Yao Shi said, "Thank you, Buddha." Then she went to the table where the strings of cash were being taken, handed over her string, took the medicine, and left.

No sooner had Yao Shi left than another little wife appeared, walking hesitantly in from outside. Now this woman was married to a man named Liu and her mother was named Li. They lived in the Liu family hamlet just to the south and outside the limits of the Kaihua district. The husband of Li Shi, as she was called, had gone away trading and for several years they had not heard from him. The family of Li Shi's mother-in-law was extremely poor, but she had been able to support herself by sewing. Two years earlier, the mother-in-law had developed a tumor, and since

Li Shi had heard that the master of the Iron Buddha was able to cure tumors, she had come, journeying on foot for a day and a night.

As she burned the incense, she said, "This small person is named Li Shi of the Liu family. My mother-in-law just beyond Kaihua has had a tumor for over two years. I beg the Iron Buddha to give me a little medicine that will make her well. When my husband returns from his trading journey, he will come to burn incense and worship."

As the demonic spirit looked at her, it realized that this illness was not caused by poison and would be incurable. Therefore it said, "Li Shi, were you able to bring cash with you?"

"No," she replied. "My home is so poor that we have no cash. I beg the Buddha to be compassionate."

"It is not possible," said the Iron Buddha. "Buddha never makes an exception. If there is no cash, there will be no medicine. Leave now."

Li Shi sighed deeply. "It is not strange that men love profit and Buddha loves wealth as well. It is just a pity that I am so devout and yet so helpless."

As she turned and went out, Ji Gong, who had been watching, realized that she was a truly good person. Going up to her, the monk said, "Do not be disturbed, my little lady. I have a piece of medicine here. Take it and give it to your mother-in-law and she will be well."

Li Shi took the medicine from him, and saying, "Thank you," she left.

Ji Gong strode into the great hall and looked at the Iron Buddha. It was a gilded figure twelve feet high, seated on a lotus flower pedestal five feet high. In front, on the huge altar that held the image, there was an incense burner and candles and fruit and many other offerings. The monk came up, took an apple and a peach, and began to eat. One of the bystanders asked, "Where did you come from, monk, taking fruit like that and eating it?"

"The offerings in a temple are supposed to be eaten," answered the monk. "You give things to Buddha to eat and to wear. Do you think that he is the son or grandson of the monks and able to eat them himself?"

When the bystander heard this, his anger was boiling, and he was about to strike the monk. The monk, however, pointed his finger and stopped him. Then the monk climbed up first onto the altar and then onto the lotus-shaped pedestal and said, "You thing! You dare to help this goblin do these strange acts to hurt the populace! Now I have found you and I will put a stop to your existence!" As he spoke, the monk slapped the image in the face twice.

Amidst the confusion, worshippers who had come to burn incense were saying, "A crazy monk has come who is slapping the Buddha's face."

The four headmen, who were standing outside the door, heard a low rumbling sound like thunder inside the belly of the image—"gu, lu, gu, lu." Suddenly there was a noise sounding like a cliff falling from a mountainside. The four headmen saw the twelve-foot high gilded image with its lotus-shaped pedestal lean forward and fall, apparently burying the monk beneath the wreckage.

The two headmen, Chai Yuanlo and She Jengying, stamped their feet in dismay and began to weep. "Teacher, you dear old fellow, we never thought you would die here! This is a bitter loss."

The other two headmen, Yang Guodang and Yin Shixiong, were also grieving. "How sad! Ji Gong, who was a really good man, crushed beneath all this!" exclaimed Yin. "Headman Chai, do not cry. Each person has a time to be born and a time to die. Let us go away from here."

Just as they were about to leave, they saw the monk come walking in, left right, left right, from outside the temple. "Headman Chai, are you all planning a funeral?" asked the monk.

"Teacher, you didn't die!" exclaimed Chai, who had stopped crying.

"No," said the monk. "Well, that evil spirit thought it could blot out the monk. I've got to drive it out of here, though. There are no two ways about it!"

"We thought you had been buried under all this," said Chai Yuanlo. "How did you manage to come in from outside?"

"It didn't hit me," answered the monk. "I was afraid and ran out." Just as he said this, the monk gave a cry. "This is dreadful! The evil is upon us!" Then there was a terrible roaring torrent of sound as a great wind uprooted trees or bent them double to the ground. It raised huge waves on the water and sent stones rolling down the hillsides. As it came into town, it shook the windows and doors and tore tiles loose from the roofs. Then, entering the temple door, it seemed to coil itself around the monk as the goblin spirit dropped down out of the sky.

Now, what was this goblin spirit? There was a reason for its existence, since nothing is without cause. The Daoist teacher of Golden Eye Jiang was named Hua, and his personal name was Qingfeng. He was sometimes called the Sorcerer of the Ninth Palace. Although Hua Qingfeng spent all his time studying Daoist lore, hoping to become an immortal, he was still an outlaw at heart. He had associations with the Greenwood and was the uncle of Cloud Dragon Hua. Some years earlier, he had murdered the

Daoist who lived in the rich shrine known as the Veiled Mountain Shrine, high up on Veiled Mountain, and had taken his place as a resident.

About thirty yards behind the shrine on a stone terrace was a pagoda just a little taller than the roof of the main building. The shrine and the pagoda were both very ancient. Before the Southern Song Dynasty (which began in 1127) and for as long as anyone knew, smoke had frequently risen from the ground near the base of the pagoda, so it was called the Smoldering Cloud Pagoda. Visitors who stayed at Veiled Mountain hoping to see the clouds of smoke gave generous donations to the shrine. This was the origin of the shrine's wealth.

People noticed that birds often flew into the clouds above the pagoda and failed to reappear. On the stone terrace around the pagoda, they would find many bones and feathers. Hua Qingfeng would have his Daoist novices sweep the terrace, making sure that the litter did not accumulate.

One morning Hua Qingfeng walked out of the north door of the shrine toward the pagoda. While he stood there, he heard someone say, "Oh, Limitless One!" Then an old man walked around from the other side of the pagoda and approached him, smiling. "Don't you recognize me?" he asked. "I am your tenant, my Daoist friend, and you are my landlord." The old man was wearing a faded dark-green Daoist robe and white shoes. His skin was the color of yellowish earth, his eyes were yellow, and his narrow beard and mustache were red.

"Yes, yes," said Hua Qingfeng. "Will my Daoist friend come into the shrine and sit down?"

The two went inside, and when they were seated the old man asked, "Daoist Hua, do you truly not recognize me?"

"Truly, I do not," replied Hua Qingfeng. "May I learn your honorable name?"

"My name is Jiang," the old Daoist said. "I have an immortal tie with you."

"From what famed mountain cave did your receive your Daoist teaching?" asked the Daoist Hua.

"I was at Pan Gu's first mountain as it issued out of chaos," the old Daoist replied.

"How many years have you been a Daoist, friend Jiang?" queried Hua Qingfeng.

"When the name of Wen Wang, the ancient literary emperor, rolled like thunder and the methods of foretelling the future first came into existence, I was there and saw everything with my own eyes. You need not ask how many years," replied old Jiang.

Hua Qingfeng began to realize that this must be an unearthly being, a phantom spirit of some kind. The two shared their thoughts and found that they were the same. Each was forever curious about unseen forces. Each was free from the feelings of loyalty, duty, pity, and other qualities that bind people to obey the laws and the rules of society.

The old Daoist Jiang was comfortable and free with Hua Qingfeng. When Hua invited him to eat, he would eat. When he invited him to drink, he would drink. As the days passed, they became more and more intimate. One day Hua Qingfeng said, "Jiang, my Daoist friend, now that we are close, I would like to see your primary shape. Is that possible?"

"What?" asked Jiang.

"I would like to see the first body that you took possession of and that you use to contain your power, and which permits you to take other forms and show yourself to men."

"You can see it if you like," said Jiang. "Just as the stars begin to fade from the sky and before the sun appears, I can let you see me. We Daoist creatures fear the light of the sun, moon, and stars, for then lightning may strike us. Open the north gate of the shrine when the sky is not fully light and look north. You will see me on the hills. I will be waiting for you."

"So be it," said Hua Qingfeng. He told the novices to prepare food and wine. The boys spread the table and the two Daoists feasted and talked intimately. As the evening wore on, Jiang at last said, "Good night. You will see me in the morning."

Hua Qingfeng walked out of the shrine with the old man, and with lifted, folded hands they parted. After the old man had gone, Hua returned. "I know that he is a spirit," he thought to himself, "but what kind? Tomorrow I will know."

"Wake me at the third watch," he told the novices. Then he lay down fully dressed and slept. The novices waited until the third watch and then called him. He went outside and looked up. The sky was still full of stars. He went inside for a while, where he had a cup of hot tea. When the first faint light appeared in the east, he opened the back gate of the shrine, walked straight to the north, and looked down from the terrace and then up at the other medium peaks. What he saw made him turn cold with fright.

CHAPTER 66

Golden Eye visits the gentry;
Cloud Dragon Hua reads a familiar verse

HUA Qingfeng, the Sorcerer of the Ninth Palace, had walked out of the back gate of the Veiled Mountain Shrine toward the pagoda. His head was erect and his eyes looked eagerly in all directions. What he saw was a huge python. Its head was resting on the topmost peak of a mountain to the east. Its tail was coiled around the peak of a mountain to the west. It was many hundreds of yards long and as large in girth as one of the largest water jars.

Hua gasped and drew in the cold air. Then the huge python was gone like a puff of smoke left hanging in the air. Then he saw the same snake close by, now only a foot long. He watched with staring eyes and open mouth as it in turn disappeared. Behind him, he heard someone say, "Oh, Limitless One! Hua, my Daoist friend, did you see it?"

Hua Qingfeng turned his head and looked. It was indeed the Daoist Jiang. "I saw," said Hua. "Will you come into the shrine and sit with me? Truly your mastery has no limits."

"Friend Hua," said Jiang, "our Daoist pursuits go well together. If you wish to use my talents, I will be with you, even unto death."

"Very good indeed!" exclaimed Hua. The two talked on, from morning to night.

One day Jiang Tianrui, nicknamed Golden Eye, came to see his former teacher Hua at the Veiled Mountain Abbey. "What brings you here?" asked Hua.

"I am now staying in the Iron Buddha Temple, where I have been cultivating my knowledge of Dao," replied Jiang. "It is an old temple very much in need of repair, but it is difficult to get enough money. I came to beg my teacher for any suggestions as to how I can do so."

Hua Qingfeng did not say anything.

"You need not be concerned about it," said the old Daoist Jiang. "How much silver would you need?"

"At least ten thousand ounces," answered Golden Eye.

"Go back," directed old Jiang. "Tomorrow I will be in Kaihua. Just put up a proclamation saying that the Iron Buddha will cure illnesses. In less than ten days I can give you eighteen thousand ounces of silver."

"Good," said Sorcerer Hua to Golden Eye Jiang. "Thank your teacher's elder brother." Jiang knelt and knocked his forehead on the floor. He then returned and posted the proclamation.

The old Daoist in his python form spit out poison into the streams and wells. Whoever drank the water would have symptoms of tumors. The old Daoist then would return to the temple and become the voice of the Iron Buddha, telling the wealthy to pay in silver and the poor to pay in cash. In the eight hundred villages of Kaihua, countless people were having the same illness, and the demonic spirit was bringing in vast amounts of money.

Who would have thought that today Ji Gong would appear? When he slapped the face of the image, the demon was frightened and fled in dismay. However, it then thought to itself, "If this poor, ragged monk drives me away, how will I maintain my connection with my Daoist friend and Sorcerer Hua? It would be better if I went back and ate this monk."

Having made this decision, it returned as a great wind and dropped down and coiled around the monk in the form of a python thirty or forty feet long, with its head lifted to bite the monk. But when the monk grasped its neck from the back, it became motionless. The python's eyes almost started from its head as it stared at the monk. The monk looked back at the snake. Meanwhile, the frightened people buying and selling in the temple were fleeing from fear.

Just as these things were happening, a voice was heard outside declaiming, "Oh, Limitless One!" The Golden Eye of Buddha had returned.

Now when Golden Eye Jiang had hurried off to the little hamlet in the west, taking Cloud Dragon Hua with him, he was met by an assembly of gentlemen who greeted the two, asking, "What are the honorable Daoists' names?"

Jiang told them, and then inquired, "Why did you ask us to come?"

The spokesman for the village gentry explained. "Just now here in our village, household after household was becoming ill with tumors. Perhaps this is Buddha's only way of showing that the temple needs to be repaired. If the honorable Daoist will persuade Buddha to be compassionate, we villagers who have now recovered would like to assist by paying for the repair of the temple. But we do not know whether we may trouble you in this our plan to help Buddha."

"Easily managed," said Golden Eye Jiang. "If you wish to come together in repairing the temple, I can certainly beg Buddha to cause all these ill-nesses to cease." Just as he was saying this, a servant came in to say that two monks from the Iron Buddha Temple had come to talk with the Dao-ist about an urgent matter.

As soon as Golden Eye Jiang heard this, he quickly took his leave from the gentlemen and went outside. There he saw the two outlaws dressed in monks' robes who had been collecting the silver and strings of cash, each of them still pale with fright. "What is it?" Jiang asked.

"Terrible things are happening," said one of them. "The monk, Ji Dian, is at the temple making trouble. You must come back and see."

Cloud Dragon Hua wanted to flee as soon as he heard this news, but Golden Eye said to him, "Second Brother, if you can control your shock, just wait until I bring an end to his life. I will take this Ji Dian and avenge you with his death."

Cloud Dragon Hua knew that Jiang had great ability, and so Cloud Dragon Hua returned to the Iron Buddha Temple with him. As soon as Jiang saw that Ji Gong was wrapped in the coils of the python, Jiang reached back and seized his precious sword saying, "Now, my good monk, you came here to seize me with no law or reason on your side."

The evil serpent glared at the monk, who was holding it by its neck. Then, as the sword came closer, the monk said, "Om Ma Ni Pad Me Hum," and the Daoist's sword fell upon the python's neck instead of Ji Gong's. There was an awful sound, and the blood came rushing out as the python's head fell to the floor. Then the demonic presence disappeared in a puff of black smoke. One stroke of the sword had destroyed hundreds of years of Daoist arts.

Ji Gong watched the python disappear and then said, "Thank you, my Daoist friend. I'm afraid you have gone to a great deal of trouble. I hope you will forgive me."

"You have destroyed my great project, and with no justice or reason," said Golden Eye. "How could I ever forgive you?"

"If there is anything more to say," said Ji Gong, "how about our going back behind the temple? Is that what you want?"

"Good!" said Golden Eye Jiang. "Come with me, my three dear friends." Cloud Dragon Hua and the two other outlaws in monks' clothing joined Golden Eye as they walked out through the back gate of the temple.

When they reached a place where they were alone, the group stopped and the monk said to Golden Eye, "Well, Jiang Tianrui, what have you to say?"

"Ji Dian," said Golden Eye Jiang, "you need to learn that your duty is to kneel and call me your ancestor three times and knock your head on the ground to me. Then by the holy Daoist deities, if I find I have an ounce of pity, I may pardon you. Otherwise, I will put an end to your life."

"Jiang Tianrui!" exclaimed the monk, "You worthless piece of trash! You are a person who leaves the world and does not know enough to fear heaven and be content with his lot. You have simply become a river pirate hiding out in a Daoist robe! You dare to use these devilish spells to delude the public and to call forth these monstrous spirits to cause harm to the populace. You did these things for mere silver, angering heaven above and mankind below. And then when you see me, the monk, you dare to be impolite. Even if you should kneel down and knock your head to me and call me your ancestor three times, as a monk I still could not forgive you!"

As Golden Eye Jiang listened, he was boiling with fury. He tried to split open the monk's head with a chop of his sword, but the monk avoided it and twisted around behind Jiang. Then Jiang aimed a thrust of his sword at the monk's heart, and again the monk avoided the thrust by twisting and turning. Slashing and stabbing, Jiang Tianrui was growing impatient. Ji Gong circled around him, pushing, pulling, pinching, and slapping! With a twist of his body the Daoist broke out of the circle and cried, "There are no two ways about it. You came here seeking your own death! You have angered the hermit and you will feel the hermit's powers!"

"Today," said the monk, "I must let you understand something."

The monk pointed and recited, "Om Ma Ni Pad Me Hum." Golden Eye Jiang began to slap his own face. "That's right. Slap a few more times," said the monk. Jiang slapped until his lips began to bleed.

"You deserved that beating," the monk said, "but stop now and straighten out your beard and mustache." Jiang stopped as he was told and began to rearrange his whiskers. "You brought this upon yourself," said Ji Gong. "Are you going to change your behavior now, or not? If you do not, you will certainly terminate your existence."

Golden Eye Jiang's pain had made him understand that the monk could indeed be dangerous. Now he said, "Teacher, have compassion for me. From now on I will behave differently. I will certainly never dare to do those things again."

"I'm afraid you don't sound sincere," said the monk. "You must swear and then I will release you."

"If I ever do such things again," said Golden Eye, "may lightning strike me dead."

"Go then, Jiang," said the monk, "but Cloud Dragon Hua, where do you think you are going?" Cloud Dragon Hua stood still in his fright, looking down. The two other outlaws, still wearing their monks' costumes, had already run away to the south. Suddenly, Cloud Dragon Hua ran off to the west, with the monk chasing after him.

Cloud Dragon Hua ran on like a dog running home to its kennel or a frightened fish in the water. Truly he ran for his life. He never dared to look back. It was very hard to put enough distance between them so that he could no longer hear the sound of the monk's straw sandals. At last he stopped. His body was covered with sweat. Before him he saw a small temple. It looked weather-beaten and deserted with tiles missing, gates and doors hanging crookedly, and weeds choking the courtyard. He thought he might hide here.

A woman's voice came screaming from inside. "Save me! A robber monk! You dare to seize a respectable woman! Let me go at once!"

"There is a wicked monk in this temple," thought Cloud Dragon Hua. "I will go and have a look." Stealthily he walked into the courtyard. There was one building with three sections on the north, a second building on the south, and a third on the west. It was from the north building that the woman's voice came.

Cloud Dragon Hua looked in through the window and saw a man dressed in monks' clothes. The man's face was turned inward. His shoulder-length hair was held in place by a gold circlet around his head. He was struggling with a rather nice-looking woman, who continued to cry for help. "If I came up behind him, I could easily kill him," Hua thought, "and I will keep this woman for myself."

He entered, and with one slash of his sword the monk's head fell to the floor. Cloud Dragon gasped as he looked at the man's face.

CHAPTER 67

Three heroes discover a dragon;
a familiar verse once more appears

AS Cloud Dragon Hua looked at the face of the dead monk he had just killed, he was shocked to see that it was, in fact, the face of a sworn brother, one of the five ghosts of Four Rivers Road in Linan. He felt sad for a while, but then he thought, "Since he is dead, there is nothing to be done about it. Once you're dead, you can't come back to life."

Now this robber had never done anything good in his life. In this story that tells about how Ji Gong passed through his time on earth, there are many loyal public servants, children who respect their parents, and faithful friends who in the end are justly rewarded. There are also grasping officials, lewd outlaws, and all sorts of wicked people who meet the fates that they deserve. People who write books hope that their readers, like the characters in the stories, will turn from evil to do good, but not everyone can be saved.

Cloud Dragon Hua had killed the man with one stroke of the sword, and the woman imagined that he was a good person. "How can I thank you for saving me?" she asked. "My name is Li and my mother's name is Liu. I had been to visit my mother, and my brother was bringing me back to my husband's home on a donkey. Just as we passed the temple gate this robber monk surprised us. He tied up my brother and put him in the west room, and then, with the worst intentions, forced me to come to this room. I do thank you for killing this robber. Now I will go home and say a prayer for you."

Cloud Dragon Hua laughed at that and said, "Let me tell you, little woman, this monk that I killed is no stranger to me. He was called Devil in the Clouds and he was my sworn brother. I did not recognize him and killed him by mistake. Now that he is dead, you need not leave. You will stay here, and after I kill your brother, we will be as man and wife. We can live here in this temple."

When the woman heard this, she realized that he was not a good person and began to scream again, "Help! Help!"

"If you call out, I will kill you," said Cloud Dragon Hua.

"Kill me, then," said the young woman, "and have it over with."

Cloud Dragon Hua looked at her, and seeing that she was atttractive he felt moved by desire. Although she had said, "Kill me, then," he hesitated.

Outside the window he heard someone laugh. "Our good friend Cloud Dragon Hua! So this is what you are doing. It's too bad that Elder Brother Yang put out a notice to the Greenwood warning us against darts and dirty pictures. You vulgar creature, a beast with a man's face! First of all, we must bring an end to your existence!"

When Cloud Dragon Hua heard this, he drew his sword, dashed out, and looked into the courtyard. Outside stood three men watching him. They were, in fact, stout fellows ready to step in on the side of the oppressed. Cloud Dragon Hua's shame quickly turned to anger. "You rascals dare to interfere with me. Today I will kill you all." The three men drew their swords and leaped forward, surrounding Cloud Dragon. "The three of them will be too much for me," he thought. "I must use my poison." With a twist of his body he broke away and ran out of the temple gate with the three men in pursuit.

Then Cloud Dragon Hua surprised them by taking out two darts. As the first man came leaping out through the temple gate, before his foot touched the ground, he was struck in the upper arm. As the second man followed, the robber hit him in the left shoulder. As the two turned and fell, the third man's face grew red with anger and he called out, "You have killed two of us, but you will die by my hand or with me!" Then he slashed with his sword at Cloud Dragon, who knocked it aside with his own sword. They continued thrusting, stabbing, and slashing at each other. Hua was hard pressed, but neither had wounded the other.

Suddenly Cloud Dragon Hua turned and ran, but the third man was unwilling to let him go. "Where are you going, Cloud Dragon Hua? Do you think you can escape me?"

When he had gone a little way, Hua turned and shook his hand as if he was about to throw something, and shouted, "Dart coming!" The man dodged, but there was no dart. Again Hua shouted, "Dart coming!" and this time the man was unprepared. The dart struck in a place that his protective clothing did not cover. He let out a cry, spun round, and fell.

Cloud Dragon Hua laughed loudly. "You three!" he exclaimed. "You rascals dared to raise your hand against me! What power did you have? You call yourselves heroes! Now you cannot even find the road to heaven or hell! You dared to anger the man with the poison and he ended your lives!"

As he finished speaking and was about to put away his sword and leave, he heard the sound of a person approaching, and a voice said, "You thing! So this is where you are, Cloud Dragon Hua. This monk has been looking for you for some time and now I have found you. This time you will not escape me!"

Before him, Cloud Dragon Hua saw Ji Gong coming toward him. The frightened outlaw was almost too shocked to move. He shook his head and then ran like lightning, like a shooting star. The monk followed left, right, left, right, his straw sandals making the familiar sound. Cloud Dragon Hua ran on without stopping until nightfall. It was very difficult to get beyond the sound of the straw sandals. At last he stopped, and when he looked around, he did not see the monk. He was exhausted and covered with sweat. There were woods ahead. He went in and sank into a sitting position, leaning against a tree. He let out a sigh and thought, "If I hadn't been so foolish, I would not have had all this trouble." He could not sit comfortably, nor sleep, nor stand.

Suddenly he saw in front of him a large gateway with a lantern above it. It was evidently the entrance to a home of wealth. He thought to himself, "Perhaps I can stay there. It will be comfortable and I can get some refreshment. Yes, I will stay there tonight and ask for a meal." As he approached the gateway and was about to knock, an old man came out with a scholar's kerchief on his head. He was dressed in a blue robe with a silken girdle. His face was kindly and he seemed to be about sixty years old. He had the appearance of one who had once been an official.

Cloud Dragon Hua approached the old man and raised his clasped hands politely in greeting. "Reverend Sir," Cloud Dragon Hua said, "I am a traveler who has lost his way to the next inn. I beg you to grant me lodging for the night, and a meal. Tomorrow, early in the morning, I will leave."

The old man lifted his head and looked at him. "What is my guest's honorable name and how many are traveling with him?"

"My name is Hua," answered Cloud Dragon, "and there is only myself."

"Please come in and sit down," said the old man. Cloud Dragon followed him inside. Cloud Dragon noticed that the parlor was furnished with great refinement. "Please be seated," the host said.

"I have not yet heard your honorable name," said Cloud Dragon Hua.

"My name is Hu," said the old man. As he spoke, another male member of the household entered the room.

"Yuanwai, sir," the man who had just entered said to the old man, "the junior *yuanwai* and many guests are waiting for you to join them at the feast."

"I'm afraid I cannot keep you company just now," the *yuanwai* told his guest. "In a little while we will have time to chat." Meanwhile, he ordered the servants to give the guest wine and food, saying, "Be careful to see to his wants."

Cloud Dragon Hua noticed that all the dishes they served were the ones he liked best to eat. Filled with happiness, he ate and drank to his heart's content, thinking to himself, "The owner of this mansion must have liked my appearance to treat me like this." His heart overflowed with gratitude. Just as he was thinking this, he heard the sound of footsteps outside.

"Is Yuanwai in the room?" Hearing the gentle tone of the speaker's voice, Cloud Dragon realized that it was the voice of a young woman, and refrained from answering. Then the bamboo curtain at the door was lifted. A beautiful girl stepped into the room. She was dressed in soft silken garments that seemed to float in the air about her. Looking at her, Cloud Dragon thought, "I have never seen such a beauty in my life before."

She drew in her breath in a gasp and looked at him as if to ask, "Who let this rough young man in here?" Then, without speaking, she turned and left the room.

Cloud Dragon Hua was, after all, a robber who felt no shame at the thought of destroying the innocence of such a young lady. He stood up, aroused by desire, and followed her out into an inner courtyard and then into the building on the north side.

She looked at him, her eyes filled with tears. "Cloud Dragon Hua," she said, "you really are very bold! Think about what you are doing! Have you any power to reason at all? Come and look there!" She pointed to the wall.

Cloud Dragon Hua looked and saw the verse he had written about himself long before on the wall of a room in the residence of Prime Minister Qin. "Strange!" he thought. "How did she know I was Cloud Dragon Hua?"

He was about to ask her when the young woman pointed and said, "Look! There is Ji Gong!" Cloud Dragon Hua turned his head and saw the monk approaching. The outlaw was nearly out of his mind with fright.

CHAPTER 68

Cloud Dragon Hua meets a ghost; the iron-shop manager talks of escorts

AS Cloud Dragon Hua looked at the monk, he began to shake with a chilling fear. Then he realized as he looked around that he was still sitting in the grove, leaning against the tree and shivering in the night air. Like the famous man who dreamed that he had been made governor of the great city of Nanko, but woke to find that the city existed only in his dream, Cloud Hua had had a dream almost more real than actual life.

What had happened was that Ji Gong had projected his presence on to Cloud Dragon Hua. It was this presence that had caused the dream, to test whether Cloud Dragon would show any signs of reforming. Ji Gong might seem terrible because of his powers, but he was really a kindly being who wished to see whether Cloud Dragon could be saved from the evil side of his own nature. Although Cloud Dragon seemed to be an altogether heartless and cruel person, the fact that he feared Ji Gong so greatly showed that a battle between good and evil was still going on somewhere in Cloud Dragon Hua's heart. This was why Ji Gong had not simply captured him long before. That would have been an easy matter. Keeping him from destroying himself and others, while trying to save his better nature, was much more difficult.

As yet, however, even in his dreams, the evil in Cloud Dragon's heart seemed to remain unchanged. As he awoke from his dream, frightened and covered with sweat, he looked up and saw that the sky was filled with stars. It was now about the second watch. He stood up and walked onward. In front of him he saw a form that proved to be human. The outlaw drew his sword, and as they came nearer together, the other spoke, "Brother Hua!" Looking more closely, Cloud Dragon saw that it was no stranger, but the Black Wind Ghost, Jiang Ying.

"Dear Brother Jiang, where are you going?" asked Cloud Dragon.

Jiang Ying, the Black Wind Ghost, came closer and raised his clasped hands in greeting. "It has been a long time, Second Brother," he said.

Now, since the time when Jiang Ying had left Yang Ming's home, where he had been a guest for some time, he had wandered about with no fixed place to stay. Then he had gone to the ancient Veiled Mountain Abbey to see the sorcerer Hua Qingfeng, the uncle of Hua Yun Long. Sorcerer Hua knew that Jiang Ying and his nephew were sworn brothers and therefore let him stay at the shrine and treated him as a friend.

On the day that Golden Eye, also called Jiang Tianrui, had fled back to the Veiled Mountain Shrine from the Iron Buddha Temple, the sorcerer Hua had stared at Golden Eye in surprise. "You look terrible," he said, "and what has happened to your beard?" he asked. In reply Golden Eye told the whole story, from start to finish, of how Ji Gong had come to exorcise the Iron Buddha Temple, and finally how Golden Eye's beard had become tangled and matted with blood when he was slapping his own face.

Sorcerer Hua's anger fairly blazed up as he listened. "That mad Ji Gong!" he exclaimed. "I will keep this in my mind until we are revenged. He has no consideration! I will have him!"

Golden Eye knelt and offered up his mystic treasure sword to the sorcerer, who stared at it for some time. After thinking it over, he decided to enlist the aid of all five of the outlaws nicknamed "the Ghosts of Four Rivers," reasoning that the mystic number of five had greater powers than any of those possessed by the ragged monk. "Together," the sorcerer said, "these five could certainly put an end to Ji Gong." And so he sent Jiang Ying, the Black Wind Ghost, down from the mountain to assemble Cloud Dragon and the other three sworn brothers. Tonight Jiang Ying had just met Cloud Dragon Hua, who was one of the five.

"Where have you been these days, dear brother Jiang?" queried Cloud Dragon.

"For a while I stayed near Dragon Ridge and Phoenix Ridge," Jiang replied, "but I was surprised that Yang Ming was not as friendly as before. After his fifteen-year-old daughter mysteriously disappeared, his manner was different and he said several things that were not very polite. You know my temperament, brother, and so I left his home and went up to the Veiled Mountain Shrine. Now your uncle has asked me to do an errand for him. Where are you going now, Second Brother?"

"Just now I have no particular place to go. The monk from the Monastery of the Soul's Retreat has been pursuing me," Cloud Dragon answered.

"Second Brother," said Jiang, "come up with me to the Veiled Mountain Shrine. Your uncle is called the Sorcerer of the Ninth Palace. He will welcome you and perhaps can intercede with Ji Gong, monk to monk, mystery to mystery, Dao to Dao. The three faiths of Confucianism, Buddhism, and Daoism are really all one family. Your uncle and Ji Gong are both people who have left the world. They are not officials and not bound by the same rules as officials. Even though you have broken the emperor's national laws, what is that to them? They are hermits. Come up with me and see your uncle and you will have a safe place to relax."

"Yes, I suppose I could go with you," said Cloud Dragon Hua, "but first I have to buy some darts. I have used up the last of mine. I depend upon poison darts for self-defense."

"If you want to buy darts," said Jiang, "there is a place at Rising Ground Village just ahead." The two walked on slowly. When they arrived at the village and the sun was a little higher, Jiang Ying said, "I will wait here for you at the entrance to the village."

"Good," said Cloud Dragon Hua. He entered the village, and when he came to the crossroad, turned east. He saw on the south side of the road a large iron shop with the name "No Mother-in-Law Iron Shop" above the door. The shop was freestanding, with no neighbors sharing a wall, and had a wide front. To the west, in an open lot, a hawker had set up shop beside the road. To the east, a fortune-teller had built a little hearth.

Cloud Dragon Hua looked up at the shop gate and saw a tall old man standing there. He was wearing a short blue outer garment and a square blue kerchief tied over the hair knot on his head. His face was a long oval, like a large date with two large eyes and snow-white hair and beard. "This must be the manager," thought Hua and so he stepped up and asked, "Manager, do you sell darts?"

The old man looked Cloud Dragon up and down, eyeing his white crane's-feather jacket of the kind fashionable with brave fellows. "We do," he replied. "What kind of darts are you looking for, sir?"

"I want the kind that will ride on the wind," answered Cloud Dragon Hua. "Do you have them?"

"We have some, but not the kind that will ride on the wind. Will you come inside and sit down? You may look at them and see whether they satisfy you or not. I can ask a craftsman to forge some for you."

Cloud Dragon nodded his head, went inside the office, and sat down. "How many would you like to buy?" the old man asked.

"Oh, eight of one and six of the other. No, twelve altogether," replied Cloud Dragon Hua. "I'll take twelve altogether, and they should weigh about three ounces each."

"Yes," said the old man. "I have some ready-made, but perhaps they are a little heavy. If you could use them, that would come to six ounces of silver. If you want them to ride on the wind, the workman could make them, especially if you would add a couple of ounces of silver for his trouble—to buy him a drink, you know."

"A few ounces of silver are nothing," Cloud Dragon Hua thought to himself, and he said, "The price is up to you. I can wait."

"Very well," said the old man, but he brought a dart to show Hua.

Hua looked at it and remarked, "It is heavy."

"Wait a bit, sir, and they will have some ready," said the old man. He called one of the servants to make a pot of tea and said to him, "We don't have any water here in the shop. Go and draw some." Meanwhile, he whispered some words into the little servant's ear. The servant nodded and went out.

The old man went on talking with Cloud Dragon Hua. "Ordinarily what do you do, sir?"

"Travelers' escort," replied Cloud Dragon Hua.

"Since you are an escort," the old man said, "let me mention a few names of people whom you may know."

"I know a good many—there are not many I don't know," said Cloud Dragon Hua.

"Well, there is Huang Yun, nicknamed 'the Swallow from South Road.' Do you know him?"

"I know the name," said Cloud Dragon Hua.

"And the escort leader Chen Xiao with the beautiful whiskers from the North Road, and his somewhat sickly, pale friend, Yang Meng? Do you know them?"

"Oh, they are like my brothers," said Cloud Dragon.

"Then there is iron-faced Chen Shengyuan, who hasn't an enemy in the world, and Zhou Shen, the escort head in West Road. You must know them."

"I do," said Cloud Dragon.

"Now there is another talented and worthy escort, Yang Ming. You probably know him, too," said the old man.

"He is no stranger to me," said Cloud Dragon.

"Well, that's about it," said the old man. "Here is the servant with the tea." The little servant gave Hua a cup of tea, and a bit later came to say that the darts had been forged. The old man brought them in and gave them to Cloud Dragon to look at.

"The points are still a little heavy," said Cloud Dragon Hua. "I'm afraid that when they are thrown, they will go wide of the mark."

"Why don't you try them out, sir?" asked the old man. "We have a place in the back courtyard. If they are not right, we can ask the workman to adjust the weight."

"Good!" exclaimed Cloud Dragon.

Carrying the darts with one hand, the old man led the way for Cloud Dragon and opened the door to the back courtyard. Cloud Dragon was surprised to see that it was so extensive. On the west and south sides were high walls, each fifty or sixty feet long. At one end of the south wall was a closed gate. There were no adjoining neighbors. The courtyard was floored with earth. It was an ideal place to try out weapons.

Cloud Dragon Hua looked around and heard a noise at the gate. It opened and two men carrying iron staves entered. The man in the lead was tall and dark with a hawklike face, and looked like a powerful opponent with an air of authority. He was named Lo Biao, and was known as "the Hawk-faced Man." The other man was somewhat similar in appearance. He was named Zhou Rui and called Evening Mound, the name given to him by a soothsayer. "Evening" was the character for his zodiac sign, and it was also associated with the word "mistake." Someone said to him jokingly, "If you find the mound, don't make a mistake." Zhou Rui never understood why the soothsayer had included the word "mound" in his name.

Both Lo Biao and Zhou Rui were beardless. Behind them came a crowd of less imposing men. The two headmen called out with one voice, "Where do you think you are going, Cloud Dragon Hua? You dare to commit murder and arson here! Don't think you can escape us!"

Now Cloud Dragon Hua had never committed any offenses in this area. However, there was a new district magistrate in Chengshan, and there had been a case of robbery and arson at a pawnshop, as well as the murder of a carter. The magistrate called his two extremely able headmen to his chambers. He gave them ten days to solve the cases, with a promise of reward if they succeeded and demotion if they failed.

CHAPTER 69

The Tangled Hair Ghost is rescued;
Headman Zhou seeks his father's advice

EACH of the headmen assembled a dozen top deputies to help. They happened to be making inquiries in the neighborhood of Wild Tiger Hill just as some travelers were returning from Linan. One of them came running up to the headmen to report that they had been stopped by a robber who demanded their money, saying that he was master of that road and that all who passed must pay him.

One of the travelers who was stopped by the highwayman was Jeng Xiong, who lived at Phoenix Hill In Linan. He was known as Iron-Faced Jeng Xiong because of the strength of his character, which matched his unusual body strength. As he looked at the outlaw who demanded payment from the travelers, Jeng Xiong thought to himself, "This is a fine-looking fellow, well built and strong, who has been driven to a life of crime by poverty. Perhaps I can help him out so that he can return to the right path."

Therefore, he said: "My friend, I can see that you are an impressive hero, straightforward and courageous. I feel that you must have taken the wrong road because of your difficulties. I would like to lend you twenty ounces of silver to set yourself up in some kind of business. I don't like to see you simply become a robber. If you have some pressing trouble, you can tell me about it and I can help you further."

The outlaw laughed loudly and said, "You can stop wagging your tongue about helping me out with twenty ounces of silver. You will have to give me whatever you have—your valuables, your donkey, everything."

When Jeng Xiong heard this, he became furious. "You think that I'm afraid of you, you ignorant beast! Today I will teach you a lesson!" As he spoke, Iron-Faced Jeng Xiong began to beat the robber's back with his bamboo staff. The outlaw leaped aside and attacked with his sword. Jeng Xiong came back at him, his blows raining down on the robber's shoulders faster than the eye could see. It was like beating a snake in the grass. After a while Jeng Xiong ceased, since he thought the outlaw had been taught a lesson. He intended to let him go rather than sending him to a yamen.

But the robber began to curse, and then said, "You may be great lords, but would you dare to tell me your name?"

The other traveler spoke up and said, "I'll tell you my name. It is Ma, you villain, Ma Ran. What about it? Are you going to send someone after me?"

"Good," said the outlaw. "Ma Ran, you had better watch out." Little did Ma Ran think that, as a result of giving the robber his name, the Ma household would be attacked and members of his family injured. The two travelers had just tied up the outlaw when the two headmen, Lo and Zhou, arrived on the scene.

"Ah! It is the official Ma," said Headman Lo. "You have taken an outlaw. Very good indeed! Just recently, at a pawnshop outside the south gate, there has been a case of arson and theft in which a good deal of clothing was lost, and outside the east gate there has been a murder. The magistrate is extremely anxious about these two cases and has asked us to solve them. You can hand over this outlaw to us."

"Good. We will give him to you," said the official Ma Ran, and he called the man who had given the alarm.

"My name is Hu Deyuan," the man said when asked. "I didn't lose anything, but I might have lost my life if you, sir, had not come along. Thank you all." With that, he went on his way. The two travelers, Jeng Xiong and the official Ma, also continued on their journey.

The two headmen, Lo and Zhou, had the deputies bring the outlaw into the yamen. The magistrate took his seat in the hall and ordered the man brought before him for questioning. The two headmen immediately did so. The outlaw glared defiantly and stood instead of kneeling.

"What is the robber's name?" demanded the magistrate from his high bench.

"My surname is Yun and my personal name is Fang," replied the outlaw, "and I am known as 'the Tangled Hair Ghost'."

"Well, my good Yun Fang," said the magistrate, "how many did you have with you at that affair at the pawnshop outside the south gate? If you speak before it is too late, you can save your skin and flesh some pain."

"I know nothing about it," said the outlaw.

"And how many of you committed that murder in the lane outside the east gate?"

"I know nothing about that, either," replied Yun Fang. "It was not I."

"How many years have you been in the Greenwood?" asked the magistrate, "and how many petty crimes have you committed?"

"I never committed any crimes previously," said Yun Fang. "This is the first time."

The magistrate flew into a rage at his statement, and startled the hall as he pounded the desk in front of him. "You robber with a beast's heart! I am surprised that you dare to lie to the district magistrate! Come, my men. He is unwilling to talk. Take him down and give him eighty blows with the bamboo!"

They gave the outlaw eighty blows, but when they had finished, he still would not talk. The magistrate ordered that he be brought back into the hall. "Yun Fang," the magistrate said, "You now have a chance to tell the truth and I will reduce your punishment. If you do not speak, investigations will continue."

"I truly do not know," said Yun Fang. The magistrate ordered that he be beaten with rods, but again this action brought no result. The magistrate threatened to apply the five punishments ending in death, but the outlaw said nothing, and while a postponement was being declared, he fell asleep. Since there was nothing more to be done, the outlaw was thrown into a jail cell.

Who would have thought that at the third watch a hundred or more river pirates would scale the walls and break into the prison to release Yun Fang! When they came to the east gate of the town, in addition to their other crimes, they killed the night watchman there as they left.

The next day the district yamen was in turmoil. The magistrate called his two headmen in. He promised that they would be rewarded with two hundred ounces of silver if they made an arrest within three days and threatened that they would be beaten with the bamboo if they failed.

The two headmen, Lo and Zhou, were not sworn brothers, nor had they been fellow students of the martial arts. Instead, Lo's teacher in the martial arts had been Zhou's father. Now, as they talked about the difficulties in the case, they decided to seek the advice of the elder Zhou, who was now living in retirement at home. Zhou Rui thought that his father might know more about the outlaw Yun Fang.

The father lived in Rising Ground Village not far from the No Mother-in-Law Iron Shop, where Cloud Dragon Hua would shortly go to buy darts. When the two headmen arrived at the father's house, he asked, "Son, what are you doing with all this crowd of deputies?"

Zhou Rui explained about the rescued outlaw and the magistrate's promises of a reward to the two headmen if they succeeded and threats of punishment if they failed.

The old man said, "These newly arrived magistrates are always difficult to work for. You say in both the cases of the arson and robbery of the pawnshop as well as the murder of the carter, that you have no suspects, and now this highwayman Yun Fang has been forcibly rescued by his friends. As for this Yun Fang, I can tell you that he is one of the river pirates who in recent times have lived at Four Rivers Road in the capital at Linan. There were a string of these ghosts, five in all, who made up what is sometimes called the Long Dragon. There were the Tangled Hair Ghost, the Rising Wind Ghost, the Cockcrow Ghost, the Black Wind Ghost, and the River Rat Ghost—Cloud Dragon Hua. Why don't you people wait here in my house while I go out and ask a few questions?"

The old man went out and walked up the street. He had just arrived in front of the iron shop as Cloud Dragon Hua was inquiring about darts. The little boy who had been sent to make tea passed on the message that the proprietor of the iron shop had whispered in his ear: "The outlaw Cloud Dragon Hua is here."

The old man immediately became excited. "Cloud Dragon Hua is asking for darts that can ride on the wind. He surely intends to poison the darts," the old man thought. "In the beginning there was only Ma Yuanzhang who knew the secret of mixing the poison, and he passed it on to Yang Ming. Yang Ming then passed the secret to Cloud Dragon Hua, not knowing what kind of a person Cloud Dragon Hua would become. Very likely Cloud Dragon Hua has some connection with the two cases about which my son told me, and certainly with the rescued outlaw Yun Fang. If my son and the other headman can capture Cloud Dragon Hua, everything may be solved."

As soon as the two headmen got the news, they surrounded the iron shop and went around to the back gate in the wall.

CHAPTER 70

Liu Tong chases a badger;
Cloud Dragon Hua escapes again

HUA Yun Long looked at the two headmen, both armed with a stout iron-tipped staff; and the deputies, each armed with some sort of weapon. The old proprietor was still holding the darts, and there was no chance for Cloud Dragon Hua to poison them. The outlaw ran to the wall, and as he reached the top, he saw that he was surrounded by a ring of armed men. There was only one thing he could do—he leaped down and ran toward them swinging his sword. They gave way and he was outside the circle.

Behind the No Mother-in-Law Iron Shop, the land rose into the long slopes of a mountain about two or three thousand feet high. A fraction of the way up, but still high above and overlooking the village that was itself on rising ground, as well as overlooking the plain far beyond, a large mound of earth protruded. It might, indeed, have been the covering for an ancient tomb. It was not very high, only about nine feet, but it was great in circumference. It presented only a slight obstacle to any climber. Beyond this mountain were other, higher, mountains, with their peaks lost in the clouds. He ran straight up the mountainside, with most of the pack falling behind.

Only Headman Zhou was able to keep up the pace. He was gaining steadily upon the outlaw as they raced up the slopes. Just ahead, Cloud Dragon saw the great mountain. He ran as he had never run before. He could hear people shouting to the headman, "Don't let him escape!" The mound was just ahead, and he wondered if he could force his body up and over this great obstacle, which was too wide to go around. There was only one way—up and over it. He could hardly move his aching legs.

"I must make these legs of mine carry me onward," he thought. "If I fall back, I will lose my life." Just as he came to the top of the mound, a large rock came flying past him, missing him by inches. He heard a cry as it struck the pursuing headman just yards behind him. A few feet more and he was over the top.

Before him he saw a group of five men standing—the impressive figure of gentlemanly Yang Ming; the short and stocky Daoist Kong Gui;
and the two young men Lei Ming and Chen Liang, the former taller and
roughly built, with his wild red-dyed hair, cheeks, and chin colored dark
blue, suggesting a close-cropped beard; and the latter slighter and almost
elegant. With them was the powerful, swift-footed but simple-minded
Liu Tong.

Less than a month earlier, the five men and Cloud Dragon Hua had
all been together at the abbey, where Lei Ming and Chen Liang had persuaded Ji Gong to allow Cloud Dragon Hua to escape despite his misdeeds. Then, as Ji Gong was leaving, he had told the five men that for
an entire month they must stay within the abbey and not go outside its
gates. If not, they would be in mortal danger. The five agreed. However,
as the days passed, while most of them found they could endure the
unaccustomed confinement, for Liu Tong it was almost impossible.
Unable to sit around like most people, he could relieve his boredom only
by spending each day practicing martial arts with his iron-tipped staff
in the courtyard.

One day Liu Tong happened to break a flowerpot with his staff. One
of the Daoist novices said, "If you want to practice, Liu Tong, why don't
you do it in the gateway?"

"Right," said Liu Tong, "I will practice in the gateway."

"I'll go with you," said Lei Ming, "and we'll practice together."

"Don't go out there," warned Yang Ming. "Remember what Ji Gong
told us. For one month we should not go through the gate. Otherwise we
will be in mortal danger. We cannot disbelieve him."

"But there is no one there in the gateway," countered Kong Gui, "and
no one here on the hilltop. What is there to worry about?"

So Lei Ming and Liu Tong went out into the abbey gateway and began
practicing, Lei Ming fencing with his sword and Liu Tong parrying with
his staff. Each had reached a state of happy excitement as the movement
loosened their bodies, which had been starved for exercise. Suddenly they
saw a badger run across the open space near the mountaintop. Liu Tong
ran after it with his staff and Lei Ming joined in the chase. The Daoist
novice who saw them went in and told Yang Ming, "Liu Tong and Lei Ming
have gone off down the other side of the mountain chasing a badger."

Yang Ming, Kong Gui, and Chen Liang were uneasy, and, taking weapons, went down the mountain after them. Who would have imagined
that Liu Tong and Lei Ming would follow the badger for almost twenty

miles! There they saw the badger enter a hole at the base of a great mound of earth.

Liu Tong peered down into the burrow and cried out, "Come out, you stubborn ball of fur, or I'll tear your den apart!" Taking his iron-tipped staff, he began to dig. It was at this point that Yang Ming, Kong Gui, and Chen Liang arrived.

"Liu Tong, you can't get away with this! If anyone sees you, they will claim that you are grave robbing and lock you up! Come back with us at once!" Chen Liang commanded.

Just as he finished speaking, the five men heard the clamor of other men's voices shouting, "Don't let the outlaw escape!"

Lei Ming looked down over the crest of the mound and saw Cloud Dragon Hua approaching below, followed by a headman. "Look, Brother Yang," he said, "Cloud Dragon is coming this way followed by some law enforcement people. I think we should help them catch him. What do you say?"

"If you ask me," replied Chen Liang, "I think we should mind our own business."

"Don't worry," said Yang Ming. "We would openly take our revenge upon him for what he did to us. Why not just throw a rock and knock him backward so that the headman can catch him? We won't even have to be seen."

"Right!" agreed Chen Liang. "Brother Yang, you're good at throwing. Why don't you throw the rock?"

With the rock in his hand, Yang Ming came to where he could just see over the edge of the mound. "Now, lightning, strike the dragon in the clouds!" he said, meaning Cloud Dragon. Yang Ming let the rock fly, but it missed Hua by less than an inch and struck headman Zhou Rui full in the chest. He fell backward and blood gushed from his mouth. Long before, the soothsayer had linked his sign wth the word "mound" and had hinted at an accident. Like most fatal warnings, part of the prophecy had a concealed meaning. The mistake was not made by Zhou Rui, but by another.

As for Cloud Dragon, he had seen Yang Ming throw the rock but was ignorant of Yang Ming's motive. He scrambled over the crest of the ridge and saw his five acquaintances standing there before him. Cloud Dragon immediately fell on his knees before Yang Ming and knocked his forehead on the ground several times in the traditional kowtow. "Thank you for saving me, my eldest brother!" exclaimed Cloud Dragon. "My feelings go beyond appreciation!"

Yang Ming could not bring himself to say, "I wasn't trying to save you—I was trying to help the headman." Instead he said, "My saving you was really nothing. Now just run for your life!"

"Eldest Brother," continued Cloud Dragon, "when you save someone, you must go all the way. I want to go to the Veiled Mountain and beg my uncle, the Sorcerer of the Ninth Palace, to let me stay there. Please go with me."

"If you want to go and stay in the shrine, just go. Why should I have to accompany you?" asked Yang Ming.

"Eldest Brother," begged Cloud Dragon Hua, "there is something that you don't know. My uncle has a terrible temper. Knowing some of the things that I have done, that I have become known for, as soon as he sees me, he will kill me. If you go with me, you can talk to him. I am kowtowing to you, Eldest Brother." And Cloud Dragon continued knocking his forehead on the ground.

Yang Ming was a compassionate man by nature. As Cloud Dragon continued to plead, he said, "Very well. I will go with you."

Lei Ming and Chen Liang were both unwilling to go with Cloud Dragon. Yet they both felt that they could not let Yang Ming go alone, so the entire group started off to the Veiled Mountain Shrine. It was a journey of about fifteen miles.

When the group reached Veiled Mountain and looked up at the shrine perched on its steep side, Liu Tong stopped. "Big Brother Yang," he said, "the rest of you can go up there. I'll wait for you here. I'm not going to see Hua Qingfeng. If I see him, I'll have to bow to that old bull's nose of a Daoist, and I don't want to do it. I'll just wait here. If you don't come back in one day, I'll wait a whole day; if you don't come back in two days, I'll wait two days. I'll keep waiting for my big brother Yang and then we'll return together."

"Very well then," said Yang Ming, "wait here." The four friends then went up the mountain with Cloud Dragon Hua.

At their knock a Daoist novice opened the shrine gate. "Ah, Elder Brother Hua," said the boy, "how are you?"

"Quite well," replied Hua Yun Long. "Greetings, greetings, Brother Teacher. Is the master teacher at home?"

"He's at home," the boy told them. As the group entered, they noticed pine trees planted here and there, and clumps of bamboo. Everything was neat and in the best of taste. There was an air of peace and refinement. Directly north was the great hall, perhaps fifty feet in length, with two smaller buildings on the east and west. The Daoist novice led them through the garden into a second courtyard that they entered by a gate in the corner. This eastern courtyard had one building about thirty feet long at the north end, and a similar one at the south end.

The novice knocked and said, "The master has been meditating, but you may go in now." Lifting a bamboo curtain at the door, they entered and saw a long wooden platform-style bed, or *kang*, carved in a cloud pattern, on which were small tables, a charcoal stove, and other ceremonially designed things. The Daoist master was seated in the lotus position at the center. His eyes were closed as if in sleep. He wore a long black Daoist robe embroidered with the trigrams in gold, and on his head, the Daoist cap that is fitted over a cloth wrapped about the head and tied with cords. He sat straight upright, with his precious sword in its fish-skin scabbard slung across his back. His face was dark red like raw liver. Thick tufts of black hair grew outward from his ears and a long black beard hung from his chin.

Yang Ming and the others stood back by the entrance while Cloud Dragon Hua approached his uncle. Falling on his knees, Cloud Dragon Hua prostrated himself flat on the tile floor. "Uncle above me, your worthless nephew greets you with the kowtow."

His uncle opened his eyes and glared at him. "You undutiful creature! How dare you go out and openly commit stupid deeds of violence that have brought dishonor to our family, which without you would still have a proud family name!" With that he drew his precious sword from its scabbard as if to strike.

Yang Ming, fearing that Cloud Dragon would be killed, rushed forward. "Most Reverend Sir! Have compassion, restrain your temper, pardon him!"

Hua Qingfeng turned his head and looked at Yang Ming. "Who are you?" he demanded to know.

"My name is Yang Ming," the other replied.

"Uncle," said Hua Yun Long, "this man has been like a kind brother to your worthless nephew. He is the Yang Ming widely known for his generous spirit!" At this point Lei Ming, Chen Liang, and Kong Gui also came forward. "These all have been like kind brothers to me," added Cloud Dragon.

"You miserable, misbegotten creature," exclaimed the sorcerer, "these are your kind brothers. Why did you not tell me at once? Everyone! Please sit down. May I ask this Daoist friend's name?"

"Oh, Limitless One," said Kong Gui, using the particular invocation referring to the founder of Daoism, "your disciple is called Kong Gui."

"And what are the names of these other two gentlemen?" asked Sorcerer Hua.

"My name is Chen," said Chen Liang.

"And mine is Lei," said Lei Ming.

"Now, may I ask why you all have come here?" asked the sorcerer.

"Since the master teacher asks," replied Yang Ming, "it is because my younger brother, your nephew, committed some serious errors in the capital, Linan. As a result, the mad monk Ji Gong from the Monastery of the Soul's Retreat follows him everywhere he goes in order to catch him and take him in. Your nephew has no place to hide. We came here with him to ask your revered self to accept him and give him refuge. Perhaps the monk Ji Gong will not think to find him here, but if he does come, the reverend teacher might persuade Ji Gong not to take him. You are both monks and know about the laws of Buddha and the ways of Dao. You both know all the mysteries of the three faiths—Confucian, Buddhist, and Daoist. I beg you, sir, to help."

When the uncle, Hua Qingfeng, heard this, he replied, "You all came here with him, to my shrine, because you were afraid that Ji Gong would take my nephew. Is that right?"

"That is so," said Yang Ming.

"And you sincerely want to help him," continued Sorcerer Hua, "or were you false in your sincerity?"

"Reverend Sir," protested Yang Ming, "what language is this? If we had been insincere about helping him, why would we have come up the mountain with him?"

"Well, since you are sincere about helping him, I want you all to lend me something to keep for a while. Will you do that or not?"

"That depends upon what it is," said Yang Ming. "If it is not something like our heads or lives, almost anything else you could certainly ask us to lend you."

"You all want to help save my nephew. If you will lend me your souls for a while to temper my sword, I will be able to cut off Ji Gong's head."

Lei Ming was the first one to let his anger break loose. "You mixed-up, addlepated old Daoist sorcerer! You are talking nonsense! We were polite to you and it meant nothing. That's enough. Brother Yang, let us leave here."

Yang Ming was so angry that his face had turned red. "You uncles and nephews!" he exclaimed. "You want it all one way and nothing the other way!" He stood up and was about to leave.

Hua Qingfeng laughed loudly. "If you little folks want to leave, you will have to get my permission," he said. "You're going to have enough trouble getting into hell, to say nothing of heaven. Golden Eye, would you come out here and help me keep these people under control?"

The Daoist Jiang, known as Golden Eye, had been waiting in the next room. He immediately came out and recited some hypnotic spells that immobilized the four friends so that they were unable to escape. They were now indeed in danger of losing their lives.

CHAPTER 71

The murderous Black Wind Ghost is murdered;
the killer, Golden Eye, is slain

WHILE Golden Eye kept the four friends motionless with his hypnotic spells, the sorcerer went out to the exercise courtyard. There on an incense table, he set out the five kinds of things necessary for tempering his sword with the blood of five men. Cloud Dragon stood to one side, watching silently.

"Well, very good, Hua," said Yang Ming. "We came here on your behalf and now we are going to die. Perhaps that's the way it should be."

When Cloud Dragon Hua heard these words spoken by Yang Ming, he finally spoke up. "Uncle, do be compassionate! These are my friends. Look me in the face. Don't kill them!"

"So, you're still begging for them, Cloud Dragon," said Sorcerer Hua. "You think them to be your friends. Did you know that there at the mountainside the one named Lei wanted to help the headmen capture you, and that the one named Yang said that he could secretly take a rock and throw it at you? It struck the headman by mistake. You are still asleep and dreaming!"

"Strange! Even the things we said," thought Yang Ming, "how could the Daoist know all that? Really, he must have the gift of foreknowledge!" Lei Ming was still uttering curses.

Sorcerer Hua Qingfeng ordered that the four men be securely bound and taken into the exercise courtyard. When they reached there, they saw the five kinds of grain all arranged upon a square "eight immortals" table, together with an incense burner and a lighted candle in a candlestick. There were also writing materials, orchid root for preparing the inkstone, clear water, square pieces of yellow paper, a writing brush, and other things. The four men were dragged toward the incense table.

"This is the end," said Chen Liang. "I never thought we could come here to die. We should have heeded Ji Gong's warning. He said that for one month we should not leave the abbey and that, if we failed to listen, we would be in danger of losing our lives. He cannot save us now. It's all because Liu Tong did not pay attention. He drew us all out of the abbey."

"Now that it has turned out this way, we need not talk about it," said Yang Ming.

Lei Ming looked at Chen Liang. "If we two die, it really doesn't matter. We have no parents or children but you, Brother Yang, have an old white-haired mother, a wife, and a young child. If you die, who will take care of them?"

These words could not help but make Yang Ming feel badly. He let out a deep sigh. "I need not say that there is a place to be born and one to die. At the third watch, who dares to say that we will live to the fifth? But death is always happy."

"How can it be happy?" asked Chen Liang.

"Have you not read the story of the three kingdoms?" asked Yang Ming. "When those three warriors took their oath in the peach orchard, they said, 'Though we three were not born together, we can die together.' Now, like those famous men, are we not all about to die together on the same date?"

The Daoist sorcerer was not listening to his victims but talking to his protégé, Golden Eye. "Now I will take their lives and with their blood imprison their souls in my sword," said Hua Qingfeng.

"Teacher," said Golden Eye, "you need five souls to temper your sword. You have only four. Without one more, the charm will not work. We should go down the mountain now and find another man."

"Why do we need to go down the mountain?" asked the sorcerer. "We'll just get that man who's out in the kitchen eating and add him."

Now the man who was out in the kitchen eating was the Black Wind Ghost, Jiang Ying. He had been waiting in the woods while Cloud Dragon Hua had gone to buy darts. Jiang Ying had waited a long time without seeing Cloud Dragon Hua return. Just as he was becoming uneasy, he saw Yang Ming, Lei Ming, Chen Liang, Kong Gui, and Liu Tong coming south down the mountain. Jiang Ying was shocked and surprised. Without showing himself, he stole toward them to watch, carefully concealing himself, for he feared for his life should he be seen.

While he watched and listened, he saw the headmen and their deputies chasing Cloud Dragon Hua. Then he heard Lei Ming say, "Let us help them catch Cloud Dragon." And he saw Yang Ming throw the rock. The rascal Jiang, still fearing Yang Ming, hurried back to the Veiled Mountain Shrine. Arriving there first, he told his story to Hua Qingfeng. Otherwise the sorcerer would not have known what really occurred. He, after all, was no immortal who could foretell the future. This was how Jiang Ying happened to be in the kitchen eating.

When Golden Eye went out to the kitchen, he said, "Jiang Ying, the master is about to temper his sword with the blood of five men, and he needs one more."

"I can go down the mountain and find one," said Jiang Ying.

"You need not go looking," said Golden Eye, while fixing him with his hypnotic glare. "The master has said you will be added. You will just have a few less years to live."

Jiang Ying's face grew white with fear. "Oh, don't add me!" he exclaimed.

"You have no choice," said Golden Eye, tying his victim's hands while he held him under his spell. He led him helpless into the courtyard.

Jiang Ying was begging, "Teacher, save my life!"

When Yang Ming saw him, he understood everything that had happened. "If Sorcerer Hua had not needed another man, I would never have known," he thought and began to curse. "Jiang Ying, you beast! I helped you once and this is how you repaid me, then and now! You miserable creature! I never expected to meet you again like this."

Jiang Ying continued begging Hua Qingfeng to spare his life. Sorcerer Hua, who was a thoroughly evil man, did not answer him. "Golden Eye," he said, "watch to see where the charm falls. Whichever person's head it falls upon will be the one from whom we will take the first soul."

The sorcerer carefully wrote out a charm on a square of yellow paper. Then he pierced it with the tip of his sword and held it in the flame of the lighted candle while he recited a spell. When the paper began to burn, he flourished the sword in the air over the heads of his five prisoners until the burning paper charm flew off from his sword point. It fell directly on the head of Jiang Ying, the Black Wind Ghost.

"That's it," said Yang Ming. "At least I will see Jiang Ying die before my eyes. I will then be glad to close my own eyes in death, even though I must go down beneath the Yellow Springs."

The sorcerer could be heard giving orders. "Now, Golden Eye," he said, "aim carefully and thrust the sword into Jiang Ying's chest." They heard a cry as the blood poured forth and life left the man's body. Then the sorcerer chanted in a loud voice, as if addressing the soul of Jiang Ying: "Now I command most strictly that this soul, as it leaves this man's body, shall enter into the sword and remain in the sword, strengthening and guiding my arm until the ragged monk is dead and his soul cut off from existence forever."

Next, the sorcerer wrote a charm on a second piece of paper, pierced it with the point of his sword, lighted it in the flame of the candle, and tossed the burning paper into the air as he recited a spell. This paper fell onto Yang Ming. "Well, my three dear brothers," said Yang Ming, "I am the next to leave. We will meet again inside the walls of the city of the dead." The others looked at him as if they had each been fatally wounded by an arrow.

Sorcerer Hua was giving orders to Golden Eye. Yang Ming closed his eyes and clenched his teeth as Golden Eye grasped his victim's jacket with his left hand and drew back his other hand, holding the sword ready to strike at Yang Ming's chest. Then there was a shout and a cry. Bright red blood shot into the air like a flash of crimson light and the dead body of Golden Eye fell to the ground. Yang Ming, who had been so close to death, was still alive and unharmed.

Down below the shrine where the footpath forked, Liu Tong had waited for a long time with no sign of Yang Ming. Simple people have simple hearts, and so Liu Tong had been thinking, "If I wait here for Big Brother Yang, what will I do if I get hungry? There's no place to eat!"

Just as Liu Tong was thinking about eating, a man selling steamed bread came walking along the pathway. When he saw Liu Tong, who carried a great iron-tipped staff, and who looked to the bread-seller almost as solid as the bottom half of a dark pagoda, the man didn't know what to think. He was so frightened that his color changed.

"What would his lordship like?" the man asked.

"His lordship would like bread," replied Liu Tong in his naturally rough voice.

"Five?" the man queried, "Ten?" He opened his hampers and spread on the ground trays each containing five small loaves. Finally the man had spread out all his wares, totaling 105 small, round steamed loaves, which everyone called "bread heads" because of their shape and size. Then without another word he took to his heels and ran, leaving everything behind.

"Come back!" cried Liu Tong.

"Do you want my clothes, too?" asked the man from a distance.

"His lordship will give you silver," said Liu Tong taking out five ounces of silver and giving it to the bread-seller, who only then realized Liu Tong was a good man.

"But these bread heads do not come to anything like this amount of silver," said the man.

"Take it," said Liu Tong, and so the man went off. Liu Tong looked at all the bread the man had left behind and let out a whistle. Saying, "Would you like me to eat you first?" he picked up the loaf he had addressed and ate it. Then he looked at another. "And do you want to be eaten, too?" and ate it as well. And so he went on talking to himself, saying, "When my companions return, there will still be enough for them all." At this point he saw the monk walking toward him with another man.

"Liu Tong!" said Ji Gong, "You still haven't gone to look for your big brother Yang. He may be killed."

"Really?" asked Liu Tong.

"Truly," replied the monk.

Liu picked up his iron-tipped staff and ran up the mountain, leaving the steamed bread abandoned on the ground. When he reached the shrine, he was tall enough to look over the wall. He could see Yang Ming tied up. Naturally, he was most alarmed and leaped inside. His staff rose and fell, cracking open Golden Eye's skull in one whirlwind motion. But then Sorcerer Hua pointed and brought Liu Tong to a standstill. The Daoist drew his precious sword and placed the tip against Liu Tong's chest.

Liu Tong laughed at him. "My body is covered with iron," he said. "I won't tell you, but I fear only fire, being buried alive, and boiling water—those three, but you don't know those three things and I won't tell." In his simple way, he had told everything while saying he wouldn't tell.

Hua Qingfeng told the novices to bring two big bundles of dry wood. "I will burn him to death," he said, "and revenge the killing of my student Golden Eye."

When Liu Tong saw them bringing the wood, he said, "This is very bad. Who told you?"

"Liu Tong is a simple person," Yang Ming told the sorcerer. "He has a Buddha heart and has never had an evil thought. How can you treat him like this?"

But heaven seemed to have turned away its eyes. "Teacher," Liu Tong cried, "come quickly and save me!"

From outside came an answering voice. "You thing! You dare to burn my follower! Do not be afraid, my disciple!" Everyone opened their eyes wide. It was indeed the *lohan*, who had come to help those in their direst need.

CHAPTER 72

Sorcerer Hua weaves his spell; the Chan master comes from the Iron Buddha Temple to save those in need

JI Gong had arrived just as Sorcerer Hua Qingfeng was lighting the fire to burn Liu Tong. Except for having encountered Liu Tong on the pathway down below the shrine shortly before, Ji Gong had not seen any of this group of friends since he left them at the abbey and went off in pursuit of Cloud Dragon Hua. Along the way he had stopped to save the lives of three young men who had been wounded by Cloud Dragon's poisoned darts. Then, after he had exorcised the python demon and driven Golden Eye and his band of outlaws from the Iron Buddha Temple, there were complaints that there was no longer any cure for those who had drunk from the wells poisoned by the python. As a result, Ji Gong had to supply a remedy of his own making.

Next he saw to the transfer of the Painted Lame Man back to the Longyou district magistrate's yamen, since it was in that district that the false cripple had been directly involved in one murder and indirectly in another. Ji Gong, having attended to all these details, said farewell to the Longyou magistrate, who thanked him profusely for his help. Then the monk went on his way down the road with the two headmen, Chai and She.

"Teacher," said Headman Chai, "since we left the capital, Linan, to capture Hua Yun Long, we have sought him hither and yon. One day you have said, 'Today we will take him.' Then on the next day you have said, 'Tomorrow we will take him.' As of today, we still have not taken him. At home we have left both old ones and young ones while spending so many days in this fruitless search. Probably we will never be able to take him."

"You two must not let yourselves be too impatient," counseled the monk. "Surely we will take him!"

There was nothing the two headmen could do. They simply walked onward. Suddenly the monk let out a cry. "Oh! Oh! I have too many lice on my belly! They're biting me terribly!" With that he scratched about with his hand and picked one off from his chest, which he then placed on his back. Then he took another from his back and put it on his chest.

"Teacher!" exclaimed Headman Chai, "don't pick lice off and put them back on again! That's a very dirty thing to do!"

"I'm helping them move from one place to another," explained the monk. "Otherwise, when they go swimming they will die."

"Teacher!" countered Headman Chai, "Don't talk nonsense! The lice on a person's body don't go swimming. I still say just get them off quickly."

"Well, these lice still need a drink of water," said the monk. Just ahead, a river came into view. "Ke tong!" The monk dived into the water.

Headman Chai then realized that the monk wanted to leave them. "Teacher is off once more," he said. "Where will we meet again?"

"Let's meet at the Changshan district yamen," the monk replied. Then he dived beneath the water and the headmen saw him no longer. Barely keeping their anger and resentment under control, the two headmen walked on.

When the monk saw that the two men had gone, he came up out of the water and went straight up to the Veiled Mountain. As he walked along the path, he saw in front of him a vagabond who was carrying on his back a gilded papier-mâché emblem almost as large as he was. It represented an antique coin in the shape of a hand. It was meant to be carried high in the air on a long pole in a procession. On it there were four lines of characters:

> Today we join in the marriage feast;
> Tonight we sleep in an ancient temple.
> If we do no evil thing,
> What fear have we from any prince?

"Where are you going to do your begging?" the monk asked.

"I am going to wish someone a happy wedding," the beggar answered.

"Let us go together, then," the monk offered.

"Oh, no," said the beggar. "What would you do there, monk?"

"I would wish them a happy wedding as well," replied the monk.

"But, if someone were getting married," said the beggar, "and you, a monk, came to the wedding, people wouldn't like your being there."

"Very well, I'll be quiet and put the lid on that idea," said the monk. The two walked along together for a while until they came to the fork in the path beneath the Veiled Mountain Shrine and saw Liu Tong, with his bread heads, talking to himself.

"Liu Tong, you still haven't gone to look!" exclaimed the monk. "Your big brother Yang may be hurt by somebody up there!"

"Really?" asked Liu Tong.

"Truly!" replied the monk. Liu Tong promptly seized his staff and dashed up the mountain, abandoning all his steamed bread.

"Gather up this bread," said the monk to the beggar.

The beggar looked at all the bread. "Don't you want it, monk?" he asked.

"No, I don't want it," replied the monk. "You take it and eat it all." The monk had given the steamed bread to the beggar because he was afraid it would be wasted. When he looked around, he could see that there was no one else to take it, and so he told the beggar to pick it up.

The monk then went up the mountain. As soon as he reached the shrine, he heard Liu Tong cry out, "Teacher, quickly save me!"

The monk immediately put his hand on top of his head and shut down the three golden lights of Buddha. As the monk leaped inside and looked around, Hua Qingfeng was just lighting the fire around Liu Tong. "You senseless Daoist necromancer! You pretend you are able to call up spirits and predict the future!" shouted the monk. "Because you intentionally and with no reason harm people, you force me, the monk, to come after you."

Hua Qingfeng was so excited that he began whining and squeaking. He rasped out, "Who are you?"

"I am Ji Dian, Mad Ji, from the Monastery of the Soul's Retreat at the West Lake," answered Ji Gong. "Since you are a person who has left the world to join the faith of those who revere the three pure ones—Lao Tzu with his teachings, Pan Gu who brought the universe out of chaos, and the Pearly Emperor who rules the unseen world as you Daoists believe— then you certainly should be against killing, obscenity, recklessness, and intemperance. Now, though, you want to take the lives of people for no reason. How can I, the monk, tolerate your doing so?"

As Hua Qingfeng listened and looked at the ragged monk, he saw that he was not very tall, with a thin body and a face streaked with the dust of the road, roughly cut hair about an inch long, and clothes all tattered and torn. Hua Qingfeng thought to himself: "He's nothing but a beggar monk, after all. Hearing is nothing like seeing, and seeing wipes out everything one has heard. I have heard people say that Ji Dian is a *lohan*. If so, there should be a golden light over his head. An immortal would have a white light and a demon would have black smoke. There is no golden light above his head, and no white light. He is just an ordinary human being." How could Hua Qingfeng know that the monk had suppressed his golden light?

"Ji Dian," said the Daoist, "you annoy me to death."

"I annoy you to death?" the monk said. "Then die!"

"Ji Dian," continued the Daoist, "you have a lot of gall, you beast! Some time ago you killed a student of mine. You burned him to death in his shrine. Then, not long ago, for no reason you disturbed things at the Iron Buddha Temple and caused the death of my friend Jiang, the python. He appeared to me in a dream and said that you had destroyed more than five centuries of his Daoist arts and that then you made my student, Golden Eye, slap his own face until he ruined his beard. Aren't you like a moth drawn into a flame? You are seeking your own death! You should know your place! Unless you get down and knock your head on the ground in the kowtow and call me your ancestor, this hermit has the power to kill you!"

The monk laughed loudly. "My good Daoist, you're talking complete nonsense. If you knelt and kowtowed to me and called me your ancestor three generations back, I couldn't pardon you either."

At those remarks, not only did the anger rise higher in the sorcerer's heart, but the evil spread into his body. He seized his sword and aimed a blow at the monk's head. The monk slipped from under it and managed to get behind his opponent, where he gave him a pinch. The Daoist was so angry that he was shouting, "Ah! Ah!" The monk's slender body made it easier for him to move about, pulling, pinching, slapping, and shoving, while the Daoist's sword could not touch him.

The Daoist was frustrated. He leaped away and said, "Ji Dian, you really are enraging me to death. Now the hermit will use one of his treasures to show you and make you know how dangerous he can be."

So saying, he took out one of his treasures and scattered it on the ground while reciting a spell. He pointed and called out: "Great One, show your power." Then, suddenly, a great wind arose. It came out of nowhere, blowing from east to west, driving boats on the rivers and on the West Lake in to the shore, filling the air with yellow dust, driving the clouds across the sky, blowing trees over, and rattling doors and windows.

The monk looked and saw that the wind was driving all sorts of wild beasts toward him. He pointed and said the six true words: "Om Ma Ni Pad Me Hum." There was a streak of golden light and the wind ceased. The wild beasts were only painted on paper.

"Well now, Monk," said the Daoist, "you have destroyed one of my treasures." He pointed again and recited another spell. This time there was a swarm of poisonous creatures about to bite and sting the monk. The monk was laughing as he again said the true words and the poisonous things disappeared.

The Daoist could see that the monk had destroyed two of his treasures, and was desperate. When he recited the next spell, a ring of fire sprang up, encircling the monk.

CHAPTER 73

Monk and Daoist match their spells; the brethren depart for Changshan

WHEN the sorcerer Hua Qingfeng created the circle of fire around the ragged monk, he hoped to burn the monk with it. Unexpectedly, when the monk said, "Om Ma Ni Pad Me Hum," the true words, and pointed, the circle of fire jumped from the monk to where the Daoist was standing and encircled him instead. Immediately the sorcerer's clothes caught on fire. He ran inside the pagoda to escape the flames. The ring of fire encircled the pagoda and sent tongues of flame inside, pursuing the sorcerer. His beard and hair, as well as his black robe with the gold embroidery, were all in flames.

The Daoist then cried out, "Holy monk, save me!" Ji Gong, after all, had a Buddhist heart. He did not enjoy harming the sorcerer—as soon as the man begged to be saved, the monk immediately pointed and extinguished the flames.

Hua Qingfeng came out of the pagoda and raced away down the mountainside. The monk did not pursue him, but went to untie Yang Ming and the others. Cloud Dragon Hua had fled some time earlier.

As dawn broke, the four Daoist novices appeared, frightened and shivering. The monk was not angry at them, but said, "You have nothing to fear, but I must ask you whether there is anyone else in the shrine."

"Yes, there are two of our novice brothers, but they are sick," replied one of the novices.

"Good," said the monk. "In a short time I shall cure them."

Yang Ming and the others approached the monk and bowed with their palms pressed together prayerfully. "Thank you for saving our lives. If you had not come, we would all have been finished."

"Yang Ming, Lei Ming, Chen Liang—there is something you three can do for me," said the monk. "I am going to give you a letter to take to Ma Jahu in the Changshan district yamen."

The body of the outlaw Chang Ying, known as the Black Wind Ghost, and that of the Daoist Golden Eye from the Iron Buddha temple had been wrapped in cloth and tied. Soon they would be carried to an open space, where it would be safe to build a large fire and burn them without causing a forest fire.

"Kong Gui," the monk asked the Daoist, "do you think that you can be spared from your own abbey at least for a few weeks? Someone needs to stay here with these novices and the Veiled Mountain Shrine needs to be made a holy and cheerful place once again!"

"There are two brother teachers at my abbey, as well as the novices, so that will not be difficult," replied Kong Gui. "I will send a letter to them to let them know that I will be here."

"And I will write a letter recommending you," said the monk, "in case you decide you would like to be the resident for a longer period."

"And what will you do?" asked Kong Gui.

"I will stay with you until Liu Tong has recovered enough from his burns to travel, and then he can go with me to Changshan," replied the monk. "Yang Ming, Chen Liang, and Lei Ming will be there at the Changshan yamen. I also told my two headmen, Chai and She, to meet me at Changshan. I think I have teased them long enough."

Cloud Dragon Hua had not followed the path in his escape from the Veiled Mountain Shrine, and found the way difficult through the tangle of growth and the twisted trees. At length he had stopped and decided to spend the night sheltered by an overhanging rock. Later, his uncle had passed him in the darkness in great leaps, as if there were no obstacles in his path. He had been so close that Cloud Dragon Hua could smell the half-burnt robe and the singed beard and hair. He did not call out to him, however. Cloud Dragon Hua had had quite enough of his company!

In the morning, the sun rose quickly, warming the chilly mountainside. Cloud Dragon Hua woke and stretched like a cat. After a while he caught a glimpse of Yang Ming, Lei Ming, and Chen Liang going down the path. For a moment Cloud Dragon Hua was tempted to call out to them. "Perhaps they might forgive me even now," he thought, but decided not to take the chance.

"I must go to some place well away from Rising Ground Village where they almost had me," he thought. Then he began to feel hungry, and he longed for a meal with a variety of the snacks called dim sum. There was a restaurant in Changshan where he had once had a breakfast that he had never forgotten. "Yes, that's where I will go," he thought. "I will go to Changshan."

Promising again that they would not fail to follow Ji Gong's instructions, the three heroes left the shrine and took the path down the steep sides of Veiled Mountain. Throughout the day they pressed onward for about thirty miles. However, just as men must have times of misery as well as times of happiness, they cannot always look through the clear air into the luminous depths of the infinite heavens. As the sun turned red, the scaly dragons stirred in the rivers, lakes, and seas; the white clouds filled the sky, and rain began to fall heavily about them. Thunder and lightning crashed and shook the earth and sky, while gales drove the rain before them.

Looking ahead, they saw a small village with a few households. As they ran into it, they saw a large gateway where they took shelter, thinking that when the storm became less violent they would go on. Then as night began to fall, the level village streets filled with water. The scene was frightening. A man came from within and said, "You three gentlemen must leave. I'm going to close this gate."

Seeing that the rain was still falling, Yang Ming asked, "Please tell us. Is there an inn close by?"

"No," answered the man. "Where would there be an inn in this small village?"

"Is there a temple?" queried Yang Ming.

"No temple, either," replied the man.

"We are travelers from far away. With no inn, where can we stay? Please ask your master if we may stay here. Give us lodging for one night," pleaded Yang Ming.

"That's impossible," countered the man. "It's a case of your having to pay for another fellow's bad behavior. The last time someone came asking to stay overnight, our master gave him a place to stay. In the morning he left before it was light, taking many things with him. He even took the bedclothes. Wasn't this a case of burning paper and finding you had called up a demon? Now, as I look at you three people, you don't seem like bad people, but I'm afraid our master won't dare to let you stay."

Yang Ming could see that it was not possible for them to leave, but he didn't know what to say. "I have to agree that you must be careful, but we three are Yangtze escorts unexpectedly caught in this downpour and we beg the master of the household to help us. We turn to him out of the common friendship of humankind and ask his sympathy. You cannot judge everybody on the basis of one case."

"If you three gentlemen will wait," said the man, "I will go and talk with the master. It is not my responsibility to answer you." With that, he turned and went back inside.

In a short time he returned and said, "The master of the household invites you in."

The three immediately followed the man in to a square courtyard. Straight ahead, they saw one building of five sections. There were also two adjoining buildings of three sections each on the east and west sides. Raising the bamboo blind at the door of the north building, the three men went inside. There they saw the household master, a silver-haired man more than seventy years old wearing the kerchief of a *yuanwai* and a robe finely embroidered with flowers. When he saw the three enter, the *yuanwai* raised his clasped hands in greeting, saying, "Please, gentlemen, be seated. I heard just now one of my household men say that you are escorts, but I have not yet learned your honorable names."

Yang Ming gave their names, saying, "And we have not yet received the honorable name of the household master whom we must have annoyed by coming today."

"What kind of words are these?" the old man rebuked him. "Within the four seas all men are brothers, and so is everyone here, both old and young. My name is Jin. Please the three of you sit."

Yang Ming looked around. The room had an atmosphere of study and refinement. The table and chairs were made from precious wood. There were pairs of scrolls with fine calligraphy and landscapes with figures, elegant vases, bronzes, and jade. It was a home of wealth.

A man entered and said, "Please have some tea. Our master Jin will soon have some wine prepared." The household man prepared a table with cups and dishes and wine and food.

Jin Yuanwai spoke to the three escorts. "There is nothing worthwhile to eat. You will find this rough fare."

"How can you say this, Yuanwai?" countered Yang Ming. "We three can hardly express our thanks." With these words, the three sat down. The food was good and they all had a cup of wine, but they could see that the *yuanwai*'s face showed signs of concern that he could not conceal.

Lei Ming, who was by nature outspoken, said, "It is not right for you to entertain us when you are so uncontrollably troubled. Please do not bother with us."

"My dear Lei Ming," the *yuanwai* said, "if I were uncontrollably troubled, I would not have asked you in."

"But I can see by your expression that it is difficult for you," rejoined Lei Ming. "Why is that?"

"You gentlemen do not understand," explained the *yuanwai*. "If my expression betrays me, it has nothing to do with our having this meal. I am troubled at heart. This year I am sixty-eight years old and I have no son, just a girl named Chiao An who is nineteen and not yet promised in marriage. An uncanny spirit has bewitched my daughter, causing her to be ill. According to her, the spirit is a female fox. I have pasted up a notice offering a reward of five hundred gold pieces to anyone who can drive it away. I have not found anyone who can do this, and that is why I am so sad."

When Lei Ming heard this, he said, "This is nothing to worry about. My teacher can perform exorcisms."

"And who is your teacher?" asked the old head of the household.

"My teacher is Ji Gong from the Monastery of the Soul's Retreat," replied Lei Ming, "and I can chase out ghosts myself."

"How did you learn to perform exorcisms?" asked the old master.

"I studied under the Iron Crown Daoist on Dragon Tiger Mountain, along the Yangtze," answered Lei Ming.

The old *yuanwai* was very happy to hear this and exclaimed, "Spirit Master Lei, since you can indeed do exorcisms, would you later on manifest your compassion? If my daughter could be saved, I would be most grateful."

"Don't be concerned about it," Lei Ming said. "In a little while we will go back and drive out this goblin for you."

The old man immediately ordered a servant to tell his daughter to leave her apartment so that the three could enter her room and drive out the uncanny spirit. The servant promised he would do so, and a little later returned to say, "The young lady has left."

The old master took the three escorts to a three-section building on the north side of a courtyard. The escorts went in and looked around. The eastern section was the girl's bedroom. In it there was an odor of perfume. The old master returned to the front part of the house.

"Brother Lei," exclaimed Yang Ming, "you are insane!"

"No, I am not!" proclaimed Lei Ming.

"If you are not insane," Yang Ming demanded, "tell me why you said you could chase ghosts."

"Don't worry about it," said Lei Ming. "It looked to me as if the old man was being a little sparing with the food, but as soon as I said I could drive out evil spirits, you saw how he put out the chickens, ducks, fish, and meat. We had a good dinner. Now you and I have one of the best rooms in the place. If the goblin comes, we will leave the room."

"How can you manage that?" asked Yang Ming.

"Don't worry," said Lei Ming. "I will stay here in this room. If the ghost doesn't come, that's it. If it does come, I'll take my sword to it and see what kind of a hobgoblin it really is."

"That's good," said Yang Ming. "As some holy person said, 'If a person's courage is steady and his heart is right, all those corrupt, magical things will go off to distant places, never to return. Harmony will be restored, everything will fall into place, and all will go well.' I think we can stand firm enough to scare this goblin off."

"Right!" said Lei Ming. "If someone has had ten years of good luck, the devils can't touch him."

"That's true," agreed Chen Liang. "I'll stand behind the door with my knife."

"And I'll get into bed and pretend to be the young lady."

"I'm still a little concerned," said Yang Ming. "I'll sit in this outer room."

"Elder Brother Yang," said Lei Ming, "you go into the west room and go to sleep. Don't bother about it."

Yang Ming went into the western section and sat down, but he did not dare go to sleep. The three waited and waited until the second watch. Then they heard a faint sound. Again they listened—this time they heard a step outside and then a voice that seemed to be coming through a wooden panel.

"Young lady, I have something to say to you, dear." Then the ghostly being was in the room, saying, "Yun! I smell a stranger! Who dares to enter this room?"

As Lei Ming heard this, he slashed toward the ghostly presence.

CHAPTER 74

Three heroes take shelter under the Jin family roof; Chen Liang questions a fellow villager

AT the time when Lei Ming and Chen Liang had heard the voice say, "I smell a stranger," Lei Ming had not answered, but had drawn his sword. Then he saw the bamboo curtain at the door move and a female form start to enter. "What is this hellish thing?" asked Lei Ming, and slashed with his sword. Then he saw a flash of light, and the being fled, but the sword had found its mark. On the floor there was blood and tawny fur. Whether it was that of a fox or a wolf he could not tell.

As soon as Lei Ming cried out, the old *yuanwai* and some household people lit the lamps and went to have a look. They saw the blood and the fur, but they also were unable to tell what sort of a beast it was.

This fox spirit, with its centuries of Daoist arts, was the same one that Ji Gong had confronted earlier. It had not changed its bad habits. Now wounded by Lei Ming, it fled back to the depths of the mountains, but it remembered the warning of Ji Gong and guessed that Lei Ming was the ragged monk's follower.

Seeing proof that Lei Ming had driven away the bestial spirit, Jin Yuanwai thanked Lei Ming profusely. Everyone talked until daylight. Then the old *yuanwai* brought out two hundred pieces of silver to give to Lei Ming. He protested, but the *yuanwai* would not accept Lei Ming's refusal. The three then divided the silver into three shares and left the village.

"You see, my brothers," said Lei Ming, "we didn't do so badly—a free meal, free lodging, and some sixty coins of silver each!"

"Yes, but after this you had better not try such a dangerous thing again," warned Yang Ming. "If that fox had had red hair, it might have eaten you. Whatever power you had came from the fact that you were still under Ji Gong's protection."

As they neared their destination, the road led through the woods. Chen Liang had dropped slightly behind. Suddenly, a tall man approached from the rear. He was wearing close-fitting dark-blue clothing and his hair was in the style of an ox heart. He had a knife in hand with which he stabbed at Chen Liang's back. Chen Liang ran forward a few steps, then turned and was easily able to overpower the man and bring him to his knees.

"You're a brave fellow," jeered Chen Liang. "You just can't get your eyes open."

The man immediately began to beg, "Honored sir, spare my life."

"You probably have been a robber for a long time and you are probably wanted in connection with some case. What's your name and where do you come from? I am ready to grant you your life if you answer my questions honestly!" responded Chen Liang.

The man answered in a frank and open manner. "I am from the Danyang district in Jenjiang prefecture."

When Chen Liang heard this and also recognized the familiar accent, he thought to himself, "There was a reason I didn't kill him! He might be a distant relative." Aloud he said, "You say that you are from Danyang—what is your surname and in what village do you live?"

"I live in the little Chen family town," the robber responded.

On hearing this, Chen wondered, "Why don't I know him if he lives in Chen family town?" Again he asked the robber's name and also asked where in the Chen family town he lived.

"I live north of the crossroads. My surname is Chen and I am called Liang. My nickname is the White Monkey with the Miraculous Hands," the robber answered.

When Chen heard this, his anger boiled over and he slapped the robber's face.

Yang Ming and Lei Ming, who had not gone very far ahead, ran back and Yang Ming asked, "What is going on, Old Third?"

"He came up behind me on the road and was about to stab me when I caught him, but that's nothing! Elder Brother, you ask him what his name is," Chen Liang replied, upset.

"So what is your name?" asked Yang Ming.

"My name is Chen Liang," answered the robber, "and I am known as the White Monkey with the Miraculous Hands."

"You borrowed yourself a name, you misbegotten liar," Lei Ming snorted. "So you're Chen Liang! Are you still Chen Liang?"

"I must be losing my eyesight. I'm from Danyang," the robber whined. "I am from Danyang, but I am not named Chen. My name is Song, Song the Eighth Immortal, but because I knew there was an honorable heroic gentleman named Chen the Third, I borrowed his name. What are your honorable names?"

"I am Yang Ming and he is Lei Ming," Yang Ming said.

"So you are the famed Yang Ming," said the robber, "and you are the honorable Lei Ming of the Whirlwind. I hope you three will pardon me!"

"Let me give you a little silver," said Yang Ming, "and you can try doing something else instead of robbing people."

"Don't bother, Elder Brother, why not snip off that calabash and let it go at that!" said Lei Ming, using the outlaw word for head. "That big gourd will make a good water holder."

"I beg you three gentlemen, spare my life! Where are you going?"

"We're going to the place of Ma Jahu, the father of Ma Ran," answered Yang Ming.

"Ah, intimate friends! Pull apart while still alive! Up over the walls for silver," said the robber in the black language of the river pirates. "The more water, the more fish"—implying that the three were going over the walls.

Lei Ming gave the still-kneeling man a kick. "Who taught you to talk like that? Be off with you!" At that the man jumped up and ran off.

The three hastened onward to the home of Ma Jahu and arrived at the village while it was still daylight. When they inquired after the official Ma, everyone knew him and said that his home was on the north side, just beyond the crossroad. As soon as they understood, they went on to the crossroad, and there it was. When they knocked, a house servant about thirty years of age came out and inquired in a very friendly manner, "Whom do you wish to see?"

"I have come on the orders of Ji Gong," said Yang Ming, "with a letter to be delivered personally."

"Of course," said the manservant. "Will you three please wait here while I go in and announce that you have arrived." He turned and quickly went inside.

Ma Ran was in the library talking with the iron-faced Zheng Xiong. He had just heard from a servant who had gone shopping at Changshan about the bandit caught there, called the Tangled Hair Ghost, and how the river pirates had come in a gang of several hundred to rescue him, killing the watchman. "Brother Xiong," said Ma Ran, "tonight we will post our guard soldiers around the place."

Just as they were talking, the manservant came to say, "There are three men who say they were sent by Ji Gong with a letter which they want to deliver personally."

"Ask them," directed Ma Ran, "whether they were coming this way and brought the letter as a favor, whether they were sent urgently with the letter, or whether they were paid by Ji Gong to deliver it."

When the servant returned and said that they were sent urgently, Ma Ran came out with the servant and led them through one courtyard into a second, where they entered a large hall. The three noticed that Ma Ran was dressed in the rich clothing of a wealthy official, with a jade ornament at the front of the kerchief on his head; he was evidently in his early thirties, with a neat, black beard. With him was an impressive man of military appearance dressed all in black. Assembled in the room were a number of men, some in uniform. The three escorts were seated with the rest. Tea was served and names were exchanged.

Ma Ran took the letter and noticed Ji Gong's mark on the outside, a cracked wine jar mended with seven rivets. After he had opened and read the letter, his face took on a serious expression.

CHAPTER 75

Yang Ming defends a country mansion;
Zhou Rui is given leave from duty

SEEING the change in Ma Ran's expression, Zheng Xiong asked, "What is it, my dear brother?"

"This is terrible!" exclaimed Ma Ran. "Look at these eight phrases!"

Zheng Xiong took the letter and read: "In valiantly coming to a traveler's aid, it seems that you have stirred up trouble. Now a great flock of robbers has gathered, intending to invade the official residence and take revenge for holding one of theirs in prison. If Ma Ran does not quickly guard against them, his entire family will be killed by these outlaws."

As Zheng Xiong read he said, "Ah, Ji Gong! He foretells with no rituals. What do you think we should do, dear brother?"

"Things do not look good," said Ma Ran.

"Brother Yang," asked Zheng Xiong, "what do you three usually do by way of occupation?"

"We have been acting as guard escorts elsewhere," replied Yang Ming. "I have not heard your honorable name."

"Really, I had forgotten," said Ma Ran. "This is my sworn brother Zheng Xiong, sometimes called the Ironfaced."

"I am happy to meet you," said Yang Ming.

"Brother Yang," said Ma Ran, "Since you are escorts, there is something I must beg you to do."

"What is that?" asked Yang Ming.

"Read this note from Ji Gong," said Ma Ran. "I recently offended a robber, a member of the Greenwood. Tonight the robbers are coming to kill this entire family. I have a few old people here with no special skills. I would beg you three to help us, but I don't know how you would feel about it."

Yang Ming took the letter. As soon as he looked at it, he understood. He thought about it for some time and then he said, "In this matter, Great Official Ma, I cannot fulfill your request unless I know which group of outlaws these are. If they are from the Jade Mountain Greenwood and I went against them, then I would be finished. If they are from the Four Rivers band, not only am I not worried, but I have a grudge against them."

When Ma Ran heard this, he replied, "I have been aware for a long time that a person named Yang Ming was generous, that he thought no more of gold than dirt, and that he valued chivalry above property. It was only because of these character traits that I dared to ask if he could help. Nevertheless, if this day we have to part, I would not expect anything else from him."

Yang Ming courteously replied, "Whatever happens, there are things beyond our control. I will certainly always respect you and feel as if we were old acquaintances at first sight. Indeed, if you are willing to accept my help, I wish to offer it but, if we do not want to fail tonight, we must make preparations."

"You are right," said Ma Ran. "We should discuss how we have to prepare."

"How many people are there in your house?" asked Yang Ming.

"Altogether, including laborers and herdsmen, about one hundred," answered Ma Ran.

"Good," said Yang Ming. "Call them all here together. I have something to say to them." Ma Ran then assembled the entire household. Yang Ming looked them over and separated the old, weak, and the very young from the rest. There were then about sixty who could be used in defense.

Yang Ming addressed them. "The head of your household has offended men of the Greenwood, and tonight a great number of outlaws are coming to make an armed attack. Do you wish to protect this house with all your strength and save the master of the household?"

They answered with one voice: "We will fight to the death against these robbers!"

When Yang Ming heard this reply, he realized Ma Ran must have treated others with great sincerity to bring forth such single-minded loyalty. He explained to them, "You must place all the wives, old women, and young girls in an empty room with no lights. How many such rooms are there in the rear courtyard?"

"There are four buildings facing the rear courtyard," answered Ma Ran.

"Then those can be defended by armed men," said Yang Ming. "Others will wait in the south courtyard in lighted rooms with the doors half open, listening for my shout. When you come out, do not try to capture any of the other robbers. Just defend yourselves with your weapons." They all nodded their heads in assent.

"Official Ma," Yang Ming continued, "You and Zheng Xiong should wait in the rear north courtyard rooms with your picked men, prepared for whatever may happen. Lock all the buildings in the western part of the estate. We three will wait in the rooms in the eastern part."

As Ma listened to Yang Ming, he could not help but feel respect. He immediately chose the ones to be with him and had food and wine prepared for everyone. When they had finished eating and drinking, it was time to light the lamps. Then Ma Ran led Yang Ming and the others into the inner courtyard. They then sat down in the various rooms assigned to them by Yang Ming with their weapons in their hands.

Yang Ming, Lei Ming, and Chen Liang blackened their faces with soot and sat in the east room with the door open, watching. At a little after the second watch they suddenly saw a figure creep down the roof opposite them. He was wearing a suit of darkness with two butterflies embroidered on his chest and a horsetail headdress. He carried a sword in his hand.

Leaping down to the ground, he stood for a moment looking around. As he saw the open door of the east room, he quickly moved toward it. Yang Ming came from behind and struck him in the face with his hand. Lei Ming struck the intruder with his sword and killed him. As yet they did not know who the robber was.

Just as the robber was killed, the three heard someone on the roof say, "There is resistance, everyone. Good! Ma Ran, you dare to oppose the men of the Greenwood! Tonight, our swords will finish your whole household! Listen, everyone, there are no defenders in the north, south, and east buildings."

Now Yang Ming shouted, "The robbers are attacking!" They could see that the courtyard was filling with robbers. Lei Ming and Chen Liang stood side by side as one of the robbers came toward them. With a sword in each hand, he slashed at Yang Ming, but Yang Ming evaded the blows and killed the robber instead.

In his place came Li Xiang, a famous outlaw. When he saw that the other outlaw had been killed, he aimed a blow at Yang Ming's head. Yang Ming was hard pressed, but brought his own sword up just as the other raised his to strike. He caught the robber off guard. Before he could recover, Yang Ming thrust his sword home and the robber fell. In a little while Yang Ming had killed four of the robbers.

Then one dressed in dark clothing approached. Yang thought he recognized him as a sworn brother. He paused, unwilling to kill him, but he was mistaken about the man, who knew him and began to laugh. The two left the courtyard and went into the woods behind. Just then another robber cried out, "This man has killed some of our people! What are you doing with him?" He dashed at Yang Ming, but fell in a pool of blood.

A voice came out of the darkness asking, "Must you kill everyone?" It was Ji Gong.

Now, when the monk had leapt into the water saying he was going to give his lice a bath, he also told his two deputies, Headman Chai and Headman She, that he would meet them in Changshan. They were extremely angry, but they walked on through the night until they reached the crossroads and saw a tall man standing in the open door of a wine shop on the west side of the road. A square blue cloth was tied over his hair knot and he was wearing a blue cotton robe. Two other men stood beside him.

"Look, Brother She," said Headman Chai. "You see those men. Those two look as though they might be headmen. Yes, that one is Zhou Rui, who was chasing Cloud Dragon a few days ago and was hit by a stone thrown by Yang Ming."

At the time Zhou Rui had been coughing up blood. When he was taken home, his father cried out, "I am so old and have only this one son. Lo Biao, you go to the magistrate's court and request a leave of absence for him."

When Lo Biao went to the yamen, surprisingly the magistrate did not believe him and said, "He wants a leave after losing such an important criminal! I want to look at him! I'll see whether he needs it or not."

There was nothing Lo Biao could do but go back to the house. Some of the household people helped Zhou Rui to the yamen. When Zhou Rui saw the magistrate, he explained, "As this inferior servant was chasing an outlaw, he was struck by a rock thrown by another outlaw and is still spitting mouthfuls of blood."

The magistrate could see that this was true, because Zhou Rui coughed up blood several times while he was at the yamen. The magistrate then gave Zhou Rui twenty ounces of silver and allowed him ten days' leave from his duties to recover. He was helped out of the yamen. Upon reaching the wine shop at the crossroads, he was thirsty and wanted to drink something, and several friends were greeting him. Suddenly a man wearing a white jacket and a cap with six sections walked out. The man, about thirty years old, was carrying a bundle in his hand, and his face was very white.

As soon as Zhou Rui saw him and realized that it was Cloud Dragon, he commanded, "You waiters, quickly seize that man! He is Cloud Dragon Hua!"

The man laughed and said, "Who do you think you are catching? You should be trying to get over your illness." And with that, he walked off to the north.

CHAPTER 76

Chai and She hear a voice from the clouds;
Ji Gong buys a dog

WHEN the two headmen, Chai and She, heard about Zhou Rui's having seen Cloud Dragon Hua, they took their iron-tipped staves and soon caught up with the outlaw. They said to him: "Go no further, my friend. You are wanted about a case. I am Headman Chai and this is Headman She. We have come from Linan to arrest you."

"Cloud Dragon," said Headman She, "do not give us more trouble. Just come along with us."

The outlaw looked at the two headmen and laughed. "You gentlemen have come especially to take me?"

"That is so," said Headman She.

The outlaw laughed again and said, "If I were Cloud Dragon Hua and you two headmen came to take me, I would certainly want to go with you, but I have a friend who is not so willing."

"And where is this friend of yours?" asked Chai.

"As far away as a thousand *li* and as close as right before your eyes," the outlaw replied mysteriously. As he said this, he drew out his sword.

Chai and She struck out with their iron-tipped staves but the flying sword of the outlaw was too much for them. They were unable to overpower him.

"His skill is very great indeed!" thought Chai to himself. "No wonder he was able to commit such crimes in Linan, even stealing the pearl coronet from the prime minister. If She and I had not been together, one of us would be dead." His resentment against the monk was particularly strong just then for his having left them and for not being there when they were trying to subdue Cloud Dragon. "Headman She, how do you feel about the monk?"

"I would not like to see him just now," he replied.

As She spoke, he heard a voice say, "I am here." The voice seemed to come from the clouds. "I am here, but I am not coming down. I might fall to my death."

Looking up, Chai saw Ji Gong standing on the top of a carved sign above the door of a drugstore. The crowd of people all looked up, and some cried out: "Oh! the monk may kill himself if he falls."

Ji Gong, after having given Liu Tong some medicine to cure his burns, set out to find Cloud Dragon Hua, stopping on the way to visit the sick Daoist, Liu Miaotong, and give him some medicine. When Ji Gong reached Changshan and the crossroads, he saw the two headmen fighting with the outlaw and used his arts to get up on the druggist's sign.

Headman Chai, seeing Ji Gong standing on the druggist's sign in mid-air, could not imagine how he could have gotten up there. Everyone was looking up and saying, "Dreadful! The monk will fall to his death!"

"Teacher, come down quickly," pleaded Chai.

"Well, I don't want to fall," said Ji Gong and simply jumped down.

The crowd of people who had been saying that the monk would fall to his death were surprised to see him land on his feet, and were now saying, "This is a strange monk!"

"Teacher! Quickly recite one of your spells and catch the outlaw!" exclaimed Chai.

"They've gone right out of my head," said the monk. Meanwhile, the outlaw was climbing across rooftops and fleeing for his life, but just then the monk said, "Oh, I remember one," and he recited, "O Mi To Fu." The outlaw slipped down and was hanging by his clothing from the eaves, right in front of Zhou Rui. The latter was about to put chains on the outlaw.

At this point Chai and She were again filled with hatred for Ji Gong, because he was allowing this invalid to take Cloud Dragon into custody. They hesitated, thinking that the crowd would not let them take the outlaw away from Zhou Rui. Then they stepped forward. "Congratulations, my friend! I am Chai Yuanlo and this is She Jengying. We two were especially sent by the yamen of the Grand Protector of Linan to bring back Cloud Dragon Hua. You must permit us to put the chains upon him."

Zhou Rui, who had a truly noble and generous spirit, was not inclined to argue with them, and simply said, "You two gentlemen may put the locks on him." Chai and She did so.

"You two must be very happy," commented the monk. "You have captured Cloud Dragon Hua and, when you get back, you will have the reward of 1,200 ounces of silver."

"Aren't you happy, Teacher?" asked Chai.

"You are happy!" said the monk again—and repeated his comment five times in all.

"Let's go, Teacher," said Chai, "and don't say that any more."

"You go ahead to the yamen," said the monk. "I will be there later."

The two headmen led the outlaw into the Changshan district yamen and reported their arrival. The magistrate immediately went to his bench and summoned the two headmen and the outlaw.

Chai and She brought the outlaw into the courtroom. Chai greeted the magistrate. "Your servant, Chai Yuanlo, repectfully hopes that your honor is well."

Headman She also greeted the magistrate and explained their going from Linan to arrest Cloud Dragon Hua for his crimes. "Now we have captured him and bring him here before you."

"And do you have a warrant?" the magistrate asked.

"We have," responded Headman Chai and immediately produced it.

The magistrate found the warrant to be correct, and then asked, "Is this the outlaw Cloud Dragon Hua?"

"My name is Hua," said the outlaw, "and I am called Cloud Dragon."

"What nicknames are you called?" queried the magistrate.

"I am known as the Water Rat of the Universe," answered the outlaw.

"What did you do in Linan?" asked the magistrate.

"I killed a young nun who refused to go away with me, as well as an old man. I also killed a man on the second floor of a restaurant. And I stole the pearl coronet from the prime minister. I did all these things."

"And what was the verse you wrote?" asked the magistrate.

The outlaw described it.

"Now," queried the magistrate further, "what did you do at the pawnshop outside the south gate? Who was it that you killed outside the east gate, and what other crimes did you commit here in my district?"

"I committed no crimes here in this district, and I know nothing about any of those things," answered the outlaw.

The magistrate became furious. "Probably you need to be questioned physically in order to make you talk! Take him down and beat him for me!"

"Your Honor," protested the outlaw, "I have committed several crimes for which I will be executed. I am already a condemned man, but I have done nothing here. You cannot punish me for what I have not done. Isn't it true, Your Honor, that you simply want to clear up your cases? If you want me to make up a story for you, you must tell me what to say."

This made the magistrate's temper explode further. "You beast! You are a real outlaw—if I do not beat you, you will never tell the truth."

The magistrate's men were about to beat the outlaw when the sound of footsteps was heard. As the sound grew louder, Ji Gong appeared. "Your Honor," announced Headman Chai, "Ji Gong has arrived."

The magistrate stood up as Ji Gong entered. Now they saw that, as he walked into the courtroom, he was leading another man. The man's eyes were staring straight ahead.

When Ji Gong had parted from the two headmen at the crossroads, he had followed them toward the magistrate's yamen. Directly opposite the yamen's gate, the monk let out an angry exclamation as he saw a wine shop and went inside. A man of about forty years old was sitting in the cashier's office. The skin of his face was a dark reddish brown and his eyes had an ugly squint. "Manager," said the monk, "lend me a writing brush."

"What for?" asked the manager.

"I'm going to drink some wine," replied the monk, "but I want to write a word or two first."

The manager handed the monk a brush, and the monk wrote something in the palm of his hand. When he had finished, he sat down and called for a pot of wine and several dishes.

Nearby a man was saying, "Today Senior Monk Ji Gong captured an outlaw near the crossroads. Didn't you see it happen?"

"No, I didn't," said a second man.

"I saw it," the first one said. "The monk was very tall. His head was like a grain measure. He was wearing a saffron-colored robe and carrying a rosary of 108 beads in his hand. Really like a *lohan*."

"Don't talk nonsense!" exclaimed the other. "That monk, Ji Gong, is a drunken madman, dirty and ragged, with parts of his sleeves torn off and his head unshaven most of the time." And pointing with his finger, he continued, "very much like that monk there."

"How do you know that?" asked the first man.

"I was a friend of Ji Dian," the other said.

"You know him?" interjected the monk. "When did you know him?"

"Last year in the spring," replied the second man. "I saw him in Linan. We ate together."

"Last year in the spring?" queried Ji Gong. "Weren't you a merchant in Jenjiang prefecture?"

The man thought that Ji Gong's question was strange. "How did he know that I was in business in Jenjiang?" he asked himself, and then he asked the monk, "How did you know I was in Jenjiang?"

"I saw you there," replied the monk.

Just as he spoke, a man called into the room, "A good dog! Who will buy it?"

"Dog seller," asked the monk, "how much do you want for this dog?"

The man heaved a deep sigh as he replied, "If the great teacher were to take it, that would be very good. There are three of us in my family. My mother is very sick. We have sold and pawned everything to buy her medicine, until there is nothing left to sell but this dog. Just give me a string of one thousand cash and you can have it."

The monk said, "I don't want it."

"Nine hundred," countered the man.

"I still don't want it," said the monk.

A hundred cash at a time, the man reduced the price to six hundred.

Another man asked, "How much are you willing to give, monk?"

"I will give you five cash," said the monk. "Are you satisfied with the price?"

"I am satisfied," said the man.

A bystander remarked, "Monk, you really are insane!"

The dog seller said, "Sold."

"Sold indeed!" said the monk. "Manager, give us five cash."

"And for what reason should I give five cash?" asked the manager.

The monk raised his open hand and showed the palm to the manager. "Look," he said, "for just this reason."

As soon as he saw what was written there, the frightened manager said, "I will give you five cash."

CHAPTER 77

Chai and She capture an outlaw at Changshan; Ji Gong reveals nine plum blossoms

WHEN the frightened manager said, "I will give you five cash," and then did so, no one could imagine what was going on.

"Dog seller," said the monk, "let the dog loose. I hear him whining. I will give you the five cash."

"The moment I let him loose he will run off," said the dog seller. "He will simply run back to my house."

"Never mind," said the monk. "If he runs off, that's my affair." The man let the dog go and the dog ran back home of its own accord. The monk handed the coins to the dog seller, who took the money and left.

"Teacher," the manager said, "don't tell anybody about this business of mine. We will keep it to ourselves and not mention it. I will pay for some dishes for you."

"Go ahead," said the monk. The manager then ordered quite a number of dishes and set them before the monk, who ate and drank.

Then the monk said, "If I do not take you into court, we will not have answered to the wronged soul of the dead man." The manager's eyes became fixed straightforward in a stare. He walked out through the restaurant after the monk, down the street and into the prefect's yamen.

The prefect stood up and greeted the monk with extreme politeness, saying, "The light of Buddha approaches me. I hope you will forgive my sins. Please be seated. What should be done with this person that you have brought here?"

"Would your honor first have someone take charge of this man," requested the monk. "We can question him a little later." The prefect immediately ordered one of his men to take the restaurant manager into custody.

"Old Chai and old She," said the monk to the two headmen, "you were very happy about bringing Cloud Dragon Hua here, and very happy that you will be getting 1,200 ounces of silver at Linan. Very happy."

"Isn't the teacher happy?" headmen Chai and She asked.

"Outlaw! What is your name?" the monk asked.

"My name is Cloud Dragon Hua," replied the outlaw.

The monk laughed loudly. "What right have you to the name Cloud Dragon Hua?" As he spoke, he pulled off the outlaw's shirt. "Come and look! This is his nickname."

When the headmen Chai and She looked, they saw on the outlaw's back nine scars the size of large coins. When the monk pointed them out, the outlaw spoke. "That's it. Monk, you know who I am. I am not named Cloud Dragon Hua."

"Then what are you called?" demanded the prefect.

"My name is Son," answered the outlaw, "and I am called Evil Tiger. My nickname is Nine Plum Blossoms. I am a Four Rivers man and I live in the Jade Emperor temple on Evil Tiger Mountain. A number of Four Rivers men of the Greenwood operate there. Outside the south gate we robbed the pawnshop and set fire to it. Altogether there were thirty people. Outside the east gate there were two, myself and Gold River Ma. Because you locked up the Tangled Hair Ghost and beat him, his Greenwood brothers came together to rescue him. There were seventy-three men in all. We did several things, including the killing of the guard soldier when we went out of the gate. The Tangled Hair Ghost's legs had been broken by the order of the magistrate. He told us the Changshan prefect and Ma Jahu were his enemies. Tonight a large number of Greenwood men will come together to kill the entire Ma family. I was to assassinate the prefect. Unexpectedly I was captured. Cloud Dragon Hua was never at the Jade Emperor's temple and is not among our number, but I know him and thought I would do him a favor by pretending to be him. I didn't expect the monk to recognize me. This is my true story."

The prefect ordered that the outlaw be kept in chains and returned to his jail cell. The prefect's underlings carried out his orders.

Chai and She were furious, but the monk said, "You two men must not get excited. Sooner or later I will surely give you two the outlaw you are looking for."

The prefect then asked again, "Holy monk, that man you brought in just now, what kind of affair is that?"

The monk put out his hand and showed the palm. "Look, Your Honor," he said. The prefect immediately understood and ordered the man brought forward.

The manager of the wine shop was named Dong Shiyuan. The original proprietor of the shop was named Kong the Fourth. He was a sworn brother of Dong. Since he was an orphan, Kong turned in times of difficulty to Dong as a friend. Kong had a wife named Zhou Shi and two young children, a boy and a girl. Dong helped out Kong in the wine shop.

Eventually Kong the Fourth became ill. When his sickness grew worse, he called Dong to his home and said, "As sworn brothers we are like hand and foot. Now I will not be in this world much longer. When I am dead, my wife and children must depend upon you for their living. They have no one to rely upon, no one to trust. I will give you my wine shop to manage. After I am dead I know that you won't let my family starve and will help my children to grow up and burn incense at my grave. Thus I can willingly close my eyes in death and go beneath the Yellow Springs."

"Elder brother," said Dong, "just try to get better and not to worry. Of course I will take care of your wife and children."

Kong the Fourth did die, and Dong took care of the funeral. Afterward he became manager of the wine shop. He often gave money to Zhou Shi.

Zhou Shi's daughter was named Xiaolan, after a fabulous bird with a beautiful song. She was seventeen years old, lovely in face and figure, and still not promised in marriage. Dong was a lustful person who had a desire for the girl from the time that Kong the Fourth had died, and in the shop he constantly thought about her. One day Zhou Shi took her son on a visit to his grandmother. She left her daughter, Xiaolan, to watch the house. Dong went to the house to bring several things that might be useful to the widow and her family. When Xiaolan started to take the things from him, he suddenly took hold of her arm. She broke away and ran out into the rear courtyard, where there was a well that had its opening level with the pavement. Preferring to die rather than have him touch her again, Xiaolan jumped into the well and drowned. Dong quickly left the house and went back to the wine shop.

When Zhou Shi came home, she did not see her daughter, and looked everywhere for her without finding her. On the third day after her disappearance, Xiaolan's body rose to the surface of the water in the well and was discovered. Zhou Shi thought that the girl had accidentally fallen into the well. She sent a note asking Dong to buy a coffin and help with the funeral. Dong said nothing about what really had happened, thinking that no one living knew and that ghosts could not talk.

How could Dong have expected that the monk would ask him for five cash, then show him his hand, on the palm of which he had written: KONG XIAOLAN DIED TO PRESERVE HER HONOR. Dong had quickly given five cash and food to the monk, thinking that the monk would overlook his crime. Instead, the monk had used his arts to bring him to the prefect's yamen.

As soon as the prefect saw the writing on the palm of the monk's hand, he understood and immediately struck the desk with his hand as he called out, "You impudent low creature! How could you dare to drive Xiaolan to suicide with your advances? Now, quickly tell the truth. If not, you will be severely punished."

Now Dong Shiyuan realized that he was in the courtroom and thought to himself, "This is strange. No one knew what I did." He said, "Your Honor above me, this small person's name is Dong Shiyuan. I am a merchant, but I do not know anyone who is called Xiaolan."

"The fellow is disrespectful," said the monk. "So you are still unwilling to admit the truth. The ghost of that dead person appeared before me and accused you."

The prefect then had Dong beaten, and he admitted his guilt. The prefect then questioned him further. Dong Shiyuan was in pain and said, "I will tell all."

"Do so," commanded the prefect.

Dong Shiyuan then told how he had promised the dying man that he would care for his family, how he had visited the family's home, and how the girl had resisted him and then thrown herself in the well to her death.

"Have him kept in irons and locked up," ordered the prefect. "Later we will have him confront the corpse, and we will then decide upon his punishment. At present we have other things to do. Let us have something to drink and discuss our plans."

As the servants prepared refreshments, the prefect said, "Holy monk, what are we going to do about all these outlaws who are about to exterminate the entire household of Ma Ran? What do you foresee?"

"Probably that is not so important as our having some refreshments," said the monk.

"You two must be very happy," he said to the two headmen, who were clearly becoming more and more angry and disgusted.

"What is there to be happy about?" Headman Chai asked. "This business has nothing to do with Cloud Dragon Hua."

"You must not get excited, you two," said the monk. "Later I will get two other men to catch Cloud Dragon Hua and give him to you so that you can get the reward."

CHAPTER 78

Yang, Lei, and Chen attack the evil Daoist; Sorcerer Hua invades Ten Li village

AS Ji Gong led the two headmen off into the hills, he saw the Sorcerer Hua Qingfeng raise his sword to kill Yang Ming, Lei Ming, and Chen Liang, who were all lying on the ground in a trance. How did this terrible situation come about?

When the Daoist Hua Qingfeng had fled from the Plum Blossom Hills, he was thinking to himself that he somehow must kill Ji Gong. He thought that, if he had the blood of a pregnant woman on his sword, he could cut through even a *lohan*'s golden light. The strongest blood would be that of a woman carrying a male child.

With a little silver he bought a medicine chest and a few pills with which he thought he could go somewhere and set himself up as a doctor. As he carried his medicine chest into a small village, he heard two old women talking. "Auntie Liu," one asked the other, "have you had breakfast yet?"

"I have," Auntie Liu replied.

The two old women were named Liu and Chen. "Look," the one named Liu continued, "wasn't that the wife of Wang the Second who just passed?

"Yes," replied old Madam Chen.

"Those two don't know how happy they are. How is it that she is still carrying his noon meal to him?" asked Grandmother Liu.

"Auntie Liu," said the other, "don't you know that the wife of Wang the Second is soon going to have a child?"

Sorcerer Hua Qingfeng walked on into the village and watched. Sure enough, the young woman was pregnant and the child would be a male. There is an old saying that telling whether a child will be a son or a daughter is the easiest thing in the world. If the woman starts to walk down the road and steps off with her left foot, the child will be a son. If she starts off with her right foot, it will be a daughter.

Hua Qingfeng saw and immediately knew. He walked up to her, chanting, "Oh, Limitless One" and said, "I see the color in your face is a little dark. Is there something wrong between you and your husband?"

The woman stopped and asked, "Daoist Master, can you read faces? Can you really tell whether there is anything wrong between my husband and me? If you see some sign that you can explain, I would thank you."

"If you would tell me the eight characters relating to your birth, I could explain everything to you," said Sorcerer Hua.

The woman gave the sorcerer the details of her birth, as requested. Hua Qingfeng heard and understood. He pointed and she became senseless. The sorcerer caught her as she fell and walked off with her.

Someone in the village saw them and called out, "A Daoist is carrying off the wife of Wang the Second." Villagers started in pursuit, but the Daoist was soon out of sight.

In the mountains, Hua Qingfeng tied the woman to a tree and drew his sword to kill her. Suddenly, three men appeared. They were Yang Ming, Lei Ming, and Chen Liang. Lei Ming, ever chivalrous, rushed to the woman's defense with his knife drawn, but Hua Qingfeng felled him with his hypnotic power. Chen Liang suffered the same fate, saying to himself, "I will save them or die with them." Yang Ming also attempted to fight the sorcerer, but he, too, fell to the ground.

The Daoist laughed and was about to kill them all when he heard a shout from Ji Gong. "You thing! You dare to harm my disciples!" As soon as the Daoist saw the monk, he was so frightened that he ran like the wind and escaped. The monk again did not follow him. He freed the three friends from the spell. Then he pointed and the woman's understanding returned.

As the monk, his disciples, and the woman came out of the mountain pass, they saw a large number of villagers approaching in pursuit of the Daoist. "The Daoist has escaped from us," Ji Gong told them. "Take this woman home." The villagers led her away.

"Yang Ming," instructed the monk, "you go back to your family." Yang Ming at once said goodbye and left. "Lei Ming and Chen Liang, come with me." The two men nodded their heads in agreement.

When the three approached Ten Li Village, they saw a teahouse by the road and outside it an area shaded by matting, raised on a framework of poles. "We will stop here and rest," said the monk. His two disciples nodded in assent. The monk did not sit down in the shade of the mats, but started walking straight into the teahouse and then sat down inside.

"Teacher, the weather is so hot," protested Chen Liang as they were walking inside. "Why do you not rest outside under the matting where it is cool? It will be very hot in the teahouse."

"You see all these men outside. In a little while, they will come inside. Find yourself seats and sit down," Ji Gong said.

"What is this?" asked Chen Liang.

"Watch," replied the monk. Then the monk went into the back courtyard, and facing toward the northeast, performed the kowtow, kneeling and touching his forehead to the ground three times.

Chen Liang thought to himself, "Since I have known Ji Gong, I have never seen him kowtow until now, nor he did I ever see him burn incense or worship Buddha." He watched the monk as he finished touching his head to the ground and came back into the room. The waiter brought them a pot of tea. After the monk had drunk two or three cups, a torrent of rain began to fall. It was as though a dark current had unrolled from the northwest.

The men who were drinking tea outside came running inside to escape the rain. A raging wind drove the rain. Crashes of thunder followed quickly, one after the other, and the lightning increasingly filled the room with a blinding light.

One of the men suddenly said, "Somebody in this room must have done a terrible wrong."

The monk, meanwhile, was speaking to himself in a low voice. Everyone seemed to be waiting for something. Suddenly, one of the men at the side of the room cried out and then came over and knelt before the monk. "Holy monk," he pleaded, "help me! Help me! My father lost his mind and once, when I was drinking, I slapped his face twice. Help me! From now on I will change."

"If you truly change," said the monk, "I can help you, but I cannot be certain you will change." The monk seemed to speak into the empty air words that could not be heard. Then he said, "I can help you if you truly change. Can you truly change?"

"I can change! I will change!" responded the man.

After a while the monk said, "There is another who drove his younger brother from their home and kept the family property."

One of the men spoke up. "It was I, not that there was much family property, but I did drive my younger brother from our home. Can you help me, holy monk?"

"I can help you, but I don't know whether it will stop this thunder and lightning. At any rate, you must bring your younger brother back within three days," ordered the monk.

"I will truly bring him back within three days," promised the man.

The rain and the thunder and the lightning continued as before. The room was like an oven, and yet there was an air of peace as every person seemed to draw around the monk.

"What would happen if Cloud Dragon's uncle repented," queried Chen Liang, who was close by Ji Gong.

"Watch," replied the monk. "In a little while we may know."

Then they saw a Daoist walking through the wind and rain. Slowly he came on toward the teahouse while the lightning flashed around him. When he had almost reached the area shaded by the matting, a great bolt of lightning struck the man. His face was brightly lit for a moment. He turned toward the north and fell to the ground dead. For a few moments, flames arose from his body. Then as suddenly as the storm had begun, it stopped. Above, the sky was clear and blue. In the west the sun sank toward the horizon, making the sky in the west red.

Chen Liang went out and looked at the dead body. He recognized the face of Cloud Dragon Hua's uncle, Hua Qingfeng.

"Lei Ming and Chen Liang," said the monk, "I have here a letter and a piece of medicine. I want you to follow the Changshan road toward Dianzhou prefecture. Five *li* before one reaches the prefecture there is a village called Five Li Marker Village. In the door of the temple there, you will see a tall man standing. Give him this medicine to take. Also give him the letter and tell him to carry out the instructions in it. On your way, be careful to mind your own business. If you do not, there may be grave consequences."

"And where shall we see you again?" asked Chen Liang.

"Probably at Dianzhou prefecture," replied the monk. "When you reach the prefecture, keep your eyes open and remember what you see—but don't try your hand at solving anything! If you act, things will no longer be in an undisturbed condition." As Lei Ming and Chen Liang listened to what the monk said, it seemed as if he were half swallowing and half spitting out his words. They took the medicine and the letter and left.

They followed the highway until they were outside the north gate of Changshan. It was growing late, and Chen Liang said, "Let us stay at the inn ahead." They went in and engaged a three-section room on the north side of the courtyard. After they had eaten and drunk, Chen Liang slept.

Lei Ming went out into the courtyard to cool off. "Everyone in the inn is sleeping and there is not a breath of wind in this courtyard," he thought. "There must be a breeze above." He leapt up onto the roof. He was just about to lie down, when suddenly he heard someone call out, "Murder! Murder!"

"It must be a highway robbery," thought Lei Ming. Blade in hand, he went to look for the source of the sound until he came to a building with courtyards on all four sides. There he saw a light in the north building. Again he heard a voice cry, "Murder!" It came from inside that building. Lei Ming leapt down, made a hole in the paper window, and looked in. His hair stood on end. He gripped the handle of his blade, ready for anything.

CHAPTER 79

Lei Ming hears a third cry for help; Chen Liang closely questions a woman's evidence

WHAT Lei Ming saw through the hole in the paper was a brick platform bed on the north side of the room. Next, on the east wall, was a tall clothes cupboard. In front of it was an "eight immortals" table with some chairs. Everything in the room was neatly arranged. On the bed lay a woman a little over twenty years old. She was wearing a simple blue gown and slippers. She had no powder or rouge on her face.

Nearby stood a young man about twenty years old, with his hair dressed in the "beef-heart" style. He was wearing white clothing. His yellowish face was somewhat ugly in features and expression. His left hand held the woman by her hair and in his right hand he held a sword. He was saying, "You must tell me the truth. If you don't tell me the truth, I will kill you slash by slash."

Lei Ming heard the woman say, "A fine one you are, Second Tiger! I was burning paper and I called up a demon! What have I done to you to make you take a sword to me?"

Lei Ming grew more and more angry as he listened. He wanted to go into the room, but he thought to himself, "I must not be too rash. Chen Liang is always telling me to be more prudent. I will go back and talk it over with him and ask him whether we should do something about this or not." Having decided, he went back over the roof and returned to their room.

There he nudged Chen Liang, saying, "Wake up."

"What are you waking me for?" asked Chen Liang.

"I saw something just now. I went up on the roof because the weather was so hot. I had been in the courtyard trying to cool off, but it was hot there, so I climbed on the roof to catch the breeze. Just as I did, I heard someone call out, 'Murder!' I thought that it was a highway robbery and I followed the sound until I reached another courtyard. There I saw a man threatening a woman. She said something, but I didn't understand what she meant. I thought of going in, but I was afraid you would say I was rash. I wanted to ask you whether we should pay attention to the matter or not. What do you say?"

"Lei Ming," responded Chen Liang, "you were wrong. You had no reason to go up on the roof and let the inn people see you, but that doesn't matter. About this other business—if you didn't know about it, it wouldn't bother us. Since we do know, however, if we don't do something about it, we will regret it. Let us go and see what's happening." Chen Liang got dressed and the two went out together without waking anybody in the inn. They crossed the roofs to the other courtyard.

Again there was a cry for help. The two went down into the courtyard, crouched by the lighted window, and looked inside. Then they heard someone say, "Second Tiger, you have cheated me and now you want to kill me. I really did burn paper and bring up a devil! Why don't you let me go? Help, someone, quickly!"

"If you shout," the man said, "I will kill you!" Bringing the sword closer, he scratched the woman's face, which became bloody. She began to cry and again called, "Help!"

Seeing this, Chen Liang jumped up and said to Lei Ming, "Come with me!" The two men pushed the door open and sprang into the room. "My friend," Chen Liang asked, "Why are you threatening this woman with a sword at the third watch near midnight?"

The man turned his head and seeing what kind of men the two were, as well as Lei Ming's red hair and blue face, he lowered his sword and asked, "What are your honorable names?"

Chen Liang answered, "Chen" and Lei Ming said, "Lei." As the man heard their names, he seemed more reasonable. "We two are originally from Jajiang," continued Chen Liang. "We are escorts passing through. We heard the call, and at first thought there was a robbery. Because we have always been helpful to other people, we burst into the room. My friend, what is your name and why are you threatening this woman with your sword?"

"So you are escort officers," commented the man. "Since you ask, my name is Son and I am called Second Tiger. Our home is in the Son Family Village, a small place of about eighty homes with the Son name. There are few outsiders. This woman is my sister-in-law. My brother had a medicine shop. He died three years ago and she was childless, but look at her big stomach now! I want to know how this came about. She cried out. It was for this reason that you two officers were disturbed."

"This is other people's business. Why should we be disturbed?"

thought Chen Liang. He said, "We are all ordinary people. Let's just for-get about this."

"Since you have no wish to call others, I'll be off and leave you two here," said Second Tiger.

When Chen Liang heard this, he thought, "How can this be? That is no way for the rascal to speak."

"Don't leave," said Lei Ming. "Why should you go and leave us here? That is no way to talk."

Looking at the two, Second Tiger did not dare to argue or seem to take offense. "Then let us leave together," he quickly said.

Lei Ming and Chen Liang started to step outside, but the woman spoke up saying, "Don't go yet, gentlemen. He is not telling the truth."

Chen Liang stopped to listen and asked, "What is not true?"

"My husband was named Son and kept a well-known medicine shop. He did die three years ago. When we were first married, I never heard anything about Second Tiger. Then something was said about a younger brother. He did not often come to see the family when my husband was alive. It was like burning paper and calling up a devil unexpectedly. One day in October, I was standing in the gateway and I saw him. He had hardly anything to wear and I asked, 'Second Tiger Son, why don't you have any warm clothing?' He replied, 'Sister-in-law, I don't have the money to buy clothes.' I thought that it was pitiful. I asked him in. Then I wrapped up my husband's clothing and gave it to him. I also gave him some money and told him to set himself up as a small merchant. Afterward, he was always out of money and he came to borrow some again and again. You open your door to do a good deed, and it goes on from there. He wanted me to sell the house to get more money. I cursed him and drove him out. Today my servant had asked leave to go home and Second Tiger came and threatened me. As for my big stomach, that is caused by illness. I called out, but no one came until you did. I don't even think he is my hus-band's actual brother."

Just then a woman said, "Did you call, mistress? What is it?"

Chen Liang saw an old gray-haired woman. Her face was covered with scars from smallpox. Her eyes were squinting and she had a misshapen nose. Some of her yellow teeth were missing.

"Second Brother Son," said Chen Liang, "come in and sit down."

"You two go back your hotel room," said Second Tiger. "I'll be off and thank you another day."

"You need not thank us," said Chen Liang. "Just go home."

"I still want to go into the city," said Second Tiger.

"How can you go through the city gate at this time of night?" asked Chen Liang.

"The wall has a weak spot," the man replied. "I can go in." Saying this, he left.

Chen Liang and Lei Ming did not knock at the inn gate, but returned to their room by the same route that they had left it.

"Well, we saved a person," said Chen Liang, "and tomorrow we will be on our way, though I fear that there may be consequences."

"It is nothing," said Lei Ming and so they both slept peacefully.

The next morning when they got up Chen Liang said to the porter, "We are going to Dianzhou prefecture. Is this the highway?"

"Yes," replied the porter.

"Quickly bring us something to eat and drink," said Chen Liang. "As soon as we finish eating, we will be on our way."

After they had finished eating and had paid their bill, they were about to leave. Meanwhile, outside two headmen had arrived bringing with them eight underlings. They were officers of the Changshan yamen. "Greetings," they had said to the manager of the inn. Then they asked, "Do you have staying in a room in your inn one named Lei and one named Chen?"

"They are in the north room," replied the manager.

"Would you call them?" asked the officer.

"Honorable Lei, Honorable Chen," the manager called out. "There is someone asking for you."

"Who is it?" the two asked as they came out.

"Are you two gentlemen named Lei and Chen?" asked the officers.

"Yes," they answered.

"You two have been accused," said the officer.

"Who accused us?" asked Chen Liang.

"You need not ask," said the officer. "Just now the prefect gave us a warrant ordering you to appear. Whatever you have to say you can say in the yamen."

The manager of the inn stepped forward and asked, "Can you tell what this is all about? I am concerned, too. These two are guests at my inn. It is my affair also. Don't leave yet."

"We cannot stay," said the headmen. "The prefect has issued a warrant. We have no choice. These two must come to court. You can find out about it later. Honorable Lei and Honorable Chen, we must go."

Lei Ming and Chen Liang still did not know what this was about. However, they were brave men and not afraid of anything that might happen to them, and they knew that one could not bargain with fate. "Manager," said Chen Liang, "you need not worry. We are not guilty of murder. There are all sorts of affairs. We don't know what this is about. There must be some mistake. Whatever it is, it will not involve your inn."

"Since you are willing to go, I will not worry, but take good care of them, headmen!"

"Yes," replied the headmen.

They left the inn and in a short time were at the yamen, where they were taken into the audience hall. The two headmen, Zhou Rui and Lo Biao, who might have recognized them, had taken leave and therefore were absent. Lei and Chen bowed to the prefect, who looked at the two angrily.

CHAPTER 80

Second Tiger Son accuses Lei and Chen; a chivalrous stalwart disturbs the court

"YOU two! What are your names? Which of you is called Chen?" The two men gave their full names. Then the prefect continued. "Lei Ming and Chen Liang, you are accused of having immoral relations with the sister-in-law of Second Tiger Son for an unknown number of days!" When Lei Ming and Chen Liang heard these words, their exasperation and anger knew no bounds.

When Second Tiger Son had left them during the night, the rascal had spent the rest of the night getting into the city. Then he took a broken rice bowl and scratched his head and clothing with it. At daybreak he was at the yamen gate making a complaint against them. This was why the prefect had called Lei and Chen to court.

"In answer to your honor," said Chen Liang, "we are Chejiang prefecture men. Lei is my sworn brother. This is the first time we have been in Changshan, and only stayed at the inn here last night. It was very hot, and we were trying to cool ourselves outside when we heard a call for help, 'Murder! Murder!' Since it is our profession to act as escorts, we try to be helpful. We thought it might be a highway robbery. We followed the sound to a courtyard. What we saw was a man threatening a woman with a sword. We then learned that it was Second Tiger Son threatening his sister-in-law. We did not know him, but we persuaded him to leave. We never thought that he would accuse us of having relations with his sister-in-law. We only stayed at the inn last night. If Your Honor does not believe us, ask the people at the inn. We have no connections with the Son family. We have not been here long and do not know them. If Your Honor would call the sister-in-law, she would tell you this is so. In addition, we come from far away and only arrived here last night. How could we have known her? If we had been here ten days or half a month, it would be a different situation."

While they were speaking, the prefect had already sent someone to bring Second Tiger's sister-in-law to the yamen. She had been weeping steadily all morning. While her maid was urging her not to cry, there was a knock at the gate. When the maid answered it, she saw a female officer and two male officers. When the maid asked what the headmen and the woman wanted, they told her that she and her mistress must come to the yamen.

On being told that, the widow said, "Good! Second Tiger has accused me. I was just about to accuse him!" She then hired a sedan chair, and with her maid went to the yamen.

When the prefect saw her, the sister-in-law, kneeling before him, he knew by her greenish complexion that she was either a widow or a woman whose husband had been absent for a long time. "What is your name?" he asked.

"My name is Son," she answered. "My mother's name was Kang. My husband left this life three years ago and I live alone in widowhood."

"Second Tiger has brought an accusation against you," the prefect said. "He says that you have been having immoral relations with Lei Ming and Chen Liang. You see Second Tiger here in court and you must speak the truth."

"I really do not know anyone named Lei or Chen, and Second Tiger is not one of my immediate family, but a demon I called up by burning paper." She went on to tell the entire story of what had happened.

The prefect then ordered that Second Tiger, Lei Ming, and Chen Liang be removed from the audience hall. "Now that there are no outsiders here, I must ask you about your big stomach. What has caused it? If you speak the truth, I must help you. Is it caused by illness or are you going to have a child?"

"Your honor, truly I am sick," she replied.

The prefect ordered that the yamen doctor be summoned. This yamen doctor was half blind, and after he had looked at her, he said, "Your Honor, I see that there is to be a happy event in the future."

When Widow Son heard this, she slapped the doctor in the face, saying, "How can you talk such rubbish! My husband has been dead for three years and I have lived alone since then as a widow. How could I be expecting a child? That is just nonsense coming out of your mouth!"

The doctor listened and replied, "I say you are going to have a child."

"Widow Son," said the prefect, "I ask you now, since you have denied Second Tiger's accusation. Why did Lei Ming and Chen Liang come to your aid?"

"I really do not know anyone named Lei or Chen," she replied, "but when Second Tiger was going to kill me, I called out 'Murder!' and Lei and Chen came. I didn't know them."

The prefect ordered that Lei Ming and Chen Liang be brought into the courtroom. When they came in, the prefect asked, "Lei Ming and Chen Liang, why were you two climbing over other people's roofs in the middle of the night and interfering in things that were none of your business?"

"We two had good intentions. How could we not act to save someone from being killed?"

"Hateful!" exclaimed the widow Son.

"What do you hate?" asked the prefect.

"I hate the fact that these two men do not have a knife!" replied the widow. "Otherwise I would cut myself open and show the court whether I am sick or whether I am going to have a child!"

"You have a lot of gall to talk that way in this court," said Lei Ming. "I have a knife here. You can cut yourself open, and if you are sick, there must be someone who will avenge you. If you are going to have a child, you will know that yourself, as well as who the person was with whom you had relations." With that, he threw the knife on the floor. Widow Son, seeing the knife, was about to seize it, but fortunately the hand of an officer standing nearby was quicker and he picked it up instead.

When the prefect heard Lei Ming's words and saw his action, he was outraged. He pounded his desk and said, "Lei Ming, you are both audacious and reckless! How dare you roar and bluster in the yamen audience hall before the prefect himself! Come men, take him and beat him for me!"

Just then, the prefect saw a note appear on his desk. He opened it and his expression changed completely. He gave a sigh, bowed his head, and said with a smile, "The prefect sees that you are a sincere person with something of a temper. I will have my men fix a table for you two and give you something to eat and drink. In a little while I will come and join you."

Lei Ming and Chen Liang thanked him and left the hall. In a nearby room, a man served them food and wine. "Second Brother," said Chen Liang to Lei Ming, "this is strange! There must be some reason why His Honor is treating us this way. He must have some secret plan to imprison us. I fear we cannot escape."

"I don't understand it at all," said Lei Ming. "Let us finish eating and then see what happens."

What had just happened was that, right after Lei Ming had lost his temper and the prefect opened the note, he saw the following message: "Lei Ming and Chen Liang used to be wicked outlaws who belonged to the numerous men of the Greenwood. Then they reformed their ways and now they have an excellent reputation." As the prefect read these words, he thought that this affair was very strange indeed, and wondered where the note had come from. As he looked at Lei Ming and Chen Liang, the prefect thought that not one of his men could compare with the two. He had Lo Biao summoned. "He would be able to deal with these two," the prefect thought. As he continued to think about the note, he also wondered whether Lei Ming and Chen Liang had been at Ma Ran's estate. He said to himself, "I will have the Tangled Hair Ghost, Yun Fang, brought out and see if he recognizes them. If he does, all the water in the Yellow River will not wash them clean."

Just as he was going to do this, he heard a voice outside say, "Your honor of the night and day! I have a wrong to declare, a bitter wrong!"

As the prefect was about to ask who was outside, he saw Ji Gong walk into the audience hall, leading a scholar. Where had Ji Gong been? After the monk had said goodbye to Lei Ming and Chen Liang, he went on with the two headmen, Chai and She. Soon they saw a sedan chair approaching at a rapid pace.

Once the monk saw it, he exclaimed, "Ai ya! O Mi To Fu! When there are such things, how can one ignore them?" The monk took his two headmen and followed the sedan chair into the village. There they saw it enter a large gate on the north side of the road.

"Old Chai and old She," said the monk, "you two wait outside." The monk entered the gate and said, "Greetings! Greetings!"

One of the household servants came out and said, "Teacher, if you want to beg, go elsewhere. This is not a good time. If you had come three days earlier, it would have been. Just now the master will have nothing to do with Daoists or Buddhists."

"What wrong has the *yuanwai* suffered?" asked the monk. "Tell me about it."

"You are a person who has left the world," replied the servant. "There is no use in telling you, but since you ask, I will tell you. It is the *yuanwai*'s third little wife. Three days ago the time came for her to have a baby, but she has been unable to give birth. We called several midwives, but it was no use. We sent her to her aunt's home in the sedan chair to see if that family could help, but that was no good either. It is often said that small women should not marry large men, but what can we do? The *yuanwai* feels terrible."

"Don't worry," soothed the monk. "Tell your *yuanwai* that I am a monk who can help with giving birth."

"Monk, you're asking a great deal," said the servant. "What family has ever asked a monk to come into the room where a child is being born?"

"You don't understand," said the monk. "I have an unusual medicine that will help in giving birth. When it is taken, the birth takes place immediately afterward."

"In that case," said the servant, "I will relay your request." He went inside and spoke to the distraught *yuanwai,* who at once asked that the monk be brought in. The servant came out and said, "The *yuanwai* invites you in."

The monk went in with the servant to the library. When the *yuanwai* saw before him a poor ragged monk, he asked him to sit down, saying, "Holy monk, do you have a medicine that helps in giving birth?"

The monk nodded his head.

CHAPTER 81

Zhao Yuanwai inquires about cause and effect; Second Tiger recognizes Dr. Xu

"WHERE do you come from, monk? And what is your honorable name?" asked the *yuanwai*.

"I come from the Monastery of the Soul's Retreat on the West Lake. The first character of my name reads Dao and the Second Ji. I am the Ji Dian about whom people often speak. What is the *yuanwai* called?"

"My surname is Zhao," replied the *yuanwai*, "and I am called Dezhong. Just now I heard one of my people say that the holy monk has some subtle medicine that can help a difficult birth. If the holy monk can help in this birth, I would be most deeply thankful."

"I have here a piece of medicine," said the monk. "If you will take it, dissolve it in hot and cold water, and give it to the mother, the child will come forth naturally."

Zhao Dezhong took the medicine and gave it to a servant, explaining clearly what the monk had said. In a little while a woman came into the library, exclaiming, "Great happiness for the *yuanwai*! When the medicine was taken, the child was born. You have a son!"

When Zhao Dezhong heard, he was most happy and said, "Holy monk, you are indeed a good spirit," and ordered that wine be prepared.

"Outside there are two headmen who came with me. They are waiting at the gate," explained the monk.

When the *yuanwai* heard this, he immediately ordered a servant to bring the two headmen inside. Then servants brought food and wine, and everyone sat eating and drinking. "There is something that I truly do not understand," said Zhou Yuanwai. "Perhaps the holy monk could explain it to me."

The monk asked what it was.

"In the beginning, I cared only for myself. I thought of myself as an important person, but in fact, my success came about through the efforts of others. I had three wives and three sons, and I was able to support my family. One day I called my three sons together to teach them about the cotton business. I explained to them such things as when prices were high, you might ask the full price of someone unknown to you but give a discount to a valued customer. I did not tell even them, however, that I had quicksilver in the hollow arm of one set of scales so that I could shift as I chose and move the balance to give short weight to a customer. Then one day, a suspicious customer got very angry during the sale of one thousand pounds of cotton. Then he caught a chill and died. I felt guilty and ashamed and changed my ways.

"Less than a month later, my oldest son died and his bride-to-be married someone else. The funeral was hardly over when my second son died as well. Less than two months later, my third son died. My three sons are all dead. Tell me, Monk, how can I become a good man and avoid evil?"

The monk laughed and told him, "Your first son was a taker of drugs. You are lucky that he died. Your second son was headed toward bankruptcy. Your third son would have brought you all sorts of harm through his evil ways and you would have been a friendless beggar in your old age. Heaven is not blind. You have turned toward good ways and this makes you the best of men. Your newborn son will now be a joy to you, and all will be well."

As Zhao Yuanwai listened, it was as if he were waking from a dream. "Holy Monk," he said, "you have taught me how to live. Now I have a son and can continue."

"Your son will lead you toward the light," the monk said. "You need only keep on in your changed condition."

"Very well," said Zhao Yuanwai, "but now please, Holy Monk, keep on eating and drinking."

When the group had finished eating it was late, and the monk, together with the headmen, were invited to stay the night. In the morning the monk rose as soon as it was light, and the three men went on their way toward Changshan.

At the crossroads just inside the Changshan city walls, they saw near the doorway of a two-story house about twenty waiting men arguing and wrangling among themselves.

"What are you doing here?" the monk asked.

"We are waiting to be examined," one of the men answered. "Master Xu, who lives here, is a famous doctor. In one day he will see twenty patients but no more. Those who come earliest get to see him. We all came early and have been waiting to be seen, but the master has not yet arisen."

"Is that so?" asked the monk. "I will go and call him." With that, he walked into the entrance and shouted, "Hasn't the master of examinations gotten up yet?"

A doorkeeper came out and said, "Don't talk nonsense, monk. Where are there any managers of medical examinations?"

"There are people waiting," said the monk.

"There are no people waiting inside," said the doorkeeper. "The master is here."

"Ask him to come out," the monk said. "I want to be examined for my illness." Just as he said this, the doctor came out. He was wearing a brilliant blue robe with a silken sash to hold it together and a blue scholar's kerchief tied over his hair knot. On his feet he wore shoes with a pattern of bamboo leaves. This was the local doctor. He had just arisen, and hearing the shouting, stepped outside. When he saw that it was a poor ragged monk, Dr. Xu asked, "Monk, what is the matter?"

"I want to be examined for my illness," replied the monk.

The doctor thought to himself, "I will give him a quick examination and that will end this." He took the monk's hand and looked at it.

"Don't look at my hand," said the monk. It's not my hands that are bothering me—it's my head."

The doctor looked at the monk's head for some time and then said, "You have no illness, monk."

"I have!" countered the monk.

"I see that everything is in order, monk—you are not sick!"

"I am sick," said the monk, "and not only that, you are sick as well. However, I have no way of curing your sickness."

"What illness do I have?" asked the doctor.

"There is a devil in your belly," answered the monk.

"Monk, you are talking nonsense!" the doctor said in an annoyed tone.

"Nonsense!" exclaimed the monk. "Now we have a disagreement that we must take to the yamen to be resolved." With that statement he grasped the doctor by the sash and dragged him away.

The crowd tried to stop him. "What is the argument?" they shouted.

"Pay no attention," said the monk. If the monk could not drag someone off, no one could. He was very strong. He went straight to the Changshan yamen, where he called out, "Your Honor, lord of the night and day, hear my grievance!"

Just as the officers were about to stop the monk, the prefect recognized Ji Gong and ordered that the Widow Son be taken from the audience chamber. He then said, "Please sit down, holy monk." He also recognized Doctor Xu, who had been at the yamen previously to treat illnesses. "What problem does the holy monk have with Dr. Xu?"

"Since Your Honor asks," replied the monk, "I will tell you. Last night I was sick while I was at the house of Zhou Yuanwai. He noticed that I was sick and told me to see the famous Dr. Xu. I walked twenty *li* by myself to reach the town walls of Changshan and went to Dr. Xu's house. It was too expensive to hire a horse—they wanted six strings of cash to start with, and twenty-four strings to go as far as Wu Lipai. I said that it was too much, that I would walk. Zhou Yuanwai gave me fifty pieces of silver. When I got to Dr. Xu's house this morning, he asked me whether I had silver. I said that I did, and took out the fifty pieces of silver on the table. He took the money and looked at me, said I was not sick, and told me to go. I asked him to return my money. He would not give it to me. That is my complaint against him."

When the prefect heard what the monk had to say, he thought it very strange and asked, "Doctor Xu, why did you cheat the monk out of his money?"

"A doctor would not dare to do such a thing," replied Dr. Xu, "and I truly did not do such a thing. I rose a little late. Just as I got up, I heard someone shout from outside that he was sick. I stepped outside and saw a monk, who asked me to examine him. He was not sick, but he said that he was and that I was sick, too, that I had a demon in my belly. He complains that I took his money, but I never saw any of his money."

"He says that he did not take my money, but he has it in the top of his gown," the monk countered. "Have him untie his sash and look."

"Dr. Xu, untie your sash," the prefect ordered. The doctor did so and a piece of paper fell to the floor. He stooped to pick it up, but the monk snatched it up first, exclaiming, "Look, your honor!"

The prefect took it and read, "Lei Ming and Chen Liang, two outlaws of the Greenwood, closely associated with the Tangled Hair Ghost." After looking at it, the prefect asked, "Dr. Xu, where did you get this? Where did it come from?"

"I picked it up," answered the doctor.

"You just got up this morning! Where did you pick up?" asked the prefect.

"I picked it up in the courtyard," responded the doctor.

"How could that have happened so conveniently!" exclaimed the prefect.

"Your Honor," said the monk, "call Widow Son into court."

The prefect had the widow summoned. As soon as she saw the doctor, she exclaimed, "Brother Xu, you are here!"

"And why are you here, Madam?" the doctor asked.

"Widow Son," asked the prefect, "How do you know the doctor?"

"In answer to your honor," the widow replied, "When my husband was alive, he kept a medicine shop. The doctor was his sworn brother. When my husband was sick, he attended him. When he died, Dr. Xu helped me with the funeral. Afterward I said to him, 'I am grateful for your help. However, I have something to ask you. Please do not visit me. Do not come to my house.' From that time on he did not come to the house. This is how I knew him."

The monk then asked that Second Tiger be brought into the audience chamber. When he came into the audience chamber, he exclaimed, "Uncle Xu, you are here!"

"Second Tiger," said the prefect, "Dr. Xu was your elder brother's sworn brother. Why do you call him uncle?"

"That's right," answered Second Tiger. "Dr. Xu was my elder brother's sworn brother. Before, I used to call him brother, but since I borrowed money from him several times I have called him uncle. I asked to borrow ten strings of cash and he lent me ten strings of cash. Then I asked for eight thousand cash and he lent me eight thousand. I couldn't call him brother after that, so I call him uncle."

"Have them all taken out of the hall," suggested the monk. After they were gone, the monk said, "Now bring in Second Tiger alone."

When Second Tiger returned alone, the monk addressed him. "Second Tiger, Dr. Xu has just made a full confession. Will you talk now? Otherwise the prefect will have you squeezed."

The prefect thought that this was a good idea and was about to have Second Tiger squeezed between boards when he started to talk. "You need not punish me. I will tell you all." Then he told the whole story of what had happened from beginning to end.

CHAPTER 82

Second Tiger explains the young doctor's illness; Lei Ming and Chen Liang lose their pants

"FIRST of all," Second Tiger explained, "I am not actually the widow's brother-in-law, but her late husband's nephew. This affair all started when I began borrowing money from Dr. Xu. One day he said to me, 'You are a rich man, Second Tiger.'

"'How am I a rich man?' I asked.

"'Your father's younger brother died,' he replied. 'You only need to persuade his widow to move. Her house is worth thirty thousand silver pieces. She would take ten thousand and give ten thousand to her relatives. You would get the remaining ten thousand. Doesn't that make you a rich man?'

"But man schemes and heaven decides. I went to my uncle's widow. As soon as I tried to talk to her about it, she cursed me and would not let me talk about the matter. Afterward, Dr. Xu kept asking me about it, and each time I told him I hadn't been able to talk her into selling her house. Then an idea came to me about what Dr. Xu must be thinking. He was thinking that now that my uncle was dead he wanted his widow. Then I approached him and said I wanted to talk with him. I told him what I thought he was thinking. He denied having such thoughts, and said that he just wanted me to be rich, that he hadn't thought of marrying my aunt. Then I questioned him further. He said, 'I'm afraid she wouldn't want me!' I told him I would be willing to talk the matter over with her, and he agreed to my doing so.

"After I had gotten that far with him, I often borrowed money from him until one day he said, 'Second Tiger, you often come to borrow money from me, but are you still talking with your brother's widow?'

"I replied, 'You might as well give up hope. My uncle's widow will never marry anyone!'

"Dr. Xu said, 'I have watched her go out to buy thread and have noticed her big stomach. There has to be a reason for this physical change. I will give you a sword. You take it with you and go and ask her the reason for her big stomach. If she tells you that it is the result of a secret affair with someone, you drive her out. Aren't you able to do something about such things?'

"I thought to myself, he is right! I took the sword and I went to my aunt's house when her maid was away. Just as I was questioning her, Lei Ming and Chen Liang came upon us and drove me away.

"When I told Dr. Xu what had happened, he said to me, 'Never mind—you can spend the night here.' Then he had me scratch my hand and clothing with a broken bowl and told me to make a complaint at the yamen against Lei Ming and Chen Liang. This is the true story from start to finish."

Second Tiger was then taken from the courtroom.

The prefect had had the clerk write down what Second Tiger was saying. The prefect next had Dr. Xu brought in to listen to the clerk read the record. The doctor's face turned pale with fright. The prefect struck his desk with his hand and exclaimed, "Dr. Xu, you are a scholar, a man of books. How dare you plot against a widow, making a relative of hers an accomplice! You know that such things are forbidden! Do you wish to be punished or do you wish to pay a fine?"

"What will happen if I ask to be punished, and what will happen if I ask to pay a fine?" queried the doctor.

"If you choose only to be punished, I will have you very, very severely beaten, one hundred strokes with a ruler, but sparing your face. If you choose to pay the fine, you must pay three thousand gold pieces to erect an arch praising the Widow Son for her chastity," explained the prefect. "But you must still be lightly beaten ten strokes with the ruler."

"Then I choose to pay the fine," replied the doctor. The prefect immediately ordered that the sentence be carried out. The doctor was beaten ten strokes and a court officer was told to collect the fine.

Next the prefect ordered that Second Tiger be brought back into court. "Second Tiger," said the prefect, "you were a party to this evil plot. You threatened this widow with a sword and you accused two people for no reason. Come, my men, give him forty blows with the big bamboo! He will then wear the wooden collar for one hundred days."

The prefect then said, "What shall we do about the widow's big stomach?"

"She is about to deliver," said the monk.

"Do not joke with me, Holy Monk. She has been a widow for three years. How can this be?" asked the prefect.

"If your honor does not believe me," said the monk, "have her sent to a special room."

"This is not to take place in court," said the prefect.

The monk gave a female officer a piece of medicine and had her take it and the woman to a separate room. The female officer gave the medicine to the widow and she immediately produced a tumor. It was as large as a melon. The female officer brought it in to the court to show to the prefect.

"Take it away," said the monk.

"What was that?" asked the prefect.

The monk explained that it was a tumor. "It grows month by month just as a child does."

The prefect finally understood, and ordered that the widow be sent home. "And what about these two men, Lei Ming and Chen Liang?" the prefect asked. "Lei Ming affronted the court and drew his knife. I was about to have the Tangled Hair Ghost brought in."

"That day I left here," said the monk, "I put a folded piece of paper in your desk. If Your Honor would look at it now, he would understand."

The prefect looked in his desk and, of course, found the folded piece paper. He opened and read what was written on it. "When Your Honor reads this, he will understand that certain men are not outlaws. They fought bravely in defense of Ma Ran's home and they are my followers, Lei Ming and Chen Liang."

When the prefect read the note, he understood everything, and said, "Oh, all the time they were followers of this holy monk. I did not know that." He at once issued an order that the false charges that had been made should be stricken from the record. He then summoned Lei Ming and Chen Liang from the interrogation room. The prefect returned to Lei Ming the knife that had been taken from him and gave ten silver coins to the two men.

Lei Ming and Chen Liang bowed to their teacher. The monk said to them, "I told you two men to go and carry out an order, but you could not mind your own business."

"If Teacher had not come forward, we two would not have escaped the rack," said Chen Liang.

Lei and Chen thanked the prefect, said goodbye to the monk, and left the yamen. They walked on until the sun was sinking in the west. Just before them they saw a village and a street stretching from east to west. On the north side were inns; on the south side were shops. The two men entered one of the inns, called the Three Benefits. A porter led them to a room on the north side of a courtyard, filled a basin with water for them to wash, and brought tea. The two asked for prepared dishes and wine. After finishing eating and drinking, since they were tired from their journey, they took off their clothes and slept.

Early the next morning they rose. When Lei Ming looked around, his pants were gone but nothing else was missing. "Old Three," Lei Ming asked Chen Liang, "did you hide my pants?"

"No," answered Chen Liang.

When he looked around, Chen Liang found that his pants were gone also. "Strange," said Chen Liang, "my pants are gone, too."

The two sat for a moment, thinking that they should call the porter but unwilling to say that their pants were missing. "Let's just call the porter and, no matter how much they cost, ask him to buy us two pairs of pants."

When they called the porter and told him what they wanted him to do, he said, "If you want to buy pants, you're in luck. Just now another guest gave me two pairs of pants and asked me to pawn them or sell them. He wanted twenty silver coins for them. I hadn't any place to sell them. I thought that he was a little crazy."

"Bring them here and we will look at them," Chen Liang said.

The porter left, and in a little while returned with the pants. When Chen Liang looked at them, he saw that they were their own. The porter thought to himself, "How is it that these two men are without their pants?"

"Porter," asked Lei Ming, "where is the room of the seller of these pants? Take us to have a look."

The porter nodded his head and took them to a nearby courtyard. As they walked into the center, they heard someone speaking with a southern accent. "Aiyah! That mixed-up porter! He's not back yet? Where did he take those pants to sell them?"

"This is the room," the porter said.

Lei Ming and Chen Liang quickly entered the room. They saw opposite the door a man in a blue gown sitting in a chair beside a table. His face was pale, and he seemed like a refined young man.

Lei Ming looked at him and said, "What do you think you are doing? Playing a joke on us two?"

This young man's surname was Liu and his personal name was Rui. He was among the thirty-six friends of the Jade Mountain and a sworn brother of Lei Ming and Chen Liang. He was refined in his behavior and elegant in his tastes, but he loved to play jokes. His mother had told him that he must attend a birthday party for Yang Ming's mother, and on his way there he had stopped at the Three Benefits inn for several days.

Because he had heard of an evil bully, Wu Kun, called the Shadow-Seizing Shining Star, Liu Rui wanted to investigate this rowdy's behavior. If Wu Kun really was an evil bully, Liu Rui wanted to rid the place of him. Although he had stayed at the inn for several days, he still had not found out anything.

When Lei Ming and Chen Liang had arrived the day before, he had intentionally played a joke on them. This morning when Lei and Chen came in, Lui Rui greeted them, saying, "Second brother Lei and Third Brother Chen, how good it is to meet you again!"

"Brother Liu," asked Chen Liang, "why are you staying here?"

"I am obeying my mother's command that I go and visit Elder Brother Yang," replied Liu Rui.

"We just parted company with him the day before yesterday at Chang-shan," explained Chen Liang. "He is going home. He will probably be there in one or two days."

"How did you three happen to be together?" asked Liu Rui.

Chen Liang let out a long sigh and said, "Words can hardly tell the story." He explained about Cloud Dragon Hua and what the three friends had been through.

Liu Rui listened to the whole account and exclaimed, "That Cloud Dragon Hua has lost all human feeling! To behave as he did after being a guest of Yang Ming, who treated him so well! Yang Ming must have suffered from his ingratitude. If I see Cloud Dragon Hua, I will bring his miserable life to a close!"

"Let's not talk about him," said Chen Liang. "What are you doing now?"

"I have heard that there is an evil bully in the neighborhood here and I would like to search him out," replied Liu Rui.

"Well, let the two of us go with you to find him," said Chen Liang.

The three went back to Lei's and Chen's room and had breakfast. Then they left the inn and walked out of the village and along the highway. They had not gone very far when they met a man trying to hang himself. He was saying to himself, "Oh cruel heaven, sightless Buddha! Heaven and earth without eyes or ears! An end to it, an end to it!"

The three saw a man not yet forty years old in a simple gown, with a four-sided kerchief tied over his topknot.

"My friend," said Chen Liang, "why do you want to die? What is the reason? Tell us."

"Life is worse than death," answered the man. "Since you ask, I will tell all."

CHAPTER 83

Lei Ming and Chen Liang rob the robber;
a journey through clouds leaves no footprints

"MY surname is Yen," began the man, "and I am called Wenhua. I came from Danzhou prefecture. From an early age I was poor at book learning. I was only able to learn to paint. This year, because of the lawlessness in the provinces, I came here and stayed at an inn, going out to peoples' houses and painting pictures for them.

"One day I went to the home of the Wu family. A senior member of the family, Wu Kun, known as the Shadow-Seizing Shining Star, called to me and asked what kind of pictures I could paint. I said that I was able to paint landscapes, people, animals, trees, birds, and flowers. He asked if I could paint people fleeing from fires. I said I could do that, too, and he asked me to paint several pictures of that sort.

"As soon as he saw the pictures, he was very pleased and asked how much I wanted for all of them. I asked for a string of cash. 'Tomorrow I will come to see you in your hotel,' he said. The next day he came riding on a horse. I had only a single room at the inn and no other place to go. When he came in, he saw my wife and daughter. My daughter turned seventeen this year and is rather attractive. Who would have thought that he had a secret evil plan in mind when he began to talk to me about my opening a shop! He let me have two hundred silver pieces to get started. I thought it was a fine idea at first, and opened a picture shop on the north side of the village street. We lived behind the shop and I sold him a great many paintings.

"Yesterday, after the shop had been open for two months, he came there again on his own horse. He had a golden coronet and a pair of golden bracelets. He asked me to keep them in my shop until he came to pick them up a little later on. 'What does it matter?' I thought. He did not come in again yesterday and I put the three pieces in a cabinet in the shop. This morning he came to get the things. I opened the cabinet and they were gone. Nothing else had been touched.

"His manner immediately changed. He said that I had taken them, and he had his men beat me. He took my wife and daughter away as security. 'Go and buy the things back,' he ordered. Otherwise, he said that he would not return my wife and daughter. I certainly had no intention of taking his things. I did not dare to provoke him. This is why I decided that death is better than living."

As the three listened, they became more and more angry. "Do not die," said Chen Liang. "Take us with you to your home. We have a way to solve your difficulty."

The artist Yen nodded his head in agreement and went with the three friends to his shop. "Put your things in order here," said Chen Liang. "Tonight we will go and get your wife and daughter and bring them back to you. We will also give you some money. Would you then be able to run away from here?"

"If you could bring back my wife and daughter, I would be glad to leave this place."

"You must wait until the third watch," said Liu Rui, "and then we will see you."

The three left and went to have a look at the walls surrounding the Wu household property. The estate was very large. Each of the four sides was about four *li* long. Sharp spikes topped the walls. Outside the walls was a moat with willow trees planted at the edge. The gate in the south wall was open. Inside they could see several evil-looking servants. Outside the gate was a drawbridge. On the north side was another small gate.

Having memorized the approach to the estate, the three returned to their inn and called for food and wine. After dinner they waited until the second watch, when everyone in the inn was asleep. The three then put on their black clothing. Each one carried at his waist a bag tightly packed with a set of ordinary clothing. Then they stealthily left the inn.

Three *li* away from the village they arrived at the Wu estate. They used a flexible ladder to scale the wall. Once on the rooftops they could see the entire estate. Everything was arranged in the best of taste. Creeping cautiously about, they came at last to a courtyard with buildings on each of its four sides. On the north and south there were buildings with three sections each and matching two-section buildings to the east and west. In the west-end windows of the northern building they could see the light of a lamp and a person's shadow.

Through small holes made in the paper covering of the lattice windows they could see a woman of about fifty years old seated on a brick platform bed. Beside her was a girl not more than seventeen or eighteen years old and unusually beautiful. Standing about the room were four old women dressed as servants. On a square table, usually called an "eight-immortals" table, there lay, as if ready for the girl to wear, a cap of golden leaves and flowers and two golden bracelets.

One of the old women was talking. "It's for your own good that I am telling you this. You should not be thinking about the fact that you are not able to escape. If you were back at your home, you would be drinking tea made from the cheapest tea leaves and wearing coarse, cheap clothing. Here you will have both fine food and clothes, but you must tell your daughter to stop crying and put on a little powder. Didn't our master really scheme to get you here! If you make the Shining Star angry with you, he will fly into a rage and kill you, both mother and daughter. Whenever Shining Star says, 'Take her!' his people just take whomever he wants. One that was brought here was very bright and lovely. I think he offered her a good many ounces of silver to submit to him. She said, 'I would rather die! Then I would become a ghost.' When she refused him, he became furious and killed her. He buried her in a back courtyard."

As Lei Ming and Chen Liang heard this and understood what was in store for the young girl, one of them pulled Liu Rui close and said, "Come with us." Knives drawn, they burst into the room. The four old women trembled with fright.

"Whichever of you screams will be the first to die!" exclaimed Liu Rui.

"We will obey your order and not scream," said one of the old women.

Liu Rui wrapped the gold jewelry into a bundle. Then the men tied and gagged two of the old women. They ordered the other two to help carry the mother and daughter away. "One scream and I will kill you," Liu Rui warned them again. The two nodded their heads. "We will first take these two home and then return here." Lei and Chen agreed, leading the mother and daughter, while Liu carried the bundle.

They went out through the back gate and straight to the picture shop, where the artist Yen was anxiously waiting. At the sound of a knock at the door Yen came out and saw Liu Rui. Liu had the old serving women bring the wife and daughter inside. He said to the old women, "Originally I had thought of killing you, but since you carried the two captives here, I will not kill you but tie you up and gag you instead. Yen Wenhua, take your wife and daughter and flee. Take this bag of gold jewelry with you. I will also give you thirty silver coins. Be off! I am going back to kill that evil old man."

The artist thanked him, but Liu Rui said, "Do not thank me. While mountains remain and water flows, I shall hope to see you again another year. Until then, the best of luck!" The artist and his family then hurried away.

Liu Rui went back to the Wu estate with Chen Liang and Lei Ming. They looked around for some time until they came to a courtyard containing a large hall of five sections. Inside, lamps were burning. When they looked through the holes in the paper window, they saw in the brightly lit room a man in an embroidered robe sitting beside a table. His oily-looking face had an unusually evil expression. He was holding a fan in his hand.

This was indeed the wicked Shadow-Seizing Shining Star, Wu Kun. He had originally been a native of Four Rivers. His nickname was a term used to describe the North Star on the night when it seemed at its brightest during the year. He had come to this village with his ill-gotten wealth to live a life of ease, and he had not changed his evil ways. Outwardly he made connections with officials and attended the yamen, all the while killing men and carrying off women. There was nothing bad that he would not do.

On this night, while Lei Ming, Chen Liang, and Liu Rui secretly watched and understood the nature of the man, they heard Wu Kun say, "Well, my children," as he called his ruffians, "How late is it?"

A servant answered, "It is not yet the third watch."

Just as this was said, the three watchers saw a rough-looking serving man enter and heard him say, "Master, outside is your old friend the Four Rivers rat, Cloud Dragon Hua. He has come to visit you."

When Wu Kun heard this, he said, "Second Brother Hua? I was just thinking about him. Open the big gate, my children, and lead me forth to meet him."

On the roof Lei Ming and the two others listened carefully. In a little while they saw Cloud Dragon Hua enter.

After Cloud Dragon Hua had fled from the Veiled Mountain, he could think of no place to stay. He thought of going back to Four Rivers, but he had no nest there. He also thought of going back to Jade Mountain prefecture, but he feared that Yang Ming would not accept him. He regretted that his use of poisoned darts had made him such an object of hatred. He felt foolish and dissatisfied. Whatever he did, he felt as if ants were biting him.

Suddenly he thought of Wu Kun and his estate. He liked the idea of spiked walls around the place and thought he could safely take refuge there. He did not dare to go there in the daylight for fear that someone would see him. Therefore he approached the estate this night seeking Wu Kun, and asked the servant to go and announce him.

Wu Kun asked him to come in and sit down, then asked him, "Second Brother Hua! Where did you come from?"

"I can hardly tell you in one word," replied Cloud Dragon. "Since we brothers parted at Four Rivers, I have been through many adventures. I was in Jade Mountain prefecture at the invitation of Yang Ming, where I made a number of friends. Then I was strolling about and I got into such a scrape that now I have nowhere I can go."

"What happened?" asked Wu Kun.

Cloud Dragon then recounted the entire story of how he had stolen the pearl coronet and the jade pendant from the prime minister's estate, how he killed the restaurant manager, and how he had gone to rape the nun but had killed two nuns instead.

"You must live here at my place," said Wu Kun. "If anyone comes to take you, I will be here. You also have an intimate friend who has made his fortune. Did you know that?"

"Who is that?" asked Cloud Dragon.

"Mountain Leopard Dian from a little town in Four Rivers—and now he is rich. He is the close friend of officials and is connected with the yamen. He has many men under him. I hear that he is to be linked to Prime Minister Qin's family by marriage. I know that you were close friends."

"If you don't mind," said Cloud Dragon Hua, "I will trouble Brother Dian with my presence for a while and then I will come back and live with you—but I need some money for expenses."

"Don't worry about that," Wu Kun reassured him. "Children, go to my strong room and get some silver."

Listening on the roof, Lei Ming was thinking that he might take Cloud Dragon and be avenged for all that he had done to them. At the same time, he knew that this was a matter for Ji Gong. Yet he clutched his knife and wanted to kill this foul criminal.

CHAPTER 84

Three sworn brothers surprise the Wu stronghold; an evil star is extinguished

L EI Ming and Chen Liang both wanted to capture Cloud Dragon, but Liu Rui countered, "What are you thinking of, brothers?"

"Come down with us!" urged Lei Ming. "We will capture Cloud Dragon."

"Slowly!" exclaimed Liu Rui. "Not this way, I think. First, there are not many of us and a good many of them; second, we are not on official business and we have no warrant. Where would we take him? Now that we have found him, why must we take him at first sight? He is not doing something evil just now. This is a matter for Ji Gong to handle and not a matter of revenge—besides, we might fail."

Liu Rui's statements seemed reasonable to Lei and Chen. Chen Liang said, "Never mind now. Let's see where he goes." Lei Ming nodded his head in agreement.

They heard Cloud Dragon say, "Brother Wu, you have given me enough. After a few days at Brother Dian's, I will come back to you. With you two I have nothing to fear."

One servant went for the sedan chair. The other passed through a gate in the corner of the courtyard, where he knocked at a door. Inside were two men, Wang the Second and the watchman whose job it was to strike the hours. The watchman and Wang came out with a lantern and unlocked the strong room. Suddenly the lantern disappeared. "Wang, why did you take my lantern?" the watchman called.

"No, I'm still in the room," said Wang. Then, as suddenly as it had disappeared, the lantern was back. In that moment the three men, Lei, Chen, and Liu, had slipped inside and hidden themselves behind a tall chest. The three observed while the watchman was getting the silver, and when the watchman and Wang had gone, helped themselves to some silver as well.

When the watchman went out he locked the door to the strong room. The three men felt about the room and discovered that there were bars on all the windows. "This is bad," said Chen Liang. "We can't get out."

"Never mind," said Liu Rui and he began to mew like a cat.

"You've locked the cat inside," said Wang.

The watchman heard the sound and came back. "I hate that cat," he said vehemently as he unlocked the door. "It's always causing trouble!" He looked about with his lantern in the center of the room, but saw nothing. When he entered the room in the west section, the three men slipped out and went up on the roof. Again Liu made the sound of a cat mewing.

"It went out and now it's on the roof," said the watchman, as he came out and again locked the door. Up on the roof, the three watched as the watchman took the silver to the guest hall and gave it to Cloud Dragon.

The outlaw expressed his thanks and said goodbye. Wu Kun accompanied him outside the big south gate, saying, "After a few days have passed, come back to us, Brother Hua."

Cloud Dragon went on his way and Wu Kun returned. As he stepped through the gate, Liu Rui, who was hiding behind it, suddenly ended the evil man's life with one stab of his knife.

The place was immediately in an uproar. People were shouting, "Catch the murderer!" But the next day they had to report that the guilty man was nowhere to be found.

The three men, having finished their task, returned to the inn and slept soundly. In the morning they rose early. Liu Rui asked, "Where will you two warriors be going?"

"We must go to Chuzhou prefecture to do something for Ji Gong," replied Chen Liang.

"I have several friends I still want to see," said Liu Rui, "so we will part here and meet another day." The three paid their bill and left the inn.

Lei Ming and Chen Liang hurried along the high road to Chuzhou prefecture. Just outside the east entrance to the village called Wuliupai, they saw a temple on the north side of the road. Standing before the gate was a tall man wearing a dark-blue jacket. He was standing unsteadily and repeating in a trembling voice, "Oh dark, dark heaven! Oh sightless gods! Oh heaven and earth! Blind and deaf! Never would I have thought that I could fall into such a condition!"

The two recognized him at once, and approaching, asked, "Brother! What happened?"

"Are you two the demons with the cow's head and the horse's face that have come to take me to hell?" asked the tall man.

"You're mad," said Lei Ming. "We are Lei Ming and Chen Liang."

"Not demons from hell?" asked the man. "Then did you come to take me to the western heaven?"

"Don't you recognize us, brother?" asked Chen Liang. "We are Lei Ming and Chen Liang."

As he began to understand, the man said, "All this time you were my brothers Lei Ming and Chen Liang. I am dying from pain." He turned as he spoke and fell to the ground, motionless.

Chen Liang went to the nearest gate on the village street and knocked. An old man came out and asked, "What do you want?"

"Would you let me have a bowl, old fellow, with a little hot water? I have a Daoist at the temple gate who is very sick. I want to dissolve some medicine and give it to him."

"So that's what it is," said the man. "That big fellow is a friend of yours, sir. He has been there at the village entrance very sick for several days. Up until two days ago we kept giving him some food, but, seeing that he was so much worse in the last two days, we did not dare to continue. If you will wait a moment, sir, I will get the bowl of water."

When he returned with the bowl of water, Chen Liang dissolved the medicine provided by Ji Gong and gave it to the man. In a short time the medicine began to take effect as the man's five organs responded.

At last he was able to sit up and speak. "Dear brothers Chen and Lei, where did you come from?"

"Is Brother Guo better now?" asked Chen Liang.

This man was none other than Guo Shun, sometimes called the Night Demon. He was one of the thirty-six friends of the Jade Mountain. Some time before he had decided to leave the fellowship of the Greenwood and become a Daoist monk, simply wandering from one place to another. He had become ill at the entrance of this old village temple. With no money to stay at an inn, he had grown worse until found by his two friends.

"We were sent by Ji Gong from Dianchang prefecture especially to help you," explained Chen Liang. "We also have a letter to give you which he asks that you read and obey."

It was only when Guo Shun took the letter and read it that he understood everything clearly. "I must go now and assist Ji Gong in carrying out some business," he said as he looked northward. "Do you two have any extra money? I will need some on my journey."

"We have," said Chen Liang and gave him an envelope with some silver.

"I have been a lot of trouble to you two," said Guo Shun. "On another day I must thank my dear brothers again." He then said goodbye and departed.

Lei Ming and Chen Liang hurried on their way to Chuzhou prefecture. Turning north at the first crossroad inside the walls of Wuliupai, they saw a wine shop where a man was raising the bamboo blind at the door. They entered the shop. Noticing a staircase, the two went upstairs. There they could see that it was very light and airy. The two found themselves a table and sat down.

"Will you gentlemen drink?" asked the waiter who approached their table.

"We will," answered Chen Liang.

"If you wish to drink wine, come downstairs," said the waiter.

"Why can't you let us sit upstairs?" asked Lei Ming.

"Today the upstairs table has been reserved for three of our great local gentlemen, whom we call the Honorable Three. Please, sirs, come downstairs to have your wine," the waiter said.

Lei Ming opened his eyes wide and said, "And we two gentlemen would also like to reserve this table."

"Don't become angry, sir," said the waiter. "This is a case of first come, first served. Of course, if you had reserved the upstairs first, we could not give it to someone else."

"Let us not be rude, brother," said Chen Liang. "It's all the same whether we drink downstairs or up."

Lei Ming then followed Chen Liang downstairs and into a room to the rear, where they found a vacant table.

The waiter quickly laid out cups and chopsticks. "And what wine and dishes would you gentlemen like?" he asked.

"What do you have?" the two responded.

"Dumplings," answered the waiter, "boiled, steamed, or fried; northern and southern style dishes of all sorts; anything you would like to order, really—and rose-flavored wine. As well as most other kinds of platters, regular plates, and side dishes. Please order anything you like."

"Fix us four dishes that will go well together, that is, something crispy fried, something steamed and so on, with two pots of old virgin wine—whatever will taste good. Don't worry about the price," ordered Chen Liang.

"Yes," replied the waiter, and immediately passed on the order. In a little while the four dishes and the wine were served.

"What is your name, waiter?" asked Chen Liang.

"My name is Liu," the waiter answered.

"I would like to ask you something," Chen Liang continued. "Is one of these three people who are coming to eat upstairs perhaps the younger brother of the prefect?"

"No," answered the waiter.

"Then why do you call them the Honorable Three?" asked Chen Liang.

"You two gentlemen are not from around here, and there are things you do not know. I will see if they have arrived and then answer your question," the waiter replied. He went out to look and then returned. "They haven't come yet. Now I will tell you what you want to know."

"Tell us then," urged Chen Liang.

In a low voice the waiter began to explain one thing after the other. As the two listened, they could feel their anger rising.

CHAPTER 85

Two heroes observe three sworn brothers; the Crane's Eye kills a man and delivers a present

"THESE men we call the Honorable Three are our local bad characters. They have connections with officials and can even go into the prefect's yamen. No one around here dares to provoke them. They have 180 servants or followers."

"And what are the names of these Honorable Three?" asked Chen Liang.

"One is surnamed Yang," answered the waiter. "His given name is Son and his nickname is the Golden Hawk."

"He must be a younger brother of the prefect—and then there are still younger brothers, aren't there?" said Chen Liang.

"No, they are sworn brothers, each with different surnames. The next is Chen Shanbao, the Mountain Leopard. The third is called the Heron, Yen Chiucheng."

Lei Ming and Chen Liang understood him. As they sat drinking their wine, a household steward came in from outside. He was wearing a cap, and thrown over his shoulders was a crane's-feather cloak. He spoke to the manager. "Are the dishes prepared?" he asked. "The Honorable Three are just about to arrive."

"They are prepared," replied the manager. "Invite the Honorable Three to enter." Lei Ming and Chen Liang looked out. They could see at once that the steward was an evil man. Another evil-looking man then came in and said, "The Honorable Three are here."

The waiter quickly announced to the people eating and drinking: "Everybody stand up! The Honorable Three have arrived!" As soon as the waiter spoke, all the other diners stood up. The waiter then said to Lei Ming and Chen Liang, "I must also ask you two brave gentlemen to stand as well. The Honorable Three have arrived!"

"Why should we stand when the Honorable Three arrive? Are they going to pay for what we eat and drink?" asked Chen Liang.

"No, they won't," replied the waiter.

"Since they are not going to pay for us, we cannot stand up," said Chen Liang.

"I intend well by what I say," said the waiter. "If you do not stand up, it will be terrible."

"I have my own life preserver," said Chen Liang, "and I have never seen anything very terrible yet. Today I would like to see what will happen here."

The waiter, fearing that they were going to provoke a fight, had the other diners stand in front of Lei Ming and Chen Liang. But the pair wanted to see what kind of people these Honorable Three were. With the other diners standing in front of them they could see nothing, so Lei and Chen stood up after all.

The first to come in were two men wearing square blue kerchiefs over their hair knots. They wore splendid blue embroidered robes, but their bent backs betrayed the fact that they had spent the early part of their lives crouched over account books.

The third man person to come in was a tall man dressed in richly embroidered clothes that were neither military nor civil in style, but a combination of each. He had a yellow face, thin eyebrows, and little triangle-shaped eyes. He did not look like a good man.

"Oh, that rascal!" whispered Lei Ming to Chen Liang. "How did he get to be so important? He was one of the Four Rivers gang in Linan."

Chen Liang watched the three as they walked up the stairs. Then he called the waiter over and asked, "Why did everyone stand up when the Honorable Three came in? Are they afraid of them?"

"I will tell you," replied the waiter. "They are related to Prime Minister Qin. Don't say they look like ordinary people. Even the prefect does not dare to cross them. If they are displeased with him, they will write a letter to the Prime Minister and the prefect will be removed and another individual sent to take his place."

"This is unthinkable!" said Chen Liang to himself. Aloud he said to the waiter, "Where do these three honorable gentlemen live?"

"Go north from this restaurant to the end of the street; turn east into the lane. Just inside the lane, the first large gate on the north side is theirs. Above the gate is a large plaque with eight trigrams on it. The place is very large."

Chen Liang had listened very carefully. After the two men had finished eating and drinking and had paid their bill, they left the restaurant, went to the north end of the street, and turned into the east lane. There was the large gate on the north side. Having made sure of their way, the two then found themselves an inn called the Best in Town. It was on the principal street within the city walls and faced east. The two men asked for a western chamber in a north courtyard. Once in their room, the porter brought a basin of water for them to wash their faces and then poured tea.

When he was gone, Chen Liang said, "Well, Brother Lei, you have seen those evildoers. Probably there is nothing bad that they would not do. Tonight let's go and look them over." Lei Ming nodded in agreement.

They waited until the second watch when everything in the inn was quiet. Then they changed into their suits of darkness. When everything was properly arranged, they left the inn and went to the gate in the east lane. There, they crept stealthily over the roofs until they came to a courtyard with a five-section building on the north and similar matching buildings to the east and west. There were four lighted lanterns hanging at the door of the north building and a light within. Lei Ming and Chen Liang came down from the eastern building and looked through the holes in the paper-covered lattice into the northern room. There they saw two servants setting a table.

One of the servants said, "A friend of our masters is coming to see them."

"Who is coming?" asked the other.

"Their sworn brother, the River Rat, Cloud Dragon Hua," replied the first servant. "In a little while our masters will be greeting His Honor Hua and then they will be having dinner in this room."

Lei Ming and Chen Liang heard this conversation distinctly. A short time afterward they saw a light at a corner gate of the north building and two servants appeared, carrying lanterns. Then came four men. The first was Cloud Dragon Hua. Just behind him was the tall man they had seen at the restaurant. Then came the two men with bent backs.

The watchers could hear the one called Dian Guoben speaking. "Brother Hua, ever since we parted so hurriedly and went our separate ways, I have thought of the day when we might meet again. After that little business of yours in Linan, if you had only come here to us right away, I could have sent a letter to the prime minister in Linan. Then the warrant would have been recalled and the monk would have been told to return. The whole case would have been over very quickly, but you didn't come. How could I know what was happening with you?"

"But how could I know where you were?" countered Cloud Dragon. "It was just now when I was with Shining Star Wu that he told me that

Elder Brother lived here. I have a couple of things with me that I would like to give Elder Brother."

"What sort of things?" asked Dian Guoben.

"One is the pearl cap known as the Phoenix Coronet, which I took from the prime minister's chamber," replied Cloud Dragon. "The other is a pair of finely carved jade pendants. These are great treasures. I could hardly sell them to anyone because they are priceless, but I would like to give them to you."

"Dear brother," said Dian Guoben, "you keep them until my birthday when several other men of the Greenwood will come here. Then you can give them to me, and that will make them open their eyes. We have known each other for so many years and have been together so seldom. I have often talked about your exploits to friends, about how you did things that astonished heaven and earth. If you stay here with us, I will write a letter to Prime Minister Qin and have the warrant for your arrest withdrawn."

"How can you associate with the prime minister?" asked Cloud Dragon.

"You don't understand," explained Dian Guoben. "I am a relative. Let me tell you that this little business of yours is nothing to speak of. The prefect before this one did not satisfy me. I sent a letter to the prime minister and he removed the prefect and sent another in his place. The present prefect is named Jiang. A little while after he came, I went to call on him. Not only would he not see me, but he said some rather impolite words. I'm going to send another letter to Prime Minister Qin about him. We are relatives. After my previous letter he sent a reply telling me to keep an eye on things and to write again. I wrote to the present prefect about some things that were happening around here, but he hasn't done anything about them. I've also thought of something else."

Then Dian turned to another person and said, "Brother Chiu, there is a worthless old man in the rear flower garden. You just go back there and nip off his calabash. We'll send it to this prefect of ours." The one named Chiu nodded and went out.

Lei Ming and Chen Liang knew that calabash gourds with their hard tough skins were used everywhere as containers, but in the black language of the outlaws, the word meant a man's head.

At that time a servant came in to report that Cheng Jiyuan and Ho Dongfeng had returned. Dian Guoben ordered that they be invited in. The servant went out and shortly came back in with the two men, one dressed in white, the other in blue.

When they arrived at the guest hall Dian Guoben said, "Dear Brothers Cheng and Ho, you have returned. Now I would like you two to go to the Monastery of the Soul's Retreat on the West Lake at Linan. Find the apartment where the abbot's guests stay and kill everyone. Then come back. Can you do that?"

Both Cheng Jiyuan and Ho Dongfeng said, "That is really a small business. We will be on our way at once."

"Good," said Dian Guoben. "Take some money for traveling expenses and then be off." The two said goodbye.

The Crane's Eye, Chiu, now entered carrying a man's head dripping with blood and saying, "See, elder brother, he is dead."

"Get something to wrap it in and wrap it up well," said Dian Guoben. "Then send it to the prefect's yamen."

In their hiding place Lei Ming and Chen Liang could hear what was being said but could not see what was being sent to the prefect. "Brother, let's follow him," said Chen Liang.

Chiu hurried off, with Chen Liang and Lei Ming secretly following him. At the prefect's yamen Chiu went up on the roofs and past one courtyard after the other. This great maze of courtyards, each surrounded by three or four buildings, contained the audience hall, the rooms for record-keeping, the prison, the guard room, the residence of the magistrate, and places for all the functions of the prefectural government. Finally, Chiu reached the residence of the prefect, a building somewhat grander than the residence of the magistrate.

The prefect slept in the east end of a good-sized building on the north side of a spacious courtyard. There were smaller matching buildings on the east and west. Chiu went to the one on the west that faced east, hung the parcel he was carrying from the eaves, and quickly departed.

Chen Liang and Lei Ming now understood what it was—a threat to the new prefect. It would be the first thing he saw when he awoke, if he looked outside. "Let's take it back and hang it on Dian Guoben's gate," suggested Lei Ming."

"No, our teacher told us to watch and take note," countered Chen Liang. "We are to see it with our eyes but avoid meddling. Let us go back now."

The two then returned to the inn.

The next day when the prefect arose, he saw the parcel hanging from the eaves and called his people to take it down. They did so and then unwrapped it and saw that it was a man's bloody head.

CHAPTER 86

The prefect sends out his men; Ji Gong goes with the magistrate to pay a social call

THE prefect naturally was furious when he saw the head. He immediately sent a message to the magistrate telling him to come at once. The magistrate bowed deeply when he arrived and saw the prefect saying, "The Great One has called for me. What are your orders?"

"Last night in this yamen, here in this courtyard of mine, an outlaw hung a package from the eaves of the west building," the prefect exploded. "Inside was a man's head, dripping with blood. So there is a robber with that kind of gall! I want you, sir, to get your men together, find the guilty man, and bring him here! Find out who was murdered and where the body has been placed!"

When the magistrate had heard the prefect out, he said, "Yes, I will find the murderer. The Great One need not trouble himself. I will have my people catch him."

"You must move quickly, sir," said the prefect. "We will also send some prefectural men."

The magistrate nodded in agreement. He quickly called his headmen together. "You must get this murderer," he ordered them. "There will be a reward of fifty ounces of silver for his capture—and punishments for failure."

The headmen bowed their heads in acknowledgement of the order. They assembled their underlings, together with the people sent by the prefect in a restaurant west of the crossroads. In the back room of the restaurant they were talking together about how to solve the case. All of the waiters were asking what had happened and were told that a man's head had been hung from the eaves of the west building that faced toward the room where the prefect slept, that there was a reward of fifty ounces of silver for success in solving the crime and punishments for failure. Everyone opened their eyes wide saying, "This is a hard case to solve."

Then they heard someone outside say, "It was you who hung that package from the eaves."

Someone else said, "Weren't you the one who told me to do it?" Everyone was silent as they listened.

Just then, in walked a poor ragged monk with two men dressed in boxy-looking, moonlight-gray gowns and jackets. The latter two looked like merchants, but they were wearing four different styles of shoes. The three individuals were, of course, Ji Gong and the headmen Chai and She, whom Ji Gong had led hither and thither in search of Cloud Dragon until their shoes were worn out and they had to put on their feet whatever they could find. However, as strange as the two headmen looked, it was what they had said before they came in that had attracted the attention of everyone.

When the monk had been at Changshan and had sent Lei Ming and Chen Liang on their way, he returned to the house of Xiao Yuanwai, where his two headmen had waited until they had become desperate.

"Holy monk, where have you been?" asked Xiao Yuanwai.

"I went out for a bit," replied the monk. "I saw a man with a bag full of money. The coins kept falling out of a hole in the bag and I followed after him, picking the coins up as I went until I had gone eight *li*."

"You must have had a lot of money by that time," said Xiao Yuanwai.

"I had been following him all this way and picking money up and putting it into a fold of my robe. When I looked to see how much I had, I found that all the coins had fallen out," explained the monk. "There wasn't a single one left."

Upon hearing this, Xiao Yuanwai laughed and ordered food and drink prepared. Then he persuaded the monk to stay overnight.

The next day the monk went to take his leave. "Why can't you stay several more days?" Xiao Yuanwai asked.

"I really have business to which I must attend," replied the monk.

Xiao Yuanwai brought out fifty silver pieces saying, "This is for wine on the road."

The monk handed it back and said, "I don't want it! I don't want it!"

Headman Chai said, "If Teacher doesn't take it, later we will want to eat and stay at an inn and there will be no money. I say we should take it!"

"If you want to, then take it," said the monk, "but wrap it up well into a parcel." Headman Chai then carefully wrapped up the money. Then the monk said, "You two want to capture Cloud Dragon Hua. What talents do you have that will help you?"

"I can fly over a wall," replied Chai.

"Then fly up to the eaves here and hang up this parcel that you wrapped so well," said the monk. "Then I will take you to capture Cloud Dragon Hua."

"That requires no effort," said Headman Chai. He then leaped up and hung the package from the eaves. "Look! It's up there."

"Then let's go," said the monk.

"Shan't we take the money down first?" asked Chai.

"Don't you have any shame?" asked the monk. "Would you really take someone else's money? That's not in the spirit of friendship! Let us go."

"If the monk does not feel hunger, do not we fear hunger?" Chai thought spitefully, but he said nothing.

The monk said goodbye and Xiao Yuanwai followed them politely outside the door. The monk led the two headmen out of Xiao Yuanwai's village, straight to Dianzhou prefecture and up to the restaurant door.

"Let's go in and have a drink," said the monk.

"Go in and have a drink!" exclaimed Chai. "Do we have money?"

"You hung the parcel from the eaves," said the monk, "and you still ask me that question."

"Didn't you ask me to hang it there?" questioned Chai.

"This is a wrong that the soul cannot shake off. I asked you to hang it there," said the monk. "When the gods make a false step, the demons use it. I asked you to hang it there!"

"What's this business about gods and demons?" asked Chai.

"Go on in!" said the monk. And so they went into the restaurant. They sat down and the monk called for food. After the monk had eaten all he could, he looked at the remaining food and said to the waiter, "Wrap it up and we'll hang it from the eaves."

The more the magistrate heard, the more interested he became. Finally he went over to the table where the monk and the two detectives were sitting and asked, "Did you hang the package there from the eaves?"

"It was I who hung it there," replied Chai.

"Good!" exclaimed the magistrate. "You are involved in the case."

Chai started to speak, but the monk interrupted him, saying, "Don't say anything! If we are involved in a case, we don't have the money to pay for the food."

One of the prefect's headmen named Liu said, "I will pay the bill."

Chai said nothing, for he realized the monk was up to his old trick of eating and getting someone else to pay for the meal. When the bill came, it was three ounces and three pieces of silver. Headman Liu again said, "I will pay it. You three come with me."

"Good!" said the monk and followed the others out of the restaurant and on to the magistrate's audience hall in the yamen.

"Friend," said Headman Liu, "tell us all now. You hung a man's head from the eaves. Whom did you kill? Where is the body? Tell us everything."

"Whose head? It wasn't a head!" said Chai. "I don't understand."

"Just now in the restaurant, didn't you say you hung a parcel from the eaves?" asked Liu.

"That's right," answered Chai. "Let me tell you what happened. My name is Chai Yuanlo. He is She Jengying. We two are detectives from Linan. The monk is Ji Gong. The prime minister had the grand protector issue a warrant for the arrest of Cloud Dragon Hua, the River Rat. Yesterday, we were at the home of Xiao Yuanwai. This morning Ji Gong asked us what abilities we had to use in catching Cloud Dragon Hua. I told him that we could fly over a wall. In order to test my ability Ji Gong asked me to hang a package containing fifty ounces of silver from the eaves. If you don't believe me, I have the warrant here."

When Headman Liu heard Chai's account, he thought to himself, "I paid that restaurant bill for nothing," and went to report what he had heard to the magistrate. The magistrate wanted to see Ji Gong at once, knowing that he was a famous monk. He sent word inviting the monk to the library. Ji Gong entered and greeted the magistrate.

"Where does the holy monk come from?" asked the magistrate.

"I come from Linan at the order of the prime minister," responded Ji Gong. "I brought two headmen, that is, detectives, with me. We were ordered to arrest the River Rat, Cloud Dragon Hua. This outlaw stole a pearl coronet and a pair of jade pendants from Prime Minister Qin's house. He killed a man in a restaurant and he also killed a nun while attempting to violate her. This robber is now in your honor's jurisdiction."

"Where?" asked the magistrate.

"In the home of Dian Guoben," answered the monk.

"Is that how it is?" said the magistrate. "My last superior, who told me that Dian Guoben was a relative of Prime Minister Qin, was removed from office. Dian Guoben came to visit me and I asked him who he was. He said he was one of the local people. I said that if he was one of the local people and not an official, he had no reason to visit me. I told him that he could, of course, bring a complaint or a petition to the audience hall and the court would hear him, but that he could not pay a social call on an official unless he were invited to do so. Later I heard that there would be an armed attack on the yamen during the night. I don't know whether that's true or false. Last night a human head was hung from eaves here in this yamen. I think there is some reason for this."

"Don't worry," said the monk. "If Your Honor wants to arrest Dian Guoben, we will arrest him. But there is one thing. If you send your officers and men to take him, you won't be able to. Dian Guoben's place is very large. As soon as word comes, the outlaws will be off like insects in the grass. Your Honor must go to visit him, and I, the monk, will go as part of your escort party. Then we will get him. I can get him myself."

"Can the holy monk do this?" the magistrate asked.

"I can," the monk stated. "Give me an official gown and I will put it on."

As soon as the monk's face was washed, removing the dust of the road that had darkened his features, he was quite handsome and his face was not shadowed at all. He tucked his monk's hat into the fold where his monk's robe crossed over his chest and put on a long black official gown over his own clothes. His hair was gathered into a knot at the back of his head and a yamen runner's black kerchief was tied over his topknot. He exchanged his sturdy monk's sandals for a pair of thin black slippers. The magistrate also changed his own clothes, donning garments suitable for a social meeting. The other yamen people who were to accompany him made similar changes in their clothing.

The magistrate then went outside and got into his sedan chair. When he and those accompanying him arrived at Dian Guoben's home, a servant went in and announced that the magistrate had come to call. Dian Guoben was in the principal reception hall talking with Cloud Dragon Hua when the servant made his announcement.

When Dian Guoben heard that the magistrate was at the gate, he said to Cloud Dragon, "My dear brother, recently I paid a visit to the magistrate, but he did not receive me. Now for no reason he appears. I fear there may be some troubling reason for this."

"Elder Brother need not be concerned," said Chiu, the Crane's Eye. "Probably the magistrate has heard that you are a relative of the prime minister. When he refused to see you recently, he evidently was not aware of that. Now he is, and has come to pay his respects."

Dian Guoben thought that Chiu's statement was reasonable. "You two dear people," he told the other two outlaws, "go into the west building and wait. If anything happens, if they make a move, you can come out and help. Brother Hua, you go into the flower garden and drink some wine while you wait until I have seen the visitors."

The three nodded in agreement and Dian Guoben prepared to meet the magistrate.

CHAPTER 87

The magistrate calls upon the outlaw;
Ji Gong cleverly seizes Cloud Dragon Hua

DIAN Guoben himself went forth to welcome the magistrate. When he reached the gate, the number of people in the magistrate's escort party surprised him. "Welcome, Your Worship," he greeted him. "This rustic person awaits your visit eagerly. You have come in your sedan chair!"

"I have long wished to make the acquaintance of the famous *yuanwai*. This is a lucky meeting," said the magistrate. "There was no need for you to meet us so ceremoniously."

"Please, Great One, enter," Dian Guoben said as he ushered in the magistrate. Ji Gong and the rest of the escort party followed. When they entered the courtyard containing the great reception hall, only the magistrate and Ji Gong entered. "Will the Great One sit down?" invited Dian Guoben when they were indoors. The magistrate sat. Dian Guoben also sat and ordered that tea be served. "Today the Great One has been so kind as to come here. Is there anything you desire?"

"We have heard about the *yuanwai*'s fame and we came to visit," replied the magistrate. Meanwhile, the monk who had been standing behind the magistrate began to nod his head and open and shut his eyes.

"Perhaps it's too late at night," said Dian Guoben. "This great one is tired. Why not go and rest?"

As soon as Ji Gong heard this, he went out of the reception room, making an apology.

To the north of the building was the flower garden. Cloud Dragon was standing at the gate. He had been drinking at a table in the garden, but he had not enjoyed the wine. He kept wondering about the reason for the magistrate's visit. "There must be another reason for his coming here besides a social visit," he thought to himself. "Could he be coming to catch me?" As he stood uneasily in the garden looking around, he saw Ji Gong in his black gown. With the monk's face washed clean, Cloud Dragon did not recognize him. He nodded his head toward him and called over. He was about to ask how many men the magistrate had brought with him and what they were doing.

"Come here, uncle," said Cloud Dragon.

Ji Gong said nothing. Cloud Dragon thought to himself, "This fellow seems rather stupid. Perhaps he is a deaf mute."

Ji Gong stepped into the flower garden, pushing back the two doors of the gate as he exclaimed, "Cloud Dragon Hua, this time you cannot run away!"

When Cloud Dragon Hua recognized Ji Gong's voice, he was more frightened than he ever had been before. "Teacher, why do you want to take me?" he asked.

"I do not actually want to take you. I could have taken you at Ma Jing's home when you were in the little cellar hiding behind the scroll, and I could have taken you a number of other times, but I didn't."

"That's right," thought Cloud Dragon, "but why does he want to take me now?"

"Dian Guoben sent a letter to the magistrate and asked us to come and take you," said the monk.

When Cloud Dragon heard this, he shouted, "That beast with a man's face, brought up by a dog!"

"You must just recognize your fate," said the monk as he pointed, and with his hypnotic power left Cloud Dragon paralyzed.

The monk turned about and left the flower garden. He passed the reception hall and went through a gate into the other courtyard, where the escort group was waiting. There he called to Chai Yuanlo and She Jingying to come to the flower garden. When they got there, he said, "I have just caught Cloud Dragon Hua. Take him and lock him in irons."

Chai and She were overjoyed. All their doubts vanished. This man really was Cloud Dragon Hua. They took their chains and locked them securely around the criminal.

Then Ji Gong went into the building where Cloud Dragon Hua had been staying and came out with the stolen pearl coronet and the jade pendants, which he gave to Headman Chai, saying, "Take these with you. Let us now go to Dian Guoben."

Dian Guoben had once been the leader of a gang in Four Rivers. After many of his men had proved to be involved in crimes, he escaped and fled to Chuzhou prefecture. He had brought a great deal of silver and with it he was able to purchase a large estate. With his two friends, Yang and Chiu, he had committed many crimes.

Prime Minister Qin's father had been named Wang, but when a eunuch who was the prime minister at the time adopted him, he naturally took the name of the eunuch and therefore was known as Qin Kui. Prime Minister Qin Kui had a brother named Wang Xien. When Wang Xien came to Chuzhou to collect taxes, Dian Guoben learned that Wang Xien had no interest in antiques or picture scrolls. He cared only for beautiful women.

Dian Guoben purchased an exquisitely beautiful young virgin named Jade Orchid for three thousand silver pieces. He had the girl brought before him and told her, "Jade Orchid, I am thinking of using you to make contact with powerful people. I would like to give you in marriage to the brother of Prime Minister Qin, but I don't know how you would feel about this."

Jade Orchid answered, "I will do whatever the *yuanwai* wishes."

"Tomorrow I shall invite Wang Xien to dinner. Put on a simple gown and come into the reception hall, pretending that you need to speak to me. Make sure that he sees you. If he asks about you afterward, I will say that you are my younger sister living here under my protection. Then, if he wishes, I will give you to him in marriage. You will be a rich woman. And I will become a powerful person with connections to the prime minister."

Jade Orchid agreed to this plan.

The next day Dian Guoben invited Wang Xien to dinner. He accepted the invitation. While they were drinking and talking together, Jade Orchid, very nicely dressed in a simple gown, came to the doorway of the room and asked, "Is the *yuanwai* here?" Just as she raised the bamboo curtain and looked into the room, she exclaimed, "Oh! There is a guest in this room! Those maids never told me!" She looked at Wang Xien and then quickly looked away and left.

"Who is that person, Dian Yuanwai?" asked Wang Xien.

"That is my younger sister," replied Dian Guoben. "Her husband died less than a month ago. Now she is staying here with me."

"Why doesn't the *yuanwai* give her to me?" asked Wang Xien. "She could be my concubine."

"It would not be proper for me. I can hardly give her to you," replied Dian Guoben.

Wang Xien said nothing more about the matter. He finished eating, said goodbye, left, and went back to the house where he was staying. There he said to one of his people. "I have never seen such a beautiful woman as that sister of Dian Guoben! I would like to have her!"

"Let me go and talk with him," said the man. "I will tell him of your wishes and no doubt he will be willing."

"Good!" exclaimed Wang Xien. "If you succeed, I will give you two hundred pieces of silver."

"I will go, then," said the man. As soon as he arrived at Dian Guoben's house and said that Wang Xien begged for his sister, Dian Guoben agreed to the arrangement.

After Wang Xien and Jade Orchid were married, Dian gave Wang Xien a letter saying that the prefect was unsuitable for his office. Wang Xien gave it to the prime minister when he next saw him. The prime minister promptly recalled the prefect and sent a new man in his place.

The new prefect did not suit Dian Guoben either, and he sent off a second letter to the prime minister. When Prime Minister Qin read it, he said to his brother, "What about this relative of yours? I changed the prefect once! Doesn't any prefect satisfy him?"

Wang Xien wrote to Dian Guoben telling of his disappointment and advising him to watch and report any improper acts of the prefect. At this point, Dien Guoben decided to send the Crane's Eye to hang the man's head in the prefect's courtyard, thinking that the prefect would be frightened.

While Dian Guoben was talking with the magistrate, he suddenly realized that something was going on in the courtyard outside. When he looked out and saw the two headmen with Cloud Dragon Hua in chains, he was enraged! "How do you dare to pretend you are making a social call while you are really pursuing a case?" he demanded springing to his feet.

He was about to attack the magistrate when Ji Gong stunned him and had him put in chains as well. When the other two outlaws heard the noise, they came rushing in with swords drawn, only to receive the same treatment as Dian Guoben.

At the magistrate's order, the party quickly returned to the yamen, where His Honor had a notice posted that court would be in session. In a short time at least twenty people came in with complaints against Dian Guoben, accusing him of theft, abduction of women, and other crimes, all of which were very serious.

Then the magistrate sent someone to call Ji Gong to the yamen to join him for a drink of wine. Afterward, the prisoners were interrogated and their confessions were written down, which the magistrate had wanted Ji Gong to hear. The prisoners were on view for all to see while the court waited for Ji Gong to appear before proceeding. Everyone knew that Ji Gong from the Monastery of the Soul's Retreat had taken Cloud

Dragon, Dian Guoben, and the three so-called Honorable Men—the first, the second, and the third.

The clamor aroused two river pirates. Who would have thought that two river pirates would hear about Cloud Dragon Hua's capture? These two were also among the men of the Greenwood. One was named Jiao Liang, the Golden-Faced Ghost. The other was Ho Jing, the Death-Decree Ghost. These two had just returned from the north and were passing through Linan when they heard the news. The two did not even know what crimes he had committed. "Since we know of this," said Jiao, "we must do something about it."

CHAPTER 88

A S the two outlaws went on walking and talking, they came to the place of execution and looked around. It was growing late in the day, but the official event had not yet occurred. Across the way was a wine shop, and the two walked in. The place was crowded. As the waiter looked at them, he saw that they were more richly dressed than most other customers. He quickly took them to a table. They sat down and ordered food and wine.

They could hear the people around them saying, "This Cloud Dragon Hua committed some terrible crimes. He killed a woman in the nunnery and also killed a man in the Tai Shan Tower restaurant. Then he stole the phoenix coronet and the jade pendants from the prime minister's bedroom. If the monk Ji Gong had not taken people with him and captured him, no one could have done anything about it."

The two outlaws were whispering one to the other, "First, we will go to the execution ground and rescue Cloud Dragon Hua. Then we will take revenge on this monk!"

Just as they were talking, in walked a poor, ragged monk. A great number of those in the restaurant knew him. One called out, "Teacher Ji has come!" Another exclaimed, "The holy monk has arrived!"

"Please, everyone, do not shout," said the monk. "I am simply the one who caught Cloud Dragon Hua—and the one who caught Cloud Dragon Hua is I. If anyone is dissatisfied with that, he can come to me."

When the outlaw named Jiao heard this, he looked at Ji Gong and thought to himself, "All the time it was just this poor, ragged monk who took our brother, Cloud Dragon Hua. After we are through at the execution ground, we will follow this monk and see what temple he goes to, and during the night we will kill him!"

The monk looked around, sat down beside the two men, and also ordered wine and food. Soon they heard the crowd outside grow noisier, and there were shouts of, "The cart is coming from the north with two officials in charge. The first one in the cart is the outlaw Dian Guoben."

Dian Guoben loudly exclaimed, "I am Dian Guoben, condemned to die at the third watch! They wouldn't dare to keep me until the fifth watch. There is a place to be born and a place to die. Even though the law condemns me to die, that is nothing!"

The second man was Wang Tong. He was cursing. "I am Wang Tong! I am not guilty of killing anyone! I wanted to kill the prefect Yang, but I didn't. There will be a ghost after I am dead!"

The third outlaw was the Chicken Thief, Liu Chang. This rascal hung his head, thinking that he shouldn't be executed with Cloud Dragon Hua. There was also a fourth outlaw and a fifth.

The sixth outlaw was Cloud Dragon Hua. He was talking and laughing to himself. "Look at this noisy crowd of people! I am Cloud Dragon Hua and I have killed over a hundred men! Perhaps after I die, there will be a ghost, but those who are here will live longer than I."

There was a great shout and those within the wine shop started to rush out. The two outlaws sitting there drew their swords as they heard that the execution was about to start. The frightened waiters hid under the table and the manager was begging for his life. The two outlaws were about to go outside, but the monk pointed at them and they became motionless. Then they heard someone shout, "A good blade!" Cloud Dragon Hua's head had fallen.

The monk got up from the table and said to the manager, "Write the charge on my account."

"Please be my guest," said the manager. "Your disciples, Yang Meng and Chen Liang, left word with me that no matter what you ordered I should not ask you for any money because they will pay for it."

"Manager, I would like to ask you for something," the monk said. "Will you give it to me?"

"What do you want?" asked the manager.

"I would like one of your melons," the monk said to him.

"Take it!" exclaimed the manager.

The monk picked out a melon and walked out of the wine shop carrying it. The two outlaws, Jiao and Ho, were now able to move again—and they still wanted to kill the monk. They paid their bill and left, following close behind the monk, who went straight to the Monastery of the Soul's Retreat.

When the monk who was the gatekeeper saw him, he said, "Old Ji is back."

"Greetings," said Ji Gong. He did not go directly to his room, but stood there in the gateway, carefully describing to the gatekeeper the location of his room. "It's on the west side of the west courtyard in the section toward the north. That's where I live. Anyone who wants to know, anyone who wants to kill this monk, can find me right there!"

"You really are half-witted," said the gatekeeper. "Who hates you that much?"

"Well, perhaps you two will remember," the monk said, but he was not speaking to the gatekeeper.

Jiao Liang and Ho Jing were listening and thinking, "This will be easy. Tonight we will find his room." The gatekeeper and the two outlaws watched as Ji Gong then went inside.

The two outlaws went off to find a wine shop. They found an inn and waited there until the second watch. Then they changed into suits of darkness. Each made a bundle of all the things he might need for the mission, slipped his broad, sharp sword into a leather scabbard, and left the inn. The two fairly flew over the road to the Monastery of the Soul's Retreat, and arriving, entered the temple over the roofs.

When they found the western courtyard, everyone seemed to be asleep. All the rooms were dark except for one in the northern section of the west building, where a lamp shone. They crept up to the window, made holes in the paper, and looked in. They could see a brick platform bed. There was nothing else in the room except for a table, a bowl half full of oil for the lamp hanging from the wall, and a stone lamp with a cotton wick. It was the custom in the monastery to give each monk a small quantity of oil in the evening. Tonight Ji Gong had asked for a bit more than usual, but was refused. Then he protested, "I have been away for many months. You should consider that." The monk in charge of the oil acceded to Ji Gong's request. He noticed that Ji Gong was carrying a melon.

The two outlaws could hear the monk talking to himself. "There is a place to be born and there is a place to die. Last night I did not have a good dream. I saw my head falling. Tonight, perhaps outlaws will come and kill me." Jiao Liang and Ho Jing were not discouraged. In a little while they saw the monk lie down and go to sleep.

Jiao Liang said, "I will kill him. You keep your nose in the wind for me." Ho Jing nodded.

Just as Jiao Liang was about to open the door, he heard the monk exclaim, "You thing! How dare you!" Jiao Liang was shocked with fright.

Then he heard the monk say, "Bite me, would you, you big old rat! You would never like the taste."

When he heard the monk say that it was a rat, he waited for a long time. He heard the monk sleeping noisily. He was again about to open the door when he heard the monk exclaim, "You things! You really are seeking your own deaths! You think you can harm me, do you?" The frightened Jiao Liang's heart was beating wildly. Then he heard the monk say, "Big bugs! Keeping me awake when I want to sleep! Terrible!"

When Jiao Liang heard that, he said to himself, "What a time for that!" There was nothing he could do but wait again until the third watch, when he heard Ji Gong snoring. Jiao Liang entered the room. He could see the lamp barely flickering, and he put it out. He then placed the bag made of strong cloth with an oiled paper lining in position to catch the monk's head. He touched the monk's short hair with his hand. Then he raised the heavy blade with its sharp edge and brought it down. Into the bag it dropped. He wrapped it up well and then rejoined Ho Jing. They went up over the roofs and returned to the inn.

"Now let's go to visit Ma Jing," said Jiao, "and tell him all about it. Cloud Dragon Hua was one of the thirty-six friends that Ma Jing had made in the Greenwood. He must see the head. Though Cloud Dragon Hua committed crimes, what would Ma Jing care!"

"Good," said Ho Jing.

They took to the road, staying overnight at inns, until they reached Phoenix Cliff Pleasant Village in the Jade Mountains and found the home of Ma Jing. Together they knocked at the gate—Jiao Liang, the Golden-Faced Ghost, and the Death-Decree Ghost, Ho Jing.

"We have a head we want to show you!" they shouted when the gate was opened.

CHAPTER 89

Two outlaws show a head to Ma Jing;
Ma Jing recalls the monk's visit

WHEN the two outlaws looked around, they saw a number of lanterns. Jiao Liang suddenly remembered the reason for them and exclaimed, "Brother Ho, we came at the right time! This is the birthday of Ma Jing's mother. I had forgotten. Today we must congratulate her and wish her a long life."

"That's right," agreed Ho.

As the two entered, a household person welcomed them, saying, "Oh, it is Jiao Liang and Ho Jing! Come in, gentlemen. The great hall is filled with people expecting you."

Jiao and Ho looked inside and saw many people they knew in the crowd. Almost every one of their friends was there. When they saw the two enter the hall, they stood and called a greeting. Ma Jing said, "Our two dear brothers have come. I have been thinking of you and was afraid you might not come, but you did not forget."

"Before we do anything else, let us wish long life to your old mother," said Jiao Liang.

"It is enough that you dear friends have come," said Ma Jing. "First, have some wine, and afterward I will convey your regards. That will suffice."

Jiao Liang and Ho Jing sat down. "Today we thirty-six friends could not all be here," said Ma Jing. "There are some who have died, some who have gone abroad, and some who have gone we know not where. We must always be several short of our whole group."

"That's natural," commented somebody.

"Where did you come from?" asked another of Jiao Liang.

"We came from the capital," replied Jiao Liang.

"And what is the news in the capital?" the man asked.

"There is sad news!" said Jiao Liang. "They have killed Cloud Dragon Hua."

"I thank heaven and I thank earth!" exclaimed Ma Jing.

"Elder Brother Jing, you introduced Cloud Dragon Hua to all the thirty-six friends of the Greenwood. If he were doing wrong, you should have been responsible for him. Now he is dead, punished by the nation's laws. How can you thank heaven and earth?"

"Dear brother Jiao," replied Ma Jing, "do you know what Cloud Dragon Hua did after my introduction?"

"No, I do not," answered Jiao.

Ma Jing then related the evil things that Cloud Dragon Hua had done in Linan. He had tried to rape a nun and then killed her when he failed; he had killed a man in a restaurant; then he had stolen the prime minister's phoenix coronet and jade pendants; he had attempted to kidnap one of the Zhou maidens; he had wounded his three friends in the Great Willow Forest with poisoned darts, and then had wounded three more friends in the same manner. Fortunately, Ji Gong had saved both the former and the latter three from death.

After Jiao Liang had heard this recitation of Cloud Dragon Hua's crimes, he burst out, "We have made a terrible mistake!"

"What kind of a mistake did you two make?" asked Ma Jing.

"Did Elder Brother know the monk Ji Dian?" asked Jiao Liang.

"I know him," replied Ma Jing.

"We two did not know all these details you have just told us," said Jiao Liang. "We wanted to avenge Cloud Dragon Hua's death, and so we killed the monk."

"Ji Gong is a living Buddha!" exclaimed Ma Jing. "How could you have killed him?"

"If you don't believe me, we brought his head here in this bag," said Jiao Liang.

"Open it and show me the head," ordered Ma Jing.

Jiao Liang opened the bag and showed what was in it. However, all this time the contents of the bag had been a melon—but there was something written on it.

> We laugh to see two friends mistake
> A melon for a monk and yet,
> Pray that no evil star may lead
> Toward a fate we'd all regret.

Everyone broke into hearty laughter.

"Ji Gong is truly a living Buddha," said Ma Jing. "He drove away a fox spirit that had been taking the form of my wife in order to destroy my friendship with my sworn brother. Ji Gong forced the spirit to reveal its fox shape and showed me that my wife was innocent of any wrongdoing with my friend."

Then Ma Jing went on to tell how he had hidden Cloud Dragon Hua, Lei Ming, and Chen Liang in the cellar behind a scroll in his east room, and how, as payment for curing his mother, Ji Gong had demanded the scroll, frightening those hiding behind it. All the company was laughing, highly amused by that incident.

"How could you possibly have killed Ji Gong?" concluded Ma Jing. "I think, though, that his written words really mean that unless you two change your ways, some calamity will befall you. You must be very careful to avoid it!"

"When we leave here, we will go home for a day or two," said Jiao Liang. "Afterward, we will return to Linan and go the Monastery of the Soul's Retreat. There, we will find Ji Gong so we can greet him respectfully, ask if we may call him our teacher, and beg him for his instruction."

"That would be a good idea," said Ma Jing and the others. For two days the company feasted. Then they thanked Ma Jing, said farewell to one another, and went their separate ways—to the north, south, east, and west.

Acknowledgments

THE Publisher and Mrs. Sara Janet Shaw would like to thank all who helped to make this publication a reality, especially Hsiao-liang (Luke) Chen, PhD, for generously sharing his knowledge of Chinese social history and the intricacies of the Chinese language; Lori L. Crouter, Dorothy Darrah, Marianna Gellert, Adam Goold, Judith Jones, Milton Levitt, Andrew Little, Donald E. McNeil, Sarah Wight, Arija Weddle and Bruce Weddle, for various forms of assistance.

Mr. Shaw would also have wanted to express his appreciation to Mr. Cal Barksdale, ex Senior Editor of Tuttle Publishing, for recognizing the worth of the translation. His advice and assistance were invaluable. A note of appreciation also goes to Bud Sperry and William Notte of Tuttle Publishing for assistance in the final stages of publication of the book.

The Tuttle Story

"Books to Span the East and West"

Many people are surprised to learn that the world's largest publisher of books on Asia had its humble beginnings in the tiny American state of Vermont. The company's founder, Charles E. Tuttle, belonged to a New England family steeped in publishing.

Tuttle's father was a noted antiquarian dealer in Rutland, Vermont. Young Charles honed his knowledge of the trade working in the family bookstore, and later in the rare books section of Columbia University Library. His passion for beautiful books—old and new—never wavered throughout his long career as a bookseller and publisher.

After graduating from Harvard, Tuttle enlisted in the military and in 1945 was sent to Tokyo to work on General Douglas MacArthur's staff. He was tasked with helping to revive the Japanese publishing industry, which had been utterly devastated by the war. After his tour of duty was completed, he left the military, married a talented and beautiful singer, Reiko Chiba, and in 1948 began several successful business ventures.

To his astonishment, Tuttle discovered that postwar Tokyo was actually a book-lover's paradise. He befriended dealers in the Kanda district and began supplying rare Japanese editions to American libraries. He also imported American books to sell to the thousands of GIs stationed in Japan. By 1949, Tuttle's business was thriving, and he opened Tokyo's very first English-language bookstore in the Takashimaya Department Store in Ginza, to great success. Two years later, he began publishing books to fulfill the growing interest of foreigners in all things Asian.

Though a westerner, Tuttle was hugely instrumental in bringing a knowledge of Japan and Asia to a world hungry for information about the East. By the time of his death in 1993, he had published over 6,000 books on Asian culture, history and art—a legacy honored by Emperor Hirohito in 1983 with the "Order of the Sacred Treasure," the highest honor Japan can bestow upon a non-Japanese.

The Tuttle company today maintains an active backlist of some 1,500 titles, many of which have been continuously in print since the 1950s and 1960s—a great testament to Charles Tuttle's skill as a publisher. More than 60 years after its founding, Tuttle Publishing is more active today than at any time in its history, still inspired by Charles Tuttle's core mission—to publish fine books to span the East and West and provide a greater understanding of each.